GLOBAL ISSUES IN HIGHER EDUCATION

GLOBAL ISSUES IN HIGHER EDUCATION

PAMELA B. RICHARDS
EDITOR

Nova Science Publishers, Inc.
New York

NOTICE TO THE READER

The Publisher has taken reasonable care in the preparation of this book, but makes no expressed or implied warranty of any kind and assumes no responsibility for any errors or omissions. No liability is assumed for incidental or consequential damages in connection with or arising out of information contained in this book. The Publisher shall not be liable for any special, consequential, or exemplary damages resulting, in whole or in part, from the readers' use of, or reliance upon, this material.

Independent verification should be sought for any data, advice or recommendations contained in this book. In addition, no responsibility is assumed by the publisher for any injury and/or damage to persons or property arising from any methods, products, instructions, ideas or otherwise contained in this publication.

This publication is designed to provide accurate and authoritative information with regard to the subject matter covered herein. It is sold with the clear understanding that the Publisher is not engaged in rendering legal or any other professional services. If legal or any other expert assistance is required, the services of a competent person should be sought. FROM A DECLARATION OF PARTICIPANTS JOINTLY ADOPTED BY A COMMITTEE OF THE AMERICAN BAR ASSOCIATION AND A COMMITTEE OF PUBLISHERS.

LIBRARY OF CONGRESS CATALOGING-IN-PUBLICATION DATA
Global issues in higher education / Pamela B. Richards (editor).
    p. cm.
  Includes index.
  ISBN-13: 978-1-60021-802-6 (hardcover)
  ISBN-10: 1-60021-802-4 (hardcover)
  1. Education, Higher. 2. Education and globalization. I. Richards, Pamela B.
  LB2322.2.G54 2006
  378--dc22
             2007022573

Published by Nova Science Publishers, Inc. ✦ New York

CONTENTS

Preface   vii

Expert Commentaries

Commentary A Applications of Universal Design in Higher Education   1
           Sheryl Burgstahler

Commentary B Management, Teaching and Research: Some Challenges for Public
           Universities in Spain at the 21st Century   5
           José Manuel Coronel Llamas

Research and Review Articles

Chapter 1 Using Developmental Research to Evaluate
           Blended Teaching in Higher Education   9
           Neal Shambaugh

Chapter 2 Higher Education and Growth in State Workforce Productivity,
           1980-2000: Evidence on the Public Benefits of College Education   37
           Michael B. Paulsen and Nasrin Fatima

Chapter 3 Academic Communities and Developing Identity:
           The Doctoral Student Journey   57
           L. McAlpine and C. Amundsen

Chapter 4 Providing Feedback on Student Writing
           Using Annotation Technology   85
           Terence C. Ahern and Judy A. Abbott

Chapter 5 A Motivational Perspective on the Self-Regulated
           Learning in Higher Education   99
           Antonio Valle, Ramón G. Cabanach, Susana Rodríguez,
           José C. Núñez, Julio A. González-Pienda,
           Paula Solano and Pedro Rosário

Chapter 6 The Changing Landscape of UK Doctoral Education   127
           Thomas F. Burgess

Chapter 7   Australian University Leaders: Agents of the Mc University,
                Entrepreneurial Transformers, or Bureaucrats?   **149**
                Deanna de Zilwa

Chapter 8   Higher Education Research Perspectives   **173**
                Alberto Amaral and António Magalhães

Chapter 9   Designing Pedagogical Models to Support Collaboration in Higher
                Education Contexts   **195**
                Raija Hämäläinen

Chapter 10   Outcomes of Project-Based Studies and Student
                Self-Regulation of Learning   **215**
                Laura Helle and Päivi Tynjälä

Chapter 11   Analysis and Decision Making Models in the Process of the
                Assimilation of Change and Innovation in Learning Systems   **237**
                Baruch Offir

Chapter 12   Higher Education: Federal Science, Technology, Engineering, and
                Mathematics Programs and Related Trends   **267**
                United States Government Accountability Office

Chapter 13   Higher Education: Schools' Use of the Antitrust Exemption Has Not
                Significantly Affected College Affordability or Likelihood of
                Student Enrollment to Date   **341**
                United States Government Accountability Office

Index   **393**

PREFACE

In most developed countries a high proportion of the population (up to 50%) now enter higher education at some time in their lives. Higher education is therefore very important to national economies, both as a significant industry in its own right, and as a source of trained and educated personnel for the rest of the economy.It follows that there are enormous stakes involved for a particular country even though the payoff of serious reforms may make decades and thus be counterproductive to the political forces responsible for designing and implimenting such reforms since their horizons tend to be very short. This new book tackles important issues in dynamic field.

Chapter 1 - Accountability of teaching in higher education has taken on greater significance given an institution's need to provide evidence supporting its overall mission and specific features of strategic plans. Evaluation of teaching beyond the limitations of student surveys is needed to support adjunct, tenure-track, and tenured faculty members in their yearly performance as well as documenting overall department and college/school performance. One way to provide systematic documentation is through developmental research. A 12-year study of a master's level course is reported. Described are data sources and data analysis procedures. The 16 deliveries are summarized in terms of the developmental research cycle phases: design, implementation, and evaluation, and evolution of the activity-participation structures that characterized the course's blended instruction. These structures include classroom activities, design activities, textbook, personal conferences, web site, Wiki, and web board. The chapter provides guidelines on the use of developmental research in terms of identifying a study focus and conducing such a study. Implications of developmental research are discussed, including improvements for student learning, methodology for research, and how iterative inquiry provides data for individual and institutional needs.

Chapter 2 - Over the past twenty-five years, the share of the burden of financing higher education borne by society has continuously decreased, while the share of that burden falling on the shoulders of students and their families has steadily increased. This raises the recurrent need to carefully examine and justify the role of society and the public sector in the finance of higher education. To the extent that investment in higher education generates public or external benefits to society—such as overall economic growth—substantial levels of public or government spending on higher education can be justified. Hence, the *purpose* of this study was to estimate the effects of initial investments in higher education on the subsequent growth in workforce productivity in the 50 individual state economies during the periods of 1980-1990 and 1990-2000.

The dependent variable in this study was the 10-year growth in state workforce productivity. The independent variables in this study were: initial state workforce productivity and initial cumulative investment in higher education at the beginning of each 10-year period of growth, and a composite measure of economic activity in ten industrial sectors in each state economy during each 10-year period of analysis. The model was first estimated with regression using data for the 10-year period from 1980-1990; again using data for the 10-year period from 1990-2000; and finally using pooled data from the two 10-year periods of analysis (1980-1990 and 1990-2000).

Findings indicated that the effect of initial cumulative investment in higher education on the subsequent 10-year growth in state workforce productivity was statistically significant and was substantial and similar in magnitude across all three samples. In addition, as expected, the initial level of state workforce productivity was significantly and negatively related to, and the expansion in economic activity in ten industrial sectors in the state economies was significantly and positively related to, the subsequent 10-year growth in state workforce productivity.

Chapter 3 - There is a substantial international literature that highlights the need to rethink doctoral pedagogies. The goal of our broad research program is to analyze the experience of doctoral students in Education and English in order to understand how they learn from engaging in the range of activities, both formal and informal, available to them in their programs. We began this program by carrying out three studies conducted in different contexts and with different research questions. As we analyzed data from these three initial studies, we noticed a clear theme emerging across all three: the development of academic identity within the shifting tensions of the discipline and the institution. To better understand this potentially significant theme of identity development, we reanalyzed the data from all three studies focusing this time on identity instead of the initial focus of investigation in each. This chapter reports the findings of this reanalysis and how we interpret them, specifically, the construction of a conceptual framework to synthesize them, and pedagogical implications that emerge.

Chapter 4 - Writing allows authors to share ideas, stories, thoughts and desires unencumbered by time and space. The process of writing is dynamic. From inspiration to dissemination the process is a give and take between author and audience. Writing is a learned skill and requires practice. Consequently, writers want readers to read their writing. They want feedback. But teaching and practicing writing are often shortchanged throughout public schooling and during the college years due to writing's time-consuming nature—time-consuming for students as they create a written piece and time-consuming for instructors as they respond to and evaluate written pieces. This project had two objectives. First, we explored the use of an Internet-based text production annotation system when developing a written assignment in an undergraduate college course. Secondly, we explored the nature of the written feedback provided by the instructor within an Internet-based text production annotation system.

Chapter 5 - Ever since the decade of the seventies, the new proposals from psychological learning theories promote a change of course that involves considering the student an active part and protagonist of the process of building knowledge. The student's mental processes (cognitive and meta-cognitive) start to be considered essential and, within them, the processes of organization, interpretation, or comprehension of information are crucial, as learning is not a copy or a mechanical recording of material, but the result of interpreting or transforming the subject matter.

This opens up new ways of reflection in the area of higher education, where the perspective of self-regulated learning could be the field that offers a broader and more dynamic approach to the comprehension of learning processes. This perspective assumes the basic principle that learners are agents who choose and make decisions about their behavior. They are the true architects and promoters of their learning. In addition to being capable of managing their own motivational and cognitive resources with the aim of achieving successful learning, self-regulated learners should have the necessary competencies to apply these resources within a plan of action that matches the demands of the specific learning situation.

As motivation plays a crucial role in learning and constitutes an essential area in all the approaches to self-regulated learning, in this chapter, an analysis is performed of the motivational components on which self-regulated learning is based, from various proposals derived from research with students of higher education.

Chapter 6 - Over the last ten years doctoral education in the UK has undergone a series of changes and a relatively stable environment has become much more dynamic. Such changes look set to continue. In this chapter past changes are identified, explored and future projections made. The chapter addresses the HE context of doctoral production, identifies the factors driving change and seeks where possible to show the connections between the various determinants, changes and consequences. Factors covered include the massification of higher education, the internalisation/globalisation (e.g. changing international markets), and the increasing encroachment of managerial and business perspectives in to higher education and research (e.g. quality assurance schemes, and the stress on business relevance of research). The nature of the changes in doctoral training include the introduction of new forms (e.g. integrated PhDs and professional doctorates) and modifications to existing structures and content (e.g. the increased emphasis on more systematic training and accents on developing transferable skills). Some speculations are made about how the landscape might change in future.

Chapter 7 - Some sociologists and higher education scholars view theory and empiricism as separate worlds, arguing that one has nothing to offer the other. This work proposes that the boundaries between theoretical conceptions and empirical realities have a transilient fluidity, that one domain informs the other. Hence this study explores connections between three theoretical conceptions of the university, Weber's bureaucracy, Ritzer's McUniversity and Clark's Entrepreneurial University and the leadership style of executives in Australian public universities. Information about executives' leadership style was gathered from case study interviews with seventeen executives from four Australian public universities. This work found that at each of the case study universities leaders' views of their university comprised elements of these three conceptions of the university, none of the three conceptions of the university were actualized in a 'pure' form. This work also identifies four different leadership styles used by these executives: entrepreneurial transformers, facilitators, bureaucrats and collegial leaders. It finds some connections between leaders' theoretical conceptions of the university and how they led their universities. However, the connections between theory and empiricism were complex, reflexive ones rather than unidirectional causes and effects.

Chapter 8 - Higher education research as a separate area of study has only recently been developed. A justification for the 'delay' of higher education research is that it has become an important focus of interest only when higher education entered the mass threshold, configuring a major financial and political issue.

This new area began to develop in the 1960s, in American universities (California at Berkeley, SUNNY Buffalo, Yale, Michigan). Only several years later has the field attracted the attention of social scientists in Europe, namely in the UK and Sweden. For Maassen there are differences in its development between the US and Europe, one of them being a strict divide in Europe between micro-level research on teaching and learning and research on organizational, political and economic aspects of higher education, the latter being the core of higher education research in Europe.

Major research efforts were aimed at the system level (Clark, Becher and Koogan, Teichler, etc.) and, in parallel, at governmental steering of the system (Neave and Van Vught, Kerr). Not only was the 'idea' of higher education discussed (Scott, Barnett, etc.), but also the issue of how to widen access of higher education for the majority of citizens. Studies on diversity and diversification were developed (Goedegebuure, Meek, Huisman).

We may argue that research on higher education reflects three different rationales: the managerial, the consulting and the social sciences approaches. The first rational, very present in international research organizations, has assumed management issues and goals, such as institutional performance, effectiveness, efficiency, etc., as privileged focus for research. The consulting approach was developed mainly in the framework of political advisors of Ministries of Education and presently also the European Commission, being the research goals mainly connected to implementation issues. The third approach, developed by social scientists, does not aim at 'solving' problems or 'advising' policy-makers and public officials responsible for policy implementation, but rather to find regularities observed when studying social objects. And as the research focus moved to the institutional level, these three approaches tended to mix.

More recently, the top-down approach of linear policy implementation has been replaced by alternative accounts that consider that organizations interact with their environment and define their own change strategies. New phenomena linked to neo-liberalism (new public management, managerialism, etc.), globalization and the emergence of new supra-national layers of authority, as observed in the EU, offer new areas of research that we will explore.

Chapter 9 - Educational research is looking for social approaches to foster virtual learning. Computer-Supported Collaborative Learning appears to be a promising approach for higher education for developing knowledge and reasoning skills. One way to enhance the process of collaboration as well as to integrate individual and group-level perspectives of learning is to structure learners' actions with the aid of scaffolding or scripted collaboration. The present study includes empirical experiments conducted in an authentic higher educational setting and leans on the design-based study approach. The leading idea in the study involved structuring the student groups' collaborative activities by means of pedagogical models (scripts), whilst they were working in learning environments. For this purpose, two different pedagogical models or scripts were designed in support of students' collaborative activities. Two different empirical studies were conducted (Escape ($N=24$) and Grid ($N28$)) to find out how effective different collaboration scripts were in guiding the learning processes. The data were collected by various means in order to capture, in a systemic manner, the complex relationships and dynamics between different variables within the diverse data. This article will discuss on the basic of the findings how scripting guided groups at the general level and helped students to find resources. Despite this positive effect scripting did not guarantee "high level" participation and there were great variations between the groups. The biggest differences occurred in the level of collaboration shown and in the roles assumed by the participants.

In: Global Issues in Higher Education
Editor: Pamela B. Richards, pp. 1-4

ISBN: 978-1-60021-802-6
© 2007 Nova Science Publishers, Inc.

Expert Commentary A

APPLICATIONS OF UNIVERSAL DESIGN IN HIGHER EDUCATION

Sheryl Burgstahler
University of Washington,USA

Postsecondary student bodies are becoming increasingly diverse with respect to race, ethnicity, age, and disability, and legislation mandates that programs and services be accessible to qualified students. In response, educators and administrators in all types of institutions are searching for a philosophical framework and a cost-effective approach to guide the creation of programs that are welcoming and accessible to all potential students. Universal design (UD), a term coined by Ronald Mace and promoted by the Center on Universal Design at North Carolina State University, is defined as "the design of products and environments to be usable by all people to the greatest extent possible, without the need for adaptation or specialized design." The Center developed seven UD principles that can be applied to the design of any product or environment: equitable use, flexibility in use, simple and intuitive, perceptible information, tolerance for error, low physical effort, and size and space for approach and use.

There are many potential applications of universal design. In the postsecondary setting, UD can be applied to physical spaces, information technology, instruction, and student services. Examples in each of these areas are listed below.

- *physical spaces.* Delivery service employees, parents with baby strollers, and individuals with disabilities benefit from curb cuts on sidewalks.
- *information technology.* Individuals with visual impairments benefit from the capability of enlarging characters on the screen, as do members of the aging population.
- *instruction.* Faculty members who use multiple modes of presentation are effective in teaching students with a wide range of learning styles, preferences, abilities, and disabilities.
- *student services.* Counters available at multiple heights are comfortable for people in both standing and sitting positions.

By being proactive, applying universal design creates more usable products and environments for everyone and minimizes the need for accommodations for students with disabilities.

Universal Design of Curriculum and Instruction

A growing body of literature is emerging to share examples of universal design to postsecondary settings. Most publications focus on the application of universal design to instruction. The Center for Applied Special Technology (CAST) has focused efforts on the application of brain research to create technological applications that can benefit all learners, including those with disabilities. Universally designed curriculum gives learners options for acquiring knowledge, demonstrating what they know, and engaging with materials, peers, and instructors by offering

- multiple means of representation
- multiple means of expression, and
- multiple means of engagement.

Universal design can be applied to all aspects of the instructional process by addressing class climate; physical access, usability, and safety; delivery methods; information resources; interaction; feedback; assessment; and accommodation. Faculty members can create a welcoming environment by encouraging students to share multiple perspectives, demonstrating and demanding mutual respect, and making statements on syllabi and in class inviting students to meet with them to discuss disability-related accommodations and other learning needs.

Universal Design of Student Services

UD principles can be applied to make student services more welcoming, accessible, and usable by postsecondary students. Such services include career centers, computer labs, libraries, recruitment and admissions, registration, financial aid, advising, student organizations learning centers, and residential life. Practitioners should consider UD as they develop policies and procedures with respect to planning and evaluation; facilities; staff training; information resources; computers, software, and assistive technology; and events.

Universal Design of Physical Spaces

UD principles can be applied to make facilities and outdoor spaces welcoming to, accessible to, and usable by all students, faculty, and staff. For example, universally designed library facilities have clear and wide aisles, large print clear signage, a range of assistive technology and electronic databases that are accessible to patrons with disabilities.

Universal Design of Information Technology

Information technology is ubiquitous on postsecondary campuses. However, some technology is inaccessible to some students with disabilities. For example, people who are blind often use text-to-speech software to read aloud text that appears on the screen. This assistive technology cannot make sense of content presented within graphic images unless the webmaster includes text-based descriptions of the content. National and international standards and guidelines have been developed to help institutions develop, procure, and use technology—including computers, software, websites, video and multimedia—that is accessible to everyone.

The Process of Universal Design

Universal design is a philosophical foundation that places high value on diversity and inclusion. It is also a process. In a postsecondary setting, once you select the application to which you want to apply universal design (e.g., a student union building, a biology class, a career center), imagine the wide range of characteristics that students, faculty, and staff using that application might possess. Then, research guidelines or standards that might be used to measure this application of universal design and apply the guidelines or standards. Develop a plan for providing additional accommodations that might be needed for some individuals with disabilities (e.g., arranging for a sign language interpreter) that assures a timely response to requests. Provide staff with the training and support they need to apply universal design and respond to requests for accommodations from individuals with disabilities, and, periodically, evaluate the effectiveness of universal design efforts.

Potential for Universal Design

Universal design holds promise for providing a philosophical framework and process for creating a campus, courses, services, and technology that is welcoming and accessible to all potential students, faculty, and staff. Researchers and practitioners should test its effectiveness for enhancing the learning environment for students with diverse characteristics.

ACKNOWLEDGEMENT

The content of this article is adapted with permission from *Universal Design in Education: Principles and Applications* at *http://www.washington.edu/doit/Brochures/Academics/ud_edu.html*. The creation of this article was funded by the National Science Foundation (Cooperative agreement #HRD0227995) and the U.S. Department of Education, Office of Postsecondary Education (#P333A050064). The opinions expressed are those of the author and do not necessarily reflect those of the funding agencies.

RESOURCES

For more information about the meaning, the process, and applications of universal design, begin by exploring the following resources.

The Center for Universal Design in Education http://www.washington.edu/doit/CUDE/
Center for Applied Special Technology (CAST)   http://www.cast.org/udl/
The Center for Universal Design http://www.design.ncsu.edu/cud/

In: Global Issues in Higher Education
Editor: Pamela B. Richards, pp. 5-7

ISBN: 978-1-60021-802-6
© 2007 Nova Science Publishers, Inc.

Expert Commentary B

MANAGEMENT, TEACHING AND RESEARCH: SOME CHALLENGES FOR PUBLIC UNIVERSITIES IN SPAIN AT THE 21ST CENTURY

*José Manuel Coronel Llamas**
Department of Education, University of Huelva
Campus del Carmen, 21007 Huelva, Spain

I would like to take advantage of this opportunity to expose my opinion about some problems and challenges that Public University in Spain has established as a Higher Education System. I am sure that these same problems can be found in other countries. Anyway, they show the evolution of the public university system and they offer, as well, a real panorama of the condition in which a main institution for the citizens' training is situated inside a "knowledge-based" society.

After the fall of the dictatorship in mid 70s, Spain experienced a growing social demand of deep reforms in the educational system and a more democratic model of school governance. These demands agreed with a period of expansion and extension of Higher Education that forced to implement new educational policies and to make a plan to improve the situation in which the university system was sunk. Moreover, an additional effort has been made to join and take part as a country member of the European Union. The last ten years, the University system has developed a process of adaptation and convergence with the so called "European Common Space of Higher Education". This adaptation leads us to face substantial changes in the university system. My commentary is going to be about three different aspects that can show the present panorama of public universities in Spain: 1) University management; 2) teaching and 3) research.

1. Nowadays, adaptation and convergence are the main policies dealing with Higher Education in European countries. The new Bologna process establishes new demands on Universities, requiring them to reorganize their curricula so as to accommodate the need for a greater portability. Universities must be conscious of the challenges that involve working under these new circumstances. Dealing with Spain, this process of adaptation means the design of a new map of degrees, that is being finished at the moment. These new degrees

* E-mail: coronel@uhu.es

should contribute to balance supply and demand .For example, in spite of the fact that there have been an increasing number of Universities, and that one of each three people decides to study, many degrees do not have an adequate number of students. We need to take decisions about how to rationalize the supply of degrees and fit it better to the new requirements and demands of our society. We need to make an urgent redistribution of the resources available and to adopt strategic measures cause a rise of student population is expected for 2014.

On the other hand, Universities present a problematic situation in financing matters. The "fiscal crisis" is attributed to government policy and the few funds assigned to assist a spreading system. The complaint at University is the shortage of funds destined to University. At this moment an increasing number of private financing is observed as an opportunity to guarantee the new challenges. We need developing social evaluation and control mechanisms of the cost in the universities. Thus, the beginning of new models for the financing appears like an opportunity that universities must incorporate to confront with greater guarantee the new raised challenges.

2. Another consequence of the process of European convergence in higher Education is that we are going to require an enabled and motivated teaching staff that must have to respond suitably to the new demands and changes. Nowadays, a formidable challenge is being considered at Spanish Universities: the need to change the way that the teaching activity had been developed. To go on from a perspective that takes the teacher and teaching as a centre, to other one that takes the student and his learning as an axis for the action. This is not simple and easy. I would emphasize the changes associated to the work at the faculty. Related to teaching staff, these changes will suppose a reorganization of teachers' work during the course of their professional activity. This reorganization affects: a) to the content of the teaching activity (extended qualitatively); b) the time needed (extended quantitatively) and, c) to the way in which we will have to work (from isolation to collaboration and collegiality). The replacement of ways of education based on the passive transmission of the knowledge on the part of the teacher for approaches that emphasize the protagonist role of the students in their own learning represents an opportunity for the change in the teaching culture and the valuation of the teachers' work. Nevertheless, in many cases, we are speaking about a process which impact will have to be valued carefully if we do not want to provoke rejections and resistances. Without fear of being wrong, we can say that a great part of our current university teaching staff does not seem to fit to the required profile and that, consistently, it is necessary to prepare the change with actions and training programs. This process should be accompanied of teachers' support policies, training programs, and structural and institutional changes at Universities.

3. If we take a look at the History of European Universities, we will find that they have traditionally kept apart from the rest of society. The institutionalized myth of autonomy and the nature of academic work have been considered as defining features of Universities. A strong tradition of self-government justifies the idea of a liberal and autonomous "academy", with a commitment to independence, neutrality, impartiality and the advance of knowledge. However, market-orientation invaded the public sector and entered into Universities.

The rising trend towards introducing market elements in Higher Education allows identifying certain problems derived from the increase of the control of neo-liberalism policies on the academy, faculty and students. Specially, University researchers who previously often worked in more autonomous working conditions were now more inclined to involve themselves closely in industrial and governmental research collaborations. The 'academic capitalism' has changed the former University habits in research, teaching and management, and has drastically changed the University climate. In FoucalThe funds of the Authority shall include:

a. assessed contributions made by members of the Authority in accordance with article 160, paragraph 2(e);
b. funds received by the Authority pursuant to Annex III, article 13, in connection with activities in the Area;
c. funds transferred from the Enterprise in accordance with Annex IV, article 10;
d. funds borrowed pursuant to article 174;
e. voluntary contributions made by members or other entities; and

payments to a compensation fund, in accordance with article 151,paragraph 10, whose sources are to be recommended by the Economic Planning Commissiondian terms the neo-liberalism creates 'conditions of domination' within academic life and obstructs the development of alternative perspectives, practices and possibilities. The marriage of corporate culture and Higher Education creates in faculty mere employees of corporate order. The research projects are discussed not in terms of their contribution to the public good or for their potential intellectual breakthroughs, but for what they produce and the potential profits they make in the commercial and business sector.

The consequences of transforming university research into a commercially driven enterprise are evident. For example, the growth of patenting by Universities has provided a strong incentive for researchers to pursue commercial projects. Social responsibility, civic discourse, and the social and intellectual role are trapped for the corporate culture. The development of intellectual and creative potential of teachers and students are undermined by bureaucracy and market forces. The uncritical thinkers increase to give special attention. Also, it is true, that classical ideals of free research and neutrality among university researchers do not disappear, but are rather competing with new norms and policies that tend to make traditional intellectual identities unsustainable. With a heavy dependence on external funding the possibilities for critique will probably decrease.

The universities must distance themselves from the demands for the new managerialism. We need to count the neo-liberal discourse. Structural and pedagogical changes are also necessary but we need a deep questioning of this situation and support a collective resistance, including faculty, students and administrators. This is a very big challenge for Universities in the 21st century.

In: Global Issues in Higher Education
Editor: Pamela B. Richards, pp. 9-36

ISBN: 978-1-60021-802-6
© 2007 Nova Science Publishers, Inc.

Chapter 1

USING DEVELOPMENTAL RESEARCH TO EVALUATE BLENDED TEACHING IN HIGHER EDUCATION

Neal Shambaugh*

Program Coordinator, Instructional Design and Technology
504N Allen Hall, PO Box 6122
West Virginia University
Morgantown, WV, USA 26506-6122

ABSTRACT

Accountability of teaching in higher education has taken on greater significance given an institution's need to provide evidence supporting its overall mission and specific features of strategic plans. Evaluation of teaching beyond the limitations of student surveys is needed to support adjunct, tenure-track, and tenured faculty members in their yearly performance as well as documenting overall department and college/school performance. One way to provide systematic documentation is through developmental research. A 12-year study of a master's level course is reported. Described are data sources and data analysis procedures. The 16 deliveries are summarized in terms of the developmental research cycle phases: design, implementation, and evaluation, and evolution of the activity-participation structures that characterized the course's blended instruction. These structures include classroom activities, design activities, textbook, personal conferences, web site, Wiki, and web board. The chapter provides guidelines on the use of developmental research in terms of identifying a study focus and conducing such a study. Implications of developmental research are discussed, including improvements for student learning, methodology for research, and how iterative inquiry provides data for individual and institutional needs.

---

* 304-293-2060; neal.shambaugh@mail.wvu.edu

INTRODUCTION

Traditional course evaluation has taken the form of institutionally-developed student surveys, which are used for promotion and tenure reviews. This data forms the basis for promotion decisions, although the quality of teaching is only a function of what students said about the teaching. No criteria exists for teaching decisions, such as appropriate learning outcomes, and alignment of teaching and assessment decisions. Issues that faculty have with student surveys may stem from fussy assessment schemes, too many objectives, unclear task and project instructions, and non-responsive attention to questions and email queries. Low teacher evaluations and faculty views of students collide and interfere with faculty members' productivity in other areas. What follows is a report summarizing my teaching of a master's level course delivered 16 times over 12 years. A developmental research methodology was used to structure data collection and analysis.

RESEARCHING ONE'S TEACHING

Nature of Teacher Inquiry

Teaching has traditionally been viewed at all educational levels as an in-person activity, with the exception of correspondence courses at the high school, college, and training levels. Distance education options have also included telephone, television, and satellite technologies. With the use of online technologies, the face-to-face (F2F) option has expanded to include what are referred to as blended learning. Blended learning can be defined as systems that "combine face-to-face instruction with computer-mediated instruction" (Graham, in press). The use of the two approaches highlights issues of what teaching consists of and what experiences instructors can provide students to support explicit learning outcomes. Studying one's teaching, whether involving F2F or blended, contributes towards improved accountability of an instructor to students (and other constituencies, such as parents), and a faculty member contribution to the mission and purposes of one's department and college or school. One of the values of blended learning and of any instructional technology is that it prompts instructors to re-examine the purposes for a course, a curriculum issue, but also what learning outcomes that course should consist of. Studying the teaching in a systematic way provides data, results, and conclusions over time that not only improve student learning but model the inquiry process for students.

A number of approaches exist for the study of teaching, depending on the overall goal of the study. Reeves (2000) suggests three broad goals for research. The first goal is to refine existing theory, and empirical research is employed where a researcher uses research hypotheses and tests those hypotheses. Often experimental or quasi-experimental studies are used to address this goal. A second goal for research is to take action. Here action research or evaluation research methodologies are called for. The purpose for action research, frequently used by public school teachers, is to study and improve some aspect of a teacher's practice (Cochran-Smith and Lytle, 1992) and can be employed by teacher candidates or practicing teachers. Bullough and Gitlin (2001) characterize action research as an integrative methodology, capable of studying personal issues using autobiography and personal teaching metaphors, as well as the context of school using school histories, ethnography, textbook and curriculum analyses. A third goal, according to Reeves (2002), is to seek an understanding of how an educational artifact, process, or intervention addresses educational objectives. The methodology applicable for this goal is developmental research, an iterative process in which the artifact is developed, tested, revised and refined based on observed outcomes, tested again, refined and revised, and so forth (Richey, Klein, and Nelson , 2003).

Developmental Research

Definition and types. Developmental research is defined by Seels and Richey (1994) as "the systematic study of designing, developing and evaluating instructional programs, processes, and products that must meet the criteria of internal consistency and effectiveness" (p. 127). Developmental research concerns itself with improving the growth, evolution, and change of the processes of instructional design, development, and evaluation (Richey, Klein, and Nelson, 2003). Development within a research context involves not only the creation of instructional products or programs, but their use and evaluation.

Developmental research lends itself to the generation of knowledge which has practical consequences. Richey, et al (2003) describe two types of knowledge that may arise out of this applied research: (1) process knowledge of dynamic systems, frequently represented by models; and (2) process understanding as a result of this knowledge. Richey, et al (2003) describe two types of developmental research. Type 1 developmental research studies specific products or programs and produces lessons learned from developing and analyzing the conditions that facilitate their use. Since specific products or programs are studied, Type 1 conclusions are context-specific. Meanwhile, Type 2 research studies design, development, or evaluation processes, tools, or models. Type 2 products include new procedures or models and the conditions that facilitate their use. Conclusions drawn from Type 2 developmental research can be generalized to other situations.

This research report documents a Type 1 developmental research study, as its emphasis is describing and documenting a context-specific teaching approach. The product from this study includes tactical "lessons learned" from implementing a course, but also the more strategic conclusions of implementing an overall teaching model across 12 years using blended delivery and how different forms of activity, described as participation structures, assist students in their learning. Although the results of Type 1 studies do not clearly transfer to courses in different contexts, the strategic conclusions of teaching model use, blended delivery, and participation structures may have implications for other content areas at different educational levels. A benefit of developmental research conducted over multiple course deliveries is the possibility that Type 2 conclusions are generated.

Characteristics. Richey, et al (2003) characterize developmental research through the use of six categories, which include: product or program focus, process focus, context of use, tools and techniques emphasized, research methods used, and the nature of conclusions. This study can then be characterized in terms of: full course (program focus); general description, development, and evaluation process (process focus); post-secondary (context use); needs assessment and learner verification (tools and techniques); descriptive case studies, observational (method); and context-specific and generalizations (nature of conclusions).

The sub-categories of process focus, according to Richey et al (1996), include description-development-evaluation process, needs assessment, content selection, design, production, formative evaluation, use and delivery, management, summative evaluation, and learner outcomes.

The second category, process focus, merits a brief discussion. The broadest process focus is the "description, development, evaluation process," which has the instructor research to describe a course's design, what occurs during the implementation of the design, and evaluates student learning and student perceptions of their learning and of the instructor. The value of this approach is to produce a descriptive summary across the entire developmental cycle: design, implementation, and evaluation. An ongoing descriptive summary provides a systematic record, a cyclical benchmark from which not only course decisions can be made but to identify research opportunities in which other methods can be used to specifically study specific phenomena in laboratory settings (design experiments) and applied back to educational settings.

12-YEAR CASE STUDY USING DEVELOPMENTAL RESEARCH

A 12-year case study of developmental research of a master's level course is presented. This developmental research describes procedures and summarizes results of yearly cycles of design, implementation, and evaluation. Summarized will be the evolution of the course in terms of various activity structures that characterize the course's blended instruction. These structures include classroom, online, textbook/readings, personal conferences, and project.

The form of inquiry is a multi-case approach used to describe *how* a teaching model was implemented across 16 deliveries of a course over 12 years. The case study is used to describe settings which include contextual issues and implementation details (Richey, et al, 2003). A "how" research inquiry deals with operational links needing to be traced over time, rather than mere frequencies or incidence (Yin, 2002). The case covers the contextual conditions inherent in teaching and relies on multiple sources of evidence to describe the same phenomena from the design, implementation, and evaluation of the teaching model used.

Course Deliveries

This study documents the implementation of the reflexive teaching model across 16 deliveries of the course over 12 years from 1994 through 2006. Table 1 summarizes each case in terms of case number, date delivered, number of students, semester-length and if the course is off-campus, institution delivered for, the number of instructors used, and the delivery type (F2F, WWW, or blended). The course was taught by the researcher at two different institutions, denoted by institution A or B. Both institutions are Research-Comprehensive universities. The first seven deliveries of the course were co-taught. In terms of delivery, 5 were delivered face-to-face (F2F), 1 was delivered totally online, and 10 were delivered using a blended approach, featuring a mix of F2F and online.

Table 1. Course deliveries

Case	Date	Students	Length	Institution	Instructors	Delivery
1	Summer 1994	13	05 week	A	2	F2F
2	Fall 1994	22	15 wk	A	2	F2F
3	Fall 1995	20	15 wk	A	2	Blended
4	Fall 1996	19	15 wk	A	2	Blended
5	Fall 1997	16	15 wk	A	2	Blended
6	Spring 1998	23	15 wk off campus	A	2	Blended
7	Summer 1997	15	05 wk off campus	A	2	WWW
8	Fall 1998	10	15 wk	A	1	F2F
9	Fall 1999	8	15 wk	B	1	F2F
10	Fall 2000	17	15 wk	B	1	F2F
11	Fall 2001	20	15 wk	B	1	Blended
12	Fall 2002	20	15 wk	B	1	Blended
13	Fall 2003	16	15 wk	B	1	Blended
14	Fall 2004	13	15 wk	B	1	Blended
15	Fall 2005	18	15 wk	B	1	Blended
16	Fall 2006	17	15 wk	B	1	Blended
		267	15 wk = 14 05 wk = 02 on campus = =15 cases off campus = = 01 case	Taught at: Inst. A = 7 Inst. B = 9	Co-taught = 7x Solo = 9x	F2F = 05 Web = 1 Blended = 10

Participants

Students. Students were characterized by their instructional design experience, teaching experience, educational level of interest, and content focus (see Table 2a). This information was acquired by self-report during the course. Students with formal ID experience totaled 24, while 243 had none. Of the 270 students in the course, 180 had teaching experience, while 87 did not. Educational levels of interest included 85 college, 54 training, 41 with an overall K12 focus, followed by 32 elementary, 32 elementary, 32 high school, and 22 middle. The largest content area focus of the participants included computing (42), science and technology (36), language arts (34), health and physical education (31), special education (22) and second language learning (20).

Instructors and institutions. Across the 16 deliveries of the course two instructors were used for this master's level course. For cases 1-7 both instructors co-taught the course at a land-grant institution, comprehensive-research university. For cases 8-16 the course was taught by the author at a second institution, also a land-grant institution, comprehensive-research university. The first instructor for cases 1-7 is a professor of educational psychology with teaching certifications in learning and behavioral disorders, and 9-years of teaching in public schools, in both general and special education settings. She also has developed two off-campus master's programs for K-12 teachers and has conducted numerous workshops for teachers.

Table 2a. Participants background

Instructional Design Experience		Teaching Experience	
Yes = 24	None = 243	Yes = 180	None = 87
Educational Level of Interest		Content Focus	
College	86	Computing	42
Training	54	Science, technology	36
K12	41	Language arts	34
Elementary	32	Health and PE	31
High school	32	Special education	22
Middle	22	Second language	20
		Mathematics	17
		Training skills	15
		Other	15
		Social studies	14
		Consumer skills	10
		Music	06
		Business	05

The second instructor for cases 1-7 and the solo instructor for cases 8-16 is an associate professor of instructional design and technology. His background includes six years of experience developing customized audiovisual and written task training, safety, and orientation materials for corporate clients, and 15 years of experience of audio/video writing and production experience. He has taught at the college level since 1994, beginning with this course.

Course Description

The course sequence, as it has evolves, begins with an examination of personal (or institutional) learning beliefs and a survey of ID tools (e.g., learning theories, ID models), followed by an overview of instructional design's analysis, design, and evaluation components (see Figure 1). "Learning Beliefs" and "Design Tools" are a distinctive feature of this sequence over other ID models used for teaching (e.g., Dick, Carey and Carey, 2005), which typically begin with a needs assessment. Implementation issues are addressed through a discussion of formative program evaluation and the "Prototype Lesson" phases. The major learning activity is a student's ID project, which addresses an instructional problem of the student's choice. Project components are structured by task sheets, including task rationale, guidelines, and performance criteria. Ongoing assessment for each student, as well as formative evaluation for the course, consist of notations on the task sheet's criteria, written and/or email feedback on learning tasks, end-of-each-class feedback (i.e., "exit slips"), webboard replies, and personal conversations. One or more individual or group conferences (Cases 2-14) have been conducted during the course to determine students' interests and backgrounds, discuss learning tasks, and progress toward project completion. Assessment of student learning involves draft and completed ID projects, personal ID models, and a self-evaluation. Evaluation of the course is obtained from students' perceptions of the course from a university course evaluation survey, in-class surveys, self- evaluation task, and conference interviews.

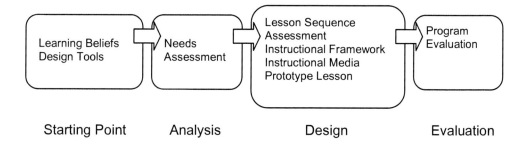

Figure 1. Course sequence.

Teaching Model Description

The reflexive teaching model consists of three components (see Figure 2). The first component visually represents students and instructor(s) in the model. The second component specifies multiple participation structures in which activity is structure. The third component is the use of dialogue between the participants and the structured activity.

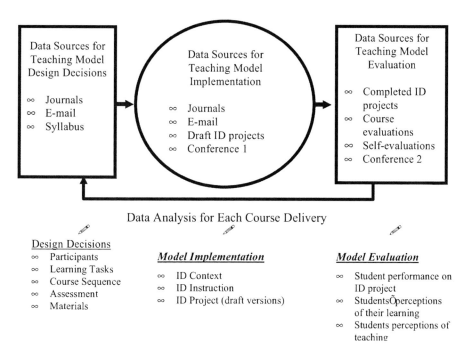

Figure 2. Reflexive teaching model

Instructor characteristics and roles. The reflexive teaching model identifies co-learners as including the instructor and the student. Both possess similar characteristics in that they are…. However, each takes on different roles. The instructor is responsible for the course content, delivery, and assessment of student learning, while the student is responsible for performing required learning tasks.

Co-participation structures. As participants within the model include both instructor and student, the forms of activity within the course are labeled as "co-participation" structures. In other words, teachers have particular roles within each structure and may include the design of the structure, implementation, and evaluation of the structure, but also performing the activity alongside the student. The co-participation structures used over 12 years have included classroom activities, design activities (out-of-class), textbook, F2F/email, personal conferences, website, wiki, and web board (see Table 2b).

Classroom activities are used to introduce, reinforce, or provide practice for students across each main topic in the course. The course assessment plan usually assigns these activities collectively as 10% of the course grade. Failure to show up for class and perform these classes results in a letter "drop" (e.g., from an A grade to a B grade). Student learning is further assisted through specific learning tasks, which are organized by task rationale, task procedures, and task assessment.

Design activities include 15 structured thinking and decision-making tasks, which together result in an instructional design document that includes analysis of an instructional problem and design decisions. Textbook use consisted of its own design activities with supporting text, reflective questions, scenario-stories, and references. These design activities were used in-class or as online activities and provided practice for the 15 structured design activities.

Table 2b. Participation Structures by Case

Case	Class Activities	Design Activities	Text	Instructor F2F/Email	Personal Conference	Web Site	Wiki	Web Board
1	X	X	X-a	X	2			
2	X	X	X-b	X	2			
3	X	X	X-b	X	2	X		
4	X	X	X	X	2	X		
5	X	X	X	X	2	X		
6	X	X	X	X	2	X		
7	X	X	X	X		X		
8	X	X	X		2			
9	X	X	X		2			
10	X	X	X		2			
11	X	X	X		2	X		
12	X	X	X		2	X		X
13	X	X	X		2		X	X
14	X	X	X		1		X	X
15	X	X	X					X
16	X	X	X					X
	16/16	16/16	16/16	7/16	13/16	7/16	2/16	4/16

Email consisted of electronic communication between the two instructors during cases 1-7, as well as email between instructor(s) and student. In addition questioning takes place on responses to posted student work on web boards. Personal conferences between instructor(s) and students were used across cases 1-14. Online participation structures have included a website for informational purposes, posting of course materials, and links to resources. Wiki or collaborative web pages have been used to enable students to post draft work along with peer critiques. A web board provides for threaded discussions, archiving of course materials, and posting of student work and peer critiques.

Dialogue. Dialogue involved assigned articles and text chapters and participating in class activities, as well as performance on the out-of-class activities. Performance in these out-of-class design activities necessitated that students make decisions, conduct research, reflect on these decisions, and provide feedback to peers and instructors. Instructor dialogue can be characterized by collaborating on course design decisions, interacting together and with students within the participation structures, and responding to student needs. Instructor actions can also be organized by multiple means of assisting student performance and include modeling, contingency managing, feeding back, instructing, questioning, cognitive structuring, and reflecting (Tharp and Gallimore, 1988). Table 3 identifies how participation structures matched these different means of assistance.

Table 3. Means of assisting student performance

	Modeling	Contingency Managing	Feeding back	Instructing	Questioning	Cognitive structuring	Reflecting
Class activities	X	X	X	X	X	X	
Design activities	X	X	X	X	X	X	X
Textbook	X			X		X	
F2F, email	X	X	X		X		X
Personal conferences	X	X	X		X		X
Web site c3-7	X			X		X	
Web site c11-12	X				X	X	X
Wiki, c12-13	X		X		X		X
Web board C13-16	X	X	X	X			X

Developmental Data Sources

The developmental research cycle consists of three phases: design, implementation, and evaluation. In terms of this study, which studies how a reflexive model helps graduate students learn instructional design, each cycle can be labeled as Teaching Model Design Decisions, Teaching Model Implementation, and Teaching Model Evaluation. Data sources that address each cycle are identified in Figure 2 and are described below.

Data sources for design decisions. Journals or working logs, email between instructors (for cases 1-7), and the course syllabus provide data sources to describe what teaching decisions were made for each delivery of the course.

Data sources for implementation. Working logs, email, draft projects, and/or personal conferences described how the teaching model was implemented. Students developed projects over the course and draft components of the project were evaluated weekly. For 12 cases, a personal conferences was held with each student. These personal conferences held about one month into the course served as a needs assessment briefing. The first six deliveries of this course the conference was audio-taped and supplemented by working log notes.

Data sources for evaluation. The major data source for this third cycle of the developmental research process involved analysis of students' final projects. A second personal conference held prior to final project submission acted as a formative one-on-one formative evaluation session. For the first six deliveries of the course the second conference was audio-taped and supplemented by working notes. In addition, students' course evaluations and perceptions of their learning provided additional data sources for this phase.

Developmental Analysis

Data analysis overview. Data were analyzed using the qualitative techniques of Miles and Huberman (1994), which consisted of data reduction from data sources and display of this reduced data in "frames" that enabled conclusions to be drawn. The data analysis sequence involves data collection, then data is analyzed, and the results are recorded into frames (i.e., tables). The data reduction documents for each course are kept in 3-ring notebooks, each divided by data sources. This strategy served to separate the data from the report and provided a means to organize the data and track the analysis sequence from data source to data reduction to data reporting.

Data analysis reporting. For each of the cases the documentation of the teaching, incorporating the reflexive teaching model, was reported in terms of the design and development cycle: design decisions, implementation, and evaluation. The needs assessment and subsequent design decisions, based on the teaching model, were reported by describing (a) participants, (b) learning tasks, (c) course sequence, (d) assessment, and (e) instructional materials. Analysis of the implementation of the model for each case described student performance and responses to instruction and instructor's assistance during (a) ID context activities, (b) ID process instruction, and (c) draft ID projects. Summative evaluation of the teaching model was reported on the basis of summarizing (a) student performance on the ID project, (b) students' self-perceptions of their learning, and (c) instructor responses to student needs.

DEVELOPMENTAL RESULTS – CASE SUMMARY

Features of the course that remained in place over the 16 cases included an instructional sequence that included (a) setting the context for ID instruction, examining one's learning beliefs, one's personal ID model, and surveying design tools, particularly other ID models; (b) ID instruction over a multi-phased set of components; and (c) self-assessment. The ID project was the principal learning task with task sheets providing students with explanation and guidance for each ID component. Assessment included weekly and final submission of an

ID project, a revised ID model, and a set of miscellaneous tasks, including a self-evaluation. Co-participation structures that remained in place across the cases included in-class activities, learning tasks, and text. The following sections summarize changes in the above features across the cases (see Table 4).

Table 4. Developmental Case Summary: Major Changes

C	N	Length	Design	Implementation	Evaluation
1	13	05 wk	8 phases	Unclear on task and instructional analyses	Lacked research, challenging terminology, draft concerns
2	22	15 wk	9 phases: added "Beliefs" Mission statement (MS)	MS task difficult	Needs assessment, project choice critical moments
3	20	15 wk	Performance criteria added to tasks	Group activities for mission, needs assessment, assessment choices	Concerns on group activities, high ratings on personal conferences
4	19	15 wk	Design Activity forms	Goal identification activity, MS workshop	
5	16	15 wk	ID competencies, web site	Issues of sequencing and assessment in online projects	Only 5 complete. Mixed reactions to groups, small room,
6	23	15 wk off	Technology focus On-campus needs assessment visit	Encouraging teachers from different grade levels to talk	9 projects complete, minimal attention to media and technology, overwhelmed by readings
7	15	05 wk off	1 week summer F2F, rest online, email, website	Email response to questions on tasks	Mixed performance on projects, participants as PE teachers and coaches difficult to engage on tasks
8	13	15 wk	First solo teaching Internet capabilities	Resistance to needs assessment research	Identifying teaching, assessment, technology decisions on sequence visual
9	8	15 wk	No changes from case 8	3/8 difficulties in handing in drafts Crowded room	3 technology projects, 3 ESL projects, effort needed for weekly drafts; stress from taking web-based ID course
10	17	15 wk	Design cycle categories chunking process Written project assessment provided	4/17 late with needs assessment	6 technology projects, minimal needs assessment research, minimal media details, time limitations on demo briefings
11	20	15 wk	Reflective web site, online activities	10/15 deficiencies in needs assessment	4.20 technology projects Too many tasks: design activities and online tasks

Table 4. (Continued)

C	N	Length	Design	Implementation	Evaluation
12	20	15 wk	Project outline links with design activity tasks Teaching and assessment combined in project Web board added	Weekly debriefs on progress and problems	12/20 technology projects, comments on too many activities (project, in-class, online), work
13	16	15 wk	Collaborative web pages added (Wiki)	3 wks teaching demos Wiki for needs assess.	7/16 technology projects Wiki improved revisions
14	13	15 wk	Scenario activity for needs assessment Only 1 personal conference	Resistance to needs assessment Peer support	2 technology projects More debriefing on other's projects
15	18	15 wk	Personal conference deleted WebQuest as mid-term Tables recorded teaching and assessment Prototype separated from teaching demo	Technology-ready room	10/18 technology projects Teachers settled on options early Low ratings to midterm
16	17	15 wk	11 of 17 teachers	Technology-ready room 4 weeks needed for demos	6/17 technology projects Clarity to prototype-demo tasks

Cases 1-7 Co-Teaching

Each case will be summarized by three paragraphs which identify design decisions, implementation, and evaluation, respectively.

Case 1 (Summer, 1994, 13 students). Case 1 used an 8-phase ID process representation (i.e., design tools, needs assessment, lesson sequence, assessment, teaching models, sample lesson, media, program evaluation). Case 1 used Smith and Ragan (1993) as the primary text because of its emphasis on learning principles and teaching models.

Nearly half (6 out of 13) of the students reported they were unclear about task and instructional analyses and did not include a task analysis but did submit an instructional analysis. Some submissions mixed the two tools. Because of the time demands of a 5-week summer session in Case 1, customized media packets were distributed to each student, in addition to brief presentations on the use of media.

Cases 1 (6 projects available) included a small number of projects and a majority of the projects exhibited completeness, consistency, and coherence. Students reported they needed more time to complete tasks, read the assigned articles and chapters. Three students commented that there was not enough time for reflection during this 5-week summer course. Students called for frequent re-visiting of the "big picture" of ID process and using more examples. Students provided a wide range of comments about the ID project. On the critical side, some students stated that there was too much to do, that it was a "struggle," some initially experienced confusion on the scope (i.e., "How long?") of the project. Three students reported being uncomfortable with handing in draft work. However, comments were largely favorable on the project: "Not as hard as I thought," and that the project was "the best way to learn instructional design."

Case 2 (Fall, 1994, 22 students). Case 2 added a Learning Beliefs component to the beginning of the ID process representation. Learning Beliefs, however, had always been in the course activities, just not in the formal representation. Students from Case 1 suggested that if we valued learning beliefs as an important issue, we should include beliefs as a component in the ID process. A structured learning task, a mission statement, was added to support students examining their beliefs on learning, learners, and teaching. The mid-term exam, used in Case 1, was replaced with individual conferences to increase one-on-one attention to student needs and as a more appropriate ongoing assessment tool. The first conference was held a month into the course and topics of discussion included student's mission statement, preliminary ID model, and project choice. During these conferences we as instructors learned more about their previous work and educational experiences. A second personal conference was held during the last week of the semester to discuss students' ID project, revised ID model, and self-evaluation.

Nine out of 20 students reported that their learning beliefs were expanded or clarified with the Learning Principles task. Students also reported struggling with the terminology of educational psychology and instructional design. The Learning Principles task was supported by a task sheet, three assigned readings, discussion, group activity, a mini-lecture on the differences between learning theories and their implication for instructional design, and a booklet of students' learning principles was distributed. The mission statement task was implemented to help students assimilate their important learning principles into a comprehensive statement of their view of learners, learning, and teaching. Twenty out of 22 mission statements had mismatches between students' learning principles and mission statement. Five students integrated their project description into their mission statement. Students described the mission statement as "hard work," that articulating and condensing their beliefs was a challenge.

Case 2 (4 projects available for analysis) included a small number of projects and a majority of the projects exhibited completeness, consistency, and coherence. Comments included "very demanding, time-wise," and "most intense, challenging course with just enough anxiety." Students, however, highly rated the value of course assignments (averaged 3.8 on a 1-4 scale). Students asked for more time in class to review peer's work on projects and complete the project. When asked what were the critical moments in the course, 7 out of 20 identified needs assessment, project selection (4 out of 20) and teaching model determination (2 out of 20).

Case 3 (Fall 1995, 20 students). We added performance criteria to each of the task sheets to clearly communicate our expectations for each task. We added an electronic Listserv to increase communications between and with students. Groups were used to introduce students to one another and share different perspectives and experiences. Mixing up the group membership several times during the first half of the course helped members to become acquainted and exposed them to different instructional problems. Grouping on the basis of project type was successful in the middle-to-later stages of the course when group members discussed design issues they had in common. Evaluating the effectiveness of groups during class meetings was difficult due to the large number of participants.

A needs assessment strategy was used to help students organize their research and prepare for their first personal conference. This strategy suggested that students identify what questions to ask, who to talk to, where to look for more information, and how to summarize their research. We added a "flexible understanding" way of thinking about content and implications for learners, teachers, and sequencing (McDiarmid, Ball, and Anderson, 1989). Initial topical lists of content remained the same throughout the course for some projects, depending on students' view of what was to be taught and learned in the course. Students who chose a thematic approach to their content used much of their project to lay out these themes with supporting activities. Task and instructional analyses were also introduced during the Sequence phase as a tool to help students analyze the complexity of learning tasks.

Three out of the 9 projects available for analysis lacked sufficient detail in a needs assessment, learner profile, what it meant to teach content, or a literature review. One project failed to supply a mission statement. Two projects lacked insufficient detail in a sample lesson to give a clear picture of what was to be accomplished by the lesson, while another project lacked sufficient detail to guide an evaluation of an implemented project. Six out of the 9 projects exhibited consistency of learning beliefs across the project. One project's institutional beliefs were not addressed in the project, a second project did not have a mission statement to track consistency, and a third project's mission statement was unclear. Only 3 out of 9 projects exhibited a coherence. Four lacked an identification of project goals in subsequent components, one project confused the project with the overall institutional program, and one program lacked sufficient detail in the sample lesson to test out any of the project's design decisions.

Student perceptions of group activity were both positive and critical. On the one hand, students generally regarded groups as positive activities, as opportunities to share ideas and take risks, making the discussion of reading more interesting, and helpful when confused on tasks. On the other hand, student comments included wanting more group opportunities that were better structured, more task focused, and more sensitive to members who did understanding "teacher language." Some students wanted more time to work in groups, some liked the same groups, and others preferred different groups. The ID process helped some students to examine their beliefs and teaching and to examine an instructional problem, provided "different ways to think about the learners," and "forces a teacher to look at lots of details." On the other hand, some students regarded the process (and course) as "very difficult," with too much information. Two students objected to our labeling of some tasks as "hard," preferring instead to discover this out for themselves.

Case 4 (Fall 1996, 19 students). Two ID components, including Sample Lesson to Instructional Frameworks and Sample Lesson as Prototype, were relabeled to match the chapter titles of a a text we had written for the course. A new activity for the first class session was used at the beginning called "Design A Lesson" to help students to think, write, and discuss important learning issues and as a means to introduce themselves in the first class. We grouped miscellaneous learning tasks together for 15% of the grade. The primary text for the course was the publisher's prototype of text, with Smith and Ragan (1993) as an optional text. In addition, supplemental readings, which had been periodically distributed in class, were available on reserve at the library. Design Activity forms, which were included in the publisher's prototype, were electronic files to help students begin their thinking on a particular design component.

"Design A Lesson" was used during the first class session and helped to reveal students' existing planning/design processes and the complexity of planning/designing instruction. In this task students identified 21 different issues. A Mission Statement Workshop was implemented to help students understand a mission statement's rationale and features, along with a range of personal, institutional, and learning examples. Goal identification, which was the major outcome from the needs assessment, was an ongoing challenge for some students. Some students resisted submitting goals. Some goals were unclear, too numerous, or were a mix of broad goals and activity objectives. An in-class group task was added that helped participants to identify goals from their research. We prompted students to identify the specific learning levels for each of their goals to gain a better understanding of what they were asking students to know (cognitive), do (psychomotor, social), or appreciate (social and other affective dimensions). Students were asked to specify what teaching methods they would use, the rationale for their choices, and how these approaches would support their project goals. A common problem in student projects was the lack of project goals identified in proposed learning activities; thus, it was unclear in draft submissions as to how their proposed instructional features supported their project intent. During this phase, 2-3 weeks were spent in having students enact teaching models. The Sample Lesson, or Prototype was a phase which allowed students to lay out the details of a lesson including its place in the overall instructional sequence, assessment, media, and teaching approaches, and an optional "Plan B." A task analysis and instructional analysis were requested for their prototype or sample lesson and frequently the same analysis, conducted during the Sequence phase, was used. However, students revealed misunderstandings about both tools.

All 5 projects available for analysis exhibited completeness, consistency, and coherence. Students also cited the changes in their thinking: "Totally changed the way I see the world" and "I can think and listen in terms of a designer".

Case 5 (Fall, 1997, 16 students). A web site was added to increase student access to course tasks and resources, including process learning hints (e.g., "How to Use the Text") and links to educational resources. Instructional Media was moved before Prototype in the ID process, so as to include media decisions in one's prototype lesson. We added a survey assessing their perceptions of their ID competencies at the beginning and end of the course. Weekly project submissions and the final project were assigned an equal percentage, 35%, of the final grade, to signal to students an equal importance for weekly work and final project. Class and text feedback were added as a miscellaneous assessment item to solicit student comments on our teaching efforts and newly published text. This requirement also modeled to students the practice of formative evaluation of instructional materials. We made conscious decisions about improving the use of groups in terms of group membership and group task structure. We mixed up the groups early in the semester to promote discussion from people with different backgrounds, while grouping students with similar projects mid-way through the course. We also improved group tasks to guide their thinking and subsequent reporting back for class discussion. Another change asked all participants to sit in a circle to increase eye contact, participation, and change the traditional "teacher up-front/student as audience" roles.

A Mission Statement Workshop was implemented to help students understand a mission statement's rationale and features, along with a range of personal, institutional, and learning examples. A book chapter from Eisner (1994) on curriculum ideologies was assigned to help participants think about different ways to view curriculum. Six ideologies or viewpoints on curriculum were summarized by groups in class. Learning taxonomies were also used as a conceptual tool to help students sequence content from simple to complex. A panel discussion on assessment was held with campus experts. Four of the 16 projects were web-based and questions were raised on how to sequence and assess learning on web sites. We experimented with the idea that students might try to demonstrate a teaching model they would propose in their prototype lesson and learn from the enactment. In Case 5 media was formally represented in our sequence before the Prototype phase to include its consideration in the Prototype Lesson. However, in practice, instructional media was addressed to varying degrees over the entire course. By Case 5 (Fall, 1997) instructional media questions had shifted from multimedia to web-based concerns. Using the Listserv, URL links to web-based teaching and other learning resources were suggested throughout the semester. The web site itself was used as an electronic access point for course learning tasks and existing links to other resources.

Only 5 of the 12 projects available for analysis had all components in place. Three lacked a literature review, two were missing instructional analysis in their prototype lesson, one project lacked a mission statement, and one project lacked an identification of a teaching model. However, 11 out of 12 projects exhibited a consistency of learning beliefs based on what students wrote in their mission statement and what was subsequently designed. Ten out of 12 projects achieved a coherence of ID components.

Case 6 (Spring, 1998, 23 teachers in a master's cohort). Design decisions in thie case were based on the fact that the participants were working teachers in an intact cohort program. We combined the teaching demonstration with the project's prototype lesson, and addressed Instructional Frameworks and Assessment together, since teachers worked with both on a daily basis. A KWL chart was used as a familiar and simpler tool to help teachers monitor their needs assessment progress than the charts we had used previously. Technology was an agreed-upon major theme for the teachers in their master's program and was discussed throughout the semester, particularly the scope and shape of the upcoming summer course in instructional technology. Shambaugh and Magliaro (1997) was adopted as the text along with a packet of supplementary readings. We mixed up group membership to include teachers from a range of grade levels, as they sat in approximately the same grade divisions, elementary, middle, and the high school. The purpose of this strategy was to encourage teachers to better understand each other's roles and challenges. Needs assessment, which was partly conducted as an on-campus visit to consult content and media experts, was another opportunity in which teachers talked with each other and came to better understand the differences they faced in their respective school.

Teachers pulled their mission statement from a teacher reflection paper conducted in a previous course. Two projects dealing with school district instructional technology support included their district's mission statement. One personal conference was held on the University campus, a needs assessment visit to conduct research and talk with University content and media experts. We had these teachers demonstrate a teaching model they would propose in their prototype lesson and learn from the enactment. The course web site was introduced to the teachers in the first class meeting using the high school's computer lab.

Nine of 13 projects had all required components in their project documents. Ten projects used the KWL strategy as a means to track their needs assessment progress. All projects did not bring forward information on teaching from their previous course in educational psychology. Two special education teachers included more detail than the other teachers on learners in their learner profile. Six out of 13 had incorrect or missing task and/or instructional analyses in their prototype lessons. Nine of the 13 projects exhibited a consistency of learning beliefs across their projects, while 11 of 13 appeared coherent across ID components. Six out of 13 projects were based on state learning standards. Three projects merged their instructional approaches, assessment, and media in their lesson sequence. All projects addressed instructional media, but with minimal details. One teacher remarked, "It would take me forever to do this for all my units." For some, needs assessment was viewed as time consuming and challenging.

Case 7 (Summer 1997 off-campus, 15 students). Case 7 involved another master's cohort, a group of health and physical education master's students from across the country. They met with us over one week during a summer session to get introduced to the course, and we provided comment to their draft submissions via email.

Cases 8-16 Solo Teaching

Case 8 (Fall 1998, 10 students). Cases 1-7 had been co-taught. Case 8 was the first delivery of the course taught solo by this researcher. The institution was the same, as the first instructor was on research leave. The design for the course remained the same as Case 8, as I was also completing my dissertation. One difference was the availability of an Internet-ready classroom, which was used to show the online web site and also refer to online references and resources.

As with the other cases, students resisted conducting research during their needs assessment and preferred to rely on their existing knowledge. Problem selection for their ID project remained a challenge. One international student refused to hand in "draft" work, until at the end of the course I asked him why this was the case, he replied that in his country he could not do so and that draft work was inferior and not worthy of my review. He produced his draft submissions and I credited him with having done the work. This student cued me into the cultural difference of "draft" submissions and of instructor-student relationships.

The major outcome from this solo teaching was having students record their design decisions regarding teaching strategies, assessment options, and media/technology use on their sequencing plans. Rather than submitting just descriptive summarizes of their proposed choices, I had them "map" these decisions along their schedule to visualize how these decisions would play out over time. I still received mixed results in terms of identifying project goals on their sequence plan and not seeing how they were addressing their goals in their design sequence.

Cases 9-16 were delivered at another institution, a land-grant and a comprehensive-research doctoral granting university. The course was still configured as a master's level instructional design course. Summary of the major changes across design, implementation, and evaluation stages of the developmental cycle are noted in Table 4.

Case 9 (Fall 1999, 8 students). As my first teaching assignment in a new institution, the course design for Case 9 remained the same as for Case 8. And as with previous cases, students experienced hallenges in responding to weekly design activity due dates and handing in draft work.

Students resisted needs assessment analysis as well as project selection. The room was small and did not have any Internet connections. To simplify my first teaching of this course in a new setting, I did not use a web site. Email, however, was used to respond to student questions and provide reminders.

A new development was an increased number of second-language learning projects (3 out of 8) and technology projects (3 out of 8). Second-language acquisition became a research focus for all of these cases, as many of the students in the course were international students. Students also commented on the amount of work needed to hand in weekly assignments. They were not used to this expectation from a new professor. They also provided the lowest rankings to the preliminary ID model task and the self-evaluation task, perhaps owing to not being used to this sort of expectation in a course. In addition, a concurrent enrollment with a web-based ID course provided anxiety for the 4 students enrolled in this course.

Case 10 (Fall 2000, 17 students). The major design decision was chunking the ID phases by categories: foundations ("setting the stage"), instructional problem identification, design formulation, design implementation, and revisiting/evaluation.

The classroom was too crowded for 17 students and no Internet capability was used, except for computer-based presentations and email. I used a "Design A Lesson" activity as a means for students to introduce themselves and to reveal the vocabulary used by them as educators. For the first time, I shared my personal learning principles and mission statement. I used an in-class activity where students paired up and prompted each other to discuss "What/Who/Where" options for needs assessment. One student commented that this activity felt "artificial" while another pair commented on how helpful it was to begin looking at options and to use someone else to "bounce ideas off of." Four out of the 17 students were late in submitting their needs assessment findings.

Six of the 17 projects focused on instructional technology, but with minimal details on its actual use across an intervention. Students commented on the 10-minute limitation for their teaching demonstrations, as only one course session was allotted to these (Election Day and personal conference limited the available time).

Case 11 (Fall 2001, 20 students). The major change was to add a new form of participation – the online reflective web site, which consisted of a cycle of activities for each ID phase. This cycle included an initial perception of the phase after reading the text chapter, answers to questions regarding the chapter, a presentation (Flash file), link to the course web board for peer critiques, a link to the relevant design activity(ies), and ending with a reflective question on student perceptions of the ID phase. The overall cycle of activity involved classroom, text, online responses, and design activity.

Students provided mixed performance on developing a strategy to gather research in a needs assessment ID phase. Ten out of 15 projects available for analysis revealed a deficiency in needs assessment as required by the design activity.

Four out of the 20 projects were technology project. Students commented that there were "too many things to do," with the addition of the reflective online activities. These provided me with a deeper view of what students were thinking about an ID phase, reactions to the text explanations, although unless prompted to do so, students did not freely critique their peers' work.

Case 12 (Fall 2002, 20 students). For the first time, the project outline items identified specific design activities, so that the connection could be made between draft work (design activities) and completed ID project. For the first time the Teaching and Assessment design activities were combined as one design activity. The online reflective prompts were continued for a second year. A web board was added.

The in-class activities were organized by collaborative groups based on their project type (mathematics, literacy, web delivery, second language, and technology). Tight scheduling limited the length of presentations by students during their teaching demonstrations.

Twelve out of 20 projects involved instructional technology. Students liked the web board over the online activities. The web board provides a means to post student work and to critique each other's work. Students commented favorably, however, on the design and features of each.

Case 13 (Fall 2003, 16 students). The major change in this case was to replace the online reflective web site with a Wiki, or collaborative web pages ("CoWebs"), which enabled students to post draft work and receive critiques from peers, from which revisions would be made. Three weeks were assigned for the prototype demos.

Three sets of scenario-descriptions and revisions were tried out. The first asked students to post an initial vision for their ID projects prior to a needs assessment, the second asked them to post a new set of goals for their project after a needs assessment, and the third asked students to post their selection of media and technology use. Each of these submissions to the CoWeb pages were reviewed by peers in their work groups, and the students made revisions based on these suggestions. The goal was to decrease the review time traditionally experienced by designers (Shambaugh, 2003; 2004).

Seven out of 16 projects were technology projects. The Wiki site improved the needs assessment content, breadth of research, and identification of project goals. All of the students produced a succinct instructional problem statement, the first case where this occurred. All of the projects were actual events students would be implementing and these choices contributed to clear problem statements.

Case 14 (Fall 2004, 13 students). The Wiki site was not used in this case, however, the scenario activities were retained and used during the needs assessment ID phase to improve the quality of research and decrease the revision time during this time-consuming phase. Only one personal conference was held at week 6.

An in-class activity prompting students to identify an instructional problem and response was used to assist student thinking. In the past the instructional problem was assigned out-of-class, the rationale being that this prompt required thinking time. However, an in-class prompt and peer feedback helped students begin clarifying what the specific instructional need was. Scenario-descriptions of their intended project outcomes helped students to redefine their initial vision and motivated them to conduct needs assessment based on a clearer scope of the options.

Only 2 of the 13 projects were technology-related. Students asked that more debriefing time with peers in-class be used and to hear the status of others' projects. Four of the 13 students commented that the course helped them learn more about themselves in terms of developing organizational skills and attitudes, and an appreciation of the iterative nature of designing. One student was disappointed that program evaluation was not given sufficient time in class and confusion between formative and summative forms of program evaluation. The deletion of the second personal conference aggravated this issue as one-on-one briefings about program evaluation used to occur during these conferences.

Case 15 (Fall 2005, 18 students). Owing to professional demands, both personal conferences were deleted from the syllabus. Three weeks were still needed for teaching demonstrations. The web board was still used. A webquest was used as a mid-term exam, facilitated by a technology-ready room which was used for the course.

The Teaching and Assessment design activity was modified in mid-course in terms of a table in which teaching strategies were identified in one column and how students were assessed was recorded in the second column. The Teaching Demonstration and Prototype design activities were separated.

Sixteen out of the 18 students had teaching experience, which reflected in their choice of projects and reflected on their design decisions. Specifically, these teachers identified a problem and settled on a course of action early. Ten projects were technology focused. Students gave the lowest end-of-the-semester ratings to the midterm exam, which had students in-class search online for definitions and examples of ID terminology.

Case 16 (Fall 2006, 17 students). No design changes were made for Case 16. Weather cancelled one session, while a power outage required a 4th class session for teaching demonstrations. The web board provided options for losing a class session. Groups were used extensively in this case to support the 5 international students who had just arrived in the United States. A technology-ready room supported computer-based presentations, media use, and online resources.

Eleven out of the 17 students had teaching experience. Six of the 17 projects were technology-focused. The teaching demonstrations addressed specific teaching strategies used in their projects, while their Prototype submissions documented the major teaching strategies proposed in their projects. This clarity improved the quality of presentations and separated the two activities, which until Case 15 had been merged into the same Design Activity.

DEVELOPMENTAL RESULTS – PARTICIPATION STRUCTURES

Overview. The previous section documents each course delivery by design decisions, implementation, and evaluation. Over the 16 deliveries different data sources were used to extract these developmental descriptions and frequently the data sources evolved to serve the needs of the students. For example, Likert-scale items and open-ended items on an end-of-the course self evaluation changed over time making comparisons across the cases problematic. The value of case descriptions when taken over time is that a more trustworthy set of conclusions can be drawn by the impact of design decisions on student performance, and reactions of students to teacher-developed learning tasks. One of the features of the course is the ongoing evolution of co-participation structures, those forms of activity in which learning takes place by both instructor and students. Table 2, earlier in this report, identifies the participation structures by case. A second way to report results of developmental research is to summarize the use of each of these participation structures.

Three structures have remained in place across the 16 deliveries: in-class activities, Design Activities, and the use of a text. A co-teaching ended with Case 8, instructor-to-instructor email ceased. Visually from Table 2, one can see that the use of online features were increasingly used; namely, the use of a web site for information and resources, the use of a Wiki to speed up the design review process, and the web board to post student work and receive critiques. Thus, blended learning, while using a web site in earlier cases (4-7), became a standard teaching option from Cases 11 forward.

In-class activities. Classroom activities were used to introduce, reinforce, or provide practice for students across each main topic in the course. The course assessment plan usually assigned these activities collectively as 10% of the course grade. Failure to show up for class and perform these classes resulted in a letter "drop" (e.g., from an A grade to a B grade). These were typically used in two ways: to introduce key points for that ID phase being discussed, and/or to provide practice for Design Activities. Classroom activities were designed as "jump-start" exercises in which students directly experienced the nature of what was asked in the out-of-class Design Activities.

The sequence of a class session could vary, but would following this sequence:

(1) Summary of what students posted to the web board.
(2) Warm-up activity to introduce students to the next ID phase.
(3) Mini-lecture/presentation.
(4) Jump-start activity to help students record thinking on paper; usually organized around random groups, early to promote meeting students, and later organized around content-specific groups, to provide peer feedback on similar projects.
(5) Scenario-descriptions where students record design decisions and peers critique resulting in an immediate design-review cycle and subsequent revisions.
(6) Explanation of the next Design Activity.

The 15 week semester was overall divided up into five sections to conceptually break-up the course. These sections included "Setting the Stage," which included three weeks for foundational knowledge about design, ID models, and learning theories. The second stage, "Instructional Problem Identification," provided three weeks for needs assessment. "Design Formulation" covered four weeks and examined sequencing issues, teaching, media/technology, and assessment decisions. "Design Implementation" covered three weeks and involved time for students to present teaching strategies that they have proposed in their projects. The final three weeks involve program evaluation, a course debrief involving revised personal ID models, and student evaluation of the course and their learning.

Design activities. Student learning was further assisted through specific learning tasks, which are organized by task rationale, task procedures, and task assessment. Over time, these modified in terms of their detail but have stabilized in terms of 15 activities which when completed produce an ID project. These Design Activities include: Initial Intent Statement, Preliminary Personal ID Model, Mission Statement, Instructional Problem and Needs Assessment Strategy, Revised Intent Statement, Instructional Sequence, Instructional Framework and Assessment Plan, Teaching Demonstration, Prototype, Program Evaluation, Revised Personal ID Model, Self Evaluation and Course Evaluation, and Final ID Project. Over the 12 years the overall format added task rationale and a reflective question designed to help us to learn more about the thinking process of each student. Students would receive feedback on the submission in writing and sometimes on the webboard where the submission was posted.

Text. Textbook use did not vary substantially, as this researcher and co-instructor wrote and published a textbook for this course. The book was organized by ID phase and 30 design activities with supporting text, reflective questions, scenario-stories, and references. The book was visually designed with font size/choice, line spacing, text organization, and summary tables to support novice learning of instructional design. The text was designed as a "tour" through the ID process phases using Design Activities to experience and think about design decisions.

Personal conference. One-on-one conferences with students were used in 13 of the 16 cases, and were designed as personalized assessment meetings. Conference 1 was scheduled around week 6 of a 15-week semester. Its purpose was to discuss project choice, mission statement, preliminary ID model, and needs assessment strategy. A second conference was scheduled around week 12 and its purpose was to help students make final ID decisions, revisions to the document, and complete the project.

F2F/Email. Email consisted of electronic communication between the two instructors during cases 1-7, frequently totally up to 500 queries, replies, and discussions. Face-to-face discussions between instructors during cases 1-7 usually consisted of several meetings prior to a course and one meeting prior to each class session. Email between instructor(s) and students also occurred and varied considerably over the 12 years. As online capabilities improved over the years, most of the email exchanges between instructor and student reduced in amount and dealt mostly with scheduling problems. Questions on tasks moved to online web boards. Personal conferences between instructor(s) and students were used across cases 1-13. These provided one-on-one formative evaluation of student performance and concerns.

Web site. A website was used for seven cases. Cases 3-6 used a website for informational purposes, but was particularly useful for Case 7 which involved an off-campus cohort of students scattered across the United States. Cases 11-12 field tested a "reflective" web site rather than as an online source for class materials and information. The site consisted of a reflective cycle of thinking activities organized by major topic and used Flash files to provide animated prompts and explanations for major topics. The purpose of this reflective structure was to learn more about students' initial reactions to an ID phase and to see how these perceptions evolved and contributed to their ID project decisions. The strategy was used for 2 years to provide some evidence on its veracity. On a pragmatic level, the additional activities proved too much for some students to handle during a semester. However, on a cognitive level, what students wrote provided some insight on the different views students had on the ID processes, particularly on how the phases relate to each other, which I believe is important for ID process understanding. The connections between the ID phases seems critical for one to use the process, although novice understanding of the process is centered on the ID phases themselves, which is how they are configured in the text and Design Activities. The iterative nature of revising the output of each ID phase is a new experience for students who are accustomed to the culture of the college classroom to more bounded and finite assignments. This reflective use for a web site merits future consideration and a reconfiguration of the technical features to take advantage of improving software and online systems.

Wiki. Cases 13-14 field tested an online "wiki," or a set of collaborative web pages which posted draft student work and required students to provide feedback on iterative design activities. The collaborative (CoWeb) pages were visually spartan and required little coding; however, students are accustomed to more interface detail. More direct instruction and experience in class sessions are needed to acquaint students with this simple online tool. Since the use of this tool, blogs have been used in some settings. Again, this is another strategy that merits reconsideration. As with the reflective online activities, the bigger issue is giving students more to do, and the course has always had plenty of steady activity configured into the course (Shambaugh, 1993, 1994).

Web board. Cases 12-16 used a web board, which provided for threaded discussions, archiving of course materials, and posting of student work and peer critiques. The primary purpose of the webboard is to post course materials and student work. Asynchronous peer critiques are possible with appropriate activity instructions. A classroom management value is that students see what other students do. In courses where there is a right answer this would be an obvious problem as students could wait to see what was posted and submit that response. However, in this course there are no right answers, just appropriate responses to student needs. The same people tend to post first and the same people post last or even late. As the system provides a time stamp to the posting late work is automatically recorded. In my assessment system late work earns 50%. Pedagogically, the web board acts as a course portfolio. The files and structure are archived weekly and the final archive record stores what students did. Frequently I distribute CDs of their work so students have a copy of what happened in the course.

METHODOLOGICAL ISSUES

Implications of developmental research will be discussed, including improvements for student learning, methodology for research, and how iterative inquiry provides a basis for how such results might be archived and retrieved and "mined" for individual and institutional needs. The chapter provides guidelines on the use of developmental research in terms of identifying a study focus, study procedures, and integrating teacher research into one's responsibilities.

Attributes and Limitations

Van den Akker (1999) has characterized research evaluating educational interventions as providing answers that are frequently "too narrow, too superficial, or too late to do any good." Developmental research addresses these issues of meaningfulness, timeliness, generalizability, and usefulness in four ways:

(1) Developmental research can involve collaborators in the analysis of practical problems and the testing of designed solutions in actual practice. These collaborators may include researchers, designers, content experts, teachers, *and* students.
(2) Developmental research uses a structured approach, consisting of design and development, implementation, and evaluation stages, to systematically collect and evaluate data. Developmental research frequently occurs over multiple cycles to provide more trustworthy results.
(3) The developmental research cycle provides a structure and path for ongoing course development.
(4) Developmental research can include whatever appropriate mix of quantitative or qualitative analyses is needed. As such, developmental research can be regarded as an integrated approach in which multiple research techniques might play a role.

Methodological Considerations

Figure 3 outlines the types of documentation that might be useful to study one's teaching. The documentation is categorized in terms of course design decisions, course implementation, and course evaluation.

Course Design Decisions	Course Implementation	Course Evaluation
Participants Learning outcomes Learning tasks Assessment plan Materials Media and Technology	Weekly plan Weekly materials Student reactions ("exit slips," comments, your observations) Student learning Instructor adjustments Mid-course survey ("temperature check")	Student learning Student perceptions of their learning Student perceptions of course Instructor course summary

Figure 3. Systematic Documentation of Teaching.

Below are guidelines to keep in mind when conducting developmental research of one's teaching.

- *Identify the research objectives for the developmental research.* These objectives will include the design objectives for the artifact, innovation, or intervention; the implementation objectives, or what occurs during instruction; and the evaluation objectives, which can include what students learn, as well as their perceptions of their learning and your teaching.
- *Develop IRB materials for each course.* If you are planning on disseminating your results, develop IRB materials, as required by your institution. Once developed, this activity becomes relatively easy to accomplish each semester.
- *Identify the data sources for each phase of the developmental research cycle.* Determine what data you need to answer the questions and how *specifically* each data source contributes to your understanding of the research objectives.
- *Document data collection and management procedures.* Determine how each form of data will be collected and stored. A 3-ring notebook works well in storing data analysis artifacts, a strategy that separates the original data from the analysis and provides a means to track the analysis sequence from data source to data reduction to data reporting. Digital files of student artifacts are optimal because they reduce the storage space requirements and provide a ready-made artifact that can be analyzed electronically. Keeping a procedural summary of how each data source is analyzed will be critical as some data sources will change over time, as teaching decisions must also change.
- *Analyze data to address research objectives.* One caution in data analysis during the implementation stage of developmental research is to remain descriptive in terms of teaching actions, how students reacted, and what adjustments were made. Remaining

descriptive helps to keep premature interpretation from entering the data reduction documents. The subsequent analysis artifacts will vary depending on the analysis method chosen, but typically will include survey results; categorical analysis of open-ended student responses, notes and interviews; structured summaries, and tables (see Miles and Huberman, 1994, for examples). This data reduction provides an analysis of the original data and allows a condensed view of the data sources. Scrutiny on this level of analysis may reveal that some further analysis is needed, such as coding of structured summaries to reveal themes as well as to identify exceptions and differences (Spradley, 1980). The analysis method may also look for contrasts, comparisons, and exemplars. The point here is that a data reduction strategy should be planned so one has a system of moving data from its original source to a more manageable form.

- *Use care in analyzing across cases.* An across-case analysis reports the changes in design decisions, implementation, and evaluation of the intervention. One should attempt to compare differences across cases but be cautioned about "averaging or filtering" out the differences inherent in each course delivery. As Huberman and Miles (1998) have commented, "each case has a specific history–which we discard at our peril–but it is a history contained within the general principles that influence its development" (p. 194).

- *Address validity and limitations of the study.* A source for bias in developmental research is the large amount of data, which may lead to missing important information or overweighting some findings due to focusing on a particular and large set of data. Personal involvement increases the possibility that recorded observations highlight particular incidents while ignoring others. The use of journals records observations or design decisions that would otherwise be lost. Personal involvement also implies a danger in being selective and overconfident with some data. One suggestion is to check descriptions and analysis of each case with students and peer review outside of the course, or with peers or co-instructors.

- *Write up the results.* Dissemination necessitates the need to transform developmental research findings to a publication audience and format. Students also appreciate this information at the beginning of a new course because your values and expectations are articulated and public – something that does not often happen in classrooms.

- *Final guideline.* If one chooses to conduct developmental research for research purposes, we encourage faculty to use the findings to improve their teaching. To ensure that developmental research "pays off" over time the design decisions must incorporate results from the evaluation stage of a previous cycle or iteration. The caveat here is to start small. Small steps allow for retreat and regrouping, as well as adaptation by both the students and the instructor. It is through the repeated iterations of this cycle that the research gathers strength, validity, and reliability.

IMPLICATIONS

Openly studying teaching enables one to model teacher inquiry for students and that one is willing to learn alongside students. One comes to better understand the content from a student's point of view, what they know and learn, and what is relevant to them. Such a stance underscores the importance of student participation in the process and the evidence that specific feedback is considered and included in the design decisions. At the beginning of each semester you can share what you have learned and what students have said about the course, as well as how to be successful in the course. In other words, data from students is shared with students up front. Results from ongoing developmental research expand teaching beyond presentations and work sheets. Student and instructor participation expands to include new forms of participation (Wenger, 1998), such as classroom activities (mini-lectures, jump-start activities), online activities, personal face-to-face conferences, textbook, and e-mail. A challenge is to analyze the implementation data as it accumulates weekly, so students might benefit from written comments and teaching adjustments during the course.

Conducting this type of inquiry forces one to become more systematic in design, collection, management, and analysis of data (Shambaugh and Magliaro, 2001). Being more systematic in describing teaching forces one to be clear about learning beliefs and the underlying theoretical basis for teaching. Over time one becomes more practiced in being systematic with course development. In developmental research, as Reeves (2000) cautions and encourages, "Expect to work very hard. Be patient and persevere. And enjoy the challenge and reward of a career worth having for its contributions to the greater good" (p. 26).

CONCLUSION

The goal for developmental research is to seek an understanding of how an educational artifact, process, or intervention addresses educational goals (Reeves, 2000). As Shulman (1986) has advocated, "Both our scientific knowledge of rules and principles ... and our knowledge of richly described and critically analyzed cases combine to define the knowledge base of teaching" (p. 32). Developmental research provides a methodology to help designers and teachers to build a personalized knowledge base for teaching. Studying one's teaching over time not only contributes to one's research portfolio but also to a discipline's pedagogical knowledge base. Developmental research suggests, too, a long-range potential. Developmental research can contribute to improvement of educational interventions, using models and other processes, courses, and media/technology artifacts, as well as adding to the knowledge about this development through generalized instructional frameworks and design principles that can be re-used and shared. Developmental research provides a vantage point for collaborators to talk about their roles, whether these roles be pragmatic (design, teaching) or knowledge-building (research). We encourage readers to consider developmental research as a systematic tool to study their teaching and to take under consideration that inquiry into teaching will prove invaluable to your professional development as well as the development of your students.

REFERENCES

Bullough, R. V., and Gitlin, A. (2001). *Becoming a student of teaching: Linking knowledge production and practice* (2nd ed). New York: RoutledgeFalmer.

Cochran-Smith, M., and Lytle, S. (1992). Communities for teacher research: Fringe or forefront? *American Journal of Education, 100*, 298-323.

Dick, W., Carey, L., and Carey, J. O. (2005). *The systematic design of instruction* (6th ed.). Boston, MA: Pearson.

Eisner, E. W. (1994). *The educational imagination: On the design and evaluation of school programs* (3rd ed.). New York: Macmillan.

Graham, C. R. (in press). Blended learning systems: Definition, current trends, and future directions. In Bonk, C. J., and Graham, C. R. (Eds.). *Handbook of blended learning: Global perspectives, local designs*. San Francisco, CA: Pfeiffer.

Huberman, A. H., and Miles, M. B. (1998). Data management and analysis methods. In N. Denzin, and Y. Lincoln (Eds.), *Collecting and interpreting qualitative materials* (pp. 179-210). Thousand Oaks, CA: Sage.

McDiarmid, G. W., Ball, D. L., and Anderson, C. W. (1989). Why staying one chapter ahead doesn't really work: Subject-specific pedagogy. In M. C. Reynolds (Ed.), *Knowledge base for the beginning teacher* (193-205). New York: Pergamon.

Miles, M. B., and Huberman, A. M. (1994). *Qualitative data analysis: An expanded sourcebook* (2nd ed.). Thousand Oaks, CA: Sage.

Reeves, T. C. (2000). Socially responsible educational technology research. *Educational Technology 40*(6), 19-28.

Richey, R. C., Klein, J. D., and Nelson, W. A. (2003). Developmental research. In D. H. Jonassen (Ed.) *Handbook of research for educational communications and technology* (2nd ed.) (pp. 1099-1130). Mahwah, NJ: Erlbaum.

Seels, B., and Richey, R. C. (1994). *Instructional technology: The definition and domains of the field*. Washington, DC: Association for Educational Communications and Technology.

Shambaugh, N. (2003). Use of CoWebs in scenario-based ID instruction. *26th Annual Proceedings – Anaheim: Selected Papers On the Practice of Educational Communications and Technology*, National Convention of the Association for Educational Communications and Technology (AECT), Research and Theory Division (pp. 400-407).

Shambaugh, N. (2004). Using student-developed scenarios to couple design and reflection. *TechTrends: Linking Research and Practice to Improve Learning, 48*(3), 26-30.

Shambaugh, R. N., and Magliaro, S. G. (1997). *Mastering the possibilities: A process approach to instructional design*. Boston, MA: Allyn and Bacon.

Shambaugh, R. N., and Magliaro, S. G. (2001). A reflexive approach for teaching and learning instructional design. *Educational Technology Research and Development, 49*(2), 69-92.

Shulman, L. (1986). Paradigms and research programs in the study of teaching: A contemporary perspective. In M. C. Wittrock (Ed.), *Handbook of research on teaching* (3rd ed.) (pp. 3-36). New York: Macmillan.

Smith, P. L., and Ragan, T. J. (1993). *Instructional design*. New York: Merrill.

Spradley (1980). *Participant observation*. Fort Worth, TX: Harcourt Brace Jovanovich.

Tharp, R. G., and Gallimore, R. (1988). *Rousing minds to life: Teaching, learning, and schooling in social context*. Cambridge: Cambridge University Press.

van den Akker, J. (1999). Principles and methods of development research. In J. van den Akker, R. Branch, K. Gustafson, N. Nieveen, and T. Plomp (Eds.). *Design approaches and tools in education and training* (pp. 45-58). Dordrecht: Kluwer.

Wenger, E. (1998). *Communities of practice: Learning, meaning, and identity*. New York: Cambridge University Press.

Yin, R. K. (2002). *Case study research: Design and methods* (3rd ed.). Thousand Oaks, CA: Sage.

In: Global Issues in Higher Education
Editor: Pamela B. Richards, pp. 37-56

Chapter 2

HIGHER EDUCATION AND GROWTH IN STATE WORKFORCE PRODUCTIVITY, 1980-2000: EVIDENCE ON THE PUBLIC BENEFITS OF COLLEGE EDUCATION

*Michael B. Paulsen** and *Nasrin Fatima*#

* The University of Iowa, USA
# Independent Research Consultant

ABSTRACT

Over the past twenty-five years, the share of the burden of financing higher education borne by society has continuously decreased, while the share of that burden falling on the shoulders of students and their families has steadily increased. This raises the recurrent need to carefully examine and justify the role of society and the public sector in the finance of higher education. To the extent that investment in higher education generates public or external benefits to society—such as overall economic growth—substantial levels of public or government spending on higher education can be justified. Hence, the *purpose* of this study was to estimate the effects of initial investments in higher education on the subsequent growth in workforce productivity in the 50 individual state economies during the periods of 1980-1990 and 1990-2000.

The dependent variable in this study was the 10-year growth in state workforce productivity. The independent variables in this study were: initial state workforce productivity and initial cumulative investment in higher education at the beginning of each 10-year period of growth, and a composite measure of economic activity in ten industrial sectors in each state economy during each 10-year period of analysis. The model was first estimated with regression using data for the 10-year period from 1980-1990; again using data for the 10-year period from 1990-2000; and finally using pooled data from the two 10-year periods of analysis (1980-1990 and 1990-2000).

Findings indicated that the effect of initial cumulative investment in higher education on the subsequent 10-year growth in state workforce productivity was statistically significant and was substantial and similar in magnitude across all three samples. In

---

* Michael B. Paulsen, Professor of Higher Education, Educational Policy and Leadership Studies, N499 Lindquist Center, The University of Iowa, Iowa City, IA 52242. michael-paulsen@uiowa.edu

addition, as expected, the initial level of state workforce productivity was significantly and negatively related to, and the expansion in economic activity in ten industrial sectors in the state economies was significantly and positively related to, the subsequent 10-year growth in state workforce productivity.

INTRODUCTION

Over the past twenty-five years, the relative proportions of public and private investment in higher education have changed substantially (Toutkoushian, 2001). In an apparent response to federal devolution, rising claims on the public purse, resistance to tax increases, budget-balancing restrictions, and recessions in the early 1990s and early 2000s, states have diverted budget shares previously committed to higher education—the largest discretionary item in state budgets—to the requisite funding of entitlements including new state priorities such as corrections and Medicaid; and most states have experienced slow growth, zero growth or even cuts in appropriations to public institutions (Mortensen, 1998, 2003; Roherty, 1997; Zemsky and Wegner, 1997; Zumeta, 2003). The effects of this ongoing diversion in budget shares have been, and continue to be, clearly manifested in persistent increases in the tuition and fees charged to students (Breneman and Finney, 1997; College Board, 2006a; Cunningham, et al., 2001; Paulsen, 1991, 2000). At the federal level, the relative proportions of available financial aid have shifted substantially from non-repayable grant assistance to repayable educational loans (College Board, 2006b; Gladieux, 2002; St. John, 1994). As a result of these changes in state appropriations, tuition charges, and growth in loan aid relative to grant aid, society now bears a smaller and decreasing share of the burden of financing higher education and a larger and growing burden now falls on the shoulders of individual students and their families—a burden that is particularly onerous for students from lower-income backgrounds (Mumper, 2001; Paulsen, 2001b; Thomas and Perna, 2004; Toutkoushian, 2001). Moreover, these decreases in the proportion of educational costs borne by society relative to students appear to have been made incrementally and with remarkably little explicit and careful public policy debate, analysis or consensus (Callan and Finney, 1997; Paulsen and Smart, 2001). Therefore, the shrinking share of educational costs now borne by society once again raises and intensifies the recurrent need to carefully examine and justify the role of society and the public sector in the finance of higher education (Fatima and Paulsen, 2004; Geske and Cohn, 1998; Johnstone, 1999; Paulsen, 1996a, 1996b, 2001b).

The rationale that is most commonly used to justify the role of government, or the public sector, in the finance of higher education is based on the existence of social, public, or external benefits associated with the decisions of individual students to invest in higher education (Baum, 2004; Carnegie Commission on Higher Education, 1973; Geske and Cohn, 1998; Paulsen, 2001b; Solmon and Fagnano, 1995; Wolfe, 1995). However, in recent years, rhetoric about the benefits of a college education has shifted substantially toward a strong emphasis on the private benefits of higher education often to the exclusion of serious consideration of the nature and importance of public or external benefits that accrue to society from investment in higher education (Baum and Payea, 2004, 2005; Institute for Higher Education Policy, 1998; Paulsen and Toutkoushian, 2006). In response to this trend, the American Council on Education—a leader among the many higher education associations actively engaged in examining key policy issues—recently initiated its *Solutions for Our*

Future program to broaden the scope of rhetoric to once again include both private *and* public benefits in explicit policy discussions of the critical outcomes of investment in higher education (American Council on Education, 2006; Paulsen and Toukoushian, 2006).

A number of taxonomies and reports of empirical evidence of the public or social benefits–both tangible and intangible--of investment in higher education have appeared in the literature (Baum and Payea, 2004, 2005; Baum, Payea and Steele, 2006; Bowen, 1977; Cohn and Geske, 1990; Institute for Higher Education Policy, 1998, 2005; Midwest Higher Education Compact, 2005; Pascarella and Terenzini, 1991; Perna, 2005; Solmon and Fagnano, 1995; Wolfe, 1995) and a number of studies have provided evidence of public benefits in terms of computed social rates of return (McMahon, 1991; McMahon and Wagner, 1982), estimates of economic impact, and estimates of the contribution of higher education to economic growth (Caffrey and Isaacs, 1971; Fatima and Paulsen, 2004; Leslie and Brinkman, 1988; Leslie and Slaughter, 1992; Pencavel, 1993).

The contribution of higher education to economic growth has been the focus of many studies documenting the public or social benefits of higher education; nevertheless, problems of measurement and estimation persist in this literature (Pencavel, 1993). However, based on his review of this literature, Pencavel (1993) concluded that the most persuasive evidence of the contribution of investment in higher education to economic growth could be documented in investigations that "examine the growth records of a cross-section of countries and determine the association between these growth rates and the educational attainment of the populations or labor forces" (p. 61). A number of well-crafted studies of this nature have now been conducted using a cross-section of national economies (Barro and Sala-i-Martin, 1992, 1995; Baumol, Blackman and Wolff, 1989). The study presented here used an approach similar to the one suggested by Pencavel (1993) to examine the nature of public or external benefits associated with investment in higher education. However, instead of studying the effects of higher education on economic growth in a cross-section of national economies, the present study examined the effects of investment in higher education on growth in workforce productivity for a cross-section of 50 state economies in the U.S. over two consecutive 10-year periods of growth, thereby building and expanding upon a relatively new line of inquiry in the higher education literature (Fatima and Paulsen, 2004; Paulsen, 1996a, 1996b). In particular, the *purpose* of this study was to estimate the effects of investments in higher education on the subsequent growth in workforce productivity in the 50 individual state economies during the periods of 1980-1990 and 1990-2000.

A study investigating the contributions of higher education to state workforce productivity is significant on several grounds. First, if the United States is to enjoy continued economic prosperity, it must continue to advance the productivity of its workforce. The findings of this study provide researchers, policy analysts, policy makers and practitioners with potentially important information and insights about how investment in higher education impacts the growth of state and national productivity in general, and the growth of state workforce productivity in particular. Second, given the existence of public or external benefits to investment in higher education, public expenditure on higher education is very important in order to maintain standards of social efficiency in the allocation of state and national resources and equity in the distribution of costs and benefits for higher education consumers. Findings of this study regarding the existence and magnitude of public benefits attributable to investment in higher education provide a potentially strong rationale or justification for sustaining or expanding public expenditure on higher education (Baum, 2004;

Paulsen, 2001b). Third, a search of the literature on economic impacts of higher education revealed that very few studies have examined the effects of investment in higher education on the subsequent growth in workforce productivity in state economies (Fatima and Paulsen, 2004; Paulsen, 1996a, 1996b). So, the findings of this study serve to advance knowledge and understanding about the existence and nature of the public benefits of investment in higher education in state economies, the magnitude of the effect of investment in higher education on subsequent growth in state workforce productivity, and as a result, the benefit-cost ratio associated with public investment in higher education.

CONCEPTUAL FRAMEWORK

The overall conceptual framework for the present study was informed by several noteworthy theoretical contributions from the discipline of economics: human capital theory, public sector economic theory, convergence theory of economic growth, and industrial differentiation. First, because the present study conceptualizes expenditure on higher education as a form of investment, the theory of human capital serves as an important and useful theoretical framework and conceptual foundation for this study. The theory of human capital asserts that human beings invest in themselves, by means of education, training, or other activities, which raises their future productivity and increases their lifetime earnings (G. Becker, 1993; Cohn and Geske, 1990; Paulsen, 2001a). However, investment in higher education by individual students can yield both private and public benefits (Baum and Payea, 2004, 2005; Baum, Payea and Steele, 2006; Cohn and Geske, 1990; Institute for Higher Education Policy, 2005; Leslie and Brinkman, 1988; Paulsen, 2001a, 2001b; Solmon and Fagnano, 1995; Wolfe, 1995). An example of a private benefit would be the additional earnings that accrue to a college graduate compared to a high school graduate (W. Becker, 1992; College Board, 2006a; Geske and Cohn, 1998), while an example of a public benefit-- also known as a social or external benefit--would be an increase in overall productivity of a state's workforce that results in additions to everyone's income rather than only the incomes of the individual students investing in higher education (Baumol, et al., 1989; Fatima and Paulsen, 2004; Leslie and Brinkman, 1988; Paulsen, 2001a; Pencavel, 1993). Consequently, if a country or a state invests in the higher education of its citizens, this would in turn, be expected to increase its economic growth (Barro, 2001) and the overall productivity of its workforce (Baumol, et al., 1989). This more productive workforce would tend to result in increases in the earnings for many other workers in the labor force—i.e., not just for the individual students who invested in higher education. Furthermore, higher earnings of the citizens of a country or a state will increase the tax revenue for government services, including subsidies to institutions or students that promote further investment in higher education.

Second, public sector economics provides another important theoretical contribution to the overall conceptual framework for this study (Hyman, 2002; Musgrave and Musgrave, 1984; Stiglitz, 2000). In relation to higher education, public sector economics deals with the government's role and public investment in higher education, particularly in the form of subsidies and other public policies that affect students' decisions about investment in higher education (Paulsen, 2001b). One of the primary functions of public investment in higher education is to allocate resources in a socially efficient manner (Hyman, 2002; Musgrave and Musgrave, 1984; Stiglitz, 2000). However, individual student investors consider only the private benefits relative to costs in their investment or enrollment decisions. If it can be demonstrated that substantial public benefits are created as a result of individual students' investments in higher education--that is, benefits that are not captured or internalized by the individual students themselves but are dispersed among the members of society in general and are "external" to the investment decisions of individual students--then public expenditure on higher education is both justified and warranted to avoid a socially inefficient underinvestment in higher education (Baum, 2004; Paulsen, 2001b; Solmon and Fagnano, 1995; Wolfe, 1995). In the presence of public or external benefits, public expenditures in the form of subsidies to institutions (e.g., state appropriations) or to students (e.g., grants) are required in order to alter, and make more attractive, the perceived benefit-cost ratios of individual student investors, thereby stimulating a greater and more socially efficient or optimal level of investment in higher education (Paulsen, 2001b).

Third, neoclassical growth theory (Barro and Sala-i-Martin, 1995) predicts that economies with constant returns to scale technology and diminishing returns to each input, demonstrate a tendency towards convergence, provided that technologies, infrastructure, human capital, savings, and population growth rates are similar. The convergence hypothesis, broadly defined, acknowledges that the economies of less developed countries tend to catch up with the economies of more advanced nations in terms of level of per capita income or product (Barro and Sala-i-Martin, 1992). Preliminary findings about economic growth in state economies, has revealed that this convergence phenomenon is also characteristic of growth in state economies over time (Barro and Sala-i-Martin, 1995; Paulsen, 1996a, 1996b). Therefore, convergence theory was also included in the overall conceptual framework for this study.

Finally, productivity growth in either a national or a state economy is also influenced by the industrial differentiation or variation in industrial structure across economies and the corresponding levels of economic activity in each of the various industrial sectors that constitute each overall economy. During any period in which economic or productivity growth is being examined, the economies of individual units–such as states or countries–can be differentially affected by aggregate shocks, either positive or negative, that affect selected industrial sectors, such as agriculture, oil, or manufacturing, during the period of analysis (Barro and Sala-i-Martin, 1995). For example, a contraction in the oil industry would have a substantial negative impact on economic activity in oil-dependent state economies such as Texas, but have much less effect on economic activity in Iowa, which has little oil-related industry. In general, the share or proportion of output emanating from specific industrial sectors varies considerably across state or national economies, and these differences must be accounted for in any examination of the determinants of economic or productivity growth across economies. Therefore, a comprehensive, detailed measure of such economic activity, following the work of Barro and Sala-i-Martin (1992), was used in the present study.

RESEARCH DESIGN

Multiple regression was used to analyze the relationships between the dependent variable—the 10-year growth in state workforce productivity—and all the independent variables—initial state workforce productivity and initial cumulative investment in higher education at the beginning of a 10-year period of growth, and economic activity in ten industrial sectors in the state economies during a 10-year period of analysis. PC-SAS version 9 was used to estimate the coefficients of the model. The basic model--and the regression equation estimated--is expressed in Equation (1). The coefficients of the model were estimated using extant data on all 50 state economies for two consecutive 10-year periods of growth—1980-1990 and 1990-2000.

$$\text{GROWTH}_{i,t+10/t} = b_0 + b_0' \, \text{PERIOD}_{t+10} + b_1 \text{PROD}_{i,t} + b_2 \text{HIGHED}_{i,t} + \\ + b_3 \text{ECONACT}_{i,j,t+10/t} + u_{i,t}$$

(Eq. 1)

where
$i = 1$ ....50 states.
$t = 1^{st}$ year and $t+10 = 10^{th}$ year of each of the two 10-year growth periods (i.e., 1980-1990 and 1990-2000) examined in this study.
$j = 1$ ....10 industries.

GROWTH $_{i,t+10/t}$ = 10-year growth in workforce productivity in state i from t to t+10. Growth in state workforce productivity (GROWTH) was measured as the percent change in inflation-adjusted gross state product per worker for state i from year t to year t+10. Data on gross state product for 1980, 1990, and 2000 were acquired from the Bureau of Economic Analysis (2003). State labor force data for 1980, 1990, and 2000 were obtained from the U.S. Bureau of the Census (1983a, 1993a, 2001a).

PERIOD $_{t+10}$ = binary variable comparing the 2nd to the 1st of the two 10-year periods of analysis and PERIOD $^-$ 0 for 1980-1990 and =1 for 1990-2000.

PROD$_{i,t}$ = the initial workforce productivity for state i in year t. Initial workforce productivity (PROD) was measured as the inflation-adjusted dollar value of the initial level of workforce productivity--i.e., gross state product per worker--for state i in year t. Data on gross state product for 1980 and 1990 were acquired from the Bureau of Economic Analysis (2003). State labor force data for 1980 and 1990 were obtained from the U.S. Bureau of the Census (1983a, 1993a).

HIGHED$_{i,t}$ = initial cumulative investment in higher education for state i in year t. Initial cumulative investment in higher education (HIGHED) was measured as the fraction of high school graduates age 25 and over who had completed four or more years of college for state i in year t. Alternatively, this variables may be viewed—in microeconomic theoretical terms—as the *initial stock of human capital* in the form college-educated members of the state's labor force at the beginning of a 10-year period of analysis. Data on high school graduates in the states for 1980 and 1990 were acquired from the U.S. Bureau of Census (1983b, 1993b). Educational attainment data by state—i.e., the number of persons age 25 and over who had completed four or more years of college—for 1980 and 1990 were obtained from the U.S. Bureau of the Census (1983b) and National Center for Education Statistics (1992).

ECONACT$_{i,j,t+10/t}$ = the weighted average of economic activity—i.e., expansion or contraction--in gross state product from industrial sectors j=1-10, in state i from t to t+10. Economic activity (ECONACT) was measured as the weighted average of the percentages of growth or decline in the gross state product per capita of the nation—from year t to year t+10-

-originating from each of 10 distinct industries, where the "weights" represent the shares of each state's own gross state product that originate from each of those 10 separate industrial sectors for state i in year t. Data on gross state product for 1980, 1990, and 2000 were acquired from the U.S. Bureau of Economic Analysis (2003). State data on population for 1980, 1990 and 2000 were acquired from the U.S. Bureau of the Census (2001b). Aggregate disturbances or shocks—that is, expansions or contractions—in economic activity of various industries on the national level can have differential effects on the gross state products of individual state economies according to differences in the industrial compositions of state economies.[1] Because of the importance of estimating and controlling for these effects, a complex and comprehensive measure of economic activity was constructed.[2] This measure captures the subtle patterns of changes in economic activity in each of ten industries that contribute to the nation's aggregated gross state product and to each state's gross state product and its growth during the period of analysis. For state i, the variable ECONACT below was calculated as expressed in Equation 2:

$$\text{ECONACT} = \sum_{j=1}^{10} W_{ijt} \log [Y_{jt+10}/ Y_{jt}] \qquad \text{(Eq 2)}$$

where i = 1...50 states, j = 1...10 industrial sectors,[3] and t is the initial or first year and t + 10 is the final or tenth year in each of the two ten-year periods of growth examined in this study, which extend from 1980 to 1990 and from 1990 to 2000. Y_{jt} is the total gross state product per capita for the national economy originating in sector j at time t (i.e., 1980 or 1990), Y_{jt+10} is the total gross state product per capita for the national economy originating in sector j at time t + 10 (i.e., 1990 or 2000), and log $[Y_{jt+10}/ Y_{jt}]$ is the percentage change in total gross state product per capita for the national economy originating in sector j between time t and time t + 10. Finally, W_{ijt} is the weight of industrial sector j in state i's gross product at time t (i.e., 1980 or 1990). Combining all these elements from Equation 2 above, this variable represents the weighted average of the percentages of growth or decline in the gross state product of the national economy originating from each of ten distinct industries, where the weights represent the shares of each state's gross state product originating in each of the ten industries.

$u_{i,t}$ = a random disturbance or error term with a mean of 0 and a variance of σ^2 that is distributed normally and independently over time periods and across state economies. Note

---

[1] For example, recessions in the manufacturing or agricultural industry during the period of analysis could suppress growth in gross state product and workforce productivity in states with heavy concentrations in these industries, while states with smaller concentrations in these industries would not be adversely affected by such recessions.

[2] This measure is derived from a similar measure used by Barro and Sala-i-Martin (1992, 1995) in their research on the economic growth—and convergence of growth—of national, regional, and state economies.

[3] For this study, the sources of gross state product in the national and state economies were disaggregated and divided into 10 industrial sectors: agriculture; mining; construction; manufacturing; transportation and public utilities; wholesale trade; retail trade; finance, insurance, and real estate; services; and government enterprises. These are the aggregated industrial categories presented in the Standard Industrial Classification used by the Bureau of Economic Analysis (e.g., see Friedenberg and Beemiller, 1997, Appendix A, p. 40) We followed Fatima and Paulsen (2004) in this regard, however, Barro and Sala-i-Martin (1992, 1995) also used a quite similar, but not identical, set of industrial sectors in their analyses.

that potential violations of assumptions of homoskedasticity due to the analysis of aggregated data for large cross-section units (i.e., state economies) is addressed below.

b_0 = the net effect on the 10-year growth in workforce productivity due to factors not specified in the equation.

b_0' = the difference in 10-year growth in workforce productivity between the 1st and 2nd 10-year periods (Hypothesis: b_0' >0).

b_1 = the effect on the 10-year growth in workforce productivity due to a one-unit increase in PROD (Hypothesis: b_1<0).

b_2 = the effect on the 10-year growth in workforce productivity due to a one-unit increase in HIGHED (Hypothesis: b_2>0).

b_3 = the effect on the 10-year growth in workforce productivity due to a one-unit increase in ECONACT (Hypothesis: b_3>0).

The hypothesized relationships between each independent variable and the dependent variable are identified in parentheses above. That is, consistent with the convergence theory of economic growth, PROD was expected to be inversely related to GROWTH (b_1< 0). Any expansion in economic activity, ECONACT, was hypothesized to have a positive effect on GROWTH (b_3 >0). And, consistent with human capital theory and public sector economic theory, HIGHED was hypothesized to have a positive effect on GROWTH (b_2>0).

Statistical Procedures, Assumptions and Limitations

Aggregate data for all variables were available for all 50 states and for both 10-year periods of analysis. Multiple regression analysis was used to estimate the effects of each independent variable on the subsequent 10-year growth in state workforce. When analyzing data on large cross-section units, such as state economies, heteroskedasticity is often problematic and could pose a potential limitation in this study. In order to address this possibility, all hypotheses in this study were tested with test statistics computed using White's heteroskedasticity-robust standard errors (White, 1980).

First, the model was estimated with regression using data for the 10-year period from 1980-1990. Second, it was estimated using data for the 10-year period from 1990-2000. Third, the two 10-year periods of analysis (1980-1990 and 1990-2000) were combined to yield a dataset with two observations for each state on all variables. Common methods for estimation with this minimal, two-period-only panel data—such as first-differencing to remove unobserved, time-constant fixed-effects—were not applicable with this data because of such inadequate variation in the independent variables after first-differencing (Wooldridge, 2003). Therefore, the two 10-year periods were pooled for the 50 states, a period-specific binary variable (PERIOD $_{t+10}$) was included in the model both additively and multiplicatively, by interacting it with all independent variables—i.e., PROD, HIGHED and ECONACT—to conduct a full test of the stability of the intercept and all regression coefficients across the two 10-year periods of analysis. Results demonstrated that all coefficients were stable across the two 10-year periods except for the intercept itself. Based on these findings, a period-specific binary variable (PERIOD $_{t+10}$) was included in the final version of the model estimated. Because the average growth in workforce productivity across the state economies was greater during the 1990-2000 period than the 1980-1990 period, the coefficient for PERIOD $_{t+10}$ was expected to be positive (i.e., $b_0' > 0$).

Initial cumulative investment in higher education (HIGHED) was measured as the fraction of high school graduates age 25 and over who had completed four or more years of college for state i in year t. In microeconomic theoretical terms this variable is conceptualized as the initial stock of human capital in the form college-educated members of the state's labor force at the beginning of a 10-year period of analysis. This is an appropriate and important definition and assumption for this study, because it is the actual number of college graduates residing in a state and participating in its workforce, instead of the number of college graduates educated in that state, that affects the state's subsequent growth in workforce productivity. Therefore, HIGHED should and does reflect the differences between states in the number of college graduates they actually had in their workforces in year t—i.e., at the beginning of each of the two 10-year period of analysis considered in this study.

Because some variables—like investment in higher education—could serve both as a cause and as a consequence of economic growth, some researchers (e.g., Pencavel, 1993) have suggested that economic growth models may be subject to a simultaneous-equations bias, thereby necessitating the estimation of a two-equation, non-recursive system in studies such as this. However, Equation (1) was carefully specified in the present study so that the estimated coefficients of Equation (1) would not be subject to such a simultaneous-equations bias. The reason for this is that the cumulative investment in higher education (HIGHED $_{i,t}$) in state i by the initial year (t) of each 10-year period of growth cannot possibly be a result of the growth in workforce productivity in the subsequent 10-year period of growth (GROWTH $_{i,t+10/t}$); instead, HIGHED $_{i,t}$ can only be the result of growth in state workforce productivity over many years *prior to* the initial year of each 10-year period of growth.

There are various forms of cumulative investments in, or stocks of, physical capital and human capital—other than higher education investments—that can affect a state's workforce productivity and growth in that productivity (GROWTH). Examples include a state's cumulative investments in literacy rates and high school education, various forms of technical and corporate training, and varieties of physical capital and new technologies in various industries. The inclusion of the variable PROD in the model addresses this issue. PROD, which represents the initial level of state workforce productivity in year t—i.e., at the beginning of a 10-year period of analysis—controls for the net effects on GROWTH of all cumulative investments (i.e., stocks of physical or human capital) due to the various non-HIGHED factors that contribute to the initial level of state workforce productivity in year t—i.e., at the beginning of a 10-year period of analysis.

Finally, changes in the values of ECONACT—even when aggregated to the level of the overall national economy, as in the present study—are contemporaneous with changes in the values of the dependent variable, growth in workforce productivity (GROWTH), in the sense that the values of both variables change between 1980 and 1990 and between 1990 and 2000. This raises a question about what could have been a potential limitation of this study—one which, under some circumstances, can lead to a possible endogeneity bias in the regression coefficients. However, because of the unique construction of the variable ECONACT, this variable can be appropriately viewed as and assumed to be exogenous with respect to the disturbance or error term $u_{i,t}$. More specifically, we follow Barro and Sala-i-Martin (1992, 1995) in making the assumption that ECONACT is an exogenous independent variable in the model for two reasons. First, the potential impact of changes in economic activity in any one individual state on changes in an aggregate measure of economic activity at the level of the overall national economy is minimal. Second, the weights, W_{ijt}, which do vary across states, are based only on 1980 or 1990 values—corresponding to the beginning year of each 10-year period—and remain constant throughout each subsequent 10-year period of analysis (Barro and Sala-i-Martin, 1992, 1995).[4] In addition, the inclusion of ECONACT in the model also helps account and control for some of the potential effects of migration of college graduates from t to t+10, because migration patterns are very responsive to state differences in economic activity (Barro and Sala-i-Martin, 1995).[5]

FINDINGS

Descriptive Statistics

The descriptive statistics in Table 1 provide useful perspectives on the nature of the dependent and independent variables when examined for the 1980-1990 period only, the 1990-2000 period only, or when the data is pooled for both 10-year periods of analysis. During the 1980-1990 period, the average growth in workforce productivity (GROWTH) for all 50 states was substantially less than it was during the more robust 1990-2000 period—i.e., from 1980-1990, average growth in workforce productivity for the 50 states was only 12.1 percent (.121), compared to 21.1 (.211) percent in the 1990-2000 period. The average growth in state workforce productivity across all 50 states when data from both 10-year periods were pooled was the arithmetic mean of the averages for the two separate 10-year periods: 16.6 percent (.166). The difference in the average growth in state workforce productivity between the two periods was 9 percent (.09). One probable reason for this difference is that the early-to-mid 1980s were characterized by quite substantial recessions in the agricultural and in the energy-related mining and extraction (oil-related) industries, which quite likely served to constrain the rate of growth in workforce productivity in the 1980s compared to the 1990s (Paulsen, 1996b; Renshaw, Trott, and Friedenberg, 1988).

In 1980—i.e., at the beginning of the 1980-1990 period of analysis—the average of the initial levels of workforce productivity (PROD, defined as gross state product per worker in the state labor force) for all 50 states was $45,075; which grew to $50,650 by 1990—i.e., the first year of the 1990-2000 period of analysis. The average of the initial levels of workforce productivity across all 50 states when data from both 10-year periods were pooled was the arithmetic mean of the averages for the two separate 10-year periods: $47,863. The standard

---

[4] See Barro and Sala-i-Martin, 1992, p. 234 and 1995, p. 391.

[5] Some migration of college graduates between states might occur during each of the 10-year periods of analysis, however, this possibility is addressed by the data and measures utilized in this study. Migration research has shown that migration of college graduates between states is consistently responsive to and correlated with job market signals associated with expansions and contractions in the sectors of state economies where the labor force typically includes substantial portions of college-educated workers (Barro and Sala-i-Martin, 1995). Therefore, the inclusion in the model of ECONACT--the comprehensive measure of expansions and contractions in ten distinct industrial sectors in each state's economy between 1980 and 1990 and between 1990 and 2000—provides a measure of control for the effects on GROWTH of migration occurring during each of the 10-year periods of analysis. An in-depth and further examination of the determinants of the migration patterns of college graduates between states is an important area for further study, but is beyond the scope of the present study.

deviation for the pooled sample was $10,624 which indicates a good deal of variation between states in terms of the initial productivity of their workforces.

Table 1. Descriptive Statistics for Dependent and Independent Variables:
1980-1990, 1990-2000, and Pooled Samples

Variable	1980-1990	1980-1990	1990-2000	1990-2000	Pooled	Pooled
	Means	S.D.	Means	S.D.	Means	S.D.
Growth	.121	.087	.211	.107	.166	.107
Prod	$45.075	10.787	$50.650	9.789	$47.863	10.624
Highed	.238	.030	.270	.045	.254	.041
Econact	.195	.016	.200	.029	.198	.024

In 1980—i.e., at the beginning of the 1980-1990 period of analysis—the average of the initial levels of cumulative investment, or stocks of human capital, in higher education (HIGHED, defined as the percent of high school graduates age 25 and over with four or more years of college) for all 50 states, was 23.8 percent (.238); which increased to 27 percent (.270) by 1990—i.e., the first year of the 1990-2000 period of analysis. The average of the initial levels of cumulative investment, or stocks of human capital, in higher education across all 50 states when data from both 10-year periods were pooled was the arithmetic mean of the averages for the two separate 10-year periods: 25.4 percent (.254). The standard deviation for the pooled sample was 4.1 percent (.041) which indicates a moderate level of variation between states in terms of their initial levels of cumulative investment, or stocks of human capital, in higher education. Finally, the overall mean of the weighted averages of the expansions or contractions in economic activity across 10 distinct industries (ECONACT) for all 50 states was similar for both 10-year periods of analysis—i.e., 19.5 percent and 20 percent, respectively for the 1980-90 and 1990-2000 periods. And the overall average value of ECONACT when data for all 50 states for the two 10-year periods were pooled was 19.8 percent (.198). In combination, these figures indicate a consistent pattern of a moderate level of net expansion in economic activity in the state economies during the two 10-year periods of analysis.

Regression Results

Table 2 presents the regression coefficients and test statistics resulting from the estimation of the model specified in Equation (1). As noted previously, the model was first estimated using data for the 10-year period from 1980-1990 only, and then the model was estimated again using data for the 10-year period from 1990-2000 only. Third, the two 10-year periods of analysis (1980-1990 and 1990-2000) were combined to create a dataset with two observations for each state. Initially, the model was estimated using the pooled data without testing for the stability of coefficients across the two time periods. First, the three sets of results from estimating the model using data from each of the two separate periods and from the combined data are presented. These results appear in the first three columns (see columns headed 1, 2, and 3) of findings in Table 2—i.e., for the 1980-1990 period, the 1990-2000 period, and for the pooled data for the two periods.

Table 2. Regression Results: Effects of PROD, HIGHED and ECONACT on GROWTH

	1	2	3	4	5
Variable	1980-1990	1990-2000	Pooled	Pooled Chow	Pooled w/Period
Intercept	.121	.211	.166	.136	.130
SE	.010*	.010*	.008*	.013*	.011*
H-R SE	.010*	.010*	.008*	.012*	.010*
Period	-	-	-	.069	.072
SE	-	-	-	.017*	.016*
H-R SE	-	-	-	.017*	.016*
Prod	-.003	-.005	-.003	-.003	-.003
SE	.001*	.001*	.001*	.001*	.001*
H-R SE	.001*	.002*	.001*	.001*	.001*
Highed	1.12	.896	1.18	1.12	.920
SE	.349*	.259*	.210*	.355*	.201*
H-R SE	.318*	.251*	.197*	.318*	.176*
Econact	1.87	1.48	1.92	1.87	1.59
SE	.786*	.426*	.383*	.799*	.358*
H-R SE	1.01+	.470*	.446*	1.01+	.389*
Prod*Period	-	-	-	-.002	-
SE/HRSE	-	-	-	.002/.002	-
Highed*Period	-	-	-	-.224	-
SE/HRSE	-	-	-	.437/.406	-
Econact*Period	-	-	-	-.390	-
SE/HRSE	-	-	-	.903/1.11	-
R^2	.372	.558	.475	.576	.566
F	9.09*	19.32*	28.89*	17.83*	30.95*
N	50	50	100	100	100

* $p<.05$ and + $p<.10$ H-RSE = Heteroskedasticity-Robust Standard Error

As shown in Table 2, the estimated effects of each of the independent variables on the dependent variable—growth in state workforce productivity over a 10-year period (GROWTH)—are similar across all three samples: for the 1980-1990 period only, the 1990-2000 period only, and the combined 1980-1990 and 1990-2000 period. The effect on GROWTH of PROD, which represents the initial level of state workforce productivity in year t—i.e., at the beginning of a 10-year period of analysis—was quite similar across the three samples, with estimates of -.003, -.005, and -.003 respectively, and was significant at the level of .05 in each case, using either ordinary standard errors or heteroskedasticity-robust standard errors (see Table 2, columns 1-3). The negative effects support the hypothesized relationship that states with lower workforce productivity at the beginning of each 10-year period experience faster rates of subsequent growth in workforce productivity than states with higher initial levels of workforce productivity.

The effect on GROWTH of ECONACT, which represents the weighted average of economic activity, including expansions or contractions in a state's gross state product originating from each of ten distinct industrial sectors, from t to t+10, was similar across the three samples, with estimates of +1.87, +1.48, and +1.92 respectively for the 1980-1990, 1990-2000, and pooled samples, and was significant at the level of .05 in each case using ordinary standard errors (see Table 2, columns 1-3). However, when heteroskedasticity-robust standard errors were used, the estimates for the 1990-2000 and for the pooled sample retained their significance at the level of .05, while the estimate for the 1980-1990 period was significant at the level of .10. These positive effects support the hypothesized relationships and indicate economic expansion in state economies is positively related to growth in workforce productivity.

Finally, the effect of greatest interest in the present study is the effect of HIGHED on GROWTH. As shown in Table 2 (columns 1-3), the effects on GROWTH of HIGHED, which represents the initial level of cumulative investment, or stock of human capital, in higher education in year t—i.e., at the beginning of a 10-year period of analysis—was also similar across the three samples, with estimates of +1.12, +.90, and +1.18 respectively for the 1980-1990, 1990-2000, and pooled samples, and was significant at the level of .05 in each case, using either ordinary standard errors or heteroskedasticity-robust standard errors. These positive effects support the hypothesized relationships and indicate that states with higher levels of cumulative investment, or stocks of human capital, in higher education at the beginning of each 10-year period experience faster rates of subsequent growth in workforce productivity than states with lower initial levels of cumulative investment, or stocks of human capital, in higher education. For the models estimated from the 1980-1990, 1990-2000, and pooled samples, the R^2 statistics were 37.2, 55.8 and 47.5 percent, respectively; and the corresponding F ratios were 9.09, 19.32 and 28.89, with each statistically significant at the level of .01.

As noted previously, typical methods for estimation of a model using panel data—such as first-differencing to remove unobserved, time-constant fixed-effects—were not applicable with this data because it represents a minimal, two-period-only panel data set, and it was characterized by inadequate variation in the independent variables after first-differencing (Wooldridge, 2003). Because of this, the two 10-year periods were pooled for the 50 states, a period-specific dummy variable ($PERIOD_{t+10}$) was included in the model both additively and multiplicatively—i.e., by interacting it with all independent variables—in order to conduct a full Chow test of the stability of the intercept and all regression coefficients across the two 10-year periods of analysis (see Table 2, column 4). Results indicated that all coefficients except the intercept were stable across the two 10-year periods (see Table 2, column 4). Based on these findings, in order to account for the shift in the intercept between the two time periods, the period-specific binary variable ($PERIOD_{t+10}$) was included additively as a new independent variable in the final version of the model estimated (see Table 2, column 5). Because the average growth in workforce productivity across the state economies was greater during the 1990-2000 period than the 1980-1990 period, the coefficient for $PERIOD_{t+10}$ was expected to be positive (i.e., $b_0' > 0$).

The findings regarding the effects of all the independent variables (PROD, HIGHED, ECONACT) on the dependent variable (GROWTH) were similar and consistent across all samples used for estimation as discussed above. Therefore, the findings discussed here are based on the final version of the model estimated (see Table 2, column 5). Overall, for the final version of the model estimated, the R^2 statistic was 56.6 percent and the corresponding F ratio was 30.95, which was statistically significant at the level of .01. First, the period-specific binary variable (PERIOD $_{t+10}$) had a positive, significant effect on GROWTH with $b_0' = .072$ or 7.2%. This was consistent with expectations, because the mean values for GROWTH across states between the 1980-1990 and the 1990-2000 periods differed by +.09 or 9%.

Second, in the final version of the model (see Table 2, column 5) the effect of PROD on GROWTH was -.003 which was significant at the level of .05 using either ordinary standard errors or heteroskedasticity-robust standard errors. This negative effect is consistent with the findings of prior research and expectations based on convergence theory (Barro and Sala-i-Martin, 1992, 1995; Baumol, et al. 1989; OECD, 2003a, 2003b; Paulsen, 1996a, 1996b), supports the hypothesized relationship, and indicates that for each $1000 increase (decrease) in a state's workforce productivity at the beginning of each 10-year period experience, the rate of subsequent growth in workforce productivity will decrease (increase) by .3 percent, all else equal. This pattern is what contributes to the tendency for economies to begin to "converge" in their productivity over time. In effect, initially-less-productive economies tend to grow at a faster rate than their more productive counterparts.

Third, in the final version of the model (see Table 2, column 5) the effect of ECONACT on GROWTH was +1.59 and was significant at the level of .05 using either ordinary standard errors or heteroskedasticity-robust standard errors. This positive effect is consistent with the results of prior research and expectations that greater expansion in a state's economic activity would be positively related to growth in workforce productivity (Barro and Sala-i-Martin, 1992, 1995; Fatima and Paulsen, 2004; Paulsen, 1996a, 1996b), supports the hypothesized relationship, and indicates that for each 1 percent expansion (contraction) in a state's economic activity the rate of growth in a state's workforce productivity would increase (decrease) by 1.6 percent, all else equal.

Finally, the central purpose of this study was to estimate the effect of the initial level of cumulative investment, or stock of human capital, in higher education in year t—i.e., at the beginning of a 10-year period of analysis—on the subsequent growth in a state's workforce productivity during a 10-year period. In the final version of the model (see Table 2, column 5) the effect of HIGHED on GROWTH was +.92 and was significant at the level of .05 using either ordinary standard errors or heteroskedasticity-robust standard errors. This positive effect is consistent with expectations based on human capital theory and public sector economics—i.e., the existence of substantial public or external benefits associated with individual investments in higher education—(Paulsen, 2001a, 2001b) and with the results of prior research on the effects of investment in various levels of schooling—including secondary and higher education—on economic growth across national and state economies (e.g., Barro, 2001; Barro and Sala-i-Martin, 1992, 1995; Baumol, et al. 1989; Fatima and Paulsen, 2004; Leslie and Brinkman, 1988; OECD, 2003a, 2003b; Paulsen, 1996a, 1996b; Pencavel, 1993). This positive effect of +.92 supports the hypothesized relationship and indicates that, all else equal, each 1 percentage-point increase in HIGHED at the beginning of a 10-year period of analysis was associated with a .92 percentage-point increase in the subsequent 10-year growth in state workforce productivity from year t to year t+10. Because the average 10-year growth in workforce productivity in the pooled sample was 16.6%, for an "otherwise average" state: each 1 percentage-point increase (< .25 SD) in HIGHED was associated with a 5.5% increase in the subsequent 10-year growth in state workforce productivity (.92/16.6 = .0554); each 1 standard deviation (1 SD = .041 = 4 percentage points) increase in HIGHED was associated with a 22.2% increase in the subsequent 10-yr growth in state workforce productivity (4 x .92 = 3.68 and 3.68/16.6 = .2217); and finally, each 10 percentage-point increase in HIGHED was associated with a 55.4% increase in subsequent 10-year growth in workforce productivity (10 x .92 = 9.2 and 9.2/16.6 = .5542).

CONCLUSION

The findings of this study suggest that initial cumulative investments or stocks of human capital, in higher education, increase the rates of subsequent growth in workforce productivity in the state economies. These findings are consistent with and supportive of previous research on the contribution of higher education to economic growth in the American economy at the national level (e.g., Institute for Higher Education Policy, 1998; Leslie and Brinkman, 1988; Pencavel, 1993) and at the state level (e.g., Fatima and Paulsen, 2004; Paulsen, 1996a, 1996b). Furthermore, this study indicates that states' investments in the higher education of its citizens--in the form of bachelor's degree education--yield substantial public or external benefits. These externalities occur through increases in a state's workforce productivity, which in turn, indicates economy-wide or state-wide increases in output and income per worker—i.e., an unambiguous public benefit (Baumol, et al. 1989). According to established theory and research in public finance and public sector economics, the existence of such externalities or public benefits due to individual students' investments in higher education is evidence of a market failure and suggests that without an appropriate level of subsidies to institutions (e.g. state appropriations) and subsidies to students (e.g. grants), an underinvestment in, and socially inefficient allocation of state resources to, higher education would occur (see e.g., Boadway, 1979; Paulsen, 2001b; Stiglitz, 2000). These findings also indicate that increased investment in higher education would yield further public benefits in the form of higher output and income per worker in the state economies, which in turn, would generate a larger volume of tax revenues for the states, and such tax revenues could then be used in appropriate proportions, to subsidize, stimulate, and expand investments in higher education toward more socially optimum levels.

These findings provide a strong rationale for public investment in higher education in the form of subsidies to institutions and students (Baum, 2004; Paulsen, 2001b). However, a series of incremental policy changes—made in large part with little discussion, debate or consensus about public financial policy (Callan and Finney, 1997; Paulsen and Smart, 2001)—have resulted in continuous and substantial decreases in the proportion of educational costs borne by society relative to students and their families during the past twenty-five years. Conversation and judgment about the nature and magnitude of the social benefits of higher education have been increasingly marginalized and ignored, while attention and logic about who should pay for higher education has been primarily focused on the individual economic benefits of higher education alone (see e.g., National Forum on Higher Education for the Public Good, 2003). The Institute for Higher Education Policy (1998) has lamented that in spite of the long-standing American tradition of an appreciation for the public benefits and public good of higher education, "Major national and state-level public policy discussions have frequently returned to the private economic benefits of a college education as the basic reason for increased public investment" (p. 8).

In light of the evidence of public or external benefits observed in the present study, coupled with extant research demonstrating the existence of a wide variety of additional forms of public benefits (see e.g., Baum and Payea, 2004, 2005; Baum, Payea and Steele, 2006; Fatima and Paulsen, 2004; Institute for Higher Education Policy, 1998, 2005; Leslie and Brinkman, 1988; Paulsen, 1996a, 1996b; Perna, 2005), the sea shift in society's views about the appropriate proportions of educational costs to be borne by society relative to students and their families may need to be re-examined (Baum and Payea, 2004, 2005; Baum, Payea and Steele, 2006; Fatima and Paulsen, 2004; National Forum on Higher Education for the Public Good, 2003; Institute for Higher Education Policy, 2005). The evidence of public or external benefits of higher education observed in the present study, based on the use of gross-state-product data as a foundation for documenting such benefits at the state level, could provide a fresh perspective and a catalyst for a more careful, deliberate, and informed public discussion of the question of what shares of educational costs should be borne by society and by students.

In combination, evidence of substantial external benefits of investment in higher education—from this study and others (e.g., Baum and Payea, 2004, 2005; Baum, Payea and Steele, 2006; Fatima and Paulsen, 2004; Institute for Higher Education Policy, 2005; Leslie and Brinkman, 1988; Paulsen, 1996a, 1996b; Perna, 2005)—and evidence of unequal rates of participation in higher education across students from different socioeconomic or racial/ethnic backgrounds (Baum and Payea, 2004; National Center for Education Statistics, 2003; Perna, 2005; St. John, 2003), constitute a strong rationale for continued and expanded public subsidization of investment in higher education. For example, in 2000, the percentages of students who completed high school during the preceding 12 months and were attending college equaled 65.7 for whites, 54.9 for blacks and 52.9 for Hispanics (National Center for Education Statistics, 2003, Table 185, p. 234). Assuming that the external or public benefits arising from black or Hispanic students attending college are equal to or greater than the public or external benefits arising from white students attending college, and that the public benefits of expanding the participation rates of blacks and Hispanics are equal to or greater than the public costs, then the substantial existing gaps in higher education participation rates across different income and racial/ethnic groups provides considerable support for the contention that society's current level of investment in higher education is less than socially optimal.

REFERENCES

American Council on Education. (2006). *American council on education launches first-of-its-kind campaign on benefits of higher education to society.* Washington, DC: American Council on Education.

Barro, R. J. (2001). Human capital and growth. *American Economics Association Papers and Proceedings* 91 (2): 12-17.

Barro, R. J. and Sala-i-Martin, X. (1992). Convergence. *Journal of Political Economy*, 100 (2): 223-251.

Barro, R. J. and Sala-i-Martin, X. (1995). *Economic growth.* New York: McGraw-Hill, Inc.

Baum, S. (2004). *A Primer on economics for financial aid professionals.* New York: The College Board.

Baum, S. and Payea, K. (2004*). Education pays: The benefits of higher education individuals and society.* New York: The College Board.

Baum, S. and Payea, K. (2005). *Education pays: Update 2005.* New York: The College Board.

Baum, S., Payea, K., and Steele, P. (2006). *Education pays: Update 2006.* New York: The College Board.

Baumol, W. J., Blackman, S., and Wolff, E. (1989). *Productivity and American leadership.* Cambridge, MA: MIT Press.

Becker, G.S. (1993). *Human capital: A theoretical and empirical analysis with special reference to education (3rd ed). Chicago:* The University of Chicago Press.

Becker, W.E. (1992). Why go to college? The value of an investment in higher education. In W.E. Becker and D.R. Lewis (Eds.), *The economics of American higher education.* Boston, MA: Kluwer Academic Publishers.

Boadway, R. W. (1979). *Public sector economics.* Cambridge, MA: Winthrop.

Bowen, H. R. (1977). *Investment in learning.* San Francisco: Jossey-Bass.

Brenneman, D. W. and J. E. Finney. (1997). The changing landscape: Higher education finance in the 1990s. In P. M. Callan and J. E. Finney (eds.), *Public and private financing of higher education.* Phoenix, AZ: American Council on Education and The Oryx Press.

Bureau of Economic Analysis (2003). Regional economic accounts. Retrieved June 6, 2003 from BEA web site via GPO Access http://www.bea.doc.gov/bea/regional/gsp/.

Caffrey, J. and Isaacs, H. (1971). *Estimating the impact of a college or university on the local economy.* Washington, DC: American Council on Education.

Callan, P. and Finney, J. (1997). Preface. In Callan and J. Finney (eds.). *Public and private financing of higher education.* Phoenix, AZ: Oryx Press.

Carnegie Commission on Higher Education. (1973). Higher education: Who pays? Who benefits? Who should pay? New York: McGraw-Hill.

Cohn, E. and Geske, T.G. (1990). *The economics of education* (3rd ed). New York: Pergamon Press.

College Board, (2006a). *Trends in college pricing.* Washington, DC: The College Board.

College Board, (2006b). *Trends in student aid.* Washington, DC: The College Board.

Cunningham, A. F., et al. (2001). *Study of college costs and prices, 1988–89 to 1997–98. Washington,* DC: U.S. Department of Education, National Center for Education Statistics.

Fatima, N. and Paulsen, M.B. (2004). Higher education and state workforce productivity in the 1990s. *Thought and Action: NEA Higher Education Journal* 20 (1): 75-94.

Friedenberg, H. L. and Beemiller, R. M. (1997). Comprehensive revision of gross state product by industry, 1977-94. *Survey of Current Business* 77 (6): 15-40.

Geske, T. G. and Cohn, E. (1998). Why is a high school diploma no longer enough? The economic and social benefits of higher education. In R. Fossey and M. Bateman (eds.), *Condemning students to debt: College loans and public policy.* New York: Teachers College Press.

Gladieux, L.E. (2002). Federal student aid in historical perspective. In D. Heller (ed.), *Condition of access: Higher education for lower income students.* Westport, CT: Prager.

Hyman, D. N. (2002). *Public finance: A contemporary application of theory to policy.* New York: Harcourt College Publishers.

Institute for Higher Education Policy (1998). *Reaping the benefits: Defining the public and private value of going to college.* Washington, DC: Institute for Higher Education Policy.

Institute for Higher Education Policy (2005). *The investment payoff: A 50-state analysis of the public and private benefits of higher education.* Washington, DC: Institute for Higher Education Policy.

Johnstone, B. (1999). Financing higher education: Who should pay? In P. Altbach, R. Berdahl, and P. Gumport (eds.). *American higher education in the twenty-first century: Social, political, and economic challenges.* Baltimore, MD: Johns Hopkins University Press.

Leslie, L.L. and Brinkman, P.T. (1988). *The economic value of higher education.* New York: ACE/Macmillan.

Leslie, L. and Slaughter, S. (1992). Higher education and regional economic development. In W. Becker, and D. Lewis, (eds.), *The economics of American higher education.* Boston, MA: Kluwer Academic Publishers.

McMahon, W.W. (1991). Relative returns to human and physical capital in the U.S. and efficient investment strategies. *Economics of Education Review* 10 (4): 283-296.

McMahon, W.W. and Wagner, A.P. (1982). The monetary returns to education as partial social efficiency criteria. In W.W. McMahon and T.G. Geske (eds.), *Financing education: Overcoming inefficiency and inequity.* Urbana, IL: University of Illinois Press.

Midwest Higher Education Compact (2005). *Investment payoff: The benefits of a higher education in the Midwestern states.* Minneapolis, MN: MHEC.

Mortenson, T. B. (2003). A nation at risk, again. *Postsecondary education opportunity.*

Mumper, M. (2001). State efforts to keep public colleges affordable in the face of fiscal stress. In M. B. Paulsen and J. Smart (eds.) (2001), *The finance of higher education: Theory, research, policy, and practice.* New York: Agathon Press.

Musgrave, R. and Musgrave, P. (1984). *Public finance in theory and practice* (4th ed), New York: McGraw-Hill.

National Center for Education Statistics (1992). *Digest of education statistics.* Years of school completed by persons age 25 years old and older, by state: April 1980 and March 1990, table-12, p. 21. Washington D. C.: Government Printing Office, U.S. Department of Education, Office of Educational Research and Improvement, National Center for Education Statistics.

National Center for Education Statistics. (2003). *Digest of education statistics*, 2003. Washington, DC: U.S. Government Printing Office.

National Forum on Higher Education for the Public Good. (2003). *Higher education for the public good: A report from the national leadership dialogues.* Ann Arbor, MI: Author.

Organization for Economic Cooperation and Development (2003a). *Financing education: Investments and return.* Paris, France: OECD.

Organization for Economic Cooperation and Development (2003b). *The sources of economic growth in OECD countries.* Paris, France: OECD.

Pascarella, E.T. and Terenzini, P.T. (1991). *How college affects students.* San Francisco: Jossey-Bass.

Paulsen, M.B. (1991). College tuition: Demand and supply determinants from 1960 to 1986. *The Review of Higher Education* 14 (3): 339-358.

Paulsen, M.B. (1996a). Higher education and productivity: An afterword. Thought and Action: *NEA Higher Education Journal* 12(2): 135-139.

Paulsen, M.B. (1996b). Higher education and state workforce productivity. Thought and Action: *NEA Higher Education Journal* 12(1): 55-77.

Paulsen, M.B. (2000). Economic perspectives on rising college tuition: A theoretical and empirical exploration. In J.C. Smart (ed.), *Higher education: Handbook of theory and research,* Volume XV. New York: Agathon Press.

Paulsen, M.B. (2001a). The economics of human capital and investment in higher education. In M. B. Paulsen and J. Smart (eds.), *The finance of higher education: Theory, research, policy, and practice.* New York: Agathon Press.

Paulsen, M.B. (2001b). The economics of the public sector: The nature and role of public policy in the finance of higher education. In M. B. Paulsen and J. Smart (eds.), *The finance of higher education: Theory, research, policy, and practice.* New York: Agathon Press.

Paulsen, M. B. and Smart, J. C. (2001). Introduction. In M. B. Paulsen and J. Smart (eds.), *The finance of higher education: Theory, research, policy, and practice.* New York: Agathon Press.

Paulsen, M. B. and Toutkoushian, R. K. (2006). Economics and institutional research: Expanding the connections and applications. In R. Toutkoushian and M. Paulsen (eds.), *Applying Economics in Institutional Research. New Directions for Institutional Research* No. 132. San Francisco: Jossey-Bass.

Pencavel, J. (1993). Higher education, economic growth, and earnings. In W.E. Becker and D.R. Lewis (eds.), *The economics of American higher education.* Boston, MA: Kluwer Academic Publishers.

Perna, L. W. (2005). The benefits of higher education: Sex, racial/ethnic, and socioeconomic group differences. *The Review of Higher Education* 29 (1): 23-52.

Renshaw, V., Trott, E. A., and Friedenberg, H. L. (1988). Gross state product by industry, 1963-1986. *Survey of Current Business* 68(5): 30-46.

Roherty, B. M. (1997). The price of passive resistance in financing higher education. In P. Callan and J. Finney (eds.). *Public and private financing of higher education.* Phoenix, AZ: Oryx Press.

St. John, E.P. (1994). Prices, productivity, and investment: Assessing financial strategies in higher education. *ASHE-ERIC Higher Education Report No.* 3. Washington, DC: The George Washington University, School of Education and Human Development.

Stiglitz, J.E. (2000). *Economics of the public sector* (3rd ed.). New York: W.W. Norton.

Solmon, L. C. and Fagnano, C. L. (1995). Benefits of education. In M. Carnoy (ed.), *International encyclopedia of economics of education,* 2nd edition. Oxford: Elsevier.

Thomas, S. L. and Perna, L. W. (2004). The opportunity agenda: A reexamination of postsecondary reward and opportunity. In J. C. Smart (ed.), *Higher education: Handbook of theory and research* Volume XIX. Dordrecht, The Netherlands: Kluwer Academic Publishers.

Toutkoushian, R. K. (2001). Trends in revenues and expenditures for public and private higher education. In M. B. Paulsen and J. C. Smart (eds.), *The finance of higher education: Theory, research, policy, and practice.* New York: Agathon Press.

U.S. Bureau of the Census (1983a). 1980 census of population: General social and economic characteristics (PC80-1-C). *Labor force characteristics,* table-67, volume 1, various parts. Washington D.C.: Government Printing Office, Department of Commerce, U.S. Bureau of the Census.

U.S. Bureau of Census (1983b). 1980 census of population: General social and economic characteristics (PC80-1-C). *Educational characteristics*, table-66, volume 1, various parts. Washington D.C.: Government Printing Office, Department of Commerce, U.S. Bureau of the Census.

U.S. Bureau of the Census (1993a). 1990 census of population: Social and economic characteristics (CP-2). *Labor force characteristics*, table-24, volume 1, various states. Retrieved August 19, 2001, from web site via GPO Access http://www.census.gov/prod/www/abs/decennial.html.

U.S. Bureau of the Census (1993b). 1990 census of population: Social and economic characteristics (CP-2). *School enrollment and educational attainment*, table-22, volume 1, various states. Retrieved August 19, 2001, from web site via GPO Access http://www.census.gov/prod/www/abs/decennial.html.

U.S. Bureau of the Census (2001a). *Statistical abstract of the United States*. Characteristics of the civilian labor force by state: 2000, table-572, p. 370. Washington D.C.: Government Printing Office, Department of Commerce, U.S. Bureau of the Census.

U.S. Bureau of the Census (2001b). *Statistical abstract of the United States*. Resident population-states: 1980 to 2000, table -18, p. 21. Washington D.C.: Government Printing Office, Department of Commerce, U.S. Bureau of the Census.

White, H. (1980). Heteroskedasticity-consistent covariance matrix estimator and a direct test for heteroskedasticity. *Econometrica* 48 (4): 817-838.

Wolfe, B. L. (1995). External benefits of education. In M.Carnoy (ed.), *International encyclopedia of economics of education, 2nd edition*. Oxford: Elsevier.

Wooldridge, J. M. (2003). *Introductory econometrics* 2nd edition. Mason, OH: South-Western.

Zemsky, R. and Wegner, G. R. (1997). Shaping the Future. In P. M. Callan and J. E. Finney (eds.), *Public and private financing of higher education*. Phoenix, AZ: American Council on Education and The Oryx Press.

Zumeta, W. (2003). Higher education finances: In recession again. *The NEA 2003 almanac of higher education*.Washington, DC: NEA.

In: Global Issues in Higher Education
Editor: Pamela B. Richards, pp. 57-83

ISBN: 978-1-60021-802-6
© 2007 Nova Science Publishers, Inc.

Chapter 3

ACADEMIC COMMUNITIES AND DEVELOPING IDENTITY: THE DOCTORAL STUDENT JOURNEY

L. McAlpine and *C. Amundsen***

*McGill University, Canada
** Simon Fraser University, Canada

ABSTRACT

There is a substantial international literature that highlights the need to rethink doctoral pedagogies. The goal of our broad research program is to analyze the experience of doctoral students in Education and English in order to understand how they learn from engaging in the range of activities, both formal and informal, available to them in their programs. We began this program by carrying out three studies conducted in different contexts and with different research questions. As we analyzed data from these three initial studies, we noticed a clear theme emerging across all three: the development of academic identity within the shifting tensions of the discipline and the institution. To better understand this potentially significant theme of identity development, we reanalyzed the data from all three studies focusing this time on identity instead of the initial focus of investigation in each. This chapter reports the findings of this reanalysis and how we interpret them, specifically, the construction of a conceptual framework to synthesize them, and pedagogical implications that emerge.

INTRODUCTION

High attrition rates, ranging from thirty to fifty percent, have been documented internationally in doctoral programs, particularly in the social sciences and humanities (for example, see Elgar, 2003). This suggests there is a problem. Previous research into doctoral education has tended to be correlational and atheoretical (Leonard et al, 2006). Often only one factor thought to effect the doctoral experience is examined (e.g., funding) rather than the

---

* E-mail: lynn.mcalpine@mcgill.ca

constellation of factors that might collectively influence the problem (Golde, 1996; McAlpine and Norton, 2006; Lee et al, 2006). Some research focuses on student characteristics rather than contextual factors, often assuming that individuals need to "integrate" into a hegemonic structure, e.g., departmental practices. The problem is often interpreted as resting with individuals and not structures (Elgar, 2003). While structures have been and undoubtedly are in need of investigation, they should not be focused on exclusively or without the perspective of the student, as doing so denies agency to the student. We submit that understanding the complexity of the issue needs be accomplished in part through the input of students. Thus, our interest lies with documenting the views of doctoral students and the ways in which they come to situate themselves in the structures in which they are working and learning.

It is within this context gleaned from the literature and from our own experiences that two years ago we undertook (along with our colleagues, Anthony Pare and Doreen Starke-Meyerring) our program of research to document the doctoral student experience in English and Education in both a research-intensive and a comprehensive university in Canada. Our focus in this chapter is on findings relevant to the theme of identity development arrived at through the reanalysis of three studies conducted earlier and reported separately elsewhere (McAlpine and Asghar, 2006; Pare et al, 2006; McAlpine et al, in press - a). To provide the reader with a context in which to understand these findings, we begin with the analytical framework that serves as a basis for our current work, and brief descriptions of the broad research program and the three independent studies upon which the reanalysis focusing on identity development was based. After discussing the results of the reanalysis, we explore them from two perspectives: the construction of a conceptual framework to synthesize the findings, and the pedagogical implications.

ANALYTICAL FRAMEWORK

The Structures in which Students Experience the Doctorate

We used a framework of nested contexts, which emerged from an analysis of previous research addressing doctoral education (McAlpine and Norton, 2006) to situate and plan our work (See Figure 1). As represented in this framework, an individual student in undertaking a doctoral program enters a department that represents only one 'outpost' of the discipline (though this may not be apparent to the individual). The department is situated within a university and a society, the expectations of both contexts can influence the doctoral experience at the level of the department, but also more broadly in terms of a student's success as an academic. The nested contexts framework integrates the six factors that have been shown to influence attrition in doctoral programs across these contexts: funding, program requirements, supervisory relationship, admission policies and practices, disciplinary mode of research, and academic climate.

Specifically, students live and work in departments; these departments strongly influence their experience of *academic climate, supervision, and disciplinary mode of research* and thus, it is argued, the ability to integrate into the disciplinary community at large. Departments are influenced by both international disciplinary concerns (e.g., theoretical conflicts, changes in knowledge production) and by institutional demands and oversight of *admissions* and *program requirements*.

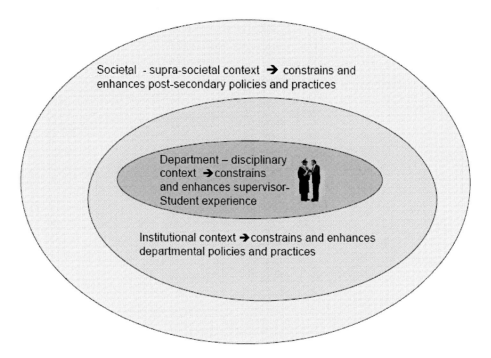

Figure 1. Nested contexts model.

Institutional policies and practices are, in turn, influenced by societal expectations and policies (e.g. *funding* council policies). Examining these factors is critical to understanding the interaction between the student's sense of agency and the structures represented in the nested contexts. In other words, the nested contexts framework enables us to conceptually situate doctoral experience as the interaction of the doctoral student – the agent – within the structures – the nested contexts of individual and group academic practices and policies. Thus, it provided a starting point for us in understanding the interaction between structures and student agency.

Voice(S) and Agency – An Expression of Identity

Given our backgrounds in academic development, we conceive of doctoral education and doctoral experience as a developmental process, and therefore our research is longitudinal in order to track this process. Thus, we were intrigued when we came across the notion put forward by Green (2005) that "doctoral pedagogy is as much about the production of identity . . . as it is the production of knowledge" (p. 162). In other words, students are coming to understand who they might be/ become in the academic world.

McAlpine et al (in press - b) describe academic identity as grounded in interrelations among individuals and disciplines, and "individual and collective values,", collective values being things such as professional autonomy and epistemic traditions (Henkel, 2005). Identity is much broader than voice, and we view an expression of identity as occurring through voice(s) (McAlpine et al, in press - b).

Voice, individual and collective, helps express identity within social interactions, influence boundaries and negotiations of roles and can maintain, resist, or disrupt the social structures that support multiple roles (Rée, 2000). Our interest is in socially oriented external representations of voice(s), those often associated with language in various modalities including spoken language, written text, or body language. Thus, while there are those who attend to voice as an internal component embodying an important sense of self that is not our concern. Rather, we are interested in the range of outer voices, some perceptible in the foreground while others are silenced in response to the roles, structures and dialectic in which we experience life and interactions with others.

Voice and agency are linked. For us, agency represents the fact that students - and individuals generally - construct their histories, 're-story' themselves, in terms of personal intentions and the ability to influence in some small ways the academic practices in which they engage. Drawing on McAlpine and Hopwood, 2006), we view these academic practices as encompassing three forms in varying degrees: inquiry, from scholarly examination of documents to empirical research; teaching, working with undergraduates, postgraduates and postdoctoral fellows; and forms of service to the institution, the discipline, profession and larger community, e.g., chair/member of a committee, organizer of a disciplinary conference, or consultant for a charity. Since the various combinations of practice shift over time and across individuals, central to our view of academic practice is a developmental perspective, including but not limited to career hopes, intentions and expectations. Experiencing agency within different aspects of these practices implies a capacity to perceive personal goals towards which one is directing action (Edwards, 2007), and to use voice(s) to negotiate these with others.

Our assumption is that much of what we know about our identities is derived from interactions with others since their verbal and non-verbal 'voices' of appraisal influence our own external voice(s), and our views of self, as well as our roles in relation to other members of the group (Stets and Harrod, 2004). This highlights the challenge of entry into social groupings; engaging in interpersonal interactions creates the context for expression of external voice(s) (expressing agency) that contribute to identity.

Tensions and Challenges

It is reasonable to expect that as students move through the range of experiences that constitute their own doctoral studies, they will have a growing sense of voice and engagement and ideally an increasing sense of disciplinary identification and membership[1] (Hasrati, 2005). This, however, is not necessarily the case. Increased engagement may lead to a deeper understanding of one's field and identification with the ideologies that underpin it (Roth, 1999); on the other hand, some ideologies may challenge a student's personal values and lead to a rejection of the field. Similarly, there may be tension between an increased sense of

---

[1] We acknowledge that not all doctoral students imagine themselves becoming academics; however, it is academic practices that we engage them in while completing the degree.

membership within a field, and the structuring influences that entering the field encompass, for example, reconciling academic demands for time against family goals.

In other words, participation in an academic community – doing academic work - is not a neutral act. The student's central task is to learn the discipline's particular values and practices, the intellectual traditions of the field, who and where the significant others are (Valimaa, 1998), and to use one's voice to participate in work that matters and might affect others. However, as Henkel (2000) notes, in doing this – in looking to one's chosen academic community for recognition - one is also learning how to reconcile potential conflicts between individual and collective values while negotiating intentions, roles and tasks, and to reconcile potential structural conflicts embedded in the nested contexts.

OUR RESEARCH PROGRAM: THE FIRST THREE STUDIES

The goals of our broad research program are twofold: a) to document and understand the experience of doctoral students in Education and English, and b) to inform and support pedagogical decision-making as it relates to development and revision of doctoral pedagogies in the departments of English and Education in which we are collecting data. In working toward our goal, we are engaging students (and professors) in examining the doctoral experience.

We began by carrying out three studies, conducted in different contexts and with different research questions. As the data from each of these three studies were analyzed, we noticed a clear theme emerging across all three: the development of academic identity within the shifting tensions of the discipline and the institution. To better understand what seemed like a significant finding, we reanalyzed the data from all three studies with a focus on identity development. We begin with a brief description of the original three studies to provide a context for the reader.

Study 1: As part of a formative process and a piece of action research, the goal of this study was to document the experience of Education doctoral students who had been members of a faculty-wide Student Committee on Doctoral Education (McAlpine and Asghar, 2006). This committee was composed principally of doctoral students – six - plus a post-doctoral fellow, and chaired by the Associate Dean Graduate Students with two faculty co-ordinators (responsible for organizing activities emerging from committee decisions), and a secretary. The mandate of the committee, arising from an external review of the Faculty, was to create a more collegial scholarly environment for graduate students - an important factor influencing doctoral success (Leonard et al, 2006). During the year before the study was done, the committee had implemented, in particular, two seminar series: one, the ABC's of the PhD (an introduction to the invisible curriculum facilitated by doctoral students and professors on, for instance, how to publish – and coordinated by the first author and students) and the Research Exchange Forum (a faculty-wide seminar series, coordinated by students and another professor). The six student members were invited to participate in a focus group (all were in Year 2 or later of their PhD). Five were able to do so, in two separate meetings.

In the focus groups, individuals were asked to describe why they had joined the committee, what the experience had been like, what they thought the impact had been, and how they felt the experience had helped them understand what they were becoming. In other words, the discussions were retrospective interpretations of a partially shared experience, the committee meetings, but situated in distinct personal histories. The taped discussions were transcribed and coded following an emergent coding process (Miles and Huberman,1994; Huberman and Miles, 2002).

In this study we were looking at the ways in which doctoral students can contribute to enhancing the academic climate. When we began this study, we had not conceived of students as their own developers. Yet, that notion emerged strongly as we documented the commitment and preparedness of students to make their own and others' experiences of the doctorate more powerful and positive. Based on student responses in the focus groups, critical to such outcomes would be a) direct access to powerful administrative structures (in this case, the Associate Dean of the Faculty chairing the committee), and b) more students than academic members on any committee so that the student voice is not diluted.

Study 2: Here, the goal was to understand the nature of the English Ph.D from the perspectives of doctoral students and professors (McAlpine et al, in press - b). As educational researchers undertaking a program of research in a Department of English, we recognized that we were entering into a community with distinct ways of thinking, valuing and acting (Becher and Trowler, 2001). We wanted to explore with both professors and students their perspectives to provide some insight into the culture we would be working in. We began by contacting our research collaborator in the Department who had previously been both Chair and Graduate Program Director. She suggested we meet with her, the present Chair and present Program Director. During that focus group meeting, they offered the names of students whom we might approach to be interviewed. These were: a first year student, a fifth year student, and a postdoctoral fellow who had just completed her degree in the Department. They all agreed to come to a focus group meeting.

In each focus group, we discussed the following: the nature of doctoral education in English today in Canada/North America; changes in the PhD that have occurred/are occurring; emerging issues and tensions, if any, across disciplinary, institutional and societal contexts. In other words, the discussions were reflective interpretations of personal histories and experiences of and in the discipline. The focus group discussions were taped and transcribed. And an emergent coding process was undertaken to answer the initial research question.

What emerged from this examination were distinct and somewhat contrasting perspectives on the factors that are influencing the English PhD in Canada and North America. In fact, the experience, as reflected in these discussions, is one of lived contradictions, pressures and resistance by both academics and students as they attempt to reconcile societal, institutional and disciplinary expectations. The academics were attempting to avoid disruption or breakdown to disciplinary knowledge production while responding to changing external environments and opposing forces within the discipline. The students were attempting to learn sufficiently about this 'shifting and fragile system' (Evans, 1990) in order not just to enter but also to contribute to change within their new community. The dilemmas emerge and are maintained in the co-construction of the discipline (a distinct culture of knowledge and ways of thinking, acting, valuing), the program (the doctorate) and the process (becoming an academic). The struggle was described as finding continuity in personal and disciplinary goals, and sustaining academic authenticity.

Study 3: In this study the focus was the nature of the conversation between student and supervisor in Education as they discussed a piece of the student's writing connected to the dissertation (Pare et al, 2006). Writing is an often overlooked aspect of the Ph.D. process, yet it is central to success, and signifies our membership in the disciplinary community (Aitchison and Lee, 2006); it is also a very academic representation of voice. In this study, discussion and reflection were not stimulated and reflective (as in the other two studies); rather, a 'fly-on the-wall' approach was taken resulting in relatively authentic conversations (in the sense that the researchers were not there, but the tape recorder might to some extent influence the interaction). Academics we felt would be interested were approached to participate in this study representing a range of educational fields; the first four approached agreed. The next step was seeking the consent of one of their students who was either writing a dissertation proposal or a dissertation draft. This was done first by each professor - with follow-up by the researchers for consent.

Once the four conversations had been taped and returned to the researchers, segments pertinent to the purpose of the original study were transcribed and analyzed to see what themes emerged. The analysis indicated that examining supervisory sessions dedicated to writing can reveal important insights into the factors that influence the success of becoming academics. Five themes emerged as particularly fruitful areas of investigation: the local culture of the department and faculty; the supervisor and committee as a microcosm of the Discipline; the supervisor as Everyreader, modeling responses to the student's text; the student's developing understanding of and participation in the discipline; and the supervisor as supporter and community co-member.

Summary: We think of the conversations and interviews that were part of these three studies as providing insight into the various aspects of academic practice referred to earlier: inquiry, teaching, service and career development. The first study examined the efforts of a committee of Education doctoral students to create a more collegial scholarly environment for students in their Faculty. In terms of academic practice, the students were taking on responsibility for an under-examined aspect of academic practice, that of *service*. The second study examined similarities and differences in student and professor perspectives on the changing expectations of the PhD in English; in retrospect, this clearly highlighted *career development* as the students analyzed their present and their potential academic practices. The third study examined the actual conversations of Education students and supervisors as they reviewed writing related to the particular student's dissertation; again, in retrospect, this was very much a focus on the *inquiry* aspect of academic practice.

A REANALYSIS OF THE FIRST THREE STUDIES: THE PROCESS

We conceived the proposed reanalysis of the data as a complex cognitive task since it involved looking across seven different transcripts, based on different protocols in the case of two studies, and in the third study naturally emerging conversations based on whatever text was under discussion. Thus, the method for the analysis was designed to enable successive levels of reduction of data. The intent in the successive stages was to refine our understanding of the essence of the embedded meaning while still preserving a direct link to the data. This gradual shift from being embedded in a particular time and place to the essence enabled us to see similarities across the quite distinct contexts. In this way, we attempted to ensure that our interpretations were representative of the totality of the data set while still attending to the influence of context.

We began with the following a priori themes taken from what had emerged from the initial analyses of the three studies: a) identity as represented in *voice*, and b) *tensions or challenges* in relation to different elements of the *nested contexts* model. These themes formed the initial scaffold for the analysis.

The goal of the reanalysis was to see a) whether, in fact, these a priori themes held when they were our specific focus, b) if so, what other themes might emerge, and c) to further clarify both a priori and emergent themes by identifying sub-themes.

The transcripts for each study were read three times, each time with a different intent as described below.

First Reading

a) For each study, the relevant transcripts were read by the first author looking for text that seemed related to identity development as represented by *voice*, *nested contexts*, and *tensions/ challenges* (the a priori themes).

b) Segments of text related to these themes were bracketed and referred to as episodes. Episodes are defined as a unit of analysis: a discrete segment of text with internal coherence that relates to one or more of the a priori themes. An episode can vary from a phrase to a page.

c) It became evident in this reading was that episodes often incorporated more than one a priori theme.

Second Reading

a) The goal in this reading was to develop descriptive summaries of each episode that preserved the context and the full meaning, but reduced the amount of text we had to work with.

b) The summary was inserted immediately above the episode in order to preserve a direct link to the actual text. These summaries made apparent the relational nature of the a priori themes. In other words, we began to see that the themes existed in relation to each other, e.g., tension and voice linked and co-occurring.

c) At this point, sub-themes that seemed to be emerging were noted, e.g., the theme 'voice' appeared to have two representations, one individual and the other collective.

d) During this reading, it was decided to replace the a priori theme *nested contexts* with the theme name of *community* in order to more specifically name the multiple communities emerging within the different nested contexts.

e) A new theme at the level of the a priori themes emerged: *pleasure* surfaced as another way in which voice was experienced in contrast with the a priori theme of *tensions/ challenges*.

Third Reading

a) The goal here was to characterize more consistently the descriptive summaries of episodes within and across the transcripts so as to name the emerging themes and sub-themes more succinctly and to enable a synthesis within and across the different transcripts and contexts.

b) Effort was made to move towards the essence of meaning, that is, to remove reference to the particular context, and to highlight the relational nature of the themes. This shift was represented in the use of consistently named themes and sub-themes across the transcripts (as represented in the codebook) instead of the descriptions that incorporated more contextual features.

c) The named themes and sub-themes were added above the descriptive summary for each episode, so that it was still possible to read the original text.

This three-step reanalysis of the data from each of the three original studies was done at different times so as to bring relatively fresh eyes to the reading of the data from each separate study and preserve whatever variation might be present in the different contexts represented by each study.

The codebook and the results of the analysis were then audited by the second author. The audit confirmed the coherence of the coding scheme. The only recoding of episodes related to whether 8 episodes coded as *larger* disciplinary community were accurately coded. The first author's assumption had been that one local individual could represent the larger disciplinary community. After discussion, it was agreed this was not the case, that these episodes were, in fact, examples of local disciplinary communities, even if only communities of one locally. In other words, individuals in the local community are linked to and thus represent an important diversity within the broader discipline and needed to be recognized as such. In addition, 4 episodes were deleted because although they were representative of identity, they did not represent voice.

THE FINDINGS

Themes and Sub-Themes

Voice: Voice was conceived as an expression of identity in social interactions, so the focus was on outer voice(s), both spoken and written. Voice was conceived as a means to influence boundaries and negotiation of roles, a means to maintain or shift structures. We conceive experiences of voice as contributing to a sense of self, agency and intention. Sub-themes: There were two sub-themes of *voice*: the *individual student voice*, and the collective. The latter manifested as either *collective student voice* or *collective disciplinary voice*. (See Table 1 for summary of themes and sub-themes.)

Communities: This theme enables a fine-grained representation of the varied communities emerging within the different nested contexts. Communities create the occasion for interactions. They are the locations (imagined and real) where purposes, roles and tasks are enacted based on often tacit rules and practices. Sub-themes: There were three sub-themes of community, two with more specific categories. The first was the *larger disciplinary community*, the virtual community that provides the foundation for more local communities to exist. The second was the *institutional community* represented in the *faculty* as well as in the *university*. The third was the *local disciplinary community* which was evident in the following forms: *dissertation committee, program/department, research team, supervisor, student groups,* and *faculty as a discipline*. There were no instances of society as community.

Table 1. Themes and sub-themes

A priori themes (First reading)	Second reading	Third reading
Voice as an expression of identity	*Voice*	*Voice* • *individual* • *collective*
Nested contexts	(changed to) *Multiple communities* within the different nested contexts	*Multiple communities* • *larger disciplinary* • *institutional* • *local disciplinary*
Tensions or challenges in relation to different elements of the nested contexts	*Tensions or challenges*	*Tensions or challenges* • *naming a challenge/ tension* • *explaining use of voice* • *practicing voice* • *using voice*
	Pleasures	*Pleasures* • *explaining use of voice* • *using voice*

Challenges/ tensions: This theme represents the results of, for instance, differences between individual and collective values, unexplained roles and expectations, structural features of the different contexts, differences in roles across different communities, and the dialectic of interactions with others. Sub-themes: Four sub-themes emerged. The first was *naming a challenge/ tension*, that is, stating what the issue is. The second was *explaining use of voice*, articulating how to deal with the challenge/ tension. The third was *practicing voice*, rehearsing how to express voice appropriately, and the last was *using voice*, actually having a say (or not) in a community.

Pleasures: This theme, which emerged during the second reading, represents a positive feature of voice within the different communities. Episodes in the transcripts demonstrated times when the students felt a sense of enhanced agency that they were contributing to a community in a positive manner. Sub-themes: There were two sub-themes or aspects to pleasures: *explaining use of voice*, articulating how to contribute; and *using voice*, actually having a say.

Intersection of themes and sub-themes: Episodes were sometimes double or triple coded; they could, for instance, refer to both local and larger disciplinary communities, or to both naming and explaining a challenge. This demonstrates the intersection of different communities and varied aspects of voice that are the lived experience of doctoral students.

Distribution of Themes and Sub-Themes

There were 70 episodes identified in the data from the original three studies that were distributed in the following manner. In the four conversations in which individual pairs of doctoral students and professors discussed a piece of the dissertation, there were 3 identified episodes in Conversation A, 8 in B, 2 in C, and 3 in D. These conversations were focused on the task of completing the dissertation, rarely broadening out to other aspects of doctoral work, and were by and large about individual student written voice. Perhaps because these were conversations between students and professors, it is here where 'explaining' principally occurred.

In the one English focus group, there were 6 identified episodes. Here students reflected on their personal histories and experiences of the doctorate and more broadly possible futures in the discipline; individual written and spoken voice – present and future - are evident with some evidence of collective voice. In the two Education focus groups, there were 30 identified episodes from focus group A and 16 in group B. These were principally individual spoken voice – present and future - with some collective voice, and it was only in these two groups that pleasure emerged as a theme.

While the third group represents two thirds of the total episodes and might be perceived to overly influence the findings, generally, the different aspects of voice and community that we report occurred in at least two of the three studies. When this is not the case, that is, a theme was only evident in one data set, we note that explicitly.

In what follows, we give a sense of both the richness of the data and the variation in experiences of voice that emerged across the episodes. The episodes included are drawn relatively equally in number from across the different data sets. Both individual and collective voice were manifested in relation to different communities – local and large disciplinary communities and institutional communities. The majority of episodes focused on tensions and challenges, with a limited number of episodes dealing with pleasures. For each example, there is a brief description.

Example Episodes Reflective of Themes and Sub-Themes

We begin with individual voice, providing examples of the different ways it emerged, and then collective voice, again with representative examples. Titles in italics make clear the link between voice and community and the nature of the relationship (tension or pleasure. As well, bold is used to signify more easily the study where the episode was found. The reference at the end of an episode refers to the source and number of the episode, and ST = student, SU = supervisor.

Individual Voice

We found instances of individual voice represented in a) the larger disciplinary community, b) different institutional communities (university, faculty) and c) distinct local disciplinary communities (supervisor, dissertation committee, department/program, research group).

1. Individual voice in larger disciplinary community: Tension/ challenge - using voice
Example from *English:*
    "I could have done a 'better' dissertation" if I had taken longer; basically I was speedy because of the money issue." (Eng 1)

In this very short episode in relation to the larger disciplinary community, we see a recently graduated PhD student referring to the tensions experienced between whether to complete her dissertation promptly or to spend more time to create and use her written voice in a way that would more substantially contribute to the discipline. Finances were important in her deciding to finish in four years although in English six years to completion is not uncommon.
Example from *English*:

    ST1 – Much has changed; now you need more pubs, and sometimes a post doc is expected. You need a lot [publications] to get a hired in a research-intensive university. And, many of them [present academics] were hired with a master's, and a few pubs.
    ST2 - Now we need to be from away, they don't hire locally, so you can't anymore use being a sessional [lecturer] as a way to get in … we have to try to get published substantially before graduation if we are to have any hope competing for a tenure-track position.(Eng 6)

This episode demonstrates an awareness of the increasing challenges for PhD students to use their voice in substantial ways – getting well published - before they complete their degrees. This is a structural constraint that is distinctly different from more senior academics, and one that these students understand to be essential if they hope to achieve their goal to hold tenure-track positions in a research-intensive university.

2. Individual voice in institutional community- university: Challenge – explaining use of voice (to prevent possible loss of voice)
    Example from *Education* conversation:

    SU – okay, let's just figure things out because you're going to run into time limitation too; you know that, right?
    ST – uh-huh
    SU – so, and that's going to come up in May or June
    ST- what do you mean? What's going to come up in May or June?
    SU – time limitation – you're in your last year that the university allows you … to stay on, you have to justify your existence … in order to do that, I would like you to have colloqued and be working on your results … so I can say 'in the past year this students has finished her internship, defended her proposal, her data is collected and she's now working on her analysis – okay that will be defensible. If you haven't defended your proposal at that

point, it's going to be not nearly so good. And what the university can ask you to do is they ask you to withdraw. And then you can work on your thesis kind of whenever you want to on your own time [continues description]

ST – I don't like the idea.

SU – okay, good I'm glad we're on the same page.

ST- I certainly hope that that's not what would happen. (EC, A3)

Here, the supervisor (SU) explained the tensions between the student's own progress on the dissertation and the university's expectations - and its ability to cut off her academic voice by asking her to withdraw. The supervisor explained the voice she would need to use (and the work this would entail for the student) in order to ensure that the student could retain her voice in the university. Interestingly, the student (ST) seemed not to have been aware of this structural aspect of academic life.

3. Individual voice in institutional community- faculty: Pleasure- using voice
Example from *Education focus group*

ST2 - so, I can see myself later in my career in the university trying to do things like that, to improve a little bit the quality of life of the students, to improve the sense of belonging, really I like being part of the Research Exchange Forum [organizing committee] - learning to organize, being able to go and ask questions of some presenters – what are you going to present? (Ed, A12)

In this episode, a student described the present pleasure of using her voice in the Faculty and also envisagedthe same thing in her future life as an academic.

4. Individual voice in local disciplinary community – supervisor: Challenge- practicing voice
Example from *Education conversation*

SU - [points out and reads two sections and asks what student means] I was a little bit lost

ST – what I'm trying to say is … [she explains, defines terms]

SU – I would object to the word 'influence' – explains confusion and rephrases

ST – [she tries to more fully explain]

SU – okay, specify that clearly because it's not what [researcher] says (EC, B4)

Here, the supervisor did not understand what the student was trying to say and challenged the student to articulate the argument more clearly. The student practiced using her voice and articulated *on the second attempt* a representation of what she wanted to say which satisfied the supervisor's concerns.

5. Individual voice in local disciplinary communities – dissertation committee member: Challenge – practicing voice

Example from *Education conversation:*

> ST and SU have a long discussion about where to put a particular piece of text; they appear to come to a decision, that it should be at the end, then the student says …
> ST – okay, my only concern about moving *that* into the concluding paragraph is that [committee member] is going to say ' well, if there's still all this research to be done on careers, then how can you say that …' so the student suggests moving the text into the section about the research question
> SU agrees (EC, B5)

Here, we see a discussion about where a section of writing – the student's written voice - should best be placed. The student and supervisor appeared to come to a decision about this, but then the student raised a concern about how a committee member might challenge the decision. This resulted in a shift of the text to another location.

6. Individual voice in local disciplinary communities – department/program: Challenge – using (losing) voice

> SU1 – there's also disciplinary culture – in [my department], there are some with a psych background and they are extremely competitive - and you get in this cycle that you are not sure what – you don't know what you can share, what you should share – are you giving something away? If you've learned something, should you tell the other person … (ED, A21)
> ST2 – I find people here very competitive – a lack of willingness to share
> ST1 – They need to learn that it's okay to share- it will actually move you forward
> ST2 – and I believe…. I'm telling it to everybody … so they know; I didn't even know - some people are just so competitive
> ST1 – And you still believe that there's this weeding out process going on
> ST2 – that thing about the people on both sides of you not being there (ED, A22)

The above two episodes followed closely one upon the other; two students described the tensions in their local disciplinary culture – the department/program, and the ways in which it constrained the use of voice (and the potential to develop collective voice).

7. Individual voice in local disciplinary communities – research team, etc.: Pleasure – using voice

Example from *Education focus group*

> ST 1 – The image I've got in my head is of a community of practice – I know when I got into the program I felt like 'oh, I'm supposed to become a member of this community of practice but the mechanisms for me to become part of it are really only informal… being on a research team … working [with local professors in faculty development activities] and working on other things - that I was moving towards becoming an academic (Ed, B44)

This last example of local disciplinary community refers to different activities – research team, other work with professors - that are available to enjoy using one's voice. However, they are informal and need to be sought out.

Collective Voice

Two kinds of collective voice surfaced. The first was student voice in the institutional community of the Faculty which only occurred in the Education focus groups. We provide examples of both challenge and pleasure. The second was disciplinary voice within the university, which only occurred in the English focus group - students as representatives of the discipline, the department as a representative of the department.

1. Collective voice in institutional community – faculty: Challenge – using voice
Example from *Education Focus group*

ST1 – It's almost like the Faculty as an organization was not equipped then to get that process of induction or socialization into a community of practice and now with activities like…[ones created by the committee] you do have mechanisms for this to happen. I mean it's moving in the right direction, I'm just wondering how much further do we need to go to make it happen more effectively. (ED, B46)

Here, the student describes the challenge the student committee faces in creating and using a collective voice for doctoral students by noting the place where the committee started and where they want to go.

2. Collective (and individual) voice in institutional community – faculty: Pleasure – using voice
Example from *Education focus group*

ST1 – I joined because you asked me – and something you said when you asked me about enhancing the culture for graduate students and it struck me that there is no culture for graduate students - what a novel idea because I haven't experienced such a culture, so being a part of something that would maybe start a culture seemed also a good way to think about my own growth and where I was in the process. A chance to resolve some of the issues probably I had with the faculty and department. Ed, A2)

In this episode, a student describes the potential pleasure of joining the student committee that had a mandate to generate a collective student voice to enhance academic climate in the Faculty. She also perceived it as a way to develop and use her individual voice.

3. Collective voice in institutional community – university: Challenge – using (losing) voice
Example from *English*

ST1 - I'm very attuned to the funding question. Last year I was grad president [in the department] so very involved, interested from a more political perspective on the issues that don't get dealt with – funding, space, resources - all of those things which contribute to attrition and completion rates which are very important and which don't get dealt with adequately because we don't bring funding into the university like the sciences do.
ST2 - I don't know about how it is allotted, but I would say that our funding situation as English students at McGill is very precarious

ST1 - The English department is the largest in Arts (maybe even on campus) and we have a completely disproportionate rate of funding; the number of students vs funding is completely out of whack ... the administration [the university] allocates resources in certain ways – it's not put into humanities ... compounds elitism of university. (Eng, 2)

In this episode, students named the challenge for those in English in relation to other disciplines which appeared to have more powerful collective voices in the university, especially as it relates to funding for students. They viewed the power differential as discriminatory.

Example from *English*

ST 1 - The "Arts Graduate Students Society" arose out of a grassroots reaction to an administrative top-down decision that resulted in a significant reduction in graduate student representation within existing university structures .... Initially, it started with a group of students meeting informally to try to find a solution to the imposition of "progress reports" which seemed, at the time, to imply that the administration was trying to find a way to kick students out of their programs. From that, a parallel movement developed to try to create an official structure so that these kinds of decisions would not happen again without us knowing, so that we would have a means to recourse within the university structure. ... The AGSS Constitution has been ratified (during a Post Graduate Student Society meeting) and an executive committee was elected to coordinate future action. A listserv has been set-up, student representatives from the 18 Arts departments have been brought on board, and the AGSS is organizing an academic conference for Arts graduate students to be held in early spring.

Here, we see the students being challenged by an institutional decision that they felt could lead to a potential loss of voice by being 'kicked out' of their programs. They responded by creating a collective voice through a structure (the AGSS) that is now formally recognized by the university; their hope was that this organization could influence future policies in positive ways.

Example Episode: Intersections of Themes

The above episodes were chosen to highlight particular expressions of voice in relation to different and distinct communities. The following was chosen because it demonstrates the potential complexity that may emerge in a single episode as multiple themes and sub-themes intersect. We have already provided some examples of relatively simple intersections, e.g., two sub-themes of voice or two different communities. We have chosen this particular one – an episode from an Education conversation - because it exemplifies a high degree of intersection. We can imagine that this episode may, in fact, be highly representative of lived doctoral experience, given that the dissertation conversations between student and supervisor were the most authentic contexts in which we collected data.

This episode represents *individual voice*. It includes evidence of *challenges* within the *larger disciplinary community* – who shares a point of view - and *two local communities – the dissertation committee, and the supervisor-student*. The aspects of voice that are evident are *naming, explaining* and *practicing*.

Example from *Education conversation*

SU – [after reviewing comments] The comments were kind of articulate, you know, well argued. But I just felt that this wasn't what your thesis was about. And so I kind of felt that, you know, I was a bit nervous about what she was saying

ST – she also said that if she were the external she would fail it

SU– really?

ST – yeah, she said 'from my experience this would fail. So that was very very different from what I had heard and I'm kind of, I'm concerned that I don't want to

SU– well, I don't feel it would fail, and I mean that the thing is, with Ph.D. theses you've got to be careful about who you choose to be external examiners. Someone like [name], for example, might fail this dissertation because, you know, I mean there's a bunch of people, of which [member] is part, and I think that she'd have huge problems with this, okay? There are other people who wouldn't and who would read it in the same way that say, me and [member 2] would read it, you know. And I think that's who we'll send it to. We'll put them down as the examiners. There's, if you like, to it, right? ...

SU –(suggests that member 2's comments are generally favourable ...)

ST – so, I'm going to incorporate some of her feedback. I'm not going to rewrite my dissertation. I'm not willing to do that

SU – no, no, no – absolutely not

ST – but what kind of

SU – I think what you should do is, I mean, what you have proposed ... makes sense. Then, broadening to adult education section – include [author] okay, because it's a bit like doing your 'hail mary', sort of thing, you gotta do it and

ST – I'll say what he's contributed and the kind of – where I diverge from what he was looking at

SU – yeah, yeah I think so. ... so that when the reader comes across this other stuff and they say 'why hasn't she done that, you've already forewarned them that's not what you're about ... also, like, in terms of the activist, like that paper you published on [name] – you've referenced that – I hope you have anyway. I think what you should say is – have a footnote to say – in that chapter – that some of this work has already been published in an international journal, or whatever – because that's gone through a peer review process, it's been published – and that tells people that you've already got the seal of approval from your academic peers.

ST – what happens if I don't satisfy [member]

SU – it doesn't matter because she's a committee member and what we'll do is we'll get ... she'll have no part in the evaluation of the thesis [explains choice re committee members at defense] (EC, D15)

The supervisor was talking to the student about feedback provided by a committee member to a draft of the dissertation. We see here a number of challenges and tensions: a) competing views in the field and the need for strategies to defend/ assert one's voice within it; b) tensions around who has power in the local and larger disciplinary communities and how to develop allegiances; c) the fact that individuals in local disciplinary communities may not share common views. The supervisor affirmed the student's stance and suggested two disciplinary strategies: the first the choice of dissertation defense members to deal with local disciplinary tensions, and the second, a way of writing to deal with the larger disciplinary community. Lastly, the student practiced a part of the writing strategy.

SUMMARY OF FINDINGS

We began with three central ideas a) factors influencing doctoral student success across nested contexts; b) various aspects of academic practice, and c) voice (and agency) as an expression of identity. We return to these now in summarizing the findings.

In the study of Education students, they were mandated to change the academic climate of their Faculty. A positive academic climate is important in reducing isolation and creating a sense of belonging. We heard students' retrospective interpretations of a partially shared experience, the committee meetings. The committee work gave them a growing sense of collective voice, not just tensions but also pleasures of being able to use their voices in order to enhance the academic climate and contribute to their local disciplinary community (the *service* aspect of academic practice). There was also some individual voice – a sense of becoming an academic. Yet, residing side-by-side with this growing collective voice was a recognition of the struggle to strengthen what they perceived as a fragile collective voice within the local disciplinary community – the faculty. Outside of the committee they might be 'heard', but not 'listened to".

The English students engaged in reflective interpretations of personal histories and experiences of and in the discipline. They expressed feelings of tension and some frustration about their future lives as academics. They noted the difficulties of lack of funding, with one making the decision to do a less excellent dissertation in order to limit debt. They believed they were being prepared for and would like to be professors at research-intensive universities, a path also promoted by their professors. Yet, what was necessary to achieve this goal, the use of their individual written voice to create an academic identity before graduation, was seen as daunting; the disciplinary expectations – the modes of research - were changing. As well, they perceived a challenge in expressing their collective disciplinary voice in the university; it was not perceived to be powerful in comparison with other disciplines. In terms of academic practice, students were struggling to reconcile their future career intentions as regards their preferred academic practice with the larger disciplinary reality.

In the Education dissertation conversations, the supervisory relationship was highlighted. Supervisors and students engaged in authentic conversations about very specific aspects of the dissertation. Again, students experienced issues related to mode of research. They expressed tensions and challenges related to developing and using their voice in the larger and local disciplinary communities, as well as the institutional community. What these conversations demonstrated because of the presence of the supervisors were a number of specific disciplinary and institutional strategies – ways of locating others/oneself amongst the academic tensions in the discipline and institutional structures - that the supervisors called on and explained to students as a way of dealing with the tensions. As well, the students had opportunities to practice their voice with a more senior member of the discipline. In terms of academic practice, students were developing their voices in relation to the inquiry aspect of academic practice.

How Might We Understand These Representations of Voice?

We move now to an exploration of the meaning of these findings, specifically, the construction of a conceptual framework to synthesize them, as well as the pedagogical implications.

A Conceptual Framework to Synthesize the Findings

The reanalysis we undertook based on three separate studies provides, we believe, greater insight into the challenges doctoral students face in developing academic identity within contexts that have inherent tensions and challenges. Tensions included lack of voice (as well as pleasure) within the local disciplinary community (Study 1), awareness of the near impossibility of reconciling personal, local and societal drivers (Study 2), and conflicts among academics in the broader community that students need to recognize and heed (Study 3). A largely invisible doctoral curriculum emerged that involved students surfacing and trying to reconcile societal drivers, institutional demands and disciplinary expectations (McAlpine and Norton, 2006) in a shifting, complex world as they participated in and learned about the workplace they were entering. We saw the students learning to use emerging voice – an expression of identity and agency. They were negotiating within and across a network of activity systems (Engestrom et al, 1999; Blackler, 1995) in order to approximate their intentions, and this involved experiencing both challenges and pleasures.

We argued initially that in order to understand the issues around doctoral student success, we needed to understand the perspectives of the students. So, in what follows we discuss first our growing understanding of identity development, particularly how we conceive students' perceptions of voice and agency in relation to community as experienced by these students. We then analyze examples from the episodes that highlight the interaction of voice and agency within community in order to better understand the relation between the structural sources of the tensions and the student as agent, attempting/ learning to forge voice(s) and role(s) within the nested contexts.

Voice, agency and community: The experienced tensions and pleasures of using voice need to be understood as emerging out of collective and established practices which have been determined by different academics communities within the nested contexts. This study highlights that within each of the nested contexts, students are engaged and negotiating within multiple communities around different activities. In fact, they are enmeshed in a network of systems. For instance, the reported range of activities in the local disciplinary community included: supervisor-student, dissertation committee, department/program, research team. If students choose to remain in their programs with the intent to become accepted as members of this range of disparate academic communities, their developing voices will need to be recognized and acknowledged in this full range of activities.

In other words, students are engaged in a process that requires learning how to reconcile perceptions of individual desired intentions within the structural practices and tensions that exist in each of these academic activities. This requires that, to some degree, they need to internalize the beliefs and ideologies of the different communities, and in the process make choices – when there are conflicts - about which communities they can most comfortably, most easily, align themselves with. Thus, in developing voice(s), some resistance or disruption to an activity is possible but the degree of personal agency is constrained by the power of one's voice. One is shaped by and shapes participation in activities since activities bring together intersecting and varying desires, responsibilities, practices and expectations. Based on the evidence which we present below, we suggest that there is greater potential for students to perceive their influence on the structural tensions in <u>local communities,</u> and it is this we return to in considering pedagogical implications.

Demonstrating the interaction of student voice, agency and community: There are a number of examples where students clearly experienced the inability to influence the structural features of a community. Their voice(s) represented frustration, but also compliance. One is the episode when time limitation would have forced the student to withdraw. There were no degrees of freedom for the student; this was made quite clear by the supervisor (the local representative of the university). The student's only means to maintain and develop her individual voice within the academy was to comply by completing a certain number of tasks within a set time period. And, the English students noted the difficulty of using their collective English voice in the University, given the power of collective disciplinary voices such as the sciences. While bemoaning the situation (as did their professors), they could not conceive strategies to change the relationship. As well, they struggled with the changing nature of the expectations of the larger disciplinary community – that they needed to publish substantially before completing – and the expectations of the university – that they needed to complete quickly. Neither their individual nor collective voices had the power to influence the practices of the larger disciplinary community or the institution.

At the same time, as reflected in some other episodes, students were finding ways to negotiate their voices. These episodes tended to occur as noted above in different local communities. Recall the Education dissertation conversation in which the student practiced how to use her voice in dealing with a committee member who was not prepared to pass her.

Another instance is the English students who were unable to use their collective voice to prevent a change in university policy (the institution of annual progress reports for every doctoral student). However, in their department they were through their collective voice (in an episode not included here) able to modify how this policy would be enacted in the department, so they wouldn't be disadvantaged by taking longer to complete than the university expected. Furthermore (as evident in an episode included here), the students took action for the future by creating the Arts Graduate Student Society (AGSS), a formal structure that they felt would have more power to present their collective voice.

A useful way of thinking about the contrast between the students' inability to influence the university policy and their hope that the new AGSS society would enable them to have a voice is to consider the Society as a representation of a 'third space' (Gutierrez et al, 1995). Third spaces are newly constructed activities that bring together people who would not previously have interacted collectively; a common motive creates a new activity system. In this new activity, roles and division of labour have not yet been established, so there are degrees of freedom for new practices and structures to be created. In these third spaces, just as in ongoing activities, individuals may have different personal intentions, but they are drawn to working together because they can perceive a collective shared motive.

Another instance of this contrast between established and third spaces in creating and using voice can be seen in the Education focus groups where students contrasted two different local communities. They noted the existence of their collective voice in a new community -

the Committee – but not necessarily in another community - the faculty. We propose they had both individual and collective voices in the Committee because the committee was created to be structurally distinct from other faculty committees and was mandated specifically to support the development of the students' voices. In the Committee, students from different departments were interacting with a limited number of academics who were intent on furthering the student's collective voice. This third space contrasts with the students' roles in their other committee work in the faculty which tends to be departmentally based with most committees having only one student representative.

What is very evident is that what we described initially in the singular - the local disciplinary context - represents, in fact, multiple outposts of the discipline, outposts that can be quite varied, and in disagreement with each other. Recall, for instance, the difficulties that the student was experiencing in the dissertation committee – trying to find a way to position herself – to find a voice - when there was clear disagreement among her committee members. The supervisor revealed practices that were unknown to the student, but well known to him that would obviate the challenges she was facing. However, in the process she would have to learn how to align herself with a certain group of people in the field, and thus not align herself with others.

What we have reported here is students experiencing the authentic academic workplace. How academics interact is guided by both complementary and competing motives and goals, such as being distinctive while also belonging (Vignoles et al., 2005). Through the perspective of identity development, individuals are shaping an understanding of the academic self, based on a constant dialogue with the communities with which they wish to become identified (Taylor, 1991), yet also influencing those communities. Thus, it is not surprising that we found a strong affective component in these reports – both negative and positive. Similar emotions have been documented in more experienced academics in relation to their academic work (Neumann, 2006): exhilaration, thrill, frustration, and depression as well as more muted ones – which would suggest that we need to be more attentive to the affective aspects of doctoral student experience.

Implications for Program Structures and Pedagogical Practices

Bieber and Worley (2006) and Austin (2002) are among the researchers who have begun to investigate the doctoral student view. Among their findings are that many doctoral students hold incomplete understandings of academic life and experience mixed messages about the relative importance of teaching and research. Many students have reported that they become increasingly aware of conflicting demands on academics and wonder if a balanced life, as an academic, is possible. Some students reported finding it easy to make sense of the values of academic practice, but more common were those who struggled, not sure if they could align their own values with those of the academy (Austin, 2002).

We have already referred to academic work or practice as encompassing in various combinations aspects of inquiry, teaching and service, and the fact that there are certainly multiple representations of academic work/ practice (McAlpine and Hopwood, 2006). At the same time, there are also, certainly, commonalities, shared notions of how academic work is distinct from other kinds of work (e.g., business, industrial, governmental, voluntary sectors). This practice is academic partly because it takes place in institutions with mandates to provide higher education, and usually to contribute to knowledge through inquiry. This impacts the structural nature of universities, which are distinct from say a business context. Further, the fact that most academics have strong loyalties to their discipline, in some cases, stronger loyalties than to their institution also makes the practice distinct. (Recall the large number of episodes in the study reported here that were focused on voice in relation to some disciplinary community.) At the same time, there are diverse disciplinary, departmental and institutional cultural-historical traditions that underlie the variation in what is understood as academic.

We move now to consider different lenses on academic work/ practice – different ways of conceiving of the nature of what we do as academics and of what we are inviting doctoral students to participate in, lenses which might be illuminating to budding academics. Our intention here is to use these different lenses to consider the ways in which we approach our doctoral pedagogies in light of the results of this analysis, particularly the range of diverse communities, the many tensions and limited reported pleasures, the opportunities for voice to be modeled, practiced and used. We first describe the lenses and then draw on episodes from the data to consider the pedagogical implications.

For us, academic practice can be viewed through the following lenses (McAlpine and Hopwood, 2006), each of which has strengths and limitations in considering pedagogical implications. Academic practice can be conceived as:

- a bundle of *skills or competencies* that academics may use in skilful ways (e.g., articulate research questions, create new curriculum or course design)
- a series of *activities* that academics can engage in to varying degrees (e.g., writing a research proposal, supervising a student, teaching a course)
- the *production of knowledge*: this is often described in terms of research productivity and its consequences for reputation and career, e.g., Brew's (2006) trading conception of research

These three lenses remind us of the scope and breadth of practice. They contribute relatively concrete characterizations of academic practice – what one knows, what one does, what one produces. Their strength lies, we argue, in providing a pedagogical perspective that is easy to articulate – the 'what' that is to be learned or done or produced as a doctoral student. The first lens was not evident in the students' descriptions of their experiences. However, evidence of the second lens emerged in the range of activities they described participating in. Evidence of the third lens can be seen in the English students' concern about publishing before graduation, and the focus on writing in the Education dissertation conversations. In fact, in an episode not reported in this chapter, a supervisor provides advice about the length of dissertation chapters in relation to making them easier to publish as papers.

In looking at the fourth and fifth lenses, there is a shift from the practice(s) to be learned to the individual engaged in doing and learning these practices.

- *identity and membership in a community* (Lave and Wenger, 1991); this encompasses taking on the discourse and behaviour of the discipline (e.g., being a 'geologist'); this may also include membership in a range of other potentially competing communities, e.g., institutional, departmental

- the *embodiment of academic values* - understanding, subscribing, and being defined by a set of values; this view goes beyond adherence to ethical standards and is concerned with the fundamental and personal commitment to the academic enterprise.

From our perspective, the strength of the fourth lens, identity, as a pedagogical framework lies in viewing doctoral education as just one part of a journey in a long career trajectory – whether from doctoral student through post-doctoral fellow, through pre-tenure academic and so on <u>or</u> from doctoral student to a range of a range of non-academic careers. This developmental perspective situates the doctorate as part of a life-long journey in which one takes up a range of different roles. Additional strengths associated with this view are that it attends to individualized views of what it is to be an academic, for instance, among members of a dissertation committee; this enables students and supervisors to explore relationships among different aspects of academic practice as they relate to and are perceived by a particular individual in a particular context. We see this lens emerging strongly in the Education dissertation conversations – where individual disciplinary differences surfaced frequently.

The strength of the fifth lens lies in foregrounding the tensions inherent in the value-laden nature of practice experienced in negotiating one's identity and community membership. It builds on the notion of practice as personal and emotional that was described in the previous lens (and that has been reported as essential experiences of academic life - Bieber and Worley, 2006; Austin, 2002). Yet, like the previous lens, it is not easy to see the actual practices in which values and purpose are brought to bear. In other words, it is a somewhat abstract or 'fuzzy' representation of what students are experiencing so it may perhaps be less easily used as an analytic pedagogical tool. However, we think this lens effectively represents the range of tensions/ challenges and pleasures that emerged in the analysis.

For us, the strength of these last two lenses combined is to integrate personal intentionality and affect with a longitudinal developmental perspective. Learning about and attempting to contribute to academic practice is an ongoing process always under construction, one in which there are complexities of emotion and conflict as well as pleasure that can be articulated and negotiated through voice.

Since we have evidence from the students' perspective of four of the five lenses (activities, knowledge production, identity, embodied values), we provide some examples of the pedagogical implications of each, linking them to the themes and sub-themes that emerged in the analysis.

In thinking pedagogically, we often focus on formal program structures. What is apparent from the reanalysis is the range of informal *activities* – distinct communities - that students participated in that we might not ordinarily attend to pedagogically. Further, as a supervisor we might not even be aware of student involvement in them, or of how they may be influencing student voice(s) – and potentially the students' perceptions of their ability to construct and use voices which they feel contribute to this range of communities. Understanding the range of communities that are available to students – both informally and formally – would appear to be an important supervisory and departmental exercise. Further, since a continued lack of voice could be conceived as influencing students' experience of involvement in the communities they are trying to enter, exploring with students how they are finding ways to negotiate these different activities – how their voices are developing – would seem to be another important supervisory task in order to differentiate those communities that are more supportive of voice and those that engender feelings of discouragement and isolation.

In considering the ways in which these activities might influence students' perceptions of personal commitment to *academic values*, it is apparent in this reanalysis that students experienced many more tensions and challenges than pleasures. The student reports actually locate tensions and challenges as central to forging their voices and academic practices. This lens highlights aspects of academic practice that we may overlook – either because we are no longer attentive to the values that we embody (having found ways to negotiate our own voices), or because we prefer to focus on the positive (presenting a relatively benign view of practice). At the same time, the absence of pleasures speaks to the need to find ways for students to experience them more – to see why we have chosen to be academics. Thus, while experiencing and learning to negotiate such tensions is central to long-term involvement in the various communities, we believe it is worthwhile to actively seek ways to create activities and informal interactions for students that provide opportunities to experience pleasure – as the Education students did in the Committee – and to articulate the positive aspects verbally with students.

The lens, *production of knowledge,* also emerged for the students. There were clearly specific difficulties experienced in using voice in ways that would gain support from some in the discipline while acknowledging difference with others in order to complete the dissertation. As well, there was a concern about the changing expectation for earlier and greater productivity. We know that productivity is important to doctoral student success (Nettles and Millett, 2006) as well as to our academic practice generally. This presents a number of pedagogical implications. For instance, to what extent do we actually address productivity as part of the formal curriculum? It is likely that are ways in which we could re-think course requirements so that writing for a course was an authentic task with the potential for publication or presentation. Further, rethinking our own research activities opens up possibilities: co-reviewing manuscripts with students, finding ways to involve students as co-authors, etc.

Lastly, we come to *identity* as a lens. This reanalysis used voice as a representation of identity development. We propose that voice proves a productive notion for thinking pedagogically since it is somewhat more concrete than identity. It is unlikely that supervisors in the Education dissertation conversations were aware of the ways in which they were modeling disciplinary voices or providing opportunities for students to practice their own voices. Yet, seeing these conversations in this way may lead to intentional shifts in pedagogy in order to explicitly highlight what voice is being modeled, and to provide more opportunities for students to practice voice. And it is likely true that this would be the case in a range of activities; we could attend to the degree to which we model, provide practice and then encourage authentic use of voice.

CONCLUSION

Universities today can be characterized as much by the internal and external pressures for change as by the traditions upon which they rest. This situation may produce tensions that are felt at all levels of the university structure (Central Administration, Faculties, Departments, Programs etc.) as well as within the scholarly disciplines represented in the university. Many new and seasoned academics, given this shifting terrain, may be struggling to understand how they can best build their own sense of worth and efficacy as it relates to their disciplines and the university itself. We acknowledge the preliminary nature of the study presented here given the small numbers of students involved and that only one institution is represented. Nevertheless, we feel that the diverse contexts in which the data were collected, the number of episodes, and the fact that the emerging themes were not the focus of the original three studies provide reason to give a central place to the developing academic identity of doctoral students in our thinking about program structures and pedagogical practices (Malfroy, 2005).

For us, as a research team, this reanalysis has challenged us to continue our investigation to shed light upon often invisible aspects of doctoral studies and to use what we learn to interrogate our own current pedagogical practices and to develop new ones that more directly address the inherent tensions that exist in the academic world.

ACKNOWLEDGEMENTS

This research was supported in part by the Social Sciences and Humanities Research Council of Canada.

ABOUT THE AUTHORS

Lynn McAlpine is a Professor of Education and former Director of the Centre for University Teaching and Learning at McGill University, Canada. She has received distinguished research awards from both the American Educational Research Association and the Canadian Society for Studies in Higher Education. She is presently on secondment to the University of Oxford as Director of the CELT Preparing for Academic Practice, and Senior Research Fellow in the Department of Education. As well, she is Co-Editor of the International Journal for Academic Development.

Cheryl Amundsen is an Associate Professor in the Faculty of Education at Simon Fraser University. Before coming to Simon Fraser University, she was a faculty member at McGill University for ten years, jointly appointed to the Centre for University Teaching and Learning (CUTL) and the Department of Educational Psychology. Her interests in teaching development in higher education and learning technologies are tightly interwoven with the focus of her research and scholarly activities. Her research focuses on how university professors develop pedagogical knowledge in relationship to their subject matter, how they come to understand teaching and make instructional decisions, and the effects of these on student attitude and learning.

REFERENCES

Aitchinson, C. and Lee, A. (2006). Research writing: problems and pedagogies. *Teaching in Higher Education, 11(3),* 265-278.

Austin, A. (2002). Creating a bridge to the future: Preparing new faculty to face changing expectations in a shifting context. *Review of Higher Education, 26(2),* 119-144.

Becher, T., and Trowler, P. (2001). *Academic Tribes and Territories* (2nd ed.). Buckingham: Open University Press.

Bieber, J., and Worley, L. (2006). Conceptualizing the academic life: Graduate students' perspectives. *Journal of Higher Education, 77(6),* 1009-1035.

Blackler, F. (1995). Knowledge, knowledge work and organizations: An overview and interpretation *Organizational Studies, 6,* 1021-1046.

Brew, A (2006) *Research and teaching: beyond the divide.* Basingstoke: Palgrave Macmillan.

Edwards, A. (2007) *Agency and activity theory: from the systemic to the relational.* Unpublished paper. Oxford University, UK.

Elgar, F. (2003). *PhD completion in Canadian universities.* Halifax: University of Dalhousie.

Engeström, Y., Miettinen, R., and Punamäki, R-L. (Eds.) (1999). *Perspectives on activity theory.* Cambridge: Cambridge University Press.

Evans, C. (1990) A cultural view of the discipline of modern languages, *European Journal of Education,* 25,3, 273-282.

Golde, C. M. (1996). *How departmental contextual factors shape doctoral attrition. Unpublished doctoral dissertation.*, Stanford University.

Green, B. (2005). Unfinished business: subjectivity and supervision, *Higher Education Research and Development, 24* (2), 151-164.

Gutierrez, K., Rymes, B., and Larson, J. (1995). Script, counterscript and underlife in the classroom: James Brown vs. Brown vs. Board of Education. *Harvard Educational Review,* 65 (3), 445-471.

Hasrati, M. (2005). Legitimate peripheral participation and supervising PhD students, *Studies in Higher Education, 30* (5), 557-570.

Henkel, M. (2005). Academic identity and autonomy in a changing policy environment. *Higher Education, 49,* 155-176.

Henkel, M. (2000). *Academic identities and policy change in higher education.* London: Jessica Kingsley.

Huberman, M., and Miles, M. (2002). *The qualitative researcher's companion.* Thousand Oaks, CA: Sage Publications.

Lave, J., and Wenger, E. (1991). *Situated learning: legitimate peripheral participation.* Cambridge: Cambridge University Press.

Lee, T., Fuller, A, Bishop, D, Felstead, A, Jewson, N, Kakavelakis, K., Unwin, L. (2006). *Reconfiguring contract research?: Career, work and learning in a changing employment landscape.* Paper presented at the Society for Research in Higher Education.

Leonard, D., Metcalfe, J., Becker, R. and Evans, J. (2006). *Review of literature on the impact of working context and support on the postgraduate research student learning experience.* London: Higher Education Academy.

Malfroy, J. (2005). Doctoral supervision, workplace research and changing pedagogic practices, *Higher Education Research and Development,* 24 (2), 165-178.

McAlpine, L., Starke-Meyerring, D., and Pare, A. (in press - a). "English" in the 21st century global village: Tensions, contradictions, pressures and resistance ... dangers ahead? In. D. Boud and A. Lee (Eds.). *Changing Practices of Doctoral Education.* London: Routledge.

McAlpine, L., Jazvak-Martek, M., and Gonsalves, A. (in press - b). The question of identity: Negotiating roles and voices in evolving academic systems. In R. Barnett and R. Di Napoli (Eds.). *Changing Identities and Voices in Higher Education.* London : Routledge.

McAlpine, L., and Norton, J. (2006). Reframing our approach to doctoral programs: A learning perspective. *Higher Education Research and Development,* 25(1), 3-17.

McAlpine, L., and Hopwood., N (2006). *Conceptualizing the research PhD: Towards an integrative perspective.* Society for Research in Higher Education. Brighton, UK.

McAlpine, L., and Asghar, A. (June, 2006). *Supporting doctoral students as their own faculty developers.* Paper presented at the conference of the International Consortium for Educational Development. Sheffield, UK.

Miles, M. B., and Huberman, A. M. (1994). *Qualitative Data Analysis (2nd Ed.).* Thousand Oaks, CA: Sage Publications.

Nettles, M., and Millett, C (2006). *Three magic letters: getting to the PhD.* Baltimore: Johns Hopkins.

Neumann, A. (2006). Professing passion: Emotion in the scholarship of professors at research universities. *American Educational Research Journal, 43(3),* 381-424.

Paré, A., Starke-Meyerring, D., and McAlpine, L., (April, 2006). *Entering the text: Learning doctoral rhetoric.* Paper presented at the American Educational Research Association, San Francisco, USA.

Rée. J. (2000). *I See a Voice.* London: Flamingo.

Roth, W.-M. (1999). "Enculturation": Acquisition of conceptual blind spots and epistemological prejudices. *British Educational Research Journal, 27*(1), 5-27.

Stets, J. E., and Harrod, M., M. (2004). Verification across multiple identities: The role of status. *Social Psychology Quarterly,* 67(2), 155-171.

Taylor, C. (1991). *The ethics of authenticity.* Cambridge, MA: Harvard University Press.

Välimaa, J. (1998). Culture and identity in higher education research. *Higher Education, 36,* 119-138.

Vignoles, V. L., Golledge, J., Regalia, C., Manzi, C., and Scabini, E. (2005). Beyond self-esteem: Influence of multiple motives on identity construction. *Journal of Personality and Social Psychology, 90(2),* 308-333.

In: Global Issues in Higher Education
Editor: Pamela B. Richards, pp. 85-98

ISBN: 978-1-60021-802-6
© 2007 Nova Science Publishers, Inc.

Chapter 4

PROVIDING FEEDBACK ON STUDENT WRITING USING ANNOTATION TECHNOLOGY

Terence C. Ahern and Judy A. Abbott
West Virginia University, USA

ABSTRACT

Writing allows authors to share ideas, stories, thoughts and desires unencumbered by time and space. The process of writing is dynamic. From inspiration to dissemination the process is a give and take between author and audience. Writing is a learned skill and requires practice. Consequently, writers want readers to read their writing. They want feedback. But teaching and practicing writing are often shortchanged throughout public schooling and during the college years due to writing's time-consuming nature—time-consuming for students as they create a written piece and time-consuming for instructors as they respond to and evaluate written pieces. This project had two objectives. First, we explored the use of an Internet-based text production annotation system when developing a written assignment in an undergraduate college course. Secondly, we explored the nature of the written feedback provided by the instructor within an Internet-based text production annotation system.

The National Commission on Writing in America's Schools and Colleges (2003) calls for "a writing revolution [that] puts language and communication in their proper place in the classroom" (p. 3). Writing allows authors to share ideas, stories, thoughts, and desires unencumbered by time and space. Writing is not limited to the marketplace of ideas but also gives authors a place for reflection where they can try out incomplete impressions and partial ideas, as well as whole thoughts. It allows authors to manipulate their thinking in order to more effectively communicate an idea. By recording partial ideas or incomplete thoughts in writing, they can be recalled, reordered, or reworked into a coherent, cohesive message directed at a specific audience. But teaching and practicing writing are often shortchanged throughout public schooling and during the college years due writing's time-consuming nature—time-consuming for students as they create a written piece and time-consuming for instructors as they respond to and evaluate written pieces (The National Commission on Writing, 2003).

Modern computer-based word-processors have decreased the drudgery of composing a document. The arduous chore of producing the text as well as the chore of editing has been simplified to a click and drag of a mouse. Additionally, help has come from the ancillary technologies of spell and grammar checkers to formatting technologies that rival Medieval monks. If the word-processor has revolutionized writing, then the Internet has revolutionized publishing. Blogs, wikis, and discussion boards have provided individual authors access to the world in which to publish their ideas. Nonetheless, even with all the wonder of technology, writing is a learned skill and is very hard to do. Policy makers and commissions have called for research that explores the potential of new and emerging technologies for teaching, development, grading, and assessment of writing (The National Commission on Writing, 2003).

Writing is a keystone for school. It is not a frill for the few, but an essential skill for the many. Larkin and Bundy (2005) noticed that the, "educational benefits of adapting a writing approach to the classroom have been widely documented. Writing serves as a tool to promote deeper and more meaningful student learning" (p. F4J-1). However, in many classrooms writing is viewed as a simple form of assessment, a snapshot of learning. Generally writing assignments outside of the language arts classroom consist of answering the questions at the end of the chapter or perhaps as a final term paper (Warschauer, 1997). Rarely do students have the opportunity, let alone the obligation, to revise a previously written assignment for increased clarity in conveying the message.

A major problem for most instructors is that written intervention strategies are resource consuming and time intensive. Even the modern word processing software or the most current online content management system requires multiple steps in order to provide feedback to a single student assignment. Further, there is no easy method to monitor the impact the feedback has had over time. This is essential in order to make sure the students are not continuing to make the same mistake time after time.

This project had two objectives. First, we explored the use of an Internet-based text production annotation system when developing a written assignment in an undergraduate college course. Secondly, we explored the nature of the written feedback provided by the instructor within an Internet-based text production annotation system.

WRITTEN COMMENTARY ON STUDENT WRITING

The process of writing is dynamic. From inspiration to dissemination the process is a give and take between the who, the what, the why, and for whom it was written. As Hyland and Tse (2004) observe "writers are clearly doing more than creating textually cohesive text; they are maneuvering themselves into line with community expectations and shaping the reader's role to give a more sympathetic hearing for their own views" (p. 163).

Writing is, first and foremost, a communicative skill that is telling or asking for information. It can, however, be more than that when it attempts to argue, explain, or describe an author's point of view. Regardless of the intent, there are linguistic resources that include an array of cohesive and interpersonal features which help relate a text to its context by assisting readers to connect, organize, and interpret material in a way preferred by the writer and with regard to the understandings and values of a particular discourse community. (Hyland & Tse, 2004, p. 157)

Writing is a learned skill and rarely do even veteran writers get it right on the first draft. Writing requires practice. Writers want readers to read their writing. They want feedback. They want to know if what they have written is understandable and makes sense. Goldstein (2004) points out that all "writers need to learn what their audiences expect and whether or not their writing is being read in the ways they would like by their audience(s)" (p. 5). The time and resources required of instructors to provide substantive feedback must be found if they are to perform their work professionally (The National Commission on Writing, 2003).

Readers in the role of editor or critic help authors refine a text so that the intended meaning becomes clear. Goldstein (2004) noticed that students needed to understand not merely the mechanical aspects of writing, but also the social-cultural needs of the target audience in order to convey meaning. She writes that students need to learn

that meaning resides in not only the words they inscribe on paper but what the audience brings to the reading of these words. This can only be understood if students get feedback from readers, feedback that shows writers were what they had intended has been achieved and where their texts have fallen short of their intentions and goals. (p. 5)

Feedback from readers can help authors clarify, organize, and guide future readers of their written messages. However, as Sprinkle (2004) noted "commenting on student writing is the most widely used method for responding to students writing, it is the least understood" (p. 273).

Providing feedback that helps students become better writers is difficult. The goal of written commentary is to provide help in improving the piece without hijacking the text, without usurping the intent of the author. Sprinkle (2004) introduced three reflective methods of examining and evaluating written commentary. The three feedback approaches were "designed to unite existing (and emerging) commenting theories" (p. 274). The goal of these models is to "help instructors become more aware of their individual commenting styles in relation to currently accepted theories" (p. 279). By understanding their own styles, instructors can become proactive in helping their students become better writers.

The Revision Responsibility Model (Sprinkle, 2004) focused on providing commentary that identifies who controls what aspect of the revision process. This approach separates feedback into six categories—correcting, emoting, describing, suggesting, questioning, and assigning. These categories are then sorted into two groups indicating revision control—teacher responsibility or student responsibility. The categories of correcting, emoting and describing are assumed to be the teacher's responsibility, whereas suggesting, questioning, and assigning repairs are centered in student revision responsibility. For example, an instructor may pose a question about the text that the author will use to repair the text. Within this model, instructors "become more like coaches than critics allowing students to take more responsibility over the revision process" (p. 276).

In contrast, the Rhetorical Situation Model (Sprinkle, 2004) provides feedback that targets the content, textual and contextual features of a document. The context features include comments addressing the focus, and the development and support of the text. The textual features include comments focused on organization and the mechanics of the text. Audience awareness comments are the focus of the contextual feature of this model. This model helps instructors balance their comments primarily between the message and the conventions of text. Finally, the Degrees of Control Model (Sprinkle, 2004) documents instructors' comments that create opportunities for the students to maintain responsibility for creating meaning in their own work.

For instructors who subscribe to the philosophy that writing is a unique mode of learning in itself, the scribal act is viewed as more than a mere display of knowledge; it is a way of creating, shaping, and discovering meaning. Thus when instructors usurp students' reasons for writing by exerting excessive control they strip them of the opportunity to make meaning for themselves and in this way can actually obstruct students' learning (Sprinkle, 2004, p. 277).

The key feature in each of these models is maintaining the integrity of the author's meaning within the text. Often it is much easier for an editor (instructor) to simply rewrite a passage based on the editor's interpreted understanding of the intent of the writer. The problem is, however, as Goldstein (2005) points out, that this can be difficult because the underlying intent of the text is clearly misunderstood by the reader. If instructors are intent upon supporting growth in student understanding of quality writing and ownership, then reflecting on the nature of their own written feedback may allow shifts that better support students to clarify their work while maintaining control of their text.

ANNOTATION TECHNOLOGIES

Creating margin notes in documents is a time-honored practice and dates back to the beginning of writing itself. In the formal correspondence from the Egyptian Pharaohs to the Hittite Kings, scribes inserted marginal comments to their counterparts. Jewish Rabbinical Scholars such as Rashi inserted textual glosses that attempted to clarify the meaning of a difficult Biblical passage. Secondary teachers and higher education instructors have marked students' papers using a red pencil or pen. Bleeding on written work with a red pencil, a cliché, suggests how students interpret feedback provided by instructors—more painful than useful. Nevertheless, advances in technology have made possible programs that permit writing communities, where students and teachers share, edit, and respond to each other's work.

Given the many different types and purposes of annotation capabilities "it is no surprise that annotation technologies are similarly based on a range of models" (Wolfe, 2002, p. 476). Wolfe (2002) identifies seven primary factors of annotation technologies: input, the interface design, base-text, anchor, storage/file, searching and filtering, as well as any other specialized behaviors that define annotation type software.

RedPencil (Ahern, 2005) was designed to reduce the complexity and the amount of time required to respond to not just one paper, but to many papers over many iterations. RedPencil was created to streamline the process of feedback through the use of Internet-based technologies. RedPencil adheres to the majority of the annotation design requirements as indicated by Wolfe (2004). For example RedPencil uses the keyboard for input and simple text file for its base-text. Currently, it has no general capabilities for filtering or searching documents.

However, there were three major design goals for the development of RedPencil. First, the design used an open system approach which requires the use of standard, non-proprietary development tools. Consequently, data storage was mapped, using standard XML in conjunction with an open source database server. Another deign goal was to make the application transparent to users for whom the software was intended. This resulted in a limited user interface. Finally, RedPencil was designed to provide document management. With these goals in mind a prototype was developed with a minimal feature set and oriented to the needs of users of online course delivery systems.

RedPencil is based around a web-based portal user-interface. A user enters the system through the main page as shown in Figure 1.

This login identifies the status of the user in order to control access to the various elements in the system. Once in the system, students, for example, can upload assignments and check their progress, while faculty can view assignments and provide feedback within the documents. The process of submitting, reviewing, and posting assignments is all done through the Internet.

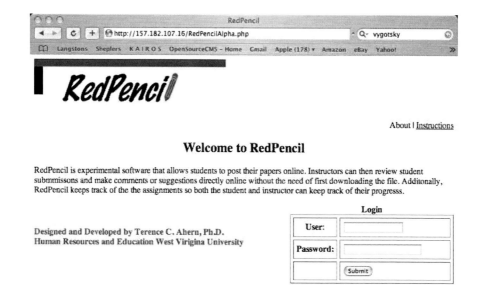

Figure 1. RedPencil login page.

One of the most important elements of RedPencil is its ability to track and manage submitted documents. Consequently, RedPencil provides a table view of submitted documents organized by class or group. Notice in Figure 2, the instructor can identify quickly which assignment students have submitted and when.

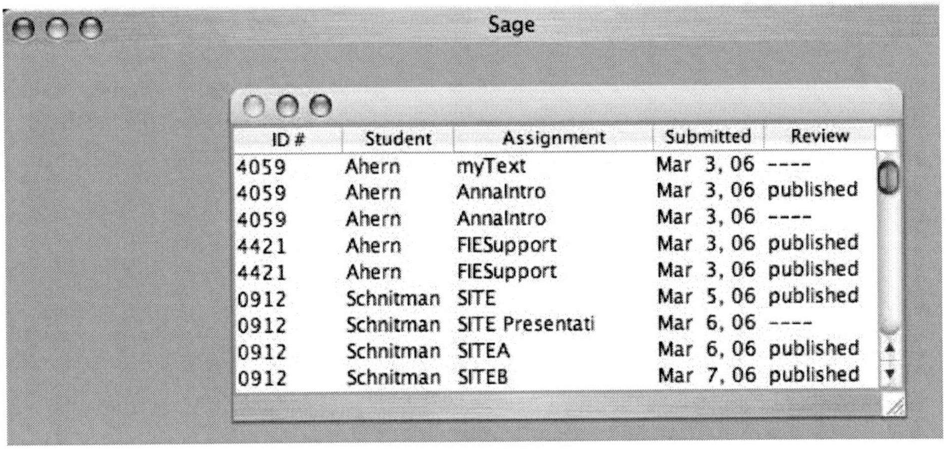

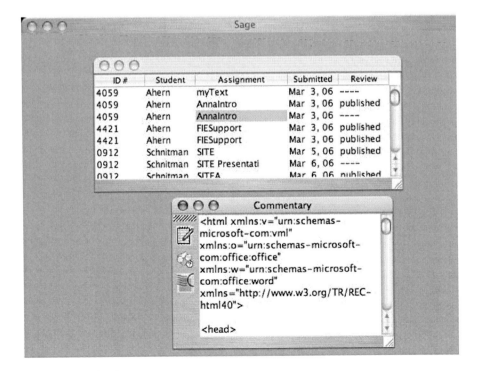

Figure 2. Document Tracking Table.

Further, instructors can also track the status of the review for each assignment. For example, if the Review column contains four dashes, a newly submitted document has been added. On the other hand, if the column reads pending, that review is incomplete. However, if the column shows published, the written comments are complete and ready for the student. From the list of assignments instructors uses the mouse to select the document they want to review. The selected document appears in a separate widow (Figure 3).

Figure 3. Document selection.

RedPencil uses a very simple feature set. The reviewer has the option of adding comments, saving the current review as pending or publishing the review. Once the written comments are saved they are stored separately in an XML file.

RedPencil supports an interlinear markup system as shown Figure 4. RedPencil uses a technique similar to "sticky notes" where a textbox is attached to a portion of the document as shown in Figure 4. The pencil icon embedded within the assignment indicates where in the text reviewer made a comments.

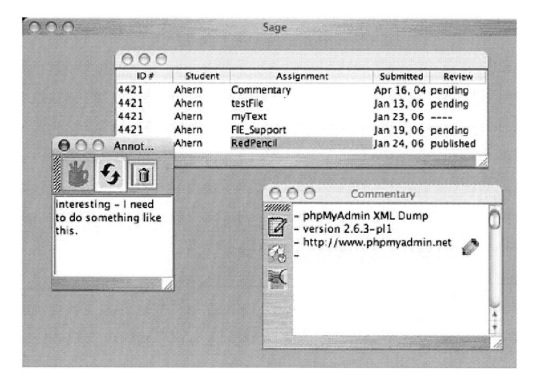

Figure 4. Markup window.

Previous Study

In the fall of 2005 a usability study for RedPencil was conducted (Ahern, 2005). The participants were programming students who were required to submit their coding assignments using RedPencil. The data revealed that RedPencil was successful in providing timely and targeted feedback. According to Ahern (2005),

> the results were overwhelmingly favorable for RedPencil. The students felt they could use RedPencil easily to submit their assignments as indicated by the high ratings reported by learnability, the ability to learn how to use the software, was also highly rated. (p. 4)

The two features the students liked about RedPencil, according to the data, was that they could locate the comment easily and the feedback was timely. They immediately saw when the instructor had completed marking the submitted text. They did not have to wait until the next class to access the feedback. Additionally, the interlinear marking system that RedPencil uses showed the students precisely where the instructor had left a comment. This prompted a student to remark that the "quick feedback in the code itself" (Ahern, 2005, p. 5) was useful. RedPencil reduced the drudgery of commenting on students' papers while keeping track of the type and number of comments.

METHODOLOGY

Writing is fundamentally a collaborative act (Elbow, 1973; Hillocks, 1995; Smith, 1994). From the correct choice of words to the right tone, authors must be aware of the intended audience. Feedback is important not only for novices, but for expert writers as well. However, school-based writing has traditionally viewed writing as a form of assessment. As many colleagues have indicated, "I don't teach writing; I grade writing."

All instructors, teachers, and educators do it. They give written commentary on student's writing, even if they are not primarily writing instructors. The typical instructor complaint is that written commentary seems to have little effect on subsequent writing. The problem is that most instructors have not been trained on how to provide meaningful written feedback. Most likely instructors comment on students' papers in much the same the way that their teachers and instructors commented on papers during their own schooling.

This study, using RedPencil as an Internet-based annotation technology, explored how undergraduate students enrolled in a university course took advantage of the software to engage in an iterative revision process. Secondly, three reflective models explored the nature of the written feedback provided by the instructor within the annotation technology system.

Participants

The participants for this study were 30 undergraduates in a proposal-writing course enrolled at a west coast university. Many of these students were non-traditional and ranged in age from their early 20s to their mid 40s.

Procedure

Data was taken from an undergraduate capstone-writing course in a college of science and technology. The course was the first course in a two-course sequence that required the student or student team to propose a project to be conducted during the second course workshop. None of these students had experience in writing project proposals.

The primary learning outcome for each student or student team was to produce a formal written proposal. The proposal was segmented into three sections and each section was presented independently. Students were required to submit at least one draft for each of the three sections: the Problem Statement, Description, and Methodology. The instructor provided written feedback on each draft. Further, students were encouraged to submit multiple iterations of the sections to strengthen the prospect of the final project proposal.

RedPencil was introduced as the software used for student submission of draft sections and for instructor feedback on each submission. RedPencil was also used to post any revisions that were submitted. Each student was assigned a unique four-digit identifier that served as the students' password. Additionally this four-digit identifier was also used by RedPencil to label and store the original submissions in individual files on a secure server.

RedPencil used an XML-based file structure to store the comment data as indicated in Figure 5.

```
<?xml version="1.0" encoding="UTF-8"?>
<!DOCTYPE commentary SYSTEM "redpencil.dtd'
<commentary>
<targetFile>Commentary_4421</targetFile>
<location>40550/published/</location>
<markup>
<notation>
<author>Terence</author>
<index>87,87</index>
<comment>this is a test </comment>
</notation>
<notation>
<author>Terence</author>
<index>27,37</index>
<comment>notice the underline</comment>
</notation>
</markup>
</commentary>
```

Figure 5. RedPencil Markup Data.

The targetFile tag identifies the name of the student-submitted file. Instructor's comments are made up of elements contained within the notation tag. Each notation includes the name of the reviewer, where the comment appears in the text, and the actual text for each comment. Each notation was stored sequentially in the file. The students were encouraged to submit as many documents for written feedback as they wanted.

Analysis

All RedPencil files related to this study were printed and documents were matched according to their unique identifier. A graduate assistant, independent of the researchers, coded the comments using the three reflective models: the Revision Responsibility Model, the Rhetorical Situation Model, and the Degrees of Control Model (Sprinkle, 2004). A second coder then reviewed the categories for consistency and accuracy. Descriptive statistics were used to analyze the submitted documents, the comments made, and the nature of each of the comments.

RESULTS AND DISCUSSION

This project examined (1) the use of an Internet-based text production annotation system when developing a written assignment in an undergraduate college course, and (2) the nature of the written feedback provided by the instructor within an Internet-based text production annotation system.

Table 1 provides an overview of data available for analysis in this study. Over the course of the semester, the 30 students submitted 116 files or documents, and the instructor provided 173 comments. Each student averaged 5.8 comments, while each submission averaged 1.5 comments.

Table 1. Data Overview

Students N	Documents Submitted N	Comments Provided N	Mean Comments per student	Mean Comments per submission
30	116	173	5.8	1.5

Further analysis of these results show that almost half the students (46.7%) sought multiple feedback by submitting more than the three required submissions of documents. This constituted more than three-fourths of the entire number of documents submitted. Within this group, as shown by Table 2, 10 students submitted 21 documents and received the lion-share of the feedback.

Table 2. Analysis of Submitted Documents

Submission Categories	Documents Submitted by Individual Students n	Frequency n	Comments Total (Mean)	Students n (%)	Documents by Category n (%)	Total Comments by Category n (%)
Less than required submissions	0	1	1 (0.1)	13 (43.3)	19 (16.4)	26 (15)
	1	5	11 (2.2)			
	2	7	14 (2)			
Minimum required submissions	3	3	8 (2.67)	3 (10)	9 (7.8)	8 (4.6)
More than required submissions	4	2	12 (6)	14 (46.7)	88 (75.9)	139 (80.4)
	5	2	8 (4)			
	6	4	47 (11.8)			
	7	2	23 (11.5)			
	8	4	49 (12.3)			

Revision responsibility, as shown in Table 3, determined whether the comment promoted the student's or the teacher's responsibility for revision. The data indicated that the teacher assumed a high level of control. Almost 30% of the 173 comments were coded as focusing on corrections provided by the instructor.

Table 3. Revision Responsibility Reflective Model

Comments N	Teacher Responsibility			Student Responsibility		
	Correct n (%)	Emote n (%)	Describe n (%)	Suggest n (%)	Questions n (%)	Assign n (%)
173	49 (28.3)	29 (16.8)	37 (21.4)	17 (9.8)	12 (6.9)	29 (16.8)
	115 (66.5)			58 (33.5)		

Notice within the student's responsibility section, the highest frequency of the type of comment was the assign type (16.8%). In other words, the instructor typically supplied the correction for the document or assigned the student to correct it. This high level of control may be due to the fact that the participants were undergraduate students with little experience writing project proposals.

The Rhetorical Situation Model, Table 4, determined whether the comments addressed primarily content, textual, or contextual features of the student writing. Notice that only 1.7 % of the comments were oriented toward audience awareness. Though a rather low percentage in comparison to content and textual features (50.9% and 47.4% respectfully), the instructor had made it clear to the participants that he was the intended audience for this project proposal. Consequently, the participants wrote specifically with him in mind, using his specific guidelines for the nature of the text. The percent of contextual feature comments is assumed to increase if the audience was less well defined than in this study.

As indicated in Table 4, the type of feedback for this model was evenly split between content features (50.9%) and text-based features (47.4%). More than one-third of the comments were related to basic grammar and mechanics (37.6%). Organizational cues (9.8%) were actually fairly low given the nature of the class. However, a high percentage (50.9%) of the comments were content oriented. Given that this was an undergraduate course, the instructor was interested in students clarifying and explaining their text to improve meaning.

Table 4. Rhetorical Situation Reflective Model

Comments N	Content Features		Textual Features		Contextual Features
	Focus n (%)	Development and Support n (%)	Organization n (%)	Mechanics n (%)	Audience Awareness n (%)
173	18 (10.4)	70 (40.4)	17 (9.8)	65 (37.6)	3 (1.7)
	88 (50.9)		82 (47.4)		3 (1.7)

The Degrees of Control Model determined the strength of control that the instructor exerts over the students' writing. These results, shown in Table 5, are consistent with the Revision Responsibility model, shown in Table 3. As indicated in Table 5, the instructor frequently took firm control of the revision process. The instructor simply offered the corrections 30% of the time in contrast to commenting on the writing. However, in contrast to the firm control, the instructor also acted as a reader 22% of the time. In the role as reader, the instructor was providing insight into what would work better for a particular reader. Overall the instructor showed a high level of restraint by offering qualified evaluations, providing advice and suggestions, or simply asking questions.

Table 5. Degrees of Control Reflective Model

	Firm Control		Moderate Control		Mild Control	
Comments N	Corrections n (%)	Comments n (%)	Qualified Evaluations n (%)	Advice / Suggestions n (%)	Questions n (%)	Reader Response n (%)
173	53 (30.6)	26 (15.0)	9 (5.2)	36 (20.8)	11 (6.4)	38 (22.0)
	79 (45.7)		45 (26)		49 (28.3)	

Though most instructors do not "teach" writing, this study demonstrates some essential truisms. First it is clear, based on our data, that when given a chance, a number of students will choose to engage in an iterative discourse about their writing. Nearly half the participants submitted more than the required number of documents, thus allowing for more feedback that could shape and sharpen their writing, strengthing the final document.

It was also found that the more submissions by students the more feedback they received; the very iterative nature of refining writing. One cautionary note is that we also found that nearly half (14) of the students failed to submit the minimum required documents of the project proposal thus limiting the opportunity for feedback. This finding may be in fact a result of the assessment model of written assignments. The technology was insufficient to overcome the students' reluctance to have their writing judged.

Written comments are meant to provide meaningful feedback for students. The idea is that students will develop an understanding of writing effectively by reflecting on the comments provided by readers. The expectation is that students will avoid errors and ineffective processes in their writing, thus future written work will be of higher quality, needing less revision or editing. However, if they do not submit the work for review then they cannot benefit from the opportunity.

When examining the nature of the comments, two models demonstrated that the instructor sought to control the revision process: Revisions Responsibility—teacher responsibility was 66.5% of comments; Degrees of Control—firm control was 45.7% of comments. However, the Rhetorical Situation Model results indicated a balance between comment focused on content features (the quality of the message) and textual features (the accuracy/correctness of the writing). This study may inform instructors that written feedback are not simply an assessment, rather written feedback can be a formative element essential for academic improvement.

RedPencil provided an archive of written comments, allowing instructors an opportunity to analyze the nature of the comment, seeking to determine if they are providing the type of feedback that may help their students develop as writers. RedPencil was also meant to provide targeted comments; though this study did not examine the response to instructor comments, it is assumed that targeted comments provided more specific information about strengthening writing.

AREAS FOR FURTHER STUDY

Providing written commentary is useful for all writers. However as the research indicates, there is little research on just what works, why does it work, and how to improve it. RedPencil was designed for providing feedback and to manage that feedback. It would be important to know what type of feedback, as indicated by three reflective models, had the most impact. Further, does the learner characteristics effect the efficacy of the type of feedback provided.

Finally, it would be very useful to track the "slope of comments." What effect does the RedPencil document management system have on the number and kind of feedback given? For example, does the number and type change depending on the number of versions submitted?

Technology can reduce the drudgery of providing feedback to student writing. It is essential that both teachers and students seize the opportunity to engage in an iterative and supportive revision cycle. In this way instructors can improve their students' writing.

REFERENCES

Ahern, T. C. (2005). Using online annotation software to provide timely feedback in an introductory programming course. *Proceedings of the 35th ASEE/IEEE Frontiers in Education Conference,* Indianapolis, IN.

Elbow, P. (1973). *Writing without teachers.* New York, NY: Oxford University Press.

Goldstein, L. M. (2005). *Teacher written commentary in second language writing classrooms.* Ann Arbor, MI: University of Michigan Press.

Hillocks, G. H., Jr. (1995). *Teaching writing as reflective practice.* New York, NY: Teachers College Press.

Hyatt, D. F. (2005). "Yes, a very good point!" a critical genre analysis of a corpus of feedback commentaries on Master of Education assignments. *Teaching in Higher Education, 10*(3): 339-353.

Hyland, K., and Tse, P. (2004) Metadiscouse in academic writing: A reappraisal *Applied Linguistics* 25(2):157-177

Larkin, T., & D. Bundy. (2005). Special Session- Writing: An active learning tool for Majors and non-majors. *Proceedings of the 35th ASEE/IEEE Frontiers in Education Conference,* Indianapolis, IN.

National Commission on Writing in American's Schools and Colleges. (2003). *The neglected "R": The need for a writing revolution.* New York, NY: College Entrance Examination Board.

Persky, H., Daane, C., & Jin, Y. (2003). *The Nation's Report Card: Writing 2002.* Retrieved February 15, 2007, from http://www.nces.ed.gov/nationsreportcard.

Smith, F. (1994). *Writing and the writer, 2nd edition.* Hillsdale, NJ: Earlbaum.

Sprinkle, R. S. (2004). Written Commentary: A systematic, theory-based approach to response. *Teaching English in Two year Colleges, 31*(3): 273-286.

Warschauer, M. (1997). Computer-mediated collaborative learning: Theory and practice. *The Modern Language Journal, 81*(4): 470-481.

Wolfe, J. (2002). Annotation technologies: A software and research reviews. *Computers and Composition, 19*: 471-497.

In: Global Issues in Higher Education
Editor: Pamela B. Richards, pp. 99-125

ISBN: 978-1-60021-802-6
© 2007 Nova Science Publishers, Inc.

Chapter 5

A MOTIVATIONAL PERSPECTIVE ON THE SELF-REGULATED LEARNING IN HIGHER EDUCATION

Antonio Valle[1], Ramón G. Cabanach[1], Susana Rodríguez[1], José C. Núñez[2], Julio A. González-Pienda[2], Paula Solano[2] and Pedro Rosário[3]
[1]University of A Coruña, Spain
[2]University of Oviedo, Spain
[3]University of Minho, Portugal

ABSTRACT

Ever since the decade of the seventies, the new proposals from psychological learning theories promote a change of course that involves considering the student an active part and protagonist of the process of building knowledge. The student's mental processes (cognitive and meta-cognitive) start to be considered essential and, within them, the processes of organization, interpretation, or comprehension of information are crucial, as learning is not a copy or a mechanical recording of material, but the result of interpreting or transforming the subject matter.

This opens up new ways of reflection in the area of higher education, where the perspective of self-regulated learning could be the field that offers a broader and more dynamic approach to the comprehension of learning processes. This perspective assumes the basic principle that learners are agents who choose and make decisions about their behavior. They are the true architects and promoters of their learning. In addition to being capable of managing their own motivational and cognitive resources with the aim of achieving successful learning, self-regulated learners should have the necessary competencies to apply these resources within a plan of action that matches the demands of the specific learning situation.

As motivation plays a crucial role in learning and constitutes an essential area in all the approaches to self-regulated learning, in this chapter, an analysis is performed of the motivational components on which self-regulated learning is based, from various proposals derived from research with students of higher education.

1. INTRODUCTION

The development of personal and professional competences in higher studies is, more or less generally, considered one of the main indicators of quality and a priority need for all the agents involved at this educational level. In order to achieve this goal, the University should facilitate routines, reconsider its mission and stance, engaging teachers and students in the process. This change is important, especially in regard to "how" students learn (Cochram–Smith, 2003) and it is urgent to promote the concept of students assuming quality as a process of continuous improvement.

To specify this goal in the field of the teaching-learning processes, it is necessary to carry out changes in teaching, in students' and teachers' roles, in the design and implementation of the syllabus, and in the evaluation methodologies, among other aspects. Competencies are understood as a sequence of knowledge, and necessary skills and attitudes to perform a certain task and solve problems autonomously and creatively. In the field of learning processes, instrumental competencies are related to the knowledge of how to cope with information and organize personal and strategic resources; systemic competencies refer to the application of knowledge to specific situations; and, lastly, personal competencies are linked to communication, cooperation, and conjoint participation. The key is that these competencies allow the task of learning to occur, promoting knowledge, knowing how, knowing how to be and how to behave, and hence, university education plays a fundamental role in effectively preparing individuals to learn throughout life.

In this context, the concept of "self-regulation of learning" becomes increasingly important, because research has shown that students participate actively in their learning process, monitoring and regulating the learning processes oriented toward products (Rosário, Mourao, Trigo, Núñez, and González-Pienda, 2005; Solano, 2006). Self-regulation of learning should not be understood as a mental aptitude, a verbal competence, but instead as a process of self-direction by which students transform their mental aptitudes into academic competencies. But perhaps the most important aspect is that each process or self-regulated behavior (such as the establishment of a goal, writing a summary, or establishing self-consequences) can be directly taught or modeled by parents, teachers, or classmates. In fact, students who self-regulate their learning seek help in order to improve the quality of their learning (Valle, Cabanach, Rodríguez, Núñez, and González-Pienda, 2006). What clearly identifies them as "self-regulators" of their learning is not so much their skill in the isolated use of learning strategies but rather their personal initiative, their perseverance at the task, and the competencies displayed, independently of the setting in which the learning takes place. Self-regulators focus on their role as agents: academic success depends particularly on what they build (Bandura, 2001). In this sense, they activate, change and maintain learning strategies in diverse settings. They treat learning as an activity that they develop "proactively," involving motivational, behavioral, and meta-cognitive processes of self-initiative, rather than mere reactive processes stimulated by their reaction to teaching.

2. SELF-REGULATED LEARNING (SRL)

Within the field of Educational Psychology, throughout its evolution, various theories and interpretations of the same phenomenon of human learning have emerged, which include different conceptions of the diverse components of learning, its functions and relations. Such theories and interpretations have greatly influenced interventions and explanations of the factors that condition learning and academic achievement. These interpretations emerge as different theories or psychological schools and related to a specific temporal context that defines precise cultural and social characteristics. But, as noted by Beltrán (1999), although each one of the various interpretations emerged because of the limitations presented by the previous interpretation with the aim of overcoming them but integrating, in turn, the previously achieved goals, currently in many cases, they still, in fact, co-exist.

As of the decade of the seventies, the new proposals of the cognitive theories of active learning and learner's information processing (Dansereau, 1985) lead to a change than implies the consideration of the student as an active part and protagonist of the process of building knowledge. At a general level, people begin to refer to learning as the construction of meanings, in which students do not limit themselves to acquiring knowledge, but instead they build knowledge using their previous experience and strategies (learning to learn) and the teacher participates in this process as facilitator. It is therefore conjointly built knowledge. Researchers begin to conceive the mental processes (cognitive and meta-cognitive) carried out by students as central processes and, within them, the processes of organization and interpretation or comprehension of the information are considered crucial, because learning is not just a mechanical copy or record of the material but the result of its interpretation or transformation. This leads to new perspectives of reflection in the area of higher education.

When research on university learning focuses on the interaction of cognitive processes and motivational processes, two lines of research or fundamental viewpoints of university learning emerge, which still currently exist (Pintrich, 2004): a viewpoint related to the *"students' approach to learning" (SAL)* and one that starts out with the perspective of information processing and that led to *self-regulated learning* (SRL).

Regarding the first viewpoint, in the 70s, a line of research emerged that focused on *student approaches to Learning (SAL)* (Biggs, 1991, 2001; Entwistle, 1988; Marton and Säljö, 1976), which developed especially in Europe and Australia. Rather than asking about the efficacy of certain behaviors and didactic strategies, the characteristic of this standpoint is that it asks why students and teachers behave in a certain way in the classroom—using data derived from qualitative in-depth interviews of students in reference to their motivation, learning, and the way they study in real university contexts (Pintrich, 2004). This research line is described as phenomenological, idiographic, or interpretative, and is concerned with knowing how educational agents experience and interpret reality, using methodologies of a qualitative, interpretative, and critical nature. The researchers that integrate the three most important groups in the development of SAL (in Sweden, United Kingdom, and Australia) agree that the approaches to learning are made up of two defining components or elements: *motivations* that reveal the intentions that move students to learn and certain *strategies* that are coherent with these intentions. Thus, the type of motivation could be significantly related to the practice of certain strategic behavioral patterns and, consequently, with the student's approach to study (Biggs, 1991, 2001; Entwistle, 1988; Rosário et al., 2005; Valle, Cabanach, Núñez, Suárez, Piñeiro, and Rodríguez, 2000).

With regard to the second research current, related to the models of information processing, the perspective of *Self-regulated Learning (SRL)* emerged in the U.S.A. (Pintrich, 2000b; Winne, and Hadwin, 1998; Zimmerman, 1998). Its main interest is to describe, explain, control, or predict objectively the cognitive and motivational processes involved in learning and achievement, using for this purpose quantitative methodologies. Within this viewpoint are Bandura's studies on self-regulation and motivational beliefs, such as self-efficacy, and the emerging works on meta-cognition that present the concept of students as active subjects who build their own learning and must therefore be capable of controlling the entire learning process (Schunk and Zimmerman, 1994, 2003). From this point of view, researchers begin to refer to people's capacity of self-regulating their learning as the only way to carry out constructive and meaningful learning. Learners should take the reins of their learning and, for this purpose, they must have a series of competencies that allow them to self-regulate their own learning and behavior. Therefore, students are conceived as autonomous, self-regulated beings who are familiar of their own cognitive processes and who control their learning by means of a series of self-regulatory strategies that involve more awareness of the strategies used and the processes followed in order to learn.

Moreover, this viewpoint incorporates not only cognitive, motivational, and affective factors, but also social and contextual factors (Pintrich, 2000b, 2004; Boekaerts, Pintrich, and Zeidner, 2000). When studying the motives that lead students to learn, it was observed that this engagement is influenced by the social and cultural setting, so support for contextual interpretations of learning were integrated into the research (Pintrich, 2000a, 2003). Although the SRL viewpoint has depended on the traditional theories of cognition and motivation, it provides a broader and more dynamic view in the sense that it contributes to understanding the dynamic processes and the contextual differences of learning.

Therefore, SRL implies the fundamental principle that learners are agents who make choices and decisions about their behavior (Winne, 2004), that is, they are the real architects and promoters of their learning.

One of the characteristics of self-regulated learners is their capacity to manage their own motivational and cognitive resources with the intention of learning successfully. This implies assuming that true learning—even considering that it is produced in a certain setting—is, above all, a personal experience that requires students' engagement and active participation.

In any case, although it is important for students to have the cognitive, motivational, and behavioral resources required to achieve satisfactory learning, what really determines the result of this learning process is their capacity to manage all these resources and articulate them as an action plan adapted to the demands of the specific learning situation.

As mentioned, SRL is a concept that integrates research on learning strategies, meta-cognition, learning goals, and, obviously, students' motivation (Valle et al., 2006). Therefore, SRL can be defined as an *active process in which students establish the goals that direct their learning, attempting to monitor, regulate, and control their cognitions, motivation, and behaviors in order to achieve these goals.*

To sum up, the various models or perspectives of SRL share four basic principles (Pintrich, 2004). Firstly, they assume a constructivist perspective that emphasizes individuals' active, and not reactive, role in their learning. Students are considered participative and active builders of their own learning, meanings, goals, and strategies, using the available information. Underlining their role as agents allows them to exert the control and regulation over their learning process and their academic achievement (Pintrich and Schrauben, 1992; Zimmerman, 2002). Secondly, students are considered capable of controlling, supervising, and regulating, to some extent, certain aspects of their own cognition, motivation, and behavior, as well as certain characteristics of the environment. Thirdly, it is assumed that there is some kind of criterion (e.g., objectives, goals, values) that act as reference point against which students can evaluate the products obtained and decide whether they need to change the direction of their academic activities. That is, when students are involved in the learning activity, they need some kind of criterion or standard, normally called goal or reference value, with which they can compare their performance to decide whether to continue to carry on as they have till then, to introduce some changes, or whether it is preferable to withdraw. Therefore, a key aspect is establishing academic learning goals and adapting their cognitive and motivational processes to achieve them. Lastly, all the models of self-regulation consider self-regulatory behaviors as mediators between personal and contextual aspects of learning, on the one hand, and the academic results, on the other. In this sense, the underlying meta-cognitive process of self-regulation of cognition, motivation, and behavior—which involve control and regulation of the activities performed—mediate the relations between person, context, and achievement. This means that a chief feature of SRL is that learning and achievement are not subject characteristics but rather the result of a dynamic process involving feedback and undergoing constant change (Boekaerts, 1999).

3. RESEARCH ON SRL IN COLLEGE STUDENTS

The SRL perspective appears as a result of the merging of various lines of research that are brought together and incorporated into its current corpus.

Firstly, the SRL model gathers the conceptions of learning that place the person-who-learns in the center of the teaching-learning process. In contrast to previous conceptions, it is assumed that the learner is an agent, underlining the processes that "mediate" in learning and, especially, the role of the person as the activator of these processes.

Secondly, this activation function refers to students' capacity to direct their cognitive and motivational processes, considering both processes as the main promoters of the quality of learning and the level of achievement.

Thirdly, and related to the above, the SRL perspective gathers motivational and cognitive aspects of research on learning in higher education. As mentioned, till then, research on the cognitive components of learning (information processing, cognitive styles, meta-cognition, strategies, etc.) and research on the motivational components (self-concept, self-efficacy beliefs, attributions, goals, etc.) had gone their different ways.

On the one hand, the studies from cognitive psychology had been concerned with the analysis of the strategies used by students in the acquisition, storing, and recall of information and the differences between "experts" and "novices" in these strategies without taking motivational variables into account (students as *motivationally inert subjects*). On the other hand, the studies on motivational variables had a conception of students as *cognitively empty* (Pintrich, Brown, and Weinstein, 1994). Although some precursor studies with an integrative conception of the cognitive and motivational variables can be found in the 70s with Bloom's theory of learning, in the 80s and the 90s, both lines of research merge. Interest is aroused because of the results of various studies in which it is observed that motivation affects the cognitive functions and that, in turn, training in cognitive strategies affects certain motivational variables such as self-efficacy, intrinsic motivation, etc. (e.g. Dweck, 1986). This aspect is especially assumed with the studies of Paul Pintrich and his collaborators, who begin to integrate both components within the framework of SRL.

Thus the exclusively cognitive models cannot explain why some students, who seem to have prior knowledge and the necessary strategies, do not use them when performing certain tasks, whereas the exclusively motivational models assume that students who have a positive motivational orientation will be more involved and will persist, which will lead them to satisfactory results. However, motivation alone cannot explain the use of adequate or inadequate strategies that affect the achievement level reached. With the perspective of SRL, the interactions of motivation and cognition in academic learning are increasingly integrated and acknowledged.

Fourthly, SRL reflects and consists of a change in the way of looking at learning with regard to why subjects do not learn. In contrast to the assumption that functioning and mental skill are determinants of academic achievement (aspects that are, moreover, relatively stable and that characterize students as reactive), SRL theories explain and describe how and in what way students can learn and achieve, "independently" of their mental capacity, environment, or the teaching quality they receive (Zimmerman, 1998, 2001). From this point of view, researchers begin to study failure or low achievement, not only in relation to the lack of capacity, intelligence, or some other kind of factor in which it is difficult to intervene, but also as a deficit of strategies or other activities and processes that can be taught, so that students can do something to improve their results.

Lastly, self-regulation in the educational field was initially approached from social psychology and, in particular, regarding Bandura's socio-cognitive perspective. This author elaborated a social learning theory, defending a triadic relation among behavior, person, and environment and for the first time mentioning the concept of self-regulation as an achievement in the socialization process. Subsequently, he elaborated a series of studies on people's beliefs, especially self-efficacy beliefs (Bandura, 1991; 1997; 2001). As of Bandura's studies, many contributions emerge (Schunk, 1981, 1983) that, continuing along the same theoretical line, conform an entire theoretical movement of self-regulation from the so-called socio-cognitive perspective, within which the importance of two more components of self-regulation appears, in addition to motivation and cognition: behavior and context.

From these five premises, many investigations and theoretical approaches to SRL have appeared, but all of them share an integrative conception of learning that emphasizes the need to combine the cognitive, metacognitive, and affective-motivational components, taking into account the context and the behavior of the person who is learning. They also share a viewpoint of students as promoters of their learning and their achievement, insofar as they are the regulators of their information processing (thanks to the use of cognitive and meta-cognitive strategies), their motivation, and their observable behavior, and they play an active and constructive role as information seekers, generators, and processors.

The results of the investigations carried out under this perspective indicate that students who are considered competent at the self-regulation level establish specific short-term goals, and prioritize their goals adequately. Moreover, whereas these students are oriented towards learning goals, the more inexpert students at the self-regulation level preferably adopt performance goals or "ego-oriented goals" (Boekaerts and Corno, 2005). These inexpert students perceive learning events as threatening experiences in which their academic performance will be evaluated and their cognitive competence questioned, so they often choose to avoid learning opportunities. In contrast, self-regulating students see academic events as occasions to increase their range of competencies and appreciate them as such. As a result, the experts normally perceive themselves as more capable than do the inexpert learners. And these self-efficacy beliefs increase not only their motivation to learn but also the self-regulation process, thereby facilitating the establishment of ambitious instructional goals and the display of self-monitoring behaviors. Contrariwise, students with low self-efficacy tend to be more anxious about learning and to avoid instructional opportunities whenever they appear. They only study what the teachers stipulate, and are very wary about displaying themselves in front of their classmates. Also in contrast to inexpert students, expert self-regulating students consider their motivation as something they can develop through school work, reading, and seeking complementary information about some topic. Inexpert students, on the contrary, have difficulty focusing on a topic and they attribute their lack of interest to external factors such as teachers with an "unappealing" discourse or uninteresting classes (Randi, 2004).

The large amount of investigation that emerged about self-regulation followed two fundamental and complementary lines of work that finally merged to give way to a third viewpoint. The first line focused on the study of theoretical aspects and the components and processes of self-regulation (Boekaerts and Corno, 2005; Zimmerman and Martínez-Pons, 1990), as well as the analysis and proof of these theoretical predictions, in order to specify and determine the impact on students of such components and processes. This tendency could be considered "descriptive." This line of investigation originated two more viewpoints of research: on the one hand, the description of the characteristics of efficient self-regulators; on the other, the description of the components of SRL.

The second research trend focused on attempting to determine how the different components interact, describing how self-regulation is carried out, and therefore considered an "explanatory" line of work. It produced, basically, the study of the development of self-regulating competence through instruction programs. Thus, from the study of how students become self-regulators of their own learning and, specifically, how certain instructional and contextual factors affect self-regulation, intervention as a means to promote self-regulation of learning is increasingly proposed.

4. CENTRAL MOTIVATIONAL TOPICS IN RESEARCH ON SRL

Motivation plays a crucial role in learning and constitutes an essential area in all the approaches to SRL. Thus, self-regulating students are characterized by their motivation and personal involvement in learning, they are capable of persisting and making an effort in the tasks to achieve their proposed goals (Zimmerman, 2000a, 1990). Such motivation is observed in students' personal choice to engage in the learning task and in the intensity of their effort and persistence in the activity (Pintrich and Schrauben, 1992).

Pintrich's (2003) conceptualization emphasizes the integration of motivational and cognitive elements as an essential aspect, a way to gain a complete view of the learning process in the school setting. More specifically, Pintrich (2000b, 2004) considers that it is possible to self-regulate motivation, in which he includes attempts to regulate both motivational beliefs and emotions by a series of regulatory strategies that help students cope with negative emotions such as fear or anxiety.

Regarding *motivational beliefs*, in his model of self-regulation, Pintrich gathers and organizes the most important constructs of the literature on academic motivation in an approach that, as he himself noted (Pintrich, 1999; Pintrich and DeGroot, 1990), is an adaptation of the expectation-value model of motivation developed by Eccles and his colleagues. Thus, in his approach to motivation, the three motivational components are included in SRL: a) the expectation component, which includes students' beliefs about their skill to perform a task, that is, their self-efficacy beliefs; b) the value component, which includes students' goals and their orientation towards them, as well as beliefs about the value and importance of the task; c) the affective component, which includes students' emotional reactions after performing the task (for example, exam anxiety) and their causal attributions of the results obtained.

In general, it is considered that self-regulating students show a series of adaptive attitudes and beliefs that lead them to engage and persist in academic tasks. Thus, these students consider themselves very efficient and they focus on increasing their learning level, appraising the material that must be learned as interesting, valuable, and useful to learn (Pintrich, 2000b; Schunk and Ertmer, 2000).

Regarding regulation of motivation, a characteristic of self-regulation, it refers to the fact that all these beliefs can be regulated and modified (Wolters, 2003a). Thus, starting with the motivational control and awareness achieved by self-observation and self-knowledge, self-regulating learners are capable of detecting maladjustments and controlling their emotions by a series of strategies aimed at regulating their motivation. Such strategies are known as *motivation-regulating strategies* (Cabanach, Valle, Rodríguez, and Piñeiro, 2002; Pintrich, 2000b; Wolters, 1998, 1999, 2003a, 2003b). One of the most essential aspects of these strategies is that they can be adopted consciously or practiced automatically, but in any case, they can be taught and learned, and, therefore, modified.

Although in this model, no explicit reference is made to volitive questions—which have been much studied in motivation, especially aspects such as persistence and effort (Valle, Cabanach, Núñez, González-Pienda, Rodríguez, and Piñeiro, 2003a)—, Pintrich (2004) includes them in the motivation-regulating strategies.

4.1. Motivational Planning and Activation

According to Pintrich (2000b), motivational planning and activation imply *adopting goals* (concerning the reasons for engaging in the task), as well as the activation of a series of motivational beliefs such as *self-efficacy beliefs* (judgments of competence about performing a task), *personal interest in the task* (with regard to task content of the, content domain or area), and the *beliefs about the value of the task* (beliefs about the importance, usefulness, relevance of the task).

4.1.1. Academic Goals

The motivational component of value integrates the motives, aims or reasons to engage in an activity, aspects that are closely related to cognitive and self-regulatory activities as well as to choice, effort, and persistence (Eccles, 1983; Pintrich, 1999).

Learning Goals Versus Performance Goals

Most of the investigations of academic goals have focused on two types of goals: (a) learning goals (also called mastery goals or task-focused goals), which concentrate on the development of competence and task mastery; and (b) performance goals (also called ego-oriented goals), which focus on displaying one's competence to others. Simply stated, it can be said that students develop learning goals to increase their capacity, and performance goals to display their capacity (Elliot, 1999; Pajares, Britner, and Valiente, 2000).

The results of research on the role of goals at the academic level coincide in noting that learning goals are beneficial for most learning-related results, including results at a motivational level, such as self-efficacy, interest, and value (see, for example, Harackiewicz, Barron, Tauer, Carter, and Elliot, 2000; Pintrich and DeGroot, 1990; Wolters, Yu, and Pintrich, 1996), emotional well-being (see, for example, Kaplan, and Maehr, 1999; Meyer, Turner, and Spencer, 1997; Middleton and Midgley, 1997), seeking help (see, for example, Nadler, 1998; Newman, 1998; Ryan and Pintrich, 1998), and cognitive engagement (Pintrich, 2000b).

Therefore, most of the works reveal that students who value learning and who are determined to learn and improve their competencies devote their efforts to academic tasks, persist at such tasks, and they usually use deep learning strategies (Suárez, Cabanach, and Valle, 2001; Valle et al., 2003a, 2003b). Moreover, these students engage more in self-regulating their learning (Ames, 1992; Pintrich, and De Groot, 1990), they make a greater effort to learn, and have more control over their comprehension, realizing what they are and what they are not learning (Middleton and Midgley, 1997).

Furthermore, when students show no interest or are not particularly motivated to learn, they may, in threatening settings and situations, choose various self-protection mechanisms such as self-handicapping and defensive pessimism (Rodríguez, Cabanach, Valle, Núñez, and González-Pienda, 2004; Valle, Cabanach, Rodríguez, Núñez, and González-Pienda, 2005) that may be beneficial for their personal self-image but which are quite detrimental at the academic level.

However, the conclusions about the advantages of adopting performance goals are not so clear, because the results from one study to another are very diverse. Given that the empirical results about the benefits or disadvantages of performance goals are fairly controversial, some authors consider that their effects on motivation and learning are more complex and require more theoretical and empirical attention (Utman, 1997) because some of the conclusions about the negative and maladaptive effects of performance goals are likely to be premature.

Approach Goals Versus Avoidance Goals

Reviewing the learning goals-performance goals dichotomy, Elliot and his collaborators (Elliot, 1999) propose a tri-dimensional framework for academic goals. In their proposal, they differentiate two tendencies within performance goals: an approach tendency and an avoidance tendency, thus defining three independent academic goals: (a) *performance-*

approach goals, focused on achieving competence in comparison to others; (b) *performance-avoidance goals*, focused on avoiding incompetence in comparison to others; and (c) *learning goals*, focused on the development of competence and task mastery.

Subsequently, a new construct, *learning-avoidance goals*, was proposed, the result of applying the differentiation between approach and avoidance tendencies to learning goals (see Pintrich, 2000b). Students with learning-approach goals are oriented to achieving the goal of learning and understanding, whereas students with *learning-avoidance goals* are concerned about not being perfect, not completely understanding the material, or failing with regard to their self-referred mastery standards (Linnenbrink and Pintrich, 2002). Some proposals suggest that the four types of goals (learning approach and avoidance, and performance approach and avoidance) constitute independent constructs that differentially predict a variety of results linked to learning.

In any case, whereas the avoidance tendency within learning goals is still scarcely studied empirically, there are many works that support the differentiation between approach tendencies and avoidance tendencies within performance goals (see, for example, Elliot, 1997, 1999; Elliot and McGregor, 1999; Elliot, McGregor, and Gable, 1999; Middleton and Midgley, 1997; Skaalvik, 1997; Rodríguez, Cabanach, Piñeiro, Valle, Núñez, and González-Pienda, 2001; Valle et al., 2006; Wolters et al., 1996). This distinction between performance-approach goals and performance-avoidance goals has led, among other things, to the reconsideration of the effects of performance-approach goals. Thus, Pintrich (2000a) noted that there may be situations in which performance goals are not maladaptive in motivational and affective terms and in terms of the use of strategies and achievement. In fact, in some works, performance-approach goals seem more closely linked to achieving goals, whereas learning goals are more related to intrinsic interest in the tasks (see, for example, Harackiewicz et al., 2000).

One Goal or Multiple Goals?

Perhaps one of the most important advances in recent years in research on goals has been to show empirically that, instead of adopting one exclusive goal, many students choose various goals—specifically, academic goals, but also social goals—to engage in learning. Thus, when facing situations in which the learning activity is not very stimulating or interesting, it might be useful to find reasons other than intrinsic interest in the task to motivate their actions. In these cases, the opportunity to choose various motives—getting others' approval, winning prizes and external rewards, etc.—may become a powerful incentive to promote and maintain academic engagement. Therefore, simultaneously choosing several goals in specific academic situations (Pintrich, 2000a; Rodríguez et al., 2001; Seifert, 1995; Valle et al., 2003b; Wentzel, 2000) is usually one of the most beneficial options at the academic level.

Students with multiple goals adapt better to the demands of the setting, especially the teaching style and the evaluation. Specifically, depending on the professor's teaching style and the evaluation criteria employed, students' way of studying and the quality of the study process will vary. The findings of the work of Suárez et al. (2001) indicate that adopting several goals simultaneously is the best option to allow students to develop direct and positive control over each and every one of the self-regulating strategies. Managing their goal orientations allows students to optimize strategic supervision in response to the demands derived from the various tasks and settings and their own interests. The results obtained by

Rodríguez et al. (2001) show that adopting multiple goals not only leads to better academic achievement, but also that coordinating various kinds of goals favors the development of self-regulation skills that allow individuals to adapt more efficiently to the demands of the learning context.

Taking as reference some of the results found in several works about the relation between performance goals and academic results and the relation between learning goals and interest, Harackiewicz et al. (2000) consider that each kind of goal (learning and performance) is associated with one relevant success indicator (interest or achievement) but not with the other, which shows that students who adopt both types of goals are probably the ones that achieve the best results in both variables, that is, high interest and high achievement. Therefore, as stated by Bouffard, Boisvert, Vezeau, and Larouche (1995), the most adequate motivational orientation for optimum academic functioning is the one in which students are not only concerned with knowledge and improving their capacities but also with achieving a certain performance level. From this perspective, the motivational orientation that best fulfills these two prerequisites is the multiple goals orientation, especially the motivational profile consisting of high learning goals and high performance-approach goals.

We consider that the articulation of both goal orientations implies putting into practice certain mechanisms of SRL for the strategic use of such orientations, with one predominating over the other in each specific situation, depending on individuals' intentions, motives, or reasons for deciding to engage in the learning task. This way of behaving requires individuals to effectively coordinate and adjust their personal values and justifications to the specific demands of the learning context. The example proposed by Paris, Byrnes, and Paris (2001) may clarify this idea: imagine a student who is solving a math problem and notices that the other classmates finish the task very quickly. If the student is having trouble solving the problem, he may attribute this situation to his own capacity (in this case, his lack of capacity for mathematics). This explanation could lead him to abandon his attempts to solve the problem successfully and, instead, copy the answer so he can give the impression of having solved the problem quickly, as this is associated with pretending in front of others that that he has the capacity to solve the task easily. In this hypothetical example, the student abandons his initial learning goals to adopt a performance-approach goal. Thus, the conditions that surround task performance can affect the way one conceives the task and the sense of one's own competence to solve it, which would be reflected in the evolution or development of the goal orientations that are adopted.

The metaphor of the "multiple pathways" used by Pintrich (2000a) is an attempt to synthesize the divergences of some of the results we have commented upon. This author proposed that learning goals and performance-approach goals can be adopted and can promote different patterns of motivation, affect, use of strategies, and achievement over time. In this sense, students who adopt different goals may follow diverse roads or trajectories over time, with some of them ending in the same place in terms of real achievement, but involving very different experiences until the final result is achieved. Thus, learning-oriented students will have a "more tranquil and pleasant" experience in terms of motivation, positive affect, effort, and use of strategies on their way towards good levels of achievement. In contrast, students with performance goals, although they can achieve equivalent and even higher levels than students with learning goals, may experience less interest, positive affect, and perhaps more anxiety or negative affect, given their concerns about doing better than others. Likewise, they might try to display less effort because of their goal of seeming smarter than their classmates and, if they have trouble or they fail on their way, this involves a cost for them in affective terms (less interest and more negative affect), or it may lead them to using strategies oriented to achieving their goal of doing better than others.

4.1.2. Motivational Beliefs

These beliefs are made up both of expectations about one's own capacity to perform a task optimally (self-efficacy beliefs) and judgments about the ease, interest, and value of the task (Pintrich, 2000a, 2000b, 2004).

Regarding *self-efficacy*, although this concept was initially elaborated and investigated by Bandura (1997), it has also received much attention in research on SRL because of its positive effect on the process of self-regulation. Thus, these beliefs about one's own skills are considered helpful to organize and carry out the necessary actions to attain the expected performance in specific tasks (Zimmerman, 2000b). These beliefs involve thoughts such as "I feel capable of performing the task," "I feel that I am good," and they have important consequences on effort, persistence, and task performance. If individuals feel capable, they will have an active attitude; otherwise, this lack of motivation will lead them to adopt a passive attitude.

Moreover, judgments and perceptions of the task, its difficulty, value, and interest are also made. Before beginning an activity, attempts are made to determine task difficulty, which Pintrich called *ease of learning judgments*, or *perceptions of task difficulty* (Pintrich, 2004). These are thoughts such as "I wonder whether the task will be easy, difficult, interesting, boring," "I consider the task easy or difficult for me," etc. Although this kind of reflections is similar to the previous ones, in the latter, emphasis is placed in the task, whereas in the former, the person is emphasized.

Beliefs about task value include perceptions about the relevance, usefulness, and interest of the task, and they can be regulated at first both consciously and unconsciously, and automatically (Pintrich, 2000a). They refer to reflections such as "I wonder why I am performing this task, what is it good for?" "I wonder whether it will be useful/useless; interesting; boring," etc. These beliefs are related to the expectation-value theory developed by Atkinson in the 50s and revised by other contemporary authors, undergoing important modifications, especially those proposed by Wigfield, Eccles, and collaborators (Wigfield and Eccles, 1992). This model proposes that the effort to achieve a good performance, such as engaging in and persisting at a task, is determined by the quality of the motives, expectations, and values. Success expectations refer to the beliefs that certain behaviors will lead to a certain result, whereas value refers to the relative suitability or the appeal of the result.

Compared with Atkinson's model, in which expectations and values were inversely related, this model tends toward a positive relation between them. The construct of value is divided into various components ; Eccles and Wigfield (2002) described task value in relation to (1) achievement value, which refers to the personal importance of doing the task well; (2) intrinsic value, which concerns the pleasure the person feels by performing the task; (3) utility value, which has to do with the relation between task and the person's goals; and (4) cost, which refers to the negative aspects that performing the task involves for the person (e.g., Wigfield, Eccles, Yoon, Harold, Arbreton, Freedman-Doan, and Blumenfeld, 1997).

The studies of this paradigm provide evidence of the critical role played by these constructs in students' engagement and maintenance of motivation and performance. These beliefs about task value have been related both to the use of strategies (Pintrich and DeGroot, 1990) and achievement (Wigfield and Eccles, 1992).

Beliefs about personal interest in the task or the specific task content are also very important when planning tasks (e.g., "I know that this task is important and useful for me and I know why."). Level of interest plays an essential role because it is related to the increase of persistence and effort (Pintrich, 2000b). It can thus provoke either positive or negative anticipatory affect, such as fear and anxiety (for example, if the task is perceived as very important but one does not perceive oneself as able to perform it successfully), which may affect subsequent processes and require active and adaptive self-regulation of cognition, motivation, and behavior. Interest in the task can be activated by the task itself (i.e., reading topic) or by contextual characteristics (i.e., social or material rewards), but it can also be controlled and regulated by the individual.

Starting with the activation of all the above-mentioned beliefs and judgments, at this stage, a dual goal is pursued. On the one hand, to promote a facilitating affective-motivational pattern that involves certain competence and controllability beliefs about the task of understanding and the assignment of high value and interest to the task, and on the other hand, planning the use of the various motivational strategies (Cabanach et al, 2002).

4.2. Control and Regulation of Motivation

While carrying out the task, people must be capable of realizing whether the task is easier or more difficult than they expected, whether they are losing interest, etc. They should also be aware of their mood, of whether they are getting nervous because a problem has come up, whether they have stopped feeling confident about their possibilities, whether they feel they are not capable of continuing, they are worried, concerned, etc. Once these aspects have been monitored, they can attempt to regulate them by choosing and adapting a series of affective-motivational strategies that allow them to go on performing the task in a relaxed and assured way (to go on or to give up, to leave it for later on, to stop and try to relax, to breathe deeply, etc.). These activities are called motivation-regulation strategies or motivational strategies, and they are the mechanisms and procedures employed to promote adaptive emotional states and/or to cope with risky situations that affect personal well-being." In general, these strategies are based on individual beliefs, justifications, and emotions and they operate through specific knowledge about the domain and the repertory of available strategies and resources, allowing individuals to maintain a positive affective and emotional climate when performing the task. More specifically, they refer to the strategies to cope with anxiety, stay engaged in the activity, and maintain adaptive beliefs and emotions.

Motivation-regulation strategies have been divided into different types, among which is notable the distinction between: (1) *motivational strategies oriented towards maintaining engagement and intentions*, whose goal is to maintain personal effort devoted to the task in the face of various sources of distraction or abandonment, or adverse experiences or difficulties, and (2) *motivational strategies to defend and protect personal well-being*, which refer to strategic behaviors designed to control negative emotions and affects, thus protecting one's emotional well-being and worth.

These strategies can be taught and modified if the individual is using them maladaptively, a very important aspect if it is taken into account that such strategies affect the choice of the procedures and resources that are put into practice in specific situations and contexts.

Below are described some of the most important motivational strategies.

Strategies Oriented towards Maintaining Engagement and Learning Intentions

These strategies allow students to control their motivation to complete a task that is becoming tiring, difficult, or boring (Pintrich, 2000b, 2004) and they are based on activities to regulate efficacy or task value.

- Strategies to control thoughts of self-efficacy using self-directed language based on positive self-affirmations (e.g., "I know I can do it.").
- Strategies to increase extrinsic motivation, promising oneself rewards if one completes the task (e.g., "If reading something is boring or difficult, I sometimes say to myself that when I finish, I can do something I like, or rest," etc.) (Wolters, 1998; Zimmerman and Martínez-Pons, 1988).
- Strategies to increase intrinsic motivation, attempting to make the task more interesting (e.g., "If the task is boring or difficult, I try to do something to make it more interesting.").
- Strategies to increase task value, reflecting and underlining its value and usefulness for the future, the career, etc. (e.g., "If I do not feel motivated to go on, I think about how important it is to understand this to pass the subject or finish the course," etc.).

Strategies Oriented towards Defense and Protection of Personal Well-Being

The goal underlying the adoption of this kind of motivational strategies is to cope with situations that are potentially aversive to the individual's emotional well-being.

On the one hand, strategic behaviors designed to protect one's value can be adopted, for example, devaluating the school with regard to its importance have in other contexts (e.g., "If it doesn't turn out right, I'll drop this activity because it was not really so important, there are other, more important things."). This kind of strategy is usually used in cases in which students achieve low performance levels and feel that their competence and beliefs of worth are threatened.

On the other hand, another group of strategies can be used to control negative emotions and affects. Specifically, they are the following:

- Self-talk aimed at controlling anxiety and negative affect (e.g., "If I don't understand some part and am getting discouraged, I try to do something to prevent myself from getting even more nervous, and feel better, such as leaving the task for later on, carrying on in case the rest of the text helps me," etc.) (Zeidner, 1998).
- Invoking negative affects (shame, guilt) to stimulate effort and persistence (e.g., "If I don't understand something and am getting discouraged about going on, I think of how disgraceful it is not to understand something like this," "I think that I must make a greater effort and keep on trying because it would be stupid if I didn't manage to do it," etc.) (Wolters, 1998).

Lastly, some defensive strategies are described:

- *Defensive pessimism*. An emotional strategy used by people to take advantage of the negative affects and anxiety that accompany a negative result in order to motivate themselves and increase their effort and engagement in the task. With this kind of strategy, people maintain low (not very realistic) expectations about the probability of success, or they underestimate the importance of the task, in the attempt to minimize the negative feelings (e.g., "I won't be able to understand this because I'm not good at it, but I'll try," "This text is really not very important but even so, I'm going to read it.") (Garcia and Pintrich, 1994).
- *Self-handicapping*. This involves reducing effort so as to justify a failure. It is characterized by the "creation of some impediment (real or imaginary)" in order for the subject to have a ready excuse for potential failure (Garcia and Pintrich, 1994). It is related to low use of cognitive and meta-cognitive strategies and resource management (Rodríguez et al., 2004).
- *Procrastination*. This is characterized by to put something off intentionally and habitually when faced with the risk of failure. Academic procrastination includes failing to perform an activity within the desired time frame or postponing until the last minute activities one ultimately intends to complete. As such, high levels of procrastination appear inconsistent with the behaviors typically attributed to self-regulated learners (Wolters, 2003b). Although conceptualizations of procrastination as self-regulation failure have received considerable empirical support, procrastination has only occasionally been examined in relation to variables emphasized in models of self-regulated learning.

4.3. Emotional Reaction and Reflection

After performing a task, students experience an emotional reaction about the result obtained (happiness about success, sadness about failure, etc.), which constitutes the affective component of motivation, as well as a reflection about the reasons for it, that is, attributions of the results obtained.

With regard to emotional reactions, when students complete a task, they experience various sensations, appraising what they achieved with regard to the proposed goal (e.g., "I feel good when I achieve my goals; I feel happy, proud of myself," "I feel bad when I do not manage to understand something; I feel sad, I feel ashamed.").

When referring to attributions, it is essential to refer to the attributional theory of Weiner (1979, 1986). This theory indicates that students have an affective reaction to any academic result (satisfaction if it is positive, frustration, sadness if it is negative) and wonder about the causes, that is, they make a series of attributions to explain the result obtained. The most frequent causes to which they attribute academic success and failure are usually ability, effort, task difficulty, and luck (Weiner, 1992). According to Weiner, the importance of causal attributions in motivation comes not from the causes themselves but from various properties and characteristics of each one of them as a function of three causal dimensions: locus of control or the internal-external dimension, stability or the stable-unstable dimension, and controllability or the controllable-uncontrollable dimension. Thus, in order to explain the fact that achievement varies from one occasion to another, students can attribute it to a series of causes that can be considered: (a) internal (that is, the causal factor is within the person, i.e., ability and effort), or external (such as luck and task difficulty); (b) stable (unchangeable over time, i.e., ability) or unstable (effort); and (c) controllable (that is, the causal factors are under one's control) or uncontrollable.

As a function of each one of these causal dimensions, a causal attribution for some result is made, which leads to a certain affective reaction that may differ depending on whether the attribution is for a successful result or a failure.

What is really crucial is not that, at some time, a result is attributed to a certain cause but that there is a more or less generalized tendency to perform certain kinds of very detrimental attributions. In this sense, various authors emphasize the existence of adaptive attributional patterns that favor motivation and maladaptive patterns that inhibit it, which has important implications for students' future achievement. When students attribute their successes to ability (internal and stable factor) or to effort (internal, unstable, and controllable factor), their motivation when faced with future tasks will increase; the same will happen if, upon failing, they make internal and controllable attributions (effort) because this way, they will feel capable of modifying the causes of this result.

An essential aspect is that attributions and the affective reactions they provoke condition future achievement. In this sense, it is noteworthy that people can actively control the kinds of attributions they make by means of motivational strategies and thus protect their self-esteem and motivation for future tasks (Pintrich, 2000b). This opens important venues for interventions to modify maladaptive patterns.

Lastly, we would like to point out that the general process of affective-emotional reaction and reflection plays such an important role that it is essential to have the suitable motivational strategies in order to control the process. On the one hand, general self-regulation of the task is affected both by the quality of the attributions and by the quality of the emotions experienced in this process (Pintrich, 2002). On the other hand, this process conditions the way in which the students will tackle, for example, the task of reading and understanding a text in the future because these reflections and reactions can provoke changes in their beliefs about self-efficacy, value, interest, and in their expectations, all of which conditions their future level of motivation.

In general, with regard to the regulation of motivation, it is clear that students are not characterized either by the presence or total absence of motivation, in terms of a general quantity, but instead there are important qualitative differences in how students become motivated and these different qualities significantly affect learning and achievement.

5. LOOKING AT THE FUTURE

In this work, we have reviewed the topics that, in our opinion, have been considered the most relevant in the configuration of the motivational dimension of the process of academic SRL. Looking at the future, we believe that it is necessary to make more effort to improve our knowledge in at least three areas of self-regulation: a) development and evaluation of efficient intervention programs to promote self-regulatory competencies; b) improvement of the principles that should govern the implementation of these programs, both in the areas of research and of teaching; and c) development of research programs and training programs to form educators who can then design instructional settings based on the principles that govern the process of self-regulated teaching-learning.

In the following pages, we approach these three areas with the aim of reflecting on what is already known and, on the basis of this, inviting everyone to work on what we must yet discover.

5.1. Intervention Programs

Simpson, Hynd, Nist, and Burrel (1997) carried out a review of the literature on programs and interventions in the area of study competencies, choosing as the organizing criterion the transfer of the learning strategies students had worked with to other contexts. In this sense, they presented a taxonomy organized in five general categories. The first one comprised courses of learning to learn, including interventions that presented a sort of development rather than an orientation with a view to reducing deficits in the area of learning strategies. The typology of courses in this category is oriented towards developing processes and promoting students who self-regulate their learning, working at repertories of learning strategies that can be modified depending on the specific school tasks. Students are trained to identify and use appropriate strategies for different tasks and learning contexts. This orientation promotes transfer of learning to other settings so that students develop a meta-cognitive awareness of the conditions associated with each specific learning task and they train the different options as a function of their aims and contextual limitations. The literature states that participants in courses coming under the general title of learning to learn improve their academic achievement (Weinstein, 1994).

The second category described comprises courses that are similar to the previous ones, but focused on a specific learning domain. These courses present an developmental orientation, training in the application of learning strategies, but in a certain study discipline or concrete knowledge area, and are not concerned about intentionally attempting to achieve transfer of the material learned to adjacent contents or contexts. Comprehensibly, there was no evidence that these competencies were transferred to other study domains (Hattie, Biggs, and Purdie, 1996; Simpson et al., 1997).

The third category includes precise interventions, summer school or bridge-programs between two study cycles (e.g., secondary school and University), oriented by the logic of filling in gaps. A "remediating" tone is notable in these interventions, focused on promoting isolated strategic aspects (e.g., reading techniques or writing competencies). Research shows that the frequency of these courses / modules does not favor transfer of the learned and trained competencies to adjacent domains. The explanations are related both to the duration of the interventions (normally short courses) and the low incidence in explicit training in applying the strategy to other domains.

The fourth category groups courses integrating the performance of reading and writing competencies. The aim is to increase the efficiency of writing and, as a consequence, academic success, but, as noted by Ackerman (1993), these programs do not present consistent results.

The last category comprises assistential services in the area of the study competencies offered by specialized centers. These services are normally isolated and atheoretical, as they do not present a theoretical framework such as the one on which precise interventions are based, or an evaluation that would allow drawing conclusions about their impact on students' academic achievement (Simpson el al., 1997).

Curricular inclusion is another method, which is not mentioned in the described typology, used to help students develop effective learning strategies. The teachers and educators that choose this methodology instruct their students in motivational aspects and cognitive strategies related to their content area (Entwistle and Tait, 1992). In the review of the literature about the different interventions in the area of learning strategies, Hattie and his collaborators (1996) suggest that these programs achieve more academic success when they are trained in a specific context or learning domain. The literature suggests that it is appropriate to incorporate the teaching of learning strategies into teachers' training programs so that they can subsequently include such strategies in the respective syllabuses of knowledge areas (Simpson et al., 1997; Hattie et al., 1996).

Another essential aspect in the architecture of the interventions in learning strategies is their design. Juxtaposed interventions provide instruction in the area of learning strategies in a specific space outside of the curriculum.

The aim of curricular inclusion is to integrate the teaching of learning strategies into the dynamics of each one of the subjects. The methodology of curricular inclusion, working with SRL strategies within the context, promotes their conceptualization as useful tools to be applied in diverse domains and not just in a specific course of "study techniques" where such techniques are usually presented isolatedly and with no theoretical anchor.

By training in the use of SRL strategies in different contexts, tasks, and content areas, curricular inclusion projects increase the probability of transfer of these learnings (Salomon and Perkins, 1989; Simpson et al., 1997; Zimmerman, Bonner, and Kovach, 1996). Although there is no solid corpus of research in this area, comparison of inclusion programs and juxtaposed (extracurricular) programs suggests that inclusion programs are more useful and efficient in basic and secondary school and the extracurricular programs are more useful in the university. The reasons for this could be related to the specificity of the different areas of knowledge chosen, the low pedagogical formation of some university teachers, the division of subjects into four-month periods, which does not allow prolonged interaction of the teachers with the students, etc.

However, from this meta-analysis, it is not sufficiently clear whether the results found are due to differences in the students' development or to specific characteristics of the interventions at the different educational levels (Hattie et al., 1996; Simpson et al., 1997).

5.2. General Principles of Teaching Learning Strategies within a Self-Regulatory Framework

In general, training programs of learning strategies (at any educational level, with any type of students, curricular setting, etc.) comprise "direct instruction" of strategies and "active construction" of knowledge by students (Swanson and Deshler, 2003). In this regard, Deshler (1998) states that, although it is possible to contemplate the different strategy instruction programs both from a reductionist viewpoint and from a constructivist viewpoint, it is probably more appropriate to consider strategic instruction a continuum between the two extremes. According to Borkowski and Muthukrishna (1992), this kind of interventions generates active students, involved in meaningful, planned, and reflective process. However, Harris and Pressley (1991) note that the term "constructivism" is not synonymous to learning by discovery. In contrast, by means of incorporating the concepts of guided discovery, strategic instruction provides sufficient opportunities to develop constructive processes and to operate effectively. In short, the interactive nature of instruction promotes SRL (Zimmerman et al., 1996).

Some of the characteristics shared by the best programs of teaching of (and by means of) cognitive strategies and self-regulation could be synthesized in the following comments.

First, strategic instruction is based on the explanation followed by an extensive and stimulating practice. Although encouraging students to be more strategic stimulates the creation and use of strategies, they need to practice the recently acquired strategies. This experience can be successful by means of guided practice in tasks of suitable difficulty, carefully controlling the successes, and offering help only when the students fail and have trouble. Moreover, failures are necessary and they are considered an opportunity to correct or perfect a strategy.

Second, the direct explanation, with the teacher's modeling, helps students to acquire meta-cognitive knowledge. That is, explicit instruction with feedback while training strategies is better than asking students to infer or summarize the characteristics of the strategies by themselves. The students have the opportunity to learn the value of the strategy employed through the explanations and practice. They understand that strategies have a facilitating effect on learning and understand when and how to use them efficiently.

Third, a good instructional program includes teaching a few strategies at once, intensively, and with meta-cognitive comprehension. To achieve comprehension, the strategies are modeled by the teacher with verbal explanations of the complete strategic sequence and with information (and examples) about the usefulness of the strategy being taught.

Fourth, it is essential that the teachers orient students to generalize the acquired strategies to new situations. Promoting generalization has the effect of stimulating the processes of reflection and planning. This approach to strategic instruction plays an important role in the autonomous use of strategies. Thus, through adequate teaching, the strategy will continue to be used in subsequent tasks, often in a different way.

Fifth, good strategic instruction implies substantial teaching and practice carried out over a long period of time and by means of multiple tasks. This sequence allows maximum exploration of strategies and provides students with sufficient opportunities to discover when and where to use particular strategies and to adapt these procedures to new situations. Teachers and students explore each learning situation in order to transfer its potential applications. Thus, they practice adapting strategies to new tasks. The long-term goal is students' construction of knowledge about the suitability of each specific strategy for a variety of tasks and to solve challenging problems.

Sixth, in contrast to what some researchers and educators consider an "imposition of static and prescribed routines on passive students," from these effective instructional approaches, good strategic instruction develops active students, engaged in a meaningful, planned, and reflexive process.

Seventh, good strategic instruction should be constructive. The purpose of the explanation and the modeling is to provide a conceptual foundation that students can extend and build on. From this framework, students are stimulated to explore new strategies. Good teachers guide students to discover the effectiveness of each sequence of strategies. The results are strategies developed by means of a process of guided discovery.

Eighth, an important component of good strategic instruction is structure. The teacher takes control to promote students' attention towards tasks and adequate strategies, to control their frustration and reduce the risk inherent in solving problems by reducing the number of steps in the process, and to underscore the discrepancies between some of the subjects' responses and the appropriate use of the strategy. Pressley and his collaborators (Pressley, Harris, and Guthrie, 1992) note that teachers should not only offer their students contents, but also strategic processing models. During extensive practical sessions, the teacher illustrates and discusses how the contents can be understood using study strategies. An important aspect of this process is that the students' responses have substantial impact on the course of the teacher-student interactions.

Finally, strategic instruction is, therefore, unique insofar as the components of the teacher-student interactions are not set down in writing, but instead are developed during instruction. The nature and contents of the teacher-student interactions are determined by the teacher's perception of the students' progress in the acquisition of each strategy.

It should also be noted that instruction in strategies should, at the same time, be strategic. That is, it should promote students' active participation, with the aim of engaging them in an instructional situation in which learning is considered a vehicle to achieve personal goals. As a macro-strategy, strategic teaching and SRL should fulfill the following prerequisites:

1. Students should be willing to learn the strategy and understand its purpose and benefits.
2. Both the physical and cognitive actions covered by the strategy should be completely described and explained, that is, students should be informed about what they are going to do and how to think about each step of the strategy, so that the strategy is meaningful for them. For this purpose, examples and relevant circumstances for the students should be included in the presentation of the strategy, and students should play an active role exploring and commenting on the strategy.
3. To facilitate the self-instruction process, students should be informed about how to use the recall system that was incorporated into the strategic intervention.
4. Students should understand the learning process of the strategy and participate in the establishment of activities in order to anticipate and control learning. Thus, students should be capable of evaluating whether they have followed each one of the steps of the strategy to determine whether they have achieved each one of the specific learning goals. Otherwise, feedback between teacher and students should be established about the aspects of the goals that were not achieved. In this way, students are taught to identify and reorient failures that occurred while learning the strategy.
5. Multiple models of the strategy should be provided and, at the same time, an adequate balance between the physical and cognitive actions involved in the strategy should be achieved. The diverse models proposed should provide a complete and clear demonstration of the strategy, and the most important procedure used for this is the teacher's "thinking out loud." By means of these models, and by thinking out loud, the association between cognitive actions and observable actions involved in the strategy should be made evident.
6. Students should be involved in the model and become active participants in the instructional process of strategies.

7. The strategy should be completely understood and memorized before being put into practice, so that students will be confident about their knowledge of the strategy and can concentrate only on its application, thus avoiding devoting part of their effort to remembering each one of the steps of the strategy.

8. Putting the strategy into practice should begin with guided and controlled practice and end with the students practicing the strategy independently.

9. A system should be used to measure as a source of information to allow the teacher and the students to determine whether the strategy was learned, how it is used, and whether the proposed demands were met. Students' progress in learning the strategy should be related to an increase in their capacity to cope with the demands made of them.

10. Once the strategy has been acquired, great effort should be devoted to generalizing it to other settings. In this stage of generalization, teachers and students should work together to identify other settings and conditions in which the strategy can be applied, the modifications it will be necessary to carry out so that it can generalize without problems, and, lastly, to plan how to use the strategy in diverse settings.

Summing up, efficient and effective strategic instruction implies teaching that has all the characteristics that help students to learn learning strategies in a meaningful and functional way. To satisfy the spirit of this kind of teaching, both the strategies that are the object of learning and the methods used to teach them should be taken into account, as well as the multiplicity of aspects that can have relevant influence on how such strategies are learned and subsequently applied by students.

5.3. Training of Trainers (through) Learning Strategies

As noted by Mayer (2002), the process that leads to meaningful learning depends both on the way in which the learner processes the information (that is, on the side of learning) and on the material presented (that is, on the side of teaching). Therefore, there are two complementary ways of promoting meaningful learning: improving the way that students process information (that is, learning and self-regulation strategies) and improving the way that the materials are presented (that is, instructional methods).

What does teaching for meaningful learning imply? Briefly, it implies providing learning experiences that allow students to use what they already know efficiently when facing a new task. In the instruction of meaningful learning, teachers create teaching and learning settings in which the students understand what they are learning. Consequently, teaching should be an active process in which students are encouraged to select the most important aspect, organize it, elaborate it, and apply it to different situations or contexts from those that served as the framework in which it was learned. Teaching for meaningful learning means that the teacher must: a) provide productive feedback; b) provide activity, concretion, and familiarity; c) explain with examples; d) guide the cognitive process during learning; e) promote learning strategies; f) promote problem-solving strategies; g) promote situated learning in the classroom; h) give priority to students' motivation to learn.

But … are teachers prepared to create this kind of context and/or conditions that are necessary to promote meaningful learning? Where have they acquired the knowledge and necessary skills to promote the development of self-regulated students, who are capable of autonomous learning? Does current training capacitate them for this activity? ... Obviously, if we expect teachers to help their students to self-regulate their learning, then we must try to promote their own self-regulation. However, traditional theories to design the instructional process point in the opposite direction.

Generally, teachers have been required to incorporate into their classrooms a whole series of innovations developed outside of the classroom. In addition, traditional training of teachers has considered teachers as "passive students" that will carry out the incorporation of the innovations by massive technical training and the help of researchers. Actually, there are possibly very few training programs for teachers that promote the notion of teachers as self-innovators. In these cases, more attention will be paid to the development of self-regulation skills in the teachers themselves and they will be invited to become "teacher-researchers."

Therefore, the great quantity of research on student's SRL, together with the new way of understanding how teachers carry out their educational task, constitutes the foundations for research on the *teachers' self-regulated teaching-learning process*.

REFERENCES

Ackerman, J. M. (1993). The promise to learn. *Written communication, 10*(3), 334-370.

Ames, C. (1992). Classrooms: Goals, structures and student motivation. *Journal of Educational Psychology, 84*, 261-271.

Bandura, A. (1991). Social cognitive theory of self-regulation. *Organizational Behavior and Human Performance, 50*, 248-287.

Bandura, A. (1997). Self-efficacy: The exercise of control. New York: Freeman.

Bandura, A. (2001). Social cognitive theory: An agentic perspective. *American Review of Psychology, 52*, 1-26.

Beltrán, J. (1999). Aprender en la Universidad [Learning in the University]. In J. R. Ruiz Carrascosa (Coord.), *Aprender y enseñar en la Universidad. Iniciación a la docencia universitaria* [Learning and teaching in the University. Initiation to university teaching]. Jaén: University of Jaén (Spain).

Biggs, J. B. (1991). *Teaching for Learning: The view from Cognitive Psychology*. Hawthorn, Australia: ACER.

Biggs, J. B. (2001). The reflective institution: Assuring and enhancing the quality of teaching and learning. *Higher Education, 42*, 221-237.

Boekaerts, M. (1999). Self-regulated learning: Where we are today. *International Journal of Educational Research, 31*, 445-457.

Boekaerts, M., and Corno, L. (2005). Self-regulation in the classroom: A perspective on assessment and intervention. *Applied Psychology: An International Review, 54*(2), 199-231.

Boekaerts, M., Pintrich, P. R., and Zeidner, M. (2000). Self-regulation: An introductory overview. In M. Boekaerts, P. R. Pintrich, and M. Zeidner (Eds.), *Handbook of self-regulation* (pp. 1-9). San Diego: Academic Press.

Borkowski, J.G., and Muthukrishna, N. (1992). Moving metacognition into the classroom: "Working models" and effective strategy teaching. In M. Pressley, K. R. Harris, and J. T.

Guthrie (Eds.), *Promoting academic competence and literacy in school* (pp. 477-501). San Diego: Academic Press.

Bouffard, T., Boisvert, J., Vezeau, C., and Larouche, C. (1995). The impact of goal orientation on self-regulation and performance among college students. *British Journal of Educational Psychology, 65*, 317-329.

Cabanach, R., Valle, A., Rodríguez, S., and Piñeiro, I. (2002). Autorregulación del aprendizaje y estrategias de estudio [Self-regulation of learning and study strategies]. In J. A. González–Pienda, J. C. Núñez, L. Álvarez, and E. Soler (Coords.), *Estrategias de aprendizaje. Concepto, evaluación e intervención* [Learning strategies. Concept, evaluation, and intervention] (pp. 17-38). Madrid: Pirámide.

Cochram-Smith, M. (2003). Teaching quality matters. *Journal of Teacher Education, 54*(2), 95-98.

Dansereau, D. F. (1985). Learning strategy research. In J. W. Segal, S. F. Chipman, and R. Glaser (Eds.), *Thinking and learning skills. Relating instruction to research. Vol. I.* (pp. 209-239). Hillsdale, NJ: Erlbaum.

Deshler, D. (1998). Grounding interventions for students with learning disabilities in "powerful ideas." *Learning Disabilities Research and Practice, 13*(1), 29-34.

Dweck, C. S. (1986). Motivational processes affecting learning. *American Psychologist, 41*, 1040-1048.

Eccles, J. S. (1983). Expectancies, values, and academic behaviors. In J. T. Spence (Ed.), *Achievement and achievement motives* (pp. 75-146). San Francisco: Freeman.

Eccles, J. S., and Wigfield, A. (2002). Motivational beliefs, values and goals. *American Review Psychology, 53*, 109-132.

Elliot, A. (1997). Integrating the "classic" and "contemporary" approaches to achievement motivation: A hierarchical model of approach and avoidance achievement motivation. In M. L. Maehr and P. R. Pintrich (Eds.), *Advances in motivation and achievement* (pp. 143-179). Greenwich, CT: JAI.

Elliot, A. J. (1999). Approach and avoidance motivation and achievement goals. *Educational Psychologist, 34*, 169-189.

Elliot, A., and McGregor, H. (1999). Test anxiety and the hierarchical model of approach and avoidance achievement motivation. *Journal of Personality and Social Psychology, 72*, 461-475.

Elliot, A. J., McGregor, H. A., and Gable, S. (1999). Achievement goals, study strategies, and exam performance: A mediational analysis. *Journal of Educational Psychology, 91*, 549-563.

Entwistle, N. J. (1988). Motivational factors in students' approaches to learning. In R. R. Schmeck (Ed.), *Learning strategies and learning styles: Perspectives on individual differences* (pp. 21-51). New York: Plenum Press.

Entwistle, N. J., and Tait, H. (1992). Promoting effective study skills. Module 8, Block A. of *Effective Learning and Teaching in Higher Education.* Sheffield, UK: Universities' and Colleges' Staff Development Agency.

Garcia, T., and Pintrich, P. R. (1994). Regulation motivation and cognition in the classroom: The role of self-schemas and self-regulatory strategies. In D. H. Schunk and B. J. Zimmerman (Eds.), *Self-regulation of learning and performance: Issues and educational applications* (pp. 127-153). Hillsdale, NJ: Erlbaum.

Harackiewicz, J. M., Barron, K. E., Tauer, J. M., Carter, S. M., and Elliot, A. J. (2000). Short-term and long-term consequences of achievement goals: Predicting interest and performance over time. *Journal of Educational Psychology, 92*(2), 316-330.

Harris, K. R., and Pressley, M. (1991). The nature of cognitive strategy instruction. *Exceptional Children, 57*, 392-404.

Hattie, J., Biggs, J., and Purdie, N. (1996). Effects of learning skills interventions on student learning: A meta-analysis. *Review of Educational Research, 66*(2), 99-136.

Kaplan, A., and Maehr, M. L. (1999). Achievement goals and student well- being. *Contemporary Educational Psychology, 24,* 330- 358.

Linnenbrink, E. A., and Pintrich, P. R. (2002). Achievement goal theory and affect: An asymmetrical bidirectional model. *Educational Psychologist, 37,* 69-78.

Marton, F., and Säljö, R. (1976). On qualitative differences in learning. I: Outcome and process. *British Journal of Educational Psychology 46,* 4-11.

Mayer, R. E. (2002). *The promise of educational psychology. Teaching for meaningful learning.* Upper Saddle River, NJ: Pearson Education, Inc.

Meyer, D. K., Turner, J. C., and Spencer, C. A. (1997). Challenge in a mathematics classroom: Students' motivation and strategies in project-based learning. *Elementary School Journal, 97,* 501-521.

Middleton, M., and Midgley, C. (1997). Avoiding the demonstration of lack of ability: An unexplored aspect of goal theory. *Journal of Educational Psychology, 89,* 710-718.

Nadler, A. (1998). Relationship, esteem, and achievement perspectives on autonomous and dependent help seeking. In S. A. Karabenick (Ed.), *Strategic help seeking: Implications for learning and teaching* (pp. 61-93). Mahwah, NJ: Erlbaum.

Newman, R. S. (1998). Adaptative help- seeking: A role of social interaction in self-regulated learning. In S. A. Karabenick (Ed.), *Strategic help seeking: Implications for learning and teaching* (pp. 13-37). Mahwah, NJ: Erlbaum.

Pajares, F., Britner, S. L., and Valiente, G. (2000). Relation between achievement goals and self-beliefs of middle school students in writing and science. *Contemporary Educational Psychology, 25,* 406-422.

Paris, S. G., Byrnes, J. P., and Paris, A. H. (2001). Constructing theories, identities, and actions of self-regulated learners. In B. J. Zimmerman and D. H. Schunk (Eds.), *Self-regulated learning and academic achievement: Theoretical perspectives* (2nd ed.). Mahwah, NJ: Erlbaum.

Pintrich, P. R. (1999). The role of motivation in promoting and sustaining self-regulated learning. *International Journal of Educational Psychology, 25,* 92-104.

Pintrich, P. R. (2000a). Multiple goals, multiple pathways: The role of goal orientation in learning and achievement. *Journal of Educational Psychology, 92,* 544-555.

Pintrich, P. R. (2000b). The role of goal orientation in self-regulated learning. In M. Boekaerts, P. R. Pintrich, and M. Zeidner (Eds.), *Handbook of self-regulation* (pp. 451-502). San Diego, CA: Academic Press.

Pintrich, P. R. (2002). Future challenges and directions for theory and research on personal epistemology. In B. K. Hofer and P. R. Pintrich (Eds.), *Personal epistemology: The psychology of beliefs about knowledge and knowing* (pp. 103-118). Mahwah, NJ: Erlbaum.

Pintrich, P. R. (2003). A motivational science perspective on the role of student motivation in learning and teaching contexts. *Journal of Educational Psychology, 95*(4), 667-686.

Pintrich, P. R. (2004). A conceptual framework for assessing motivation and self-regulated learning in college students. *Educational Psychology Review 16*(4), 385-407.

Pintrich, P. R., and DeGroot, E. V. (1990). Motivational and self-regulated learning components of classroom performance. *Journal of Educational Psychology, 82*, 33-40.

Pintrich, P. R., and Schrauben, B. (1992). Students' motivational beliefs and their cognitive engagement in classroom tasks. In D. Schunk and Meece (Eds.), *Student perceptions in the classroom: Causes and consequences* (pp. 149-183). Hillsdale, NJ: Erlbaum.

Pintrich, P.R., Brown, D. and Weisntein, C.E. (1994). *Student motivation, cognition and learning. Essays in Honor of W.J. McKeachie.* Hillsdale, NJ: Lawrence Erlbaum Associates

Pressley, M., Harris, K. R., and Guthrie, J. T. (1992). *Promoting academic competence and literacy in school.* San Diego: Academic Press.

Randi, J. (2004). Teachers as self-regulated learners. *Teachers College Record, 106(9),* 1825-1853.

Rodríguez, S., Cabanach, R. G., Piñeiro, I., Valle, A., Núñez, J. C., and González-Pienda, J. A. (2001). Approach goals, avoidance goals and multiple academia goals. *Psicothema, 13*, 546-550.

Rodríguez, S., Cabanach, R. G., Valle, A., Núñez, J. C., and González-Pienda, J. A. (2004). Differences in use of self-handicapping and defensive pessimism and its relation with achievement goals, self-esteem, and self-regulation strategies. *Psicothema, 16*, 626-632.

Rosário, P., Mourao, R., Trigo, J., Núñez, J. C., and González-Pienda, J. A. (2005). SRL Enhancing Narratives: Testas´ (Mis)adventures. *Academic Exchange Quarterly, 9 (4)*, 73-77.

Ryan, A. M., and Pintrich, P. R. (1998). Achievement and social motivational influences on help seeking in the classroom. In S. A. Karabenick (Ed.), *Strategic help seeking: Implications for learning and teaching* (pp. 117-139). Mahwah, NJ: Erlbaum.

Salomon, G., and Perkins, D. (1989). Rocky roads to transfer: Rethinking mechanisms of a neglected phenomenon. *Educational Psychologist, 24*, 113-142.

Schunk, D. H. (1981). Modelling and attributional effects on children's achievement. A self-analysis. *Journal of Educational Psychology, 73*, 93-105.

Schunk, D. H. (1983). Progress self-monitoring: Effects on children's self-efficacy and achievement. *Journal of Experimental Education, 51*,89-93.

Schunk, D. H., and Ertmer, P. A. (2000). Self-regulation and academic learning: Self-efficacy enhancing interventions. In M. Boekaerts, P. R. Pintrich, and M. Zeidner (Eds.), *Handbook of self-regulation* (pp. 631-651). London: Academic Press.

Schunk, D. H., and Zimmerman, B. J. (1994). Self-regulation in education: Retrospect and prospect. In D. H. Schunk and B. J. Zimmerman (Eds.), *Self-regulation of learning and performance: Issues and educational applications* (pp. 181-199). Hillsdale, NJ: Erlbaum.

Schunk, D. H., and Zimmerman, B. J. (2003). Social origins of self-regulatory competence. *Educational Psychologist, 32*, 195-208.

Seifert, T. L. (1995). Characteristics of ego -and task-oriented students: A comparison of two methodologies. *British Journal of Educational Psychology, 65*, 125-138.

Simpson, M. L, Hynd, C. R., Nist, S. L., and Burrel, K. I. (1997). College assistance programs and practices. *Educational Psychology Review, 9*(1), 39-87.

Skaalvik, E. (1997). Self-enhancing and self-defeating ego orientation: Relations with task and avoidance orientation, achievement, self- perceptions, and anxiety. *Journal of Educational Psychology, 89*, 71- 81.

Solano, P. (2006). *Elaboración y evaluación de un programa de mejora de la competencia en estrategias de autorregulación* [Elaboration and evaluation of a program to enhance competence in self-regulation strategies]. Oviedo, Spain: University of Oviedo.

Suárez, J. M., Cabanach, R. G., and Valle, A. (2001). Multiple-goal pursuit and its relation to cognitive, self-regulatory, and motivational strategies. *British Journal of Educational Psychology, 71,* 561- 572.

Swanson, H. L., and Deshler, D. (2003). Instructing adolescents with learning disabilities : Converting a meta-analysis to practice. *Journal of Learning Disabilities, 36*(2), 124-135.

Utman, C. (1997). Performance effects of motivational state: A meta- analysis. *Personality and Social Psychology Review, 1,* 170-182.

Valle, A., Cabanach, R., Núñez, J. C., González-Pienda, J. A., Rodríguez, S., and Piñeiro, I. (2003a). Cognitive, motivational, and volitional dimensions of learning: An empirical test of a hypothetical model. *Research in Higher Education, 2003, 44,* 557-580.

Valle, A., Cabanach, R. G., Núñez, J. C., González-Pienda, J. A., Rodríguez, S., and Piñeiro, I. (2003b). Multiple goals, motivation and academic learning. *British Journal of Educational Psychology, 73,* 71-87.

Valle, A., Cabanach, R. G., Rodríguez, S., Núñez, J. C., and González-Pienda, J. A. (2005). Self-Worth protection strategies in higher educational students: Exploring a model of predictors and consequences. In R. Nata (Ed.), *New directions in higher education* (pp. 99-126). New York: Nova Science.

Valle, A., Cabanach, R. G., Rodríguez, S., Núñez, J. C., and González-Pienda, J. A. (2006). Academic goals, cognitive and self-regulatory strategies. *Psicothema, 18,* 165-170.

Valle, A., Cabanach, R., Núñez, J.C., Suárez, J.M., Piñeiro, I., and Rodríguez, S. (2000). Approaches to learning in university students. *Psicothema, 12,* 368-375.

Weiner, B. (1979). A theory of motivation for some classroom experiences. *Journal of Educational Psychology, 71,* 3-25.

Weiner, B. (1986). *An attributional theory of emotion and motivation,* New York: Springer-Verlag.

Weiner, B. (1992). *Human motivation: Metaphors, theories, and research.* Newbury Park, CA: Sage.

Weinstein, C. E. (1994). Students at risk of academic failure: Learning to Learn classes. In K. W. Prichard and R. M. Sawyer (Eds.), *Handbook of college teaching: Theory and applications* (pp. 375-474). Westport, CT: Greenwood Press.

Wentzel, K. R. (2000). What is it that I'm trying to achieve? Classroom goals from a content perspective. *Contemporary Educational Psychology, 25,* 105-115.

Wigfield, A., and Eccles, J. S. (1992). The development of achievement task values: A theoretical analysis. *Developmental Review, 12,* 265-310.

Wigfield, A., Eccles, J. S., Yoon, K. S., Harold, R. D., Arbreton, A. J., Freedman-Doan, C., and Blumenfeld, P. C. (1997). Change in children´s competence beliefs and subjetive task values across the elementary school years: A 3-year study. *Journal of Educational Psychology, 89,* 451-469.

Winne, P. H. (2004). Identificando retos en la investigación sobre el aprendizaje autorregulado: Contribuciones de Paul R. Pintrich [Identifying challenges in research on SRL: Contributions of Paul R. Pintrich]. *Revista Electrónica de Investigación Psicoeducativa, 2*(1), 185-188.

Winne, P. H., and Hadwin, A. F. (1998). Studying as self-regulated learning. In D. J. Hacker, J. Dunlosky, and A. C. Graesser (Eds.), *Metacognition in educational theory and practice* (pp. 277-304). Hillsdale, N.J: Erlbaum.

Wolters, C. A. (1998). Self–regulated learning and college students' regulation of motivation. *Journal of Educational Psychology, 90*(2), 224–235.

Wolters, C. A. (1999). The relation between high school students' motivational regulation and their use of learning strategies, effort, and classroom performance. *Learning and Individual Differences, 3*(3), 281–299.

Wolters, C. A. (2003a). Regulation of motivation: Evaluating an underemphasized aspect of self–regulated learning. *Educational Psychologist, 38*(4), 189–205.

Wolters, C. A. (2003b). Understanding procrastination from a self–regulated learning perspective. *Journal of Educational Psychology, 95*(1), 179–187.

Wolters, C. A., Yu, S. L., and Pintrich, P. R. (1996). The relation between goal orientation and students' motivational beliefs and self-regulated learning. *Learning and Individual Differences, 8,* 211- 238.

Zeidner, M. (1998). *Test anxiety: The state of the art.* New York: Plenum Press.

Zimmerman, B. J. (1990). Self-regulated learning and academic achievement: An overview. *Educational Psychologist, 25,* 3-17.

Zimmerman, B. J. (1998). Developing self-fulfilling cycles of academic regulation: An analysis of exemplary instructional models. In D. H. Schunk and B. J. Zimmerman (Eds.), *Self-regulated learning. From teaching to self-reflective practice* (pp. 1-19). Hillsdale, NJ: Erlbaum.

Zimmerman, B. J. (2000a). Attaining self-regulation. A social cognitive perspective. In M. Boekaerts, P. Pintrich, and M. Zeidner (Eds.), *Handbook of self-regulation.* New York (pp. 13-39). San Diego: Academic Press.

Zimmerman, B. J. (2000b). Self-efficacy: An essential motive to learn. *Contemporary Educational Psychology, 25,* 82-91.

Zimmerman, B. J. (2001). Theories of self-regulated learning and academic achievement: An overview and analysis. In B. J. Zimmerman and D. H. Schunk (Eds.), *Self-regulated learning and academic achievement: Theoretical perspectives* (pp. 1-37). London: Erlbaum.

Zimmerman, B. J. (2002). Becoming a self-regulated learner: An overview. *Theory into practice, 41*(2), 64-70.

Zimmerman, B. J., Bonner, S., and Kovach, R. (1996). *Developing self-regulated learners: Beyond achievement to self-efficacy.* Washington, DC: American Psychological Association.

Zimmerman, B. J., and Martinez-Pons, M. (1988). Construct validation of a strategy model of student self-regulated learning. *Journal of Educational Psychology, 80*(3), 284-290.

Zimmerman, B. J., and Martinez-Pons, M. (1990). Student differences in self-regulated learning: Relating grade, sex, and giftedness to self-efficacy and strategy use. *Journal of Educational Psychology, 82*(1), 51-59.

In: Global Issues in Higher Education
Editor: Pamela B. Richards, pp. 127-147

ISBN: 978-1-60021-802-6
© 2007 Nova Science Publishers, Inc.

Chapter 6

THE CHANGING LANDSCAPE OF UK DOCTORAL EDUCATION

Thomas F. Burgess

Leeds University Business School, Leeds, UK

ABSTRACT

Over the last ten years doctoral education in the UK has undergone a series of changes and a relatively stable environment has become much more dynamic. Such changes look set to continue. In this chapter past changes are identified, explored and future projections made. The chapter addresses the HE context of doctoral production, identifies the factors driving change and seeks where possible to show the connections between the various determinants, changes and consequences. Factors covered include the massification of higher education, the internalisation/globalisation (e.g. changing international markets), and the increasing encroachment of managerial and business perspectives in to higher education and research (e.g. quality assurance schemes, and the stress on business relevance of research). The nature of the changes in doctoral training include the introduction of new forms (e.g. integrated PhDs and professional doctorates) and modifications to existing structures and content (e.g. the increased emphasis on more systematic training and accents on developing transferable skills). Some speculations are made about how the landscape might change in future.

Keywords: *doctoral education, PhD production.*

INTRODUCTION

In 1919 the first UK PhD graduated at Oxford University (Simpson, 1983) (p. 140). The PhD's UK introduction and its rapid take-up by many universities was a reaction to perceptions that the UK was lagging behind research developments in USA and German universities. A further key factor was the desire to attract quality overseas students from the US and countries associated with the British Empire. Although other doctorates existed previously, and still exist today, the PhD now dominates the doctoral scene in the UK. Recent pressures have buffeted doctoral education, as with many areas of Higher Education (HE), stimulating changes in the PhD and fostering development of new doctoral forms. This chapter explores these pressures and their consequent impact on the UK doctoral production system. My role as Director of Doctoral Programmes within a large Business School colours my viewpoint as does involvement in programme management at institutional level in a large, research-intensive University. However, as far as possible a broad view of the UK landscape is conveyed and linked to the wider international situation.

The first section deals with features of the current HE system that establish the context for doctoral education. The next section concentrates on an overview of doctoral supply and demand, and covers criticisms made of the doctoral production system. The main changes occurring, mainly instigated by government, in response to these criticisms are covered in the following section. Comments are then made about changes encountered at the doctoral programme level. The penultimate section addresses the appearance of new doctoral forms and the chapter then finishes with the conclusion.

HE CONTEXT OF DOCTORAL EDUCATION

This section deals with the HE context of doctoral education and covers various environmental features and key driving forces that link to broader societal pressures.

Massification of HE

In the UK HE expansion has been substantial with the creation of the new universities in 1992 standing out as a significant milestone. Schofer and Meyer (2005) show that the growth in HE is a global phenomena and has accelerated sharply from 1960 onwards. They examine the forces at work leading to a new model of society where more young people are considered necessary to participate in HE. Strong trends have led to a global participation rate of 20% of the eligible cohort. Gamage and Mininberg (2003) identify issues that apply to USA and Australia, and presumably to other countries. These issues include: costs to students, technology and instructional delivery, faculty roles and rewards.

Internationalisation/Globalisation

A growth in international/ global interchange and competition has accompanied the growth in HE across the globe. For example, Currie and Newson (1998) in their edited book recognise globalisation as a major imperative that is affecting universities. From their viewpoint this phenomena can be conceptualised as "a market ideology with a corresponding material set of practices drawn from the world of business" (p. 1). According to Marginson (2006) national and global competition in HE are distinct but feed in to each other. He shows that a mass market has developed rapidly that is led by, amongst others, the UK since English Language is important and links to uni-directional flows of students. He identifies the emergence of elite US/UK universities to service the high end of the market in contrast to mass institutions. Within the European Union HE an ongoing campaign to set up a common European HE Area assists the globalisation pressures for a supra-national marketplace. However, some countervailing factors are apparent that need to be taken in to account, e.g. cultural and regional differences (Kivinen and Nurmi, 2003).

Impact of Technology

Information and Communication Technologies (ICT) comprise a factor supporting closer meshing of HE across the globe but also impacting locally by affecting such as course delivery. The Internet assists potential students in identifying and evaluating provision globally and also provides a distinct channel to support their distance and flexible learning. However, a downside to the new technology is the reduced barriers to plagiarism, a topic of increasing concern across HE.

Changing Role of Universities in Society

Grubb and Lazerson (2005) argue that American HE has seen a greater emphasis on vocational purposes in addition to the expansion of access; an emphasis also apparent in the UK. HE is increasingly a mechanism providing individuals with access to income and professional status. More and more people see HE as a commodity with students stereotyped as consumers. These substantial shifts in the perceived teaching mission of universities have also been accompanied by shifts in the other key mission area, of research. Policy makers have looked to get more value for money from research, an approach epitomised by the sequence of Research Assessment Exercises in the UK. Practitioners and policy makers increasingly require university research to be relevant to their needs (Lambert, 2003).

Increased Accountability and Public Scrutiny

HE went through a period when performance indicators became a major issue (Johnes and Taylor, 1990). Subsequently, University league tables have become prominent and receive more coverage in the media although their usefulness is under question (Bowden, 2000; Goldstein and Spiegelhalter, 1996). Such league tables deal with both national and international rankings thus reflecting HE's greater global reach. Quality has formed a major part of a performance discourse across the public sector including education (Vidovich and Porter, 1999). They observe that this is symptomatic of a "culture of performativity" that progressively pervades HE in many OECD countries. The roots of this quality discourse can be traced to the substantial push for privatisation and deregulation that surfaced in developed economies during the eighties.

Financing of HE and Increased Cost Consciousness

The expansion in HE described above has implications for government and other forms of public expenditure (Barr, 2004). Mayhew, Deer and Dua (2004) point out that the HE expansion has occurred alongside tight public spending since the early 1980s. Greenaway and Haynes (2003) state that UK funding per student has halved in 20 years while aggregate student numbers have doubled. Major changes have occurred in the UK with the introduction of top-up fees and the reshaping of the loans and grant system with the major outcome that the burden of financing HE has shifted to students and parents. The UK government initiatives to investigate costing within HE, e.g. the cost transparency review (*Transparency review of research: proposal for a new uniform approach to the costing of research and other activities in universities and colleges of higher education*, 1999), have culminated in the introduction of full economic costing for research.

Research Intensification

In the USA the last 25 years has seen the development of research universities to focus on national wealth development rather than primarily a vehicle for liberal education of undergraduates (Mendoza, 2007). Some would argue that it is part of the UK government agenda to polarise HE in to research-intensive and teaching-focused universities. For example, Willmott (2003) argues that the RAE has primarily contributed to legitimise the restructuring of HE rather than rationalising resources allocated to research or improving accountability of such resources.

Managerial/Business Ethos in Universities

Deem (2001) includes "new managerialism" as one of three key concepts that she examines as explaining change in universities (the other two are academic capitalism and entrepreneurial universities). She (Deem, 1998) describes new managerialism as "the adoption by public sector organisations of organisational forms, technologies, management practices and values more commonly found in the private business sector". Some see managerialism as a phenomenon that owes its growth to the reluctance of academics to display leadership in universities because of the low regard accorded this activity (Dearlove, 2006).

The Working Environment of Academics

Kinman (1998) reports on a UK survey into occupational stress suffered by academics and related staff. She found a disturbing situation with respondents suffering a heightened degree of work pressure arising from various sources that are features of the national educational policy and of individual organisational climates. These sources lead to work overload, long hours of work and job insecurity among a variety of other factors leading to stress. The sources include: rising student numbers, increased administrative burdens, more intrusive requirements from outside bodies, rising pressure to engage in high quality research, reduced administrative support and lowered resourcing. Respondents see too much change in HE, most of it unnecessary, eroding traditional values. Changes in management style are seen by many as the major cause of stress in the workplace. Other, more recent, reports have shown that stress is a continuing issue in academic jobs and in addition is making itself felt in all categories of staff employed in HE (Kinman and Jones, 2003; Tytherleigh, Webb, Cooper, and Ricketts, 2005). Research in other countries demonstrate similar concern about workload and stress in universities, e.g. in New Zealand (Chalmers, 1998). Kimber (2003) writes about the significant managerial agenda and its considerable impact on academic work. In particular she focuses on casualisation of the academic workforce in Australian universities. A further set of issues relate to gender balance and inequality in HE (Kulis, Sicotte, and Collins, 2002).

DOCTORAL PRODUCTION AND CRITICISMS

Golde and Walker (2007) highlight some of the important changes in the doctoral landscape (p. 4):

- Time-to-career (in academia) continues to grow. PhDs have to take on temporary posts before gaining a permanent post.
- Disciplines continue to evolve and boundaries are in a state of flux
- Financial support for students is "a complex and dynamic ecosystem" affected by changing priorities of federal governments, state governments and individual universities.
- Student inflows and outflows are subject to federal (government) policies and international competition.

Doctoral Demand and Supply

A comprehensive report (*What do PhDs do? 2004 analysis of first destinations for PhD graduates*, 2004) claiming to be the first detailed look at where UK PhDs go after graduation points out that final year PhD students had grown by 31% over the five years prior to the report with the majority of this growth coming from overseas students and UK part-time students. UK doctoral production grew by 109% over a longer period of ten years from 1994 (see Table 1) while the comparable growth in first degrees was 29% (Table 2). Table 1 also shows that growth in doctoral students from overseas was higher than home, with 137% vs. 94% respectively. The report also mentions the rise of new doctoral forms such as the professional doctorate.

According to Moyer, Salovey and Casey-Cannon (1999) although increasing representation of women and minorities is a widely held goal, their numbers remain small in the US. The emphasis must be placed on minorities other than females since their numbers have grown from 5,000 to nearly 20,000 in a 40 year period during which US production has roughly doubled.

Table 1. UK Doctoral Output by Mode, Gender and Origin from 1994 to 2004

1994/95

		UK	Non-UK	Total
Full-time	Female	243	131	374
	Male	557	454	1011
	Total	800	585	1385
Part-time	Female	1399	554	1953
	Male	2770	1451	4221
	Total	4169	2005	6174
Both modes	Female	1642	685	2327
	Male	3327	1905	5232
	Total	4969	2590	7559

2000/2001

		UK	Non-UK	Total
Full-time	Female	2665	1435	4100
	Male	3735	2680	6415
	Total	6400	4115	10515
Part-time	Female	1155	320	1475
	Male	1585	545	2130
	Total	2740	865	3605
Both modes	Female	3820	1755	5575
	Male	5320	3225	8545
	Total	9140	4980	14120

2004/05

		UK	Other EU	Non-EU	Total
Full-time	Female	3145	755	1230	5130
	Male	3730	940	2230	6900
	Total	6870	1700	3460	12030
Part-time	Female	1335	145	220	1700
	Male	1435	220	390	2045
	Total	2770	365	610	3745
Both modes	Female	4480	910	1450	6830
	Male	5165	1160	2620	8945
	Total	9640	2065	4070	15775

Source: Higher Education Statistics Agency Limited (2006)

http://www.hesa.ac.uk

Accessed 16th February 2007

Note: A major change to the definitions of categories occurred in 2000/01. Prior to that date those gaining their qualification whilst writing up (i.e. outside the standard period of 3 years for full-time) were classified as part-time. After this date those that were full-time prior to writing up were put in to the full-time category and part-time in to the part-time figures. This change accounts for the substantial differences between full-time and part-time students when comparing the beginning (94/95) and later periods.

Table 2. UK Higher Education Output by Subject for 1994/95 and 2004/05

Subject area	1994/95			2004/05			Doctorate growth %
	First Degree	Docto-rates	Percent	First Degree	Docto-rates	Percent	
Medicine and dentistry	5619	544	9.68	7445	1565	21.02	188
Subjects allied to medicine	11106	350	3.15	27880	930	3.34	166
Biological sciences	12378	1114	9.00	27200	2505	9.21	125
Veterinary science	472	55	11.65	690	95	13.77	73
Agriculture and related subjects	1828	216	11.82	2225	215	9.66	0
Physical sciences	13440	1457	10.84	12530	2335	18.64	60
Mathematical sciences	4069	232	5.70	5270	415	7.87	79
Computer science	8274	222	2.68	20095	545	2.71	145
Engineering and technology	22083	1327	6.01	19575	2015	10.29	52
Architecture, building and planning	8166	93	1.14	6565	240	3.66	158
Social studies (was Social, economic and political studies)	19757	501	2.54	28825	1320	4.58	163
Law	9598	76	0.79	13735	200	1.46	163
Business and administrative studies	25916	215	0.83	42190	580	1.37	170
Mass communications and documentation (was Librarianship and information sciences	2490	27	1.08	8890	75	0.84	178
Languages	15728	386	2.45	20025	895	4.47	132
Historical and philosophical studies (was Humanities)	10094	389	3.85	15480	925	5.98	138
Creative arts and design	14633	60	0.41	30610	275	0.90	358
Education	13810	170	1.23	10615	655	6.17	285
Combined	38337	125	0.33	6510	5	0.08	-96
Total	237798	7559	3.18	306365	15780	5.15	109

Source: Higher Education Statistics Agency Limited (2006)
http://www.hesa.ac.uk/
Accessed 16th February 2007

Thurgood, Golladay and Hill (2006) state the proportion of women graduating with a doctorate was just over 40% of the total in 1999 with women exceeding men in non-science and engineering subjects. The gender mix in UK doctorates has equalised substantially over the ten years from 1994/95 to 2004/05 with the female proportion increasing from 31% to 43% of the total (see Table 1).

Table 2 gives some idea of the differential growth in subjects through two measures. One is a straight growth in the output of doctorates (the end column) over ten years while the second measure involves the change in a crude conversion ratio, the percentage of doctorates to first degrees, given for the start and end of the period. Using the first measure a pattern that can be discerned is the growth in science and engineering subjects generally lagging behind growth in non-science subjects. This is not that surprising in one sense since the substantially higher conversion ratios for (natural) sciences make it more difficult to increase these cf. to those for social sciences. The sluggishness in increase may also connect with the crisis in the UK where science departments are under threat of closure due to poor recruitment but the second measure shows that the conversion ratio is rising in most subjects including science subjects.

The balance between "hard" and "soft" sciences, which can be gleaned from Tables 2 and 3, and between supply and demand seems to fluctuate over time and by the subject concerned. Kumar (2004) highlights a decline in science doctorates and shift towards commerce, arts and education in India. In some areas of the USA there is oversupply, e.g. biomedical sciences (Triggle and Miller, 2002) which they put down to unlimited supply of talented foreign students. Freeman, Jarvenpaa and Wheeler (2000) cite "a large and growing lack of supply to meet current and future demand" in relation to supply and demand of IS doctorates.

Finn (2001) sketches a picture of increases in supply and, less reliably, increases in demand for PhD scientists and engineers in the US over the 1990s. Again the increase in supply is put down to the availability of foreign students. Nerad (2004) points out that students recognise that engineering and life science PhDs excel in terms of non-academic job opportunities. An examination of employment experiences of recently-qualified social science doctors concluded no significant demand could be identified outside of academia (Pearson, Secombe, Pike, and Connor, 1993).

Table 3. US Doctorates Awarded, by Major Field in 1999

Field	Doctorates
Education	6,557
Engineering	5,337
Biological sciences	5,600
Humanities	5,045
Social sciences	4,060
Physical sciences	3,582
Psychology	3,667
Professional fields/other	2,175
Mathematics and computer sciences	1,935
Health sciences	1,410
Agricultural sciences	965
Earth, atmospheric, and ocean sciences	807
All fields	41,140

Source: National Science Foundation
http://www.nsf.gov/statistics/nsf06319/tables.cfm
Accessed 27th February 2007

Mangematin (2000) examined the hiring of PhD graduates in academia vs. private sector. His view was of a slowing down of PhD production to match the reducing job opportunities in science. He also looked at relationships between supervisor and student and found that this was shaped by the candidate's intention as to which sector they were targeting, i.e. whether they were focused on a career in academia or the private sector.

Criticisms of Doctoral Education

Nerad (2004) summarised the following criticisms to be found in the literature (text in brackets is main source of the criticism):

- Too narrowly educated and trained (industry, business and government)
- Lacking professional skills associated with employment (industry, business and government)
- Ill-prepared to teach (HE institutions mainly teaching ones)
- Take too long to complete (various including policy makers)
- Ill-informed about non-academic employment (current and former students)

And he adds a further personal, criticism about the transition between PhD study and stable employment being too long.

Golde and Walker (2007) also refer to the studies and reports in the nineties that point to conventional doctoral education failing students, employers and society in general. They highlight three particular issues: lack of PhD preparedness for work, under-representation of women and minorities, and the high attrition rates associate with doctoral study – in some cases exceeding 50%.

The comments above, although emanating from North America, are matched by similar views in other developed countries. For example, Noble (1994) lists ten problems as evidence of the "international disharmony and discontent surrounding doctoral programmes" (p.25). Examples of UK concern with doctoral education can be seen in the Roberts report (Roberts, 2002) and the government action in allocating funds to implement his recommendations.

Harman (2002) looked at research intensive universities producing PhD graduates for the knowledge economy. He found low student satisfaction with their learning experiences and particularly negative views about careers in academia. This stemmed from perceptions of reduced government support for academia and the increased workload pressures on academics. Of concern to governments, and business, is the contribution of PhDs to economic development. In the USA it is claimed that many states fail to capture the economic development advantages that come from training a skilled work force (Stephan, Sumell, Black, and Adams, 2004)

Concern continues about the length of doctoral study and with completion rates. It can be argued that degree completion is necessarily taking a longer time because of the expansion of knowledge that requires greater effort on the part of the candidate to get to grips with both subject and methodological developments (Nerad, 2004). Notwithstanding this point, it has often been remarked that completing a PhD takes longer in the humanities and social sciences than science and engineering. Nerad (2004) points out this occurs because students have a "double burden of limited funding resources and long courses of study". UK completion rates have been linked to a variety of factors (*PhD research degrees: Entry and completion*, 2005). The following were found to correlate with higher completion rates: full-time mode of study, financial backing, overseas origin, student aged 30 and under, good performance on first degree and studying in the natural sciences.

Nerad (2004) states that the criticisms of doctoral education have led to a variety of initiatives to modify existing or create new styles of doctoral programmes. He also highlights the role of student dissatisfaction in generating responses to the criticisms.

HIGH LEVEL RESPONSES TO CRITICISMS

This section aims to capture the main system level responses to criticisms over the last ten years in the UK. The majority of these stem from government initiatives.

Concentration in Research-Intensive Universities

Earlier comments have referred to the concentration of research occurring recently in the UK as a consequence of the RAEs. This concentration also applies to doctoral production. Nerad (2004) remarks that PhD production in the US is concentrated in a few institutions, mainly the major research universities that are members of the American Association of Universities. Fifty of the 406 institutions that are eligible to award doctorates produce about 50% of the annual production, which was over 40,000 at the time of his review. Table 4 illustrates that concentration in the UK is higher with the top 20 universities out of more than 100 producing 59% of the annual total of around 16,000 doctorates. The largest US producer is the University of California at Berkeley with between 750 and 800 PhDs annually while Table 4 shows that the largest producers in the UK are comparable in size.

Table 4. UK Top 20 Universities by Production of Doctorates for 2004/05

University	Doctorates	Percent of UK total	Cumulative percent
Cambridge	920	5.90	5.90
Manchester	775	4.97	10.88
Oxford	755	4.84	15.72
Birmingham	595	3.82	19.54
University College London	585	3.75	23.29
Nottingham	520	3.34	26.63
Imperial College	485	3.11	29.74
Edinburgh	470	3.02	32.76
Leeds	430	2.76	35.51
Southampton	415	2.66	38.18
Sheffield	400	2.57	40.74
Glasgow	395	2.53	43.28
Bristol	355	2.28	45.56
King's College London	340	2.18	47.74
Liverpool	330	2.12	49.86

Table 4. (Continued)

University	Doctorates	Percent of UK total	Cumulative percent
Newcastle-upon-Tyne	325	2.09	51.94
Cardiff University	305	1.96	53.90
Queen's University of Belfast	250	1.60	55.50
Reading	235	1.51	57.01
Warwick	235	1.51	58.52
Total UK	15585		

Source: Higher Education Statistics Agency Limited (2006)
http://www.hesa.ac.uk/
Accessed 16th February 2007

Cost of Doctoral Education

The report by JM Consulting (*Costs of training and supervising postgraduate research students*, 2005) for the Higher Education Funding Council for England (HEFCE) raises important questions about why UK institutions are active in doctoral research. This is claimed to be the first time that costs of postgraduate research students have been calculated on a systematic full economic cost basis. In their words the results will come as an "unwelcome surprise to many in the [HE] sector" since there are significant levels of under-recovery of costs. However, as the report points out, this under-recovery has to be balanced against "significant and unquantifiable benefits" that include:

- Regenerating the profession by training the next generation of researchers
- Contributing to the research environment of institutions
- Conferring benefits on individual academics in various ways such as the presence of PhDs serves to validate academics as good researchers while providing a deployable resource
- PGR numbers and the outputs of their research, such as papers, figure in the measures of departmental and institutional performance used by the various governmental bodies, e.g. in the RAE

Financing of PhDs

PhD study in the UK is funded by the government through a dual support system. One leg of this support comprises funding directed by Research Councils (RCs) to students while the other leg involves funding flows through the Higher Education Funding Councils to universities. Table 5 shows the sources of UK student sponsorship to assist with tuition fees and maintenance.

Over the past ten years UK RCs have moved from selecting recipients of studentships through national competitions, to a situation where funding is devolved to individual universities for them to allocate to students according to specified guidelines. This funding devolution has coincided with increased selectivity of outlets recognised for doctoral training that is linked to recent changes in the dual support system concentrating funds in departments scoring highly in the RAE.

Table 5. Source of Student Sponsorship for Students Starting in 1996/97

Source of sponsorship	Full-time		Part-time		All	
	No. of students	% of students	No. of students	% of students	No. of students	% of students
Research Council	3,381	25%	29	1%	3,410	18%
Charity/British Academy	768	6%	50	1%	818	4%
Institution	2,130	16%	617	13%	2,747	15%
Government	622	5%	243	5%	865	5%
UK industry	860	6%	587	12%	1,447	8%
Overseas	2,046	15%	69	1%	2,115	11%
Other	821	6%	450	9%	1,271	7%
No financial backing	3,044	22%	2,806	58%	5,850	32%
All	13,672	100%	4,851	100%	18,523	100%

Source: PhD research degrees: Entry and completion (2005)
http://www.hefce.ac.uk/
Accessed 27th February 2007

Research councils in the UK, in reaction to various factors including the Roberts report, have substantially increased stipends generally but also introduced, not without some controversy, additional support for "shortage" areas such as Economics and Management. RCs have recognised that the time to obtain a PhD is often extended beyond the standard three years for full-time students and are providing funding for three and a half years or, even in some cases, four years.

Regeneration of the Academic Profession

As mentioned under the Cost of Doctoral Education one of the key acknowledged benefits of doctoral education is its role in regenerating the academic profession. Over the last few years a number of bodies have recognised and become concerned that in some areas, such as Business Schools, there is an impending crisis in that the current levels of doctoral production are not sufficient to meet this regeneration task (*Sustaining scholarship in Business Schools. Report of the Doctoral Faculty Commission to AACSB International's Board of Directors*, 2003). Basil and Basil (2006) examined the situation in the management discipline of marketing and concluded that undersupply of PhDs is a major factor in the shortfall of faculty.

Doctoral Programme Management and Supervision

The pervasive influence of quality as a discourse in HE was referred to in an earlier section. In some respects undergraduate and masters levels have been subject to this first but a substantial application of this discourse to doctoral level in the UK was apparent with the publication of the Quality Assurance Agency (QAA) for Higher Education Code of Practice (*Code of practice for the assurance of academic quality and standards in higher education. Section 1: Postgraduate research programmes*, 2004). The updating of this code in 2004, and the subsequent audit provision, has had a major impact on UK HE institutions. The code lays down 27 precepts (system-wide principles) that are considered important for assurance of quality and academic standards in doctoral programmes. An individual institution is expected to be able to demonstrate that they are addressing the principles effectively through their own processes.

Training of PhDs

The UK RCs play a substantial role in setting standards and promoting good practice in doctoral training. A key articulation of this role is through their Joint Statement on training requirements for research students. Over and above this joint statement individual RCs have specific guidelines. The Economic and Social Research Council (ESRC) has a system whereby departments and courses apply to be "recognised" as providing the required level of training to do a PhD and thereby become eligible to receive studentship funding. Although their guidelines apply primarily to the students they support, the RC's expectation is for them to apply to all students in the recognised department.

Various changes were introduced by the ESRC in the 1980s including restricting the time limit for thesis submission and a compulsory research methods training. Other initiatives since then have included the emphasis on the 1+3 approach, i.e. one year of training on a recognised research masters followed by a three year PhD. However, the 1+3 approach is now receiving reduced emphasis and other approaches, e.g. 2+2 in Economics, are being considered.

In the past ten years RCs have enhanced their requirements for skills development, partly as a consequence of various government stimulated initiatives. The report of Sir Gareth Roberts (Roberts, 2002) has had a significant effect on skills development for doctoral students with money channelled to institutions. One key initiative is concerned with developing general, transferable skills to improve employability rather than research skills.

RCs support PhD training workshops and courses across the UK, e.g. the ESRC supports a substantial Research Methods Summer School open to doctoral students and other researchers. In addition to RCs other bodies support doctoral training. The UK Grad School is instrumental in this, as are professional institutions such as the British Academy of Management. Regional cooperation is also growing, e.g. the Northern Doctoral Training Network comprises the research-intensive Management and Business Schools in the North of England that have joined together to promote advanced training of doctoral students through regional workshops and an annual colloquium.

CHANGES AT THE DOCTORAL PROGRAMME LEVEL

This section concentrates on changes occurring at the level of the doctoral programme.

Management and Supervision of PhDs

An earlier section commented on recent changes in the academic work environment. These impact on how academics see the attractions or otherwise of supervising doctoral candidates and on how they engage with students. According to Evans, Lawson, McWilliam and Taylor (2005) "few academics would argue with the proposition that the work of supervising doctoral studies is vastly different from that of a decade ago". The implicit contract between supervisor and supervisee is changing, although this differs from country to country (Lanciano-morandat and Nohara, 2003). Joint supervision, which the QAA Code of Practice recommends, means that supervisor-student relationships are open to closer scrutiny and are no longer as intimate, or secretive, as they might have been in the past.

Training of PhDs

Supervisor responses to the ESRC changes of the 1980s mentioned above were not particularly positive and included complaints that these held back the fostering of research creativity in students (Hockey, 1995). More recent changes are not necessarily welcomed by academics. The additional demands for training, particularly for employability, are not received wholeheartedly by students either. Many involved in doctoral education would recognise that tension exists between training needs of a broad nature and that needed for the specific thesis. Students often focus in on the need to get their specific research project and thesis completed and any distractions from this to try to develop them in to an autonomous researcher, with skills and knowledge across a broad front, are not always appreciated.

Changing Content and Process of Doctoral Research

Research topics are changing as disciplines emerge and mutate but also in reaction to the tests of relevancy being applied by government and business. More fundamental views on the changing nature of knowledge production have surfaced such as Mode 2 (Enders, 2005). Access and environments are changing. Increasing difficulties are attached to survey research with industry and commerce as response rates reflect "questionnaire fatigue". Research methods are changing with one of the main factors being the ongoing march of IT and Communications technology. Other factors include the changing nature of society and the environment (Bardsley and Wiles, 2006). The world-wide web is not only a mechanism for facilitating access to knowledge and data but has become a major source of study in its own right. Moutinho, Hutcheson and Rita (2006) attempt to capture some of this change within the meta-discipline of management but cannot claim to be a comprehensive and systematic view. The availability of PC software to support methods such structural equation modelling, qualitative data analysis and social network analysis have meant that barriers to their use have dropped substantially.

Examining PhDs

Although great reliance is still placed on the viva voce examination, its position is being eroded by pressures to recognise the growing importance of other forms of assessment on the doctoral programme. For example, the increased emphasis on employment-related skills and the introduction of more systematic, taught research training requires that accompanying assessment in these areas should be taken account of. On a different front, low financial rewards for external examining exacerbate the difficulties of finding suitable and willing examiners.

Dissemination

The ubiquity of ICT now means that there is considerable pressure to move to publishing electronically PhD theses. This raises concern about plagiarism given its growth elsewhere in HE that has been driven by the expansion of the Internet.

CHANGING DOCTORAL FORMS

Here trends and changes the form of the doctoral programme are highlighted.

Remote Learning

The growth of the Internet has led to online doctoral programmes and their numbers can be expected to grow. Examples of programmes include nursing (Halter, Kleiner, and Hess, 2006) and in HE leadership (Ivankova and Stick, 2007). The use of online support may be specifically appropriate to part-time doctoral programmes and to professional doctorates. In the UK the Knowledge Media Institute of the Open University is particularly looking, in its e-PhD Project, at the use of ICT and how this relates to those research skills that are "picked up by osmosis when physically co-located in a research group" (http://kmi.open.ac.uk/projects/e-phd/).

New Route PhDs

The New Route or Integrated PhD is an initiative that was launched in 2003 with 34 universities across the UK offering doctorates of the new style in over 120 subject areas (http://www.newroutephd.ac.uk/). The New Route PhD typically is a four year programme with substantial taught input in the first and second years. It is seen as an alternative to the traditional UK PhD whereby the systematic development of research and generic transferable skills forms a major element. The New Route can be seen as positioned somewhere in between traditional UK and US style doctorates and was originally conceived to appeal to the overseas market.

Professional Doctorates

Bourner, Bowden and Laing (2001) reviewed the introduction of Professional Doctorates (PDs) in the UK during the 1990s and their subsequent rapid growth so that they now can be found in the majority of universities and in a wide variety of subjects. These include education, business and engineering as established subjects and burgeoning interest is apparent in other areas, e.g. nursing. In Business and Management the upsurge in the number of PDs in that area, usually designated Doctor in Business Administration (DBA), has been recognised by the various professional bodies establishing guidelines, e.g. Association of MBAs (AMBA), ESRC and the Association of Business Schools (ABS).

Bourner, Bowden and Laing (2001) identify various common features that identify PDs and distinguish them from other doctoral types. Scott, Brown, Lunt and Thorne (2004) (p.1) remark on PDs as existing in the twilight zone between the university and the workplace. Characteristically these doctorates focus on a contribution to practical knowledge and include professionally developing the student-practitioner. Typically a PD might include a structured training programme with substantial assessments that then lead on to a thesis of the same standard as a traditional PhD but of shorter length. The research project for the thesis usually focuses on some workplace-based topic. Wellington and Sikes (2006) explore the motivations of students on professional doctorates. The idea of second generation professional doctorates has been proposed (Maxwell, 2003) and Lester (2004) refers to these second generation schemes as "practitioner doctorates" but argues for their conceptualisation as academically robust despite the terminology.

Practice-based Doctorates

More and more, practice-based doctorates are appearing in the UK in areas where "performance" is important, such as music or the performing arts in general. Macleod and Holdridge (2004) examine the "troubled history" of the doctorate in Fine Art and examine the "making/writing" and "theory/practice" debate.

Collaborative Schemes

A number of collaborative schemes have been established between academia and business to encourage PhDs doing work relevant to business but also to develop the student's knowledge and exposure to the world of work. ESRC Collaborative Awards in Science and Engineering (CASE) studentships are supported by both the RC and a collaborating organisation to research a topic of mutual interest to the three parties: the student, academic institution and organisation. The organisation doing the collaborating can be drawn from industry, government or other public sector including charities and voluntary bodies. Similar arrangements for PhD sponsorship can be set under the Knowledge Transfer Partnership initiative (formerly called Teaching Company Schemes). In addition to university-industry collaboration there is a move toward cooperation between HE institutions, e.g. setting up joint doctorates or exchanging students. This move arises from a number of pressures, e.g. to collaborate internationally or a reaction to the concentration of PhD production in research-intensive universities.

CONCLUSION

Although doctoral education has probably never been in a state of stasis, the last ten years in the UK have seen some major changes compared to previous eras. However, it is worthwhile reflecting that the key impetus driving the first introduction of the PhD in to the UK is still apparent today, namely the need to attract overseas students. On the other hand an issue stressed more today is the need to build capacity and ensure the next generation is there to succeed the ageing academics of today. What is different today from the start of the last century is the context that surrounds doctoral education. The tremendous expansion in HE numbers, the intense global competition, research intensification and concentration, the impact of managerialism, the demand for economic and business relevance and the advent of ICT have all made, and are still making, their presence felt. Doctoral education, like undergraduate and masters education before it, is subject increasingly to pressures to be relevant to business and economic needs and to display resource efficiency. These pressures appear to impinge more severely on the social sciences. PhDs in (natural) sciences and engineering already adhere more closely to an instrumental paradigm where students pursue, in teams, objectives that are often more closely linked to the needs of society's economic advance and emerge post-PhD in to a reasonably well-defined employment marketplace. The impact of these pressures can be seen, particularly in the social sciences, in the move toward the professional doctorate which some see as the dilution of the research tradition by the morals of the market. Despite reservations and some opposition, it would seem that these pressures will continue to impact on HE. The future presumably holds out doctorates that are more varied in form, more closely linked to managerial perceptions of economic needs, more concentrated in individual or collaborating groups of research-intensive university departments, and that involve more closely specified and monitored training paths. It may be that the UK tradition of PhD as students will change somewhat to accommodate the more European tradition of PhDs as employees. The implications of the Bologna process for UK doctoral education are not yet clear. A major growth in part-time doctorates might be proposed as a way of linking doctoral education to business needs and resolving some of the funding difficulties but the major deficiencies of completion rates and timescales for part-time students demonstrate that there are some substantial problems to solve in this area.

REFERENCES

Bardsley, N., and Wiles, R. (2006). *A consultation to identify the research needs in research methods in the UK social sciences*. ESRC National Centre for Research Methods.

Barr, N. (2004). Higher education funding. *Oxford Review of Economic Policy*, 20(2), 264-283.

Basil, M. D., and Basil, D. Z. (2006). The marketing market: A study of PhD supply, demand, hiring institutions, and job candidates. *Journal of Business Research*, 59(4), 516-523.

Bourner, T., Bowden, R., and Laing, S. (2001). Professional Doctorates in England. *Studies in Higher Education*, 26(1), 65-83.

Bowden, R. (2000). Fantasy Higher Education: university and college league tables. *Quality in Higher Education,* 6(1), 41-60.

Chalmers, A. (1998). *Workload and stress in New Zealand Universities in 1998.* Wellington: New Zealand Council for Educational Research.

Code of practice for the assurance of academic quality and standards in higher education. Section 1: Postgraduate research programmes. (2004). Gloucester: Quality Assurance Agency for Higher Education.

Costs of training and supervising postgraduate research students. (2005). Bristol: JM Consulting Ltd.

Currie, J., and Newson, J. (Eds.). (1998). *Universities and globalization: critical perspectives.* Thousand Oaks: Sage Publications.

Dearlove, J. (2006). Collegiality, managerialsim and leadership in English universities. *Tertiary Education and Management*, 1(2), 161-169.

Deem, R. (1998). 'New managerialism' and higher education: the management of performances and cultures in universities in the United Kingdom. *International Studies in Sociology of Education,* 8(1), 47-70.

Deem, R. (2001). Globalisation, New Managerialism, Academic Capitalism and Entrepreneurialism in Universities: is the local dimension still important? *Comparative Education,* 37(1), 7-20.

Enders, J. (2005). Border crossings: Research training, knowledge dissemination and the transformation of academic work. *Higher Education*, 49(1-2), 119-133.

Evans, T., Lawson, A., McWilliam, E., and Taylor, P. (2005). Understanding the management of doctoral studies in Australia as risk management. *Studies in Research*, 1, 1-11.

Finn, M. G. (2001). Market heats up for S/E doctorates. *Research-Technology Management*, 44(3), 39-43.

Freeman, L. A., Jarvenpaa, S. L., and Wheeler, B. C. (2000). The supply and demand of information systems doctorates: Past, present, and future. *MIS Quarterly*, 24(3), 355-380.

Gamage, D. T., and Mininberg, E. (2003). The Australian and American higher education: Key issues of the first decade of the 21st Century. *Higher Education*, 45(2), 183-202.

Golde, C., and Walker, G. E. (Eds.). (2007). *Envisioning the future of doctoral education: preparing stewards of the discipline*. San Francisco: Josey Bass.

Goldstein, H., and Spiegelhalter, D. J. (1996). League tables and their limitations: statistical issues in comparisons of institutional performance. *Journal of the Royal Statistical Society,* 159(3), 385-443.

Greenaway, D., and Haynes, M. (2003). Funding higher education in the UK: The role of fees and loans. *Economic Journal*, 113(485), F150-F166.

Grubb, W. N., and Lazerson, M. (2005). Vocationalism in higher education: The triumph of the education gospel. *Journal of Higher Education*, 76(1), 1-25.

Halter, M. J., Kleiner, C., and Hess, R. F. (2006). The experience of nursing students in an online doctoral program in nursing: A phenomenological study. *International Journal of Nursing Studies*, 43(1), 99-105.

Harman, G. (2002). Producing PhD graduates in Australia for the knowledge economy. *Higher Education Research and Development*, 21(2), 179-190.

Hockey, J. (1995). Change and the social science PhD: supervisors' responses. *Oxford Review of Education,* 21(2), 195-206.

Ivankova, N. V., and Stick, S. L. (2007). Students' persistence in a distributed doctoral program in educational leadership in higher education: A mixed methods study. *Research in Higher Education*, 48(1), 93-135.

Johnes, J., and Taylor, J. (1990). *Performance indicators in higher education: UK universities.* Milton Keynes: Open University Press.

Kimber, M. (2003). The Tenured 'Core' and the Tenuous 'Periphery': the casualisation of academic work in Australian universities. *Journal of Higher Education Policy and Management*, 25(1), 41-50.

Kinman, G. (1998). *Pressure points: a survey into the causes and consequences of occupational stress in UK academic and related staff.* London: Association of University Teachers.

Kinman, G., and Jones, F. (2003). 'Running Up the Down Escalator': stressors and strains in UK academics. *Quality in Higher Education*, 9(1), 21-38.

Kivinen, O., and Nurmi, J. (2003). Unifying higher education for different kinds of europeans. Higher education and work: a comparison of ten countries. *Comparative Education*, 39(1), 83-103.

Kulis, S., Sicotte, D., and Collins, S. (2002). More than a pipeline problem: Labor supply constraints and gender stratification across academic science disciplines. *Research in Higher Education,* 43(6), 657-691.

Kumar, N. (2004). A comparative analysis of shifting of doctorates. *Current Science*, 86(1), 33-36.

Lambert, R. (2003). *Lambert Review of Business-University Collaboration*: *Final Report.* London: Her Majesty's Stationery Office.

Lanciano-morandat, C., and Nohara, H. (2003). *The new production of young scientists (PhDs): a labour market analysis in international perspective - DRUID working paper 03-04.* Aalborg: Danish Research Unit for Industrial Dynamics: Aalborg University.

Lester, S. (2004). Conceptualising the practitioner doctorate. *Studies in Higher Education*, 29(6), 757-770.

Macleod, K., and Holdridge, L. (2004). The doctorate in fine art: The importance of exemplars to the research culture. *International Journal of Art and Design Education*, 23(2), 155-168.

Mangematin, V. (2000). PhD job market: professional trajectories and incentives during the PhD. *Research Policy*, 29, 741-756.

Marginson, S. (2006). Dynamics of national and global competition in higher education. *Higher Education*, 52(1), 1-39.

Maxwell, T. (2003). From first to second generation professional doctorate. *Studies in Higher Education,* 28(3), 279-291.

Mayhew, K., Deer, C., and Dua, M. (2004). The move to mass higher education in the UK: many questions and some answers. *Oxford Review of Education*, 30(1), 65-82.

Mendoza, P. (2007). Academic capitalism and doctoral student socialization: A case study. *Journal of Higher Education*, 78(1), 71-96.

Moutinho, L., Hutcheson, G., and Rita, P. (Eds.). (2006). *Advances in doctoral research in managment - volume 1.* Singapore: World Science Publishing.

Moyer, A., Salovey, P., and Casey-Cannon, S. (1999). Challenges facing female doctoral students and recent graduates. *Psychology of Women Quarterly*, 23(3), 607-630.

Nerad, M. (2004). The PhD in the US: criticisms, facts and remedies. *Higher Education Policy*, 17, 183-199.

Noble, K. A. (1994). *Changing doctoral degrees: an international perspective.* Buckingham: Society for Research into Higher Education.

Pearson, R., Secombe, I., Pike, G., and Connor, H. (1993). Employer demand for doctoral social-scientists. *Studies in Higher Education*, 18(1), 95-104.

PhD research degrees: Entry and completion. (2005). London: Higher Education Funding Council for England.

Roberts, G. (2002). *SET for success. The supply of people with science, technology, engineering and mathematics skills. The report of Sir Gareth Roberts' Review.* London: HM Treasury.

Schofer, E., and Meyer, J. W. (2005). The worldwide expansion of higher education in the twentieth century. *American Sociological Review*, 70(6), 898-920.

Scott, D., Brown, A., Lunt, I., and Thorne, L. (2004). *Professional Doctorates: integrating professional and academic knowledge.* Maidenhead: Open Unversity Press.

Simpson, R. (1983). *How the PhD came to Britain: a century of struggle for postgraduate education.* Guildford: Society for Research into Higher Education.

Stephan, P. E., Sumell, A. J., Black, G. C., and Adams, J.D. (2004). Doctoral education and economic development: The flow of new Ph.D.s to industry. *Economic Development Quarterly*, 18(2), 151-167.

Sustaining scholarship in Business Schools. Report of the Doctoral Faculty Commission to AACSB International's Board of Directors. (2003). St Louis: The Association to Advance Collegiate Schools of Business.

Thurgood, L., Golladay, M. J., and Hill, S. T. (2006). *US Doctorates in the 20th Century.* Arlington: National Science Foundation.

Transparency review of research: proposal for a new uniform approach to the costing of research and other activities in universities and colleges of higher education. (1999). Bristol: JM Consulting Ltd.

Triggle, D. J., and Miller, K. W. (2002). Doctoral education: Another tragedy of the commons? *American Journal of Pharmaceutical Education*, 66(3), 287-294.

Tytherleigh, M. Y., Webb, C., Cooper, C. L., and Ricketts, C. (2005). Occupational stress in UK higher education institutions: a comparative study of all staff categories. *Higher Education Research and Development*, 24(1), 41-61.

Vidovich, L., and Porter, P. (1999). Quality policy in Australian higher education of the 1990s: university perspectives. *Journal of Education Policy*, 14(6), 567-586.

Wellington, J., and Sikes, P. (2006). 'A doctorate in a tight compartment': why do students choose a professional doctorate and what impact does it have on their personal and professional lives? *Studies in Higher Education*, 31(6), 723-734.

What do PhDs do? 2004 analysis of first destinations for PhD graduates. (2004). Cambridge: UK GRAD Programme.

Willmott, H. (2003). Commercialising higher education in the UK: the state, industry and peer review. *Studies in Higher Education*, 28(2), 129-141.

In: Global Issues in Higher Education
Editor: Pamela B. Richards, pp. 149-172

ISBN: 978-1-60021-802-6
© 2007 Nova Science Publishers, Inc.

Chapter 7

AUSTRALIAN UNIVERSITY LEADERS: AGENTS OF THE MC UNIVERSITY, ENTREPRENEURIAL TRANSFORMERS, OR BUREAUCRATS?

*Deanna de Zilwa**

Sociology, School of Political Science,
Criminology and Sociology, University of Melbourne,
Victoria, 3010, Australia

ABSTRACT

Some sociologists and higher education scholars view theory and empiricism as separate worlds, arguing that one has nothing to offer the other. This work proposes that the boundaries between theoretical conceptions and empirical realities have a transilient fluidity, that one domain informs the other. Hence this study explores connections between three theoretical conceptions of the university, Weber's bureaucracy, Ritzer's McUniversity and Clark's Entrepreneurial University and the leadership style of executives in Australian public universities. Information about executives' leadership style was gathered from case study interviews with seventeen executives from four Australian public universities. This work found that at each of the case study universities leaders' views of their university comprised elements of these three conceptions of the university, none of the three conceptions of the university were actualized in a 'pure' form. This work also identifies four different leadership styles used by these executives: entrepreneurial transformers, facilitators, bureaucrats and collegial leaders. It finds some connections between leaders' theoretical conceptions of the university and how they led their universities. However, the connections between theory and empiricism were complex, reflexive ones rather than unidirectional causes and effects.

* Email: ddezilwa@unwired.com.au

INTRODUCTION

Australian public universities are currently subjected to a myriad of environmental pressures. Some pressures are economic: intensified levels of competition in global student, staff and research funding markets, declining levels of public funding and increasing operating costs from the massification of student cohorts (increasing numbers and diversity of students), rising salary and infrastructure costs and costs of compliance with accountability measures set by regulatory authorities. These economic pressures have a profound impact on the university as an organization posing significant challenges for universities and their academic units to adapt to this situation and on the social and cultural identity and values of academics (faculty). Other studies have explored these issues (de Zilwa, 2006; Harman, 2005; Marginson, 2006; Meek, 2002, 2003) so this study has a different focus. It explores how executives[1] in Australian universities deal with this situation.

This study has three objectives. First, it seeks to discover how Australian university leaders conceive their universities as organizations. Do these leaders view their university as a Weberian bureaucracy, as Ritzer's McUniversity, or as Clark's Entrepreneurial University (Clark, 2004; Ritzer, 1998, 2006; Roth and Wittich, 1978)? Second, how do these leaders conceive their role in leading and managing their universities? Third, is there any association between how leaders conceive their university and how they approach their leadership and management role? In précis this study's research methods entail answering its research questions by contrasting the three theoretical conceptions of the university with empirical data (interviews with Australian university leaders); a more detailed account of research methods follows.

This chapter has three parts. First the three conceptions of the university are introduced; this is done at some length for the benefit of readers who are unfamiliar with this work. These theories are not critiqued in this section of the chapter because this is not the task at hand, analysis occurs later. Second notes are provided about how the interviews with the university leaders were conducted. Third is the data analysis section of this study. This analysis contrasts empirical findings with theoretical perspectives evaluating the relevance and explanatory power of these theories in relation to the study's empirical findings. Finally conclusions and reflections on the study are made.

THREE CONCEPTIONS OF THE UNIVERSITY

The three conceptions of the university chosen for this study were selected because they are well known and provide diverse representations of the university. Each conception of the university reflects a particular political position, a worldview that privileges certain norms and values over others. This work does not offer a normative view; it does not endorse any of these conceptions of the university. Instead it seeks to discover whether Australian university leaders support any of these conceptions of the university and whether these leaders view their role as aligned with any of these conceptions of the university.

---

[1] Executives refers to vice-chancellors, deputy and pro-vice chancellors, directors and general managers, sometimes known as presidents in United States universities.

WEBER – THE UNIVERSITY AS A BUREAUCRACY

Weber's work spans an enormous gamut of empirical and theoretical topics in Sociology. Our primary interest is his work on bureaucracy, authority, and rationality. Weber observed that many public and private organizations are bureaucracies including political structures, the military, judiciary, banks, commercial firms, schools and universities. Indeed Weber argued that universities were typical bureaucracies. Therefore before examining some of Weber's specific comments on the university as a bureaucracy it is helpful to examine how Weber defined the characteristics of a bureaucracy and how he interpreted its advantages and disadvantages. As with many theorists Weber's work has been interpreted in vastly different ways by various scholars. Classical organizational theorists 'read' Weber as advocating the virtues of bureaucracy whereas some contemporary sociologists and organizational theorists (Edles and Applerouth, 2005 pp.181-182; Morgan, 2006 pp.17-18, 294, 371-372) argue that Weber viewed bureaucracies as dehumanizing organizations that denied people freedom, individuality and led to the homogenization of society. Because of this debate surrounding how Weber's work on bureaucracy should be interpreted this work uses Weber's actual texts rather than later commentaries on his work[2].

Weber's famous essay on bureaucracy was included in *Economy and Society*, a work published posthumously in 1925. Two authoritative translations of this work are (Henderson and Parsons, 1947; Roth and Wittich, 1978). Weber stated that a bureaucratic organization functions in the following manner:

> There is the principle of official *jurisdictional areas,* which are generally ordered by rules, that is by laws or administrative regulations.
>
> This means:
>
> (1) The regular activities required for the purposes of the bureaucratically governed structure are assigned as official duties.
>
> (2) The authority to give the commands required for the discharge of these duties is distributed in a stable way and is strictly delimited by rules concerning coercive means, physical, sacerdotal, or otherwise which may be placed at the disposal of the officials.
>
> (3) Methodical provision is made for the regular and continuous fulfillment of these duties and for the exercise of the corresponding rights; only persons who qualify under general rules are employed. ...
>
> 11. The principles of *office hierarchy* and of channels of appeal (*Instanzenzug*) stipulate a clearly established system of super- and subordination in which there is a supervision of the lower offices by the higher ones. ....
>
> 111. The management of the modern office is based upon written documents (the "files"), which are preserved in their original or draft form, and upon a staff of subaltern officials and scribes of all sorts. ...
>
> 1V. Office management, at least all specialized office management – and such management is distinctly modern – usually presupposes training in a field of specialization. ...
>
> V. When the office is fully developed, official activity demands the *full working capacity* of the official, irrespective of the fact that the length of his obligatory working hours in the bureau may be limited....

---

[2] I have used translations of Weber's texts because his original work was written in German and I do not read German.

VI. The management of the office follows *general rules*, which are more or less stable, more or less exhaustive, and which can be learned. Knowledge of these rules represents a special technical expertise which the officials possess. It involves jurisprudence, administrative or business management.... (Roth and Wittich, 1978 pp.957-958).

Weber states that the bureaucratic office is a "vocation" that requires special training, is a full-time job, office holders are paid a salary but do not "own" the position which they occupy (Roth and Wittich, 1978 p.959). Weber notes that officials in bureaucracies are held in high esteem by others in their society because of their technical expertise (Roth and Wittich, 1978 p.960).

Weber's distinction between three ideal or pure types of authority[3] is integral to his conception of the bureaucratic organization. Weber identified three types of authority: rational-legal, traditional and charismatic. Rational-legal authority 'rests on a belief in the legality of enacted rules', traditional authority 'rests on an established belief in the sanctity of immemorial traditions and the legitimacy of those exercising authority under them', charismatic authority 'rests on devotion to the exceptional sanctity, heroism or exemplary character of an individual person, and of the normative patterns or order revealed or ordained by him' (Roth and Wittich, 1978 p.215). For Weber the bureaucratic organization was an exemplar of rational authority. According to Weber a monocratic bureaucracy (where power and authority is held by an individual) was a superior form of organization to a collegial form of organization (where power and authority is shared amongst a group) of people.

> Once fully established, bureaucracy is among those social structures which are the hardest to destroy. Bureaucracy is the means of transforming social action into rationally organized action. Therefore as an instrument of rationally organizing authority relations, bureaucracy was and is a power instrument of the first order for one who controls the bureaucratic apparatus. Under otherwise equal conditions, rationally organized and directed action (Gessellschaftshandeln) is superior to every kind of collective behavior (Massenhandeln) and also social action (Gemeinschaftshandeln) opposing it. Where administration has been completely bureaucratized, the resulting system of domination is practically indestructible (Roth and Wittich, 1978 p.987).

For Weber a bureaucratic organization was also an extremely efficient organization that was technically superior to other types of organization, its officials made informed, impartial decisions quickly.

> The decisive reason for the advance of bureaucratic organization has always been its purely *technical* superiority over any other form of organization. The fully developed bureaucratic apparatus compares with other organizations exactly as does the machine with the mechanical modes of production. Precision, speed, unambiguity, knowledge of the files, continuity, discretion, unity, strict subordination, reduction of friction and of material and personal costs – these are raised to the optimum point in the strictly bureaucratic administration, and especially in its monocratic form. As compared with all collegiate,

---

[3] Weber used the word herrschaft in the original text of *Economy and Society* to refer to why subordinates in an organization accept the authority of superiors. It is interesting to note that Parsons in his 1947 edition of *Economy and Society* translated herrschaft as legitimate authority , (Henderson and Parsons, 1947), p.297. Whereas in Roth's 1968 translation of *Economy and Society* Roth translates herrschaft as legitimate domination (Roth and Wittich, 1978), p.53 and p.212.

honorific, and avocational forms of administration, trained bureaucracy is superior on all these points. And as far as complicated tasks are concerned, paid bureaucratic work is not only more precise but, in the last analysis, it is often cheaper than even formally unremunerated honorific service (Roth and Wittich, 1978 pp.973-974).

Although Weber acknowledged the efficiency of a bureaucratic organization he also noted that a bureaucratic organization has a tendency of dehumanizing its officials and the people affected by its rules and decisions, he stated that bureaucracies operate 'without regard for persons':

> Bureaucracy develops the more perfectly, the more it is "dehumanized", the more completely it succeeds in eliminating from official business love, hatred, and all purely personal, irrational, and emotional elements which escape calculation. This is appraised as its special virtue by capitalism (Roth and Wittich, 1978 p.975).

Next some comments that Weber made about universities as bureaucracies are noted. Weber argued that universities play a key role in providing the training and specialized expertise for bureaucratic officials:

> Educational institutions on the European continent, especially the institutions of higher learning – the universities, as well as technical academies, business colleges, gymnasia, and other secondary schools –, are dominated and influenced by the need for the kind of "education" which is bred by the system of specialized examinations or tests of expertise (*Fachprüfungswesen*) increasingly indispensable for modern bureaucracies (Roth and Wittich, 1978 p.999).

Especially pertinent to this work are Weber's comments that bureaucratic organizations such as universities tend to concentrate resources at the apex of their hierarchy, leading to a concentration of power and privileges:

> In the field of scientific research and instruction, the bureaucratization of the inevitable research institutes of the universities is also a function of the increasing demand for material means of operation. Liebig's laboratory at Giessen University was the first example of big enterprise in this field. Through the concentration of such means in the hands of the privileged head of the institute the mass of researchers and instructors are separated from their "means of production" in the same way as the workers are separated from theirs by the capitalist enterprises (Roth and Wittich, 1978 p.983).

Another example of the bureaucratization of the university for Weber related to the appointment of academics (faculty). Weber stated that "the freedom of science, scholarship and teaching" in a university certainly does not exist where appointment to a teaching post is made dependent on the possession –or simulation – of a point of view which is "acceptable in the highest circles" of church and state" (Shils, 1973 p.19). Weber remarked:

> Universities do not have it as their task to teach any outlook or standpoint which is either "hostile to the state" or "friendly to the state". They are not institutions for the inculcation of absolute or ultimate moral values. They analyse facts, their conditions, laws and interrelations; they analyse concepts, their logical presuppositions and content. They do not and they cannot

teach what should happen – since this is a matter of ultimate personal values and beliefs, a fundamental outlook, which cannot be "demonstrated" like a scientific proposition (Shils, 1973 p.21).

For Weber further evidence of the bureaucratization of universities is demonstrated by university leaders' desire to maximize the efficiency and productivity of academics' work. In a paper written in 1919, Weber mentions two signs of the bureaucratization of universities. First he notes that academics in United States Universities had "heavy" teaching loads (many hours of classes) and second that junior academics do not have tenure (contract staff could easily be dismissed or not have their contract renewed):

> In Germany the career of a scientist or scholar depends on his having private means, for it is extremely hazardous for a young scholar, who has no financial resources of his own, to expose himself to the conditions of an academic career… In the United States, on the contrary there, is a bureaucratic system in which the young man is paid from the very beginning – although moderately to be sure. Usually his salary barely corresponds to the wages of a not entirely unskilled labourer. Nevertheless, he begins with an apparently secure position, for he receives a definite salary. The rule is that like the German assistant, he may be dismissed, and he has to be ready for this should he fall short of expectations. However, this threat disappears if he packs the house" This threat of dismissal does not exist for the German Privatozent. Once he is appointed he remains permanently (Shils, 1973 pp.54-55).

> In America things are organized on a different principle. It is indeed in his earlier years that the assistant is heavily overburdened, precisely because he is *paid*. In a German department, for instance, a full professor will give a three hour course on Goethe and that is all – while the younger assistant is lucky if his assignment is 12 hours per week …. (Shils, 1973 p.55).

RITZER – THE MC UNIVERSITY

Ritzer a contemporary sociologist argues that the dominant paradigm of many modern societies is rationalization. For Ritzer, the fast food restaurant, Mc Donalds epitomizes this process of rationalization. Ritzer's Mc Donaldization thesis draws from Weber's concept of rationalization and his view that rationalized systems such as bureaucracies become "iron cages" restricting and controlling people (Weber, 1930). Ritzer initially outlined his McDonaldization thesis in an article published in 1983. Later he revised and extended this work (Ritzer, 1993, 1998, 2000, 2004, 2006). Ritzer stated:

> Mc Donaldization involves an increase in efficiency, predictability, calculability and control through the substitution of non-human for human technology. While undoubtedly bringing with it many positive developments, Mc Donaldization also involves a wide range of irrationalities, especially dehumanization and homogenization. It is these irrationalities of rationality (and associated problems) which represent the true heart of the McDonaldization thesis (Ritzer, 1998 p.vii).

Ritzer defines the four elements that he views as the primary means of attaining Mc Donaldization: efficiency, predictability, calculability and control in the following way.

Efficiency refers to the fastest means or optimum method of attaining a goal, 'for consumers, Mc Donalds offers the best available way to get from being hungry to being full' (Ritzer, 2004 p.12). Predictability refers to the assurance that a product or service will always be the same over time and in all places, that 'The Egg McMuffin in New York will be, for all intents and purposes, identical to those in Chicago and Los Angeles' (Ritzer, 2004 p.14). 'Calculability is an emphasis on the quantitative aspects of products sold (portion size, cost) and services offered (the time it takes to get the product). In McDonaldized systems, quantity has become equivalent to quality; a lot of something, or the quick delivery of it, means it must be good' (Ritzer, 2004 p.13). Control means programming and controlling peoples actions through non-human technology especially computers 'Mc Donalds has lines, limited menus, few options, customers do what management wants them to – eat quickly and leave' (Ritzer, 2004 p.15). The way McDonalds' employees perform tasks such as preparing hamburgers, cooking fries or pouring beverages is also regulated and controlled in work manuals and automatically by machines. Ritzer argues that the process of Mc Donaldization applies to many fields including universities, credit cards, Disney world, health care, travel, leisure and dieting (Ritzer, 2004 p.2; 2006). (Alfino, Caputo, and Wynward, 1998; Hartley, 1995; Hayes and Wynward, 2002; Parker and Jary, 1995) provide critiques of the McDonaldization thesis.

At the heart of Ritzer's conception of the McUniversity is the idea that the 'university can be conceived of as a means of educational consumption, one that allows students to consume educational services and eventually to obtain important "goods" – degrees and credentials' (Ritzer, 1998 p.151). According to Ritzer students and parents now have a consumerist orientation and expectations of universities, they want them to operate like their banks and fast food restaurants – to be conveniently located and to operate during convenient hours, they expect personnel to offer professional services, they want high quality products at low cost and are prepared to comparison shop for the best deal (Ritzer, 1998 p.152). Ritzer adds that in addition universities now operate with less government funding (Ritzer, 1998 p.154). According to Ritzer prestigious and wealthy universities such as Harvard and Oxford are largely able to ignore these pressures but most universities are forced to try to adapt to this situation (Ritzer, 1998 pp.152-153). Ritzer contends that this later group of universities have become McUniversities – these universities have borrowed ideas on how to attract and process more students/customers and reduce operating costs by emulating business practices developed by McDonalds, shopping malls and banks (Ritzer, 1998 pp.152-159).

Ritzer identifies several strategies employed by McUniversities to attract more students, generate more revenue and reduce operating costs including opening satellite or branch campuses overseas, increased reliance on computers for online teaching, student administration, access to information for research and assignments (Ritzer, 1998 pp.154-155). According to Ritzer McUniversities deliver modularized, standardized curriculum to reduce costs, cheaper teaching assistants deliver the curriculum whilst assessment costs are reduced by using multiple choice tests that are graded by computers (Ritzer, 1998 pp.157-158). He observes that McUniversities increase management's control over academics (faculty), they no longer devise courses, their performance in teaching and research is evaluated often using quantifiable measures to ensure efficiency and quality control (Hartley, 1995 pp.411-412). Ritzer also notes that McUniversities like many corporations are heavily engaged in downsizing – reducing staff numbers and streamlining processes to make them more efficient and to reduce operating costs (Ritzer, 1998 p.155). Other theorists refer to these sorts of changes implemented by universities as strategies and actions associated with 'new public management' or managerialism (Considine and Painter, 1997; Currie, 2004; Meek, 2003).

More recently Ritzer has called for universities to resist McDonaldization suggesting that in order to attract more students thereby increasing their revenue, universities should emulate the spectacular aspects of the cathedrals of consumption (mega malls, Disney World, Las Vegas) (Ritzer, 2002 p.20). Ritzer observes that the cathedrals of consumption create spectacles to enchant and attract customers such as the simulation of Venice in Las Vegas(Ritzer, 2002 p.21). He also suggests that the cathedrals of consumption use implosion of space and time – 'the elimination of boundaries between extant phenomena so that they collapse in on one another' to attract more customers (Ritzer, 2002 pp.21-22). Ritzer acknowledges that universities are subject to regulatory and financial constraints that restrict their capacity to use implosion to attract more students (Ritzer, 2002 p.22). He recommends that universities can attract and retain more students, generating more income if they make their 'quotidian' (core activities of teaching and learning) spectacular (Ritzer, 2002 p.22-28). Ritzer suggests several ways universities can do this: reinstate small tutorials so that students have direct contact with their professors, ensure that star professors teach undergraduate classes, customize the curriculum and make it unpredictable, focus on the quality of teaching and research not on quantity (Ritzer, 2002 pp.26-30). In Ritzer's view if universities take such 'spectacular' actions they will overcome the 'irrationality of rationality', the dehumanizing affects of McDonaldization.

CLARK – THE ENTREPRENEURIAL UNIVERSITY

Clark trained as a sociologist yet much of his work has focused on higher education. Clark argued that from the 1990s universities many countries faced an imbalanced situation where 'the demands on universities outran their capacity to respond' (Clark, 1998b p.6). He identified four particular demands on universities. First, universities have to teach more students and more different types of students (Clark, 1998b p.6). Second, more employers demand more university graduates trained for highly specialized occupations at different degree levels, in addition graduates require retraining throughout their professional careers (Clark, 1998b p.6). Third, universities are now subjected to pressures from a diverse range of stakeholders and are accountable to these groups for funding received, governments expect universities to do more at lower unit cost, industry also wants to see healthy returns for its investments (Clark, 1998b p.6). Fourth, expanding areas of knowledge require more resources, new research centers – departments always want more funding, personnel, students and space (Clark, 1998b p.6). Clark argued that national governments made some efforts to deal with these pressures that universities faced by trying to introduce system wide differentiation between universities but this strategy had limited success (Clark, 1998b p.8). Clark argued that in the past universities had been too passive that they had displayed inertia in the face of these pressures. According to Clark universities should take a more active entrepreneurial and innovative approach to survive these pressures (Clark, 1998b p.8). Clark defined an entrepreneurial university as a university that:

> Actively seeks to innovative how it goes about its business. It seeks to work out a substantial shift in organizational character so as to arrive at a more promising posture for the

future. Entrepreneurial universities seek to become "stand-up" universities that are significant actors on their own terms. Institutional entrepreneurship can be seen as both a process and outcome (Clark, 1998a p.4).

In the 1990s Clark conducted case studies of how five European universities transformed themselves to become entrepreneurial universities: University of Warwick (England), University of Twente (Netherlands), University of Strathclyde (Scotland), Chalmers University of Technology (Sweden) and the University of Joensuu (Finland). Clark reported his findings from this study in *Creating Entrepreneurial Universities* published in 1998. In this work Clark identified five pathways that these universities took to attain entrepreneurial transformation: a strengthened steering core, an expanded development periphery, a diversified funding base, a stimulated academic heartland; and an integrated entrepreneurial culture (Clark, 1998a p.5). Clark's definitions of these pathways for entrepreneurial transformation follow. A strengthened steering core refers to universities enhancing their management's capacity to respond more quickly and with greater flexibility and focus to changing environmental demands, to refashion and change its courses, organisational structure and mode of operating (Clark, 1998a p.5). Clark also identified stronger line authority (between rectors – deans – department heads) as a key facet of this strengthened steering capacity (Clark, 1998b p.8). An expanded development periphery refers to increasing numbers of organizational units outside the boundaries of traditional academic departments engaged in outreach activities such as knowledge transfer, developing industrial partnerships, intellectual property, continuing education, fundraising, alumni and marketing, interdisciplinary project oriented research centers working on applied, practical research problems (Clark, 1998a p.6). The diversified funding base refers to widening the sources of revenue from independent (non-government) sources such as industrial firms, local governments, philanthropic foundations, royalty income from intellectual property, earned income from campus services, student fees and alumni (Clark, 1998a pp.6-7). This independent income, Clark called it second and third stream income gave universities greater autonomy. It reduced their dependence on government funding – which was being significantly reduced and was accompanied by stringent rules anyway. The stimulated academic heartland refers to academic units (departments, schools and faculties) becoming entrepreneurial units 'reaching more strongly to the outside with new programs and relationships and promoting third stream income' (Clark, 1998a p.7). Clark added that successful entrepreneurial transformation was dependent upon staff from academic units accepting stronger lines of management authority, these staff should also participate in central steering groups (Clark, 1998a p.7). The integrated entrepreneurial culture refers to the blending of traditional collegial academic cultures and values held by academics from academic units with the new entrepreneurial culture and values (Clark, 1998a p.7). Clark identified the rigidity and path-dependence of traditional academic cultures as one of the most significant obstacles to successful entrepreneurial transformation, arguing that universities needed to develop the capacity to embrace change ((Clark, 1998a p.7).

Clark revisited his work on the entrepreneurial transformation of universities in 2004 when he published *Sustaining Change in Universities: Continuities in Case Studies and Concepts*. In this later work, Clark revisited the European universities in his 1998 study adding fourteen additional case study universities from Latin America, Africa, Australia and the United States[4]. His primary research question for this later study was to discover how universities sustained the process of entrepreneurial transformation. Clark argued that the case study universities sustained entrepreneurial transformation when they attained a 'steady state of change' (Clark, 2003 p.111; 2004 p.178). For Clark universities attain a 'steady state of change' when they have three forms of dynamism – the 'dynamism of reinforcing interaction': where all units and people within the university are change oriented, the 'dynamism of perpetual momentum': where there is cumulative incremental change and the 'dynamism of collegial volition': where academics are committed to proactive change and willing to take risks to be self-reliant (Clark, 2003 pp.110-115; 2004 pp.90-95). It is interesting to note that Clark observes that when universities embark upon processes of entrepreneurial transformation the 'bureaucracy grows. But it is based on a change orientation very different from the old rule-enforcing, state-mandated bureaucracy that gets left behind. The old bureaucracy looked to the prevention of error; the new bureaucracy looks to the stimulation of initiative' (Clark, 2003 pp.108-109). Finally it is important to mention Clark's observation that not all universities will undertake entrepreneurial transformation, for some levels of inertia are too strong, others are too wary of the risks associated with new ventures, some believe that government will eventually increase funding, and in others there is active resistance to entrepreneurialism (Clark, 2004 pp.170-171).

RESEARCH METHODS

I wanted to conduct an empirical inquiry to investigate whether Australian university leaders subscribed to any of the three conceptions of the university and whether there was any association between the leaders' perceived leadership style and their conception of the university. I had the opportunity to explore these questions when I interviewed leaders from four Australian public universities as part of a project investigating how academic units in Australian public universities were adapting to changing operating environments. The universities were: Monash University, Queensland University of Technology, Murdoch University and The University of Sydney[5]. The interviews were conducted between 1999 – 2002.

These four universities are very different. They are located in different states of Australia; vary in age, resource capacity, research activity and strengths, course profile and reputation amongst stakeholders including potential domestic and international students, graduate employers, firms and government agencies seeking research partners. Useful insights about the different attributes of Australian universities are provided by Marginson's typology of Australian public universities (Marginson and Considine, 2000 pp.189-202). Marginson identified five types of Australian public universities:

---

[4] Clark did not conduct these later case studies himself he used data collected by other researchers.

[5] There are 39 Australian public universities. Australia's universities are almost all public. Only 5 of the 44 institutions that are eligible for funds under the *Higher Education Funding Act 1988* are private and four of these receive limited funds. In 1999 there were 86 registered private higher education institutions. They are typically single-purpose institutions such as colleges of theology and business institutes. Together they account for approximately 3 per cent of higher education students (DEST 2002).

1.   Sandstones

- the oldest universities in each state,
- with superior economic resources,
- capacity to attract leading academics,
- strong networks with alumni, professions, international scholars
- strong discipline based academic cultures
- do not need to be entrepreneurial

2.   Redbricks

- second university in capital city[6],
- less traditionally academic than sandstones,
- more corporate and modernist than sandstones,

3.   Gumtrees

- founded between the late 1960s and 1975,
- modern and nationalistic, reflected in their native tree plantings,
- inter-disciplinary,
- democratic governance and informal management style,
- weaker links to alumni and professions,
- school leavers second, third or fourth choice,

4.   Unitechs

- formed from institutes of technology,
- weaker discipline based cultures than in pre-1986 universities,
- strong graduate professional cultures,
- teach occupational skills, strong links to industry,
- move quickly into new markets,
- innovative curriculum – new media, communications, creative industries,
- committed to mass access for students regardless of age, or background
- corporate, market oriented culture,

5.   New universities

- developed from merger of expansion of Colleges of Advanced Education
- post 1986 establishment,
- a heterogeneous sub-sector that may eventually fragment,
- some are regional, rural universities with branch campuses in metropolitan cities

Source: (Marginson and Considine, 2000 pp.189-202).

---

[6] This applies to Monash and the University of New South Wales but not to the Australian National University.

Monash University, classified as a Redbrick by Marginson was founded in 1958; it was the second university in the southern state of Victoria, after The University of Melbourne. Monash's original campus is at Clayton, an industrial suburb situated approximately twenty kilometers south of the central business district of Melbourne. Monash University enrolls more students than any other Australian public university, approximately 50,000 students (DEST, 2005). Monash University has undertaken considerable global expansion with campuses in South Africa, Malaysia and centres in Prato, Italy and London in addition to its six domestic campuses (Monash University, 2000). Queensland University of Technology (QUT) classified as a Unitech by Marginson was established when the Queensland Institute of Technology was redesignated as a university in 1989, the following year it was amalgamated with the Brisbane College of Advanced Education. QUT's main campus is situated at Garden's Point within walking distance of Brisbane's central business district, providing easy access for mature age students to attend classes after work. Brisbane is the capital city of the state of Queensland. Murdoch University classified as a gumtree by Marginson is one of five universities in the state of Western Australia. Murdoch University was established in 1973 however it did not enroll students until 1975. Murdoch University has three campuses, its main campus – South Street, is fifteen kilometers from Perth, the capital city of the state of Western Australia and eight kilometers from the port of Fremantle. In 1996 Murdoch University opened its third campus at Rockingham, forty-five kilometers from Perth. Rockingham is an industrial area with many people from low socio-economic groups. Prior to Murdoch University establishing a campus at Rockingham few people in this area had the opportunity of attaining higher education. The University of Sydney was established in 1850, it is the oldest public university in Australia. Marginson classifies The University of Sydney as a sandstone university; it is a wealthy and prestigious institution with strong networks with its alumni, the professions, government and industry.

Semi-structured face-to-face interviews were conducted with seventeen vice chancellors, deputy and pro-vice chancellors and directors of planning and resources from these four universities[7]. These university leaders were asked questions about their university's strengths and weaknesses, to identify factors in its environment that were influencing its operations, to identify its major competitors in local and global research and teaching markets and to describe how they perceived themselves as leaders, how they thought their staff perceived their leadership style and how their leadership style influenced their approach to managing change. The interviews were tape-recorded; the tapes were transcribed, coded and analyzed using the software package ATLAS ti. The analysis identified patterns and trends within the data, points of similarity and contrast between the leader's responses to questions. More specifically the data analysis sought answers to three questions. First, how did each participant perceive their university, was their perception of their university aligned with Weber's bureaucratic university, Ritzer's Mc University or Clark's Entrepreneurial University, or did these leaders hold totally different views about their university? Second, how did these executives perceive their role as leaders? Third was there any association between the way an executive viewed their university and their chosen leadership style and approach to managing change?

---

[7] Sixteen of these seventeen executives were male and all were aged over 50.

LIMITATIONS OF THE STUDY

It is important to acknowledge that this is an exploratory study. Therefore the study's findings are tentative pronouncements rather than definitive statements. This study focuses on the traits and skills of university leaders. However if one uses an alternative definition of leadership, if leadership is defined as a relationship between leaders and followers then it can be argued that leaders may perceive themselves as using one leadership style and followers may view their leadership style in a different way. Those who support this later definition may view this study as limited because it does not report followers' perceptions of their leaders. For insights on how employees in these universities viewed their leaders, see (de Zilwa, 2006).

A further limitation is that this study's findings' refer only to this specific empirical context. Whilst a consequence of globalization is that universities situated in different countries now display greater levels of homogeneity in some facets of their operations. It is self-evident that universities situated in different countries are subjected to different state resource and regulatory policy that create heterogeneity in their operations. Therefore a similar study conducted in a different empirical setting could yield markedly varied findings. Despite these caveats I hope that this preliminary work can serve as a useful foundation for further work.

DATA ANALYSIS

To recap Ritzer's McUniversity thesis suggests that how universities operate including how they undertake their core functions such as teaching students has been rationalized and standardized: that education is now just another commodity for mass consumption. Ritzer identifies a primary cause of the McDonaldization of universities as reduced government funding. Ritzer identifies a key outcome of the McDonaldization of universities as the diminution of the quality of teaching and research conducted by universities. Further the McUniversity thesis suggests that the raison d'etre of contemporary universities is purely economic. That they are fordist factories whose primary goal is to increase their revenue by increasing production throughput (teach more students more cheaply) and improve levels of operational efficiency (reduce costs). Thus Ritzer's conception of the McUniversity represents a strong critique of the norms, values and goals of the contemporary university. However university leaders play a significant role in developing and sustaining the enculturation of their university's norms, values and goals. Their leadership role entails acting as the 'spokesperson', or salesperson for their university's values, goals and strategic directions. University leaders are largely responsible for motivating, encouraging and supporting staff to attain these things. Yet even more significantly the claim that McDonaldization leads to the diminution in the quality of university 'outputs', of its teaching and research is problematic for universities currently pushed towards marektization. As an integral aspect of marketization is intensified levels of competition between universities for students, staff and research funding in local, regional and global markets. Given that a university's capacity to attract students, research investors and partners, to gain a competitive advantage over rival universities in its markets is influenced by its reputation, 'its brand image', then it would probably not be prudent for key spokespeople responsible for 'selling the brand' (university leaders) to acknowledge that the quality of its teaching and research had diminished. Therefore it seems unlikely that university leaders would support Ritzer's McUniversity thesis which critiques the norms, values, goals and outputs of the university. Hence it is not surprising that this study found that only three of the seventeen Australian university leaders interviewed for this study made statements that acknowledged that Australian universities were affected by the process of McDonaldization or that any Australian universities were McUniversities.

One of the vice chancellors[8] interviewed for this study who agreed with the McDonaldization thesis stated that reduced government funding had resulted in reduced quality of teaching and research, referring to this process as 'everybody colluding with the spiraling down'. This vice chancellor suggested that in the future an Australian public university may actually refuse to accept government funding arguing that the level of this funding is inadequate to provide an acceptable education for students:

> Although we don't complain about declining government money, we do complain about a government that basically under-funds the students that we deliver programs for, that's unforgivable. If they want to cut funding, fine, but they should still fund what they buy appropriately. There will come a time that a university will turn around and say we are terribly sorry but we can not in all consciousness take the money that you are offering in the contract that we have with you because we can not deliver a quality education on the money that you are willing to pay. At the moment everybody is colluding with the spiraling down, it has been going on for twenty years it did not happen last week. For the last twenty years in most developed countries the real student dollar per student provided by governments to pay for the education of their citizenry has gone down. Sooner or later an Australian university will just turn around and say to the government that the money you are paying to buy the students' education isn't enough and we will demean our reputation as an institution by taking your money (vice chancellor).

Even though this statement suggests that Australian universities are affected by McDonaldization it is interesting to note that the vice chancellor who suggested that 'everybody was colluding with the spiraling down' of Australian universities did not suggest that the quality of teaching and research and at his university had diminished, it was a generic statement referring to the Australian higher education system as a whole. In a somewhat oblique reference to the McDonaldization of universities another vice chancellor stated that 'we have got to be careful about fast food and slow food, we have got to be careful about fast education and slow education'. Another university leader acknowledged the McDonaldization of Australian universities, yet this leader used McDonaldization as a competitive tool, attempting to strengthen his university's reputation by attacking the quality of a rival university's teaching:

> You have the 'sandstone university'[9] which is old and elite, you have the 'university of technology' which perceives itself as being very industry focused and job oriented and XXXX

---

[8] The quotes provided in this study list the interviewee's position title but not their university to provide anonymity for the participants.
[9] University types have been inserted in the quotation in place of university names to protect anonymity.

University which is frequently described as Kmart University. Except if you get a degree from there and you don't like it, you can't go and get your money back (pro-vice chancellor).

Only one of the leaders interviewed for this study described his university as a Weberian bureaucracy. This deputy vice-chancellor was asked how decisions about the university's strategic plan were made and his response reinforced important aspects of the Weberian conception of decision-making in a bureaucratic organization: a vertical hierarchical structure, an established chain of command, with each level having a designated function, and budgetary authority.

> The main practical way where that gets worked through is in discussions with the Vice Chancellor's group, particularly though in the Committee of Deans- which is the ten Deans and the Vice Chancellor's group that is probably in a sense the major priority setting group and where most big decisions stand or fall at the Committee of Deans. They are discussed at Academic Board, reviews coming in other ways but that is really the group, the Deans and the Vice Chancellor's group decide if something is going to happen and if they don't it doesn't by and large at the big strategy level (deputy vice-chancellor).

This deputy vice-chancellor was asked to explain how leaders at his university decided how to allocate resources to academic units when there were insufficient resources and hence intense competition between units for resources. His response reinforced his conception of his university as a Weberian bureaucracy. He mentioned another two key indicators of a traditional Weberian bureaucratic mode of decision-making - the formation of sub-committees and working parties to investigate issues and decisions being made according to codified policies and procedures, in an impartial apolitical fashion:

> The Committee of Deans receives submissions from different faculties and then decisions are made according to established policies, procedures and precedence. It is the Committee's job to keep vested interests in check. So within the Deans themselves load is very scarce now that DETYA has cut back. New programs are coming and wanting load, every now and again we have had a process where we have said 3000 or 200 or some number of places available bids come in to have a new program in Biomedical Ethics or a new program in Information Technology Networking or something or other we usually then form a working party from the Committee of Deans to look at the issue and write a report so that the Committee of Deans can make a recommendation to the Academic Board, sometimes the matter may need to be referred to the Vice Chancellors Group (deputy vice-chancellor).

Most of the leaders interviewed for this study (thirteen of the seventeen) stated that their universities were in a transitionary or uneven state with some parts (academic units, marketing and commercial units) displaying characteristics associated with entrepreneurialism – an external orientation, risk taking, diversified revenue streams, quick decisions made by executives) and other parts of their universities functioning as conventional bureaucratic organizations (central administration offices – such as student administration – internal orientation, focus on policies, procedures, precedence, decisions made by committees). It was interesting to note that this group of university leaders described the organizational units concerned with purely administrative functions as monocratic bureaucracies, whereas they identified some academic units in their university as collegial bureaucracies. Several university leaders said that the co-existence of these two organizational types 'the entrepreneurial university' and the 'bureaucratic/collegial university' was problematic, a point of great tension within their university. A general manager of resources articulated his views on the co-existence of the entrepreneurial university and the bureaucratic/collegial university:

> Well I think there are two groups here there are those that are more comfortable with yesterday. The life where the Commonwealth government provided 80 per cent of your money and didn't have to go out and earn your bread, your bread was always there and the only issue was how you digested it. Thankfully that group is in the minority at our university otherwise we would not be where we are today. Then we have the other group, the real go getter entrepreneurs out there. The biggest difficulty that I face is getting those that are looking back to the past to realize that they are responsible for their own future they have to be financially self-reliant (general manager resources).

A pro-vice chancellor at another university spoke about the difficulties that he encountered trying to get academics to move towards entrepreneurialism describing this process as 'herding cats'. Another pro-vice chancellor of resources mentioned that he was familiar with Burton Clark's work and that he 'had been to Warwick University three or four times to look at how they set up their earned income group' and that is why his university had decided to use OPTs (operational performance targets) to reward academic units that generated independent income. This pro vice-chancellor suggested that the bureaucratic aspects of his university impeded its efforts to become more entrepreneurial 'I think that we have been a bit slow in getting our act together with commercialization and entrepreneurship in a structured and supportive way. I think that we have too much policing of policies, this is anti-entrepreneurial and it is done by people who are supposed to be facilitating entrepreneurialism'.

This study's findings support Burton Clark's findings that not every university has the capacity to be entrepreneurial, or wants to be entrepreneurial. A pro-vice chancellor of resources who had previously worked in a commercial firm spoke about the resistance that he faced from some academic units and academics when he tried to implement some entrepreneurial initiatives to generate independent revenue (third stream revenue):

> When you come in from the private sector and you have a short term appointment you have got to do something pretty quickly. I brought forward to the university some big commercial things which I believed had a lot of up side to them. But it was a pretty hard slog for me. I had to tackle the cultures head on and it has been like banging your head against a brick wall. It has been very difficult to get some of the academics to embrace some of the changes in the Senate. They sabotage the Senate by vested interests (pro vice-chancellor resources).

One of the vice chancellors in this study stated that he wanted to encourage academic units and academics at his university to be entrepreneurial but that some academic units in Arts and Sciences lacked the capacity to be entrepreneurial adding that they needed to be cross-subsidized by those academic units that were capable of being entrepreneurial. According to this vice- chancellor one of the main impediments that some academics and academic units had constraining their capacity to be entrepreneurial was a low degree of comfort and acceptance of risk taking:

> If you always want to be on certainties you will never do anything, you will never cross the road. So if we are risk taking I say to University Council and I say to my staff occasionally at some point we are going to make a real boo boo and we will fall over and graze our knee but that is what taking risks is all about. And we don't want to recriminate on who made the decision we will just get out of it as best we can because we have to make many decisions without total information. So as long as the strike rate is okay, nine things out of ten succeed and one thing falls over disastrously well that is okay, that's life that's the penalty for risk taking. We are trying to be increasingly risk taking, investment and return, risk and reward that is the rhetoric (vice chancellor).

Here the vice chancellor's use of the phrase 'risk and reward that is the rhetoric' is noteworthy as it suggests an awareness that there may be dissonance between the espoused or theoretical conceptions of the entrepreneurial university and the reality that for some universities becoming an entrepreneurial university is not an easy task. In closing this discussion reporting findings about how the leaders interviewed for this study conceived their universities it is important to emphasize that a university leaders' preferred way of conceiving his university was not necessarily shared by other leaders, nor by staff in central administration units, nor by academic units. One of the consequences of this dissonance in views over what type of organization a university should aspire to become was that these three theoretical conceptions remained as ideal types in the Weberian sense they were not fully realized or actualized by the leaders in the case study universities. In this regard we can conclude that conceptual views of the university are largely aspired to rather than actually attained. Our next task is to explore how the university executives interviewed for this study viewed their role as leaders before concluding by investigating whether there was any association between leaders' conceptions of their university and how they conducted their roles as leaders and managers.

Defining leadership is not an easy task. Some theorists define leadership as a skill or ability, others as an action, others as an influencing relationship between leaders and followers, whilst some theorists question whether there even is such a thing as leadership (Barker, 1997; Lakomski, 2005). There is an equally spirited debate amongst theorists about whether leadership and management are dichotomous concepts (Drucker, 2001; Hooijberg, 1996; Kotter, 1999). Whilst it is important to acknowledge that these debates exist I will not enter into them here. Rather than arbitrarily selecting definitions of leadership and management from the plethora of options available this work presents data that depicts how the university leaders interviewed for this study defined leadership and management and described their style or approach as leaders and managers. When analyzing this data a clear theme emerged: the university executives described themselves as using one of four different leadership/management styles:

- Entrepreneurial transformers
- Facilitators
- Bureaucrats
- Collegial

Further it was possible to identify a number of characteristics or traits that were associated with the different styles of leadership (Avery, 2004; Bryman, 1996). This is a useful task because it provides insights into the different ways that the university executives understood what it meant to be a leader and manager. It will also help us to explore our last research question whether there is any link between leadership style and leaders' conception of the university. I found nine leaders in this study who described themselves as entrepreneurial transformers (ETs). They stated that they were risk-takers, innovative and creative thinkers, that they were flexible, not path-dependent. They described themselves as having a sense of urgency, they wanted to act quickly which in practice meant that they often bypassed the traditional decision-making forums such as committees, and processes such as consultation and consensus preferring executive decisions. These comments made by a vice chancellor articulate the traits of an ET:

> My job is to provide the framework and encouragement that enables academic units to be entrepreneurial. I facilitate transformation I do not enact it. I have got to set the tone, I have got to constantly reinforce the views in our strategic plan so people are confident to make decisions. I keep telling people to make decisions. Don't put a paper to a committee make a decision (vice chancellor).

This vice chancellor was asked what lessons he had learnt in his role as vice chancellor, he responded:

> Intestinal fortitude is one of the things that you need, you have got to get used to the fact that the buck stops with you and that all of the problems, the big ones, eventually all really come onto your desk and then everybody just sits back and says well. Ninety-nine per cent of the key decisions have to be yours. And there is absolutely no doubt about it those are the decisions that there is no right answer to. If there was a right answer that's easy, so its all about judgment, its about being confident in your judgment and the more you do it the more you realize that the world doesn't fall over. I mean I used to wake up in the middle of the night in cold sweats (vice chancellor).

ETs seemed to perceive themselves as charismatic leaders who motivated and inspired their staff to strive to become successful entrepreneurs. Yet it was also evident that ETs could display an authoritarian command and control management style, with little time, patience and tolerance to listen to alternative points of view, or to tolerate resistance from staff:

> I say to people quite openly in meetings. If you don't agree with the route that we are taking with the strategic directions that we are heading towards with our push to be entrepreneurial, there are plenty of other universities, find one that you are happy in (vice chancellor).

Another example of the ET style of leadership and management is this response from a deputy vice-chancellor from another university in the study when asked to describe how he viewed his role as a leader and manager he stated:

> This can be quite a conservative university and my job is to push, push, push. Every now and again the VC says no more, or stop that, or its too fast, or I don't want to go there but I have an incredibly strong relationship with him based on the fact that we actually don't agree

with each other on almost anything but there can only be one boss and he gives me very wide discretion to do what I want in terms of running the place and that is great, it works well (deputy vice-chancellor).

I found four leaders who were Facilitators. Facilitators led through others. They did not perceive their role as the sole locus of power, authority and innovative ideas. Facilitators actively delegated decision-making responsibilities to staff and sought the counsel of staff. In contrast to ETs who sometimes 'ruled with an iron fist' , facilitators were more willing to entertain alternative points of view and to broker comprise deals with staff that opposed or resisted proposed strategic changes such as opening a new campus, changing course profile or introducing tuition fees. A deputy vice-chancellor articulated the role of a facilitator: 'I see my role is to facilitate the work of all of our stars out there so that they can achieve without hindrance whatever they can achieve'. A vice-chancellor said 'I do the job because I enjoy drawing out the capacity of others, rather than running my own race. That is what sucks anybody into a management role and that is a very rewarding thing, trying to produce effective outcomes and get people to reach their full potential'. The following response from a deputy vice-chancellor illustrates how a facilitator deals with resistance to the university's proposed strategic directions:

> We all resist change except when it is initiated by ourselves but if it is initiated by somebody else then you will find resistance. So resistance to change is just human nature. Dealing with resistance comes down to leadership and team work, the management of change. You need a leader who is knowledgeable, who is empathetic and who is to an extent charismatic, they can communicate the need for change well and build a team behind themselves who will sing the same song (deputy vice-chancellor).

When another deputy vice-chancellor was asked how he coped with resistance to change from staff he said 'jaw, jaw not war, war' I mean endless talking, endless persuasion, endless meetings. Just demonstrating that at all times that you know what they want and that you are there to support them and to remove all of the impediments towards them achieving what they want to achieve'.

Three leaders in this study displayed many of the characteristics of Weber's ideal type of bureaucrat. These leaders viewed their prime responsibility as fulfilling the tasks specified in their position description within the established boundaries of codified policies, procedures and established precedents. Hence bureaucrats focused on maintaining established order and modes of operating, they did not see it as their role or responsibility to transform the university or even to 'manage change'. This group of leaders did not strive to be charismatic figures instead they derived their authority and staff complied with their decisions because staff accepted that their appointments had been made in accordance with due process. As long as these leaders did not seek to expand their power and authority beyond the boundaries of their designated role their authority was deemed to be legitimate, exemplifying Weber's rational-legal mode of authority. The remarks made by a registrar (director) when asked how he managed change illustrate the bureaucratic leadership style: 'I have put in place a very comprehensive continuous improvement project now. The coordinator works with major divisions and departments and examines whether they have particular problems and how we could improve them. So she has looked at sixty or seventy processes now and written new policies and procedures to manage change'.

For a considerable period of time collegial leadership was the dominant mode of leadership for Australian universities (Marginson and Considine, 2000 p.62). Vice Chancellors, deputy vice- chancellors, deans and heads of department were viewed as 'the first amongst equals' and most of the significant decisions that were made within the university were debated at length in university councils and academic boards. Yet since the Dawkins reforms of 1987-90 there has been a shift to a more corporate managerialist style of executive leadership (Harman, 2005; Marginson and Considine, 2000; Meek, 2003). Hence it is not surprising that only one of the seventeen leaders in this study used a collegial style of leadership. This leader (a deputy vice-chancellor) did not see himself as the sole agent of power and authority. He sought to share decision-making authority for resource allocation, strategic goals and the priorities for goals amongst a group of senior colleagues and academics. When asked to describe how he viewed his role as a leader and manager and what his priorities were, this deputy vice chancellor responded:

> I think that it is important to show the staff that we care about them, that we value them and their contribution to the university. We must interact with staff in a meaningful way, we have to try and engage them. We are extremely fortunate we have an extremely loyal staff that are committed to the university; they see it as their university.

When this collegial leader was asked how he managed change he said that 'the most important thing is to have a lot of consultation, to involve as many people as possible in making decisions, and to deal with resistance by explaining to academics about the changes in the environment and why the changes are necessary, otherwise people will just go off completely disillusioned'. To conclude this discussion about the leadership style of the university executives in this study I will add the observation that there was no definitive association between a leader's seniority and leadership style, that is senior leaders (vice chancellors) were not necessarily ETs and lower ranked executives (directors and general managers) were not necessarily collegial leaders. The following conclusion explores the issue of whether it is possible to identify any links or connections between how the university executives conceived their university and their leadership style and offers some reflections on the study.

CONCLUSIONS

This work identifies several links between the theoretical conceptions of the university and university executives' leadership style. The strongest link between theory and empiricism demonstrated in this study is that most of the university executives described their leadership style as an entrepreneurial transformer (ET) and this leadership style illustrates many key aspects of Clark's conception of the entrepreneurial university. These aspects included accepting and striving for change in organizational structure, modes of operating, types of research undertaken, research partners, types of courses taught, modes of delivery, risk taking – entering new markets, changing hiring and pricing strategies, having a greater focus on competition, diversifying revenue streams, and making decisions quickly so as to respond to changes in markets rather than relying on more traditional committee and consultative decision-making patterns. This link is significant because it stands as evidence that several Australian universities are currently aspiring to become entrepreneurial universities. Of course Clark's observation stands, not every university has the capacity to be entrepreneurial and indeed not every university wants to be entrepreneurial.

A second link between theory and empiricism suggested by this study's findings is that because only one of the seventeen university executives in this study described himself as a bureaucratic leader, this implies that Australian universities may no longer be bureaucratic organizations. Yet we must be cautious, the sample size is small so it is not legitimate to offer definitive statements. It would be premature to declare the death of bureaucracy in the Australian university. Indeed a case can be made that the rise of managerialist initiatives such as quality assurance and key performance indicators for strategic planning have spurred growth in the number of bureaucrats working in Australian universities, and that there has been a shift of power from academics to bureaucrats, see (Meek, 2003). Indeed this points to an interesting paradox noted by Clark – whilst the emergence of the entrepreneurial university seems to have modified the traditional Weberian bureaucracy, a new form of bureaucracy has emerged, a bureaucracy that is more closely integrated with entrepreneurial initiatives in universities rather than one that operates in opposition to entrepreneurial goals (Clark, 2003 pp.108-109).

An absence in the data provides the third finding for this study. The fact that only three of the seventeen university leaders in this study acknowledged the existence of Ritzer's McDonaldization thesis and none of these leaders admitted to being agents for McDonaldization suggests that the McDonaldization thesis requires a codicil when applied to universities. Those who consume the products of the university (students) and those who deliver those products and services (employees) may support the McDonaldization thesis, yet it seems that university leaders who manage and control universities and their means of production are unlikely to acknowledge that their universities are being 'McDonaldized'.

Even though this research project was small scale and exploratory its findings demonstrate the complexity of the university. None of the leaders interviewed for this study viewed their university as completely aligned with any of the three theoretical conceptions of the university investigated in this work. Each of the universities displayed aspects of all three conceptions of the university. In addition this study focused on reporting executives' perceptions of their leadership style, identifying four styles of leadership: entrepreneurial transformers, facilitators, bureaucrats and collegial leaders. The study also pointed out that there can be a mixture of leadership styles within a university's executive groups and noted that even though leaders may believe they are using a particular leadership style their followers (employees) may view their leadership in a totally different way.

In disciplines such as Sociology and its specializations such as Higher Education Studies there is a distinct chasm between those who work with empirical realities and those who explore theoretical conceptions. All too often there is a lack of understanding and value of each type of work. Theoreticians often harshly critique empiricists' work asserting that it is merely descriptive and not explanatory. And in turn empiricists often view theoreticians' work as impenetrable, and devoid of all connections with reality. Some scholars hold an entrenched view that by definition theory is separate from empiricism. Yet this work illustrates that there are connections between theory and empiricism. Although it is important to note that these connections were complex and reflexive rather than unidirectional causes and effects. I contend that the boundaries between theoretical conceptions and empirical realities have a transilient fluidity, that they are indeed permeable. It is my view that integrating theory and empiricism is a useful endeavor because it enriches both domains. This project enables practitioners to operate with enhanced knowledge of theoretical conceptions that seek to explain situations and issues. While theoreticians who test their theories in empirical contexts can evaluate the analytical and explanatory power of their theories and modify, enhance or reject their theoretical conceptions in the light of knowledge gained from empirical contexts.

REFERENCES

Alfino, M., Caputo, J. S., and Wynward, R. (eds.). (1998). *McDonaldization Revisited:Critical Essays on Consumer Culture*. Westport: Praeger.

Avery, G. C. (2004). *Understanding Leadership: Paradigms and Cases*. London: Sage Publications.

Barker, R. A. (1997). How Can We Train Leaders if We Do Not Know What Leadership Is? *Human Relations, Vol.50* (No.4), pp. 343- 362.

Bryman, A. (1996). Leadership in Organizations. in S. Clegg, C. Hardy and W. Nord (eds.), *Handbook of Organization Studies* (pp. pp.276-292). London: Sage Publications.

Clark, B. (1998a). *Creating Entrepreneurial Universities: Organizational Pathways of Transformation*. Oxford: Pergamon.

Clark, B. (1998b). The Entrepreneurial University: Demand and Response. *Tertiary Education and Management, Vol.4* (No.1), pp.5-16.

Clark, B. R. (2003). Sustaining Change in Universities: Constituencies in Case Studies and Concepts. *Tertiary Education and Management, Vol.9* (No.2), pp.99-116.

Clark, B. R. (2004). *Sustaining Change in Universities: Continuities in Case Studies and Concepts*. Maidenhead: Society for Research into Higher Education and Open University Press.

Considine, M., and Painter, M. (1997). *Managerialism: The Great Debate*. Melbourne: Melbourne University Press.

Currie, J. (2004). The Neo-Liberal paradigm and Higher Education: A critique. In J. Odin and P. Manicus (eds.), *Globalization and Higher Education*. Honolulu: University of Hawaii Press.

de Zilwa, D. K. (2006). *Academic Units in the era of the Entrepreneurial University*. Melbourne: University of Melbourne.

DEST. (2005). *Selected Higher Education Statistics, Students*, from http://www.dest/highereducation/publications/selected statistics.

Drucker, P. (2001). Leadership as Work. In P. Drucker (Ed.), *The Essential Drucker* (pp. pp.268-271). Oxford: Butterworth Heinemann.

Edles, L. D., and Applerouth, S. (2005). *Sociological Theory in the Classical Era: Texts and Readings*. Thousand Oaks: Pine Forge Press (Sage Publications).

Harman, G. (2005). Introducing Comprehensive National Higher Education Reforms:The Australian Reforms of Education Minister John Dawkins, 1987-90. In A. Gornitzka, M.

Kogan and A. Amaral (eds.), *Reform and Change in Higher Education: Analyzing Policy Implementation* (Vol. Vol.8, pp. pp.169-185). Dordrecht: Springer.

Hartley, D. (1995). The 'McDonaldization' of Higher Education: Food for Thought. *Oxford Review of Education, Vol. 21*(No.4), pp.409-423.

Hayes, D., and Wynward, R. (eds.). (2002). *The McDonalization of Higher Education*. Westport: Bergin and Garvey.

Henderson, A. R., and Parsons, T. (1947). *The Theory of Social and Economic Organization: By Max Weber*. London: William Hodge and Company Limited.

Hooijberg, R. (1996). A multidimensional approach toward leadership: an extension of the concept of behavioral complexity. *Human Relations, Vol.49* (No. 7), pp.917-946.

Kotter, J. P. (1999). *John.P Kotter on What Leaders Really Do*. Boston: Harvard Business Review.

Lakomski, G. (2005). *Managing without Leadership: Towards a Theory of Organizational Functioning*. Oxford: Elsevier.

Marginson, S. (2006). Dynamics of National and Global Competition in Higher Education. *Higher Education, Vol. 52*(No. 4), pp.1-39.

Marginson, S., and Considine, M. (2000). *The Enterprise University: Power, Governance and Reinvention in Australia*. Cambridge: Cambridge University Press.

Meek, V. L. (2002). On the Road to Mediocrity? Governance and Management of Australian Higher Education in the Marketplace. In A. Amaral, G. A. Jones and B. Karseth (Eds.), *Governing Higher Education:National Perspectives on Institutional Governance* (pp. pp.235-260). Dordrecht: Kluwer.

Meek, V. L. (2003). Governance and Management of Australian Higher Education: Enemies Within and Without. In A. Amaral, V. L. Meek and I. M. Larsen (eds.), *The Higher Education Managerial Revolution?* (Vol. Vol.3, pp. pp.179-201). Dordrecht: Kluwer Academic Publishers.

Monash University. (2000). *Global Development Framework*. Melbourne: Monash University.

Morgan, G. (2006). *Images of Organization*. Thousand Oaks: Sage.

Parker, M., and Jary, D. (1995). The McUniversity:Organization, Management and Academic Subjectivity. *Organization, Vol.2* (No.2), pp.319-338.

Ritzer, G. (1993). *The Mc Donaldization of Society*. Thousand Oaks: Pine Forge Press.

Ritzer, G. (1998). *The McDonaldization Thesis: Explorations and Extensions*. London: Sage.

Ritzer, G. (2000). *The McDonaldization of Society*. Thousand Oaks, California: Pine Forge Press.

Ritzer, G. (2002). Enchanting McUniversity: Toward a Spectacularly Irrational University Quotidian. In D. Hayes and R. Wynward (Eds.), *The McDonaldization of Higher Education*. Westport: Bergin and Garvey.

Ritzer, G. (2004). *The McDonaldization of Society*. Thousand Oaks: Pine Forge Press.

Ritzer, G. (2006). *McDonaldization: The Reader*. Thousand Oaks: Pine Forge Press.

Roth, G., and Wittich, C. (eds.). (1978). *Max Weber Economy and Society: An Outline of Interpretative Sociology* (Vol. Vol.2). Berkeley: University of California Press.

Shils, E. (ed.). (1973). *Max Weber: On Universities: The Power of the State and the Dignity of the Academic Calling in Imperial Germany*. Chicago: The University of Chicago Press.

Weber, M. (1930). *The Protestant Ethic and the Spirit of Capitalism.* London: Allen and Unwin.

In: Global Issues in Higher Education
Editor: Pamela B. Richards, pp. 173-193

ISBN: 978-1-60021-802-6
© 2007 Nova Science Publishers, Inc.

Chapter 8

HIGHER EDUCATION RESEARCH PERSPECTIVES

Alberto Amaral and António Magalhães
CPIES and University of Porto, Portugal

ABSTRACT

Higher education research as a separate area of study has only recently been developed. A justification for the 'delay' of higher education research is that it has become an important focus of interest only when higher education entered the mass threshold, configuring a major financial and political issue.

This new area began to develop in the 1960s, in American universities (California at Berkeley, SUNNY Buffalo, Yale, Michigan). Only several years later has the field attracted the attention of social scientists in Europe, namely in the UK and Sweden. For Maassen there are differences in its development between the US and Europe, one of them being a strict divide in Europe between micro-level research on teaching and learning and research on organizational, political and economic aspects of higher education, the latter being the core of higher education research in Europe.

Major research efforts were aimed at the system level (Clark, Becher and Koogan, Teichler, etc.) and, in parallel, at governmental steering of the system (Neave and Van Vught, Kerr). Not only was the 'idea' of higher education discussed (Scott, Barnett, etc.), but also the issue of how to widen access of higher education for the majority of citizens. Studies on diversity and diversification were developed (Goedegebuure, Meek, Huisman).

We may argue that research on higher education reflects three different rationales: the managerial, the consulting and the social sciences approaches. The first rational, very present in international research organizations, has assumed management issues and goals, such as institutional performance, effectiveness, efficiency, etc., as privileged focus for research. The consulting approach was developed mainly in the framework of political advisors of Ministries of Education and presently also the European Commission, being the research goals mainly connected to implementation issues. The third approach, developed by social scientists, does not aim at 'solving' problems or 'advising' policy-makers and public officials responsible for policy implementation, but rather to find regularities observed when studying social objects. And as the research focus moved to the institutional level, these three approaches tended to mix.

More recently, the top-down approach of linear policy implementation has been replaced by alternative accounts that consider that organizations interact with their environment and define their own change strategies. New phenomena linked to neo-liberalism (new public management, managerialism, etc.), globalization and the emergence of new supra-national layers of authority, as observed in the EU, offer new areas of research that we will explore.

HIGHER EDUCATION AS A SEPARATE AREA OF STUDY

When compared to other areas of research, higher education as a separate area of study is quite recent. In the US, the development of research in higher education has been closely linked to graduate programs on higher education, specializing in areas such as administration, leadership, organizational change, student services, etc. The first research centers were established in the late 1950's: The Center for Studies in Higher Education (CSHE) at the University of California, Berkeley and the Center for the Study of Higher and Postsecondary Education (CSHPE) at the University of Michigan (Ann Harbor) were both founded in 1957. The Institute of Higher Education founded was in 1964 at the University of Georgia.

In Europe the development of higher education research was even more recent. A possible justification for this 'delay' of the European higher education research is that it has become an important focus of interest only when higher education entered the mass threshold, thus configuring a major financial, administrative and political issue. In the late 1960's some social science researchers in the United Kingdom and Sweden have focused their attention in the area of higher education, and in 1964 the Society for Research into Higher Education (SRHE) was established in London. The SRHE is a "UK-based international learned society concerned to advance understanding of higher education, especially through the insights, perspectives and knowledge offered by systematic research and scholarship" (SRHE 2007). Contrary to the US, the European higher education research centers have been predominantly research centers not linked to graduate programs.

On the other hand, research on higher education is frequently defined by the object of research rather than by the disciplines that focus on it. In spite of the fact that research on higher education has been developed by disciplines such as sociology, psychology, economics, history and law, and interdisciplinary fields such as public administration or organizational studies, neighboring not only educational research[1], but also science and labor market research to mention only these, they did not achieve a stable place in the framework of the established knowledge and within the disciplinary bounds. This is probably the reason why higher education research has a hybrid and flexible institutional basis, ranging from department based research to applied research units or institutes. As Altbach *et al.* recognize, "in part because higher education has no disciplinary base, it has never had a clear academic home" (2006: 2).

Due to its late development, research on higher education is probably still in the first phase of discipline development (Van den Daele, Krohn and Weingart 1977). For Maurice Kogan and Mary Henkel "higher education research may generally be assumed to be at a pre-paradigmatic stage if, indeed, it is ever likely to create paradigms" (Kogan and Henkel 2000:

---

[1] In the US, Canada, United Kingdom and Australia higher education research was initially developed in the framework of schools of education.

29-30). And more recently Malcolm Tight (2004), after analyzing "a database with 406 articles published in 2000 in 17 specialist higher education journals outside North America (ibid: 395), concluded not only that:

> Higher education researchers, for the most part, do not appear to feel the need to make their theoretical perspectives explicit, or to engage in a broader sense in theoretical debate (Tight 2004: 409).

but also that when they do so, their theoretical perspectives "tend to be based more often in social science disciplines or academic development units, rather than education departments or higher education research centers" (*ibid.*: 409).

Teichler, in 1992, wrote: "higher education as a field of knowledge, study, and research is closely related to specific national contexts of higher education systems and higher education policies" (1992: 37). Additionally, he argued that the links to specific national contexts and political debates must be considered as a characteristic of a newly emerging field "still in its infancy" (*ibid.*). Therefore, in his forecast once the field has reached a certain degree of maturity, institutional instability and dependency on national contexts would decrease or even disappear. However, in 2000 Teichler still conceded that "the institutional basis of higher education is heterogeneous and often shaky" (Teichler 2000: 23).

Fifteen years later, we can say that this forecast has not been fully accomplished. However, as a field of research higher education has been developing, important research units were created (and, those already existing, consolidated) and associations, consortia, journals, publication series, resource books, etc. are producing work and creating an important critical mass. At the institutional level, governments all over the world, as higher education becomes a central ingredient of economic development in the framework of knowledge society paradigm and passes the mass threshold, are becoming increasingly aware of the need of expertise in the political steering of the sector and of the need to improve institutional management. However, in spite of this growth, the field is far from being stable, or clearly defined as a knowledge field, and perhaps it never will. Disciplinary anarchy and a Mode 2 attitude, i.e., the definition of the research priorities based on their object/application, are features that probably will endure, not because this is a new field of research, but because it was created, with very few exceptions, outside of disciplinary tribes and territories to use Tony Becher's expression (1989). And while some consider that "higher education has legitimized itself as a research area within educational studies, gaining acceptance among those who are responsible for the leadership of higher education" (Altbach *et al.,* 2006: 20), others conclude:

> … that higher education research is not a single community of practice but, rather, a series of, somewhat overlapping, communities of practice. … there is a need for more theoretical engagement so that the field (or community of practice) can develop further, and gain more credibility and respect. (Tight 2004: 409)

It is usually assumed that only in the US higher education has become a well-established field of knowledge. The longer tradition of the American research on higher education is probably linked to the fact that the American system had to deal, before Europe, with the administration and management issues that mass higher education imposes. Firstly, the administration and management of the very autonomous American higher education institutions, characterized by a heavy and strong central administration, have made imperative a very professional administration to be carried out by college-trained staff and, secondly, the need to provide data to support decision-making processes, were at the roots of the enhancement of the quantitative and institutional-driven research in US. These features, have marked, and still mark, higher education research in US. In Europe, most universities had much lower degree of autonomy and their administration was traditionally weak. As we will argue, these characteristics are changing with the emergence of market regulation and increasing institutional autonomy. Consequently, institutional-level research is becoming also more and more visible in European higher education research. It is also true that in Europe there has always been a distinction between research on teaching and learning in general linked to pedagogical and educational research and research on organizational, economic and political research, which is considered as the area of higher education research.

Teichler (1992), in the work we have already quoted, has characterized research on higher education in Western European countries as being decentralized (differently from what appears to be the tendency in Eastern European countries); very heterogeneous, as far as its institutional base, disciplines and links to the practice are concerned; paying stronger emphasis to macro approaches, rather than to institutional problems; and being performed in small size and fragile institutional locations (*ibid.*: 39-40). Additionally, important differences between countries can also be identified in different European countries in line with different regional and national traditions:

> We note, first of all, substantial differences in the role higher education plays. It might be justified to state that research on higher education in Sweden, Britain, the Netherlands, and possibly in the Federal Republic of Germany is relatively well established whereas in Latin countries it is in a more shaky position. The lesser role of higher education research in Latin countries might be due to the Napoleonic administrative tradition of the powerful enlightened administrators who consider themselves so knowledgeable that externalized problem-solving and reflection by means of research is hardly to be needed. In Britain, Sweden, and the Netherlands social scientists are somewhat more successful in their claim that a distinct knowledge base nourished by research is helpful for decision-making. (*ibid.*: 40)

However, in spite of the overall differences between American, Western and Eastern European perspectives on research on higher education, a common concern appears to be related with political steering, and administrative and managerial issues imposed by mass higher education. In fact, as higher education has been transformed into a multi-billion euro business, strategically assumed as a key factor for economic development, involving millions of students and thousands of academic and non-academic staff, higher education broke through the research agendas of the governments and of the institutions (Altbach *et al.*, 2006). *A contrario*, one can strengthen this argument by stressing the secondary role that educational research, *stricto sensu*, has played (and still plays) in the general landscape of higher education research. If higher education research had been imposing itself from within the academy, this kind of research, or research field would have emerged earlier. In fact, to give just an example, periodicals on pedagogical and didactic research in higher education, even though they are starting to emerge, are not competing with the visibility that journals such as Higher Education Policy, Higher Education, Higher Education in Europe, European Journal in Higher Education, Higher Education Management, to cite only these, have. This is, in many senses, a paradox, i.e., as education and knowledge become central in an unprecedented way, educationalists and pedagogues are marginalized.

Assuming that the quantitative expansion of higher education has been the main propulsion force promoting the strengthening of higher education research, we can say this research field echoed the problems raised by the growth paths of the higher education systems, at least in Western European countries. After the middle of the XXth century, the expansion has become essentially quantitative and the political management of resources appeared as the main issue. A macro research drive was added, focusing on the problems raised by the mass assault to the ivory tower, i.e., research on systems' organization and its political steering, institutional reconfiguration and, last but not least, on equality of opportunities. The concept and the purposes of higher education, on the one hand, and system and institutional reforms to deal with mass higher education, on the other hand, have assumed the front stage. Clark Kerr (1983) with *The Uses of University* and Burton Clark's (1983) classic *The Higher Education System: Academic Organization in Cross-National Perspective* can be pointed out as examples coming from the United States.

The expansion of higher education systems in Europe has taken different paths according to the models and patterns of university education that each country assumed. The Humboldtian model, the Oxbridge model and the Napoleonic model led to different massification paths. In the United Kingdom, for instance, even the idea of a higher education system, i.e., a set of institutions politically integrated by the state, is quite recent. Actually, in the British case we can hardly speak of a national higher education system before the end of the world wars. Until then, the state's involvement with higher education was quite limited, and universities and colleges were, essentially, private institutions (Scott 1995: 14)[2]. In spite of this 'delay', the search for political and institutional devices to deal with mass higher education was quite fertile in the old Albion. In fact, the research on political, institutional and philosophical dimensions involved in the mass configuration of higher education, ranging from the decline of donnish dominion (Halsey 1995) to the meanings of mass higher education (Scott 1995) and to the idea of higher education (Barnett 1994), via research on processes and structures on higher education (Becher and Kogan 1992; Becher 1989) flourished in the United Kingdom.

Nevertheless, any effort to give a unified and complete general view of the research in higher education from an international perspective is doomed to failure. Not only because the field is object-driven and multi and trans-disciplinary, but also due to its youth and institutional location. Its youth makes difficult the availability of this type of studies to policy-makers and practitioners, and even more so to the general public, as literature search systems lack categories for the field (Teichler 1994). Its institutional location, ranging from departments to newly created centers, let alone the language divide in the European context, is far from being well established. Curiously enough, what seems to be consolidating is a diversified pattern with regard to disciplinary bases and institutional location.

---

[2] The reason being that "Guild control flourished in this British pattern of remote state supervision, especially in the two oldest universities, whose historical primacy and prestige have subtly defined for all universities a towering British style of academic control" (Clark & You 1976: 7).

HIGHER EDUCATION RESEARCH IN A CONTEXT OF FINANCIAL STRINGENCY: THE IMPACT OF THE EFFICIENCY PARADIGM ON HIGHER EDUCATION RESEARCH

In Europe, the late 1970s and the 1980s was the period of increasing financial crisis of the traditional welfare state model and when financial stringency imposed changes in the relationship between the state and higher education. Prometheus was to be unbounded (Neave and van Vught 1991 and 1994), meaning that higher education was to be regulated and governed differently. Research on higher education drifted from dwelling on the macro and 'noble' concept and purposes of higher education and their systems, to become dominated by the political concern of how to steer the sector effectively and simultaneously how to meet the political goal of equality of opportunities. It is worth mentioning the research on implementation policies in higher education (Cerych 1980; Cerych and Sabatier 1986) and the pioneering research in Germany on the relationship of higher education and the labor market (Teichler 1988). CHEPS, founded in 1984 in the Netherlands, was to become an important reference with regard to the development of knowledge on higher education and its dissemination all over the world.

As the systems increased enrolments towards the mass threshold, institutions were forced to deal with decreasing *per capita* funding in the name of economies of scale. At the same time, an expanding army of non-academic staff and non-academic tasks demanded expertise and, apparently, business-like treatment. If in the US this institutional, managerial and administrative drive developed earlier, in Western Europe it only came out when the development of the institutions and the emergence of New Public Management imposed a more professional perspective of institutional management. It has been within this framework that research at institutional level challenged the grandiose trend of research around the idea of higher education by giving emphasis to a more pragmatic theme: how to manage institutions in a time of financial stringency? And Teichler stated: " higher education research does not seem to move any balance regarding theories, disciplines, and themes, but rather research linked to management and policy issues seem to take over the scene" (1992: 45).

In the 1990s the focus of higher education research was shifted to managerialism and political steering, which have assumed an increasing relevance in the higher education panorama. It was as if the higher education research paradigms were to be traced externally and higher education researchers were loosing the capacity of defining their own research agenda.

In Western Europe, governments had consolidated the move from the mode of State control to the mode of State supervision, while awarding increasing autonomy to institutions. Quality assessment systems were introduced as a regulation tool – the emergence of the "evaluative state, which appears to be more effective in enforcing systems of accountability (the other face of institutional autonomy)" (Neave 1996: 37). This shift in the traditional modes of relationship between the government and institutions was coincident with a similar shift in the higher education research agenda. The management philosophies coming from the US invaded the research agendas and even the way higher education was conceived, i.e., in many senses the entrepreneurial paradigm became the matrix of higher education itself (see, for instance, B. Clark's work on the entrepreneurial universities, 1998a, 1998b): universities in order to be efficiently managed must act, not as institutions, but as organizations in order to survive. This imposed organizational characteristics such as sensitiveness to external changes, assumption of demand-driven patterns and, consequently, permeable organizational boundaries with labor market business-like organizations.

The popularization of neo-liberal policies has put emphasis on the 3Es of Margaret Thatcher (**E**conomy in the use and acquisition of resources, **E**fficiency in the use of resources and **E**ffectiveness in the achievement of objectives (Sizer 1990)), while New Public Management policies were introduced trying to replace the slow, inefficient decision making processes of academic collegiality by the "fast, adventurous, carefree, gung-ho, open-plan, computerized, individualism of choice, autonomous enterprises and sudden opportunity" (Ball 1998: 124).

Governments are increasingly using market and quasi-market mechanisms as instruments of public policy (Dill *et al,* 2004), aiming at increasing efficiency and the responsiveness of services to the public (now seen as clients). This search for efficiency was also extended to higher educations systems forcing market-like competition (for students, for research projects, for additional resources) between institutions as market regulating instruments. Therefore, an important layer was added to research on higher education inspired on the political and ideological agenda of the New Public Management. Deem used the concept of "new managerialism" to refer to these ideas about changes in the way that "publicly funded institutions are managed, following the widespread restructuring of welfare services in Western societies" (2001: 10), and she referred to them both as 'ideology' and in terms of the 'actual use' of those techniques and practices in publicly funded organizations. She concluded:

> Those promoting new managerialist discourses, whether politicians, management gurus or managers themselves, frequently claim that the ideas of new managerialism are purely based on an objective search for efficiency, effectiveness and excellence, with assumptions about continuous improvement of organizations often a further underlying theme. New managerialism is used to refer to the desirability of a variety of organizational changes. (*ibid.*: 10)

On the one hand, this managerialist inspiration has driven at least part of higher education research to organizational perspectives on higher education. Theories and analytical instruments coming from organizational studies populated the field and were functionally articulated with the entrepreneurial/managerial trend (Santiago, Magalhães and Carvalho 2005). On the other hand, it has inspired research focused on institutions in order to provide solid information to decision-making, planning and policy choices.

The European Association for Institutional Research (EAIR), founded in 1989[3], was an initially an extension of the American Association for Institutional Research, intending to develop "research conducted within an institution of higher education in order to provide information which supports institutional planning, policy formulation, and decision making". Its goals were to encourage professional interests among its members; to encourage studies into the functioning of higher education establishments; to enhance collaboration between researchers and institutional planners, managers and policy makers and to encourage comparative research. Even the Consortium of Higher Education Researchers (CHER),

---

[3] EAIR, in fact, started in 1979 as a branch of AIR (Association for Institutional Research), which was based in the United Sates. Only in 1989 it became an independent organization.

founded in 1988, in spite of the fact that it is a network of both individual and groups of researchers that does not intend to compete with networks focusing on more practical issues, but rather to enhance and support the exchange of theories and approaches aiming at the development of the research field, was caught by this trend. Neave and Teichler, expressed in the 1988 CHER meeting in Kassel, the view that there were many obstacles conditioning the development of the field, and they named as main barriers the small size of the research community, the rapid change of topics and issues, the multitude of disciplines involved and the heavy commitment of many scholars in consulting and advising (1989).

RESEARCH RATIONALES IN HIGHER EDUCATION: DIFFERENT ACTORS WITH DIFFERENT CULTURES

As higher education has become more and more economically relevant, the managerial, institutional-driven and efficiency oriented research became dominant. However, we cannot say that this is the only research rational of the field. The sociologist of education Roger Dale (1986) identified three 'projects'[4] in the study of education policy: the 'social administration project'; the 'policy analysis project' and the 'social science project'.

The social administration project aimed at improving the conditions of living of the populations, at social amelioration. Consequently, this approach was frequently focused on national policies and issues; it assumed an interventionist and prescriptive perspective and, by concentrating on 'facts' rather than on theories and interpretation of the welfare, it tended to delimit a 'field' and not adopting a disciplinary view. The 'policy analysis project' aimed "not in trying to change the content of the social policy in a particular direction, but in the search for ways of ensuring the efficient and effective delivery and implementation of social policies, irrespective of their content" (ibid.: 58). Finally, there was the 'social science project' whose scope is not functional, i.e., "Social scientists are concerned with finding out how things work rather than putting them to work" (ibid.: 61). Therefore, the goal of this project was to produce better explanatory theories rather than more efficient decision-making processes or more welfare. And, as Martin Trow has emphasized, researchers, usually performing at universities and not in governmental agencies and/or business organizations, "operate at a high level of training and specialization, which means that they tend to isolate a 'slice' of a problem area that can be more readily handled than more complicated global problems" (Trow 1984: 5).

One may find these three projects, or rationales, also structuring higher education research. However, for the reason we have explained before, the concerns and goals of the social administration project appear as dominant in the field. The second is probably the most rapidly growing research rational in higher education. The third project, in spite of its high status, is the less privileged one.

Teichler (2000: 17) has proposed that the institutional settings of higher education research can be described using five dimensions: the functional setting describing whether research takes place in a research unit, a research and teaching unit or a unit with a mixture of diverse functions (research, administration, services, etc.); the thematic setting describing if

---

[4] Dale clarifies his concept of 'project': "What I have in mind here is the purpose of the enterprise, the students' or researcher' conception of why they are doing what they are doing" (Dale 1986: 56).

higher education is the only research theme or if other themes are considered or if research addresses the relationship of higher education with other areas (higher education and the labor market for instance); the application setting, i.e., pure research, applied research, etc.; the stakeholders: governments, university administration, students, employers, international organizations, etc.; and the modes of control, i.e., academic self-regulation, national agency, control by a board, etc.

Teichler (2000) has also referred to Elaine El-Khawas (2000) who following John Kingdon's description (1984) of the policy process as composed of three mainly unrelated "streams" – problem, policy and political – identified three separated bases of higher education research by "regarding research, policy and practice as separated functional spheres" (El-Khawas 2000: 46). The first basis (research) referred to higher education research with an institutional academic base, such as a chair, a department, a centre or institute; the second basis (policy) included policy research or information units linked to supra-institutional agencies, namely governments; the third basis (practice) included institutional research in the US, performed by some higher education units and linked to the management of higher education institutions.

Teichler (2000) has considered that this type of classification was not restricted to the US and mentioned the use in Western Europe of a classification proposed by Frackman (1997) based on the same three functional types although using a different terminology:

- "the national and system wise decision support,
- institutional research and institutional decision support,
- research on higher education as reflexion." (Teichler 2000: 18)

In 1979, Maurice Kogan wrote:

> I assume that it is the task of social scientists to take things apart. I assume that it is the task of politicians and administrators to make sure that things are brought together again. Social scientists are right to detect the ambiguities and the multiplicity of contests, impacts, values and structures. They can, indeed, go further by showing what might be the consequences of building alternative systems or maintaining existing ones. They are merchants in ambiguity. Administrators cannot ignore those ambiguities but have to make a constructive use of them. Keeping the options open is, after all, making a constructive use of ambiguity but ultimately they have to decide and the word 'decide' means, literally, cutting off. Whilst the social scientist has license to engage in the study of phenomena for its own sake, the creed of the administrator has to be 'I must act', therefore I must think'. It is not the other way around. (Kogan 1979: 8)

But in spite of the clarity and legitimacy of the different rationales, one might argue that in the last ten years the applied projects, the social administration project and the policy analysis project assumed a clear supremacy and, paradoxically enough, within the social science project itself. The emphasis, for instance, on organizational and management studies, the focus on ('costumer'?) satisfaction and dissatisfaction and the centrality given to policy design (rather than to policy analysis…) are invading the social science project. The 'sacrificial offering' to relevance also reflected in the institutional profile of higher education research centers and institutes, as we argued before. It is not that the social science project is homogeneous; it is not that it should pursue identical perspectives and issues, but that the field and the research agenda has been strongly pressured by both ideological and pragmatic forces. These pressures are organized around the increasing individualization of citizens and educational opportunities – see, for instance, the relevance that 'choice' issues have assumed in the literature –; and the urgent need to provide quality mass higher education in the name of economic development.

Altbach *et al.* (2006), after asserting that in the industrialized world mass access has been achieved, that a few countries (USA and Canada, South Korea, Finland, Japan, etc) have even moved to semi-universal access enrolling half of the relevant age group or more, and that in Europe and the Pacific Rim some countries educate 40% of the age group concerned, emphasized:

> In this context, there is a great need for expertise and data about all aspects of higher education and for a sophisticated understanding of the nature of academic institutions. Academic institutions require thoughtful and competent leadership. Research on higher education and training in the art and science of administration and institutional leadership are critical to the future of the university. Policy makers outside academic institutions, in government and in the private sector, who increasingly wield power over the future of academe, need knowledge and analysis in order to effectively coordinate complex institutions and system (Altbach *et al.*: 2).

This pragmatic pressure is an important drive for the field of higher education research and for the development of its weaknesses and strengths. Actually, it seems that its object-driven and interdisciplinary features are enhanced by the need to act, to use Kogan's words (see the quotation already made in this chapter). The interdisciplinary approach to methodology whilst, on the one hand, hinders the creation of a more consistent research community, on the other hand, creates the conditions for innovative and inventive research perspectives. Conversely, the relevance vertigo that presently pervades higher education research induces also weaknesses and strengths. The strengths are linked to the increasing visibility of the field as its relevance is stressed, the weakness are linked to the increasing tendency to focus on micro issues and on 'how to do?' questions. If we consider the comparative studies, for example, in higher education, it is also possible to identify at their root the need to respond to demands for providing policymakers with a basis for international comparisons, benchmarking, etc. This comparative trend in higher education research is not only visible in the activities of the research centers and publications within the field, but also in the reviews led by the World Bank (e.g. 1994, 2000) and Unesco (e.g.1993).

Probably one of the major weaknesses brought by the relevance hegemony and the practical drift in higher education research is that it can become an obstacle to the construction of broad and explanatory theory or theories. In spite of the fact that the field has managed to built up a sizable literature and important research networks,

> Those responsible for planning and administering higher education institutions and systems are beginning to recognize the need for data and interpretation. Yet, the field has no widely accepted theories. Policymakers and administrators often say that they do not find research produced by the research community directly applicable to 'practical' problems of higher education management. (Altbach, *et al.,* 2006: 5)

The quest for relevance may have a negative influence over the development of this new research area. Kogan and Henkel (2000) considered that research in higher education was still in a pre-paradigmatic phase, which allowed for inputs of functional research to the discipline. And Teichler recognized that "the shaky institutional and financial basis for higher education research, due to the pressures of application and practical problem-solving, leads the key researchers in this field to take over applied research and consultancy roles" (Teichler 2000: 21). However, these pressures for application and consultancy, although providing opportunities for higher education research are not without danger and Teichler considered that there was "an application and consultancy drift in academically based higher education research" (*ibid:* 21). When policy-makers are the "customers" for research we need to pay attention to the fact that:

> If research is bounded by criteria of demonstrated method and openness, policy-making and practice are related to criteria of relevance and in that pursuit will take account of Ordinary Knowledge (Cohen and Lindbolm 1979 as cited by Kogan and Henkel 2000: 27).

For Teichler those dangers might include lowering theoretical and methodological standards to offer useful pragmatic knowledge, following political fads or allowing the quest for relevance leading to subordination to the prevailing norms: "for example, higher education in recent years often tended to preach the gospel of managerialism and evaluative steering" (Teichler 2000: 22). It is also evident that policy-makers are looking for "useful knowledge" meaning knowledge that provides solutions for actual problems, which is more compatible with positivist modes of research rather than with the traditional modes of academic enquiry (Kogan and Henkel 2000). However, "the research most highly prized by academics assumes that all questions are open and are likely to remain so after the research is completed" (*ibid.*: 39), which might explain that policy-makers "may favor knowledge created by inspectors, auditors and consultants who start with the premises of policy-makers" (*ibid.*).

And Teichler (2000) recognized that the European tradition of organizing higher education research based predominantly on research centers not linked to graduate programs had the disadvantage that it might be:

> ...tempted to polarize between disciplinary research that lacks field knowledge and practical relevance on the one hand and applied research which is unconsciously embedded in the prevailing norms on the other. (Teichler 2002: 23)

To counteract these dangers Teichler (*ibid.*) recommended that higher education researchers should engage in "meta-research and continuous reflection on its conditions" and to "embark more systematically on a critique of research", while "collaborative projects of researchers from various countries" might help challenging "the national idiosyncrasies of public debates and research traditions".

The proceedings of a meeting organized by the American Council on Education (2001) report the outcomes of a meeting of education policy analysts, education scholars, college and university presidents and foundation executives aiming at exploring the possibility of agreeing on a research agenda that "is rewarding and exciting for researchers, sustainable and mission-driven for foundations, and applicable and relevant to practitioners". The report reveals that college and university leaders complained that research was not relevant and that researchers complained that good research results were not fully utilized. And the discussions held at the meeting led to the conclusion:

> Researchers tend to develop questions that come from historic strands of research based on existing conceptual models. Practitioners tend to ask questions that come from real life problems and contexts that do not fit into research models. Foundations tend to ask questions that reflect their values and missions. ...the types of questions asked may be messy and overly complex, whereas research-driven questions often are tailored to fit cleaner, neater methodologies (American Council on Education 2001: 2-3)

The participants in the meeting have agreed on a number of viable research topics but they also identified three main types of barriers that impede better linkages between research and action/practice. Firstly, there was what we may call a mismatch between academic (research) time and policy-maker time. While researchers in general needed a long time to develop their work and to produce the necessary analysis and debates, policy-makers and practitioners needed fast-responses to meet their needs. This mismatch might result in legislation being passed without paying attention to the "broader philosophical tenets of higher education" (*ibid.*: 4) in the debates over higher education policy. Secondly, the participants recognized that in the US other significant barrier was the "promotion and tenure policies at colleges and universities" (*ibid.*: 4) as current reward systems did not encourage higher education policy research. Thirdly, participants recognized that communication strategies of the results of research addressing practitioners and policy-makers were not effective.

Elaine El-Khawas (2002) discussed in detail the patterns of communication and miscommunication between research, policy and practice recognizing that these worlds operated with "different purposes and modes of communication" (*ibid.*: 51), which frequently resulted in a "major disjunction" between them. And she recommended that researchers should contribute to improved communication by paying attention to the best modes of delivery, paying attention to the audience by taking the time "to hear the concerns of policy makers and to learn about the constraints they face" (*ibid.*: 53) and by accepting the random aspects of policy formulation.

MAPPING OUT THE RESEARCH FIELD

As the systems and institutions have expanded, more and more specialized knowledge became necessary and higher education research shifted from education and from theory on higher education to focus on information on enrolments trends, students' performance, institutional missions, financing and budgeting, the relevance of higher education to post-industrial societies, academic and non-academic staff. In the Anglo-Saxon world, as already stressed, institutional research has proliferated in the first place, but in countries like China, a significant part of the now established 400 research centers on higher education are already focusing on institutional research.

On the other hand, as governments required national data for planning and decision making processes, research centers were created and supported by the state, like for instance in Norway, NIFU- STEP, Norwegian Institute for Studies in Research and Education – Centre for Innovation Research, established in 1969[5], in the Netherlands CHEPS – Centre for Higher Education Policy Studies, established in 1984 or, more recently, CIPES – Centre for Research in Higher Education Policy, established in 1998, in Portugal, and CHES – Centre for Higher Education Studies, established in 1995, in the Czech Republic.

To map out the research field of higher education, the first landmark that one evidently has is the shift from research *of* higher education to research *for* higher education to paraphrase John Codd (1988)[6]. While research *of* higher education focused on the exam and analysis of the processes and transformations that occur in the field and on the effects of these processes, research *for* higher education focused on the need to make specific recommendations and to provide policy-makers, administrators and managers information and data to assist them in the governance processes. An archetypical example of this shift is provided by the comparison of the objectives of the recently established (2002) HEPI – Higher Education Policy Institute – in the United Kingdom: "The aim of the Higher Education Policy Institute is to improve the formation of higher education policy by providing research and other evidence to inform the development policy" (Altbach, *et al.*, 2006: 108), with the objectives of SRHE – Society for Research into Higher Education, founded in 1964, whose aims are to stimulate new forms of research and inquiry, to assist in developing research capacity, to offer *fora* for the presentation of research and scholarship in the field and to develop opportunities for researchers to engage with policy makers, practitioners in order "that policy and practices may be shaped by research" (*ibid.*: 111).

This trend is also evident in the research activities of international and regional organizations such as UNESCO, Word Bank and OECD – which sponsors IMHE, Institutional Management in Higher Education, and in non-governmental institutes such as CHET – Centre for Higher Education Transformation, in South Africa, established in 1995.

This tendency towards research for higher education has been lately enriched by the contribution of sociology of science. This sub-area has developed dramatically as the focus of analysis became research networks, scientists and researchers productivity – bibliometry included –, articulation between knowledge production, property and dissemination and the nature of knowledge itself (Ziman 1994). Discussions on Mode 1 and 2 (Gibbons *et al.*, 1997) of knowledge production have proliferated, linking more closely research on science and knowledge production and dissemination to political management and steering of research. As academic capitalism (Slaughter and Leslie, 1999) has been reconfiguring the research function of the higher education institutions and higher education systems, this sub-area of research developed in the field of higher education research (Magalhães 2004) at the same pace that the rhetoric on knowledge society became hegemonic in the political discourses.

The globalized economic and political landscape is also an important factor for the configuration of higher education as a research field. Internationalization and globalization are presently at the centre of the political and managerial concerns of governments and higher

---

[5] The mission of NIFU STEP is to be a national resource centre for studies on the relationships between competencies and technological development on the one hand, and cultural, social and economic change on the other hand (Altbach *et al*, 2006: 94).

[6] Codd referred this distinction with regard to policy analysis: "Policy analysis is a form of enquiry which provides either the information base upon which policy is constructed, or the critical examination of existing policies. The former has been called analysis for policy, whereas the latter has been called analysis of policy" (Codd 1988: 235).

education institutions. About 2.5 million students are studying abroad, which makes higher education simultaneously a business and an academic political issue.

However, and to bring together our argument, the move from research *of* ... to research *for* higher education, has been concomitant with the move to the micro level, meaning the institutional level. In fact, concerns with science, research productivity and science social relevance, teaching-learning efficiency, knowledge property, internationalization and attraction of new students (that the new market-friendly rhetoric characterizes as market niches), etc. has proliferated at the same pace that institutional management demanded data and information that could assist in their search for accountability and improved performance. Even at government level, higher education systems are increasingly being configured as a set of organizations (rather than institutions) that need to be governed to ensure their capacity to survive in a competitive environment. It is interesting to notice that in China, a country where state regulation matters (!), institutional research has been assuming the front stage of research into higher education. (Altbach 2006)

The managerial revolution (Amaral, Meek and Larsen 2003) did not happen only because academics do not typically have specific training for the administrative and managerial roles they are supposed to perform, but also because higher education entered a new paradigm. As it consolidated its mass character, other features gathered to reconfigure higher education and, consequently, higher education as a field of research: entrepreneurialism, managerialism, neo-liberal and market-driven policies, re-conceptualization of students and their families as clients and the academic staff as resources to be managed, accountability and social responsibility are the ingredients that the emerging paradigm is bringing together.

The National Center for Postsecondary Improvement at Stanford University has produced a report (NCPI 2002) aiming at defining research priorities for redirecting American Higher Education. The NCPI intended to complete "a fresh assessment of higher education's purposes and effectiveness" (NCPI 2002: 2), which was based on the idea that higher education institutions live today in an environment that is "both changed and uncharted" (*ibid.*) due to a range of new forces including "globalization, changing demographics, the growth of knowledge, technological advancements, the rise of market forces and growing accountability demands" (*ibid.*: 24). By recognizing this changing context surrounding higher education, NCPI has made salient the relevance of the proposed research agenda:

> As they navigate what increasingly appear to be uncharted waters, American colleges and universities, along with the public agencies that support and monitor their efforts, find themselves relying on a kind of dead reckoning to plot their future course. The result, too often, is a reactive improvisation that allows untried organizational forms and incomplete information to mask potential risks while overstating likely benefits. (NCPI 2002: 2)

NEW GOVERNANCE AND POSSIBLE FUTURE DEVELOPMENTS OF HIGHER EDUCATION RESEARCH

Governance theory "wrestles with the problem of how to govern complex and differentiated societies, societies in which the local and the global interact in dynamic processes of structural change" (Newman 2003: 3). In recent years the structure of modern government has changed dramatically in a number of countries, and especially in the US. The questioning of the cost and effectiveness of government programs and the emergence of neo-liberal theories has resulted in governments "being challenged to be reinvented, downsized, privatized, devolved, decentralized, deregulated, delayered, subject to performance tests, and contracted out" (Salamon 2002: 1).

This "new governance" approach (Salamon 2002) is characterized by the massive proliferation that has occurred "in the tools of public action, in the instruments or means used to address public problems" (Salamon 2002: 1-2), while attention was shifted "from hierarchic agencies to organizational networks" (*ibid.:* 11). The state is no longer considered as having the monopoly of expertise and resources to govern (Newman 2003). However, the increasing complexity of using the multitude of tools of public action may result in "the strong possibility that the reforms they are espousing may be the source, rather than the cure, for the problems they are seeking to remedy" (Salamon 2002: 7).

For a better understanding of the characteristics and consequences of the use of the new tools of public action it will be necessary to shift the unit of analysis by refocusing research from government agencies and individual programs to the tools used to respond to public problems (Salamon 2002: 600). It will also be necessary:

> ...to call the attention to the quite different management skills and accountability requirements that many of these tools entail, and thereby to improve the design and management of public problem solving and the citizenry's comprehension of what public action now involves (Salamon 2002: 610)

For Lascoumes and Le Galès (2006) the tools of public action may become strong compliance instruments, dramatically changing the behavior of social actors that will be forced to respond to "uncertain, floating parameters, changing with time but always forcing them to move in an one-way direction, that of economic effectiveness and cost reduction" (*ibid.:* 368).

New governance assumes interesting and very complex characteristics in the European Union (EU) where it is combined with an intricate multi-level structure. In the EU the dispersion of authority away from the central government resulting form the reallocation of power upwards (to EU), downwards (to the regions, local authorities) and sideways (to public/private networks) (Hooghe and Marks 2001), has led to the development of multi-level governance which describes the dispersion of authority across multiple territorial levels.

In the traditional mode of European integration, the so-called "Community method", member states transfer authority to the European Union, European-wide laws are passed, a supranational organ, the European Commission, is in charge of its application and the European Court of Justice is called to intervene whenever a member state breached the law (Dehousse 2002). This has been the method used for building the European Monetary Union (EMU). However, the further expansion of European Union policies to areas reserved for the exclusive authority of the member states by the treaties of the Union provoked "an increasing number of criticisms raised against what rightly or wrongly appeared to be an unlimited erosion of the member states' powers" (*ibid.:* 2). This has led to the development of a new "soft law" instrument, the Open Method of Co-ordination (OMC), which is a new governance mode based on "mutual leaning, participation and decentralized decision-making" (Amitsis *et al.,* 2003: 86).

Under the OMC there are no European laws. Governments agree on common objectives and a timetable for implementation and then each national government will pass the necessary national laws to attain those objectives. The OMC shares a set of common features with other modes of new governance, including multi-level interactions, participation of a broad range of actors including pools of experts, exchange of information and experience and peer review. Benchmarks and performance indicators are used to assess the progress of the fulfillment of agreed objectives (Kroeger 2004).

On the other hand, in parallel with the OMC, new governance at the EU level relies on the extensive use of "comitology" which is a form of control of national governments over the Commission:

> The innovation, as far as new governance is concerned, lies in the introduction of implementation committees into the decision-making process; this with a view to facilitating a degree of continuing Council [7] control over the Commission in the exercise of its executive functions. As is well known, comitology operates according to a variety of guises, the specificities of each manifestation determining the precise power relations between the actors concerned; the Commission, Council, and the committees themselves. (Scott and Trubek 2002: 2)

The Commission also makes extensive use of experts both hired by the Commission or appointed by national governments to the very large number of committees that proliferate in Brussels. This is consistent with the OMC's explicit intention to involve a wide range of different types of actors aiming at increasing legitimacy through enlarged participation. However, apparently this objective is far from being accomplished some even considering that "the permissive character of open coordination allows for window-dressing: the process by which open coordination remains an administrative formality of dressing-up existing policy" (The Netherlands Council for Social Development 2004).

The use of an OMC-type method for the implementation of the Bologna process raises the question of the "tools" and "networks" of new governance. The implementation of Bologna relies on the use of several tools of public policy (benchmarks, progress indicators, peer review, periodic reporting) that allowing for naming and shaming of the laggards tries to coordinate the process in the absence of effective legal constraints. The tools or instruments of public policy used to implement the Bologna process, are supposed to influence the behavior of organizational actors (leadership, academics, non-academics, students) participating in the implementation process. The use of this type of method in the implementation of the Bologna process presents coordination problems that do not allow for the full coherence of the results:

> As the process is quite complex, involving three different levels (European, national and local) and as the final actors in the implementation process higher education institutions (HEIs) have considerable degree of autonomy, assuming that the implementation of Bologna is a top–down linear policy implementation process does not account for the developments

---

[7] The European Council brings together the heads of state or government of the European Union and the president of the Commission. It defines the general political guidelines of the European Union. The decisions taken at the European Council meetings are a major impetus in defining the general political guidelines of the European Union. The meetings of the European Council usually take place in Brussels, in the Justus Lipsius building.

taking place, which produce implementation difficulties at several different levels. (Veiga and Amaral 2006: 283).

The difficulties of implementing multi-level policy open a new promising field of research. The implementation of the Bologna process involves the European, national and local levels (at the level of higher education institutions). The environment influences all actors involved in the process of decision-making and policy implementation. The complexity of these relations and the creation of feedback loop interactions could be responsible for unanticipated consequences that are not acknowledgeable by policy and decision makers (Pierson 1996). So we believe that the emergence of new governance, either in its American version or in the EU version will create new and interesting opportunities for higher education research, from the supra-national level down to the institutional level.

CONCLUSION

Sadlak and Altbach (1997) have considered that higher education research developed substantially over the last two decades and the same is true in the present decade. Massification of higher education and concerns about the quality of provision has certainly contributed to this expansion. As Guy Neave recognizes, "the mass university both generates and consumes information" (Neave 2000: 72). In the US the development of research has been embedded in strong graduate programs while in Europe higher education research was mainly conducted in research centers.

Neave has referred that the expanding "consultancy nexus":

> ... may be seen as part of that broader phenomenon which some are pleased to identify with the 'post modern' university, namely the blurring of operational and definitional boundaries around functions and fields of study once clearly demarcated. (Neave 2000: 73)

However, the relationship of researchers with policy-makers and practitioners, representing two different cultures with different needs, different purposes and different communication styles, is not in general easy, being frequently afflicted with miscommunication problems. Kogan and Henkel (2000: 27) have referred that Mrs. Thatcher used to say of one of her ministers, Lord Young: "The others bring me problems; he brings me solutions". And they provided another example from the UK, as "British policy-makers complained that they lacked the time and other resources to act as efficient receptors of commissioned research" (*ibid.*: 35).

In the US we listed the efforts of the American Council on Education to increase communication between researchers, policy-makers and practitioners, and the attempt of Stanford's NCPI to define a research agenda for American higher education. In Europe, the new governance being implemented at the level of the European Union, with its extensive use of pools of experts, may well contribute to an increasing demand for consultancy.

Therefore we might expect a further development of the field that will take into consideration "that many of the maps and navigation instruments that were once effective guides are now obsolete" (NCPI 2002: 2). Despite this foreseeable development it is unlikely, at least in the present decade, that higher education research will cross the boundaries of the pre-paradigm phase into the phase of paradigm articulation. The combined effects of the pressure for increased research relevance, the likely increase of the application and consultancy drift and the strong dependence on commissioned research to ensure financial sustainability are strong barriers to the development of the discipline. Teichler (2000) has presented several recommendations to overcome problems of counterbalancing the drifts, pressures and biases impinging on higher education research. El-Khawas (2000) and the American Council on Education (2001) have reflected on the barriers between higher education researchers, policy-makers and practitioners. And Malcolm Tight (2004:410) has proposed:

> … for higher education research to so develop, it needs to recognize itself, and be recognized, as an interdisciplinary field of research in which multiple communities of practice operate. … [it requires] for those with a major involvement in higher education research to engage with different disciplinary perspectives, and for the field as a whole to find more effective means of bringing researchers from these perspectives together. (Tight 2004: 410)

REFERENCES

Altbach, P., Bozeman, L., Janashia, N. and Rumbley, L. (2006). *Higher Education: a Worldwide Inventory of Centers and Programs*. Massachusetts: Boston College.

Amaral, A., Meek, L. and Larsen, I. (Eds.) (2003). *The Higher Education Managerial Revolution?* London: Kluwer Academic Publishers.

American Council on Education (2001). *Seeking a Common Agenda: Priorities for Research on Higher Education.*
http://www.acenet.edu/AM/Template.cfm?Section=CPAandTemplate=/CM/ContentDisplay.cfmandContentFileID=641.

Amitsis, G., Berghman, J., Hemerijck, A., Sakellaropoulos, T., Stergiou, A. and Stevens, Y. (2003). *Connecting Welfare Diversity within the European Social Model*. Background Report, presented 22-23 May at the International Conference of the Hellenic Presidency of the European Union "The Modernization of the European Social Model and EU policies and instruments".

Ball, S. J. (1998). Big Policies/Small World: an introduction to international perspectives in education policy. *Comparative Education, 34* (2), 119-130.

Barnett, R. (1994). *The Idea of Higher Education*. Buckingham: The Society for Research into Higher Education and Open University Press.

Becher, T. (1989). *Academic Tribes and Territories*. Buckingham: The Society for Research into Higher Education and Open University Press.

Becher, T., and Kogan, M. (1992). *Process and Structure in Higher Education*. London: Routledge.

Cerych, L. (1980). Retreat from Ambitious Goals? *European Journal of Education, 15* (1), 5-13.

Cerych, L. and Sabatier, P. (1986). *Great Expectations and Mixed Performance. The Implementation of Higher Education Reforms in Europe*. Stoke-on-Trent: Trentham Books.

Clark, B. (1983). *The Higher Education System: Academic Organisation in Cross-National Perspective*. Berkeley: University of California Press.

Clark, B. and Youn, T. (1976). *Academic Power in the United Sates: Comparative Historic and Structural Perspectives*, ERIC/Higher Education Research Report nº 3, Washington: The American Association for Higher Education.

Clark, B. (1998a). *Creating Entrepreneurial Universities*. Oxford: Pergamon Press.

Clark, B. (1998b). The Entrepreneurial University: Demand and Response. *Tertiary Education and Management, 4* (1), 5-16.

Codd, J. (1988). The Construction and Deconstruction of Educational Policy Documents. *Journal of Education Policy, 3* (3), 235-247.

Cohen, D. and Lindblom, C.E. (1979). *Usable Knowledge*. New Haven: Yale University Press.

Dale, R. (1986). *Perspectives on Policy-Making*. London: Open University.

Deem, R. (2001), Globalisation, New Managerialism, Academic Capitalism and Entrepreneurialism in Universities: is the Local Dimension Important*? Comparative Education,* 1, 7-20.

Dehousse, R. (2002). The Open Method of Coordination: A New Policy Paradigm? Paper presented at the First Pan-European Conference on Union Politics *The Politics of European Integration: Academic Acquis and Future Challenges",* Bordeuax, 26-28 September.

de la Porte, C. and Pochet, P. (2004). The European Employment Strategy: existing research and remaining questions. *Journal of European Social Policy, 14* (1), 71–78.

Dill, D., Teixeira, P., Jongbloed, B. and Amaral, A. (2004). Conclusion. In Teixeira, P., Jongbloed, B., Dill, D. and Amaral, A. (Eds.), *Markets in Higher Education: Rhetoric or Reality* (pp. 327-352). Dordrecth, Kluwer and Springer.

El-Khawas, E. (2000). Patterns of Communication and Miscommunication between research and Policy. In Schwarz, S. and Teichler, U. (Eds.), *The Institutional Basis of Higher Education Research* (pp: 45-56). Dordrecht: Kluwer Academic Publishers.

Frackmann, E. (1997). Research on higher education in Western Europe: From policy advice to self-reflection. In Sadlak, J. and Altbach, P. (Eds.). *Higher education research at the turn of the century: Structures, issues and trends* (pp: 107-126). New York: Garland.

Gibbons, M., Limoges, C., Nowotny, H., Schwartzman, S., Scott, P. and Trow, M. (1997). *The New Production of Knowledge: The Dynamics of Science and Research in Contemporary Societies*. London: Sage.

Halsey, A. H. (1995). *Decline of Donnish Dominion: The British Academic Professions in the Twentieth Century*. Oxford: Clarendon Press.

Hooge, L. and Marks, G. (2001). Types of multi-level governance. *European Integration online Papers, 5* (11), http://eiop.or.at/eiop/pdf/2001-011.pdf

Kingdon, J. (1984). *Agendas, Alternatives, and Public Policies*. Boston: Little, Brown and Co.

Kogan, M. (1979). Different Frameworks for Educational Policy-Making and Analysis. *Educational Analysis, 1* (2), 5-14.

Kogan, M. and Henkel, M. (2000). Future Directions for Higher Education Policy Research. In Schwarz, S. and Teichler, U. (Eds.), *The Institutional Basis of Higher Education Research* (pp: 25-43). Dordrecht: Kluwer Academic Publishers.

Kerr, C. (1983). *The Uses of University*. Cambridge, Mass: Harvard University Press.

Kroeger, S. (2004). Let's talk about it – Theorizing the OMC (inclusion) in light of its real life application. Paper prepared for the doctoral meeting of the Jean Monet chair of the Institut d'Ètudes Politiques, Paris, section "Public Policies in Europe", 11 June.

Lascoumes, P. and Le Galès, P. (2006). De l'Innovation Instrumentale à la Recomposition de l'État. In Lascoumbes, P. and Le Galès, P. (Eds.), *Gouverner par les instruments* (pp: 357-370). Paris: Les Presses Sciences Po.

Magalhães, A. M. (2004). *A Identidade do Ensino Superior: Política, Conhecimento e Educação numa Época de Transição*. Lisboa: Fundação Calouste Gulbenkian/Fundação para a Ciência e Tecnologia.

NCPI – National Center for Postsecondary Improvement (2002). *Beyond Dead Reckoning: Research Priorities for Redirecting American Higher Education*. Stanford: Stanford University.

Neave, G., and Teichler, U. (eds.) (1989). Research on Higher Education in Europe. *European Journal of Education, 24* (3).

Neave, G. and Van Vught, F. (Eds.) (1991). *Prometheus Bound: The Changing Relationship Between Government and Higher and Higher Education in Western Europe Relationships*. Oxford: Pergamon Press.

Neave, G. and Van Vught, F. (Eds.) (1994), *Government and Higher and Higher Education Relationships Across Three Continents: The Winds of Change*, Oxford: Pergamon Press.

Neave, G. (1996). Homogenization, integration and convergence. In Meek, V.L., Goedegebuure, L., Kivinen, O. and Rinne, R. (Eds.), *The Mockers and the Mocked: Comparative Perspectives on Differentiation, Convergence and Diversity in Higher Education* (pp: 26-41). London, Pergamon Press.

Neave, G. (2000). On Fate and Intelligence: The Institutional Base of Higher Education Research. In Schwarz, S. and Teichler, U. (eds). *The Institutional Basis of Higher Education Research* (pp: 57-71). Dordrecht: Kluwer Academic Publishers.

Newman, J. (2003). Rethinking governance: critical reflections on theory and practice, paper prepared for the 2003 ESPAnet Conference, „Changing European Societies – The Role for Social Policy", 13–15 November 2003, Copenhagen, www.sfi.dk/sw2031.asp

Pierson, P. (1996). The path of European integration: A historical institutionalist analysis. *Comparative Political Studies*, 29, 123–163.

Sadlak, J. and Altbach, P. (Eds.) (1997). *Higher education research at the turn of the century: Structures, issues and trends*. New York: Garland.

Salamon, L. M. (Ed.) (2002). *The Tools of Government: A Guide to the New Governance*, Oxford: Oxford University Press.

Santiago, R., Magalhães, A. and Carvalho, T. (2005). *O Surgimento do 'Managerialismo' no Sistema de Ensino Superior Português*. Matosinhos: CIPES.

Scott, J. And Trubek, D. M. (2002). Mind the Gap: Law and New approaches to Governance in the European Union.
http://wage.wisc.edu/uploads/Articles/dt_mindgap.pdf

Scott, P. (1995). *The Meanings of Mass Higher Education*. Buckingham: The Society for Research into Higher Education and Open University.

Sizer, J. (1990). Funding Councils and Performance Indicators in Quality Assessment in the United Kingdom. In Goedegebuure, L., Maassen, P. and Westerheijden, D. (Eds.). *Peer Review and Performance Indicators – Quality Assessment in British and Dutch Higher Education,* Utrecht, Lemma.

Slaughter, S. and Leslie, L. (1999). *Academic Capitalism: Politics, Policies, and the Entrepreneurial University*. London: John Hopkins University Press.

SRHE (2007), SRHE Mission statement, http://www.srhe.ac.uk/about.asp

Teichler, U. (1988). Higher education and Work in Europe. In Smart, J. (Ed.). *Higher Education Handbook of Theory and Practice*. (pp. 109-182) New York: Agathon Press.

Teichler, U. (1992). Research on Higher Education in Europe – Some Aspects of Recent Developments. In Frackmann, E. and Maassen, P. (Eds.). *Towards Excellence in European Higher Education*. (pp. 37-61) Utrecht: Lemma.

Teichler, U. (1994). Research on Academic Mobility and International Cooperation in Higher Education. In Smith, A., Teichler, U. and Van der Wende, M. (Eds.). *The International Dimension of Higher Education: Setting the Research Agenda* (pp: 10-21). Wien: IFK Materialien.

Teichler, U. (2000). Higher Educational Research and its Institutional Basis. In Schwarz, S. and Teichler, U. (eds). *The Institutional Basis of Higher Education Research* (pp: 13-24). Dordrecht: Kluwer Academic Publishers.

The Netherlands Council for Social Development (2004), *European Coordination, Local Effects? Towards an Effective Implementation of the European Social Inclusion Strategy in the Netherlands*. The Hague: The Netherlands Council for Social Development.

Tight, M. (2004). Research into higher education: an a-theoretical community of practice? *Higher Education Research and Development, 23* (4), 395-411.

Trow, M. (1984). Researchers, Policy Analysts and Policy Intellectuals. In Husén, T. and Kogan, M. (Eds.). *Educational Research and Policy: How Do They Relate?* (pp: 261-282). Oxford: Pergamon.

UNESCO (1993). World Education Report. Paris: UNESCO.

Veiga, A. and Amaral, A. (2006), "The open method of coordination and the implementation of the Bologna process". *Tertiary Education and Management*. 12: 283-295.

World Bank (1994). *Higher Education: the Lessons of Experience*. Washington, DC: World Bank

World Bank (2000). *Higher Education in Developing Countries: Peril and Promise*. Washington, DC: World Bank.

Van den Daele, W., Krohn, W. and Weingart, P. (1977). The Political Direction of Scientific Development. In Mendelson, E., Weingart, P. and Whitley, R. (Eds.). *The Sociological Production of Scientific Knowledge* (pp: 219-242). Dordrecht and Boston/USA: Reidel Publishing Co.

Ziman, J. (1994). *Prometheus Bound: Science in a Dynamic Steady State*. Cambridge: Cambridge Press.

In: Global Issues in Higher Education
Editor: Pamela B. Richards, pp. 195-213

ISBN: 978-1-60021-802-6
© 2007 Nova Science Publishers, Inc.

Chapter 9

DESIGNING PEDAGOGICAL MODELS TO SUPPORT COLLABORATION IN HIGHER EDUCATION CONTEXTS

*Raija Hämäläinen**

University of Jyväskylä, Institute for Educational Research,
P.O. Box 35, FI-40014, Finland

ABSTRACT

Educational research is looking for social approaches to foster virtual learning. Computer-Supported Collaborative Learning appears to be a promising approach for higher education for developing knowledge and reasoning skills. One way to enhance the process of collaboration as well as to integrate individual and group-level perspectives of learning is to structure learners' actions with the aid of scaffolding or scripted collaboration. The present study includes empirical experiments conducted in an authentic higher educational setting and leans on the design-based study approach. The leading idea in the study involved structuring the student groups' collaborative activities by means of pedagogical models (scripts), whilst they were working in learning environments. For this purpose, two different pedagogical models or scripts were designed in support of students' collaborative activities. Two different empirical studies were conducted (Escape ($N=24$) and Grid ($N28$)) to find out how effective different collaboration scripts were in guiding the learning processes. The data were collected by various means in order to capture, in a systemic manner, the complex relationships and dynamics between different variables within the diverse data. This article will discuss on the basic of the findings how scripting guided groups at the general level and helped students to find resources. Despite this positive effect scripting did not guarantee "high level" participation and there were great variations between the groups. The biggest differences occurred in the level of collaboration shown and in the roles assumed by the participants.

---
* E-mail: raija.hamalainen@ktl.jyu.fi. Tel: +358407442611; Fax: +358 14 260 3201

INTRODUCTION

There is a growing need for distance learning and virtual settings in higher education. At their best, virtual environments enable flexible learning arrangements independent of time and place. However, it is critical to consider how such arrangements could best benefit learning. Virtual learning may vary from individual distance learning (e.g. Beyth-Marom, Chajut, Roccas and Sagiv, 2003) to different variations of group learning (e.g. Baker, 2002). Even within the same type of virtual setting the conditions for distance learning may vary depending on the learner characteristics (Dillenbourg and Self, 1995). Group size can range from small groups to hundreds of people, and the time span from brief one-time sessions to multi-semester courses. The processes may also differ by the type and time of communication. In synchronous interaction learners are expected to interact at the same time without technical or non-technical delay, whereas asynchronous communication involves some delay between participants (Koschmann, 1996).

Educational research is looking for social approaches to foster virtual learning. Computer-Supported Collaborative Learning (CSCL) appears to be a promising approach for higher education for developing knowledge and reasoning skills (e.g. Stahl, 2005). In a collaborative learning process, a group of people construct a new understanding of the topic they are working on. Thus, collaborative learning can be seen as a process of meaning construction. The main idea of collaborative learning is that collaborative knowledge construction, co-ordination of different perspectives, commitment to joint goals, and shared evaluation of group activities enable a group to create something that goes beyond what any one individual could achieve alone (Bereiter, 2002; Stahl, 2003; 2004). However, computer-supported collaborative learning is a complex phenomenon and often difficult to realise in authentic educational settings. Researchers have pointed out various kinds of problems in collaboration at virtual learning environments, such as difficulties to build common ground and shared understanding (Järvelä and Häkkinen, 2002; Mäkitalo, Häkkinen, Leinonen and Järvelä, 2002; Strijbos, Kirschner and Martens, 2004).

In order to achieve productive interactions and to improve the quality of learning, different pedagogical models and technology-based learning tools have been developed to support collaborative learning processes between participants. One way to enhance the process of collaboration as well as to integrate individual and group-level perspectives of learning is to structure learners' actions with the aid of scaffolding or scripted collaboration (Kobbe, Weinberger, Dillenbourg, Harrer, Hämäläinen, Häkkinen and Fischer, 2007). Current research on scripting CSCL is derived partly from earlier work on the approach based on scripted co-operation (Derry, 1999; O'Donnell, 1999).

Collaboration scripts can be compared with a drama manuscript (designed for an educational setting) (Hämäläinen and Häkkinen, 2006). In practice, (collaboration) scripts are sets of instructions prescribing, for instance, how the students should form groups, interact with each other, and solve the problem together (Dillenbourg, 2002; Weinberger, Ertl, Fischer and Mandl, 2005). Through scripting, learners are introduced to activities they would not otherwise engage in on their own (Häkkinen and Mäkitalo-Siegl, 2006). Furthermore, scripts particularly aim to enhance the probability of knowledge generative collaborative activities such as argumentation that triggers the solving of cognitive conflicts (Kobbe *et al.*, 2007).

Collaboration scripts can be differentiated according to whether collaboration is supported by specific instructional means or by technology (Hämäläinen and Arvaja, 2007). According to Lipponen (2001), collaborative technology refers to specific technological support for collaboration built in computer networks. In the case of computer-mediated communication the technology may be used collaboratively, for example, so that people's ideas are restored on the shared platform, which serves as a shared workplace for long term.

The level of scripting can vary, ranging from micro-scripts (direct facilitation of specific activities) to macro-scripts, which typically set the conditions for collaborative learning prior to the actual collaboration phase (Dillenbourg and Jermann, 2006). In "micro-level" scripting, students are assigned with detailed guidance, which is expected to produce specific activities such as asking thought-provoking questions or constructing arguments through which certain learning outcomes are expected. On the other hand, macro-level scripting concentrates on more general ideas, such as what kind of activities should take place in a scripted learning situation and how to set up conditions in which argumentation should occur (Dillenbourg and Jermann, 2006; Kobbe *et al.*, 2007).

According to Dillenbourg and Tchounikine (2007), the purpose of a script is to shape collaborative interactions. If this scaffolding is too lax, it will not produce the expected interactions; if it is too strict, it will spoil the natural richness of free collaboration. When designing scripts, finding the appropriate degree of coercion is therefore critical. The flexibility of the activities or leeway given to students is defined by the script. Macro-scripts offer some flexibility because they rely on indirect constraints generated by the sequence of activities, the form of grouping or the CSCL interface. Micro-scripted structures and interfaces are designed to be rather directive (Dillenbourg and Tchounikine, 2007).

Different pedagogical models serve as a basis for collaboration scripts. Within scripted collaborations different types of schemata can be identified based on the pedagogical model of the script, such as Jigsaw schemata, conflict schemata, reciprocal schemata, project schemata, problem-based learning schemata and science making schemata (Kobbe *et al.*, 2007). The particular scripts used in this study leaned on problem-based learning schemata (Escape) and Jigsaw schemata (Grid). These schemata will be described next in more detail.

Problem-based learning (e.g. Hmelo-Silver and Barrows, 2006; Dochy, Segers, Van den Bossche and Gijbels, 2003) schemata are driven by challenging, open-ended problems. Students work in small groups outlining the problem and striving for shared solutions. Pedagogically the idea is to create meaningful contexts and provide the students with adequate resources, guidance, and instruction as they develop content knowledge and problem-solving skills (Mayo, Donnelly, Nash, and Schwartz, 1993).

The jigsaw type of script leans on the idea of complementary knowledge (e.g. Brown and Campione, 1994). In practice this typically means providing students with different pieces of information and/or distributing the knowledge among the students (see Aronson, Blaney, Stephan, Sikes and Snapp, 1978). Dillenbourg and Jermann (2006) have taken the Jigsaw schemata further to so-called "ConceptGrid". In the first phase of the "ConceptGrid" script each participant reads background information related to his/her personal role, after which all participants together decide on how to distribute the sixteen different concepts to be addressed in their roles. In the third phase, each participant writes a definition of the concepts allocated to his/her role. After that they will have a discussion and decide how to arrange the concepts into a grid table and how to relate them to each other. In the final phase, the tutor reviews the grids and points out possible omissions, inconsistencies and errors (Dillenbourg and Jermann, 2006).

AIMS

The present study leans on the design-based study approach (Brown 1992; Cobb, Confrey, diSessa, Lehrer and Schauble, 2003). In essence, it involves structuring of student groups' collaborative activities by means of pedagogical models (scripts) – whilst they were working on an assignment in specific learning environments – and empirical experiments conducted in an authentic higher education setting. For this purpose, two different pedagogical models or scripts were designed in support of students' collaborative activities. A general aim of this undertaking is to gain insight into scripted collaboration processes in different higher education settings. More precisely, this included designing two different theoretically founded scripted tasks to support collaboration in higher education contexts, analysing how these different types of collaboration scripts guide groups' processes in a higher education setting, and also describing the problems of collaboration occurring during the scripted assignment. In addition, the study describes differences in collaboration in scripted settings of different types.

Instructional Design of the Scripts

At its best, careful pedagogical design such as structuring learners' interactions seems an effective way to improve the outcomes of collaboration (Lehtinen, 2003; Lipponen, 2000). However, according to latest research, it seems that independent development of educational theories and putting them to practice is not enough for the learning needs. Therefore something more needs to be done to empower virtual learning. The design-based research approach is one promising way to integrate research and traditional instructional design (ID) (or instructional system design, ISD) into a shared process in which different types of expertise enable reciprocal development of theory, implementation of the virtual environments and practice in the field of education (Wang and Hannafin, 2005). In this experiment two different types of scripts were designed to make collaboration more effective. Of the scripts discussed in this article, one (Escape) is built in an online 3D game, while the other one (Grid) makes use of a pre-existing platform (Optima), which is used collaboratively. The Escape script is based on problem-based learning (e.g. Hmelo-Silver and Barrows, 2006), whereas the Grid script represents the jigsaw family and ConceptGrid type of scripts (see above). The scripts were mainly the epistemic type (which gives guidance on how to solve the learning task itself, but does not regulate social interaction; cf. Weinberger, Ertl, Fischer and Mandl, 2005) and gave macro level (cf. Dillenbourg and Jermann, 2006) guidance to student work.

Synchronous Escape Script

The Escape script (Table 1) is based on problem-based learning schemata and includes puzzles, or scripted problem scenarios that can be solved only through the effort and commitment of every participant (Price, Rogers, Stanton and Smith, 2003). This was meant to prevent "secret master plans" (Fisher and Mandal, 2001). The purpose of these problem scenarios was to establish the significant key points where collaboration was expected to emerge. In essence, shared workspace collaboration revolves around certain core activities that must be supported: 1) communication and negotiation between group members, 2) keeping track of other group members' work, and 3) stimulated physical activities such as moving tools and objects (Pinelle, Gutwin and Greenberg, 2002).

Table 1. Description of the Escape script

Features	
Script Name	Escape game
Reference	Hmelo-Silver & Barrows, 2006; Dochy, Segers, Van den Bossche and Gijbels, 2003; Mayo, Donnelly, Nash, & Schwartz, 1993
Objectives	Social tasks in which players are expected to practise collaborative learning mechanisms
Target Audience	Higher education students
Context	Includes different collaboration tasks: − open problem − different sets of activities, which were based on participants' interdependency and co-ordination
Locus of representation	External
Granularity	Medium − The script forces students to make decisions together.
Coercion Degree/ Degree of freedom -> moderate	Medium / High − The design task gives guidelines for activities, which are predetermined. Problems are set in fixed order, but teams may create different ways to solve problems. Subtasks need to be solved in the previous phase to be able to move on to the next level.
Duration	1 hour
Environment	3D game (online) Escape is a virtual game for four players. It can be defined as a social and problem-based learning oriented computer game. The role management and player-to-player communication is supported by voice-over-IP speech systems.
Design Principle	− Uses the features of illustrative environment provided by the virtual game − Contains problem-based open problems requiring teamwork − Gameplay emphasises collaboration and co-ordination between the players. − Includes individual puzzles and puzzles designed so that the effort and commitment of many or all players is required for successful completion.

The Escape script includes nine phases, which students were supposed to solve in linear order. First, in the orientation phase the students were expected to establish contacts to each other and they were also provided with some overall status information about the environment. In the second phase the students were expected to solve an open problem (Hmelo-Silver, 2004) wherein they had two alternative ways to solution. Phases 3-8 of the script included four different sets of activities, which were based on participants' interdependency and co-ordination (Barron, 2000). In the end of the script students were expected to work as a team to complete the task.

Asynchronous Grid Script

The jigsaw type script leans on the idea of complementary knowledge (e.g. Brown and Campione, 1994). In practice this typically means providing students with different pieces of information and/or distributing the necessary knowledge among students (Aronson *et al.,* 1978). In the first phase of the "ConceptGrid" script each participant reads background information related to his/her personal role, after which all participants together decide on how to distribute the sixteen different concepts to be addressed in their roles. In the third phase, each participant writes a definition of the concepts allocated to his/her role. After that they will have a discussion and decide how to arrange the concepts into a grid table and how to relate them to each other. In the final phase, the tutor reviews the grids and points out possible omissions, inconsistencies and errors (Dillenbourg and Jermann, 2006). The asynchronous Grid script is based on ConceptGrid. Some context-specific modifications were made to the original "ConceptGrid", and instead of concepts, the students were to work on interrelated topics. However, the phases of the script were quite similar to the original "ConceptGrid" model, like also the resources (theoretical background reading material and the table) used in the study. Also the composition of participants (small groups of 3-5 students) followed the original model.

During the Grid script (Table 2), students were expected to go through five different steps. Moving from one stage to the next presupposed that the previous task was completed. However, the students were not penalised in any way, even if they failed to go through all the steps in the script. First, the groups *received different theoretical background information* (for each participant) to create distinctive personal roles for each student, *which the students themselves allocated within the group.* In the second phase *each student read his/her theory material and made a visit* to a related pre-primary education learning centre so as to strengthen the personal roles created in the first phase. In the third phase *each student filled in a table his/her views and definition concerning the topic* on the basis of the background information and the visit. Combining their individual contributions the table gave the group members a well-rounded picture of the various aspects concerned. In the fourth phase *each group had a shared discussion in which they had to formulate final statements around the topic accounting for opposite points of view.* In the final phase each *group had an analytic discussion* about how well they had been able to construe the task and complete the final statement.

Table 2. Description of the Grid script

Features	
Script Name	Grid
Reference	Dillenbourg & Jermann, 2006; Dillenbourg, 1999; Brown & Campione, 1994; Aronson, Blaney, Stephan, Sikes & Snapp, 1978;
Objectives	Epistemic tasks of designing personal learning plans for students with special needs
Target Audience	Higher education students
Context	Designing personal learning plans for students with special needs. For this assignment students are expected to read theory and make a visit to a related pre-primary education learning centre, fill in a table his/her views and definition concerning the topic and have shared discussion in which they have to formulate final statements around the topic accounting for opposite points of view. Finally the groups enter in analytic discussion
Locus of representation	External
Granularity	Medium – The script encourages students to make decisions together.
Coercion Degree / Degree of freedom -> moderate	Medium / High – The design task gives guidelines for activities, which are predetermined. Problems are set in fixed order, but teams may create different ways to solve problems. Subtasks in the previous phase need to be solved to be able to move on to the next level – students are not penalised on skipping phases.
Duration	3 months
Environments	Optima platform with discussion and shared files
Design Principle	– Uses the features of an existing platform – Contain authentic problems – Emphasises collaboration

METHODS

This study is a design experiment (e.g. Cobb *et al.,* 2003) encompassing both the process of designing two different scripts for a higher education setting and a parallel empirical study where data are collected by various methods. The findings and conclusions of subsequent analysis serve as a basis for further design work.

Subjects

The subjects of the study comprise two sets of higher education students (N=52) (see Table 3). In the online game project (Escape), we had six groups of four students (N=24). On the first day the students were given a half an hour's training session in the game environment. On the second day they played the game, immediately followed by a stimulated recall interview. The online web-based project (Grid) involved seven small groups with 3 to 5 students in each (N=28, including 8 sign language students) and lasted about a month. The leading idea in both studies involved structuring the student groups' collaborative activities by means of a pedagogical model (script), whilst they were working.

Table 3. The subjects and main elements of the studying process for two different scripts (Escape and Grid)

Script	Escape	Grid
N	24	28
type of environment	3D online game	web-based environment
Phases of the script*	the progress structured – open problems – variations in role distribution	the progress and task structured – students distributed the roles in the beginning of the task
Size of the group	4	3-5
Duration	1 hour	1 month

Data Collection

In both experiments the data were collected by various means (see Table 4) in order to capture, in a systemic manner, the complex relationships and dynamics between different variables within the diverse data (Salomon, 1997).

Table 4. Data sources of the Escape and Grid experiments

Script	Escape	Grid
Number of Utterances / Messages	4868	352
Type of communication	spoken dialogue	postings
Timing	synchronous	asynchronous
Data	– background information questionnaires – audio recordings of spoken dialogue (4886 utterances) – observation notes – the players' personal notes + stimulated recall interviews	– background information questionnaires – asynchronous web-based discussions (352 messages) – log data on student activities – a self-report questionnaire – - material used and produced in the computer-based activity

In both experiments background information about the students' previous experiences were collected. Spoken dialogues during the Escape script were audio recorded (4868 utterances), and asynchronous web-based discussions (352 messages) were stored during the Grid task. Moreover, to learn more about students' actions during the scripts, two types of data were gathered. For the Escape experiment, observation notes were made and then verified after the game (by cross-checking the notes of four different observers) and sorted into categories. Correspondingly, the log data on student activities for the Grid script were stored. To find out how students experienced the scripted tasks, stimulated recall interviews were conducted and the players' personal notes were collected for the Escape exercise, and a self-report questionnaire (Järvenoja, Volet and Järvelä, 2005) was administered for the Grid task. In addition, also other materials used and produced in the computer-based activity during the Grid script were collected.

Data Analysis

The focus of data analysis was on determining how the scripts guide the collaboration processes during different tasks. The analysis involved three levels. First, all the data were verified and students' activity levels were categorised in terms of the overall activity of all the students during the Escape exercise and the Grid exercise (how many of students were active in each phase of the scripts and how many times they participated).

The second level of analysis concentrated on how well the groups proceeded through the different steps from the collaboration point of view. The qualitative analysis was driven both by theory (Berger and Calabrese, 1975; King, 1999) and by the data (Rennie and Fergus, 2006), yielding two data classifications. This second analysis was based on the key points scripted into the environments. As an initial step of the classification process, all the different kinds of data were categorised according to the key collaboration points (phases of the script) scripted into the environments. This step involved, for example, analysing the first key problem of each experiment (Escape and Grid) by a) reading the game transcripts and web-discussions several times; b) comparing student experiences (self-report questionnaire, interviews and personal notes) with the logged activities and web discussions, video material and observation notes. At this stage, different teams were identified by the main features of their collaboration. Groups identified as collaborative were active and engaged in high-level discussions. Such engagement showed, for example, in elaborative questioning, explaining and reasoning (e.g. Van Boxtel, Van der Linden, and Kanselaar, 2000). Finally, the categories of different experiments (Escape and Grid) were cross-compared from the viewpoint of collaboration.

RESULTS OF THE EMPIRICAL STUDY

This section will first describe how two different types of collaboration scripts guide student groups' processes in a higher education setting. Further, some differences in collaboration processes in different type of scripted settings (i.e. the game environment and the web-based learning environment) will be illustrated. The last part of this section will focus on problems occurred during scripted task solving.

Groups' Processes Supported by Scripts

Despite obvious differences in the type of communication pertinent to the two different scripts - the Escape exercise consisting of synchronous communication with numerous short utterances, while the Grid script typically featured long contributions with several content items in one message – comparison of the data revealed also similarities in terms of collaboration. In both experiments scripting guided groups at the general level and helped students to find necessary resources. Scripting also guided group processes so that students knew how to proceed during the exercise. During the scripted exercises the students neither got lost nor spent much time in formulating the problem. By the same token, in both experiments scripting directed players towards information sharing, shared knowledge construction, giving feedback to other players and co-ordination of the group's work, as shown in the following excerpts.

Excerpt 1. Information sharing

Escape	Grid
1: Listen everybody, I have something reasonable here [4: I don't have a thing.] that in case you want to get high and here is also like... [TS: mitä tarkoittaa "get high"? Ei kai tässä huumeita kokeilla?]	Sani: Ritu, could you please explain the following clause more precisely; "The role of the child wasn't perhaps always the role of a prestudent but at times also that of a first-grader." So what are the roles of a prestudent and a preschooler? This "prestudent" is quite a new term to me. Learning, Sani-Kaneli Ritu: By prestudent I refer here to a child in preschool education, not a first-grader, for example. I don't know how official this term is, but I've heard it. Maybe that 'role' word is a bit poor choice in this connection,, but I'll use it anyway because I can't think of any better. Let me know if you come up with a better term. Well, by these roles I mean mainly that a first- grader is often expected to be able to concentrate for a while e.g. on learning letters, writing etc. In my opinion a preschooler cannot be expected to be able to concentrate on textbook exercises for a whole lesson. Among preschoolers playing and functional activities in general are more essential than among first-graders. So, if preschoolers and first-graders share the same space, the prestudents have to stay too much at their seats and the activity is very "school-like", which in my view shouldn't necessarily belong to prestudents' daily life. I wonder if this was even more confusing. Made any sense? Asking Ritu

Researcher's Interpretation

In the above examples, the students' information sharing shows firstly in the case of Escape script while Minttu tells that she has some extra information, which may be important for solving the problem, while Santtu comments that he has no information for this task. And secondly, in the case of the Grid script it can be seen while Sani asks Ritu to explain further the roles of prestudents and preschoolers. Then Ritu explains her understanding about the issue and in turn inquires the other group members for better knowledge about the definitions.

Excerpt 2. Giving feedback

Escape	Grid
Pike: Oh, it's Lilli Lilli: So what should we do now? Pike: Push that drum. I was here a moment ago and now... Hanna: Good, good	Conclusion The goal of the collaboration is flexible and safe transition from preschool education to the elementary level. This can be achieved through familiarisation with the school and by discussion with the new teacher, which gives information about the child's learning abilities and personal characteristics. Preschoolers could visit the school on a regular basis, which would make the start of the school easier. There can also be some shared teaching arrangements and various projects in co-operation with the nearby school. Other possible partners include child welfare clinics, hospitals, other day-care centres etc... Nice summary, Simo! I suppose that we two are the only ones in our group who have participated in the discussion and made the summaries. But that's fine with me, or what do you think, Simo? -Manna

Researcher's Interpretation

In the above examples giving feedback shows as Lilli asks what to do and Pike advises her, followed by Hanna's positive acknowledgement. In the Grid example Simo has drawn together the main idea of collaboration in the transition from preschool to primary school. Then Manna gives feedback to Simo about his well-done summary and also comments on the other members' inactivity during the task.

Excerpt 3. Co-ordination

Escape	Grid
Markku: Should we each go to a different direction so as not to waste time? That thing up there shows the points of the compass. I can go north, for instance. Minna: Miia is going south. Jani: I'm heading east, approximately. Markku: Yeah.	Choosing an article Caro: Hello my group. We all were supposed to choose an article we wanted to read. So I'm asking if I could pick the one titled Learning based on play and immediate surroundings Assi: Howdy! I don't know if this is the right place to write but if no one else hasn't taken that text "Co-operation for the child's best interest ...", then I could take it. And one other thing, should anyone have any info about the exam, I mean what are the books to be read, I'd appreciate it very much. Nina: Hi! I read the article" "Co-operation for the child's best interest in Norway" and already completed the assignment, as well... Vera: Hi there! I think I'm lagging behind the deadline but... ☺ I could take that "Preschool education culture from the children's point of view" by A. Brotherus. Nobody taken it yet, have you?

Researcher's Interpretation

In the above Escape excerpt, co-ordination shows as Markku suggests spreading out and the team agrees on the directions accordingly. In the excerpt from Grid, the participants negotiate a solution as regards their respective choices for an article to be read.

In both experiments students set themselves rules and used self-scripting on those parts of the exercise that were not guided by the script. In Escape this showed as low-level action plans during the play, and Grid students developed strategies for role distribution within their groups. The Escape experiment involved plenty of student negotiation, whereas the Grid students resorted to shared knowledge construction rather than negotiation.

Group-Based Variations in Collaboration

Since the scripts were used in settings of different types, there were also variations in the forms of collaboration, not only between the two different scripts but also between the different groups following the same script. In other words, group and individual actions varied a great deal despite the scripted environments (Escape and Grid). The groups differed in terms of the time spent on the task, the degree of collaboration shown, the roles assumed and attitudes displayed by their members. Typical of the Escape experiment was that all the groups set themselves goals and used humour during the game process. In contrast, the Grid script did not invoke any goal setting (other than completing the task) and the amount of humour in student communication was very low.

Variation in Synchronous Interaction

In the Escape script, five of the six groups achieved collaboration at some points of the game at least. The five collaborative groups followed the predefined, scripted order of sequences, which ensured successful completion and also made all students contribute to the efforts at each stage of the script. During the experiment, the groups used different modes of interaction to solve the game problems. All groups set themselves goals, but the actual decision-making process ranged from group decisions to leader-oriented ones. The group decisions affected the game and the process of team formation in different ways at different stages of the game session.

The time spent on the game varied from about 45 minutes to 1 hour and 20 minutes. A total of 4868 utterances were sent during the script, but the number of utterances varied between the groups from 495 (Group 2) to 1077 (Group 6). As shown in Table 5 below, the groups varied also in terms of their discussion activity in different phases of the script.

Table 5. Discussion activity in different phases of the Escape script

Gr.	Phase 1	Phase 2	Phase 3	Phase 4	Phase 5	Phase 6	Phase 7	Phase 8	Phase 9	Total	Proportion of all utterances
	(%)	(%)	(%)	(%)	(%)	(%)	(%)	(%)	(%)		(%)
G1	2.8	9.7	12.8	11.5	5.9	15.5	11.6	28.2	2.0	100%	17.1
G2	4.8	6.5	5.5	14.9	11.7	8.5	17.6	12.1	18.4	100%	10.2
G3	4.4	19.6	17.9	9.7	10.0	9.9	12.2	13.1	3.1	100%	21.9
G4	1.8	17.4	13.7	15.6	7.2	13.9	22.3	5.0	3.0	100%	15.1
G5	4.4	5.9	14.2	3.6	15.7	8.2	17.9	26.5	3.6	100%	13.6
G6	2.8	3.6	4.4	11.3	7.1	31.2	25.3	12.3	1.9	100%	22.1

Variation in Asynchronous Interaction

During the Grid exercise, scripting guided collaboration on a general level, ensuring that all the groups were able to carry through the task and that all students contributed to the effort. The activity level of participants varied between the different steps both in terms of the number of active participants and the degree of activity in each phase of the script, as shown in Table 6 below. All postings (N=352) were sent in the 4th and 5th phase, but the number of messages varied between the groups from 29 (Group 4) up to 92 (Group 7). As regards the time limits, six groups kept in pace with the timeline set by the script, while one of the groups (Group 3) exceeded it by over a week. A total of 30 students started the course, but two of them dropped out. While all groups followed the Grid script, 4 out of the 28 participants skipped one or more of the steps of the script. However, all groups completed the task successfully. The widest variation in the rate of participation of individual learners occurred in phase 4 (web-discussion), where the most active member of Group 7 sent 34 messages while a "free-rider" from Group 6 sent only 2 messages.

Problems In Scripted Collaboration Processes

Despite the positive effects of scripting described above, there were some problems as well. Within both experiments student groups solved problems in mutual understanding and conflict situations during the scripted exercise were rare. Thus, the scripting actually failed to create significant cognitive conflicts. Both of the scripts required individual efforts from each student, so that such contribution was necessary in order to complete the task. However scripting did not guarantee equal and "high level" participation within the groups.

Table 6. Participation rate and discussion activity in phases 4 and 5 of the Grid script

Group	Phase 1	Phase 2	Phase 3	Phase 4	Phase 5	Proportion of all postings
G1 active participants	3/3	3/3	3/3	3/3	(3/3 =)	
% of messages	-	-	-	*89.7%*	*10.1%*	11.1%
G2 active participants	4/4	4/4	4/4	4/4	4/4	
% of messages	-	-	-	90.7%	9.3%	12.2%
G3 active participants	4/4	4/4	3/4	4/4	2/4	
% of messages	-	-	-	91.7%	8.3%	13.6%
G4 active participants	4/4	4/4	4/4	4/4	3/4	
% of messages	-	-	-	86.2%	13.8%	8.2%
G5 active participants	4/4	4/4	4/4	4/4	4/4	
% of messages	-	-	-	90%	10%	14.2%
G6 active participants	5/5	5/5	4/5	5/5	4/5	
% of messages	-	-	-	90.2%	9.8%	14.5%
G7 active participants	5/5	5/5	5/5	5/5	4/5	
% of messages	-	-	-	93.5%	6.5%	26.1%
Total						100%

There were problems in both experiments with regard to group members' attitudes towards collaborative work. A special problem with the Grid script was the low level of learning activities in three of the groups, and more specifically the extensive use of copy-pasting text from individual tables to the conversations. Besides, in one group there was one particular member with a very dominating attitude towards the work, who repeatedly indicated in his messages that the level of working did not reach his standards for virtual working. Problems occurred when he tried to ask the others' opinions; he was not able to formulate his messages in a way that the other members would have found appreciative.

While there were great variations between the groups within same phases of the Escape script, a particular problem was attributable to non-collaborative attitudes towards other group members, which obviously hindered collaboration. For instance, in one group three out of the four players behaved in a way that was counter-effective in terms of collaboration. One of the group members failed to share information, another one can be characterised as a "lonely rider", who always tried to solve the problems by himself, whereas the third one tried very hard to work collaboratively and was extremely supportive towards her fellow players. The problem was that she did not really listen to other people's suggestions, with the result that she was very supportive about their ideas even when the game environment did not work as she expected.

CONCLUSION

This study involved an attempt to design two different theoretically founded scripted tasks to support collaborative learning in higher education contexts and to investigate how these different types of collaboration scripts guide groups' processes in such settings and what kind of problems would possibly occur during scripted task solving. In addition, the aim was to study differences in collaboration in different types of scripted setting. Although the forms of communication differed (asynchronous and synchronous), scripting guided working in both experimental exercises at the general level; for example, helping the students find necessary resources and proceed through the exercise. During the scripted exercises the students neither got lost nor spent much time in formulating the problem. By the same token, in both experiments scripting directed players towards information sharing, shared knowledge construction, giving feedback to other players and co-ordination of the group's work. The forms of collaboration varied not only between the two different scripts, but also between different groups following the same script. According to Arvaja (2007), collaborative learning is achieved under unique circumstances, the significance of which is interactively constructed by the learners and cannot be directly predicted. When designing contexts for future learning, it is therefore essential to also account for individuals' needs during collaboration processes.

On the other hand, there seemed to be problems in collaboration as well. For example, in both experiments there were groups dominated by one of the members. Hence, scripting ought to have guided students' social interactions more strongly, which has been indicated as an effective way to support collaborative problem solving (e.g. with the aid of an argumentative script) (Stegmann, Weinberger, Fischer and Mandl, 2005). Despite the problems in collaboration processes, latest studies have indicated that minimally guided instruction is less effective than instructional approaches that emphasise the guidance of the student learning processes (Kirschner, Sweller and Clark, 2006). Therefore collaboration scripts can be seen as a promising way to give instructional support, to trigger productive collaborative activities and to provide structure and support for otherwise open learning environments (Dillenbourg, 2002; Hämäläinen, 2007; Hämäläinen, Manninen, Järvelä and Häkkinen, 2006; Weinberger, 2003).

ACKNOWLEDGMENTS

This study is supported by the Academy of Finland (project no. 200167). Special thanks to Dr. Maarit Arvaja, Prof. Päivi Häkkinen and Mr Tuomo Suontausta (University of Jyväskylä), Prof. Sanna Järvelä's research group and Prof. Tony Manninen's research group (University of Oulu).

REFERENCES

Aronson, E., Blaney, N., Stephan, C., Sikes, J. and Snapp, M. (1978). *The Jigsaw classroom*. Beverly Hills, CA: Sage Publications, Inc.

Arvaja, M. (2007). Contextual perspective in comparing meaning negotiations of two small groups' web-based discussion in university settings. *ijCSCL*, in press.

Baker, M. (2002). Forms of cooperation in dyadic problem-solving. In P. Salembier and H. Benchekroun (Eds.) *Cooperation and complexity* (pp.587-620). Sociotechnical Systems,Vol. 16. Paris: Hermès.

Barron, B. (2000). Achieving coordination in collaborative problem-solving groups. *The Journal of the Learning Sciences, 9*(4), 403-436.

Bereiter, C. (2002). *Education and mind in the knowledge age*. Hillsdale, NJ: Erlbaum.

Berger, C. R. and Calabrese, R. (1975). Some explorations in initial interaction and beyond: Toward a developmental theory of interpersonal communication. *Human Communication Research,* 1, 99-112.

Beyth-Marom, R., Chajut, E., Roccas, S. and Sagiv, L. (2003). Internet-assisted versus traditional distance learning environments: factors affecting students´ preferences. *Computers and Education*, 41, 65-76.

Brown, A. (1992). Design experiments: Theoretical and methodological challenges in creating complex interventions in classroom settings. *Journal of the Learning Sciences, 2*(2), 141-178.

Brown, A. and Campione, J. (1994). Guided discovery in a community of learners. In K. McGilly (Ed.) *Classroom lessons: Integrating cognitive theory and classroom practice.* (pp. 227-270). Cambridge, MA: MIT Press.

Cobb, P., Confrey, J., diSessa, A., Lehrer, R. and Schauble, L. (2003). Design Experiments in Educational Research. Web version of *Educational Researcher, 32*(1), 9-14.

Derry, S. J. (1999). A fish called peer learning: Searching for common themes. In A. M. O'Donnell, and A. King (Eds.), *Cognitive perspectives on peer learning* (pp. 197-211). Mahwah, NJ: Erlbaum.

Dillenbourg, P. and Self, J.A.. (1995). Designing human-computer collaborative learning, in C. O'Malley (Ed.), *Computer-Supported Collaborative Learning*, Springer-Verlag, Berlin, 245-264.

Dillenbourg, P. (2002). Over-scripting CSCL: The risks of blending collaborative learning with instructional design. In P. A. Kirschner (Ed.), *Three worlds of CSCL. Can we support CSCL* (pp. 61-91). Heerlen, Open Universiteit Nederland.

Dillenbourg, P., and Jermann, P. (2006). Designing integrative scripts. In F. Fischer, H. Mandl, J. Haake, and I. Kollar (Eds.), *Scripting computer-supported collaborative learning: Cognitive, computational and educational perspectives.* New York: Springer.

Dillenbourg, P. and Tchounikine, P. (2007). Flexibility in macro-scripts for computer-supported collaborative learning. *Journal of Computer Assisted Learning, 23*(1), 1-13.

Dochy, F., Segers, M., Van den Bossche, P. and Gijbels, D. (2003). Effects of problem-based learning: a meta-analysis. *Learning and Instruction, 13*(5), 533-568.

Fischer, F., and Mandl, H. (2001). Facilitating the construction of shared knowledge with graphical representation tools in face-to-face and computer-mediated scenarios. In P. Dillenbourg, A. Eurelings, and K. Hakkarainen (Eds.), *European perspectives on computer-supported collaborative learning* (pp. 230-236). Maastricht, Netherlands: McLuhan Institute.

Hmelo-Silver, C. E. (2004). Problem-based learning: What and how do students learn? *Educational Psychology Review*, 16, 235-266.

Hmelo-Silver, C. E. and Barrows, H. S. (2006). Goals and strategies of a problem-based learning facilitator. *Interdisciplinary Journal of Problem-based Learning*, 1. 21-39.

Häkkinen, P. and Mäkitalo-Siegl, K. (2006). Educational Perspectives to Scripting CSCL. In F. Fischer, H. Mandl, J. Haake, and I. Kollar (Eds.), *Scripting Computer-Supported Collaborative Learning – Cognitive, Computational, and Educational Perspectives.* Computer-Supported Collaborative Learning Series, New York: Springer.

Hämäläinen, R. Manninen, T. Järvelä, S. and Häkkinen, P. (2006). Learning to Collaborate: Designing Collaboration in a 3-D Game Environment. *The Internet and Higher Education, 9*(1), 47-61.

Hämäläinen, R. (2007). Designing and evaluating collaboration in a virtual game environment for vocational learning. *Computers and Education,* in press.

Hämäläinen, R and Häkkinen, P. (2007) Verkkotyöskentelyn vaiheistaminen yksilöllisen ja yhteisöllisen oppimisen tukena. In S. Järvelä, P. Häkkinen and E. Lehtinen (Eds.) Oppimisen teoria ja teknologian opetuskäyttö. (pp. 230-246). Finland: WSOY.

Hämäläinen, R. and Arvaja, M. (2007). Scripted collaboration and group-based variations in a higher education CSCL context, submitted.

Järvelä, S. and Häkkinen, P. (2002). Web-based cases in teaching and learning – the quality of discussions and a stage of perspective taking in asynchronous communication. *Interactive Learning Environments, 10*(1), 1-22.

Järvenoja, H., Volet, S., and Järvelä, S. (2005). *Investigating self-, other- and shared-regulation in socially challenging learning situations: An instrument to assess dynamics of students' emotion and motivation regulation processes.* Manuscript submitted for publication.

King, A. (1999). Discourse patterns for mediating peer learning. In A. M. O'Donnell, and A. King (Eds.), *Cognitive perspectives on peer learning* (pp. 87-115). Mahwah, NJ: Erlbaum.

Kirschner, P.A., Sweller, J., and Clark, R.E. (2006). Why minimal guidance during instruction does not work: An analysis of the failure of constructivist, discovery, problem-based, experiential, and inquiry-based teaching. *Educational Psychologist, 41*(2), 75-86.

Kobbe, L., Weinberger, A., Dillenbourg, P., Harrer, A., Hämäläinen, R., Häkkinen, P and F. Fischer (2007). Specifying Computer-Supported Collaboration Scripts. *ijCSCL*, in press.

Koschmann, T. (1996). CSCL: Theory and practice of an emerging paradigm. Mahwah, NJ: LEA.

Lehtinen, E. (2003). Computer-supported collaborative learning: An approach to powerful learning environments. In E. de Corte, L. Verschaffel, N. Entwistle, and J. van Merriëboer (Eds.), *Powerful learning environments: Unravelling basic components and dimensions* (pp. 35-54). Amsterdam: Pergamon.

Lipponen, L. (2000). Towards knowledge building discourse: From facts to explanations in primary students' computer mediated discourse. *Learning Environments Research, 3*(2), 179-199.

Lipponen, L. (2001) *Computer-supported collaborative learning: From promises to reality.* Dissertation. University of Turku.

Mayo, P., Donnelly, M.B., Nash, P.P., and Schwartz, R.W. (1993). Student perceptions of tutor effectiveness in a problem-based surgery clerkship. *5*(4), 227-233.

Mäkitalo, K., Häkkinen, P., Leinonen, P., and Järvelä, S. (2002) Mechanisms of common ground in case-based web-discussions in teacher education. *The Internet and Higher Education* 5(3), 247-265.

O'Donnell, A. M. (1999). Structuring dyadic interaction through scripted cooperation. In A. M. O'Donnell, and A. King (Eds.), *Cognitive perspectives on peer learning* (pp. 179-196). Mahwah, NJ: Lawrence Erlbaum.

Pinelle, D., Gutwin, C. and Greenberg, S. (2002). The task analysis for groupware usability evaluation: Modeling shared-workspace tasks with the mechanics of collaboration. *Human Computer Interaction*. Retrieved November 11, 2005, from http://www.cpsc.ucalgary.ca/grouplab/papers/2002/02-Task-Analysis.Report/task-analysis-report.pdf.

Price, S., Rogers, Y., Stanton, D., and Smith, H. (2003). A New Conceptual Framework for CSCL: Supporting Diverse Forms of Reflection through Multiple Interactions. In (eds) B. Wasson, S. Ludvigsen, U. Hoppe, *Designing for Change in Networked Learning Environments. Proceedings of the International Conference on Computer Supported Collaborative Learning* 2003.

Rennie, D.L. and Fergus, K. (2006). Embodied Categorizing in Grounded Theory Method. Methodical Hermeneutics in Action. *Theory and Psychology, 16* (4), 483–503.

Salomon, G. (1997). Novel constructivist learning environments and novel technologies: Some issues to be concerned with. Invited Keynote Address presented at the 7th European Conference for Research on Learning and Instruction, Athens, Greece, August 26-30.

Stahl, G. (2003). *Meaning and interpretation in collaboration. Design for change in networked learning environments*. Retrieved November 11, 2005, from http://www.cis.drexel.edu/faculty/gerry//publications/conferences/2003/cscl/cscl2003.doc

Stahl, G. (2004). Building collaborative knowing. Elements of a social theory of CSCL. In P. Dillenbourg (Series Ed.) and J. W. Strijbos, P. A. Kirschner and R. L. Martens (Vol Eds.) Computer-supported collaborative learning, Vol 3. *What we know about CSCL... and implementing it in higher education* (pp. 53-85). Boston, MA: Kluwer Academic Publishers.

Stahl, G. (2005). *Group Cognition: Computer Support for Collaborative Knowledge Building*. Cambridge, MA: MIT Press.

Stegmann, K., Weinberger, A., Fischer, F., and Mandl, H. (2005). Scripting Argumentation in computer-supported learning environments. In P. Gerjets, P. A. Kirschner, J. Elen and R. Joiner (Eds.), *Instructional design for effective and enjoyable computer-supported learning. Proceedings of the first joint meeting of the EARLI SIGs "Instructional Design" and "Learning and Instruction with Computers"* (pp. 320-330) [CD-ROM]. Tübingen: Knowledge Media Research Center.

Strijbos, J.-W., Kirschner, P.A. and Martens, R.L. (2004). What we know about CSCL and what we do not (but need to) know about CSCL. In J. W. Strijbos, P. A. Kirschner and R. L. Martens (Eds.), *What we know about CSCL: And implementing it in higher education* (pp. 245-261). Boston, MA: Kluwer Academic/Springer Verlag.

Van Boxtel, C., Van der Linden, J., and Kanselaar, G. (2000) Collaborative learning tasks and the elaboration of conceptual knowledge. *Learning and Instruction* 10 (4), 311-330.

Wang, F. and Hannafin, M.J. (2005). Design-based research and technology-enhanced learning environments. *Educational Technology Research and Development, 53*(4), 5-23.

Weinberger, A. (2003). *Scripts for Computer-Supported Collaborative Learning Effects of social and epistemic cooperation scripts on collaborative knowledge construction.* Dissertation an der Fakultät für Psychologie und Pädagogik der Ludwig-Maximilians-Universität München.

Weinberger, A., Ertl, B., Fischer, F., and Mandl, H. (2005). Epistemic and social scripts in computer-supported collaborative learning. *Instructional Science, 33*(1), 1-30.

In: Global Issues in Higher Education
Editor: Pamela B. Richards, pp. 215-235

ISBN: 978-1-60021-802-6
© 2007 Nova Science Publishers, Inc.

Chapter 10

OUTCOMES OF PROJECT-BASED STUDIES AND STUDENT SELF-REGULATION OF LEARNING

*Laura Helle** and *Päivi Tynjälä***

* University of Turku, Faculty of Education, 20014 Turku, Finland
** University of Jyväskylä, Institute for Educational Research
P.O. Box 35, 40014 Jyväskylän yliopisto, Finland

INTRODUCTION

Why is it that some students succeed in their studies better than others? Are they smarter? Do they study more? Do they use more and better learning strategies? Do they hold certain beliefs about learning that make them more resilient to challenges? Or were they so precocious that they have in a sense had an academic mind set for significantly longer than others? There have been studies and entire lines of research exploring all of these questions and they most likely all contribute to partially explaining success in higher education. For instance, research on epistemological beliefs has shown that academic performance is related to styles or ways of knowing and especially to the belief that learning does not occur instantaneously, but takes time ($r = 0.31$) (Schommer-Aikins and Easter, 2006). According to studies on expertise, there is a general rule that attaining a high performance level in just about any field requires at least 10 years of intense preparation; this applies at least to the domains of chess, musical composing and science (Ericsson, Krampe and Tesch-Römer, 1993). Recently, it has been suggested that it is the time spent on certain study strategies that distinguishes the best (science) students from the others although the best students also were shown to study more (Nandagopal and Ericsson, 2007). In a study concerning engineering education, it was similarly found that a deep study strategy was the most important predictor of study success, while surface strategy and doubt about one's abilities were negatively related to study success Tynjälä et al., 2005). Also intelligence has a role in at least in inductive science learning as evidenced by a recent study by Prins et al. (2006). However, the correlation between intelligence or other ability measures and learning is surprising low – in

---

* Telephone number: +358-2-333 8612; Fax number: +358-2-333 8830.

the range of 0.2-0.35 and its role appears to decline with experience (Ericsson et al., 1993). The starting point of this chapter backed by a growing amount of evidence is that what really counts is metacognitive activity or student self-regulation of learning, i.e. way the students actually go about studying (Boekaerts and Cascallar, 2006; Nieminen, Lindblom-Ylänne and Lonka, 2004; Veenman, 1997).

In our view, *self-regulated students are characterised by the fact that they are coordinated in their actions*: they know what it takes to learn the essential parts of a course, they are totally self-motivated, they plan and invest the time needed to carry out learning activities and finally they carry out with discipline all the activities necessary to gain the objectives while monitoring time and progress and making adjustments in the course of action if necessary. Since the process of self-regulation is very holistic, certain authors have resorted to the study of larger patterns of learning incorporating not only the monitoring and control of learning processes but also motivation and epistemological beliefs. Such models have been found to account for approximately 25 % of variance in means exam scores across different domains. (See also Alexander, 2003).

Although it cannot be denied that self-regulated activity is a whole, for analytical purposes, it may be useful to define self-regulation is terms of how students actually go about studying. It may also be helpful to distinguish between an inner and outer layer of self-regulation. The inner layer involves "regulation of the study process": goal setting, planning and implementing plans. It is emphasized that meta-cognitive activity can focus on *any* of these activities (Kaldeway and Korthagen, 1995). The outer layer has to do with the setting of personal (study related) priorities and time management (cf. Pintrich, 1999; Boekaerts, 1999).

Student self-regulation is likely to be even more important in the context of *project-based learning*, which has been argued to pose more demands on student self-regulation than conventional lecture-based instruction (see Vermunt, 2003). The essence of project-based learning is that a question or problem serves to organise and drive activities; and these activities culminate in a final product that addresses the driving question (Blumenfeld et al., 1991). In addition, it involves student initiative and it goes on for a considerable length of time (cf. Thomas, 2000, 1). For example, students taking a project-based introductory course in astronomy addressed the (implicit) question: "How are the planets in the solar system positioned relative to one another and the sun?" To answer this question, they were instructed to construct a three-dimensional model of the solar system and to provide explanations on how the model differs from reality. In more vocational domains projects are typically *work-based*: for example, Vaz (2000) reported on a number of students and their supervisors investigating whether it would be feasible to implement a vacuum sewer system in Venice. The basic idea – and challenge - in different types of project-based learning is that as students solve complex real life problems they are pressed to either to apply or to figure out concepts related to one or several domains (cf. Olesen and Jensen, 1999; Thomas, 2000; Markowitsch and Messerer, 2006). Projects pose additional demands on student self-regulation due to the fact that resources have to be sought out. Projects also pose high demands on time (and resource) management since projects are by definition extensive. In fact, a study by Ertmer, Newby and MacDougall (1996) indicated that students low in self-regulation of learning neither profited from nor enjoyed case-based instruction as much as students higher in self-regulation of learning.

RESEARCH ON WORK-RELATED PROJECT-BASED LEARNING AND STUDENT SELF-REGULATION

The purpose of this chapter is to explore affective and learning outcomes of university-level project-based learning. Learning outcomes refer to knowledge and skill acquisition, whereas affective outcomes refer to feeling-related outcomes, such as intrinsic study motivation (ie. perception that studies have intrinsic meaning vs. extrinsic or no meaning at all), course satisfaction and perceived impact. The work is based on two series of studies conducted in work-based project learning environments in the context university education, regular and extension training. The contribution of the studies is that they provide novel and partly unexpected findings to help promote understanding of self-regulation in context. In addition, implications for organizing project-based learning for regular students and adult students are discussed.

The first series to be presented involved a project-based course for university students in the middle phase of their studies in the field of information systems design (Case ISD). The basic idea of the course, which has been running and continually developed since the 70's, was that small groups of students complete commissioned assignments for authentic clients. The course has also been a topic of research since the late nineties, studies indicating that it may serve to promote acquiring strategic competence in using domain-specific methods, an overall view of project work, social skills such as co-operation and communication skills, and resource management skills (e.g. resources allocation and time management) (Eteläpelto, 2000; Tynjälä, 2001). The most recent results to be presented in this chapter stem from data collected at the turn of the millennium[1].

The second series of case studies concerned a university extension training program for human resource development personnel (Case ET) funded by the European Social Fund. It was a one-shot pilot training program, in which the participants worked on projects stemming from their own work. It has also been the topic of a line of studies exploring the process and products of learning (see Tuominen, 2003; Leppänen, 2005; Helle, Tuominen & Olkinuora., 2006). A synthesis and refinement of the results is presented in this chapter. Data in both Case ISD and ET included questionnaires administered to the students at the beginning and end of training (including self-regulation items from the ILS by Vermunt (1994) as well as student and teacher interviews. The research questions are the following:

(1) What were the learning outcomes?
(2) What were the affective outcomes?
(3) How was student self-regulation manifest in the course of training?
(4) To what extent was it related to affective or cognitive outcomes?

---

[1] They are presented in more detail by Helle et al. (2007a) and Helle et al. (2007b).

CASE INFORMATION SYSTEMS DESIGN (ISD)

Instructional Procedure

The subject of the study was a mandatory work-based project course in information systems design at the University of Jyväskylä, Finland. During the course, students worked on a commissioned information systems design assignment, which they were to complete in teams of 4-5 students in the course of seven months (400 hours). At the beginning of the project studies, the coordinator gave a series of lectures on project management, which was the focus of the course. Then teams were formed: students were introduced to a series of possible clients and assignments (i.e. projects), after which students self-selected a topic of interest. During the unit, the students were mentored or coached by a university teacher and, ideally, by a representative of the client. Teams and individual students also had an external counsellor at their service. Teams, instead of individual team members, were graded on the basis of a three-way assessment partnership. In other words, teachers, client representatives and the students themselves all met on a regular basis and contributed to the grading procedure, in which both process and product were assessed, the product accounting for only 20 % of the final grade.

The objectives of the course were a) to provide an integrating experience especially in terms of programming and design, b) to provide the students an authentic and holistic experience of the work of an information systems designer, and c) to provide the students with an experience of project work and project management.

Participants

The students (N=58) who participated in the mandatory project-based course were mainly third-year students majoring in information systems design. Since we were concerned over the fact that observable effects might in fact be due to maturation or to learning from the first two questionnaires, we decided to use a comparison group (N=51). The median age for the project group was 23 years; 43 were male and 8 female. The students' previous working experience in the field of information technology was in general rather limited, 17 % having no previous experience, but there were some exceptions, as 14 % reported having had more than three years of working experience. Data were obtained, depending on data collection (and analysis) method, on 41 to 48 students. The comparison group was composed of Finnish computer science students in the same phase of their studies without a project component.

Data Collection Instruments, Procedures, Analysis

The project students were administered a questionnaire at the beginning and end of the project-based course and the comparison group at the same interval of seven months. The first questionnaire dealt with themes such as motives with respect to the project-based course, conceptions of expertise and general study orientations related to *studying the subject one is majoring in*. The students were requested to answer the items dealt with in this study on a five-point Likert scale. There were two central constructs: *intrinsic study motivation* and *self-regulation*. The former was measured with six items from the Task Booklet of Learning by Lonka and Lindblom-Ylänne (1996) on the basis of the Inventory of Learning Strategies (ILS) (Vermunt, 1994), whereas the latter by four items from the Inventory of General Study Orientations (IGSO) (Mäkinen, 2003). For more detail, see Table 1.

Table 1. An overview of the central constructs of Case ISD

Name and meaning of construct	Source, number of items and reliability
-*Self-regulation of learning* referring to the quality and amount of cognitive or metacognitive learning activity the student selects to engage in	Three items out of six lack of regulation items (reversed) and three out of eleven self-regulation items from the Task Booklet of Learning by Lonka & Lindblom-Ylänne on the basis of the Inventory of Learning Styles (ILS); Cronbach α=0.59 (in the project group: α=0.73)
- *Intrinsic study motivation* referring to the perception that studies and learning have intrinsic meaning (vs. extrinsic meaning or no meaning at all)	Two items from the deep orientation scale and two items from the lack of meaning scale from the IGSO (Mäkinen, 2003; Mäkinen et al., 2004, Cronbach α=0.63

In the second questionnaire, which was administered at the end of the course, the wording of the items was modified, to explicitly pertain to the project-based course, or in the case of the comparison group, to the previous seven month period.

In addition, the students were interviewed directly after the course. The themes of the one-hour semi-structured interviews were as follow: motivational orientations and learning experiences, development of expertise, group dynamics and use of information technology. In the beginning of the interview the students were asked in an open-ended manner how they experienced the course. Later on they were asked whether they found the course motivating, and why or why not. Students were also asked to select one or several work roles describing their own work role in the student team.

A between-groups repeated-measures ANOVA was carried out on self-report measures of intrinsic study motivation and cognitive processing. A similar analysis was performed in the comparison group. The results obtained from the ANOVA analysis were double checked by a regression model, in which increase in intrinsic motivation was the dependent variable and self-regulation of learning was the predictor.

RESULTS

Affective Outcomes and Their Relation to Student Self-Regulation of Learning

The course in general was perceived as an overwhelmingly positive experience. Intrinsic study motivation increased from M=3.77 (SD=0.52) to M=4.35 (SD=0.46) in the project group, and this effect was statistically significant, $F(1,38)=39.0$, $p<0.001$, $\eta^2=0.51$. This result was corroborated by interview results.

When the students were asked how they had experienced the course, they typically said that the course had been hard work, but for the most part a positive and rewarding experience, and many expressed relief and a sense of accomplishment once it was over. Several students perceived the course as exceptionally valuable working experience, even those students who had other working experience: the special arrangements had allowed them to experience more responsibility and more prestigious work roles than are typically offered to novices. Nine of the 44 students interviewed described the course in terms of superlatives such as the best course or one of the best courses in the department, at the university, or in terms of what the university can possibly offer, and an additional three students found the course "very motivating" when asked whether the course had been motivating. In addition, it was found that especially the group of students who scored low in self-regulation seemed to benefit from the project-based course in terms of intrinsic study motivation. The interaction effect was statistically significant, $F(2,34)=5.9$, $p=0.007$, $\eta^2=0.26$. See Figure 1.

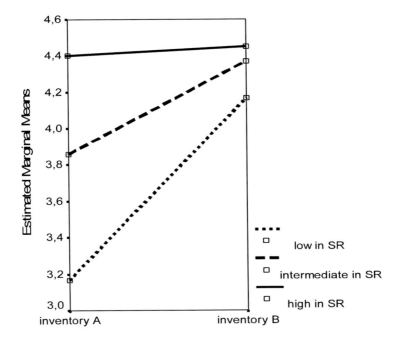

Figure 1. The development of intrinsic study motivation in the project group by students who scored low, moderate and high in self-regulation of learning.

Learning Outcomes

As for learning outcomes, the students *reported* to be learning domain-specific skills (e.g. established ways of describing systems and programming), dealing with the client, communication with different people and project management. In addition, it was reported to strengthen professional self-concept and to clarify career goals and to help build an integrative view of constructing an information system. It is worth noting that these self-reported learning outcomes are strikingly similar to those reported by Tynjälä (2001).

In order not to take self-reports at face value, the self reports were examined more carefully for depth and frequency. It appeared that the increase in domain-specific skills and strengthening of professional self-concept were the outcomes that were mentioned most frequently, whereas there was substantially less evidence on the building of an integrative view of constructing an information system. Over 80 % of the students (40 out of 48) could pinpoint some aspect of domain-specific knowledge or skill that they had applied during the course. Approximately three out of four students (37 out of 49) could, when explicitly asked to do so, name new domain-specific knowledge or skills that they had learnt. Most of these students reported to have learnt to use new tools. As for strengthening of self-concept, approximately 40 % of the students clearly stated that the course had a beneficial effect on (professional) self-concept despite the fact that they were not asked directly about self-concept. Some students reported gaining in self-confidence while others reported being surprised discovering what they were able to do or learn. The teachers also reported that the students' gain in self-confidence was one of the major outcomes of the course. It was expected that students would report that the course had helped build an integrative view of constructing an information system, since this was one of the main objectives of the course. However, this types of reports were mainly casual references to "project phases". Four students were judged to provide articulate accounts related to building an information system. Thus, is there any evidence that students are actually learning more than some ICT tools and some features of interacting with other people?

In order to answer the question, it is necessary to take a look at results from a preceding cohort of students using an alternative methodology. Eteläpelto (2000) explored ISD learning by using a carefully constructed pretest and posttest design. The participants, who consisted of 33 students on the project-based course and 40 "experts" with at least two years of working experience as teachers or systems analysts after graduation, were asked to solve the task of developing a micro-computer based information system that would help families plan and monitor their domestic finances. Thus, the main data consisted of participants' solutions to the design task. The data was analysed according to "systematic content analysis" and resulted in a categorisation system with four categorical variables (scope of solution, solution structure, strategy of IS development and identification with client), two of which were analysed by two independent evaluators as two variables were considered self-evident. The final categorisation is presented in APPENDIX 3. Results indicated that the students differed from the professionals in their solution patterns both on the pretest and the posttest. The students used the initial work phase model more often, whereas the professionals used the comprehensive and interactive approach more often both on the pretest and on the posttest. The analysis of the shifts among the students indicated that 37 % of the students did not change their solution pattern. The most notable change was that 17 % of the students shifted from the first pattern, the initial work-phase model, to the second one, the individualised and interactive prototyping model. The shifts and the distribution of the solution pattern of the experts is presented in Table 2.

Table 2. Solutions patterns among novices and experts and shifts among novices during project-based course (Eteläpelto, 2000) (reprinted with permission of Elsevier)

Frequencies of the five solution patterns among novices and experts

Solution pattern	Professional Client	Novices (N=30)		Experts (N=39)
		Beginning	End	
I. Initial work-phase model		33.3%	33.3%	2.6%
II. Individualised and interactive prototyping		13.3%	43.3%	38.5%
III. Customer-centred identification		10.0%	6.7%	10.3%
IV. Dialogue-oriented marketing strategy		26.7%	10.0%	17.9%
V. Comprehensive and interactive approach		0.0%	3.3%	18.9%
Unclassifiable		16.7%	3.3%	12.8%

CASE EXTENSION TRAINING (ET)

Instructional Procedure

The main objective of the 10 credit point[2] university extension training program was to provide the participants with knowledge and skills of competence development and competence evaluation. The main topics were the following: competence and learning, transformative learning environments, methods of learning (work-based learning, problem-based learning), evaluation and assessment, using the scenario technique and networking.

The structure of the training program was the following:

- work-based project (undertaken as a part of the participant's normal work) including a final report
- eleven individual assignments intended to support the learning of subject matter and the successful completion of the project
- eight days of residential sessions (including lectures and workshops)
- written material (c. 500 pages) placed on the web + list of suggested readings
- collective learning in a web-based learning environment
- tutorials (the group of participants was subdivided into five heterogeneous tutorial groups)

---

[2]To be more precise, participants received 8-12 credit points. Each credit point is equal to 40 hours of full time study.

Participants

There were 23 participants attending the Competence Development training program who completed the program and five participants who failed to do so and were not included in this study. They were all employed, in the public as well as the private sector, and working full time. The mean age of the participants was 44 years and they were predominantly female. The work, or in some cases the work prospectives, of the participants dealt directly or indirectly with human resource development (HRD). Over half of the participants held typical HRD positions including titles such as training manager, training designer, trainer and (adult) educator and 16 of them had at least a master's level degree. According to Hytönen (2002) HRD professionals can be characterized as "progressives" promoting individual growth, as "guerrillas" creating a new or better order, as "organizational maintainers" promoting effectiveness or, most currently, as "change agents" working in the interests of organizations, industry, or the economy. Thus, although promoting the competence development of the personnel is at the core of HRD practitioners' work, the work is driven by a variety of interests and requires problem solving in diverse situations and contexts, resulting in demand for competence development programs for HRD practitioners.

Data Collection Instruments and Procedures

The participants (N=23) of the training program were administered a questionnaire at the very beginning of training and during the last residential session. Based on *reactions* (satisfaction and perceived impact), seven participants were selected for a follow-up interview in order to explore learning outcomes in more depth. These seven participants were selected to represent the whole training program as well as possible: satisfied and dissatisfied participants covering different types of work organisations. Interviews were conducted approximately four months after the completion of the training program. The one-hour interviews were semi-structured and they covered the following themes: the process of completing the project, learning results and attainment of personal objectives. (See APPENDIX 2). The interviews were recorded and transcribed verbatim.

The central constructs of the questionnaire consisted of reactions (satisfaction, perceived impact) and factors that were presumed to predict reactions (e.g. mental models of learning, study motive, lack of regulation, deep processing). *Satisfaction with the training program* was measured on a seven point scale familiar to the participants from school: "4" is the worst grade which represents unacceptable performance and "10" represents outstanding performance. *Perceived impact* consisted of the average score of three self-report variables: general competence development (1 item), development of evaluation competence (3 items) and prediction of future competence requirements (1 item). The original items were measured on a four point scale (0="no impact whatsoever … 3="great impact").

The pre-structured part of the first questionnaire contained four scales measuring *mental models of learning,* which were expected to predict reactions and learning outcomes: learning as *knowledge construction, externally regulated dualism, cookbook view of learning* and *learning as collaboration and exchange of ideas.* The participants were instructed to answer these items on a six point Likert scale (1="I definitely disagree … 6="I definitely agree").

In the questionnaire administered during the last residential session, *instead* of scales on conceptions of learning and knowledge, there were scales concerning the *study motives, lack of regulation, deep processing* and several scales measuring the *perceived impact of the training program.*

Study motives (adopted *during* the training program) defined as training program specific personal meaning of studying were measured on a four point scale (1="of very little significance" … 4= "of great significance") on the *second* questionnaire. The specific motives each measured by a single indicator were the following: *learning motive* (motive to learn and to develop one's professional expertise), *credit point motive, motive to gain contacts* and *the motive to cope with job requirements.*

The *lack of regulation scale*, a metacognitive regulation subscale, consisted of four out of five items from the Student Task Booklet of Learning by Lonka and Lindblom-Ylänne (1996) adopted from the Inventory of Learning Styles (ILS, Vermunt and Rijswijk, 1988). In addition it contained three self-constructed items designed to lessen social desirability. The content of the items was the same as for the original items, but in reverse form. Thus, the scale contained 7 items, three of which were reversed. For all of these items the participants were asked to answer on a five point Likert scale (1="I definite disagree" … 5="I definitely agree").

The *deep processing scale* consisted of two items from the generalized study orientation scale (IGSO) by Mäkinen, Olkinuora & Lonka (2004) adopted from the SIAS (Entwistle, 1988). For a synthesis of the main constructs, see Appendix 1.

Analysis Procedures

The *statistical analysis* was carried out as follows. In order to determine which factors were related to reactions (satisfaction and perceived impact), zero-order correlations were calculated. For the *qualitative analysis* of learning outcomes interview transcripts were read and reread numerous times and notes were taken on the quality of learning outcomes and possible explanatory factors until the idea of a hierarchical three level coding category emerged. The resulting coding scheme of learning outcomes was essentially influenced by two sources of inspiration: the phenomenographic method (Marton & Booth, 1997) and the four-level framework for evaluating training programs (Kirkpatrick, 1998). To complete the analysis, the categories of learning outcomes and amount of reading, an explanatory variable, were attached numerical codes, and their zero-order correlation was calculated.

RESULTS

Reactions to Training Program

To start off, participant reactions are presented. As can be seen in Table 3, the training program was not experienced as an overwhelmingly positive (learning) experience. On a scale from 4 to 10, satisfaction with the training program was 6.9 on the average. As can be seen in Table 4, learning was also rated rather mediocre: on a scale from 0 to 3, the median ratings on four variables ranged from 1.5 to 3.

Table 3. Participant reactions to the training program (Helle et al., 2006) Reprinted with permission of Elsevier

Scale	General reaction
Minimum	5
Maximum	9
Median	7
Mode	8
Mean	6.9
Standard deviation	1.2

Table 4. Perceived impact as measured by three indicators on a scale from 0 to 3 (Helle et al., 2006) Reprinted with permission of Elsevier

Scale	General competence development	Development of evaluation competence	Prediction of future competence requirements
Minimum	0.0	0.3	0.0
Maximum	3.0	3.0	3.0
Median	2.0	1.7	1.5
Mode	2.0	-	1.0
Mean	1.5	1.6	1.5
Standard deviation	0.9	0.7	1.0

Since there was considerable variance in the reactions, an attempt was made to find factors which would account for the variance. Certain interesting findings can be seen in Table 5: The knowledge construction view of learning, which was measured in the beginning of learning, is negatively correlated (rho=-0.53) with lack of regulation during training (measured at the end). This indicates that the knowledge construction view of learning may have served to *prevent* problems in self-regulation of learning.

Table 5. Zero-order correlations (Spearman's rho) among six constructs (correlations, which are significant (p<0.05 are colored gray)

Scale	1	2	3	4	5	6
1. Learning motive	—	-.18	.14	-.47	.31	.38
2. Cookbook view of learning		—	-.02	.16	-.15	-.02
3. Knowledge construction view of learning			—	-.53	.30	.06
4. Lack of regulation				—	-.60	-.32
5. Deep processing					—	.45
6. Perceived impact						—

Learning Outcomes Based on Participant Interviews

The three-level taxonomy of learning outcomes that emerged from data analysis of interviews is presented in Table 6. Level I (the reactive level of learning outcomes) refers to a situation in which only affective level outcomes are articulated or the participant reports having learnt something, but without knowing if it was something he or she knew before. Here is an excerpt from a participant expressing learning outcomes at the reactive level:

> *"There was one lecture, I cannot remember who's, but it took two to three hours, some consultant from some firm and, er, he had very good material and he clearly had a lot of experience and a lot of good slides. Actually I have the material somewhere there, but that was something that I recall."*

Level II (identification of learning outcomes) refers to a situation in which cognitive level outcomes are identified and attributed to the training program, but not put directly into use. For example, one participant reported that a specific lecture had been a significant learning experience, because she realised that competence development is tied to the organisational strategy. When asked later on if she had come up with a specific idea as a result of training she replied:

> *"I just talked yesterday - - to my boss and to a colleague --, about this competence development at a longer perspective. Not just about needing a competent person for some line today, who can use something, but about what that competence should be in three or five years. What is the development plan that supports corporate strategy? I mean competence development is long term, not just according to today's needs. "*

At Level III, learning outcomes are clearly a result of training, learning outcomes are articulated and put to use in an organisational context. For example, one participant described what she had done during the project in the following way:

> *"Well, I naturally started off from our vision and strategy and then I bumped into the strategy for our sector and that was something I worked on for long, because our strategy definitely needs some revisions. - - Then for a long time I searched for a framework, because I felt that it is difficult to recognise competence in an organisation composed of rather autonomous professionals, then I started thinking "Do I have measures?" and then there was talk about developing measures and everything and after a really painful process I ended up using the Balanced Scorecard System and primitive attempts to find measures, to draw up strategic maps and learn these things and use them here.."*

When asked if the training program changed the way she goes about her work she replied:

> *"... I really have the intention to carry out my project, to start to looking for these competence areas with my team and to start evaluating them and if it turns out that we have deficits, then we will look and see..."*

Table 6. Taxonomy of learning outcomes

Level I: reactions	Level II: identification of learning outcomes	Level III: applying learning outcomes into work practice
-outcomes that are articulated are at an affective level -cognitive outcomes are not specified -if cognitive outcomes are mentioned they remain at a very general level ("the course was useful as it helped me understand competence development better") -it is not specified that the outcomes are due to training events	-cognitive outcomes are *specified* and *articulated* -it is specified that the outcomes are due to training events	level II PLUS -learning outcomes are not just learning for the purpose of learning, but they are perceived to provide value-added for the work organisation -the development project continues (clear plan for the course of action) -cognitive learning outcomes are put into practice

For the purpose of statistical analysis, Level I was coded "1", level II "2" and level III "3". Since several participants expressed that reading was a significant learning experience, the reports on reading were also coded (1=minimal reading, 2=serious reading). The criteria for serious reading was specifying to have read extensively at least one book although all of the participants who engaged in serious reading were actually able to name several of books.

The zero-order correlation between Reading and Learning outcome turned out 0.88 and statistically significant.

CASE INFORMATION SYSTEMS DESIGN AND EXTENSION TRAINING AND TEACHER FACILITATION OF LEARNING

Comparing data from Case ISD and ET indicated that all of the tutors in Case ET and an experienced supervisor from Case ISD emphasised the importance of establishing a certain working culture with certain rules from the very beginning. In addition, in Case ET, all parties appeared to agree on one thing: time was a problem. Participant interviews also revealed that time management in many cases was very problematic: participants had problems freeing up time from work and family responsibilities. Some participants were even involved in other training programs. Tutors expressed that there were problems "working in an academic way" in three out of five tutorial groups (Leppänen, 2005). Helle (2007) concluded that based on participant and tutor interviews, the participants appeared to have problems in the outer layer of self-regulation related to time management.

As for Case ISD, two challenges related to facilitation were identified in a previous study (Helle et al., 2007a). First of all, in some student groups, it was obvious that knowledge was unequally distributed inside the group. Secondly, student group had varying access to social and conceptual resources outside the group.

How can it be explained that the outer level of self-regulation was a problem in extension training, but not a problem for the students in information systems design? Helle (in press) argued that this could be attributed to three factors: 1) the information systems design students were full-time students, whereas the extension training participants were studying only part-time (and working full time) 2) the information systems students were required to design and implement a system for time management, whereas the extension training students were not, and 3) the work-related aspect of the course seemed to serve as a powerful motivator for the information systems students, whereas for the extension training participants work projects were "business as usual".

PRACTICAL IMPLICATIONS FOR DESIGNING WORK-BASED PROJECT LEARNING

The practical implication of the studies is that although work-based project learning holds considerable promise for the integration of conceptual knowledge with the practices of daily work as evidenced by the results of several studies, a close look at the results reveals that there is a significant proportion of regular and extension training students who do not show expected progress or learning.

The extension training participants who made major progress in learning emphasised that the value of training was that it forced them to stop and to think. Judging from the results of this study, engaging in serious reading appeared to reinforce this effect. Thus, it is recommended that course designers pay special attention to the issue of *time*. Extending a 400-hour course over an extended period of time should be considered as well as creating some form of time management scaffolds (e.g. discussions before the training on how to find the required 400 hours for deliberate study). Since the list of suggested readings appeared to promote learning, the use of such lists is encouraged. However, since it is unlikely that all extension training participants will engage in active reading and elaboration of course content, activities to support such activity could be built into training (e.g. collective discussions directly after residential sessions in which theoretical concepts are used for understanding work practice). As a matter of fact, the training program appeared to reflect rather painfully the historical tension between the vision of distance or extension training as opportunistic learning and the vision of it as a substitute for on-campus learning (see Larreamendy-Joerns and Leinhardt, 2006) with some participants viewing extension training from a more opportunistic view than others.

As for regular students, it is recommended that tutors pay special attention to the distribution of work. The most demanding tasks are easily given to the most advanced students, which may not result in optimal learning for less advanced students. The authors also agree with the conclusion put forward by Eteläpelto (2000): it is recommended to complement work-based project learning with more academic instruction focused on, for example, the analysis of different design solutions. In other words, also regular students would profit from learning to use conceptual tools as well as concrete ones and from integrating practical and scientific knowledge. (Cf. Tynjälä et al., 2006, pp. 84-86.)

Finally, it is recommended that teachers or tutors discuss "rules and regulations of project work" at the very beginning in order to establish a good working culture. Actually, such a practice has been incorporated into the practical training of pharmacists. Rules and regulations that have been jointly agreed upon, are documented into the trainees' workbook.

The workbook itself is a product of the collaboration of different stakeholders including different faculties of pharmacy, university pharmacies, a student union and a labor union.

APPENDIX 1

Table A1. Description of the main scales of the questionnaire, sample items and sources

Construct			
Conceptions of learning and knowledge	Description	Source	Reliability
– knowledge construction view of learning	Viewing as one's task in learning: taking initiative in making up one's own questions and examples, looking for relationships and consulting other books	Task Booklet of Learning (TBL) adopted on the basis of the ILS	0.60 (5 items)
– cookbook view of learning	Viewing one's task as acquiring directly applicable theories and "facts"	CLKQ by Lonka et al. (2001)	0.60 (5 items)
– collaborative learning	Viewing collaborative learning as worthwhile	CLKQ by Lonka et al.	0.59 (6 items)
– externally regulated dualism	Viewing the teacher's role as that of regulator and provider of the "right" answers	CLKQ by Lonka et al.	0.77 (7 items)
Lack of regulation	Noticing difficulties with the regulation of one's own study processes	Task Booklet of Learning adopted on the basis of the ILS	0.75 (7 items)
Deep processing	Making serious efforts to understand while studying through trying to make connections and trying to see the big picture.	IGSO adopted on the basis of the SIAS	0.62 (2 items)
Perceived impact	"development of competence and expertise"	Three of the impact items developed on the basis of the sponsor's objectives	0.67 (three items)

APPENDIX 2

1) Structure of "Learning Interview" (Translated into English from Finnish)

1 A) Background

It has been approximately four months since the end of the Competence Development Training Program. What are the first thoughts that come into your mind / How do you generally feel about the training program?

1 B) The project and its progress

Your project dealt with… could you please elaborate on it? What exactly did you do in relation to the training programme?

- Was it your idea or was it from your boss…
- Did your project fit in with your work?
- Was there anything that promoted the progress in your project?
- Was there anything that interfered with the progress in your project?
- Was the organisation committed to the project?
- How would you describe your contribution to the project? What is your estimate of the time spent on the project? How much of this was on your free time?)
- How did you utilise the list of suggested readings? To what extent? Did find information from other sources? To what extent?

2) Learning and Applying What Has Been Learnt

2 A) Learning experiences and conflicts
- What was the most significant learning experience or situation during the training program? Could you please describe what made it special from the learning point of view?
- Can you recall an especially frustrating situation during the training program. Could you please describe what you did in that situation?
- Did the training program or the project cause any kind of conflict in the organisation, workplace or in terms of work tasks?

2 B) Learning outcomes

If you think of this training program, there have been tutorials, learning assignments and this project, can you tell me what you have learnt and can you specify in which situations learning occurred?

The interviewee is shown the four categories of learning outcomes by Robinson and Robinson, 1989, 209, and learning is discussed on the basis of them. Do you think the training program had an impact on one or several of these categories? Where was the impact greatest?

(1) Affective learning outcomes
- Did the training program change the way you experience e.g. your work, colleagues, organization? Could you please provide an example? Can you describe the situation in which the learning occurred?
(2) Cognitive learning outcomes such as concepts, principles and facts
- Do you understand something related to your work better now? Could you please give me an example? Can you describe the situation in which the learning occurred?

(3) Behavioral or skill learning outcomes: What are you able to do, something others can see, "new skills"? Could you provide an example? Do you have any idea how you learned it?

(4) Operational outcomes: Did the training programme change your way of doing your work? How? Could you please provide an example? Can you tell me how you learned?

3) Subjective Impact: Interviewees Are Shown Results from the Questionnaire and Are Asked to Comment

Subjective personal impact, subjective organisational impact

Can you tell me what interfered or promoted the spreading of the impact to the organisational level?

Subjective impact by sector: do have any idea why the participants from the polytechnics appear to have profited less from training than the others?

3 A) Reaching goals

- goals of the training program
- personal goals
a) What were your goals and expectations towards the training program?
b) Did you reach your goals? Did your goals change during the training program?

B) Plans for the future

- Have you thought about how to promote your professional development in the future?
- Do you have plans for the competence development of your organisation?
- What about your project, how is it going?
- Have you come up with a concrete idea that you would like to develop further as a result of this training?
- Organisational support: do you have the opportunity to pursue that course of action?

4) Finally

Is there something you would like to ask or add?

APPENDIX 3

Table A2. The five solution patterns and the four variables that define them (Eteläpelto, 2000) Reprinted with the permission of Elsevier

Variables			Scope of solution	Solution structure	Strategy of IS development	Identification with clients
Solution pattern	Professional	Client				
I. Initial work-phase model			Limited to *how-* level	Procedural or definition-based	Professional-centred construction	No identification
II. Individualised and interactive prototyping			*How-* or *what-* levels included	Procedural or definiton-based	Interactive prototyping	No or some identification
III. Customer-centred identification			Any scope	Procedural or definition-based	Purchasing and tailoring	High identification
IV. Dialogue-oriented marketing strategy			Any scope	Any structure	Purchasing and tailoring	No or some identification
V. Comprehensive and interactive approach			Comprehensive scope	Any structure	Interactive prototyping or purchasing and tailoring	Some identification

REFERENCES

Alexander, P.A. (2003). The Development of Expertise: the journey from acclimation to proficiency. *Educational Researcher, 32*(8), 10-14.

Blumenfeld, P. C., Soloway, E., Marx, R. W., Krajcik, J. S., Guzdial, M. and Palincsar, A. (1991). Motivating project-based learning: sustaining the doing, supporting the learning. *Educational Psychologist, 26*(3 and 4), 399-427.

Boekaerts, M. (1999). Self-regulated Learning: where we are today. *International Journal of Educational Research, 31*, 445-457.

Boekaerts, M. and Cascallar, E. (2006). How far have we moved toward the integration of theory and practice in self-regulation? *Educational Psychology Review, 18*, 199-210.

Entwistle, N. (1988). *Styles of Learning and Teaching. An integrated outline of Educational Psychology for students, teachers and lecturers.* London: David Fulton.

Ericsson, K. A., Krampe, R. Th. and Tesch-Römer, C. (1993). The role of deliberate practice in the acquisition of expert performance. *Psychological Review, 100*(3), 363-406.

Ertmer, P. A., Newby, T. J. and MacDougall, M. (1996). Students' responses and approaches to case-based instruction: The role of reflective self-regulation. *American Educational Research Journal, 33*(3), 719-752.

Eteläpelto, A. (2000). Contextual and strategic knowledge in the acquisition of design expertise. *Learning and Instruction, 10,* 113-136.

Helle, L. (in press) Exploring project-based learning: the interplay between teacher regulation and student self-regulation of learning. Annales universitatis turkuensis.

Helle, L., Tuominen, T. and Olkinuora, E. (2006). Learning in project-based extension training? In P. Tynjälä, J. Välimää and G. Boulton-Lewis (Eds.) Advances in Learning and Instruction, *Higher Education and Working Life: Collaborations, Confrontations and Challenges.* (pp. 209-229). Amsterdam: Elsevier.

Helle, L., Tynjälä, P. and Olkinuora, E. (2007a). Where's the learning in work-based project learning? Case study in information systems design. Rinne, R., Heikkinen, A. and Salo, P. (Eds.) (2007a). *Adult Education - Liberty, Fraternity, Equality. Nordic Views on Lifelong Learning.* (pp. 297-321). Turku: Finnish Educational Research Association.

Helle, L., Tynjälä, P., Olkinuora, E, and Lonka, K. (2007b). "Ain't Nothin' Like the Real Thing". Motivation and Study Processes on a work-based project course in information systems design. *British Journal of Educational Psychology, 77*(2).

Hytönen, T. (2002). *Exploring the practice of human resource development as a field of professional expertise.* Jyväskylä Studies in Education, psychology and social research 202. University of Jyväskylä.

Kaldeway, J. and Korthagen, F. A. J. (1995). Training in studying in higher education: objectives and effects. *Higher Education, 30,* 81-98.

Kirkpatrick, D. L. (1998). *Evaluating training programs.* The four levels. San Francisco: Berrett-Koehler.

Larreamendy-Joerns, J. and Leinhardt, G. (2006). Going the distance with online education. *Review of Educational Research, 76* (4), 567-605.

Leppänen, R. (2005). OSKE:sta verkostoksi? Tapaustutkimus täydennyskoulutuksen tutor-ryhmätoiminnasta ja sen yhteyksistä verkostoitumiseen. Pro gradu –tutkielma. Kasvatustieteen laitos, Turun yliopisto. (In English: From the Competence Development training program to a network? A case study on extension training tutorials and networking. Master's thesis. Department of Education, University of Turku).

Lonka, K. and Lindblom-Ylänne, S. (1996). Epistemologies, conceptions of learning, and study practices in medicine and psychology. *Higher Education, 31,* 5-24.

Markowitsch, J. and Messerer, K. (2006). Practice-oriented methods in teaching and learning in higher education. In P. Tynjälä, J. Välimaa and G. Boulton-Lewis (Eds.), *Higher Education and Working Lifee. Collaborations, confrontations and challenges. Advances in Learning and Instruction Series* (pp. 177-194). Amsterdam: EARLI, Elsevier.

Marton, F. and Booth, S. (1997). Learning and Awareness. Mahwah, N.J.: Lawrence Erlbaum Associates.

Mäkinen, J. (2003). *University Students' General Study Orientations. Theoretical background, measurements, and practical implications.* Annales universitatis turkuensis B:262.

Mäkinen, J., Olkinuora, E. and Lonka, K. (2004). Students at risk: how to predict study problems in higher education? Students' general study orientations and abandoning the course of their studies. *Higher Education, 48*(2), 173-188.

Nandagopal, K. and Ericsson, K. A. (2007) An expert performance approach to measuring self-regulated learning strategies in college students. *AERA 2007 paper.*

Nieminen, J., Lindblom-Ylänne, S. and Lonka, K. (2004). The development of study orientations and study success in students of pharmacy. *Instructional Science, 32,* 387-417.

Olesen, H.S. and Jensen, J.H. (Eds.) (1999). *Project studies – a late modern university reform?* Roskilde university press.

Pintrich, P. R. (1999). The role of motivation in promoting and sustaining self-regulated learning. The role of motivation in promoting and sustaining self-regulated learning. *International Journal of Educational Research, 31*, 459-470.

Prins, F. J., Veenman, M. V. J. and Elshout, J. J. (2006). The impact of intellectual abilility and metacognition on learning: New support for the threshold of problematicity theory. *Learning and Instruction,16*, 374-387.

Robinson, D. G. & Robinson, J. C. (1989). *Training for Impact. How to link training to business needs and measure the results.* San Francisco: Jossey-Bass.

Schommer-Aikins, M. and Easter, M. (2006). Ways of knowing and epistemological beliefs: combined effect on academic performance. *Educational psychology, 26*(3), 411-423.

Thomas, J. W. (2000). A Review of Research on Project-based Learning. Available from: *http://www.bie.org/pdf/researchreviewPBL.pdf* [cited 7 March 2007].

Tuominen, T. (2003). Projektiopiskelu ja sen vaikuttavuus täydennyskoulutuksessa. Tapaustutkimus Osaamisen kehittäjäksi – valmennusohjelmassa. Pro gradu –tutkielma. Kasvatustieteen laitos, Turun yliopisto. (In English: Project-based learning and its impact in extension training. Case study on the Competence Development Training Program. Master's Thesis. Department of Education, University of Turku.)

Tynjälä, P. (2001). Writing, Learning and the Development of Expertise. In P. Tynjälä, L. Mason and K. Lonka (Eds.), *Writing as a Learning Tool. Integrating Theory and Practice.* (pp. 37-56). Dordrecth: Kluwer Academic Publishers.

Tynjälä, P., Salminen, R.T., Sutela, T., Nuutinen, A. and Pitkänen, S. (2005). Factors related to study success in engineering education. *European Journal of Engineering Education, 30*(2), 221-231.

Tynjälä, P., Slotte, V., Nieminen, J., Lonka, K. and Olkinuora, E. (2006). From university to working life: graduates' workplace skills in practice. In P. Tynjälä, J. Välimää and G. Boulton-Lewis (Eds.), *Higher Education and Working Life: Collaborations, Confrontations and Challenges.* (pp. 73-88). Amsterdam: Elsevier.

Vaz, R. F. (2000). Connected learning. Interdisciplinary projects in international settings. *Liberal Education, 86*(1), 24-31.

Veenman, M. V. J., Elshout, J. J. and Meijer, J. (1997). The generality vs. domain-specificity of metacognitive skills in novice learning across domains. *Learning and Instruction, 7*(2), 187-209.

Vermunt, J. D. (1994). *Inventory of Learning Styles in Higher Education.*

Vermunt, J. D. (2003). The Power of Learning Environments and the Quality of Student Learning. In E. De Corte, L. Verschaffel, N. Entwistle and J. van Merriënboer (Eds.),

Powerful Learning Environments: Unravelling basic components and dimensions. Advances in Learning and Instruction Series (pp. 109-124). Amsterdam: Pergamon.

Vermunt, J. D. (2005). Relations between student learning patterns and personal and contextual factors and academic performance. *Higher Education, 48*, 205-234.

Vermunt, J. D. H. M. and van Rijswijk, F. A. W. M. (1988). Analysis and development of students' skill in self-regulated learning. *Higher Education, 17*, 647-682.

In: Global Issues in Higher Education
Editor: Pamela B. Richards, pp. 237-266

ISBN: 978-1-60021-802-6
© 2007 Nova Science Publishers, Inc.

Chapter 11

ANALYSIS AND DECISION MAKING MODELS IN THE PROCESS OF THE ASSIMILATION OF CHANGE AND INNOVATION IN LEARNING SYSTEMS

Baruch Offir

Bar-Ilan University, School of Education, Israel

Research has shown that a relation exists between the level of learning in the schools and universities and a country's strength. A relation also exists between education and the level and quality of life. Education today is a significant factor for ensuring society's normal existence, development and prosperity. However, major cities can afford the student the opportunity to acquire knowledge more than cities found in the periphery. A gap therefore exists between the level of learning in the major cities and the level of learning in the peripheral settlements. Students with high learning abilities who live in the cities can participate in university courses and other learning centers, whereas students with learning abilities who live in the periphery do not have a framework which can afford them knowledge in accordance with their talents and abilities.

This reality was the basis for our research on the integration of technological systems for the advancement of students in the periphery towards academic studies. Our research aims to investigate how technological systems can be used to advance populations of students who live in distant areas, to afford them the opportunity to learn academic courses and to be university students while still learning in high school.

A proper combination of this means during the learning process requires a change in the teaching method. This process of change is very complex, since it must take numerous educational and pedagogical factors which are involved in the process into account. It must recognize the teachers' and students' personal attitudes, must evaluate the student's level, analyze the sociological processes taking place in the classroom, formulate an appropriate teaching method, recognize the teacher's position and status in the classroom, etc. Proper activation of technological systems in order to reduce gaps between populations is a very complex system and its successful implementation depends on the understanding and control of numerous diverse and complex parameters.

The function of the education system today is indeed complex. It must educate towards values and mold each student's behavior, afford the student the ability to crystallize his viewpoint and attitude while concomitantly leading him towards achievements and affording him the tools with which he will be able to learn and acquire a profession so that he will be able to earn a living for himself and his family and will be able to contribute to the society in which he lives. These goals are not identical, and are sometimes not compatible, since the strict and demanding educational framework which accurately evaluates and judges the student's achievements is not necessarily the same educational framework which is soft, encouraging, educating and guiding.

The education system is not static. History shows that its goals, methods of operation and structure have changed during different periods of history, according to sociological influences and society's goals . The goals of education have undergone changes according to the particular period, from a framework whose function was to watch over the children and thus enable the parents to join the workforce, to a framework which affords the student knowledge and skills in order to enable him to become integrated in society and contribute to his environment.

Education systems must develop the ability to change in order to cope with the goals set by society. The education system today needs to prove its effectiveness. Today's society demands that education systems prove that their methods and modes of operation are effective in achieving the goals of education as formulated by the society. These demands, of meeting standards set by the society, require that the education system develop instruments of evaluation and measurement, that it formulate more accurate methods for collecting and analyzing data and that it develop methods for reaching conclusions.

These processes will comprise the basis for a change in the methods of learning, for improvement in existing teaching approaches, for the construction of appropriate tests for evaluation, while affording more accurate and effective instruments for guiding the education system towards the effective achievement of its goals, as currently takes place in other fields such as medicine, engineering, agriculture and economics.

For this purpose the education system must undergo a process of change. Do we know how to generate a change in the education system? Are there mechanisms that can be used to generate change? Does education research afford us with tools to cope with these demands? Do the information and data supplied by education research join the body of knowledge that comprises an instrument for navigating in and improving the education system? Is education research identical to research in the other sciences in the ways in which it collects data and formulates theories, or does education research have unique goals, research methods and ways of reaching conclusions? If so, we must formulate the goals and determine the extent to which these goals are indeed achieved by education research. It is possible that the research approach in the field of education requires change. This requires the consolidation of a method which will enable the systematic achievement of this change.

Three terms which should be considered when referring to the process of consolidating a unique research approach in the field of education are:

1. Conceptualization: To what extent are the concepts which we use in the education research process indeed identical concepts?

2. Collecting and handling scientific knowledge: How can scientific knowledge be accumulated? How should the knowledge be handled and how should conclusions be reached?

3. Rules for constructing a body of knowledge: Can a body of knowledge be constructed? It may be appropriate to carry this out only for defined and limited sections in the field of education, whereas for others we will agree that they have no rules or that other rules apply to them .

It may be assumed that there exist factors in the education system which accelerate processes of change and others which decelerate these processes: Do we know which factors affect the process of change within the education system? What are the mechanisms which enable effective change? Can these changes be measured and evaluated?

EVALUATING A PROCESS OF CHANGE

We have carried out research on the integration of technological systems in the education system for the past three decades. However, our interest did not focus on the technological systems and their integration in the education system. Rather, we examined processes of change within the education system. The advanced technological systems comprised a tool by whose means we created a research situation that enabled examination of the mechanisms which characterize and accompany processes of change. For example, integration of computers in schools in the 1970's or systems for transmission of information via broadband lines on the internet today, require changes in the education system. The researches we performed monitored these attempts and tried to assess and measure the various variables related to this process and thus to contribute to a better understanding of the process of change: What factors affect this process? How does it occur in the education system? What variables slow the process of change?

A better understanding of the processes of change will make it possible to guide and direct these processes. It will enable assessment of their effectiveness and measurement of the change's contribution to the achievement of the education system's goals.

In this chapter we will deal with the integration of technological systems in the learning process. Integration of technological systems in the learning system is a change. Research on the various variables involved in this change will enable a better understanding of how the process of change takes place in the education system. It will also elucidate the factors and rules that affect this process.

Integration of a technological system must enable the education system to achieve its goal of educating and imparting knowledge to the student. It must therefore take into account the abilities, feelings, attitudes, wishes, personalities and worldviews of all factors involved in the process of change. Integration of technological systems in teaching and education requires making a change. A longitudinal research which will accompany the process of the integration of these systems in teaching and education may therefore afford measurement and evaluation tools and a better understanding of the process of change.

Our occupation with the subject of integrating technological systems is only the framework and research field through which we wish to study and understand processes, mechanisms and variables accompanying the process of change in the education system in order to consolidate ways in which to generate a change in the field of education and learning. The results of the investigations afford tools for generating and guiding change within the education system.

Any change in education which tries to become integrated in the school encounters a teacher who is found in the classroom. The teacher is therefore a most significant factor for the success or failure of the introduction of change into the learning process . The presence of a flesh and blood teacher is essential in some fields of the education system, where the teacher has no substitute. It will be more complicated and less justified to integrate technological systems in these fields. However, there are other fields in the learning process in which it will be easier to integrate technological systems. Technological systems can be used to relieve the teacher of some of his responsibility, especially in the transmission of knowledge. This will enable the teacher to invest more time and to concentrate on the promotion of processes in which his presence comprises an advantage, fields in which he cannot be substituted.

An accepted and consolidated process for analyzing education systems will assist us in evaluating and quantifying various variables that take part in the process of integrating a new technology system. The integration of a technology system in learning necessitates a determination of which measurable components of the learning process can be most easily transferred to the technology system and which subjective non-measurable components should be left to the teacher. We thus wish to design a map of the optimal division of roles between the teacher's contribution, the student's activity and the help afforded by the technology system and other variables in order to achieve a more effective teaching system.

According to this approach we will not measure whole learning systems. Rather, we will divide the super-goal of the system into secondary goals. Some of these goals can be accurately measured and evaluated while others cannot be measured. The Firm Effects Model statistical method enables division between the general investment and a goal-directed investment. In the analysis of a learning system we will also separate between the general learning goals and secondary learning goals which can be measured at different levels. The resultant evaluation is then composed of a measurement of different goals. Some of the secondary goals can be measured accurately, some can be measured less accurately and some can only be evaluated subjectively.

Integrating computers in the school is a process of change which depends on several factors, such as: the learning method, the teacher's role in the classroom, the student's contribution. Research which is directed towards reaching conclusions and understanding processes of change in the school can monitor the processes of integrating computers in the school.

Although many predicted that the integration of computers in teaching will lead to a revolution in the learning system, the appearance of computers within the learning framework did not lead to the expected change. This raised the following questions: Why was this process not realized? Why it did not generate a revolution in teaching? Indeed, expectations were high whereas the changes that took place were negligible.

The process of integrating computers in teaching in the 1980's comprised a research field for our team. It comprised a framework in which to investigate and understand the variables related to the process of change and to elucidate the reason why the expected change did not take place. (Offir , 1987 ; 1993 Offir etal 1998 ;1990a ; 1990b ;1995 ;1999 , Katz and Offir 1988; 1990a; 1990b ; 19911 ;1993;1994)

Since the 1990's we have focused on the subject of distance learning. Examination and evaluation of distance learning processes also serve as a framework for understanding processes of change and renewal in the school. Our research on distance learning attempts to assess those factors which promote change and those which interfere and prevent change.

Understanding the variables involved in the assimilation of distance learning systems, which are based on the results of field experiments, may contribute to a more in-depth understanding of the process of change within the teaching and learning frameworks. Evaluating the attitudes of the teachers and the students, the teacher's personality, examining the teaching methods, achievements and other variables and their integration within a comprehensive theory will help us understand the process of integrating advanced technologies in the school. Their integration and evaluation will afford a better understanding of the process of change.

The subject of the process of change, from the 1980's to the 1990's, was the computer and its integration in the teaching process. Since the 1990's, the subject of the process of change has become the distance learning system. Researches dealing in the integration of computers in teaching as well as those dealing in distance learning aim at affording a better description and understanding of the processes of generating a change in the school . We need language. We need concepts that are as accurate as possible, which can be used to produce meaningful information in order to describe and evaluate a process and reach conclusions. The desired direction of development cannot be described without concepts, and research hypotheses cannot be hypothesized or proven. Progress cannot take place without a pool of concepts.

Concepts are formulated by asking questions that are as accurate as possible and affording answers to these questions. Concepts accumulate during generations of ongoing research. One research is the continuation of a previous research. Every research helps make the concept more accurate and differentiates it from other similar concepts.

Scientific research helps us differentiate between concepts which appear similar and defines the differences between similar concepts. A collection of concepts and elucidation of the connections between them affords a body of information which is essential for describing processes in any scientific field. A body of information is effective only when it is constructed of clear and defined concepts, with clear relations between them.

We must assess and measure the change in order to monitor and describe a change. This will enable the production of information on this change. Terms and concepts are necessary in order to define essential elements that comprise the process of change. Thus, scientific research deals in the definition of concepts and their classification. It affords tools for quantifying concepts. This process has been ongoing in scientific research for decades.

Concepts which are defined and clear to everyone are an essential condition in the processes of analyzing and understanding a process. The defined concept has a measurable quantitative value, and can be integrated in the process. Its intensity can be calculated and its effect can be evaluated. Defined concepts enable the achievement of results. They enable evaluation of the effectiveness of a process. Above all, concepts are tools which can be used to explain the past, analyze the present and predict the future. Science defines concepts and thus enables calculations, formulations of hypotheses as well as conclusions pertaining to the effectiveness of the process.

When we deal in learning, the task is much more complex. Not all concepts that are related to the learning process can be defined accurately and measured. The concepts brilliance, creativity, thinking ability and conclusion ability are concepts which are related to learning but are difficult to quantify. In contradistinction, concepts such as "achievement" can be defined, and can be used to judge the success of the process. They can be calculated and quantified more accurately. Measuring and quantifying is even more difficult when discussing and investigating changes in behavior.

Learning and educational theories contain measurable concepts as well as concepts which are difficult to measure. Reaching conclusions will be enabled when the definition of the concepts is more accurate. It will be possible when a larger number of concepts in the process are defined and a more accurate connection between concepts is found.

The need for conceptualization exists in all fields of science. It is, therefore, an essential condition for the development of an education and learning system, as it is essential for the development of any information system. The field of learning, of behavior, has indeed remained a field in which is it difficult to consolidate a paradigm, compared to the natural sciences or even compared to economics, where the result is usually measured by an economic profit. Three main reasons for this are:

The sample size: The sample in the natural sciences is very large. A researcher who bases his conclusions on a milliliter of material actually has a sample with an immense number of molecules. For example, a milliliter of water contains 3.3×10^{22} molecules. The researcher controls this immense sample, and learns from a sample with a large number of items. In contradistinction, the sample in the behavioral sciences is small and limited.

The research population: The research samples in the natural sciences are identical. An experiment can be performed on a chemical substance. This experiment can be repeated and will yield an identical result. The equation in the natural sciences presents the bottom line of the process. In contradistinction, in the behavioral sciences the individual student is also taken into consideration. Understanding the individual is a necessary and essential condition for understanding processes in the behavioral sciences.

The research and measurement tools: The research and measurement tools in the natural sciences are identical during all experimental and information collection processes. The research tools collect objective and measurable data (such as temperature, pressure, etc.). The situation is different in behavior research, where the concepts are subjective. The measurement tools are not identical and the collected data can be manipulated such that their conclusions are not identical.

Theories in the behavioral sciences which referred to the concept "learning" referred to the level of behavior that can be shaped, directed, behavior that can be controlled and evaluated and whose results could be measured. The behaviorist theory, when using the concept "learning", refers to a level of behavior that has rules, learning that can be directed and guided, learning that can be evaluated and judged. However, there exist additional levels of learning, such as discovery, invention, conclusion, etc. (Offir 2000b; 2003a ; 2006 ; Offir etal 2000b; 2005 ; 2002 ;2007 ; 2003b ;2000c ; 2004)

THE OCCURRENCE OF LEARNING

Attempts to understand the learning process have been made for centuries, beginning already with Aristotle, Socrates and Plato and on through the philosophical approaches of Hume, Luke and Kant.

How does learning occur? The answer to this question may be obtained by observing man in nature. In ancient times man was a nomad, migrating from place to place in order to find food for his family and livestock. Man then discovered, by asking the right questions and answering them, that there is no need to migrate. He discovered that he could grow his food near his home. He learned to grow wheat in the correct season, he learned to transport water in a canal in order to water this wheat, how to reap the wheat, grind it and bake bread. Man learned to control nature and direct it to his needs. The ability to ask questions, the ability to relate to his environment, the ability to investigate and reach conclusions converted man from a nomad into a wheat grower.

The entire process began when for the first time, by chance, water fell on a pile of wheat grains. The wheat germinated and man was not indifferent to this event. He asked questions: What factors led to the germination of the wheat? Can we ourselves promote the germination of the wheat? Can I grow a field of wheat?

A natural environment is a stimulus-rich environment. Stimuli arouse questions. An environment which supplies the student with questions at the appropriate level is an essential condition for learning. Curiosity, alertness, asking the right questions, logical thinking, an environment that stimulates the asking of questions, trial and error, these are the conditions that enable learning.

This approach emphasizes the importance of the interaction between the student and the learning environment. A student who is naturally curious tries to afford meaning to everything he sees. Knowledge and understanding are processes that are related to the student's tendency to afford meaning, to understand his surroundings. This is learning. The natural environment in which man lives is rich in stimuli and encourages asking questions and answering them. An environment that arouses curiosity is the most suitable environment for learning. Based on this viewpoint, efforts are made to create a learning environment in the classroom which is as natural as possible, an environment that stimulates the asking of questions.

The modern constructivist theory adopted this approach. The constructivist theory believes that knowledge is constructed by the student and is not transmitted by the teacher. Jerome Bruner calls this process "meaning making". This is a process of affording meaning which is the fundament of the constructivist theory. Development of thinking is carried out by thinking. Learning does not occur without understanding. Knowledge is acquired by power of the student as a result of contact with the learning material. Each student's interpretation of the learning material will comprise a stimulus according to his knowledge from the past and according to his intellectual abilities. Learning is the product of activity, response and referral to the material at the student's disposal. Every person has different wishes and therefore a different and complex behavior. Every person needs to be treated uniquely.

The constructivist theory claims that there is limited room for a system of rules in the learning process, the education process and the change in behavior. Every child and every person learns in a method that is unique to him. He learns from the environment, from a collection of stimuli which is appropriate for his ability, his perception and his knowledge. The contact and the relations with the environment, the thinking, the person's ability to cope with the learning material, are essential conditions for the occurrence of learning. Therefore, learning will occur in the classroom only if we supply the student with an environment rich in stimuli which are suitable and significant for his level, interest and knowledge.

Thus, the student does not learn from his teacher. The student learns from the actual thinking process. The student thinks about what he does, what he believes, what others are doing. Thinking is aroused by action, by creating contact. A different action creates different thinking. A different thinking requires use of memory, remembering prior knowledge, reading, learning, experiencing. We learn from experience, from cases, events and activities, from processes in which we were involved. The interpretation of our experience is influenced by what we know. Knowledge is created by thinking and is not transmitted by teaching. Knowledge is acquired by the student's activity and is influenced by his prior knowledge and experience.

Knowledge is influenced and explained by the environment in which it is acquired. The explanation takes place in the student's mind. Problems, questions, deliberations or agreement, striving to acquire knowledge, the student's personality, motivation, all these are intervening variables and influence the knowledge acquisition process. The learning process is, therefore, an individual process. The student acquires knowledge by contact with a rich environment which is meaningful to his prior knowledge. The student acquires knowledge by thinking. The constructivist approach distances itself from any attempt to direct and consolidate regularity in learning.

According to this approach the student must be supplied with a stimulus-rich environment. The learning process must be left to different influences – external influences from the environment or internal influences created by the student's thinking process. These influences are different in every individual and every student absorbs, collects and sorts the meanings which are suitable for him through his contact with the environment.

Direct contact with the environment is the basis for learning according to the constructivist approach. The open school tries to implement this approach. The role of the teacher in the open school is to allow learning to occur by light, careful and positive intervention which will enable the interaction between the student and the environment to take place and develop. The teacher promotes and creates a close and warm atmosphere and turns the student's attention to information which is meaningful to the learning process.

This approach distances itself from any attempt to formulate learning programs and strategies, except for the obligation to supply the appropriate conditions and environment and information which will enable and promote the existence of the learning process. Therefore the teacher's role also changes. It is less fixed and defined. It depends on the teacher's personality and considerations and on the student's feelings. Any action by the teacher is intended to meet the student's thinking and needs.

The constructivist approach aims to create an environment similar to the natural environment in which man discovered how to grow wheat. An education system that affords the student a learning environment which is compatible with his level and with the interest he exhibits in the learning subject, an open learning environment, a learning environment which enables the student to raise questions and find solutions to these questions by himself using a trial and error method, is a more effective method. However, this method is also more expensive, and requires more resources and manpower. A system which enables constant and free interaction with the teacher, with the learning environment and with the knowledge sources is a necessary condition for the realization of the constructivist approach. This is the way for ideal learning, learning which has its own rate and development stage. A learning system in which every student is afforded an environment which is challenging and suitable for him is very expensive, requires many resources that will enable each student to learn at his own rate.

The constructivist approach is based on a theory that claims that the motive driving the learning process is the person himself – the knowledge and interest, the talent and the student's motivation. A learning method according to the constructivist approach will supply every student with the means for expressing his ability. This should be achieved without pressure, without direction and without competition. Every individual will be judged against himself, and not against his friends' achievements. Every student will invest according to his ability, and the environment will stimulate him to express his latent potential.

The student's development is smooth and continuous and takes place one stage after the other, i.e. a continuous growth of knowledge. This method does not claim to understand and control the laws of learning and the process of the acquisition of knowledge by the student. The environment supplies the learning needs and learning takes place.

The constructivist approach comprised the basis for the evolution of teaching methods: active learning, experiential learning and self-regulated learning. These learning processes enable the student to cope with data taken from the situation with which he is faced and creates an interaction with the knowledge he accumulated in prior experiences. The person acquires knowledge via problem solving and shaping. Learning occurs by doing, where the student and the teacher are active. This is learning which involves the students in doing and in thinking about what they are doing. The students are encouraged to experience things and understand them beyond the basic facts. They are encouraged to analyze the ideas and carry out synthesis while working. This led to the development of curricula adapted to the student's fields of interest. The major characteristics of these curricula are:

- The student is involved in doing.
- Less emphasis is placed on transmitting information and more on the development of the student's skills and abilities.
- The student creates a connection between activities by discussion, writing and presenting.
- Emphasis is on the student. The student is afforded the possibility of researching the approaches and values he chooses.

Learning is not effective if it does not include the acquisition of knowledge while developing skills, experience and doing. Learning is a skill that includes training, instruction, trial and correction of errors while learning. These curricula emphasize the acknowledgement of the variance of the individual and his development as a student. An interpersonal relation evolves, which emphasizes the importance of democracy as an existential need in the individual's worldview. The goal is to achieve a balance between the needs of the individual and care for the society. The needs of the individual are expressed in the development of the ability to learn, the development of moral judgment, the development of personal abilities and the development of tools that will enable the individual to act and learn autonomously. The needs of the society are expressed in the development of tolerance, cooperation, social skills and improved interpersonal communication. The principles of learning are:

- Emphasizing human and warm relations between those participating in the learning and emphasizing the student's activity in directing independent learning.
- Developing a flexible curriculum which is adapted to the student.
- Developing and organizing materials and resources in the learning environment which stimulate learning and investigation.
- Using alternative teaching and a diversity of social designs for developing learning experiences.

Meaningful learning occurs via methods which develop activity that combines learning tasks, learning and education experiences that promote in-depth learning. Experience in social roles is very important in the moral and spiritual development of those experiencing the process.

These approaches are based on the assumption that meaningful learning occurs via the manner of experiencing or the personal experience or the teamwork. These teaching methods are based on maximal activity by the student. The teacher's role is to direct and organize the learning experience. It includes affective and psychomotor components which are integrated into a complete whole. This type of learning is suitable for the development of high levels of thinking and problem solving.

In his book *The Third Way*, Anthony Giddens analyzes the trends existing today in the Western World. Today the state passes as much authority and responsibility as possible to its citizens. In order to serve this goal, the education system must educate citizens who will be able to take their fate into their own hands. The goal of the education system is therefore to develop the student's ability, so that he will be able to fulfill his needs. Give the people the ability to solve their problems. Do not supply them with the solutions themselves! The education system thus needs to afford the student with the means and the ability by which he will be able to become integrated in society and will be able to earn a living for himself and his family.

According to this approach we can define the goals of learning, analyze the way and stages by which we will achieve these goals and finally judge the extent to which the goals were achieved. Giddens' approach is based on the assumption that we can direct, guide and lead the students towards goals that we shall define.

A similarity exists between the behaviorist approach and the approach of Hobbes, Luke and Hume. Their approach assumes that man is born a *tabula rasa* (clean slate) and all information reaches him from experiences and that the experience can be measured and directed and influenced. In contradistinction, the philosopher Immanuel Kant claims that a process of thinking can be found behind behavior. The individual's behavior is influenced and directed by the events that take place in his internal world, in his awareness and in his thought. These occurrences are not always understood and are not given to simple evaluation and measurement.

These are two approaches to learning with two methods for activating them. The policy makers must decide which method to use. This is an almost impossible task. It is difficult to use both methods. They are not always complementary and are sometimes even contradictory. The constructivist approach will dictate freedom in the classroom, an open learning system, a stimulating learning environment, inquiry and experience. On the other hand, the behaviorist approach will demand discipline, presentation of goals, measurements, evaluation, judgment of the teacher and his achievements, constant evaluation of the student, giving grades, giving prizes and encouraging excellence, control of the learning process and making changes in it according to the students' performances.

Which approach will the education system choose? Do we have the tools to decide which method is preferable? Will we afford the teacher or the education system a tool by which they can make decisions in the field of teaching? When should one method be used and not the other? Can the accumulation of knowledge through research in the field of curricula help us improve the manner of collecting information, analyzing and making decisions?

JUDGING AND EVALUATING LEARNING PROCESSES

The school system must therefore judge itself. It must evaluate the education and teaching methods. An objective and clear scale which will enable the assessment of processes must be formulated using a systematic and reliable method that will enable measurement, evaluation, control and conclusions.

A system of concepts is required in order to succeed in measuring a process and reaching conclusions about the process. The chances of evaluating and reaching conclusions about a process improve when the process contains more defined and measurable concepts.

The learning process is a complex process. Not all variables that participate in this process are measurable. Not every variable in the field of learning and teaching can be evaluated objectively. Some variables are subjective and cannot be measured. Nonetheless, when discussing these fields we should strive to as clear and accurate a definition as possible of as many variables of the variables which take part in the process as possible.

Data collection, defining concepts and their accuracy is identical in all sciences. This process is essential for increasing knowledge in the field. The concepts become more accurate as more information is supplied by research. This process enables the development of knowledge.

In order to guide a learning process we must define different methods of teaching and the differences between them as well as which goals can be achieved by each method. A series of researches which we carried out during the 1980's helped us differentiate between different methods of activating technological systems in teaching.

The teaching methods are a factor that should be taken into account during the process of planning an effective curriculum (Offir, 2003b; 2004; 2005). A method of learning by computer may be considered along a spectrum. The "traditional method" is at one end of the spectrum and the "open method" is at the other end. The traditional method provides the student with information. The computer directs the student according to his particular level and in response to his answers. The learning processes and stages are well-defined and documented and all possible correct answers are known. In contradistinction, the open method enables the student to operate independently. The student can use different methods and applications in different subjects according to his interests, inclinations and abilities. The computer serves as an information store, and a broad variety of information can be presented to the student.

The concepts of open and traditional methods can be regarded as being derived from the definition of the open and traditional classroom. There is no consistent way of defining open classrooms. Amabile (1983) cites several definitions or views. Openness can be viewed as "a style of teaching involving flexibility of space, student choice of activity, richness in learning materials, integration of curriculum areas, and more individual or small-group instruction", or one can emphasize the open classroom atmosphere as being conducive to developing curiosity, exploration and self-directed learning. This is in contrast to the traditional classrooms which are characterized by authoritative teaching, examinations, grading, large group instruction and strict adherence to curricula. We adopted Blitz's (1973) definition of the open classroom. This definition includes several fundamental characteristics:

- The open classroom stresses the need to be actively engaged with the environment as a means for achieving meaningful learning.
- The open classroom is tailored to individual interests and activities, and learning must therefore take place at an individual pace and style.
- The open classroom content is relevant to the student's environment, the environment is important in structuring learning.
- The open classroom is designed to be used according to the individual student's particular pace and learning style.
- The open classroom strives to achieve learning which is exciting and enjoyable.
- The open classroom promotes learning which is diagnostic, guiding and stimulating, rather than authoritative.

However, as Blitz points out, additional elements exist which may vary greatly, in addition to the above-mentioned basic characteristics. These elements depend on the teacher's particular philosophy and personality as well as on the teaching facilities.

Research supports the prediction that the open classroom contributes to creativity to a greater extent than the traditional classroom. Amabile (1983), in a review of studies performed on open classrooms and creativity, reports that most of the evidence supports the open classroom:

- The open classroom leads to a consistent and maintained superiority among children.
- Children in the open classroom achieve higher scores on creativity tests.
- The open classroom contributes to higher scores in open-ended tests.

The open method follows the same guidelines as the open classroom. The most frequent activities in the traditional classroom are group reading and mathematics drills. In contradistinction, the most frequent activities in the open classroom are creative writing, group projects and independent reading. The traditional method thus typically consists of drills and practice, whereas the open method usually includes tools for supporting creative writing and exploration.

The open method may include other elements, such as fewer or no constraints on performance, team effort, etc. The open classroom may be designed as such, or may be used in a special way as a standard tool. A database may be introduced as a useful tool in the technological world, and the student can learn to use this database, collect and analyze data (which are traditional applications of the tool). Alternately, the database may be used as a tool for exploration.

According to Schank and Farell (1990), the fastest way to change a traditional classroom into an open classroom is via computer technology. For example, the biggest obstacle to proposing and introducing new and original ideas is the fear of failure. The computer creates an environment which allows for failure and encourages originality. The student asks questions, formulates a hypothesis and examines the hypothesis using a computer simulation or database. The student can make as many mistakes as necessary in order to find the answer, without fear of embarrassment.

Previous research has shown that different variables influence the computer's effectiveness. It is assumed that the presence of certain factors will improve the effectiveness of the open classroom, whereas the presence of others will improve the effectiveness of the traditional classroom. The student's level of creativity should apparently be taken into consideration when using either the open or the traditional method (Crawford, 1988).

We carried out a research with a sample of 140 high school students aged 16 from two socio-economic statuses. Different methods were used as an integral part of their learning process. The different methods were divided according to their degree of openness. The open method was at one end of the scale and the traditional method was at the other end. Two research instruments were used in this study. The first was a 15-item questionnaire designed to examine the students' computer-related attitudes. The items form a general factor, i.e. computer-related attitudes, which explained at least 10% of the variance. The second instrument was the "Torrance Test" for measuring the "level of creativity". Socio-economic information about each participating student was also collected. Statistical analysis of the data did not indicate any significant differences between the "flexibility" and "originality" scores received by students from a low socio-economic status and those from a high status. However, significant differences were found in the scores obtained by the two groups in "fluency". Students from the high socio-economic group received higher scores than those from the low socio-economic status.

Significant differences were also found between the attitudes of these two groups of students towards the methods of using computers in the learning process. The students from the low socio-economic status preferred to work with word processors. In contradistinction, students from the high socio-economic status expressed no preference. The open method was preferred by students with high scores in "originality", whereas the traditional method was preferred by students with low scores in "originality". Thus, differences were found between the creativity level of students from a low and high socio-economic status. Furthermore, the students' level of creativity influenced their attitudes towards different teaching methods in the classroom.

Significant differences were found between three aspects of creativity: "fluency", "flexibility" and "originality". The level of originality was found to be significantly related to the type of computer method preferred by the students. The open method was preferred by students with a high level of originality, whereas the traditional method was preferred by students with a low level of originality. This correlation was found in both groups, i.e. those with a low and those with a high socio-economic status. Significant differences were also found in the level of fluency of students with a low and a high socio-economic status, with those with a low status exhibiting a lower level of fluency.

The computer stores information in a databank and a wide variety of information may be presented to the student for analysis or for searching for information. The student needs to perform the difficult task of assessing the information and reaching conclusions. It may be concluded that the level of originality is significantly related to the student's attitude towards using technology during the process of learning. As the level of originality increases, so does the preference for an open method of learning. This conclusion is also supported for the level of fluency.

This connection between the level of originality and the preference for an open method of teaching is found only when the level of fluency is high. When this level is low, the influence of originality is not related to the preference for an open teaching method. When the level of originality is low, the influence of other factors, such as the student's attitude towards the subject matter, increases. The research results prove that the concept "open method" is not similar to the concept "traditional method".

Any method proves its effectiveness in different populations in order to achieve different goals. Each method has a different definition. This research helped us define concepts and understand the difference between them. As we define more concepts, we will have more tools to construct a model that will help us make decisions in the process of activating technological systems.

The introduction of instructional technology into the classroom has not always met with success. Technology itself is obviously just another tool with the potential to revolutionize the education system. However, a revolution in education will occur only if the correct educational steps and decisions are taken in order to ensure the successful introduction of technology into the learning and instruction process. Thus, decision making is a major variable that must be taken into account when deciding on the introduction of any instructional technology methodology into the education framework (Offir, 1993; 2000b).

THE TEACHER'S ROLE IN INSTRUCTIONAL TECHNOLOGY

The method for operating instructional technology depends mainly on the goal of learning. Instructional technology can contribute towards achieving the learning goal only when the teacher is not essential for learning. Decision making on the part of the teacher demands a clear definition of the different aims of learning and the different methods of operating a technological system in learning.

In the first phase of defining the goal of learning, different psychology theories, such as Bloom's (1956) taxonomy of the cognitive domain, can be used. The lowest cognitive level is knowledge. The students must remember and recall information. The highest level is evaluation. The students must be able to assess the value of a method for attaining a particular purpose.

Guilford (1959) presented a model for representing separate mental abilities which collectively form a map of structure, of intelligence. His theory can also be used for defining the method of teaching. One aspect of his model, called operations, is particularly relevant to the present discussion. Guilford suggested that retrieval of information from storage in memory basically involves two kinds of operations, divergent production and convergent production. When divergence is high, or the level on Bloom's scale is high (for example, evaluation), the role of instructional technology is minimal since it cannot fully cope with this task given the present state of the art in software. The teacher must take the dominant role in teaching such a subject. However, when the subject matter is low in divergence (convergent) or is mainly a transfer of knowledge, instructional technology can replace the teacher to a higher extent. The teacher's role becomes less effective.

The accuracy of the goal definition increases as more information is collected by the system. Instructional technology can be operated by different methods for establishing different levels of teacher-student interactions. These levels have been found to affect the student's needs for the teacher's presence. These findings directed us in our effort to try and define different methods for operating instructional technology.

OPERATING INSTRUCTIONAL TECHNOLOGY

The teacher is an important factor in the introduction of instructional technology into the schools. Instructional technology will be used in a school if the teacher considers it to be a more effective method for achieving the aim of teaching. Two extreme methods can be found on the continuum of instructional technology methods. These extremes are the two extremes mentioned above, i.e. the open and the traditional method.

With the traditional method, the material and process of learning are well-defined. All possible answers are known and the aim of the method is solely to transfer information. The "teaching machine", for example, is a traditional method. In contradistinction, the "open method" aims to develop the student's way of thinking and his ability to analyze material, to draw conclusions and present original ideas. The teacher makes a different contribution to the process of learning in these two extreme methods of teaching. In the traditional method the teacher transfers knowledge, i.e. delivers information to the student. This task can be accomplished by lectures, books or other sources of information. In the open method the teacher asks the students open questions, discusses ideas and encourages the students to present their own original conclusions. The teacher's presence in the classroom is more important in the open method. This method of learning is suitable for achieving the aim of "evaluation".

The method of operating instructional technology should be directed by the goals of teaching. In the traditional method, when the aim of learning is mainly the transfer of information, instructional technology can control the learning process. In this situation the student can even obtain information at home via the Internet, television, satellite, book or fax. The effectiveness of the teacher-student interaction in this case is less critical.

In the open method, instructional technology should be operated so that it leaves the teacher in the classroom with enough space for expressing himself. The teacher-student interaction is important in this method. The student should have the opportunity to express his or her ideas and comments, whether the teacher is in the instructional technology studio or in the classroom.

The different systems for operating instructional technology can be classified according to the level of interaction which they enable, with each possessing advantages and disadvantages. Videoconferencing enables full interaction between the teacher and the student. Both can see and hear each other. Learning by satellite enables limited teacher-student interactions. The students can see the teacher, but the teacher cannot see the students. The students can ask and answer questions mainly in writing. Television and fax enable unidirectional delivery of information. Therefore, the aim of learning will affect the method of learning. The method of learning will affect the type of instructional technology that will be used and this technology will affect the level and quality of the teacher-student interaction.

We found that the teacher-student interaction is an important factor affecting the level of learning. The interaction is important mainly in the open method. However, the instructional technology system is limited in constructing a teacher-student interaction. It may be concluded that when the importance of the teacher-student interaction increases, the importance of the teacher's presence in the classroom also increases.

We have constructed a model for analyzing the messages in instructional technology. The validity and reliability of our research tool for analyzing interactions was developed as an integral part of operating our instructional technology system (Offir and Lev, 2000). During the past twenty years our research has directed us towards developing a model for decision making, i.e. where, when and how to use different instructional technology means for achieving defined aims of education (Katz and Offir, 1990; Offir, 1988; Offir and Katz, 1990a,b,c)

The teacher must be taken into account when generating a change in the learning and teaching system. The model which was consolidated enables the analysis of the goals of the learning process which will be achieved by the teacher and those which will be achieved by technological systems: Which teaching method is suitable for achieving a defined measurable and objective aim? Which teaching method is suitable for achieving a less defined and subjective aim?

According to this model, the teacher will concentrate mainly on imparting ability, developing thinking and tasks that involve individual attention. The technological systems will be operated mainly in order to impart information to the student. A combination and integration between technological systems and a flesh and blood teacher will lead to an improvement in the learning and teaching framework and will thus increase their effectiveness.

RESEARCH PROCESS FOR EVALUATING THE INTEGRATION OF TECHNOLOGIES IN LEARNING

The process of integrating technological systems in teaching and learning thus requires a unique research strategy which includes four stages, as presented in the following diagram:

The concepts which we use for discussing and making decisions in the field of the "integration of technological systems in learning" are concepts that were created and formulated in various disciplines: psychology, sociology, curricula, business administration, economics, etc. Some of these concepts will be found to be relevant to the research and will be able to help in the process of assimilating and evaluating technological systems in learning. Other concepts will be found unsuitable for the assimilation and evaluation process. The theoretical research must locate the concepts relevant to the field. It affords tools for formulating and defining the goal which we wish to achieve with the learning process.

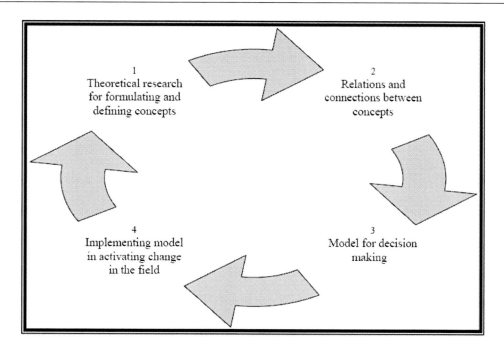

Defining the concepts and determining their use in the process of assimilating and evaluating technologies is the first stage, i.e. the theoretical research for formulating and defining concepts, some of which will be found relevant to the assimilation process. Some innovative technological systems will be found appropriate, and some will be found unsuitable.

The second stage of the research will deal in defining relations and connections between the concepts. For example, the research methods were defined on a continuum, where the "open method" is at one end and the "traditional method" is at the other end. Determining the methods on this continuum enables reference to methods found between these two extremes, i.e. an open method which also contains fixed objective elements, for example a simulation or model. The concept of "goal" in the second stage of our research can be found to have a relation and connection to different types of "goals". Different theories can be used in order to define the goals, as defined in the previous section.

The third stage will deal in the presentation of a model which will demonstrate complex relations between the various concepts and the relations between the teaching method and the goal which we are planning to achieve. The model will present the relation between the teaching method, the goal, and the teacher's contribution to the teaching process. The model that is constructed in the third stage is three-dimensional and presents relations between various variables.

The validity of the model which is constructed in the third stage will be examined in the fourth stage of the process, i.e. the implementation stage. This is the stage in which we activate the project in the field, make decisions according to the model which we designed and examine the model's effectiveness in improving the discussion and the decision making process. The model's effectiveness is examined by the extent of its contribution to improving the achievement of the project's aims.

STAGES OF RESEARCH AND IMPLEMENTATION IN THE FIELD OF INSTRUCTIONAL TECHNOLOGY

Thus, the first stage of research is theoretical and attempts to understand the relations and effects between diverse variables. A major part of this research will we found to be non-relevant, i.e. no relations will be found between the variables. However, some variables with significant relations and effects will be found. These variables will comprise the basis for continuing research.

In our research the teacher was found to comprise a significant factor in the process of change. We therefore asked: Does a relation exist between any of the teacher's characteristics, personality or abilities and his willingness to carry out a change in his teaching habits? We carried out investigations in an attempt to discover significant relations between the teacher's willingness to assimilate change and his personality traits. The teacher's personality trait as a risk-taker was found to be significant. The teacher's risk-taker trait can predict his willingness to cope with change.

In the next stage of our research we tried to understand the relation between the level of the teacher's willingness to take risks (risk-taker) and his attitudes towards the use of technological systems in his teaching process. An investigation was carried out with the aim of examining the relations between the concepts and their contribution to the consolidation of a model that will help in the decision making process (Offir, 1990). Two questionnaires were designed especially for this study:

1. Risk-taking questionnaire: This questionnaire was comprised of 12 items and was intended for assessing the subjects' risk-taking level. A principal components analysis with VARIMAX rotation, designed to rotate the initial factors such that each item loads high on one factor but almost zero on others, yielded one significant factor comprising six questionnaire items (this factor had an eigenvalue greater than 1.0, indicating that it consisted of homogeneous content and explained at least 10% of the variance). A higher score in this aspect of the factor indicated that the subject indulged more in high level risk-taking behavior. The second aspect of the factor included these 6 risk-taking experiences where the subjects were asked to predict the number and levels of risk-taking behavior which they thought they would undertake in the future. A higher score on this aspect indicated a higher number and level of future risks chosen. The compound risk-taking score was based on the cumulative score achieved on both of the risk-taking aspects.
2. Attitude to computers questionnaire: This questionnaire contained one significant factor (eigenvalue greater than 1.0 and explaining at least 10% of the variance) and was comprised of 13 items. The subjects were asked to state their computer-related attitudes on a scale from 1 (low level attitude) to 5 (high level attitude). The final score was based on a summation of the answers to all 13 items.

The subjects were divided into three levels of risk-taking according to their responses in the risk-taking questionnaire. Analysis of variance performed for the risk-taking attitude towards computer variables indicated the existence of a significant difference between the three risk-taking level groups. A *post hoc* Scheffe test, designed to examine the significance of inter-group differences resulting from the significant main effects was performed. The results indicated that high level risk-takers have a significantly more positive attitude towards computers than medium level risk-takers, who in turn have a significantly more positive attitude towards computers than low level risk-takers.

These results can help us make a decision regarding the suitable method for carrying out a change in the education system. Instructional technology is generally accepted by teachers as being an innovation in the field of education and instruction (Katz and Offir, 1988). When technology is introduced into the classroom, the teachers must carry out changes in their instructional and teaching methods in order to effectively accommodate instructional technology in the instructional process. However, any institutional, curriculum or instructional change is only as effective as the teaching staff's ability to implement the change effectively. The effectiveness of any staff development policy can only be considered in light of the manner in which the teachers respond to this policy. Understanding the teachers' behaviors and attitudes is therefore a prerequisite for the implementation of any reform in the teaching and instruction methods.

The relation between change and personality variables is well-known in society in general and in education in particular. When society feels that a fundamental change is necessary, it calls upon innovative leaders to initiate the necessary change. This is also the case in education (Duke, 1987). Technology is a new instructional aid and only those teachers whose personalities are comfortable with innovative teaching methods will respond positively to technology and will make a firm decision to use instructional technology in the classroom (Glasman and Nevo, 1988).

The results of our investigation clearly demonstrate that a positive attitude towards using technology in the classroom is significantly related to the personality trait of risk-taking. High level risk-takers are apparently more likely to be capable of making the transition to using instructional technology than are medium or low level risk-takers. The risk-taking trait appears to be necessary for the adoption of a new and innovative instructional and teaching method and can be used to predict successful introduction of novelty into the classroom. In contradistinction, low level risk-takers appear to reflect traditionalism in the teachers' perceptions of teaching methods. This impairs their ability to accept novel teaching methods in the classroom. These results confirm findings that certain personality traits are necessary for the successful implementation of novel situations in the classroom (Katz, 1984).

When use of instructional technology in the classroom is universally perceived as successful, all teachers (low, medium and high level risk-takers) will agree to implement this technology within their instructional activities. However, if instructional technology is perceived as only about 50% successful, then the low level risk-takers will agree to implement it in only about 10% of their teaching activities. Medium level risk-takers will use this technology in 50% of their instruction, whereas the high level risk-takers will use instructional technology in 80% of their teaching.

These results indicate that schools which are intent on introducing instructional technology into their classrooms should do so only with teachers who are classified as high level risk-takers. After instructional technology is demonstrated as being useful in teaching by these risk-taking teachers, it can be introduced into the classrooms of medium and low level risk-takers. These teachers will then be more inclined to accept instructional technology as a new, but not threatening, teaching method.

Further research should be carried out in order to examine whether the findings of this research are unique to the field of instructional technology.

With the development of the computer in the 1980's, many believed that the computer would become integrated in the teaching process and would comprise an effective tool. Some even predicted that it would replace the teacher. Many believed that the change in the education system would result from a flooding of the school with computers. The model which we consolidated as a result of our researches indicates and directs towards a different method for integrating technological systems in education:

1. The system must take the teacher's needs and wishes into account.
2. The teacher's personality is an important factor in his willingness to cope with new systems in teaching.
3. Success in using instructional technology systems in the past influences the teacher's attitudes towards the change.

A teacher who experienced more successful and tangible success in integrating instructional technology systems in the past will have less resistance to the integration of such systems in the classroom.

The model therefore guides us to the decision to integrate instructional technology systems in slow steps. If we wish to succeed, instructional technology should at first be introduced into a limited number of schools. Concentrating the efforts to a limited number of schools will increase the chances for success. Evidence of success will enable the introduction of more technological systems into the education process. Integration of technological systems in additional schools will be carried out only in places where the chances for success are high. Acting according to this model will lead to greater assurance of success. This method is contradictory to the method that was customary in the past, i.e. "flooding the school with technology" and stems from the research which we carried out and which is based on research results and models that were consolidated in order to make decisions based on these models.

ASSIMILATING DISTANCE LEARNING AS AN ENVIRONMENT FOR INVESTIGATING THE GENERATION OF CHANGES IN THE EDUCATION SYSTEM

We have been investigating distance learning systems since the 1990's. Activation of a distance learning system within the framework of the classroom is a change and an innovation which evoke responses by the teachers who must cope with this change.

Distance learning today is similar to the integration of computers in the teaching of the 1980's. Both are innovative systems which are supposed to become integrated within the teaching system and are under the authority and influence of the teacher. It is therefore natural that the teacher's attitudes and willingness to cooperate with this process of change are important and dominant variables that must be taken into account in the decision making process when deciding on the most suitable method for integrating technological systems in education.

Our research on distance learning, similarly to our research on the integration of computers in teaching, focuses on the investigation, measurement, assessment and becoming familiar with the process of change generated in the learning systems. It aims to elucidate factors which influence the teacher's place, role and status in the classroom. The evaluation and research process of distance learning systems indicated the importance of the concept "interaction", since in distance learning contact between the teacher and the student is not face to face. Rather, learning is carried out at a distance. The teacher is found in a distant location and the issue of contact with the student is significant, dominant and important.

Teacher-student interactions have always been regarded as a crucial variable for determining learning and attitudinal outcomes in distance learning environments. Many of the recent studies reviewed by Liaw and Huang (2000) are based on the "interaction quality hypothesis" (Trentin, 2000). These studies assume the existence of a direct correlation between the quality of the teacher-student interaction and positive learning outcomes. However, the term "quality" is not always defined. Furthermore, the "interaction quality hypothesis" is not always supported when empirically examining the nature of the relationship that exists between specific types of teacher-student interactions and learning outcomes.

Our interaction research therefore focused on the development and validation of instruments that can be used to analyze the content of verbal and nonverbal teacher-student interactions (Offir and Lev, 1999; 2000). These instruments enabled a comparison of teacher-student interaction patterns in conventional as opposed to distance learning environments. These interaction patterns were used to elucidate how interaction patterns change across contents, using content analysis for establishing empirical links between different types of interactions and student attitudinal outcomes (Offir, Lev and Barth, 2002).

A content analysis instrument which was developed and validated in our studies (Offir and Lev, 2000) was used in order to calculate the frequencies and ratios of different teacher-student interaction categories. This instrument was based on Henri's (1992) content analysis framework, which was subsequently modified by Oliver and McLoughlin (1996). The instrument's coding scheme contained the following categories:

- Social interaction: Teachers interact with students in order to create social relations and support affective-motivational aspects of the learning process.
- Procedural interaction: Statements containing information about administrative and technical issues related to the lesson or course.
- Expository interaction: Statements which present knowledge content.
- Explanatory interaction: Teachers use the students' reactions to explain content.
- Cognitive task engagement: Teachers present a question or learning task which requires the students to engage in information processing.

Data generated by interaction content analysis was used online to supply the teacher with formative evaluation and data-based recommendations regarding his interaction management. After each lesson, the teacher received a "map" which reflected his use of interactions during the lesson. This objective feedback helped the teacher identify the specific interactions which should be increased or decreased during the next lesson. Ongoing research on the teacher's interactions enabled us to feed information directly "back into the loop" in order to help the teacher make more effective use of interactions.

However, when the number of students in the project increased, it became apparent that the question "effective for whom?" needed further investigation. We had a situation in which students with similar levels of ability (as indicated by their teachers' recommendations) and motivation (self-selection) were producing very diverse learning outcomes. We realized that instead of asking which interaction patterns were effective, we should establish the types of interaction that worked effectively for specific students. We would have to establish what works for which types of students and why. Only then could we use interaction analysis in order to help us design and deliver an effective distance learning program. We began to track the students' performance and learning outcomes in each lesson, so as to understand the diversity in learning outcomes. Multiple criteria were used to collect data on each student's learning outcomes.

As we shall see, when educational research moves from the laboratory to the field, it becomes almost impossible to isolate and control the numerous variables involved. Researchers who focus on content analysis can adopt a systematic and integrative approach in order to examine how person, process or product variables interrelate in a distance learning environment. Online data collection on the students' performance, combined with analysis of the teacher's interactions during each lesson, enable researchers to identify patterns of teacher interactions that support effective learning. Significant correlations between types of interaction patterns and positive learning outcomes can be immediately "fed back into the loop" in order to help teachers manage their interactions more effectively. The objective "map" generated by content analysis helps teachers understand which specific interactions they should increase or decrease. Use of content analysis as a formative evaluation tool, as opposed to summative evaluation at the end of the course, helps both researchers and practitioners maximize the potential of the distance learning environment.

Examination of the data indicated that the category "teacher's explanatory interactions" should be re-divided into the following three sub-categories:

- Learning assistance interactions: The teacher's explanatory interactions which are designed to facilitate the students' comprehension and retention of content. This sub-category contains the teacher's use of advance organizers, overviews and summaries, explicit definition of the lesson's objective and structure, emphasis on the relevance of the target content and other teaching strategies designed to gain and maintain the student's attention. This sub-category was subsequently defined as a category in order to enable the user to differentiate between expository statements which present content and statements which facilitate students' information-processing (Offir and Barth, 2002).
- Superficial teacher feedback: The teacher's responses which do not contain an informative explanation of why the student's answer or comment is incorrect. Teachers' responses such as: "Incorrect, anyone else?" and "You are in the right direction, try again", can be included in this category.
- In-depth teacher feedback: In-depth explanatory feedback in response to students' questions and comments. Statements in this sub-category supply students with a detailed explanation of why their comments or answers are correct or incorrect. Teacher statements such as: "Your argument leaves out data relating to ..." or "You are assuming that a correlation necessarily implies causality", can be included in this category.

After the category of explanatory interactions was sub-divided, a significant positive correlation was found between the teachers' social interactions and learning assistance interactions. A larger correlation was found at the end of the teaching process than at the beginning.

One of the main aims of interaction content analysis research is to systematically observe and categorize types of teacher-student interactions in order to illuminate interaction patterns that might otherwise be overlooked (Stubbs and Delamont, 1986). Interaction content analysis helps researchers "tease apart" the essential elements of the interaction and investigate which interactions correlate with positive learning and attitudinal outcomes. Empirical examination of interaction patterns which exhibit a significant correlation with positive outcomes facilitates data-based decisions on the quality of the interaction and enables researchers to supply teachers with an effective formative evaluation.

For example, as the course progressed, the correlation between social interactions and learning assistance interactions increased. No such correlation was found at the beginning of the course, whereas later it became significant. The correlation increased even further during the last part of the learning process (Offir 2003a; 2006; 2007). However, no correlations were found between the other categories of teacher interactions. The increased correlation between social interactions and learning assistance interactions was accompanied by a concomitant increase in the percentage of students who confirmed that they understood the content of the unit.

The category of social interactions included all non-content related teacher statements that support motivational-affective aspects of the learning process. This category includes instructors' attempts to increase student confidence and mediate a feeling of competence. For example, statements such as: "Come on guys, this just looks complicated – when you begin using it you will see that you have already mastered much more complicated material", may be classified in this category. When teacher-related findings were correlated with student-related findings, a correlation of $r=.9582$ was found between the percentage of students who thought they understood the content of the unit and the teacher's social interactions. Furthermore, a correlation of $r=.8357$ was found between the percentage of students who indicated that they thought they understood the content of the unit and the teacher's learning assistance interactions. The significant increase in the number of students who confirmed that they understood the content when the teacher's learning assistance interactions were correlated with the teacher's social interactions emphasizes three basic assumptions on which this study was based:

1. Non-intellective factors play a key role in determining the extent to which talented students realize their learning potential. The significance of a cluster of non-intellective factors was identified by Terman and Oden (1959) in their thirty year follow-up study of high IQ persons. Their study clearly indicates that traits such as persistence, integration towards goals, self-confidence and freedom from inferiority complexes differentiated between achieving and non-achieving persons. Feuerstein and Tannenbaum (1993) also examined the relationship between non-intellective dispositions and underachievement among highly talented students.

2. Students with a high learning potential who live in peripheral areas must be taught non-intellective dispositions together with the subject content. Acquisition of content alone, without these enabling dispositions, will not necessarily empower these

students to maximize their full potential. High school students' participation in a university course within the framework of their own school creates a challenging but supportive learning environment that also focuses on the acquisition of enabling dispositions. In our project, one of the main functions of the on-site facilitator is to identify and prevent potential obstacles to effective learning. These obstacles have been reviewed by Tzuriel (1991). They include rapid loss of persistence in the face of failure, interpretation of errors as indicative of insufficient ability and expectation of future failure.

3. In a conventional learning environment, effective instructors constantly use verbal and nonverbal messages in order to encourage and reassure their students that they are capable of learning the material. In a distance learning environment, the students do not have access to the teacher's nonverbal expressions and gestures. According to Cookson and Chang (1995), distance learning instructors must compensate for the loss of this visual dimension. Our findings regarding concomitant improvements in students' self-evaluations of content comprehension when the teacher's social interactions correlate with learning assistance interactions reinforce this position.

This field project was designed to identify and enrich students whose psychometric scores and school grades did not reflect their high levels of learning potential. The student sample therefore did not contain the full range of ability levels. The findings regarding the correlation between types of teacher interactions and students' evaluation of content comprehension reinforce our previous findings (Offir and Lev, 2000). However, our conclusions remain limited to samples consisting of students with relatively high ability levels. Furthermore, our findings regarding the impact of teacher interactions remain limited to students' subjective feelings and attitudes towards content comprehension. Future research should focus on clarifying when and under what conditions the teachers' interactions significantly affect the students' objective scores.

Our findings regarding the use of objective feedback to modify teaching behaviors reflect previous research on feedback and behavior modifiability as reviewed by Mory (1996). Thus, our future research will focus on teacher-related variables which affect the modifiability of teacher interactions. Further research is also necessary in order to establish the extent to which teacher interactions influence student outcomes when the content's difficulty level is increased. We hope to include additional courses in future studies in order to investigate how teacher interactions affect student outcomes in a distance learning environment across subject-content areas and across varying levels of student ability.

In the first stage of our research we always try to define and examine concepts. This is how we defined the concept of interaction. The research helped us differentiate between different types of teacher-student interactions. Definition of the different types of interaction enabled investigation of the differences between the interactions that exist in a distance learning environment and interactions which exist in the traditional classroom. This will enable us to assess which interactions should be left to the teacher in the classroom and which interactions can be operated in a distance learning environment. The results of the research will help in the process of training teachers. The teacher in the classroom will fulfill the same tasks and will help achieve those goals of the curriculum which are difficult or impossible to achieve via distance learning systems. Defining the concepts helps us understand a model for operating a distance learning system as an auxiliary aid and will help the teacher's activity in the teaching and learning processes. The results of this investigation direct us to those interactions which are beneficial in different teaching situations.

CONCLUSION

The education system must achieve two main goals. One is to shape the student's behavior, to impart habits, to shape his attitudes, to increase his willingness to integrate in the society in which he lives and to contribute from his abilities and skills, to develop the student's thinking and motivation and to educate him to become an independent learner. The other goal is to impart as much knowledge as possible to the student. Some of these goals can be achieved by individual education and direction. When our goal is to transmit knowledge we will ask: What are the efforts? What is the investment which we are willing to make and which it is correct to invest in order to reach a defined achievement? In such systems the investment will be measurable and the products quantifiable.

When we activate a distance learning system we turn to a large population of students. Hundreds of students who are dispersed over the entire country can participate in a distance learning lesson. Here we will measure: What is the investment, the input? To what achievements have we led the students? What is the profit gained from activating the distance learning system, i.e. the output?

When referring to large populations of students, the considerations systems are not measurable. In such cases we refer to the mean achievements of the population. Decision making models are therefore models that measure and characterize quantitative products.

The overall goals of learning cannot be achieved solely by measurable and objective processes. There exist subjective variables such as the teacher's contribution, education to moral behavior, attitudes, thinking and learning ability, motivation and interest. These concepts are not measurable and cannot be judged in terms of objective measures. The cooperation, integration between the distance learning system and a flesh and blood teacher are parameters which must be taken into account when constructing and designing an education and teaching system. The quantitative concepts cannot be used solely to appropriately and accurately describe the learning process, and neither can the qualitative concepts.

Our research began with an attempt to define concepts taken from the field of the social sciences (psychology, sociology). Our aim was to quantify and define these concepts as accurately as possible. These concepts comprise basic elements for a model which helps us in decision making and deliberations processes.

The learning process can be described on a continuum which begins at a particular point and ends when the learning goals have been achieved. Parts of this continuum can be described using objective concepts. Parts of this continuum can be quantified. However, such a model does not afford an accurate picture since some of its parts cannot be defined in objective terms. This fact does not absolve us of attempting to consolidate models and trying and make them as accurate as possible. The most accurate picture is described using objective concepts. However, where objective concepts are limited, subjective concepts will be added in order to understand and describe the picture. This combination of objective and subjective concepts will present the true picture. Accurate mathematical models cannot describe and explain the decision making process. This process includes objective evaluation along with subjective concepts. In our research we use psychological, i.e. subjective, concepts and try to define them as accurately as possible. We then try to use these concepts in order to predict processes.

This chapter detailed three fields which have developed during the years of this ongoing research. The first field enables definition of the method of operating technological systems according to the teaching goals. Different teaching goals were achieved using different methods (Offir, 1995; 2000). The second field helps determine a method for the assimilation of innovative systems within the education system. This method indicated that the preferable method for activating a "change" is to first activate it within a limited environment where it can be controlled and where its non-failure can be ensured. Success of this change reduces resistance to the change to a minimum and enables its growth and expansion (Offir, 1990). The third field in which our research concentrates is the field of teacher-student interactions. First we invested an effort in an attempt to define various teacher-student interactions. Then we attempted to examine which interactions are suitable for face to face teaching in the classroom and which interactions can be completed by distance learning (Offir, 1999; 2000c; 2002; 2003a, 2003b; 2004; 2005; 2006; 2007).

The results of this research help define the division of roles in the teaching process between the teacher and the technological system. It defines which teaching goals will be achieved by a flesh and blood teacher and which will be achieved by the technological system. The research process in these fields began with an attempt to define concepts and variables which are relevant to the learning process via technological systems. We then tried to find connections and influences between these variables and to present a model which will comprise a basis for analysis and decision making processes in this field.

There is general agreement that the field of learning and education is a most important field in modern society. Few will disagree with the assumption that a relation exists between the level of learning and the effectiveness of the education systems and the strength of the society in which we live. Shaping the behavior of tomorrow's citizens is carried out within today's schools. However, the learning and education systems must undergo a process of change in order to achieve these goals.

The fields of business administration, economics and sciences have models for collecting and classifying information. These models are directed towards and aid in the analysis of processes and making decisions. However, in spite of the great importance of the field of learning and education, this field has not adopted and assimilated these ways of thinking, discussion and analysis: How are changes generated in the learning systems? What are the mechanisms which promote change? What are the dominant variables in the process of consolidating models for evaluation and measurement of change in learning systems? These are subjects that have been investigated by our research team for approximately twenty-five years.

In contradistinction to economic and business systems, judgment and evaluation in the field of education and learning are mainly intuitive. Analysis of research data demonstrated that the integration of computerized systems within the school framework is a process of change. However, this process of change is not identical to processes of change in economical systems and therefore cannot use the same models.

A change in the field of learning systems must take many data that belong to the field of education and learning into account, including attitudes and the teachers' and students' ability and personality, psychological and sociological processes that accompany a process of change, the teaching method, the learning goals as well as cost versus effectiveness (Offir, 1999). However, these concepts are not accurate and it is difficult and complex to quantify them. The researches that were carried out and published by our research team deal in this issue. The complexity of the issue increases because economic models as a sole means are not effective. Nonetheless, knowledge on learning and education is also not sufficiently quantified to comprise a basis for analysis and decision making. We must find a method that will use an accurate quantitative model but will at the same time leave some room for subjective considerations.

These conclusions were reached by our team already in the 1980's, in light of the fact that computers were not generating the expected revolution in the education system. Since the 1980's the team has investigated and published articles dealing in the issue of the integration of technological systems in learning. The aim of these researches is to consolidate models for the assimilation of change in learning and education systems.

Computers and distance learning systems are only means which bring the change to the learning frameworks. Integration of these systems within learning systems creates a situation of change. Evaluation and research on the processes of assimilation of innovative technologies enables evaluation research and elucidates the process of change in learning systems.

The research method which was used is the "ongoing research". The experimental fields in which data are collected are the schools that decided to join the research and assimilate a change. The collected data comprise the basis for decisions for improving methods of operating the project in the following stages of its development. As the project progresses, the decision making model becomes more accurate and effective. The research process thus aspires to:

- Formulate a definition that is as accurate as possible of psychological and sociological concepts that appear to be relevant to the evaluation of the process of assimilation of innovative systems in teaching, according to the literature.
- Examine connections between variables and the accuracy of their definition by researches carried out within the framework of the project in the schools.
- Find relations between the variables. Relations and connections between the variables may help present a holistic model which will contribute to the decision making process.
- Confirm the model, i.e. examine the accuracy of the model in the decision making process.

The teaching and learning system cannot waive the teacher's contribution, the personal human contact between the student and the teacher. The research results indicate that the teacher's contribution is not fixed and changes according to the learning goals. The model defines those goals for which the teacher can use teaching means.

The research team is interested mainly in increasing the effectiveness of the teaching and learning system. The teacher is mainly a mediator. His contribution is mainly in those complex fields of education, development of thinking ability, crystallization of attitudes and moral behaviors in which the teacher's contribution as having a personal-human approach is critical. There is no technological system that can exchange the teacher and which can replace the personal human teacher-student contact. The fact that technological systems fulfill some of the teacher's functions (such as the transmission of information) enables the teacher in the classroom to pay greater attention to individual education in small groups. This enables the teacher to contribute from his ability and uniqueness as a person and as a teacher. With this approach the level of teaching and the transmission of information is carried out in a more professional and strict manner.

The process of the confirmation of the objectivity of the model is a process that has been taking place for years. It is based on the relation between the investment and the product. The model is more effective when the investment is smaller and the product is greater. Our aspiration is, of course, to make a small investment and achieve a high output. Investment when implementing a model in an educational learning environment is measured by concepts which have a varying value in terms of being quantifiable. For example, the investment includes the type of teacher involved in operating the system, the effort invested by the teacher, the teacher's willingness and ability, etc. On the other hand, the products include, for example, the student's motivation, his willingness to contribute to the environment in which he lives, his ability, his skill, the knowledge he acquired and the achievements he attained.

REFERENCES

Amabile, T.M. (1983). *The Social Psychology of Creativity*. New York: Springer Verlag.

Blitz, B. (1973). *The Open Classroom: Making it Work*. Boston: Allyn and Bacon.

Bloom, B.S. (1956). *Taxonomy of Educational Objectives, Handbook 1: Cognitive Domain*. New York: Longman.

Cookson, P.S. and Chang, Y. (1995). The multidimensional audio conferencing classification system. *American Journal of Distance Education*, 9 (3), 18-35.

Crawford, R. (1988). Computer and curriculum in 1999 computers in education. In: F. Lovis and E.D. Tagg (eds.) *Proceedings of the IFIP TC3, European Conference on Computers in Education*, pp. 645-650.

Duke, D.L. (1987). *School Leadership and Instructional Improvement*. New York: Random House, pp. 40-47.

Feuerstein, R. and Tannenbaum, A.J. (1993). Mediating the learning experiences of gifted underachievers. In: B. Wallace and H.B. Adams (eds.) *Worldwide Perspective on the Gifted Disadvantaged*. Natal: AB Academic Publishers.

Giddens, A. (1999). *The Third Way: The Renewal of Social Democracy*. Melden MA: Polity Press.

Glasman, S.L. and Nevo, D. (1988). *Evaluation in Decision Making*. Boston: Kluwer Academic Publishers, pp. 71-112.

Guildford, J.P. (1959). Three faces of intelligence. *American Psychologist*, 14, 469-479.

Henri, F. (1992). Computer conferencing and content analysis. In: A.R. Kaye (ed.) *Collaborative Learning through Computer Conferencing: The Najaden Papers*. New York: Springer, pp. 115-136.

Katz, Y.J. and Offir, B. (1988). Computer oriented attitudes as a function of age in an elementary school population. *Computers in Education*. Elsevier Science Publishers, pp. 371-373.

Katz, Y.J. and Offir, B. (1990a). Computer assisted instruction and students' social orientations. *Proceedings of the 5th Jerusalem Conference on Information Technology*. Los Alamitos CA IEEE: Computer Society Press, pp. 660-664.

Katz, Y.J. and Offir, B. (1990b). Learning and teaching with computers: psychological and counseling considerations. *Educational Counseling*, 1 (2), 124-130.

Katz, Y.J. and Offir, B. (1991). The relationship between personality and computer related attitudes of Israeli teachers. *Education and Computing*, 7, 249-252.

Katz, Y.J. and Offir, B. (1993). Computer assisted learning and cognitive abilities: hardware and software planning implications. In: A. Knierzinger and M. Moser (eds.) *Informatics and Changes in Learning*. Linz, Austria: IST Press, pp. 11-13 (section I).

Katz, Y.J. and Offir, B. (1994). Computer games as motivators for successful computer end-use. In: J. Wright and D. Benzie (eds.) *Exploring a New Partnership: Children Teachers and Technology*. Amsterdam: Elsevier Science Publishers, pp. 81-87.

Liaw, S. and Huang, H. (2000). Enhancing interactivity in Web-based instruction: a review of the literature. *Educational Technology*, 40, 41-45.

Mory, E.M. (1996). Feedback research. In: D.H. Jonassen (ed.) *Handbook of Research for Educational Communications and Technology*. New York: Simon and Schuster Macmillan, pp. 919-956.

Offir, B. and Cohen-Fridel, S. (1998). Psychological factors in conducting an interactive distance learning system. *Teleteaching*, Edited by the Austrian Computer Society, pp. 779-787.

Offir, B. and Katz, Y.J. (1990a). Learning-curve as a model for analyzing the cost-effectiveness of a training system. *Education and Computing*, 6 (1-2), 161-164.

Offir, B. and Katz, Y.J. (1990b). Computer oriented attitudes as a function of risk-taking among Israeli elementary school teachers. *Journal of Computer Assisted Learning*, 6, 168-173.

Offir, B. and Katz, Y.J. (1995). The teacher as initiator of change: fact or fiction. *Curriculum and Teaching*, 10 (1), 63-66.

Offir, B. and Lev, J. (1999). Teacher-learner interaction in the process of operating D.L. (distance learning) system. *Educational Media International*, 36 (2), 132-138.

Offir, B. and Lev, J. (2000a). Constructing an aid for evaluating teacher-learner interaction in distance learning. *Educational Media International*, 37 (2), 91-98.

Offir, B. (1987). Application of psychology theory in computer-based instruction. *Educational Technology*, XXII (4) , 47-49.

Offir, B. (1993). C.A.I. as a factor in changing the self image of pre-school children. *Computer in Education*, Pedagogical and Psychological Implications, UNESCO Publishers, pp. 68-74.

Offir, B. (2000b). Map for decision making in operating distance learning – research results. *Educational Media International*, 37 (1), 8-15.

Offir, B. (2003a). Analyzing of teacher-students interaction. *Proceedings of the Fourth International Conference on Teacher Education – Teacher Education as a Social Mission – A Key to the Future*. Achva College of Education, Mofet Institute.

Offir, B. (2006). Influence of a distance learning environment on university students' attribution of success and failure factors. *Computers in Education Journal*, 16 (1), 82-94.

Offir, B., Barth, I., Lev, J. and Shteinbok, A. (2005). Can interaction content analysis research contribute to distance learning. *Educational Media International*, 42 (2), 161-171.

Offir, B., Bezalel-Rosenblatt, R. and Barth, I. (2007). Introverts, extroverts, and achievement in a distance learning environment. *The American Journal of Distance Education*, 21 (1).

Offir, B., Golub, M.R. and Cohen-Fridel, S. (1993). Attitude towards courseware as a function of high schools' creative level. *Information and Changes in Learning*, Elsevier Science Publishers, 7, 211-218.

Offir, B., Katz, Y.J. and Schmida, M. (1991). Do universities educate towards a change in teacher attitudes? The case of computer attitudes. *Education and Computing*, 7, 289-292.

Offir, B., Lev, J., Harpaz, Y. and Barth, I. (2002). Using interaction content analysis instruments to access distance education. Special issue of the journal *Computer in Schools*, 18 (2/3), 27-42.

Offir, B., Lev, J., Lev, Y., Barth, I. and Shteinbok, A. (2003b). Teacher-student interactions and learning outcomes in a distance environment. *Internet and Higher Education*, 6 (1), 65-75.

Offir, B., Lev, Y. and Lev, Y. (2000c). Matrix for analyzing verbal and non-verbal teacher-learner interactions in distance learning. In: D. Benzie and D. Passey (eds.) *Educational uses of Information and Communication Technology*. Publishing House of the Electronics Industry, pp. 319-326.

Offir, B., Lev. Y., Lev, Y., Barth, I. and Shteinbok, A. (2004). An integrated analysis of verbal and nonverbal interaction in conventional and distance learning environments. *Journal of Educational Computing Research*, 31 (2), 101-118.

Oliver, R. and McLoughlin, C. (1996). An investigation of the nature and form of interaction in live interactive television. *ERIC Document* Number 396738.

Schank, R.C. and Farell, R. (1990). *Creativity in Education: New Standard for Teaching with Computers*. New Haven: Yale University.

Stubbs , E and Delamont , S . (1986) *Explorations in classroom Observation* , in . P. Croll (ED) Systematic classroom Observation (London . The falmer Press) .

Terman, L.M. and Oden, M.H. (1959). *Genetic Studies of Genius: The Gifted Group at Mid-life*. Stanford CA: Stanford University Press.

Trentin, G. (2000). The quality-interactivity relationship in distance education. *Educational Technology*, January/February, 17-27.

Tzuriel, D. (1991). Cognitive modifiability, mediated learning experience and affective-motivational processes: a transactional approach. In: R. Feuerstein, P.S. Klein and A.J. Tannenbaum (eds.) *Mediated Learning Experience: Theoretical, psychological and Learning Implications*. London: Freund Publishing House.

In: Global Issues in Higher Education
Editor: Pamela B. Richards, pp. 267-339

ISBN: 978-1-60021-802-6
© 2007 Nova Science Publishers, Inc.

Chapter 12

HIGHER EDUCATION: FEDERAL SCIENCE, TECHNOLOGY, ENGINEERING, AND MATHEMATICS PROGRAMS AND RELATED TRENDS*

United States Government Accountability Office

WHY THIS STUDY?

The United States has long been known as a world leader in scientific and technological innovation. To help maintain this advantage, the federal government has spent billions of dollars on education programs in the science technology, engineering, and mathematics (STEM) fields for many years. However, concerns have been raised about the nation's ability to maintain its global technological competitive advantage in the future. This report presents information on(1) the number of federal programs funded in fiscal year 2004 that were designed to increase the number of students and graduates pursuing STEM degrees and occupations or improve educational programs in STEM fields, and what agencies report about their effectiveness; (2) how the numbers, percentages, and characteristics of students, graduates, and employees in STEM fields have changed over the years; and (3) factors cited by educators and others as affecting students' decisions about pursing STEM degrees and occupations, and suggestions that have been made to encourage more participation.

GAO received written and/or technical comments from several agencies. While one agency, the National Science Foundation, raised several questions about the findings, the others generally agreed with the findings and conclusion and several agencies commended GAO for this work.

ABBREVIATIONS

BEST   Building Engineering and Science Talent

---

* Excerpted from http://www.gao.gov/new.items/d06114.pdf

BLS   Bureau of Labor Statistics
CGS   Council of Graduate Schools
CLF   civilian labor force
COS   Committee on Science
CPS   Current Population Survey
DHS   Department of Homeland Security
EPA   Environmental Protection Agency
HHS   Health and Human Services
HRSA   Health Resources and Services Administration
IPEDS   Integrated Postsecondary Education Data System
NASA   National Aeronautics and Space Administration
NCES   National Center for Education Statistics
NCLBA   No Child Left Behind Act
NIH   National Institutes of Health
NPSAS   National Postsecondary Student Aid Study
NSF   National Science Foundation
NSTC   National Science and Technology Council
SAO   Security Advisory Opinion
SEVIS   Student and Exchange Visitor Information System
STEM   science, technology, engineering, and mathematics

The United States has long been known as a world leader in scientific and technological innovation. To help maintain this advantage, the federal government has spent billions of dollars on education programs in the science, technology, engineering, and mathematics (STEM) fields for many years. Some of these programs were designed to increase the numbers of women and minorities pursuing degrees in STEM fields. In addition, for many years, thousands of international students came to the United States to study and work in STEM fields. However, concerns have been raised about the nation's ability to maintain its global technological competitive advantage in the future. In spite of the billions of dollars spent to encourage students and graduates to pursue studies in STEM fields or improve STEM educational programs, the percentage of United States students earning bachelor's degrees in STEM fields has been relatively constant—about a third of bachelor's degrees— since 1977. Furthermore, after the events of September 11, 2001, the United States established several new systems and processes to help enhance border security. In some cases, implementation of these new systems and processes, which established requirements for several federal agencies, higher education institutions, and potential students, made it more difficult for international students to enter this country to study and work.

In the last few years, many reports and news articles have been published, and several bills have been introduced in Congress that address issues related to STEM education and occupations. This report presents information on (1) the number of federal civilian education programs funded in fiscal year 2004 that were designed to increase the numbers of students and graduates pursuing STEM degrees and occupations or improve educational programs in STEM fields and what agencies report about their effectiveness; (2) how the numbers, percentages, and characteristics of students, graduates, and employees in STEM fields have changed over the years; and (3) factors cited by educators and others as influencing people's decisions about pursuing STEM degrees and occupations, and suggestions that have been made to encourage greater participation in STEM fields. To determine the number of programs designed to increase the numbers of students and graduates pursuing STEM degrees and occupations, we identified 15 federal departments and agencies as having STEM programs, and we developed and conducted a survey asking each department or agency to provide information on its education programs, including information about their effectiveness [1]. We received responses from 14 of them, the Department of Defense did not participate, and we determined that at least 13 agencies had STEM education programs during fiscal year 2004 that met our criteria.

To describe how the numbers of students, graduates, and employees in STEM fields have changed, we analyzed and reported data from the Department of Education's (Education) National Center for Education Statistics (NCES) and the Department of Labor's (Labor) Bureau of Labor Statistics (BLS). Specifically, as shown in table 1, we used the National Postsecondary Student Aid Study (NPSAS) and the Integrated Postsecondary Education Data System (IPEDS) from NCES and the Current Population Survey (CPS) data from BLS. We assessed the data for reliability and reasonableness and found them to be sufficiently reliable for the purposes of this report.

To obtain perspectives on the factors that influence people's decisions about pursuing STEM degrees and occupations, and to obtain suggestions for encouraging greater participation in STEM fields, we interviewed educators and administrators in eight colleges and universities (the University of California Los Angeles and the University of Southern California in California; Clark Atlanta University, Georgia Institute of Technology, and Spelman College in Georgia; the University of Illinois; Purdue University in Indiana; and Pennsylvania State University). We selected these colleges and universities to include a mix of public and private institutions, provide geographic diversity, and include a few minority-serving institutions, including one (Spelman College) that serves only women students.

Table 1. Sources of Data, Data Obtained, Time Span of Data, and Years Analyzed

Department	Agency	Database	Data obtained	Time span of data	Years analyzed
Education	NCES	NPSAS	College student enrollment	9 years	Academic years 1995-1996 and 2003-2004
Education	NCES	IPEDS	Graduation/degrees	9 years	Academic years 1994-1995 and 2002-2003
Labor	BLS	CPS	Employment	10 years	Calendar years 1994 through 2003

Sources: NCES's National Postsecondary Student Aid Study (NPSAS) and Integrated Postsecondary Education Data System (IPEDS) and BLS's Current Population Survey (CPS) data.

Note: Enrollment and employment information are based on sample data and are subject to sampling error. The 95-percent confidence intervals for student enrollment estimates are contained in appendix V of this report. Percentage estimates for STEM employment have 95-percent confidence intervals of within +/- 6 percentage points and other employment estimates (such as wages and salaries) have confidence intervals of within +/- 10 percent of the estimate, unless otherwise noted. See appendixes I, V, and VI for additional information.

In addition, most of the institutions had large total numbers of students, including international students, enrolled in STEM fields. We also asked officials from the eight universities to identify current students to whom we could send an e-mail survey. We received responses from 31 students from five of these institutions. In addition, we interviewed federal agency officials and representatives from associations and education organizations, and analyzed reports on various topics related to STEM education and occupations. Appendix I contains a more detailed discussion of our scope and methodology. We conducted our work between October 2004 and October 2005 in accordance with generally accepted government auditing standards.

RESULTS IN BRIEF

Officials from 13 federal civilian agencies reported having 207 education programs funded in fiscal year 2004 that were designed to increase the numbers of students and graduates pursuing STEM degrees and occupations or improve educational programs in STEM fields, but they reported little about the effectiveness of these programs. The 13 agencies reported spending about $2.8 billion in fiscal year 2004 for these programs. According to the survey responses, the National Institutes of Health (NIH) and the National Science Foundation (NSF) sponsored 99 of the 207 programs and spent about $2 billion of the approximate $2.8 billion. The program costs ranged from $4,000 for a national scholars program sponsored by the Department of Agriculture (USDA) to about $547 million for an NIH program that is designed to develop and enhance research training opportunities for individuals in biomedical, behavioral, and clinical research by supporting training programs at institutions of higher learning. Officials reported that most of the 207 programs had multiple goals, and many were targeted to multiple groups. For example, 2 programs were identified as having one goal of attracting and preparing students at any education level to pursue coursework in STEM areas, while 112 programs had this as one of multiple goals. Agency officials also reported that evaluations were completed or under way for about half of the programs, and most of the completed evaluations reported that the programs had been effective and achieved established goals. However, some programs that have not been evaluated have operated for many years.

While the total numbers of students, graduates, and employees have increased in STEM fields, changes in the numbers and percentages of women, minorities and international students varied during the periods reviewed. From the 1995-1996 academic year to the 2003-2004 academic year, the number of students increased in STEM fields by 21 percent—more than the 11 percent increase in non-STEM fields. Also, students enrolled in STEM fields increased from 21 percent to 23 percent of all students. Changes in the numbers and percentages of domestic minority students varied by group. For example, the number of African American students increased 69 percent and the number of Hispanic students increased 33 percent. The total number of graduates in STEM fields increased by 8 percent from the 1994-1995 academic year to the 2002-2003 academic year, while graduates in non-STEM fields increased 30 percent. Further, the numbers of graduates decreased in at least four of eight STEM fields at each education level. The total number of domestic minority graduates in STEM fields increased, and international graduates continued to earn about one-third or more of the master's and doctoral degrees in three fields. Moreover, from 1994 to 2003, employment increased by 23 percent in STEM fields as compared with 17 percent in non-STEM fields. African American employees continued to be less than 10 percent of all STEM employees, and there was no statistically significant change in the percentage of women employees.

Educators and others cited several factors as influencing students' decisions about pursuing STEM degrees and occupations, and they suggested many ways to encourage more participation in STEM fields. Studies, education experts, university officials, and others cited teacher quality at the kindergarten through 12th grade levels and students' high school preparation in mathematics and science courses as major factors that influence domestic students' decisions about pursuing STEM degrees and occupations. In addition, university officials, students, and studies identified mentoring as a key factor for women and minorities. Also, according to university officials, education experts, and reports, international students' decisions about pursuing STEM degrees and occupations in the United States are influenced by yet other factors, including more stringent visa requirements and increased educational opportunities outside the United States. We have reported that several aspects of the visa process have been improved, but further steps could be taken. In order to promote participation in the STEM fields, officials at most of the eight universities visited and current students offered suggestions that focused on four areas: teacher quality, mathematics and science preparation and courses, outreach to underrepresented groups, and the federal role in STEM education. The students who responded to our e-mail survey generally agreed with most of the suggestions and expressed their desires for better mathematics and science preparation for college. However, before adopting such suggestions, it is important to know the extent to which existing STEM education programs are appropriately targeted and making the best use of available federal resources.

We received written comments on a draft of this report from the Department of Commerce, the Department of Health and Human Services, and the National Science and Technology Council. These agencies generally agreed with our findings and conclusions. We also received written comments from the National Science Foundation which questioned our findings related to program evaluations, interagency collaboration, and the methodology we used to support our findings on the factors that influenced decisions about pursing STEM fields. Also, the National Science Foundation provided information to clarify examples cited in the report, stated that the data categories were not clear, and commented on the graduate level enrollment data we used. We revised the report to acknowledge that the National Science Foundation uses a variety of mechanisms to evaluate its programs and we added a bibliography that identifies the reports and research used during the course of this review to address the comment about our methodology related to the factors that influenced decisions about pursuing STEM fields. We also revised the report to clarify the examples and the data categories and to explain the reasons for selecting the enrollment data we used. However, we did not make changes to address the comment related to interagency collaboration for the reason explained in the agency comments section of this report. The written comments are reprinted in appendixes VII, VIII, IX, and X. In addition, we received technical comments from the Departments of Commerce, Health and Human Services, Homeland Security, Labor, and Transportation, and the Environmental Protection Agency and National Aeronautics and Space Administration, which we incorporated when appropriate.

BACKGROUND

STEM includes many fields of study and occupations. Based on the National Science Foundations' categorization of STEM fields, we developed STEM fields of study from NCES's National Postsecondary Student Aid Study (NPSAS) and Integrated Postsecondary Education Data System (IPEDS), and identified occupations from BLS's Current Population Survey (CPS). Using these data sources, we developed nine STEM fields for students, eight STEM fields for graduates, and four broad STEM fields for occupations. Table 2 lists these STEM fields and occupations and examples of subfields. Additional information on STEM occupations is provided in appendix I.

Many of the STEM fields require completion of advanced courses in mathematics or science, subjects that are introduced and developed at the kindergarten through 12th grade level, and the federal government has taken steps to help improve achievement in these and other subjects. Enacted in 2002, the No Child Left Behind Act (NCLBA) seeks to improve the academic achievement of all of the nation's school-aged children. NCLBA requires that states develop and implement academic content and achievement standards in mathematics, science and the reading or language arts. All students are required to participate in statewide assessments during their elementary and secondary school years. Improving teacher quality is another goal of NCLBA as a strategy to raise student academic achievement. Specifically, all teachers teaching core academic subjects must be highly qualified by the end of the 2005-2006 school year [2]. NCLBA generally defines highly qualified teachers as those that have (1) a bachelor's degree, (2) state certification, and (3) subject area knowledge for each academic subject they teach.

The federal government also plays a role in coordinating federal science and technology issues. The National Science and Technology Council (NSTC) was established in 1993 and is the principal means for the Administration to coordinate science and technology among the diverse parts of the federal research and development areas. One objective of NSTC is to establish clear national goals for federal science and technology investments in areas ranging from information technologies and health research to improving transportation systems and strengthening fundamental research. NSTC is responsible for preparing research and development strategies that are coordinated across federal agencies in order to accomplish these multiple national goals.

In addition, the federal government, universities and colleges, and others have developed programs to provide opportunities for all students to pursue STEM education and occupations [3]. Additional steps have been taken to increase the numbers of women, minorities, and students with disadvantaged backgrounds in the STEM fields, such as providing additional academic and research opportunities. According to the 2000 Census, 52 percent of the total U.S. population 18 and over were women; in 2003, members of racial or ethnic groups constituted from 0.5 percent to 12.6 percent of the civilian labor force (CLF), as shown in table 3.

In addition to domestic students, international students have pursued STEM degrees and worked in STEM occupations in the United States. To do so, international students and scholars must obtain visas [4]. International students who wish to study in the United States must first apply to a Student and Exchange Visitor Information System (SEVIS) certified school. In order to enroll students from other nations, U.S. colleges and universities must be certified by the Student and Exchange Visitor Program within the Department of Homeland Security's Immigration and Customs Enforcement organization.

Table 2. List of STEM Fields Based on NCES's NPSAS and IPEDS Data and BLS's CPS Data

Enrollment–NCES' NPSAS data	Degrees–NCES1P EDS data	Occupations–BLS' CPS data
Agricultural sciences	Biological/agricultural sciences	Science
	Botany	Agricultural and food scientists
	Zoology	Astronomers and physicists
	Dairy	Atmospheric and space scientists
Biological sciences	Forestry	Biological scientists
	Poultry	Chemists and materials scientists
	Wildlife management	Environmental scientists and geoscientists
		Nurses
	Earth, atmospheric, and ocean sciences	Psychologists
	Geology	Sociologists
	Geophysics and seismology	Urban and regional planners
Physical sciences	Physical sciences	
	Chemistry	
	Physics	
Psychology P sychol	ogy	
	Clinical	
	Social	
Social sciences	Social sciences	
	Political science	
	Sociology	
Technology T echnol	ogy	Technology
	Solar	Clinical laboratory technologists and technicians
	Automotive engineering	Diagnostic-related technologists and technicians
		Medical, dental, and ophthalmic laboratory technicians
Enrollment–NCES' NPSAS data	Degrees–NCES1P EDS data	Occupations–BLS' CPS data
Engineering E ngineerin	g	Engineering
	Aerospace, aeronautical, and astronautical	Architects, except naval
	Architectural	Aerospace engineers
	Chemical	Chemical engineers
	Civil	Civil engineers
	Electrical, electronics, and communication	Electrical and electronic engineers
	Nuclear	Nuclear engineers
Computer sciences	Mathematics/computer sciences	Mathematics and computer sciences
Mathematics	Actuarial science	Computer scientists and systems analysts
	Applied mathematics	Computer programmers
	Mathematical statistics	Computer software engineers
	Operations research	Actuaries
	Data processing	Mathematicians
	Programming	Statisticians

Sources: NCES for NPSAS and IPEDS data; CPS for occupations.

Note: This table is not designed to show a direct relationship from enrollment to occupation, but to provide examples of majors, degrees, and occupations in STEM fields from the three sources of data.

Table 3. Percentage of the U.S. Population for Selected Racial or Ethnic Groups in the Civilian Labor Force, Calendar Years 1994 and 2003

	Percentage of U.S. population in the CLF, 1994	Percentage of U.S. population in the CLF, 2003
Race or ethnicity		
Hispanic or Latino origin	8.9	12.6
Black or African American	10.8	10.7
Asian	2.8	4.4
American Indian or Alaska Native	0.5	0.5

Source: GAO calculations based upon March 1994 and March2003 CPS data.

As of February 2004, nearly 9,000 technical schools and colleges and universities had been certified. SEVIS, is an Internet-based system that maintains data on international students and exchange visitors before and during their stay in the United States. Upon admitting a student, the school enters the student's name and other information into the SEVIS database. At this time the student may apply for a student visa. In some cases, a Security Advisory Opinion (SAO) from the Department of State (State) may be needed to determine whether or not to issue a visa to the student. SAOs are required for a number of reasons, including concerns that a visa applicant may engage in the illegal transfer of sensitive technology. An SAO based on technology transfer concerns is known as Visas Mantis and, according to State officials, is the most common type of SAO applied to science applicants [5]. In April 2004, the Congressional Research Service reported that State maintains a technology alert list that includes 16 sensitive areas of study. The list was produced in an effort to help the United States prevent the illegal transfer of controlled technology and includes chemical and biotechnology engineering, missile technology, nuclear technology, robotics, and advanced computer technology [6].

Many foreign workers enter the United States annually through the H-1B visa program, which assists U.S. employers in temporarily filling specialty occupations [7]. Employed workers may stay in the United States on an H-1B visa for up to 6 years. The current cap on the number of H-1B visas that can be granted is 65,000. The law exempts certain workers, however, from this cap, including those who are employed or have accepted employment in specified positions. Moreover, up to 20,000 exemptions are allowed for those holding a master's degree or higher.

More than 200 Federal Education Programs are Designed to Increase the Numbers of Students and Graduates or Improve Educational Programs in STEM Fields, but Most Have Not Been Evaluated

Officials from 13 federal civilian agencies reported having 207 education programs funded in fiscal year 2004 that were specifically established to increase the numbers of students and graduates pursuing STEM degrees and occupations, or improve educational programs in STEM fields, but they reported little about the effectiveness of these programs [8]. These 13 federal agencies reported spending about $2.8 billion for their STEM education programs. Taken together, NIH and NSF sponsored nearly half of the programs and spent about 71 percent of the funds. In addition, agencies reported that most of the programs had multiple goals, and many were targeted to multiple groups. Although evaluations have been done or were under way for about half of the programs, little is known about the extent to which most STEM programs are achieving their desired results. Coordination among the federal STEM education programs has been limited. However, in 2003, the National Science and Technology Council formed a subcommittee to address STEM education and workforce policy issues across federal agencies.

Federal Civilian Agencies Reported Sponsoring over 200 STEM Education Programs and Spending Billions in Fiscal Year 2004

Officials from 13 federal civilian agencies provided information on 207 STEM education programs funded in fiscal year 2004. The numbers of programs ranged from 51 to 1 per agency with two agencies, NIH and NSF, sponsoring nearly half of the programs—99 of 207. Table 4 provides a summary of the numbers of programs by agency, and appendix II contains a list of the 207 STEM education programs and funding levels for fiscal year 2004 by agency.

Table 4. Number of STEM Education Programs Reported by Federal Civilian Agencies

Federal agency	Number of STEM education programs
Department of Health and Human Services/ National Institutes of Health	51
National Science Foundation	48
Department of Energy	26
Environmental Protection Agency	21
Department of Agriculture	16
Department of Commerce	13
Department of the Interior	13
National Aeronautics and Space Administration	5
Department of Education	4
Department of Transportation	4
Department of Health and Human Services/Health Resources and Services Administration	3
Department of Health and Human Services/Indian Health Service	2
Department of Homeland Security	1
Total	207

Source: GAO survey responses from 13 federal agencies.

Federal civilian agencies reported that approximately $2.8 billion was spent on STEM education programs in fiscal year 2004 [9]. The funding levels for STEM education programs among the agencies ranged from about $998 million to about $4.7 million. NIH and NSF accounted for about 71 percent of the total—about $2 billion of the approximate $2.8 billion.

NIH spent about $998 million in fiscal year 2004, about 3.6 percent of its $28 billion appropriation, and NSF spent about $997 million, which represented 18 percent of its appropriation. Four other agencies, some with a few programs, spent about 23 percent of the total: $636 million. For example, the National Aeronautics and Space Administration (NASA) spent about $231 million on 5 programs and the Department of Education (Education) spent about $221 million on 4 programs during fiscal year 2004. Figure 1 shows the 6 federal civilian agencies that used the most funds for STEM education programs and the funds used by the remaining 7 agencies.

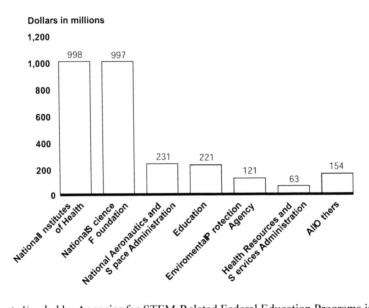

Figure 1. Amounts Funded by Agencies for STEM-Related Federal Education Programs in Fiscal Year 2004.

Table 5. Funding Levels for Federal STEM Education Programs in Fiscal Year 2004

Program funding levels	Numbers of STEM education programs	Percentage of total STEM education programs
Less than $1 million	93	45
$1 million to $5 million	51	25
$5.1 million to $10 million	19	9
$10.1 million to $50 million	31	15
More than $50 million	13	6
Total	207	100

Source: GAO survey responses from 13 federal agencies.

The funding reported for individual STEM education programs varied significantly, and many of the programs have been funded for more than 10 years. The funding ranged from $4,000 for an USDA-sponsored program that offered scholarships to U.S. citizens seeking bachelor's degrees at Hispanic-serving institutions, to about $547 million for a NIH grant program that is designed to develop and enhance research training opportunities for individuals in biomedical, behavioral, and clinical research by supporting training programs at institutions of higher education. As shown in table 5, most programs were funded at $5 million or less and 13 programs were funded at more than $50 million in fiscal year 2004. About half of the STEM education programs were first funded after 1998. The oldest program began in 1936, and 72 programs are over 10 years old [10]. Appendix III describes the STEM education programs that received funding of $10 million or more during fiscal year 2004 or 2005 [11].

Federal Agencies Reported Most STEM Programs Had Multiple Goals and Were Targeted to Multiple Groups

Agencies reported that most of the STEM education programs had multiple goals. Survey respondents reported that 80 percent (165 of 207) of the education programs had multiple goals, with about half of these identifying four or more goals for individual programs [12]. Moreover, according to the survey responders, few programs had a single goal. For example, 2 programs were identified as having one goal of attracting and preparing students at any education level to pursue coursework in the STEM areas, while 112 programs identified this as one of multiple goals. Table 6 shows the program goals and numbers of STEM programs aligned with them.

Table 6. Program Goals and Numbers of STEM Programs with One or Multiple Goals

Program goal	Programs with only this goal	Programs with multiple goals including this goal	Total programs with this goal and other goal(s)
Attract and prepare students at any education level to pursue coursework in STEM areas	2	112	114
Attract students to pursue degrees (2-year through Ph.D.) and postdoctoral appointments	6	131	137
Provide growth and research opportunities for college and graduate students in STEM fields	3	100	103
Attract graduates to pursue careers in STEM fields	17	114	131
Improve teacher education in STEM areas	8	65	73
Improve or expand the capacity of institutions to promote or foster STEM fields	3	87	90

Source: GAO survey responses from 13 federal agencies

The STEM education programs provided financial assistance to students, educators, and institutions. According to the survey responses, 131 programs provided financial support for students or scholars, and 84 programs provided assistance for teacher and faculty development [13]. Many of the programs provided financial assistance to multiple beneficiaries, as shown in table 7.

Most of the programs were not targeted to a specific group but aimed to serve a wide range of students, educators, and institutions. Of the 207 programs, 54 were targeted to 1 group and 151 had multiple target groups [14] In addition, many programs were targeted to the same group. For example, while 12 programs were aimed solely at graduate students, 88 other programs had graduate students as one of multiple target groups. Fewer programs were targeted to elementary and secondary teachers and kindergarten through 12th grade students than to other target groups. Table 8 summarizes the numbers of STEM programs targeted to one group and multiple groups.

Table 7. Numbers of STEM Programs with One or Multiple Types of Assistance and Beneficiaries

Type of assistance	Programs that provide only this type of assistance	Programs that provide this type and other types of assistance	Total programs that provide this type of assistance
Financial support for students or scholars	54	77	131
Institutional support to improve educational quality	6	70	76
Support for teacher and faculty development	12	72	84
Institutional physical infrastructure support	1	26	27

Source: GAO survey responses from 13 federal agencies

Table 8. Numbers of STEM Programs Targeted to One Group and Multiple Groups

Targeted group	Targeted to only this group	Targeted to this and other groups	Total programs targeted to this group
Kindergarten through grade 12 students			
Elementary school students	0	28	28
Middle or junior high school students	1	33	34
High school students	3	50	53
Undergraduate students			
2-year college students	1	57	58
4-year college students	4	92	96
Graduate students and postdoctoral scholars			
Graduate students	12	88	100
Postdoctoral scholars	12	58	70
Teachers, college faculty and instructional staff			
Elementary school teachers	0	39	39
Secondary school teachers	3	47	50
College faculty or instructional staff	4	75	79
Institutions	5	77	82

Source: GAO survey responses from 13 federal agencies.

Some programs limited participation to certain groups. According to survey respondents, U.S. citizenship was required to be eligible for 53 programs, and an additional 75 programs were open only to U.S. citizens or permanent residents [15]. About one-fourth of the programs had no citizenship requirement, and 24 programs allowed noncitizens or permanent residents to participate in some cases. According to a NSF official, students receiving scholarships or fellowships through NSF programs must be U.S. citizens or permanent residents. In commenting on a draft of this report, NSF reported that these restrictions are considered to be an effective strategy to support its goal of creating a diverse, competitive, and globally-engaged U.S. workforce of scientists, engineers, technologists, and well-prepared citizens. Officials at two universities said that some research programs are not open to non-citizens. Such restrictions may reflect concerns about access to sensitive areas. In addition to these restrictions, some programs are designed to increase minority representation in STEM fields. For example, NSF sponsors a program called Opportunities for Enhancing Diversity in the Geosciences to increase participation by African Americans, Hispanic Americans, Native Americans (American Indians and Alaskan Natives), Native Pacific Islanders (Polynesians or Micronesians), and persons with disabilities.

Agency Officials Reported That Evaluations Were Completed or under Way for about Half of the Federal Programs

Evaluations had been completed or were under way for about half of the STEM education programs. Agency officials responded that evaluations were completed for 55 of the 207 programs and that for 49 programs, evaluations were under way at the time we conducted our survey. Agency officials provided us documentation for evaluations of 43 programs, and most of the completed evaluations reviewed reported that the programs met their objectives or goals. For example, a March 2004 report on the outcomes and impacts of NSF's Minority Postdoctoral Research Fellowships program concluded that there was strong qualitative and quantitative evidence that this program is meeting its broad goal of preparing scientists from those ethnic groups that are significantly underrepresented in tenured U.S. science and engineering professorships and for positions of leadership in industry and government.

However, evaluations had not been done for 103 programs, some of which have been operating for many years. Of these, it may have been too soon to expect evaluations for about 32 programs that were initially funded in fiscal year 2002 or later. However, of the remaining 71 programs, 17 have been operating for over 15 years and have not been evaluated. In commenting on a draft of this report NSF noted that all of its programs undergo evaluation and that it uses a variety of mechanisms for program evaluation. We reported in 2003 that several agencies used various strategies to develop and improve evaluations [16]. Evaluations play an important role in improving program operations and ensuring an efficient use of federal resources. Although some of the STEM education programs are small in terms of their funding levels, evaluations can be designed to consider the size of the program and the costs associated with measuring outcomes and collecting data.

A Subcommittee Was Established in 2003 to Help Coordinate STEM Education Programs among Federal Agencies

Coordination of federal STEM education programs has been limited. In January 2003 the National Science and Technology Council (NSTC), Committee on Science (COS), established a subcommittee on education and workforce development. The purpose of the subcommittee is to advise and assist COS and NSTC on policies, procedures, and programs relating to STEM education and workforce development. According to its charter, the subcommittee will address education and workforce policy issues and research and development efforts that focus on STEM education issues at all levels, as well as current and projected STEM workforce needs, trends, and issues. The members include representatives from 20 agencies and offices—the 13 agencies that responded to our survey as well as the

Departments of Defense, State, and Justice, and the Office of Science and Technology Policy, the Office of Management and Budget, the Domestic Policy Council, and the National Economic Council. The subcommittee has working groups on (1) human capacity in STEM areas, (2) minority programs, (3) effective practices for assessing federal efforts, and (4) issues affecting graduate and postdoctoral researchers. The Human Capacity in STEM working group is focused on three strategic initiatives: defining and assessing national STEM needs, including programs and research projects; identifying and analyzing the available data regarding the STEM workforce; and creating and implementing a comprehensive national response that enhances STEM workforce development.

NSTC reported that as of June 2005 the subcommittee had a number of accomplishments and projects under way that related to attracting students to STEM fields. For example, it has (1) surveyed federal agency education programs designed to increase the participation of women and underrepresented minorities in STEM studies; (2) inventoried federal fellowship programs for graduate students and postdoctoral fellows; and (3) coordinated the Excellence in Science, Technology, Engineering, and Mathematics Education Week activities, which provide an opportunity for the nation's schools to focus on improving mathematics and science education. In addition, the subcommittee is developing a Web site for federal educational resources in STEM fields and a set of principles that agencies would use in setting levels of support for graduate and postdoctoral fellowships and traineeships.

Numbers of Students, Graduates, and Employees in STEM Fields Generally Increased, but Percentage Changes Varied

While the total numbers of students, graduates, and employees have increased in STEM fields, percentage changes for women, minorities, and international students varied during the periods reviewed.

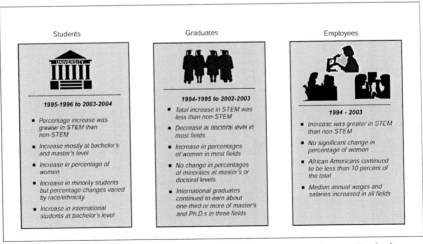

Source: GAO analysis of CPS, IPEDS, and NPSAS data; graphics in part by Art Explosion.

Figure 2. Key Changes in Students, Graduates, and Employees in STEM Fields.

The increase in the percentage of students in STEM fields was greater than the increase in non-STEM fields, but the change in percentage of graduates in STEM fields was less than the percentage change in non-STEM fields. Moreover, employment increased more in STEM fields than in non-STEM fields. Further, changes in the percentages of minority students varied by race or ethnic group, international graduates continued to earn about a third or more of the advanced degrees in three STEM fields, and there was no statistically significant change in the percentage of women employees. Figure 2 summarizes key changes in the students, graduates, and employees in STEM fields.

Numbers of Students in STEM Fields Grew, but This Increase Varied by Education Level and Student Characteristics

Total enrollments of students in STEM fields have increased, and the percentage change was greater for STEM fields than non-STEM fields, but the percentage of students in STEM fields remained about the same. From the 1995-1996 academic year to the 2003-2004 academic year, total enrollments in STEM fields increased 21 percent—more than the 11 percent enrollment increase in non-STEM fields. The number of students enrolled in STEM fields represented 23 percent of all students enrolled during the 2003-2004 academic year, a modest increase from the 21 percent these students constituted in the 1995-1996 academic year. Table 9 summarizes the changes in overall enrollment across all education levels from the 1995-1996 academic year to the 2003-2004 academic year.

The increase in the numbers of students in STEM fields is mostly a result of increases at the bachelor's and master's levels. Of the total increase of about 865,000 students in STEM fields, about 740,000 was due to the increase in the numbers of students at the bachelor's and master's levels. See table 23 in appendix IV for additional information on the estimated numbers of students in STEM fields in academic years 1995-1996 and 2003-2004.

Table 9. Estimated Changes in the Numbers and Percentages of Students in the STEM and Non-STEM Fields across All Education Levels, Academic Years 1995-1996 and 2003-2004

	Academic year1995-1996		Academic year 2003-2004	
	STEM	Non- STEM	STEM	Non- STEM
Enrollment measures				
Students enrolled (in thousands)	4,132	15,243	4,997	16,883
Percentage of total enrollment	21	79	23	77

Source: GAO calculations based upon NPSAS data.

Note: The totals for STEM and non-STEM enrollment include students in bachelor's, master's, and doctoral programs as well as students enrolled in certificate, associate's, other undergraduate, first-professional degree, and post-bachelor's or post-master's certificate programs. The percentage changes between the 1995-1996 and 2003-2004 academic years for STEM and non-STEM students are statistically significant. See appendix V for confidence intervals associated with these estimates.

The percentage of students in STEM fields who are women increased from the 1995-1996 academic year to the 2003-2004 academic year, and in the 2003-2004 academic year women students constituted at least 50 percent of the students in 3 STEM fields—biological sciences, psychology, and social sciences. However, in the 2003-2004 academic year, men students continued to outnumber women students in STEM fields, and men constituted an estimated 54 percent of the STEM students overall. In addition, men constituted at least 76 percent of the students enrolled in computer sciences, engineering, and technology [17]. See tables 24 and 25 in appendix IV for additional information on changes in the numbers and percentages of women students in the STEM fields for academic years 1995-1996 and 2003-2004.

While the numbers of domestic minority students in STEM fields also increased, changes in the percentages of minority students varied by racial or ethnic group. For example, Hispanic students increased 33 percent, from the 1995-1996 academic year to the 2003-2004 academic year. In comparison, the number of African American students increased about 69 percent. African American students increased from 9 to 12 percent of all students in STEM fields while Asian/Pacific Islander students continued to constitute about 7 percent. Table 10 shows the numbers and percentages of minority students in STEM fields for the 1995-1996 academic year and the 2003-2004 academic year.

Table 10. Estimated Percentage Changes in the Numbers and Percentages of Domestic Minority Students in STEM fields for All Education Levels for Academic Years 1995-1996 and 2003-2004

Race or ethnicity	Numbers of students, 1995-1996 (in thousands)	Numbers of students, 2003-2004 (in thousands)	Percentage change in the numbers of students between academic years 1995-1996 and 2003-2004	Minority group as a percentage of students in STEM fields, academic year 1995-1996	Minority group as a percentage of students in STEM fields, academic year 2003-2004
Black or African American	360	608	+69	9	12
Asian/Pacific Islander	289	345	+19	7	7
Hispanic or Latino origin	366	489	+33	9	10
American Indian	18	38	+107	0	1
Other/Multiple minorities	29	166	+475	1	3

Source: GAO calculations based upon NPSAS data.

Note: All percentage changes are statistically significant. See appendix V for confidence intervals associated with these estimates.

From the 1995-1996 academic year to the 2003-2004 academic year, the number of international students in STEM fields increased by about 57 percent solely because of an increase at the bachelor's level. The numbers of international students in STEM fields at the master's and doctoral levels declined, with the largest decline occurring at the doctoral level. Table 11 shows the numbers and percentage changes in international students from the 1995-1996 academic year to the 2003-2004 academic year.

According to the Institute of International Education, from the 2002-2003 academic year to the 2003-2004 academic year, the number of international students declined for the first time in over 30 years, and that was the second such decline since the 1954-1955 academic year, when the institute began collecting and reporting data on international students [18].

Table 11. Estimated Changes in Numbers of International Students in STEM fields by Education Levels from the 1995-1996 Academic Year to the 2003-2004 Academic Year

Education level	Number of international students, 1995-1996	Number of international students, 2003-2004	Percentage change
Bachelor's	31,858	139,875	+339
Master's	40,025	22,384	-44
Doctoral	36,461	7,582	-79
Total	108,344	169,841	+57

Source: GAO calculations based upon NPSAS data.

Note: Changes in enrollment between the 1995-1996 and 2003-2004 academic years are significant at the 95 percent confidence level for international students and for all education levels. See appendix V for confidence intervals associated with these estimates.

Moreover, in November 2004, the Council of Graduate Schools (CGS) reported a 6 percent decline in first-time international graduate student enrollment from 2003 to 2004. Following a decade of steady growth, CGS also reported that the number of first-time international students studying in the United States decreased between 6 percent and 10 percent for 3 consecutive years.

Total Numbers of Graduates with STEM Degrees Increased, but Numbers Decreased in Some Fields, and Percentages of Minority Graduates at the Master's and Doctoral Levels Did Not Change

The number of graduates with degrees in STEM fields increased by 8 percent from the 1994-1995 academic year to the 2002-2003 academic year. However, during this same period the number of graduates with degrees in non-STEM fields increased by 30 percent. From academic year 1994-1995 to academic year 2002-2003, the percentage of graduates with STEM degrees decreased from 32 percent to 28 percent of total graduates. Table 12 provides data on the changes in the numbers and percentages of graduates in STEM and non-STEM fields.

Table 12. Numbers of Graduates and Percentage Changes in STEM and Non-STEM Fields across All Degree Levels from the1994-1995 Academic Year to the 2002-2003 Academic Year

Graduation measures	STEM fields			Non-STEM fields		
	1994-1995	2002-2003	Percentage change	1994-1995	2002-2003	Percentage change
Graduates (in thousands)	519	560	+8	1,112	1,444	+30
Percentage of total graduates	32	28	-4	68	72	+4

Source: GAO calculations based upon IPEDS data.

Decreases in the numbers of graduates occurred in some STEM fields at each education level, but particularly at the doctoral level. The numbers of graduates with bachelor's degrees decreased in four of eight STEM fields, the numbers with master's degrees decreased in five of eight fields, and the numbers with doctoral degrees decreased in six of eight STEM fields. At the doctoral level, these declines ranged from 14 percent in mathematics/computer sciences to 74 percent in technology. Figure 3 shows the percentage change in graduates with degrees in STEM fields from the 1994-1995 academic year to the 2002-2003 academic year.

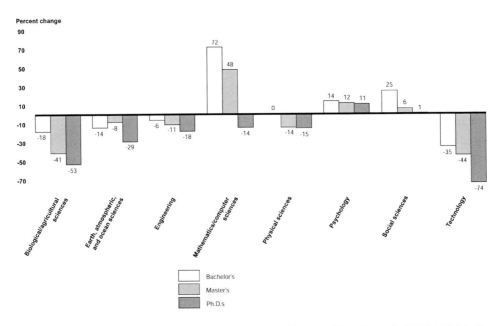

Figure 3. Percentage Changes in Bachelor's, Master's, and Doctoral Graduates in STEM Fields from Academic Year 1994-1995 to Academic Year 2002-2003.

From the 1994-1995 academic year to the 2002-2003 academic year, the total number of women graduates increased in four of the eight fields, and the percentages of women earning degrees in STEM fields increased in six of the eight fields at all three educational levels. Conversely, the total number of men graduates decreased, and the percentages of men graduates declined in six of the eight fields at all three levels from the 1994-1995 academic year to the 2002-2003 academic year. However, men continued to constitute over 50 percent of the graduates in five of eight fields at all three education levels. Table 13 summarizes the numbers of graduates by gender, level, and field. Table 26 in appendix IV provides additional data on the percentages of men and women graduates by STEM field and education level.

The total numbers of domestic minority graduates in STEM fields increased, although the percentage of minority graduates with STEM degrees at the master's or doctoral level did not change from the 1994-1995 academic year to the 2002-2003 academic year. For example, while the number of Native American graduates increased 37 percent, Native American graduates remained less than 1 percent of all STEM graduates at the master's and doctoral levels. Table 14 shows the percentages and numbers of domestic minority graduates for the 1994-1995 academic year and the 2002-2003 academic year.

Table 13. Numbers and Percentage Changes in Men and Women Graduates with STEM Degrees by Education Level and Field for Academic Years 1994-1995 and 2002-2003

Education level	STEM field	Number of men graduates		Percentage change in men graduates	Number of women graduates		Percentage change in women graduates
		1994-1995	2002-2003		1994-1995	2002-2003	
Bachelor's level	Biological/agricultural sciences	36,108	23,266	-36	35,648	35,546	
	Earth, atmospheric, and ocean sciences	2,954	2,243	-24	1,524	1,626	+7
	Engineering	52,562	48,214	-8	10,960	11,709	+7
	Mathematics and computer sciences	25,258	46,381	+84	13,651	20,436	+50
	Physical sciences	9,607	8,739	-9	5,292	6,222	+18
	Psychology	19,664	18,616	-5	53,010	64,470	+22
	Social sciences	56,643	63,465	+12	56,624	77,701	+37
	Technology	14,349	9,174	-36	1,602	1,257	-22
Master's level	Biological/agricultural sciences	4,768	2,413	-49	4,340	2,934	-32
	Earth, atmospheric, and ocean sciences	1,032	805	-22	451	552	+22
	Engineering	24,031	20,258	-16	4,643	5,271	+14
	Mathematics and computer sciences	10,398	14,531	+40	4,474	7,517	+68
	Physical sciences	2,958	2,350	-21	1,283	1,299	+1
	Psychology	4,013	3,645	-9	10,319	12,433	+20
	Social sciences	11,952	11,057	-7	11,398	13,674	+20
	Technology	927	467	-50	222	173	-22
Doctoral level	Biological/agricultural sciences	3,616	1,526	-58	2,160	1,161	-46
	Earth, atmospheric, and ocean sciences	488	315	-35	134	125	-7
	Engineering	5,401	4,159	-23	728	839	+15
	Mathematics and computer sciences	1,690	1,378	-18	434	439	+1
	Physical sciences	2,939	2,396	-18	922	892	-3
	Psychology	1,529	1,380	-10	2,511	3,086	+23
	Social sciences	2,347	2,111	-10	1,463	1,729	+18
	Technology	24	7	-71	3	0	-100

Source: GAO calculations based upon IPEDS data.

Table 14. Numbers and Percentage Changes in Domestic Minority Graduates in STEM Fields by Education Levels and Race or Ethnicity for Academic Years 1994-1995 and 2002-2003

Race or ethnicity	Degree Level	Number of graduates in STEM fields, 1994-1995	Number of graduates in STEM fields, 2002-2003	Percentage change in graduates	Percentage of total graduates in STEM fields, 1994-1995	Percentage of total graduates in STEM fields, 2002-2003
Black or African American	Total	33,121	44,475	+34	6	8
	Bachelor's	28,236	37,195	+32	5	7
	Master's	4,358	6,588	+51	1	1
	Doctoral	527	692	+31	0	0
Hispanic or Latino origin	Total	25,781	37,056	+44	5	7
	Bachelor's	22,268	32,255	+45	4	6
	Master's	3,015	4,121	+37	1	1
	Doctoral	498	680	+37	0	0
Asian/Pacific Islanders	Total	37,393	46,941	+26	7	8
	Bachelor's	29,389	39,030	+33	6	7
	Master's	6,064	6,814	+12	1	1
	Doctoral	1,940	1,097	-43	0	0
Native Americans	Total	2,488	3,409	+37	0	1
	Bachelor's	2,115	2,903	+37	0	1
	Master's	320	425	+33	0	0
	Doctoral	53	81	+53	0	0

Source: GAO calculations based upon IPEDS data.

Table 15. Changes in Numbers and Percentages of International Graduates in STEM fields at the Master's and Doctoral Degree Levels, 1994-1995 and 2002-2003 Academic Years

	1994-1995		2002-2003	
Masters' level	Number	Percentage of all graduates	Number	Percentage of all graduates
Agriculture/biological sciences	1,549	17	633	12
Earth, atmospheric, and ocean sciences	285	19	192	14
Engineering	9,720	34	11,512	45
Mathematics/computer sciences	5,105	34	10,335	47
Physical sciences	1,467	35	1,171	32
Psychology	493	3	704	4
Social sciences	3,749	16	4,795	19
Technology	169	15	118	18
Total	22,537		29,460	
Doctoral level				
Agriculture/biological sciences	1,616	28	743	28
Earth, atmospheric, and ocean sciences	183	29	140	32
Engineering	3,001	49	2,853	57
Mathematics/computer sciences	927	44	895	49
Physical sciences	1,290	33	1,281	39
Psychology	186	5	202	5
Social sciences	1,123	29	1,192	31
Technology	9	33	4	57
Total	8,335		7,310	

Source: GAO calculations based upon IPEDS data.

International students earned about one-third or more of the degrees at both the master's and doctoral levels in several fields in the 1994-1995 and the 2002-2003 academic years. For example, in academic year 2002-2003, international students earned between 45 percent and 57 percent of all degrees in engineering and mathematics/computer sciences at the master's and doctoral levels. However, at each level there were changes in the numbers and percentages of international graduates. At the master's level, the total number of international graduates increased by about 31 percent from the 1994-1995 academic year to the 2002-2003 academic year; while the number of graduates decreased in four of the fields and the percentages of international graduates declined in three fields. At the doctoral level, the total number of international graduates decreased by 12 percent, while the percentage of international graduates increased or remained the same in all fields. Table 15 shows the numbers and percentages of international graduates in STEM fields.

STEM Employment Rose, but the Percentage of Women Remained About the Same and Minorities Continued to be Underrepresented

While the total number of STEM employees increased, this increase varied across STEM fields. Employment increased by 23 percent in STEM fields as compared to 17 percent in non-STEM fields from calendar year 1994 to calendar year 2003. Employment increased by 78 percent in the mathematics/computer sciences field and by 20 percent in the science field over this period. The changes in number of employees in the engineering and technology fields were not statistically significant. Employment estimates from 1994 to 2003 in the STEM fields are shown in figure 4.

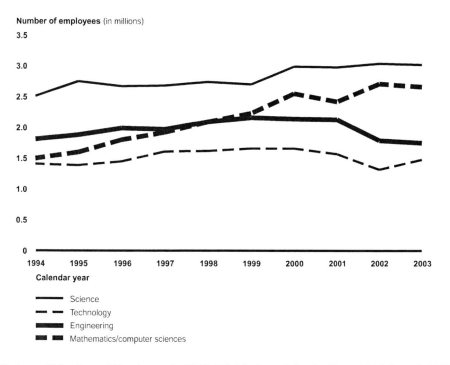

Figure 4. Estimated Numbers of Employees in STEM Fields from Calendar Years 1994 through 2003.

From calendar years 1994 to 2003, the estimated number of women employees in STEM fields increased from about 2.7 million to about 3.5 million. Overall, there was not a statistically significant change in the percentage of women employees in the STEM fields. Table 16 shows the numbers and percentages of men and women employed in the STEM fields for calendar years 1994 and 2003.

Table 16. Estimated Numbers and Percentages of Employees in STEM Fields by Gender in Calendar Years 1994 and2003(numbers in thousands)

STEM field	1994				2003			
	Men		Women		Men		Women	
	Number	Percent	Number	Percent	Number	Percent	Number	Percent
Science	792	32	1,711	68	829	28	2,179	72
Technology	955	68	445	32	1,050	71	425	29
Engineering	1,658	92	*141	8	1,572	90	*169	10
Mathematics/ computer sciences	1,056	71	432	29	1,952	74	695	26
Total	4,461	62	2,729	38	5,404	61	3,467	39

Source: GAO calculations based upon CPS data.

Note: Estimated employee numbers noted by an asterisk have a 95 percent confidence interval of within +/- 25 percent of the estimate itself. All other estimated employee numbers have a 95 percent confidence interval of within +/- 16 percent of the estimate. See appendix VI for confidence intervals associated with these estimates. Calculations of percentages and numbers may differ due to rounding.

In addition, the estimated number of minorities employed in the STEM fields as well as the percentage of total STEM employees they constituted increased, but African American and Hispanic employees remain underrepresented relative to their percentages in the civilian labor force [19]. Between 1994 and 2003, the estimated number of African American employees increased by about 44 percent, the estimated numbers of Hispanic employees increased by 90 percent, as did the estimated numbers of other minorities employed in STEM fields [20]. In calendar year 2003, African Americans comprised about 8.7 percent of STEM employees compared to about 10.7 percent of the CLF. Similarly, Hispanic employees comprised about 10 percent of STEM employees in calendar year 2003, compared to about 12.6 percent of the CLF. Table 17 shows the estimated percentages of STEM employees by selected racial or ethnic groups in 1994 and 2003.

International employees have filled hundreds of thousands of positions, many in STEM fields, through the H-1B visa program. However, the numbers and types of occupations have changed over the years. We reported that while the limit for the H-1B program was 115,000 in 1999, the number of visas approved exceeded the limit by more than 20,000 because of problems with the system used to track the data [21]. Available data show that in 1999, the majority of the approved occupations were in STEM fields. Specifically, an estimated 60 percent of the positions approved in fiscal year 1999 were related to information technology and 5 percent were for electrical/electronics engineering. By 2002, the limit for the H-1B program had increased to 195,000, but the number approved, 79,000, did not reach this limit. In 2003, we reported that the number of approved H-1B petitions in certain occupations had declined. For example, the number of approvals for systems analysis/programming positions declined by 106,671 from 2001 to 2002 [22].

Table 17. Estimated Percentages of STEM Employees by Selected Racial or Ethnic Group for Calendar Years 1994 and 2003

Race or ethnicity	Percentage of total STEM employees, 1994	Percentage of total STEM employees, 2003
Black or African American	7.5	8.7
Hispanic or Latino origin	5.7	10.0
Other minorities[a]	4.5	6.9

Source: GAO calculations based upon CPS data.

Note: Estimated percentages have 95 percent confidence intervals of +/- 1 percentage point. Changes for African Americans between calendar years 1994 and 2003 were not statistically significant at the 95-percent confidence level. Differences for Hispanic or Latino origin and other minorities were statistically significant. See appendix VI for confidence intervals associated with these estimates. aOther minorities include Asian/Pacific Islanders and American Indian or Alaska Native.

Although the estimated total number of employees in STEM fields increased from 1994 to 2003, according to an NSF report, many with STEM degrees were not employed in these occupations. In 2004, NSF reported that about 67 percent of employees with degrees in science or engineering were employed in fields somewhat or not at all related to their degree [23]. Specifically, 70 percent of employees with bachelor's degrees, 51 percent with master's degrees, and 54 percent with doctoral degrees reported that their employment was somewhat or not at all related to their degree in science or engineering.

In addition to increases in the numbers of employees in STEM fields, inflation-adjusted median annual wages and salaries increased in all four STEM fields over the 10-year period (1994 to 2003). These increases ranged from 6 percent in science to 15 percent in engineering. Figure 5 shows trends in median annual wages and salaries for STEM fields.

University Officials and Others Cited Several Factors That Influence Decisions about Participation in STEM Fields and Suggested Ways to Encourage Greater Participation

University officials, researchers, and students identified several factors that influenced students' decisions about pursuing STEM degrees and occupations, and they suggested some ways to encourage more participation in STEM fields. Specifically, university officials said and researchers reported that the quality of teachers in kindergarten through 12th grades and the levels of mathematics and science courses completed during high school affected students' success in and decisions about STEM fields. In addition, several sources noted that mentoring played a key role in the participation of women and minorities in STEM fields. Current students from five universities we visited generally agreed with these observations, and several said that having good mathematics and science instruction was important to their overall educational success. International students' decisions about participating in STEM education and occupations were affected by opportunities outside the United States and the visa process. To encourage more student participation in the STEM fields, university officials, researchers, and others have made several suggestions, and four were made repeatedly. These suggestions focused on teacher quality, high school students' math and science preparation, outreach activities, and the federal role in STEM education.

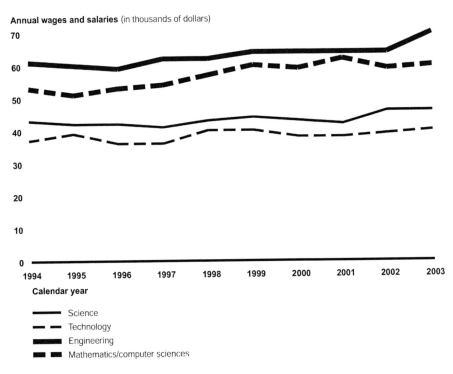

Figure 5. Estimated Median Annual Wages and Salaries in STEM Fields for Calendar Years 1994 through 2003.

Teacher Quality and Mathematics and Science Preparation Were Cited as Key Factors Affecting Domestic Students' STEM Participation Decisions

University officials frequently cited teacher quality as a key factor that affected domestic students' interest in and decisions about pursuing STEM degrees and occupations. Officials at all eight universities we visited expressed the view that a student's experience from kindergarten through the 12th grades played a large role in influencing whether the student pursued a STEM degree. Officials at one university we visited said that students pursuing STEM degrees have associated their interests with teachers who taught them good skills in mathematics or excited them about science. On the other hand, officials at many of the universities we visited told us that some teachers were unqualified and unable to impart the subject matter, causing students to lose interest in mathematics and science. For example, officials at one university we visited said that some elementary and secondary teachers do not have sufficient training to effectively teach students in the STEM fields and that this has an adverse effect on what students learn in these fields and reduces the interest and enthusiasm students express in pursuing coursework in high school, degree programs in college, or careers in these areas.

Teacher quality issues, in general, have been cited in past reports by Education. In 2002, Education reported that in the 1999-2000 school year, 14 to 22 percent of middle-grade students taking English, mathematics, and science were in classes led by teachers without a major, minor, or certification in these subjects—commonly referred to as "out-of-field" teachers [24]. Also, approximately 30 to 40 percent of the middle-grade students in biology/life science, physical science, or English as a second language/bilingual education classes had teachers lacking these credentials. At the high school level, 17 percent of students enrolled in physics and 36 percent of those enrolled in geology/earth/space science were in classes instructed by out-of-field teachers. The percentages of students taught by out-of-field teachers were significantly higher when the criteria used were teacher certification and a major in the subject taught. For example, 45 percent of the high school students enrolled in biology/life science and approximately 30 percent of those enrolled in mathematics, English, and social science classes had out-of-field teachers. During the 2002-2003 school year, Education reported that the number and distribution of teachers on waivers—which allowed prospective teachers in classrooms while they completed their formal training—was problematic. Also, states reported that the problem of underprepared teachers was worse on average in districts that serve large proportions of high-poverty children—the percentage of teachers on waivers was larger in high-poverty school districts than all other school districts in 39 states. Moreover, in 2004, Education reported that 48 of the 50 states granted waivers [25].

In addition to teacher quality, students' high school preparation in mathematics and science was cited by university officials and others as affecting students' success in college-level courses and their decisions about pursuing STEM degrees and occupations. University officials at six of the eight universities we visited cited students' ability to opt out of mathematics and science courses during high school as a factor that influenced whether they would participate and succeed in the STEM fields during undergraduate and graduate school. University officials said, for example, that because many students had not taken higher-level mathematics and science courses such as calculus and physics in high school, they were immediately behind other students who were better prepared. In July 2005, on the basis of findings from the 2004 National Assessment of Educational Progress, the National Center for Education Statistics reported that 17 percent of the 17-year-olds reported that they had taken calculus, and this represents the highest percentage in any previous assessment year [26]. In a study that solicited the views of several hundred students who had left the STEM fields, researchers found that the effects of inadequate high school preparation contributed to college students' decisions to leave the science fields [27]. These researchers found that approximately 40 percent of those college students who left the science fields reported some problems related to high school science preparation. The underpreparation was often linked to problems such as not understanding calculus; lack of laboratory experience or exposure to computers, and no introduction to theoretical material or to analytic modes of thought. Further, 12 current students we interviewed said they were not adequately prepared for college mathematics or science. For example, one student stated that her high school courses had been limited because she attended an all-girls school where the curriculum catered to students who were not interested in STEM, and so it had been difficult to obtain the courses that were of interest to her.

Several other factors were mentioned during our interviews with university officials, students, and others as influencing decisions about participation in STEM fields. These factors included relatively low pay in STEM fields, additional tuition costs to obtain STEM degrees, lack of commitment on the part of some students to meet the rigorous academic demands, and the inability of some professors in STEM fields to effectively impart their knowledge to students in the classrooms. For example, officials from five universities said that low pay in STEM fields relative to other fields such as law and business dissuaded students from pursuing STEM degrees in some areas. Also, in a study that solicited the views of college students who left the STEM fields as well as those who continued to pursue STEM degrees, researchers found that students experienced greater financial difficulties in obtaining their degrees because of the extra time needed to obtain degrees in certain STEM fields. Researchers also noted that poor teaching at the university level was the most common complaint among students who left as well as those who remained in STEM fields. Students reported that faculty do not like to teach, do not value teaching as a professional activity, and therefore lack any incentive to learn to teach effectively [28]. Finally, 11 of the students we interviewed commented about the need for professors in STEM fields to alter their methods and to show more interest in teaching to retain students' attention.

Mentoring Cited as a Key Factor Affecting Women's and Minorities' STEM Participation Decisions

University officials and students said that mentoring is important for all students but plays a vital role in the academic experiences of women and minorities in the STEM fields. Officials at seven of the eight universities discussed the important role that mentors play, especially for women and minorities in STEM fields. For example, one professor said that mentors helped students by advising them on the best track to follow for obtaining their degrees and achieving professional goals. Also, four students we interviewed—three women and one man—expressed the importance of mentors. Specifically, while all four students identified mentoring as critical to academic success in the STEM fields, two students expressed their satisfaction since they had mentors, while the other two students said that it would have been helpful to have had someone who could have been a mentor or role model.

Studies have also reported that mentors play a significant role in the success of women and minorities in the STEM fields. In 2004, some of the women students and faculty with whom we talked reported a strong mentor was a crucial part in the academic training of some of the women participating in sciences, and some women had pursued advanced degrees because of the encouragement and support of mentors [29]. In September 2000, a congressional commission reported that women were adversely affected throughout the STEM education pipeline and career path by a lack of role models and mentors [30]. For example, the report found that girls rejection of mathematics and science may be partially driven by teachers, parents, and peers when they subtly, and not so subtly, steer girls away from the informal technical pastimes (such as working on cars, fixing bicycles, and changing hardware on computers) and science activities (such as science fairs and clubs) that too often were still thought of as the province of boys. In addition, the commission reported that a greater proportion of women switched out of STEM majors than men, relative to their representation in the STEM major population. Reasons cited for the higher attrition rate among women students included lack of role models, distaste for the competitive nature of science and engineering education, and inability to obtain adequate academic guidance or advice. Further, according to the report, women's retention and graduation in STEM graduate programs were affected by their interaction with faculty, integration into the department (versus isolation), and other factors, including whether there were role models, mentors, and women faculty.

International Students' STEM Participation Decisions Were Affected by Opportunities Outside the United States and the Visa Process

Officials at seven of the eight universities visited, along with education policy experts, told us that competition from other countries for top international students, and educational or work opportunities, affected international students' decisions about studying in the United States. They told us that other countries, including Canada, Australia, New Zealand, and the United Kingdom, had seized the opportunity since September 11 to compete against the United States for international students who were among the best students in the world, especially in the STEM fields. Also, university officials told us that students from several countries, including China and India, were being recruited to attend universities and get jobs in their own countries. In addition, education organizations and associations have reported that global competition for the best science and engineering students and scholars is under way. One organization, NAFSA: Association of International Educators reported that the international student market has become highly competitive, and the United States is not competing as well as other countries [31].

According to university officials, international students' decisions about pursuing STEM degrees and occupations in the United States were also influenced by the perceived unwelcoming attitude of Americans and the visa process. Officials from three of the universities said that the perceived unwelcoming attitude of Americans had affected the recruitment of international students to the United States. Also, officials at six of the eight universities visited expressed their concern about the impact of the tightened visa procedures and/or increased security measures since September 11 on international graduate school enrollments. For example, officials at one university stated that because of the time needed to process visas, a few students had missed their class start dates. Officials from one university told us that they were being more proactive in helping new international students navigate the visa system, to the extent possible. While some university officials acknowledged that visa processing had significantly improved, since 2003 several education associations have requested further changes in U.S. visa policies because of the lengthy procedures and time needed to obtain approval to enter the country.

We have reported on various aspects of the visa process, made several recommendations, and noted that some improvements have been made. In October 2002 we cited the need for a clear policy on how to balance national security concerns with the desire to facilitate legitimate travel when issuing visas and we made several recommendations to help improve the visa process [32]. In 2003, we reported that the Departments of State, Homeland Security, and Justice could more effectively manage the visa function if they had clear and comprehensive policies and procedures and increased agency coordination and information sharing [33]. In February 2004 and February 2005, we reported on the State Department's efforts to improve the program for issuing visas to international science students and scholars. In 2004 we found that the time to adjudicate a visa depended largely on whether an applicant had to undergo a security check known as Visas Mantis, which is designed to protect against sensitive technology transfers. Based on a random sample of Visas Mantis cases for science students and scholars, it took State an average of 67 days to complete the process [34]. In 2005, we reported a significant decline in Visas Mantis processing times and in the number of cases pending more than 60 days [35]. We also reported that, in some cases, science students and scholars can obtain a visa within 24 hours.

We have also issued several reports on SEVIS operations. In June 2004 we noted that when SEVIS began operating, significant problems were reported [36]. For example, colleges and universities and exchange programs had trouble gaining access to the system, and when access was obtained, these users' sessions would "time out" before they could complete their tasks. In that report we also noted that SEVIS performance had improved, but that several key system performance requirements were not being measured. In March 2005, we reported that the Department of Homeland Security (DHS) had taken steps to address our recommendations and that educational organizations generally agreed that SEVIS performance had continued to improve [37]. However, educational organizations continued to cite problems, which they believe created hardships for students and exchange visitors.

Several Suggestions Were Made to Encourage More Participation in the STEM Fields

To increase the number of students entering STEM fields, officials from seven universities and others stated that teacher quality needs to improve. Officials of one university said that kindergarten through 12th grade classrooms need teachers who are knowledgeable in the mathematics and science content areas. As previously noted, Education has reported on the extent to which classes have been taught by teachers with little or no content knowledge in the STEM fields. The Congressional Commission on the Advancement of Women and Minorities reported that teacher effectiveness is the most important element in a good education [38]. The commission also suggested that boosting teacher effectiveness can do more to improve education than any other single factor. States are taking action to meet NCLBA's requirement of having all teachers of core academic subjects be highly qualified by the end of the 2005-2006 school year.

University officials and some students suggested that better preparation and mandatory courses in mathematics and science were needed for students during their kindergarten through 12th grade school years. Officials from five universities suggested that mandatory mathematics and science courses, especially in high school, may lead to increased student interest and preparation in the STEM fields. With a greater interest and depth of knowledge, students would be better prepared and more inclined to pursue STEM degrees in college. Further, nearly half of the students who replied to this question suggested that students needed additional mathematics and science training prior to college. However, adding mathematics and science classes has resource implications, since more teachers in these subjects would be needed. Also this change could require curriculum policy changes that would take time to implement.

More outreach, especially to women and minorities from kindergarten through the 12th grade, was suggested by university officials, students, and other organizations. Officials from six of the universities we visited suggested that increased outreach activities are needed to help create more interest in mathematics and science for younger students. For example, at one university we visited, officials told us that through inviting students to their campuses or visiting local schools, they have provided some students with opportunities to engage in science laboratories and hands-on activities that foster interest and excitement for students and can make these fields more relevant in their lives. Officials from another university told us that these experiences were especially important for women and minorities who might not have otherwise had these opportunities. The current students we interviewed also suggested more outreach activities. Specifically, two students said that outreach was needed to further stimulate students' interest in the STEM fields. One organization, Building Engineering and Science Talent (BEST), suggested that research universities increase their presence in prekindergarten through 12th grade mathematics and science education in order to strengthen domestic students' interests and abilities. BEST reported that one model producing results entailed universities adopting students from low-income school districts from 7th through 12th grades and providing them advanced instruction in algebra, chemistry, physics, and trigonometry. However, officials at one university told us that because of limited resources, their efforts were constrained and only a few students would benefit from this type of outreach.

Furthermore, university officials from the eight schools and other education organizations made suggestions regarding the role of the federal government. University officials suggested that the federal government could enhance its role in STEM education by providing more effective leadership through developing and implementing a national agenda for STEM education and increasing federal funding for academic research. Officials at six universities suggested that the federal government undertake a new initiative modeled after the National Defense Education Act of 1958, enacted in response to the former Soviet Union's achievement in its space program, which provided new funding for mathematics and science education and training at all education levels. In June 2005, CGS called for a renewed commitment to graduate education by the federal government through actions such as providing funds to support students trained at the doctoral level in the sciences, technology, engineering, and mathematics; expanding U.S. citizen participation in doctoral study in selected fields through graduate support awarded competitively to universities across the country; requiring recruitment, outreach, and mentoring activities that promote greater participation and success, especially for underrepresented groups; and fostering interdisciplinary research preparation. In August 2003, the National Science Board recommended that the federal government direct substantial new support to students and institutions in order to improve success in science and engineering studies by domestic undergraduate students from all demographic groups. According to this report, such support could include scholarships and other forms of financial assistance to students, incentives to institutions to expand and improve the quality of their science and engineering programs in areas in which degree attainment is insufficient, financial support to community colleges to increase the success of students in transferring to 4-year science and engineering programs, and expanded funding for programs that best succeed in graduating underrepresented minorities and women in science and engineering. BEST also suggested that the federal government allocate additional resources to expand the mathematics and science education opportunities for underrepresented groups. However, little is known about how well federal resources have been used in the past. Changes that would require additional federal funds would likely have an impact on other federal programs, given the nation's limited resources and growing fiscal imbalance, and changing the federal role could take several years.

Concluding Observations

While the total numbers of STEM graduates have increased, some fields have experienced declines, especially at the master's and doctoral levels. Given the trends in the numbers and percentages of students pursuing STEM degrees, particularly advanced degrees, and recent developments that have influenced international students' decisions about pursuing degrees in the United States, it is uncertain whether the number of STEM graduates will be sufficient to meet future academic and employment needs and help the country maintain its technological competitive advantage. Moreover, it is too early to tell if the declines in international graduate student enrollments will continue in the future. In terms of employment, despite some gains, the percentage of women in the STEM workforce has not changed significantly, minority employees remain underrepresented, and many with degrees in STEM fields are not employed in STEM occupations.

To help improve the trends in the numbers of students, graduates, and employees in STEM fields, university officials and others made several suggestions, such as increasing the federal commitment to STEM education programs. However, before making changes, it is important to know the extent to which existing STEM education programs are appropriately targeted and making the best use of available federal resources. Additionally, in an era of limited financial resources and growing federal deficits, information about the effectiveness of these programs can help guide policy makers and program managers.

Agency Comments and Our Evaluation

We received written comments on a draft of this report from Commerce, the Department of Health and Human Services (HHS), NSF, and NSTC. These comments are reprinted in appendixes VII, VIII, IX, and X, respectively. We also received technical comments from the Departments of Commerce, Health and Human Services, Homeland Security, Labor, and Transportation; and the Environmental Protection Agency and National Aeronautics and Space Administration, which we incorporated when appropriate.

In commenting on a draft of this report, Commerce, HHS, and NSTC commended GAO for this work. Commerce explicitly concurred with several findings and agreed with our overall conclusion. However, Commerce suggested that we revise the conclusion to point out that despite overall increases in STEM students, the numbers of graduates in certain fields have declined. We modified the concluding observations to make this point. HHS agreed with our conclusion that it is important to evaluate ongoing programs to determine the extent to which they are achieving their desired results. The comments from NSTC cited improvements made to help ensure that international students, exchange visitors, and scientists are able to apply for and receive visas in a timely manner. We did not make any changes to the report since we had cited another GAO product that discussed such improvements in the visa process.

NSF commented about several of our findings. NSF stated that our program evaluations finding may be misleading largely because the type of information GAO requested and accepted from agencies was limited to program level evaluations and did not include evaluations of individual underlying projects. NSF suggested that we include information on the range of approaches used to assure program effectiveness. Our finding is based on agency officials' responses to a survey question that did not limit or stipulate the types of evaluations that could have been included.

To help improve the trends in the numbers of students, graduates, and employees in STEM fields, university officials and others made several suggestions, such as increasing the federal commitment to STEM education programs. However, before making changes, it is important to know the extent to which existing STEM education programs are appropriately targeted and making the best use of available federal resources. Additionally, in an era of limited financial resources and growing federal deficits, information about the effectiveness of these programs can help guide policy makers We received written comments on a draft of this report from Commerce, the Department of Health and Human Services (HHS), NSF, and NSTC. These comments are reprinted in appendixes VII, VIII, IX, and X, respectively. We also received technical comments from the Departments of Commerce, Health and Human Services, Homeland Security, Labor, and Transportation; and the Environmental Protection Agency and National Aeronautics and Space Administration, which we incorporated when appropriate.

In commenting on a draft of this report, Commerce, HHS, and NSTC commended GAO for this work. Commerce explicitly concurred with several findings and agreed with our overall conclusion. However, Commerce suggested that we revise the conclusion to point out that despite overall increases in STEM students, the numbers of graduates in certain fields have declined. We modified the concluding observations to make this point. HHS agreed with our conclusion that it is important to evaluate ongoing programs to determine the extent to which they are achieving their desired results. The comments from NSTC cited improvements made to help ensure that international students, exchange visitors, and scientists are able to apply for and receive visas in a timely manner. We did not make any changes to the report since we had cited another GAO product that discussed such improvements in the visa process.

NSF commented about several of our findings. NSF stated that our program evaluations finding may be misleading largely because the type of information GAO requested and accepted from agencies was limited to program level evaluations and did not include evaluations of individual underlying projects. NSF suggested that we include information on the range of approaches used to assure program effectiveness. Our finding is based on agency officials' responses to a survey question that did not limit or stipulate the types of evaluations that could have been included.

Nonetheless, we modified the report to acknowledge that NSF uses various approaches to evaluate its programs.

NSF criticized the methodology we used to support our finding on the factors that influence decisions about pursuing STEM fields and suggested that we make it clearer in the body of the report that the findings are based on interviews with educators and administrators from 8 colleges and universities, and responses from 31 students. Also, NSF suggested that we improve the report by including corroborating information from reports and studies. Our finding was not limited to interviews at the 8 colleges and universities and responses from 31 current students but was also based on interviews with numerous representatives and policy experts from various organizations as well as findings from research and reports—which are cited in the body of the report. Using this approach, we were able to corroborate the testimonial evidence with data from reports and research as well as to determine whether information in the reports and research remained accurate by seeking the views of those currently teaching or studying in STEM fields. As NSF noted, this approach yielded reasonable observations. Additional information about our methodology is listed in appendix I, and we added a bibliography that identifies the reports and research used during the course of this review.

NSF also commented that the report mentions the NSTC efforts for interagency collaboration, but does not mention other collaboration efforts such as the Federal Interagency Committee on Education and the Federal Interagency Coordinating Council. NSF also pointed out that interagency collaboration occurs at the program level. We did not modify the report in response to this comment. In conducting our work, we determined that the NSTC effort was the primary mechanism for interagency collaboration focused on STEM programs. The coordinating groups cited by NSF are focused on different issues. The Federal Interagency Committee on Education was established to coordinate the federal programs, policies, and practices affecting education broadly, and the Federal Interagency Coordinating Council was established to minimize duplication of programs and activities relating to children with disabilities.

In addition, NSF provided information to clarify examples related to their programs that we cited in the report, stated that some data categories were not clear, and commented on the graduate level enrollment data we used in the report. NSF pointed out that while its program called Opportunities for Enhancing Diversity in the Geosciences is designed to increase participation by minorities, it does not limit eligibility to minorities. Also, NSF noted that while the draft report correctly indicated that students receiving scholarships or fellowships from NSF must be U.S. citizens or permanent residents, the reason given for limiting participation in these programs in the draft report was not accurate. According to NSF, these restrictions are considered to be an effective strategy to support its goal of creating a diverse, competitive and globally engaged U.S. workforce of scientists, engineers, technologists and well prepared citizens. We revised the report to reflect these changes. Further, NSF commented that the data categories were not clear, particularly the technology degrees and occupations, and that the data did not include associate degrees. We added information that lists all of the occupations included in the analysis, and we added footnotes to clarify which data included associate degrees and which ones did not. In addition, NSF commented that the graduate level enrollment data for international students based on NPSAS data are questionable in comparison with other available data and that this may be because the NPSAS data include a relatively small sample for graduate education. We considered using NPSAS and other data but decided to use the NPSAS data for two reasons: NPSAS data were more comprehensive and more current. Specifically, the NPSAS data were available through the 2003-2004 academic year and included numbers and characteristics of students enrolled for all degree fields—STEM and non-STEM—for all education levels, and citizenship information.

APPENDIX I:
OBJECTIVES, SCOPE, AND METHODOLOGY

Objectives

The objectives of our study were to determine (1) the number of federal civilian education programs funded in fiscal year 2004 that were specifically designed to increase the number of students and graduates pursuing science, technology, engineering, and mathematics (STEM) degrees and occupations, or improve educational programs in STEM fields, and what agencies report about their effectiveness; (2) how the numbers, percentages, and characteristics of students, graduates, and employees in STEM fields have changed over the years; and (3) factors cited by educators and others as influencing people's decisions about pursuing STEM degrees and occupations, and suggestions to encourage greater participation in STEM fields.

Scope and Methodology

In conducting our review, we used multiple methodologies. We (1) conducted a survey of federal departments and agencies that sponsored education programs specifically designed to increase the number of students and graduates pursuing STEM degrees and occupations or improve educational programs in STEM fields; (2) obtained and analyzed data, including the most recent data available, on students, graduates, and employees in STEM fields and occupations; (3) visited eight colleges and universities; (4) reviewed reports and studies; and (5) interviewed agency officials, representatives and policy experts from various organizations, and current students. We conducted our work between October 2004 and October 2005 in accordance with generally accepted government auditing standards.

Survey

To provide Congress with a better understanding of what programs federal agencies were supporting to increase the nation's pool of scientists, technologists, engineers, and mathematicians, we designed a survey to determine (1) the number of federal education programs (prekindergarten through postdoctorate) designed to increase the quantity of students and graduates pursuing STEM degrees and occupations or improve the educational programs in STEM fields and (2) what agencies reported about the effectiveness of these programs. The survey asked the officials to describe the goals, target population, and funding levels for fiscal years 2003, 2004, and 2005 of such programs. In addition, the officials were asked when the programs began and if the programs had been or were being evaluated.

We identified the agencies likely to support STEM education programs by reviewing the Catalog of Federal Domestic Assistance and the Department of Education's Eisenhower National Clearinghouse, Guidebook of Federal Resources for K-12 Mathematics and Science, 2004-05. Using these resources, we identified 15 agencies with STEM education programs. The survey was conducted via e-mail using an ActiveX enabled MSWord attachment. A contact point was designated for each agency, and questionnaires were sent to that individual. One questionnaire was completed for each program the agency sponsored. Agency officials were asked to provide confirming documentation for their responses whenever possible.

The questionnaire was forwarded to agencies on February 15, 2005, and responses were received through early May 2005. We received 244 completed surveys and determined that 207 of them met the criteria for STEM programs. The following agencies participated in our survey: the Departments of Agriculture, Commerce, Education, Energy, Homeland Security, Interior, Labor, and Transportation. In addition, the Health Resources and Services Administration, Indian Health Service, and National Institutes of Health, all part of Health and Human Services, took part in the survey. Also participating were the U.S. Environmental Protection Agency; the National Aeronautics and Space Administration; and the National Science Foundation. Labor's programs did not meet our criteria for 2004 and the Department of Defense (DOD) did not submit a survey. According to DOD officials, DOD needed 3 months to complete the survey and therefore could not provide responses within the time frames of our work. We obtained varied amounts of documentation from 13 civilian agencies for the 207 STEM education programs funded in 2004 and information about the effectiveness of some programs.

Because we administered the survey to all of the known federal agencies sponsoring STEM education programs, our results are not subject to sampling error. However, the practical difficulties of conducting any survey may introduce other types of errors, commonly referred to as nonsampling errors. For example, differences in how a particular question is interpreted, the sources of information available to respondents in answering a question, or the types of people who do not respond can introduce unwanted variability into the survey results. We included steps in the development of the survey, the collection of data, and the editing and analysis of data for the purpose of minimizing such nonsampling errors. To reduce nonsampling error, the questionnaire was reviewed by survey specialists and pretested in person with three officials from agencies familiar with STEM education programs to develop a questionnaire that was relevant, easy to comprehend, unambiguous, and unbiased. We made changes to the content and format of the questionnaire based on the specialists' reviews and the results of the pretests. To further reduce nonsampling error, data for this study returned electronically were entered directly into the instrument by the respondents and converted into a database for analysis. Completed questionnaires returned as hard copy were keypunched, and a sample of these records was verified by comparing them with their corresponding questionnaires, and any errors were corrected. When the data were analyzed, a second, independent analyst checked all computer programs. Finally, to assess the reliability of key data obtained from our survey about some of the programs, we compared the responses with the documentation provided, or we independently researched the information from other publicly available sources.

Analyses of Student, Graduate, and Employee Data

To determine how the numbers and characteristics of students, graduates, and employees in STEM fields have changed, we obtained and analyzed data from the Department of Education (Education) and the Department of Labor. Specifically, we analyzed the National Postsecondary Student Aid Study (NPSAS) data and the Integrated Postsecondary Education

Data System (IPEDS) data from the Department of Education's National Center for Education Statistics (NCES), and we analyzed data from the Department of Labor's Bureau of Labor Statistics' (BLS) Current Population Survey (CPS). Based on National Science Foundation's categorization of STEM fields, we developed STEM fields of study from NPSAS and IPEDS, and identified occupations from the CPS. Using these data sources, we developed nine STEM fields for students, eight STEM fields for graduates, and four broad STEM fields for occupations.

For our data reliability assessment, we reviewed agency documentation on the data sets and conducted electronic tests of the files. On the basis of these reviews, we determined that the required data elements from NPSAS, IPEDS and CPS were sufficiently reliable for our purposes. These data sources, type, time span, and years analyzed are shown in table 18.

NPSAS is a comprehensive nationwide study designed to determine how students and their families pay for postsecondary education, and to describe some demographic and other characteristics of those enrolled. The study is based on a nationally representative sample of students in postsecondary education institutions, including undergraduate, graduate, and first-professional students. The NPSAS has been conducted every several years since the 1986-1987 academic year. For this report, we analyzed the results of the NPSAS survey for the 1995-1996 academic year and the 2003-2004 academic year to compare student enrollment and demographic characteristics between these two periods for the nine STEM fields and non-STEM fields.

Table 18. Sources of Data, Data Obtained, Time Span of Data, and Years Analyzed

Department	Agency	Database	Data obtained	Time span of data	Years analyzed
Education	NCES	NPSAS	College student enrollment	9 years	Academic years 1995-1996 and 2003-2004
Education	NCES	IPEDS	Graduation/degrees	9 years	Academic years 1994-1995 and 2002-2003
Labor	BLS	CPS	Employment	10 years	Calendar years 1994 through 2003

Sources: NPSAS, IPEDS, and CPS data.

Because the NPSAS sample is a probability sample of students, the sample is only one of a large number of samples that might have been drawn. Since each sample could have provided different estimates, confidence in the precision of the particular sample's results is expressed as a 95-percent confidence interval (for example, plus or minus 4 percentage points). This is the interval that would contain the actual population value for 95 percent of the samples that could have been drawn. As a result, we are 95 percent confident that each of the confidence intervals in this report will include the true values in the study population. NPSAS estimates used in this report and the upper and lower bounds of the 95 percent confidence intervals for each estimate relied on in this report are presented in appendix V.

IPEDS is a single, comprehensive system designed to encompass all institutions and educational organizations whose primary purpose is to provide postsecondary education. IPEDS is built around a series of interrelated surveys to collect institution-level data in such areas as enrollments, program completions, faculty, staff, and finances. For this report, we analyzed the results of IPEDS data for the 1994-1995 academic year and the 2002-2003 academic year to compare the numbers and characteristics of graduates with degrees in eight STEM fields and non-STEM fields.

To analyze changes in employees in STEM and non-STEM fields, we obtained employment estimates from BLS's Current Population Survey March supplement for 1995 through 2004 (calendar years 1994 through 2003). The CPS is a monthly survey of households conducted by the U.S. Census Bureau (Census) for BLS. The CPS provides a comprehensive body of information on the employment and unemployment experience of the nation's population, classified by age, sex, race, and a variety of other characteristics. A more complete description of the survey, including sample design, estimation, and other methodology can be found in the CPS documentation prepared by Census and BLS [1].

This March supplement (the Annual Demographic Supplement) is specifically designed to estimate family characteristics, including income from all sources and occupation and industry classification of the job held longest during the previous year. It is conducted during the month of March each year because it is believed that since March is the month before the deadline for filing federal income tax returns, respondents would be more likely to report income more accurately than at any other point during the year [2].

Table 19. Classification codes and Occupations, 2002-2003

Science	Technology	Engineering	Mathematics/Computer Science
1600 – Agricultural and food scientists	1540 – Drafters	1300 – Architects, except naval	1000 – Computer scientists and systems analysts
1610 – Biological scientists	1550 – Engineering technicians, except drafters	1310 – Surveyors, cartographers, and photogrammetrists	1010 – Computer programmers
1640 – Conservation scientists and foresters	1560 – Surveying and mapping technicians	1320 – Aerospace engineers	1020 – Computer software engineers
1650 – Medical scientists	1900 – Agricultural and food science technicians	1330 – Agricultural engineers	1040 – Computer support specialists
1700 – Astronomers and physicists	1910 – Biological technicians	1340 – Biomedical engineers	1060 – Database administrators
1710 – Atmospheric and space scientists	1920 – Chemical technicians	1350 – Chemical engineers	1100 – Network and computer systems administrators
1720 – Chemists and materials scientists	1930 – Geological and petroleum technicians	1360 – Civil engineers	1110 – Network systems and data communications analysts
1740 – Environmental scientists and geoscientists	1940 – Nuclear technicians	1400 – Computer hardware engineers	1200 – Actuaries
1760 – Physical scientists, all other	1960 – Other life, physical, and social science technicians	1410 – Electrical and electronic engineers	1210 – Mathematicians
1800 – Economists	3300 – Clinical laboratory technologists and technicians	1420 – Environmental engineers	1220 – Operations research analysts
1810 – Market and survey researchers	7010 – Computer, automated teller and office machine repairers	1430 – Industrial engineers, including health and safety	1230 – Statisticians
1820 – Psychologists	8760 – Medical, dental, and ophthalmic laboratory technicians	1440 – Marine engineers and naval architects	1240 – Miscellaneous mathematical science occupations
1830 – Sociologists		1450 – Materials engineers	
1840 – Urban and regional planners		1460 – Mechanical engineers	
1860 – Miscellaneous social scientists and related workers		1500 – Mining and geological engineers, including mining safety engineers	
2010 – Social workers		1510 – Nuclear engineers	
3130 – Registered nurses		1520 – Petroleum engineers	
6010 – Agricultural inspectors		1530 – Engineers, all other	

We used the CPS data to produce estimates on (1) four STEM fields, (2) men and women, (3) two separate minority groups (Black or African American, and Hispanic or Latino origin), and (4) median annual wages and salaries. The measures of median annual wages and salaries could include bonuses, but do not include noncash benefits such as health insurance or pensions. CPS salary reported in March of each year was for the longest held position actually worked the year before and reported by the worker himself (or a knowledgeable member of the household). Tables 19 and 20 list the classification codes and occupations included in our analysis of CPS data over a 10-year period (1994-2003). In developing the STEM groups, we considered the occupational requirements and educational attainment of individuals in certain occupations. We also excluded doctors and other health care providers except registered nurses. During the period of review, some codes and occupation titles were changed; we worked with BLS officials to identify variations in codes and occupations and accounted for these changes where appropriate and possible.

Table 20. Classification codes and occupations, 1994-2001

Science	Technology	Engineering	Mathematics/Computer Science
069 – Physicists and astronomers	203 – Clinical laboratory technologists and technicians	043 – Architects	064 – Computer systems analysts and scientists
073 – Chemists, except biochemists	213 – Electrical and electronic technicians	044 – Aerospace engineers	065 – Operations and systems researchers and analysts
074 – Atmospheric and space scientists	214 – Industrial engineering technicians	045 – Metallurgical and materials engineers	066 – Actuaries
075 – Geologists and geodesists	215 – Mechanical engineering technicians	046 – Mining engineers	067 – Statisticians
076 – Physical scientists, n.e.c.	216 – Engineering technicians, n.e.c.	047 – Petroleum engineers	068 – Mathematical scientists, n.e.c.
077 – Agricultural and food scientists	217 – Drafting occupations	048 – Chemical engineers	229 – Computer programmers
078 – Biological and life scientists	218 – Surveying and mapping technicians	049 – Nuclear engineers	
079 – Forestry and conservation scientists	223 – Biological technicians	053 – Civil engineers	
083 – Medical scientists	224 – Chemical technicians	054 – Agricultural engineers	
095 – Registered Nurses	225 – Science technicians, n.e.c.	055 – Electrical and electronic engineers	
166 – Economists	235 – Technicians, n.e.c.	056 – Industrial engineers	
167 – Psychologists	525 – Data processing equipment repairers	057 – Mechanical engineers	
168 – Sociologists		058 – Marine and naval architects	
169 – Social scientists, n.e.c.		059 – Engineers, n.e.c.	
173 – Urban planners		063 – Surveyors and mapping scientists	
174 – Social workers			
489 – Inspectors, agricultural products			

Note: For occupations not elsewhere classified (n.e.c.).

Because the CPS is a probability sample based on random selections, the sample is only one of a large number of samples that might have been drawn. Since each sample could have provided different estimates, confidence in the precision of the particular sample's results is expressed as a 95 percent confidence interval (e.g., plus or minus 4 percentage points). This is the interval that would contain the actual population value for 95 percent of the samples that could have been drawn. As a result, we are 95 percent confident that each of the confidence intervals in this report will include the true values in the study population. We use the CPS general variance methodology to estimate this sampling error and report it as confidence intervals. Percentage estimates we produce from the CPS data have 95 percent confidence intervals of plus or minus 6 percentage points or less. Estimates other than percentages have 95 percent confidence intervals of no more than plus or minus 10 percent of the estimate itself, unless otherwise noted. Consistent with the CPS documentation guidelines, we do not produce estimates based on the March supplement data for populations of less than 75,000.

GAO's internal control procedures provide reasonable assurance that our data analyses are appropriate for the purposes we are using them. These procedures include, but are not limited to, having skilled staff perform the analyses, supervisory review by senior analysts, and indexing/referencing (confirming that the analyses are supported by the underlying audit documentation) activities.

College and University Visits

We interviewed administrators and professors during site visits to eight colleges and universities—the University of California at Los Angeles and the University of Southern California in California; Clark Atlanta University, Georgia Institute of Technology, and Spelman College in Georgia; the University of Illinois; Purdue University in Indiana; and Pennsylvania State University. These colleges and universities were selected based on the following factors: large numbers of domestic and international students in STEM fields, a mix of public and private institutions, number of doctoral degrees conferred, and some geographic diversity. We also selected three minority-serving colleges and universities, one of which serves only women students. Clark Atlanta University and Spelman College were selected, in part, because of their partnerships with the College of Engineering at the Georgia Institute of Technology. During these visits we asked the university officials about factors that influenced whether people pursue a STEM education or occupations and suggestions for addressing those factors that may influence participation. For example, we asked university officials to identify (1) issues related to the education pipeline; (2) steps taken by their university to alleviate some of the conditions that may discourage student participation in STEM areas; and (3) the federal role, if any, in attracting and retaining domestic students in STEM fields. We also obtained documents on programs they sponsored to help support STEM students and graduates.

Reviews of Reports and Studies

We reviewed several articles, reports, and books related to trends in STEM enrollment and factors that have an effect on people's decisions to pursue STEM fields. For two studies, we evaluated the methodological soundness using common social science and statistical practices. We examined each study's methodology, including its limitations, data sources, analyses, and conclusions.

- *Talking about Leaving: Why Undergraduates Leave the Sciences,* by Elaine Seymour and Nancy Hewitt.[3] This study used interviews and focus groups/group interviews at selected universities to identify self-reported reasons for changing majors from science, mathematics, or engineering. The study had four primary objectives: (1) to identify sources of qualitative differences in educational experiences of science, mathematics, and engineering students at higher educational institutions of different types; (2) to identify differences in structure, culture, and pedagogy of science, mathematics, and engineering departments and the impact on student retention; (3) to compare and contrast causes of science, mathematics, and engineering students' attrition by race/ethnicity and gender; and (4) to estimate the relative importance of factors found to contribute to science, mathematics, and engineering students' attrition. The researchers selected seven universities to represent the types of colleges and universities that supply most of the nations' scientists, mathematicians, and engineers. The types of institutions were selected to test whether there are differences in educational experiences, culture and pedagogy, race/ethnicity and gender attrition, and reasons for attrition by type of institution. Because the selection of students was not strictly random and because there is no documentation that the data were weighted to reflect the proportions of types of students selected, it is not possible to determine confidence intervals. Thus it is not possible to say which differences are statistically significant. The findings are now more than a decade old and thus might not reflect current pedagogy and other factors about the educational experience, students, or the socioeconomic environment. It is important to note that the quantitative results of this study are based on the views of one constituency or stakeholder—students. Views of faculty, school administrators, graduates, professional associations, and employers are not included.

- NCES's *Qualifications of the Public School Teacher Workforce: Prevalence of Out-of-Field Teaching*, 1987-1988 to 1999-2000 report. This study is an analysis based upon the Schools and Staffing Survey for 1999-2000. The report was issued in 2004 by the Institute of Education Sciences, U.S. Department of Education. NCES's Schools and Staffing Survey (SASS) is a representative sample of U.S. schools, districts, principals, and teachers. The report focusing on teacher's qualifications uses data from the district and teacher portion of SASS. The 1999-2000 SASS included a nationally representative sample of public schools and universe of all public charter schools with students in any of grades 1 through 12 and in operation in school year 1999-2000. The 1999-2000 SASS administration also included nationally representative samples of teachers in the selected public and public charter schools who taught students in grades kindergarten through 12 in school year 1999-2000. There were 51,811 public school teachers in the sample and 42,086 completed public school teacher interviews. In addition, there are 3,617 public charter school teachers in the sample with 2,847 completed interviews. The overall weighted teacher response rate was 76.7 percent for public school teachers and 71.8 percent for public charter school teachers. NCES has strong standards for carrying out educational surveys. The Office of Management and Budget vetted the questionnaire and sample design. The Census Bureau carried out survey quality control and data editing. One potential limitation is the amount of time it takes the Census Bureau to get the data from field collection to public release, but this is partly due to the thoroughness of the data quality steps followed. The SASS survey meets GAO standards for use as evidence in a report.

Interviews

We interviewed officials from 13 federal agencies with STEM education programs to obtain information about the STEM programs and their views on related topics, including factors that influence students' decisions about pursuing STEM degrees and occupations, and the extent of coordination among the federal agencies. We also interviewed officials from the National Science and Technology Council to discuss coordination efforts. In addition, we interviewed representatives and policy experts from various organizations. These organizations were the American Association for the Advancement of Science, the Commission on Professionals in Science and Technology, the Council of Graduate Schools, NAFSA: Association of International Educators, the National Academies, and the Council on Competitiveness.

We also conducted interviews via e-mail with 31 students. We asked officials from the eight universities visited to identify students to complete our e-mail interviews, and students who completed the interviews attended five of the colleges we visited. Of the 31 students: 16 attended Purdue University, 6 attended the University of Southern California, 6 attended Spelman College, 2 attended the University of California Los Angeles, and 1 attended the Georgia Institute of Technology. In addition, 19 students were undergraduates and 12 were graduate students; 19 students identified themselves as women and 12 students identified themselves as men. Of the 19 undergraduate students, 9 said that they plan to pursue graduate work in a STEM field.

APPENDIX II:
LIST OF 207 FEDERAL STEM EDUCATION PROGRAMS

Based on surveys submitted by officials representing the 13 civilian federal agencies, table 21 contains a list of the 207 science, technology, engineering, and mathematics (STEM) education programs funded in fiscal year 2004.

Table 21. Federal STEM Education Programs Funded in FY 2004

Program number	Program name	Fiscal year 04 funding
Department of Agriculture		
1.	1890 Institution Teaching and Research Capacity Building Grants Program	$11.4 million
2.	Higher Education Challenge Grants Program	$4.6 million
3.	Hispanic-Serving Institutions Education Grants Program	$4.6 million
4.	Alaska Native-Serving and Native Hawaiian-Serving Institutions Education Grants Program	$3 million
5.	Food and Agricultural Sciences National Needs Graduate and Postdoctoral Fellowships *Grants Program*	$2.9 million
6.	Tribal Colleges Endowment Program	$1.9 million
7.	Tribal Colleges Education Equity Grants Program	$1.7 million
8.	Tribal Colleges Research Grant Program	$1.1 million
9.	Higher Education Multicultural Scholars Program	$986,000
10.	International Science and Education Competitive Grants Program	$859,000

Table 21. (Continued)

Program number	Program name	Fiscal year 04 funding
11.	Secondary and Two-Year Postsecondary Agricultural Education Challenge *Grants Program*	$839,000
12.	Agriculture in the Classroom	$623,000
13.	Career Intern Program	$272,000
14.	Veterinary Medical Doctoral Program	$140,000
15.	1890 National Scholars Program	$16,000
16.	Hispanic Scholars Program	$4,000
Department of Commerce		
17.	Educational Partnership Program with Minority Serving Institutions	$7.4 million
18.	National Marine Sanctuaries Education Program	$4.4 million
19.	National Sea Grant College Program	$4 million
20.	Chesapeake Bay Watershed Education and Training Program	$2.5 million
21.	Coral Reef Conservation Program	$1.8 million
22.	Exploration, Education and Outreach	$1.3 million
23.	National Estuarine Research Reserve Graduate Research Fellowship Program	$1 million
24.	Bay Watershed Education and Training Hawaii Program	$500,000
25.	Monterey Bay Watershed Education and Training Program	$500,000
26.	Dr. Nancy Foster Scholarship Program	$494,000
27.	EstuaryLive	$115,000
28.	Teacher at Sea Program	$95,000
29.	High School-High Tech	$11,000
Department of Education		
30.	Mathematics and Science Partnerships Program	$149 million
31.	Upward Bound Math and Science Program	$32.8 million
32.	Graduate Assistance in Areas of National Need	$30.6 million
33.	Minority Science and Engineering Improvement Program	$8.9 million
Department of Energy		
34.	Science Undergraduate Laboratory Internship	$2.5 million
35.	Computational Science Graduate Fellowship	$2 million
36.	Global Change Education Program	$1.4 million
37.	Laboratory Science Teacher Professional Development	$1 million
38.	National Science Bowl	$702,000
39.	Community College Institute of Science and Technology	$605,000
40.	Albert Einstein Distinguished Educator Fellowship	$600,000
41.	QuarkNet	$575,000
42.	Fusion Energy Sciences Fellowship Program	$555,000
43.	Pre-Service Teacher Fellowships	$510,000
44.	National Undergraduate Fellowship Program in Plasma Physics and Fusion Energy Sciences	$300,000
45.	Fusion Energy Postdoctoral Research Program	$243,000
46.	Faculty and Student Teams	$215,000
47.	Advancing Precollege Science and Mathematics Education	$209,000
48.	Pan American Advanced Studies Institute	$200,000
49.	Trenton Community Partnership	$200,000
50.	Fusion/Plasma Education	$125,000
51.	National Middle School Science Bowl	$100,000
52.	Research Project on the Recruitment, Retention, and Promotion of Women in the Chemical Sciences	$100,000
53.	Used Energy Related Laboratory Equipment	$80,000

Table 21. (Continued)

Program number	Program name	Fiscal year 04 funding
54.	Plasma Physics Summer Institute for High School Physics Teachers	$78,000
55.	Pre-Service Teacher Program	$45,000
56.	Wonders of Physics Traveling Show	$45,000
57.	Hampton University Graduate Studies	$40,000
58.	Contemporary Physics Education Project	$23,000
59.	Cooperative Education Program	$17,000
Environmental Protection Agency		
60.	Science to Achieve Results Research Grants Program	$93.3 million
61.	Science to Achieve Results Graduate Fellowship Program	$10 million
62.	Post-Doctoral Fellows Environmental Research Growth Opportunities	$7.4 million
63.	Intern Program	$3 million
64.	Environmental Science and Engineering Fellows Program	$2.5 million
65.	Greater Research Opportunities Graduate Fellowship Program	$1.5 million
66.	Environmental Risk and Impact in Communities of Color and Economically Disadvantaged Communities	$824,000
67.	Research Internship for Students in Ecology	$698,000
68.	National Network for Environmental Management Studies Fellowship Program	$589,000
69.	Cooperative Agreements for Training Cooperative Partnerships	$352,000
70.	University of Cincinnati/EPA Research Training Grant	$300,000
71.	P3 Award: National Student Design Competition for Sustainability	$150,000
72.	Environmental Protection Agency and the Hispanic Association of Colleges and Universities Cooperative Agreement	$121,000
73.	Environmental Science Program	$100,000
74.	Environmental Career Organization's Internship Program	$89,000
75.	EPA—Cincinnati Research Apprenticeship Program	$75,000
76.	Environmental Protection Internship Program Summer Training Initiative	$72,000
77.	Tribal Lands Environmental Science Scholarship Program	$60,000
78.	Internship Program for University of Arizona Engineering Students	$50,000
79.	Teacher Professional Development Workshop for Teachers Grade 6-12	$18,000
80.	Saturday Academy, Apprenticeships in Science and Engineering Program	$6,000
Department of Health and Human Services/Health Resources and Services Administration		
81.	Scholarships for Disadvantaged Students Program	$45.5 million
82.	Nursing Workforce Diversity	$16 million
83.	Faculty Loan Repayment Program	$1.1 million
Department of Health and Human Services/Indian Health Service		
84.	Indian Health Professions Scholarship	$8.1 million
85.	Health Professions Scholarship Program for Indians	$3.7 million
Department of Health and Human Services/National Institutes of Health		
86.	Ruth L. Kirschstein National Research Service Award Institutional Research Training Grants	$546.9 million
87.	Ruth L. Kirschstein National Research Service Awards for Individual Postdoctoral Fellows	$72.6 million
88.	Research Supplements to Promote Diversity in Health-Related Research	$70 million
89.	Postdoctoral Visiting Fellow Program	$64.8 million
90.	Clinical Research Loan Repayment Program	$40.6 million
91.	Ruth L. Kirschstein National Research Service Awards for Individual Predoctoral Fellows, Predoctoral Minority Students, and Predoctoral Students with Disabilities	$33.8 million

Table 21. (Continued)

Program number	Program name	Fiscal year 04 funding
92.	Minority Access to Research Careers Program	$30.7 million
93.	Postdoctoral Intramural Research Training Award Program	$30.2 million
94.	Science Education Partnership Award	$16 million
95.	Pediatric Research Loan Repayment Program	$15.9 million
96.	Post-baccalaureate Intramural Research Training Award Program	$9.1 million
97.	Ruth L. Kirschstein National Research Service Award Short-Term Institutional Research Training Grants	$9 million
98.	Health Disparities Research Loan Repayment Program	$8.7 million
99.	Graduate Program Partnerships	$7.4 million
100.	Student Intramural Research Training Award Program	$6.3 million
101.	Career Opportunities in Research Education and Training Honors Undergraduate Research Training Grant	$5 million
102.	General Research Loan Repayment Program	$4.9 million
103.	Ruth L. Kirschstein National Research Service Awards for Individual M.D./Ph.D. Predoctoral Fellows	$4.7 million
104.	Science Education Drug Abuse Partnership Award	$3.1 million
105.	Pharmacology Research Associate Training Program	$2.7 million
106.	Technical Intramural Research Training Award	$1.9 million
107.	Fellowships in Cancer Epidemiology and Genetics	$1.8 million
108.	Clinical Research Loan Repayment Program for Individuals from Disadvantaged Backgrounds	$1.7 million
109.	Contraception and Infertility Research Loan Repayment Program	$1 million
110.	Medical Infomatics Training Program	$853,000
111.	Undergraduate Scholarship Program for Individuals from Disadvantaged Backgrounds	$838,000
112.	Curriculum Supplement Series	$788,000
113.	National Science Foundation and the National Institute of Biomedical Imaging and Bioengineering	$782,000
114.	Summer Institute for Training in Biostatistics	$694,000
115.	Summer Institute on Design and Conduct of Randomized Clinical Trials Involving Behavioral Interventions	$622,000
116.	Clinical Research Loan Repayment Program for Individuals from Disadvantaged Background	$551,000
117.	Clinical Research Training Program	$407,000
118.	NIH Academy	$385,000
119.	Health Communications Internship Program	$340,000
120.	NIH/National Institute of Standards and Technology Joint Postdoctoral Program	$338,000
121.	Summer Genetics Institute	$323,000
122.	AIDS Research Loan Repayment Program	$271,000
123.	Intramural NIAID Research Opportunities	$271,000
124.	Cancer Research Interns in Residence	$250,000
125.	Comparative Molecular Pathology Research Training Program	$199,000
126.	Office of Research on Women's Health-funded Programs with the Office of Intramural Research	$179,000
127.	Summer Institute for Social Work Research	$144,000

Table 21. (Continued)

Program number	Program name	Fiscal year 04 funding
128.	Office of Research on Women's Health-funded Programs with the Office of Intramural Training and Education	$119,000
129.	CCR/JHU Master of Science in Biotechnology Concentration in Molecular Targets and Drug Discovery Technologies	$111,000
130.	Introduction to Cancer Research Careers	$96,000
131.	Fellows Award for Research Excellence Program	$61,000
132.	Office of Research on Women's Health-funded Programs Supplements to Promote Reentry into Biomedical and Behavioral Research Careers	$60,000
133.	Translational Research in Clinical Oncology	$28,000
134.	National Institute of Environmental Health Sciences Office of Fellows' Career Development	$20,000
135.	Mobilizing for Action to Address the Unequal Burden of Cancer: NIH Research and Training Opportunities	$10,000
136.	Sallie Rosen Kaplan Fellowship for Women in Cancer Research	$5,000
Department of Homeland Security		
137.	Scholars and Fellows Program	$4.7 million
Department of the Interior		
138.	Cooperative Research Units Program	$15.3 million
139.	Water Resources Research Act Program	$6.4 million
140.	U.S. Geological Survey Mendenhall Postdoctoral Research Fellowship Program	$3.5 million
141.	Student Educational Employment Program	$1.8 million
142.	EDMAP Component of the National Cooperative Geologic Mapping Program	$490,000
143.	Student Career Experience Program	$177,000
144.	Cooperative Development Energy Program	$60,000
145.	Diversity Employment Program	$30,000
146.	Cooperative Agreement with Langston University	$15,000
147.	Mathematics, Science, and Engineering Academy	$15,000
148.	Shorebird Sister Schools Program	$15,000
149.	Build a Bridge Contest	$14,000
150.	VIVA Technology	$8,000
National Aeronautics and Space Administration		
151.	Minority University Research Education Program	$106.6 million
152.	Higher Education	$77.4 million
153.	Elementary and Secondary Education	$31.3 million
154.	E-Education	$9.7 million
155.	Informal Education	$5.5 million
National Science Foundation		
156.	Math and Science Partnership Program	$138.7 million
157.	Graduate Research Fellowship Program	$96 million
158.	Integrative Graduate Education and Research Traineeship Program	$67.7 million
159.	Teacher Professional Continuum	$61.5 million
160.	Research Experiences for Undergraduates	$51.7 million
161.	Graduate Teaching Fellows in K-12 Education	$49.8 million

Table 21. (Continued)

Program number	Program name	Fiscal year 04 funding
162.	Advanced Technological Education	$45.9 million
163.	Course, Curriculum, and Laboratory Improvement	$40.7 million
164.	Research on Learning and Education	$39.4 million
165.	Computer Science, Engineering, and Mathematics Scholarships	$33.9 million
166.	Louis Stokes Alliances for Minority Participation	$33.3 million
167.	Centers for Learning and Teaching	$30.8 million
168.	Instructional Materials Development	$29.3 million
169.	Science, Technology, Engineering, and Mathematics Talent Expansion Program	$25 million
170.	Historically Black Colleges and Universities Undergraduate Program	$23.8 million
171.	Interagency Education Research Initiative	$23.6 million
172.	Information Technology Experiences for Students and Teachers	$20.9 million
173.	Enhancing the Mathematical Sciences Workforce in the 21st Century	$20.6 million
174.	Centers of Research Excellence in Science and Technology	$19.8 million
175.	ADVANCE: Increasing the Participation and Advancement of Women in Academic Science and Engineering Careers	$19.4 million
176.	Federal Cyber Service: Scholarship for Service	$15.8 million
177.	Alliances for Graduate Education and the Professoriate	$15.3 million
178.	Research on Gender in Science and Engineering	$10 million
179.	Tribal Colleges and Universities Program	$10 million
180.	Model Institutions for Excellence	$9.7 million
181.	Grants for the Department-Level Reform of Undergraduate Engineering Education	$8.2 million
182.	Robert Noyce Scholarship Program	$8 million
183.	Research Experiences for Teachers	$5.8 million
184.	Nanoscale Science and Engineering Education	$4.8 million
185.	Research in Disabilities Education	$4.6 million
186.	Opportunities for Enhancing Diversity in the Geosciences	$4 million
187.	Mathematical Sciences Postdoctoral Research Fellowships	$3.7 million
188.	Minority Postdoctoral Research Fellowships and Supporting Activities	$3.2 million
189.	Partnerships for Research and Education in Materials	$3 million
190.	Undergraduate Research Centers	$3 million
191.	Centers for Ocean Science Education Excellence	$2.8 million
192.	Undergraduate Mentoring in Environmental Biology	$2.2 million
193.	Director's Award for Distinguished Teaching Scholars	$1.8 million
194.	Astronomy and Astrophysics Postdoctoral Fellowship Program	$1.6 million
195.	Geoscience Education	$1.5 million
196.	Internships in Public Science Education	$1.2 million
197.	Discovery Corps Fellowship Program	$1.1 million
198.	East Asia and Pacific Summer Institutes for U.S. Graduate Students	$1 million
199.	Pan-American Advanced Studies Institutes	$800,000
200.	Distinguished International Postdoctoral Research Fellowships	$788,000
201.	Postdoctoral Fellowships in Polar Regions Research	$667,000
202.	Arctic Research and Education	$300,000
203.	Developing Global Scientists and Engineers	$172,000

Table 21. (Continued)

Program number	Program name	Fiscal year 04 funding
Department of Transportation		
204.	University Transportation Centers Program	$32.5 million
205.	Dwight David Eisenhower Transportation Fellowship Program	$2 million
206.	Summer Transportation Institute	$2 million
207.	Summer Transportation Internship Program for Diverse Groups	$925,000

Source: GAO survey responses from 13 federal agencies.

APPENDIX III: FEDERAL STEM EDUCATION PROGRAMS FUNDED AT $10 MILLION OR MORE

The federal civilian agencies reported that the following science, technology, engineering, and mathematics (STEM) education programs were funded with at least $10 million in either fiscal year 2004 or 2005. However, programs that received $10 million or more in fiscal year 2004 but were unfunded for fiscal year 2005 were excluded from table 22. Agency officials also provided the program descriptions in table 22.

Table 22. Federal STEM Education Programs Funded at $10 Million or More during Fiscal Year 2004 or Fiscal Year2005

Program	Description	Funding (in millions of dollars)[a]		
		First year	2004	2005
Department of Agriculture				
1890 Institution Teaching and Research Capacity Building Grants Program	Is intended to strengthen teaching and research programs in the food and agricultural sciences by building the institutional capacities of the 1890 Land-Grant Institutions and Tuskegee University and West Virginia State University through cooperative linkages with federal and nonfederal entities. The program supports projects that strengthen teaching programs in the food and agricultural sciences in the targeted educational need areas of curriculum design and materials development, faculty preparation and enhancement of teaching, student experiential learning, and student recruitment and retention.	1990	$11.4	$12.5
Department of Education				
Mathematics and Science Partnerships Program	Is intended to increase the academic achievement of students in mathematics and science by enhancing the content knowledge and teaching skills of classroom teachers. Partnerships are between high-need school districts and the science, technology, engineering, and mathematics faculties of institutions of higher education.	2002	$149	$180
Upward Bound Math and Science Program	Designed to prepare low-income, first-generation college students for postsecondary education programs that lead to careers in the fields of math and science.	1990	$32.8	$32.8
Graduate Assistance in Areas of National Need	Provides fellowships in academic areas of national need to assist graduate students with excellent academic records who demonstrate financial need and plan to pursue the highest degree available in their courses of study.	1988	$30.6	$30.4
EnvironmentalP rotection Agency				
Science to Achieve Results Research Grants Program	Funds research grants in numerous environmental science and engineering disciplines. The program engages the nation's best scientists and engineers in targeted research. The grant program is currently focused on the health effects of particulate matter, drinking water, water quality, global change, ecosystem assessment and restoration, human health risk assessment, endocrine disrupting chemicals, pollution prevention and new technologies, children's health, and socio-economic research.	1995	$93.3	$80.1
Science to Achieve Results Graduate Fellowship Program	The purpose of this fellowship program is to encourage promising students to obtain advanced degrees and pursue careers in environmentally related fields.	1995	$10	$10

Table 22. (Continued)

Program	Description	Funding (in millions of dollars)[a]		
		First year	2004	2005
Department of Health and Human Services/Health Resources and Services Administration				
Scholarships for Disadvantaged Students Program	Funds are awarded to accredited schools of allopathic medicine, osteopathic medicine, dentistry, optometry, pharmacy, podiatric medicine, veterinary medicine, nursing, public health, chiropractic, or allied health, and schools offering graduate programs in behavioral and mental health practice. Priority is given to schools based on the proportion of graduating students going into primary care, the proportion of underrepresented minority students enrolled, and graduates working in medically underserved communities. Schools select qualified students and provide scholarships that cannot exceed tuition and reasonable educational and living expenses.	1991	$45.5	Not avail.
Nursing Workforce Diversity	To increase nursing education opportunities for individuals who are from disadvantaged backgrounds (including racial and ethnic minorities underrepresented among registered nurses) by providing student stipends, pre-entry preparation, and retention activities.	1989	$16	$16
Department of Health and Human Services/National Institutes of Health				
Ruth L. Kirschstein National Research Service Award Institutional Research Training Grants	Is designed to develop and enhance research training opportunities for individuals in biomedical, behavioral, and clinical research by supporting training programs at institutions of higher education. These institutional training grants allow the director of the program to select the trainees and to develop a curriculum of study and research experiences necessary to provide high-quality research training. The grant helps offset the cost of stipends and tuition for the appointed trainees. Graduate students, postdoctoral trainees, and short-term research training for health professional students can be supported by this grant.	1975	$546.9	Not avail.
Ruth L. Kirschstein National Research Service Awards for Individual Postdoctoral Fellows	To support the advanced training of individual students who have recently received doctoral degrees. This phase of research education and training is performed under the direct supervision of a sponsor who is an active investigator in the area of the proposed research. The training is designed to enhance the fellow's understanding of the health-related sciences and extend his/her potential to become a productive scientist who can perform research in biomedical, behavioral, or clinical fields.	1975	$72.6	Not avail.
Research Supplements to Promote Diversity in Health-Related Research	To improve the diversity of the research workforce by recruiting and supporting students, postdoctoral fellows, and eligible investigators from groups that have been shown to be underrepresented, such as individuals from underrepresented racial and ethnic groups, individuals with disabilities, and individuals from disadvantaged backgrounds.	1989	$70	$70
Postdoctoral Visiting Fellow Program	To provide advanced practical biomedical research experience to individuals who are foreign nationals and are 1 to 5 years beyond obtaining their Ph.D. or professional doctorate (e.g., M.D., DDS, etc.).	1950	$64.8	$70.7

Program	Description	Funding (in millions of dollars)[a]		
		First year	2004	2005
Clinical Research Loan Repayment Program	To attract health professionals to careers in clinical research. Clinical research is defined as "patient-oriented clinical research conducted with human subjects, or research on the causes and consequences of disease in human populations involving material of human origin (such as tissue specimens and cognitive phenomena) for which an investigator or colleague directly interacts with human subjects in an outpatient or inpatient setting to clarify a problem in human physiology, pathophysiology or disease, or epidemiologic or behavioral studies, outcomes research or health services research, or developing new technologies, therapeutic interventions, or clinical trials."	2002	$40.6	$42.6
Ruth L. Kirschstein National Research Service Awards for Individual Predoctoral Fellows, Predoctoral Minority Students, and Predoctoral Students with Disabilities	Provides predoctoral fellowships to students who are candidates for doctoral degrees and are performing dissertation research and training under the supervision of a mentor who is an active and established investigator in the area of the proposed research. The applicant and mentor must provide evidence of potential for a productive research career based upon the quality of previous research training, academic record, and training program. The applicant and mentor must propose a research project that will enhance the student's ability to understand and perform scientific research. The training program should be carried out in a research environment that includes appropriate resources and is demonstrably committed to the student's training.	1975	$33.8	Not avail.
Minority Access to Research Careers Program	Offers special research training support to 4-year colleges, universities, and health professional schools with substantial enrollments of minorities such as African Americans, Hispanic Americans, Native Americans (including Alaska Natives), and natives of U.S. Pacific Islands. Individual fellowships are also provided for graduate students and faculty.	1972	$30.7	$30.7
Postdoctoral Intramural Research Training Award Program	To provide advanced practical biomedical research experience to individuals who are 1 to 5 years beyond obtaining their Ph.D. or professional doctorate (e.g., M.D., DDS, etc.).	1986	$30.2	$33.3
Science Education Partnership Award	Provides funds for the development, implementation, and evaluation of innovative kindergarten through 12th grade (K-12) science education programs, teaching materials, and science center/museum programs. This program supports partnerships linking biomedical, clinical researchers, and behavioral scientists with K-12 teachers and schools, museum and science educators, media experts, and other interested organizations.	1992	$16	$16
Pediatric Research Loan Repayment Program	A program to attract health professionals to careers in pediatric research. Qualified pediatric research is defined as "research directly related to diseases, disorders, and other conditions in children."	2002	$15.9	$16

Table 22. (Continued)

Program	Description	First year	2004	2005
		Funding (in millions of dollars)[a]		
Post-baccalaureate Intramural Research Training Award Program	To provide (1) recent college graduates (graduated no more than 2 years prior to activation of traineeship), an introduction early in their careers to biomedical research fields; encourage their pursuit of professional careers in biomedical research; and allow additional time to pursue successful application to either graduate or medical school programs or (2) students who have been accepted into graduate, other doctoral, or medical degree programs, and who have written permission from their school to delay entrance for up to 1 year.	1996	$9.1	$12.3
Department of Homeland Security				
University Programs	Provides scholarships for undergraduate and fellowships for graduate students pursuing degrees in mission-relevant fields and postdoctoral fellowships for their contributions to Department of Homeland Security research projects. Students receive professional mentoring and complete a summer internship to connect academic interests with homeland security initiatives. Postdoctoral scholars are also mentored by DHS scientists.	2003	$4.7	$10.7
Department of the Interior				
Cooperative Research Units Program	The program links graduate science training with the research needs of state and federal agencies, and provides students with one-on-one mentoring by federal research scientists working on both applied and basic research needs of interest to the program. Program cooperators and partners provide graduate training opportunities and support.	1936	$15.3	$15
Department of Labor				
Community College/Community Based Job Training Grant Initiative	To build the capacity of community colleges to train in high-growth, high-demand industries and to actually train workers in those industries through partnerships that also include workforce investment boards and employers.	2005	$0	$250
National Aeronautics and Space Administration				
Minority University Research Education Program	To expand and advance NASA's scientific and technological base through collaborative efforts with Historically Black Colleges and Universities (HBCU) and other minority universities (OMU), including Hispanic-serving institutions and Tribal colleges and universities. This program also provides K-12 awards to build and support successful pathways for students to progress to the next level of mathematics and science, through a college preparatory curriculum, and enrollment in college. Higher-education awards are also given that seek to improve the rate at which underrepresented minorities are awarded degrees in STEM disciplines through increased research training and exposure to cutting-edge technologies that better prepare them to enter STEM graduate programs, the NASA workforce pipeline, and employment in NASA-related industries.	2002	$106.6	$73.6

Program	Description	First year	2004	2005
		Funding (in millions of dollars)[a]		
Post-baccalaureate Intramural Research Training Award Program	To provide (1) recent college graduates (graduated no more than 2 years prior to activation of traineeship), an introduction early in their careers to biomedical research fields; encourage their pursuit of professional careers in biomedical research; and allow additional time to pursue successful application to either graduate or medical school programs or (2) students who have been accepted into graduate, other doctoral, or medical degree programs, and who have written permission from their school to delay entrance for up to 1 year.	1996	$9.1	$12.3
Department of Homeland Security				
University Programs	Provides scholarships for undergraduate and fellowships for graduate students pursuing degrees in mission-relevant fields and postdoctoral fellowships for their contributions to Department of Homeland Security research projects. Students receive professional mentoring and complete a summer internship to connect academic interests with homeland security initiatives. Postdoctoral scholars are also mentored by DHS scientists.	2003	$4.7	$10.7
Department of the Interior				
Cooperative Research Units Program	The program links graduate science training with the research needs of state and federal agencies, and provides students with one-on-one mentoring by federal research scientists working on both applied and basic research needs of interest to the program. Program cooperators and partners provide graduate training opportunities and support.	1936	$15.3	$15
Department of Labor				
Community College/Community Based Job Training Grant Initiative	To build the capacity of community colleges to train in high-growth, high-demand industries and to actually train workers in those industries through partnerships that also include workforce investment boards and employers.	2005	$0	$250
National Aeronautics and Space Administration				
Minority University Research Education Program	To expand and advance NASA's scientific and technological base through collaborative efforts with Historically Black Colleges and Universities (HBCU) and other minority universities (OMU), including Hispanic-serving institutions and Tribal colleges and universities. This program also provides K-12 awards to build and support successful pathways for students to progress to the next level of mathematics and science, through a college preparatory curriculum, and enrollment in college. Higher-education awards are also given that seek to improve the rate at which underrepresented minorities are awarded degrees in STEM disciplines through increased research training and exposure to cutting-edge technologies that better prepare them to enter STEM graduate programs, the NASA workforce pipeline, and employment in NASA-related industries.	2002	$106.6	$73.6

Table 22. (Continued)

Program	Description	First year	2004	2005
		Funding (in millions of dollars)[a]		
Higher Education	The Higher Education Program focuses on supporting institutions of higher education in strengthening their research capabilities and providing opportunities that attract and prepare increasing numbers of students for NASA-related careers. The research conducted by the institutions will contribute to the research needs of NASA's Mission Directorates. The student projects serve as a major link in the student pipeline for addressing NASA's human capital strategies and the President's management agenda by helping to build, sustain, and effectively deploy the skilled, knowledgeable, diverse, and high-performing workforce needed to meet the current and emerging needs of government and its citizens.	2002	$77.4	$62.4
Elementary and Secondary Education	To increase the rigor of STEM experiences provided to K-12 students through workshops, summer internships, and classroom activities; provide high-quality professional development to teachers in STEM through NASA programs; develop technological avenues through the NASA Web site that will allow families to have common experiences with learning about space exploration; encourage inquiry teaching in K-12 classrooms; improve the content and focus of grade level/science team meetings in NASA Explorer Schools; and share the knowledge gained through the Educator Astronaut Program with teachers, students, and families.	2002	$31.3	$23.2
Informal Education	The principal purpose of the informal education program is to support projects designed to increase public interest in, understanding of, and engagement in STEM activities. The goal of all informal education programs is an informed citizenry that has access to the ideas of science and engineering and understands its role in enhancing the quality of life and the health, prosperity, welfare, and security of the nation. Informal learning is self-directed, voluntary, and motivated mainly by intrinsic interests, curiosity, exploration, and social interaction.	2002	$5.5	$10.2
National Science Foundation				
Math and Science Partnership (MSP) Program	The MSP is a major research and development effort that supports innovative partnerships to improve kindergarten through grade 12 student achievement in mathematics and science. MSP projects are expected to both raise the achievement levels of all students and significantly reduce achievement gaps in the mathematics and science performance of diverse student populations. Successful projects serve as models that can be widely replicated in educational practice to improve the mathematics and science achievement of all the nation's students.	2002	$138.7	$79.4
Graduate Research Fellowship Program (GRFP)	The purpose of the GRFP is to ensure the vitality of the scientific and technological workforce in the United States and to reinforce its diversity. The program recognizes and supports outstanding graduate students in the relevant science and engineering disciplines who are pursuing research-based master's and doctoral degrees. NSF fellows are expected to become knowledge experts who can contribute significantly to research, teaching, and innovations in science and engineering.	1952	$96	$96.6

Program	Description	First year	2004	2005
		Funding (in millions of dollars)[a]		
Integrative Graduate Education and Research Traineeship Program	This program provides support to universities for student positions in interdisciplinary areas of science and engineering. Traineeships focus on multidisciplinary and intersectoral research opportunities and prepare future faculty in effective teaching methods, applications of advanced educational technologies, and student mentoring techniques.	1998	$67.7	$69
Teacher Professional Continuum	The program addresses critical issues and needs regarding the recruitment, preparation, induction, retention, and lifelong development of kindergarten through grade 12 STEM teachers. Its goals are to improve the quality and coherence of teacher learning experiences across the continuum through research that informs teaching practice and the development of innovative resources for the professional development of kindergarten through grade 12 STEM teachers.	2004	$61.5	$60.2
Research Experiences for Undergraduates	This program supports active participation by undergraduate students in research projects in any of the areas of research funded by the National Science Foundation. The program seeks to involve students in meaningful ways in all kinds of research—whether disciplinary, interdisciplinary, or educational in focus—linked to the efforts of individual investigators, research groups, centers, and national facilities. Particular emphasis is given to the recruitment of women, minorities, and persons with disabilities.	1987	$51.7	$51.1
Graduate Teaching Fellows in K-12 Education	This program supports fellowships and associated training that enable graduate students in NSF-supported STEM disciplines to acquire additional skills that will broadly prepare them for professional and scientific careers. Through interactions with teachers, graduate students can improve communication and teaching skills while enriching STEM instruction in kindergarten through grade 12 schools. This program also provides institutions of higher education with an opportunity to make a permanent change in their graduate programs by including partnerships with schools in a manner that will mutually benefit faculties and students.	1999	$49.8	$49.9
Advanced Technological Education (ATE)	With an emphasis on 2-year colleges, the ATE program focuses on the education of technicians for the high-technology fields that drive our nation's economy. The program involves partnerships between academic institutions and employers to promote improvement in the education of science and engineering technicians at the undergraduate and secondary school levels. The ATE program supports curriculum development, professional development of college faculty and secondary school teachers, career pathways to 2-year colleges from secondary schools and from 2-year colleges to 4-year institutions, and other activities. The program also invites proposals focusing on applied research relating to technician education.	1994	$45.9	$45.1
Course, Curriculum, and Laboratory Improvement	This program emphasizes projects that build on prior work and contribute to the knowledge base of undergraduate STEM education research and practice. In addition, projects should contribute to building a community of scholars who work in related areas of undergraduate education.	1999	$40.7	$40.6

Table 22. (Continued)

Program	Description	Funding (in millions of dollars)[a]		
		First year	2004	2005
Research on Learning and Education	The program seeks to capitalize on important developments across a wide range of fields related to human learning and to STEM education. It supports research across a continuum that includes (1) the biological basis of human learning; (2) behavioral, cognitive, affective, and social aspects of STEM learning; (3) STEM learning in formal and informal educational settings; (4) STEM policy research; and (5) the diffusion of STEM innovations.	2000	$39.4	$38.2
Computer Science, Engineering, and Mathematics Scholarships	This program supports scholarships for academically talented, financially needy students, enabling them to enter the high-technology workforce following completion of an associate, baccalaureate, or graduate-level degree in computer science, computer technology, engineering, engineering technology, or mathematics. Academic institutions apply for awards to support scholarship activities and are responsible for selecting scholarship recipients, reporting demographic information about student scholars, and managing the project at the institution.	1999	$33.9	$75
Louis Stokes Alliances for Minority Participation	The program is aimed at increasing the quality and quantity of students successfully completing STEM baccalaureate degree programs and increasing the number of students interested in, academically qualified for, and matriculated into programs of graduate study. It also supports sustained and comprehensive approaches that facilitate achievement of the long-term goal of increasing the number of students who earn doctorates in STEM, particularly those from populations underrepresented in STEM fields.	1991	$33.3	$35
Centers for Learning and Teaching	The program focuses on the advanced preparation of STEM educators, as well as the establishment of meaningful partnerships among education stakeholders, especially Ph.D.-granting institutions, school systems, and informal education performers. Its goals are to renew and diversify the cadre of leaders in STEM education; to increase the number of kindergarten through undergraduate educators capable of delivering high-quality STEM instruction and assessment; and to conduct research into STEM education issues of national import, such as the nature of learning, teaching strategies, and reform policies and outcomes.	2000	$30.8	$28.4
Instructional Materials Development	This program contains three components. It supports (1) the creation and substantial revision of comprehensive curricula and supplemental materials that are research-based, enhance classroom instruction, and reflect standards for science, mathematics, and technology education developed by professional organizations; (2) the creation of tools for assessing student learning that are tied to nationally developed standards and reflect the most current thinking on how students learn mathematics and science; and (3) research for development of this program and projects.	1983	$29.3	$28.5

Program	Description	Funding (in millions of dollars)[a]		
		First year	2004	2005
Science, Technology, Engineering, and Mathematics Talent Expansion Program	The program seeks to increase the number of students (U.S. citizens or permanent residents) receiving associate or baccalaureate degrees in established or emerging fields within STEM. Type 1 proposals that provide for full implementation efforts at academic institutions are solicited. Type 2 proposals that support educational research projects on associate or baccalaureate degree attainment in STEM are also solicited.	2002	$25	$25.3
Historically Black Colleges and Universities (HBCU) Undergraduate Program	This program provides awards to enhance the quality of STEM instructional and outreach programs at HBCUs as a means to broaden participation in the nation's STEM workforce. Project strategies include curriculum enhancement, faculty professional development, undergraduate research, academic enrichment, infusion of technology to enhance STEM instruction, collaborations with research institutions and industry, and other activities that meet institutional needs.	1998	$23.8	$25.2
Interagency Education Research Initiative	This is a collaborative effort with the U.S. Department of Education. The goal is to support scientific research that investigates the effectiveness of educational interventions in reading, mathematics, and the sciences as they are implemented in varied school settings with diverse student populations.	1999	$23.6	$13.8
Information Technology Experiences for Students and Teachers	The program is designed to increase the opportunities for students and teachers to learn about, experience, and use information technologies within the context of STEM, including information technology courses. It is in direct response to the concern about shortages of technology workers in the United States. It has two components: (1) youth-based projects with strong emphasis on career and educational paths and (2) comprehensive projects for students and teachers.	2003	$20.9	$25
Enhancing the Mathematical Sciences Workforce in the 21st Century	The long-range goal of this program is to increase the number of U.S. citizens, nationals, and permanent residents who are well prepared in the mathematical sciences and who pursue careers in the mathematical sciences and in other NSF-supported disciplines.	2004	$20.6	$20.7
Centers of Research Excellence in Science and Technology	This program makes resources available to significantly enhance the research capabilities of minority-serving institutions through the establishment of centers that effectively integrate education and research. It promotes the development of new knowledge, enhancements of the research productivity of individual faculty, and an expanded diverse student presence in STEM disciplines.	1987	$19.8	$15.9
ADVANCE: Increasing the Participation and Advancement of Women in Academic Science and Engineering Careers	The program goal is to increase the representation and advancement of women in academic science and engineering careers, thereby contributing to the development of a more diverse science and engineering workforce. Members of underrepresented minority groups and individuals with disabilities are especially encouraged to apply.	2001	$19.4	$19.8

Table 22. (Continued)

Program	Description	Funding (in millions of dollars)[a]		
		First year	2004	2005
Federal Cyber Service: Scholarship for Service	This program seeks to increase the number of qualified students entering the fields of information assurance and computer security and to increase the capacity of the United States' higher education enterprise to continue to produce professionals in these fields to meet the needs of our increasingly technological society. The program has two tracks: provides funds to colleges and universities to (1) award scholarships to students to pursue academic programs in the information assurance and computer security fields for the final 2 years of undergraduate study, or for 2 years of master's-level study, or for the final 2 years of Ph.D.-level study, and (2) improve the quality and increase the production of information assurance and computer security professionals.	2001	$15.8	$14.1
Alliances for Graduate Education and the Professoriate	This program is intended to increase significantly the number of domestic students receiving doctoral degrees in STEM, with special emphasis on those population groups underrepresented in these fields. The program is interested in increasing the number of minorities who will enter the professoriate in these disciplines. Specific objectives are to develop (1) and implement innovative models for recruiting, mentoring, and retaining minority students in STEM doctoral programs, and (2) effective strategies for identifying and supporting underrepresented minorities who want to pursue academic careers.	1998	$15.3	$14.8
Research on Gender in Science and Engineering	The program seeks to broaden the participation of girls and women in all fields of STEM education by supporting research, dissemination of research, and extension services in education that will lead to a larger and more diverse domestic science and engineering workforce. Typical projects will contribute to the knowledge base addressing gender-related differences in learning and in the educational experiences that affect student interest, performance, and choice of careers, and how pedagogical approaches and teaching styles, curriculum, student services, and institutional culture contribute to causing or closing gender gaps that persist in certain fields.	1993	$10	$9.8
Tribal Colleges and Universities Program	This program provides awards to enhance the quality of STEM instructional and outreach programs, with special attention to the use of information technologies at Tribal colleges and universities, Alaskan Native-serving institutions, and Native Hawaiian-serving institutions. Support is available for the implementation of comprehensive institutional approaches to strengthen STEM teaching and learning in ways that improve access to, retention within, and graduation from STEM programs, particularly those that have a strong technological foundation. Through this program, assistance is provided to eligible institutions in their efforts to bridge the digital divide and prepare students for careers in information technology, science, mathematics, and engineering fields.	2001	$10	$9.8

Program	Description	Funding (in millions of dollars)[a]		
		First year	2004	2005
Department of Transportation				
University Transportation Centers Program (UTC)	The UTC program's mission is to advance U.S. technology and expertise in the many disciplines comprising transportation through the mechanisms of education, research, and technology transfer at university-based centers of excellence. The UTC program's goals include (1) developing a multidisciplinary program of coursework and experiential learning that reinforces the transportation theme of the center; (2) increasing the numbers of students, faculty, and staff who are attracted to and substantially involved in the undergraduate, graduate, and professional programs of the center; and (3) having students, faculty, and staff who reflect the growing diversity of the U.S. workforce and are substantially involved in the undergraduate, graduate, and professional programs of the center.	1998	$32.5	$32.5

Source: GAO survey responses from 13 federal agencies.

[a]The dollar amounts for fiscal years 2004 and 2005 contain actual and estimated program funding levels.

APPENDIX IV: DATA ON STUDENTS AND GRADUATES IN STEM FIELDS

Table 23 provides estimates for the numbers of students in science, technology, engineering, and mathematics (STEM) fields by education level for the 1995-1996 and 2003-2004 academic years. Tables 24 and 25 provide additional information regarding students in STEM fields by gender for the 1995-1996 and 2003-2004 academic years. Table 26 provides additional information regarding graduates in STEM fields by gender for the 1994-1995 and 2002-2003 academic years. Appendix V contains confidence intervals for these estimates.

Table 23. Estimated Numbers of Students in STEM Fields by Education Level for Academic Years 1995-1996 and 2003-2004

Education level/STEM field	Academic year 1995-1996	Academic year 2003-2004	Percentage change
Bachelor's level			
Total	2,218,510	2,876,721	30
Agricultural sciences	101,885	87,025	b
Biological sciences	407,336	351,595	-14
Computer sciences	261,139	456,303	75
Engineering	363,504	422,230	16
Mathematics	57,133	64,307	b
Physical sciences	107,832	129,207	b
Psychology	309,810	409,827	32
Social sciences	536,487	825,495	54
Technology	73,384	130,733	78
Master's level			
Total	321,293	403,200	25
Agricultural sciences	a	12,977	a
Biological sciences	34,701	19,467	-44
Computer sciences	49,071	58,939	b
Engineering	66,296	90,234	b
Mathematics	a	12,531	a
Physical sciences	a	22,008	a
Psychology	30,008	31,918	b
Social sciences	82,177	144,895	76
Technology	a	10,231	a
Doctoral level			
Total	217,395	198,504	b
Agricultural sciences	a	5,983	a
Biological sciences	a	33,884	a
Computer sciences	a	9,196	a
Engineering	32,181	35,687	b
Mathematics	a	9,412	a
Physical sciences	38,058	24,973	b
Psychology	30,291	33,994	b
Social sciences	54,092	42,464	b
Technology	a	2,912	a

Source: GAO calculations based upon NPSAS data.

Note: Enrollment totals differ from those cited in table 9 because table 9 includes students enrolled in certificate, associate's, other undergraduate, first-professional degree, and post-bachelor's or postmaster's certificate programs.

aSample sizes are insufficient to accurately produce estimates.

bChanges between academic years 1995-1996 and 2003-2004 are not statistically significant at the 95-percent confidence level. See table 30 for significance of percentage changes.

Table 24. Estimated Percentages of Students by Gender and STEM Field for Academic Years 1995-1996 and 2003-2004

	Male		Female	
Agricultural sciences	Percent: 1995-1996	Percent: 2003-2004	Percent: 1995-1996	Percent: 2003-2004
Total	58	55	42	45
Bachelor's	56	54	44	46
Master's	a	a	a	a
Doctorate	a	61	a	39
Biological sciences				
Total	46	42	54	58
Bachelor's	45	42	55	58
Master's	a	26	a	74
Doctorate	a	50	a	50
Computer sciences				
Total	67	76	33	24
Bachelor's	69	77	31	23
Master's	a	69	a	31
Doctorate	a	72	a	28
Engineering				
Total	83	83	17	17
Bachelor's	83	83	17	17
Master's	a	81	a	19
Doctorate	a	78	a	22
Mathematics				
Total	62	55	38	45
Bachelor's	57	54	43	46
Master's	a	a	a	a
Doctorate	a	68	a	32
Physical sciences				
Total	62	56	38	44
Bachelor's	56	53	44	47
Master's	a	a	a	a
Doctorate	a	68	a	32
Psychology				
Total	26	26	74	74
Bachelor's	26	26	74	74
Master's	a	21	a	79
Doctorate	a	30	a	70
Social sciences				
Total	54	41	46	59
Bachelor's	52	42	48	58
Master's	51	35	49	65
Doctorate	83	46	17	54
Technology				
Total	89	81	11	19
Bachelor's	88	81	12	19
Master's	a	a	a	a
Doctorate	a	a	a	a

Source: GAO calculations based upon NPSAS data.

aSample sizes are insufficient to accurately produce estimates.

Table 25. Estimated Number of Women Students and Percentage Change by Education Level and STEM Field for Academic Years 1995-1996 and 2003-2004

	Education level/STEM field	Number of women students		Percentage change in women students
		1995-1996	2003-2004	
Bachelor's level	Agricultural sciences	44,444	39,702	b
	Biological sciences	222,323	203,038	b
	Computer sciences	82,013	104,824	b
	Engineering	59,985	70,353	b
	Mathematics	24,597	29,791	b
	Physical sciences	47,421	60,203	b
	Psychology	229,772	304,712	+33
	Social sciences	258,023	475,544	+84
	Technology	8,871	25,227	+184
Master's level	Agricultural sciences	a	a	a
	Biological sciences	a	14,415	a
	Computer sciences	a	18,000	a
	Engineering	a	17,042	a
	Mathematics	a	5,562	a
	Physical sciences	a	8,497	a
	Psychology	23,857	25,342	b
	Social sciences	40,395	94,169	+133
	Technology	a	1,280	a
Doctoral level	Agricultural sciences	a	2,353	a
	Biological sciences	a	17,074	a
	Computer sciences	a	2,556	a
	Engineering	a	7,868	a
	Mathematics	a	3,042	a
	Physical sciences	a	8,105	a
	Psychology	a	23,843	a
	Social sciences	9,440	22,931	+143
	Technology	a	692	a

Source: GAO calculations based upon NPSAS data.

a Sample sizes are insufficient to accurately produce estimates.

bChanges between academic years 1995-1996 and 2003-2004 are not statistically significant at the95-percent confidence level. See table 29 for confidence intervals.

Table 26. Comparisons in the Percentage of STEM Graduates by Field and Gender for Academic Years 1994-1995 and 2002-2003

	Percentage graduates, men, 1994-1995	Percentage graduates, men, 2002-2003	Percentage graduates, women 1994-1995	Percentage graduates, women 2002-2003
STEM Degree/field				
Bachelor's degree				
Biological/agricultural sciences	50	40	50	60
Earth, atmospheric, and ocean sciences	66	58	34	42
Engineering	83	80	17	20
Mathematics and computer sciences	65	69	35	31
Physical sciences	64	58	36	42
Psychology	27	22	73	78
Social sciences	50	45	50	55
Technology	90	88	10	12
Master's degree				
Biological/agricultural sciences	52	45	48	55
Earth, atmospheric, and ocean sciences	70	59	30	41
Engineering	84	79	16	21
Mathematics and computer sciences	70	66	30	34
Physical sciences	70	64	30	36
Psychology	28	23	72	77
Social sciences	51	45	49	55
Technology	81	73	19	27
Doctoral degree				
Biological/agricultural sciences	63	57	37	43
Earth, atmospheric, and ocean sciences	78	72	22	28
Engineering	88	83	12	17
Mathematics and computer sciences	80	76	20	24
Physical sciences	76	73	24	27
Psychology	38	31	62	69
Social sciences	62	55	38	45
Technology	89	100	11	0

Source: GAO calculations based upon IPEDS data.

APPENDIX V:
CONFIDENCE INTERVALS FOR ESTIMATES OF STUDENTS AT THE BACHELOR'S, MASTER'S, AND DOCTORAL LEVELS

Because the National Postsecondary Student Aid Study (NPSAS) sample is a probability sample of students, the sample is only one of a large number of samples that might have been drawn. Since each sample could have provided different estimates, confidence in the precision of the particular sample's results is expressed as a 95-percent confidence interval (for example, plus or minus 4 percentage points). This is the interval that would contain the actual population value for 95 percent of the samples that could have been drawn. As a result, we are 95 percent confident that each of the confidence intervals in this report will include the true values in the study population. The upper and lower bounds of the 95 percent confidence intervals for each estimate relied on in this report are presented in the following tables.

Table 27. Estimated Changes in the Numbers and Percentages of Students in the STEM and Non-STEM Fields across All Education Levels, Academic Years 1995-1996 and 2003-2004 (95 percent confidence intervals)

Lower and upper bounds of 95 percent confidence interval	STEM field	Non-STEM field
Lower bound: number of students: 1995-1996	3,941,589	14,885,171
Upper bound: number of students: 1995-1996	4,323,159	15,601,065
Lower bound: percentage of students: 1995-1996	20	78
Upper bound: percentage of students: 1995-1996	22	80
Lower bound: number of students: 2003-2004	4,911,850	16,740,049
Upper bound: number of students: 2003-2004	5,082,515	17,025,326
Lower bound: percentage of students: 2003-2004	22	77
Upper bound: percentage of students: 2003-2004	23	78
Lower bound: percentage change: 1995/96-2003/04	15	8
Upper bound: percentage change: 1995/96-2003/04	26.9	13.5

Source: GAO calculations based upon 1995-1996 and 2003-2004 NPSAS data.

Note: The totals for STEM and non-STEM enrollments include students in addition to the bachelor's, master's, and doctorate education levels. These totals also include students enrolled in certificate, associate's, other undergraduate, first-professional degree, and post-bachelor's or post-master's certificate programs. The percentage changes between the 1995-1996 and 2003-2004 academic years for STEM and non-STEM students are statistically significant.

Table 28. Numbers of Students by Education Level in all STEM Fields for Academic Years 1995-1996 and 2003-2004 (95 percent confidence intervals)

		Total	Bachelors	Masters	Doctorate
Total	Lower bound: Number of Students: 1995-1996	2,633,867	2,114,316	271,208	171,824
	Upper bound: Number of Students: 1995-1996	2,880,529	2,322,704	377,821	271,230
	Lower bound: Number of Students: 2003-2004	3,411,004	2,819,206	366,141	185,230
	Upper bound: Number of Students: 2003-2004	3,545,844	2,934,236	442,938	212,471
Agricultural Sciences	Lower bound: Number of Students: 1995-1996	93,346	78,241	a	a
	Upper bound: Number of Students: 1995-1996	151,132	130,144	a	a
	Lower bound: Number of Students: 2003-2004	93,543	76,472	7,296	4,661
	Upper bound: Number of Students: 2003-2004	119,613	98,590	21,202	7,553
Biological Sciences	Lower bound: Number of Students: 1995-1996	416,315	360,553	18,883	a
	Upper bound: Number of Students: 1995-1996	524,615	454,119	57,066	a
	Lower bound: Number of Students: 2003-2004	383,277	330,834	13,728	30,401
	Upper bound: Number of Students: 2003-2004	427,502	372,355	26,694	37,367
Computer Sciences	Lower bound: Number of Students: 1995-1996	275,804	224,616	31,634	a
	Upper bound: Number of Students: 1995-1996	363,084	297,662	71,242	a
	Lower bound: Number of Students: 2003-2004	495,359	428,927	47,669	7,427
	Upper bound: Number of Students: 2003-2004	554,747	483,679	70,210	11,243
Engineering	Lower bound: Number of Students: 1995-1996	411,868	321,464	45,912	16,620
	Upper bound: Number of Students: 1995-1996	516,391	405,544	90,768	54,155
	Lower bound: Number of Students: 2003-2004	514,794	400,252	63,632	32,113
	Upper bound: Number of Students: 2003-2004	583,058	444,208	116,835	39,261
Mathematics	Lower bound: Number of Students: 1995-1996	68,083	42,910	a	a
	Upper bound: Number of Students: 1995-1996	119,165	74,456	a	a
	Lower bound: Number of Students: 2003-2004	75,705	55,314	7,869	7,687
	Upper bound: Number of Students: 2003-2004	97,848	74,318	18,867	11,392
Physical Sciences	Lower bound: Number of Students: 1995-1996	139,416	87,966	a	21,279
	Upper bound: Number of Students: 1995-1996	214,274	130,658	a	60,546
	Lower bound: Number of Students: 2003-2004	160,895	116,479	14,944	22,043
	Upper bound: Number of Students: 2003-2004	192,534	142,894	31,092	27,903
Psychology	Lower bound: Number of Students: 1995-1996	327,359	271,188	17,600	16,929
	Upper bound: Number of Students: 1995-1996	416,804	348,432	47,037	48,601
	Lower bound: Number of Students: 2003-2004	449,858	385,660	24,218	27,846
	Upper bound: Number of Students: 2003-2004	502,696	433,995	41,116	40,142
Social Sciences	Lower bound: Number of Students: 1995-1996	608,199	478,659	60,792	33,489
	Upper bound: Number of Students: 1995-1996	742,107	594,315	103,562	79,414
	Lower bound: Number of Students: 2003-2004	974,279	791,462	125,457	38,291
		Total	Bachelors	Masters	Doctorate
	Upper bound: Number of Students: 2003-2004	1,052,506	859,527	164,333	46,636
Technology	Lower bound: Number of Students: 1995-1996	63,910	57,446	a	a
	Upper bound: Number of Students: 1995-1996	104,308	92,251	a	a
	Lower bound: Number of Students: 2003-2004	130,347	118,492	5,556	1,814
	Upper bound: Number of Students: 2003-2004	158,418	143,848	17,158	4,421

Source: GAO calculations based upon 1995-1996 and 2003-2004 NPSAS data.
aSample sizes are insufficient to accurately produce estimates.

Table 29. Estimated Numbers and Percentage Changes in Women Students in STEM Fields, Academic Years 1995-1996 and 2003-2004 (95 percent confidence intervals)

	Lower bound: Number of Students: 1995-1996	Upper bound: Number of Students: 1995-1996	Lower bound: Number of Students: 2003-2004	Upper bound: Number of Students: 2003-2004	Lower bound: Percentage Change: 1995/96-2003/04	Upper bound: Percentage Change: 1995/96-2003/04
Total						
Total	1,100,766	1,260,962	1,546,340	1,638,269	24.9	44.8
Agricultural sciences	33,541	67,797	39,678	56,710	-41.2	31.4
Biological sciences	215,624	293,386	217,669	251,384	-23.4	7.7
Computer sciences	78,956	129,858	110,119	140,642	-12.6	52.8
Engineering	60,568	100,683	84,556	105,970	-14.3	55
Mathematics	21,805	46,907	31,207	45,593	-34.1	57.6
Physical sciences	42,352	91,230	66,408	87,203	-29.9	59.9
Psychology	236,730	311,792	331,616	376,179	9.6	48.5
Social sciences	267,155	348,561	562,529	622,759	65.2	119.8
Technology	5,136	13,993	21,339	33,060	52.3	361
Bachelor's						
Total	909,030	1,045,868	1,271,939	1,354,847	24.1	44.7
Agricultural sciences	27,943	60,945	32,293	47,111	-47.8	26.4
Biological sciences	188,204	256,442	187,283	218,793	-24.4	7
Computer sciences	61,719	102,307	90,851	118,798	-8.1	63.7
Engineering	45,013	74,957	61,142	79,563	-15.8	50.3
Mathematics	16,558	32,636	23,487	36,094	-26	68.3
Physical sciences	32,641	62,201	51,259	69,147	-16.9	70.8
Psychology	197,530	262,014	284,138	325,287	12	53.3
Social sciences	220,004	296,042	449,103	501,985	55.3	113.3
Technology	5,185	13,867	19,582	30,872	40.2	328.6

	Lower bound: Number of Students: 1995-1996	Upper bound: Number of Students: 1995-1996	Lower bound: Number of Students: 2003-2004	Upper bound: Number of Students: 2003-2004	Lower bound: Percentage Change: 1995/96-2003/04	Upper bound: Percentage Change: 1995/96-2003/04
Master's						
Total	109,116	183,302	170,116	210,777	-5.6	66.1
Agricultural sciences	a	a	a	a	a	a
Biological sciences	a	a	11,330	16,806	a	a
Computer sciences	a	a	11,907	24,093	a	a
Engineering	a	a	10,989	24,604	a	a
Mathematics	a	a	2,979	8,336	a	a
Physical sciences	a	a	4,713	12,802	a	a
Psychology	15,901	28,488	21,284	28,384	-58.1	70.5
Social sciences	26,605	54,185	79,619	108,720	45.8	220.5
Technology	a	a	235	3,485	a	a
Doctorate						
Total	38,103	79,875	81,553	95,377	-6.3	115.6
Agricultural Sciences	a	a	1,441	3,265	a	a
Biological Sciences	a	a	14,455	19,692	a	a
Computer Sciences	a	a	1,745	3,503	a	a
Engineering	a	a	5,870	9,867	a	a
Mathematics	a	a	1,999	4,085	a	a
Physical Sciences	a	a	6,298	9,913	a	a
Psychology	a	a	19,198	28,489	a	a
Social Sciences	4,098	17,371	19,778	26,083	4.2	281.6
Technology	a	a	254	1,339	a	a

Source: GAO calculations based upon NPSAS data.

aSample sizes are insufficient to accurately produce estimates.

Table 30. Estimated Percentage Changes in Bachelor's, Master's, and Doctoral Students in STEM Fields, Academic Years 1995-1996 and 2003-2004 (95 percent confidence intervals)

STEM fields	Percentage change in academic years 1995-1996 and 2003-2004	Lower and upper bounds of 95 percent confidence interval			
		Total	Bachelor's	Master's	Doctoral
Agricultural sciences	Lower bound: percentage change	-34.8	-38.7	a	a
	Upper bound: percentage change	11.9	9.5	a	a
	Statistically significant	no	no	a	a
Biological sciences	Lower bound: percentage change	-24.4	-24.8	-79.6	a
	Upper bound: percentage change	-2.6	-2.5	-8.3	a
	Statistically significant	yes	yes	yes	a
Computer sciences	Lower bound: percentage change	41.1	48.1	-34.8	a
	Upper bound: percentage change	89.5	101.3	75	a
	Statistically significant	yes	yes	no	a
Engineering	Lower bound: percentage change	3.5	1.4	-27.5	-55.4
	Upper bound: percentage change	33.8	30.9	99.7	77.2
	Statistically significant	yes	yes	no	no
Mathematics	Lower bound: percentage change	-33.5	-21.8	a	a
	Upper bound: percentage change	23	46.9	a	a
	Statistically significant	no	no	a	a
Physical sciences	Lower bound: percentage change	-21.7	-6.6	a	-70.2
	Upper bound percentage change	24.4	46.3	a	1.4
	Statistically significant	no	no	a	no
Psychology	Lower bound: percentage change	11.7	14	-51.2	-48.8
	Upper bound: percentage change	45.4	50.5	63.9	73.3
	Statistically significant	yes	yes	no	no
Social sciences	Lower bound: percentage change	34.6	36.1	24.7	-59.3
	Upper bound: percentage change	66.5	71.6	127.9	16.3
	Statistically significant	yes	yes	yes	no
Technology	Lower bound: percentage change	30	33.4	a	a
	Upper bound: percentage change	119.6	122.9	a	a
	Statistically significant	yes	yes	a	a
Total	Lower bound: percentage change	20	23.1	1.8	-29.5
	Upper bound: percentage change	32.3	36.3	49.2	12.1
	Statistically significant	yes	yes	yes	no

Source: GAO calculations based upon 1995-1996 and 2003-2004 NPSAS data.
aSample sizes are insufficient to accurately produce estimates.

Table 31. Estimates of STEM Students by Gender and Field for Academic Years 1995-1996 and 2003-2004 (95 percent confidence intervals)

STEM fields	Men: 1995-1996 academic year		Men: 2003-2004 academic year			Women: 1995-1996 academic year		Women: 2003-2004 academic year		
	Lower bound	Upper bound	Lower bound	Upper bound	Statistically significant	Lower bound	Upper bound	Lower bound	Upper bound	Statistically significant
Agricultural sciences										
Bachelor's	44	69	48	61	no	31	56	39	52	no
Master's	[a]	[a]	[a]	[a]	[a]	[a]	[a]	[a]	[a]	[a]
Doctoral	[a]	[a]	49	72	[a]	[a]	[a]	28	51	[a]
Biological sciences										
Bachelor's	40	51	39	45	no	49	60	55	61	no
Master's	[a]	[a]	14	46	[a]	[a]	[a]	54	89	[a]
Doctoral	[a]	[a]	44	55	[a]	[a]	[a]	45	56	[a]
Computer sciences										
Bachelor's	62	75	74	80	no	25	38	20	26	no
Master's	[a]	[a]	61	78	[a]	[a]	[a]	22	39	[a]
Doctoral	[a]	[a]	62	81	[a]	[a]	[a]	19	38	[a]
Engineering										
Bachelor's	80	87	81	85	no	13	20	15	19	no
Master's	[a]	[a]	73	88	[a]	[a]	[a]	12	27	[a]
Doctoral	[a]	[a]	73	83	[a]	[a]	[a]	17	27	[a]
Mathematics										
Bachelor's	44	70	46	61	no	30	56	39	54	no
Master's	[a]	[a]	[a]	[a]	[a]	[a]	[a]	[a]	[a]	[a]
Doctoral	[a]	[a]	59	77	[a]	[a]	[a]	23	41	[a]
Physical sciences										
Bachelor's	46	66	48	59	no	34	54	41	52	no
Master's	[a]	[a]	[a]	[a]	[a]	[a]	[a]	[a]	[a]	[a]
Doctoral	[a]	[a]	62	73	[a]	[a]	[a]	27	38	[a]
Psychology										
Bachelor's	20	32	23	28	no	68	80	72	77	no
Master's	[a]	[a]	10	35	[a]	[a]	[a]	65	90	[a]
Doctoral	[a]	[a]	20	39	[a]	[a]	[a]	61	80	[a]
Social sciences										
Bachelor's	46	57	40	45	yes	43	54	55	60	yes
Master's	38	64	28	42	no	36	62	58	72	no

STEM fields	Men: 1995-1996 academic year		Men: 2003-2004 academic year			Women: 1995-1996 academic year		Women: 2003-2004 academic year		
	Lower bound	Upper bound	Lower bound	Upper bound	Statistically significant	Lower bound	Upper bound	Lower bound	Upper bound	Statistically significant
Doctoral	70	91	41	51	yes	9	30	49	59	yes
Technology										
Bachelor's	81	93	77	85	no	7	19	15	23	no
Master's	[a]	[a]	[a]	[a]	[a]	[a]	[a]	[a]	[a]	[a]
Doctoral	[a]	[a]	[a]	[a]	[a]	[a]	[a]	[a]	[a]	[a]
Total students										
Total	55	60	53	55	yes	40	45	45	47	yes
Bachelor's	54	58	53	55	no	42	46	45	47	no
Master's	46	63	48	57	no	37	54	43	52	no
Doctoral	63	82	53	58	yes	18	37	42	47	yes

Source: GAO calculations based upon 1995-1996 and 2003-2004 NPSAS data.

aSample sizes are insufficient to accurately produce estimates.

Table 32. Estimates of Students for Selected Racial or Ethnic Groups in STEM Fields for All Education Levels and Fields for the Academic Years 1995-1996 and 2002-2003 (95 percent confidence intervals)

Race or ethnicity	Lower bound: number of students, academic year, 1995-1996	Upper bound: number of students, academic year, 1995-1996	Lower bound: number of students, academic year, 2003-2004	Upper bound: number of students, academic year, 2003-2004
African American	303,832	416,502	577,854	639,114
Hispanic	285,381	446,621	461,738	515,423
Asian/Pacific Islander	247,347	330,541	322,738	367,377
Native American	11,464	28,103	30,064	47,694
Other/multiple minorities	17,708	44,434	150,264	183,174

Lower bound: percentage change	Upper bound: percentage change	Lower bound: percentage of students, academic year 1995-1996	Upper bound: percentage of students, academic year 1995-1996	Lower bound: percentage of students, academic year 2003-2004	Upper bound: percentage of students, academic year 2003-2004
41	97	7	10	12	13
3	64	7	11	9	10
1	38	6	8	6	7
8	206	0	1	1	1
219	732	0	1	3	4

Source: GAO Calculations based upon 1995-1996 and 2003-2004 NPSAS data.

Table 33. Estimates of International Students in STEM Fields by Education Levels for Academic Years 1995-1996 and 2003-2004 (95 percent confidence intervals)

Education level	Lower bound: number of students, 1995-1996	Upper bound: number of students, 1995-1996	Lower bound: number of students, 2003-2004	Upper bound: number of students, 2003-2004	Lower bound: percentage change	Upper bound: percentage change
Total	80,812	142,192	154,466	186,322	12	102
Bachelor's	20,254	47,684	125,950	154,911	155	523
Master's	23,063	64,587	16,359	29,899	-76	-13
Doctoral	20,525	59,861	5,168	10,735	-90	-68

Source: GAO calculations based upon 1995-1996 and 2003-2004 NPSAS data.

APPENDIX VI:
CONFIDENCE INTERVALS FOR ESTIMATES OF STEM EMPLOYMENT BY GENDER, RACE OR ETHNICITY, AND WAGES AND SALARIES

The current population survey (CPS) was used to obtain estimates about employees and wages and salaries in science, technology, engineering, and mathematics (STEM) fields. Because the current population survey (CPS) is a probability sample based on random selections, the sample is only one of a large number of samples that might have been drawn. Since each sample could have provided different estimates, confidence in the precision of the particular sample's results is expressed as a 95 percent confidence interval (e.g., plus or minus 4 percentage points). This is the interval that would contain the actual population value for 95 percent of the samples that could have been drawn. As a result, we are 95 percent confident that each of the confidence intervals in this report will include the true values in the study population. We use the CPS general variance methodology to estimate this sampling error and report it as confidence intervals. Percentage estimates we produce from the CPS data have 95 percent confidence intervals of plus or minus 6 percentage points or less. Estimates other than percentages have 95 percent confidence intervals of no more than plus or minus 10 percent of the estimate itself, unless otherwise noted. Consistent with the CPS documentation guidelines, we do not produce estimates based on the March supplement data for populations of less than 75,000.

Table 34. Estimated Total Number of Employees by STEM Field between Calendar Years 1994 and 2003

STEM fields		Lower bound: calendar year 1994	Upper bound: calendar year 1994	Lower bound: calendar year 2003	Upper bound: calendar year 2003	Statistically significant
Science		2,349,605	2,656,451	2,874,347	3,143,071	yes
Technology	1,285,	321	1,515,671	1,379,375	1,568,189	no
Engineering	1,668,	514	1,929,240	1,638,355	1,843,427	no
Mathematics/ computer sciences		1,369,047	1,606, 395	2,520,858	2,773,146	yes

Table 35. Estimated Numbers of Employees in STEM Fields by Gender for Calendar Years 1994 and 2003

STEM fields	Lower bound: calendar year 1994, women	Upper bound: calendar year 1994, women	Lower bound: calendar year 2003, women	Upper bound: calendar year 2003, women	Statistically significant	Lower bound: calendar year 1994, men	Upper bound: calendar year 1994, men	Lower bound: calendar year 2003, men	Upper bound: calendar year 2003, men	Statistically significant
Science	1,594,527	1,827,685	2,031,124	2,327,390	yes	708,673	875,171	733,358	925,548	no
Technology	385,433	505,329	357,805	489,899	no	863,785	1,046,445	941,960	1,157,900	no
Engineering	107,109	174,669	126,947	210,407	no	1,538,198	1,777,778	1,440,510	1,703,920	no
Mathematics/ computer sciences	372,953	491,053	610,649	779,525	yes	959,765	1,151,681	1,805,505	2,098,325	yes

Table 36. Estimated Changes in STEM Employment by Gender for Calendar Years 1994 and 2003

STEM fields	Lower bound: calendar year 1994	Upper bound: calendar year 1994	Lower bound: calendar year 2003	Upper bound: calendar year 2003	Statistically significant
	Men		Men		
Science	28.87	34.40	24.84	30.30	yes
Technology	64.50	71.90	67.29	75.19	no
Engineering	90.28	94.05	87.93	92.69	no
Mathematics/ computer sciences	67.46	74.46	70.87	76.61	no
	Women		Women		
Science	65.71	71.01	69.81	75.05	yes
Technology	28.26	35.35	24.97	32.55	no
Engineering	6.03	9.64	7.41	11.97	no
Mathematics/ computer sciences	25.69	32.39	23.51	29.01	no

Table 37. Estimated Percentages of STEM Employees for Selected Racial or Ethnic Groups for Calendar Years 1994 and 2003

Race or Ethnicity	Lower bound: calendar year 1994	Upper bound: calendar year 1994	Lower bound: calendar year 2003	Upper bound: calendar year 2003	Statistically significant
Black or African American	6.49	8.46	7.66	9.79	no
Hispanic or Latino origin	4.76	6.60	8.83	11.09	yes
Other minorities	3.64	5.28	5.89	7.81	yes

Table 38. Estimated Changes in Median Annual Wages and Salaries in the STEM Fields for Calendar Years 1994 and 2003

STEM fields	Lower bound: calendar year 1994	Upper bound: calendar year 1994	Lower bound: calendar year 2003	Upper bound: calendar year 2003	Statistically significant
Science	$42,212	$45,241	$44,650	$47,008	yes
Technology	$36,241	$39,769	$38,554	$41,286	yes
Engineering	$59,059	$63,134	$67,634	$71,749	yes
Mathematics/computer sciences	$51,922	$55,905	$58,801	$61,679	yes

APPENDIX VII:
COMMENTS FROM THE DEPARTMENT OF COMMERCE

THE DEPUTY SECRETARY OF COMMERCE
Washington, D.C. 20230

September 23, 2005

Ms. Cornelia M. Ashby
Director
Education, Workforce,
 and Income Security Issues
U.S. Government Accountability Office
Washington, D. C. 20548

Dear Ms. Ashby:

Thank you for the opportunity to review and comment on the Government Accountability Office's draft report, *Higher Education: Federal Science, Technology, Engineering, and Mathematics Programs and Related Trends* (GAO-05-887).

I enclose the U.S. Department of Commerce's recommended changes regarding factual or technical information.

Sincerely,

David A Sampson

Enclosure

As a result of these changes, there should be no programs listed under the Department of Commerce for Table 20.

Editorial Comments

Pages 3-4, Results in Brief, second paragraph:
The *Results in Brief* states the numbers and percentages of student and graduates increased in most science, technology, engineering, and mathematics (STEM) fields. However, Figure 3 (page 22) shows significant declines in biological sciences; earth, atmospheric and ocean sciences; engineering; and technology. As the Department of Commerce (National Oceanic and Atmospheric Administration (NOAA)) relies particularly on students in the biological, earth, ocean and atmospheric sciences, we recommend the conclusion point to these declines, despite overall increases in STEM students.

U.S. Department of Commerce Response to Key GAO Conclusions

Page 9, More than 200 Federal Education Programs Are Designed to Increase the Numbers of Students and Graduates or Improve Educational Programs in STEM Fields, but Most Have Not Been Evaluated:

We concur with the importance of evaluation. Evaluation is established as a standard in the NOAA Education Plan and education programs throughout the agency are working to achieve this standard.

Page 30, Teacher Quality and Mathematics and Science Preparation Were Cited as Key Factors Affecting Domestic Students' STEM Participation Decisions:

We concur with the importance of improving teacher content knowledge. The NOAA Education Plan identifies teacher professional development as a key strategy and several education programs are focused on this effort.

Page 33, Mentoring Cited as a Key Factor Affecting Women's and Minorities' STEM Participation Decisions:

We concur. Mentoring and internships are required under NOAA's Ernest F. Hollings Undergraduate Scholarship Program, Nancy Foster Scholarship Program, and the scholarship programs of NOAA's Education Partnership Program with Minority Serving Institutions.

Page 39, Concluding Observations, first paragraph:
GAO reports university officials and others suggested increasing the federal commitment to STEM education programs, but adds the importance of understanding the extent to which existing STEM programs are appropriately targeted. We agree with the conclusion regarding targeting. Our STEM education programs within NOAA are specific to NOAA-related mission goals.

APPENDIX VIII: COMMENTS FROM THE DEPARTMENT OF HEALTH AND HUMAN SERVICES

 DEPARTMENT OF HEALTH & HUMAN SERVICES   Office of Inspector General

Washington, D.C. 20201

SEP **3 0** 2005

Ms. Cornelia M. Ashby
Director, Education, Workforce,
  And Income Security Issues
U.S. Government Accountability Office
Washington, DC 20548

Dear Ms. Ashby:

Enclosed are the Department's comments on the U.S. Government Accountability Office's
(GAO's) draft report entitled, "HIGHER EDUCATION: Federal Science, Technology, Engineering,
and Mathematics Programs and Related Trends" (GAO-05-887). These comments represent the
tentative position of the Department and are subject to reevaluation when the final version of this
report is received.

The Department provided several technical comments directly to your staff.

The Department appreciates the opportunity to comment on this draft report before its publication.

Sincerely,

Larry Goldberg
for Daniel R. Levinson
       Inspector General

Enclosure

> The Office of Inspector General (OIG) is transmitting the Department's response to this draft
> report in our capacity as the Department's designated focal point and coordinator for U.S.
> Government Accountability Office reports. OIG has not conducted an independent
> assessment of these comments and therefore expresses no opinion on them.

**COMMENTS OF THE U.S. DEPARTMENT OF HEALTH AND HUMAN
SERVICES ON THE U.S. GOVERNMENT ACCOUNTABILITY OFFICE'S
DRAFT REPORT ENTITLED, "HIGHER EDUCATION: FEDERAL SCIENCE,
TECHNOLOGY, ENGINEERING, AND MATHEMATICS PROGRAMS AND
RELATED TRENDS" (GAO-05-887)**

General Comments

The U.S. Department of Health and Human Services (HHS) thanks the U.S. Government
Accountability Office (GAO) for providing us the opportunity to review and comment on the
draft report.

The education and training of future generations of science, technology, engineering, and
mathematics (STEM) professionals is an important investment in the nation's future. This
expertise will help provide the personnel devoted to the technological innovation needed to
address the research and development requirements of industry and Government. HHS
commends GAO for collaborating with 13 departments and agencies to assemble a partial
compendium of Federal STEM and related education and training programs that directly and
indirectly help lead students to pursue degrees or careers in STEM fields. This information has
the potential for further collaborations that will enhance synergy across the Federal departments
and agencies that support STEM related education and training.

We agree with GAO that it is important to evaluate ongoing programs to determine the extent to
which they are achieving their desired results. HHS, under the auspices of the National Institutes
of Health (NIH) and the Agency for Healthcare Research and Quality, supports nearly 17,000
individuals pursuing graduate and postdoctoral research training annually as part of the Ruth L.
Kirschstein National Research Service Award (NRSA) Programs noted in the report. NRSA
programs were established by an act of the Congress of the United States in 1974 in order to help
support and produce a diverse pool of highly trained scientists to perform the nation's biomedical,
behavioral, and clinical research.

NRSA programs have been systematically evaluated twelve times by the National Research
Council (NRC) of the National Academies. The most recent evaluation, *Advancing the Nation's
Health Needs—NIH Research Training Programs*, was completed earlier this year. This report
indicated that NRSA institutional training grants, which fund the education and training of the
majority of NRSA participants, are widely regarded as one of the best vehicles for learning the
theories and techniques of biomedical and behavioral research. In addition, the report noted that
the NRSA program has successfully produced high-quality research personnel and has been
important for the upgrading of research training in general.

We believe that the NRC evaluations and the HHS responses to them serve important roles in
assessing and responding to the changing needs in the education and training of biomedical,
behavioral, and clinical research personnel. These evaluations have resulted in the
implementation of improvements in NRSA programs in order to better meet the nation's evolving
research and research training needs.

APPENDIX IX:
COMMENTS FROM THE NATIONAL SCIENCE FOUNDATION

NATIONAL SCIENCE FOUNDATION
4201 WILSON BOULEVARD
ARLINGTON, VIRGINIA 22230

NSF

OFFICE OF THE
ASSISTANT DIRECTOR
FOR EDUCATION AND
HUMAN RESOURCES

TO: Cornelia M. Ashby
            Director, Education, Workforce and Income Security Issues
            U.S. Government Accountability Office

FROM: Donald Thompson, Assistant Director (Acting)
            NSF Directorate for Education and Human Resources

RE: Response to Draft GAO Report: *Federal Science, Technology,*
            Engineering, and Mathematics Programs and Related Trends

DATE: September 21, 2005

Thank you for the opportunity to respond to the draft of the GAO Report: *Federal Science, Technology, Engineering, and Mathematics Programs and Related Trends.* This report summarizes an impressive amount of information obtained from federal agencies, workforce data from numerous sources, and results from interviews GAO conducted with several students and university officials. This was a formidable task, especially considering the tight timeline GAO had to conduct its work. The resulting report will be useful.

Below are a few specific comments that are submitted for your consideration.

1. Evaluation of program effectiveness

The report contains several statements such as "most [programs] have not been evaluated" and "the agencies report little about the effectiveness of these programs". NSF believes this conclusion, which is presented without definition of what criteria GAO accepted as evidence of evaluation, may be misleading largely because of the type of information GAO requested and accepted from the agencies. Although given the time constraints under which GAO was operating it is understandable that only program level evaluation was collected, evaluation of individual projects is very valuable in determining program effectiveness. Given the alternative approaches that projects develop to achieve the overall program goals, the evaluation of individual projects provides valuable information about the effectiveness and impact of the program. NSF programs require that the individual projects supported be evaluated, but this information was not included in the GAO analysis.

Telephone (703) 292-8600   FAX (703) 292-9179

In addition, NSF conducts Committee of Visitor (COV) reviews for each of its program every three years. GAO studied the COV process and reported on its value as an evaluation process in the previous GAO report 03-454.

In summary, all NSF programs undergo evaluation. This evaluation includes COV review, project evaluations, and, in many cases, third party program evaluation. Other Federal agencies also have a variety of mechanisms for program evaluation. If time permits, we would appreciate having this range of approaches to ensure program effectiveness addressed in more detail in the document.

2. Study of factors impacting studying/entering S&E fields

The report includes recommendations that are based on interviews with educators and administrators from eight colleges and universities as well as responses from 31 students at five of these institutions. Although GAO includes reasonable observations based on these interviews, a "pilot study" with this design and scope seems a rather weak basis for significant findings and recommendations. Because the data are relegated to the appendix, the design and scope are not readily apparent. It should be made clearer in the body of the text that the conclusions reached are based on these limited numbers of interviews. Also, the report could be improved by referencing corroborating information from other available reports and studies or findings from research conducted on these topics.

3. Eligibility for NSF program

There appears to be a simple misunderstanding regarding NSF program eligibility. Page 15 of the report states; "In addition to these restrictions, some programs limit eligibility to minorities in order to increase their representation in STEM fields. For example, NSF sponsors a program called Opportunities for Enhancing Diversity in the Geosciences to increase participation by African Americans, Hispanic Americans, Native Americans (American Indians and Alaskan Natives), Native Pacific Islanders (Polynesian or Micronesians), and persons with disabilities." Please note that, although the goal of the program is to broaden participation in the geosciences, the program does not limit eligibility to minorities.

4. US citizen/permanent resident requirement for recipients of scholarships or fellowships

Another apparent misunderstanding also appears on page 15 of the report. The report states that "According to an NSF official, students receiving scholarships or fellowships through NSF programs must be U.S. citizens or permanent residents." This is correct, but the report goes on with the conjecture that "such restrictions limit may reflect concerns about access to sensitive areas." In fact, this restriction to U.S. citizens and permanent residents is considered primarily to be an effective strategy to support the

NSF People Goal: "a diverse, competitive, and globally engaged U.S. workforce of scientists, engineers, technologists and well-prepared citizens."

5. Interagency collaboration

The report only mentions the NSTC efforts for interagency collaboration. Other mechanisms for coordination of federal STEM programs exist. Operating with the Secretary of Education as its chair, the Federal Interagency Committee on Education studies and makes recommendations for assuring effective coordination of Federal programs, policies, and administrative practices affecting education. Similarly, the Federal Interagency Coordinating Council, in order to minimize duplication of programs and activities, coordinates Federal early intervention and preschool programs and policies across Federal agencies; the provision of Federal technical assistance and support activities to States; and identifies gaps in Federal programs and services and barriers to Federal interagency cooperation. Also, when the National Science and Technology Council (NSTC) Committee on Science (COS) established the Subcommittee on Education and Workforce Development (EWD), it assumed the responsibilities of its predecessor, the Interagency Working Group on S&T Workforce of the Future, which, in turn, was the successor of earlier coordinating bodies. The new EWD Subcommittee puts greater emphasis on the interagency coordination of federal education programs.

Interagency collaboration also occurs at the program level. For example, the NSF Federal Cyber Service: Scholarship for Service (SFS) program partners with the Department of Homeland Security (DHS) through an ongoing MOU and contracts with OPM to provide the operational support for placing students in Federal jobs in IT security.

6. Enrollment and degree data

The data taxonomy used for the report is not clear. For example, the report includes some, but not all, technology degrees and some, but not all, technology occupations. Also, the report does not appear to include associates degrees in the enrollment and degree analysis. The particular data in Table 11 on international student enrollment are based on GAO analysis of NPSAS data. The graduate level enrollment data in the table are questionable in comparison with other available data. The difficulty may be that the NPSAS data include a relatively small sample for graduate education.

Donald Thompson
Assistant Director (Acting)

3

APPENDIX X:
COMMENTS FROM THE NATIONAL SCIENCE AND TECHNOLOGY COUNCIL

EXECUTIVE OFFICE OF THE PRESIDENT
OFFICE OF SCIENCE AND TECHNOLOGY POLICY
WASHINGTON, D.C. 20502

September 22, 2005

Ms. Cornelia M. Ashby
Director, Education, Workforce,
 and Income Security Issues
Government Accountability Office (GAO)
441 G Street, N.W.
Washington, D.C. 20548

Dear Ms. Ashby:

Thank you for providing a copy of your draft report entitled "Higher Education: Federal Science, Technology, Engineering, and Mathematics Programs and Related Trends" (GAO-05-887). I applaud your efforts to provide an overview of the state of Federal support for attracting and retaining students in STEM disciplines.

We understand that any such report will reflect the situation at one point in time and, given a rapidly changing world, research conducted even a short time ago may not fully reflect current conditions. Given this situation we have one comment regarding the discussion of international students' STEM participation decisions, particularly in regards to obtaining visas.

Recent policy changes implemented by the United States Government have resulted in significant reductions in the time it takes to process visas for entry into the U.S. The U.S. government has made and continues to make a concerted effort to ensure that international students, exchange visitors and scientists are able to apply for – and receive – their visas in a timely manner. The State Department and the Department of Homeland Security have implemented a policy that gives priority processing to international students and research scholars, leading to shorter waits to begin the visa application process. In addition, the vast majority of applicants who are approved for student visas get them within two days. The approximately two percent of visa applications that are referred for additional screening are now, on average, processed within 14 days. This represents a significant improvement from the 67 day average processing time reported in the 2004 GAO report entitled *"Border Security: Improvements Needed to Reduce Time Taken to Adjudicate Visas for Science Students and Scholars."* In February of 2005, Mantis SAO validity periods were extended by up to four years for students and up to two years for exchange visitors. These extensions improve the ability of scientists and students to be able to leave and re-enter the United States as part of their normal course of scientific activities. Another important policy change was announced in May 2005, which will extend the initial duration of visas for certain long-term researchers from three to five years and also allows for extensions of up to five years.

Again, thank you for the opportunity to review this document.

Sincerely,

John H. Marburger, III
Director

ACKNOWLEDGMENTS

Cornelia M. Ashby, Carolyn M. Taylor, Assistant Director; Tim Hall, Analyst in Charge; Mark Ward; Dorian Herring; Patricia Bundy; Paula Bonin; Scott Heacock; Wilfred Holloway; Lise Levie; John Mingus; Mark Ramage; James Rebbe; and Monica Wolford made key contributions to this report.

BIBLIOGRAPHY

Congressional Research Service, *Foreign Students in the United States: Policies and Legislation*, RL31146, January 24, 2003, Washington, D.C.

Congressional Research Service, Immigration: *Legislative Issues on Nonimmigrant Professional Specialty (H-1B) Workers*, RL30498, May 5, 2005, Washington, D.C.

Congressional Research Service, *Monitoring Foreign Students in the United States: The Student and Exchange Visitor Information System (SEVIS)*, RL32188, October 20, 2004, Washington, D.C.

Congressional Research Service, *Science, Engineering, and Mathematics Education: Status and Issues*, 98-871 STM, April 27, 2004, Washington, D.C.

Council on Competitiveness, *Innovate America*, December 2004, Washington, D.C.

Council of Graduate Schools, *NDEA 21: A Renewed Commitment to Graduate Education*, June 2005, Washington, D.C.

Institute of International Education, *Open Doors: Report on International Educational Exchange*, 2004, New York.

Jackson, Shirley Ann, *The Quiet Crisis: Falling Short in Producing American Scientific and Technical Talent*, Building Engineering and Science Talent, September 2002, San Diego, California.

NAFSA: Association of International Educators, *In America's Interest: Welcoming International Students*, Report of the Strategic Task Force on International Student Access, January 14, 2003, Washington, D.C.

NAFSA: Association of International Educators, *Toward an International Education Policy for the United States: International Education in an Age of Globalism and Terrorism*, May 2003, Washington, D.C.

National Center for Education Statistics, *Qualifications of the Public School Teacher Workforce: Prevalence of Out-of-Field Teaching 1987-88 to 1999-2000*, May 2002, revised August 2004, Washington, D.C.

National Science Foundation, *The Science and Engineering Workforce Realizing America's Potential*, National Science Board, August 14, 2003, Arlington, Virginia.

National Science Foundation, *Science and Engineering Indicators*, 2004, Volume 1, National Science Board, January 15, 2004, Arlington, Virginia.

Report of the Congressional Commission on the Advancement of Women and Minorities in Science, Engineering and Technology Development.

Land of Plenty: Diversity as America's Competitive Edge in Science, Engineering, and Technology, September 2000.

A Report to the Nation from the National Commission on Mathematics and Science Teaching for the 21st Century, *Before It's Too Late*, September 27, 2000.

Seymour, Elaine, and Nancy M. Hewitt, *Talking about Leaving: Why Undergraduates Leave the Sciences*, Westview Press, 1997, Boulder, Colorado.

The National Academies, *Policy Implications of International Graduate Students and Postdoctoral Scholars in the United States*, 2005, Washington, D.C.

U.S. Department of Education, National Center for Education Statistics, Institute of Education Sciences, *The Nation's Report Card, NAEP 2004: Trends in Academic Progress*, July 2005, Washington, D.C.

U.S. Department of Education, *The Secretary's Third Annual Report on Teacher Quality*, Office of Postsecondary Education, 2004, Washington, D.C.

U.S. Department of Homeland Security, *2003 Yearbook of Immigration Statistics*, Office of Immigration Statistics, September 2004, Washington, D.C.

REFERENCES

[1]   For the purposes of this report, we will use the term "agency" when referring to any of the 13 federal departments and agencies that responded to our survey.

[2]   Core subjects include English, reading or language arts, mathematics, science, foreign languages, civics and government, economics, arts, history, and geography.

[3]   Other federal programs that are not specifically designed to attract students to STEM education and occupations, such as Pell Grants, may provide financial assistance to students who obtain degrees in STEM fields.

[4]   There are several types of visas that authorize people to study and work in the United States. F, or student, visas, are for study at 2- and 4-year colleges and universities and other academic institutions; the exchange visitor, or J, visas are for people who will be participating in a cultural exchange program; and M visas are for nonacademic study at institutions, such as vocational and technical schools. In addition, H-1B visas allow noncitizens to work in the United States.

[5]   GAO, *Border Security: Streamlined Visas Mantis Program Has Lowered Burden on Foreign Science Students and Scholars, but Further Refinements Needed*, GAO-05-198 (Washington, D.C.: Feb. 18, 2005).

[6]   Congressional Research Service, *Science, Engineering, and Mathematics Education: Status and Issues*, 98-871 STM, April 27, 2004, Washington, D.C.

[7]   A specialty occupation is defined as one that requires the application of a body of highly specialized knowledge, and the attainment of at least a bachelor's degree (or its equivalent), and the possession of a license or other credential to practice the occupation if required.

[8]   GAO asked agencies to include STEM and related education programs with one or more of the following as a primary objective: (1) attract and prepare students at any education level to pursue coursework in STEM areas, (2) attract students to pursue degrees (2-year degrees through post doctoral) in STEM fields, (3) provide growth and research opportunities for college and graduate students in STEM fields, such as working with researchers and/or conducting research to further their education, (4)

attract graduates to pursue careers in STEM fields, (5) improve teacher (pre-service, in-service, and postsecondary) education in STEM areas, and (6) improve or expand the capacity of institutions to promote or foster STEM fields.

[9]   The program funding levels, as provided by agency officials, contain both actual and estimated amounts for fiscal year 2004.

[10] Six survey respondents did not include the date the program was initially funded.

[11] Fiscal year 2005 funding levels were not available for all of the 207 STEM education programs.

[12] Three survey respondents did not identify the program goals.

[13] One survey respondent did not identify the type of assistance supported by the program.

[14] Two survey respondents did not identify the group targeted by the program.

[15] Lawful permanent residents, also commonly referred to as immigrants, are legally accorded the privilege of residing permanently in the United States. They may be issued immigrant visas by the Department of State overseas or adjusted to permanent resident status by the Department of Homeland Security in the United States.

[16] GAO, *Program Evaluation: An Evaluation Culture and Collaborative Partnerships Help Build Agency Capacity,*G AO-03-454 (Washington, D.C.: May 2, 2003).

[17] In 2004, we reported on women's participation in federally funded science programs. Among other issues, this report discussed priorities pertaining to compliance with provisions of Title IX of the Education Amendments of 1972. For additional information, see GAO, *Gender Issues: Women's Participation in the Sciences Has Increased, but Agencies Need to Do More to Ensure Compliance with Title IX,* GAO-04-639, (Washington, D.C.: July 22, 2004).

[18] Institute of International Education, *Open Doors: Report on International Educational Exchange*, 2004, New York.

[19] On the basis of March 2004 CPS estimates, the Pew Hispanic Research Center reported that over 10 million unauthorized immigrants resided in the United States and that people of Hispanic and Latino origin constituted a significant portion of these unauthorized immigrants.

[20] Other minorities include Asian/Pacific Islanders and American Indian or Alaska Native.

[21] GAO, *H-1B Foreign Workers: Better Controls Needed to Help Employers and Protect Workers,* GAO/HEHS-00-157 (Washington, D.C.: Sept. 7, 2000).

[22] GAO, *H-1B Foreign Workers: Better Tracking Needed to Help Determine H-1B Program's Effects on U.S. Workforce,* GAO-03-883 (Washington, D.C.: Sept. 10, 2003).

[23] National Science Foundation, *Science and Engineering Indicators*, 2004, Volume 1, National Science Board, January 15, 2004.

[24] National Center for Education Statistics, *Qualifications of the Public School Teacher Workforce: Prevalence of Out-of-Field Teaching 1987-88 to 1999-2000*, May 2002, revised August 2004,Washington, D.C.

[25] U.S. Department of Education, *The Secretary's Third Annual Report on Teacher Quality*, Office of Postsecondary Education, 2004, Washington, D.C.

[26] U.S. Department of Education, National Center for Education Statistics, Institute of Education Sciences, *The Nation's Report Card, NAEP 2004: Trends in Academic Progress*, July 2005, Washington, D.C.

[27] [27]Seymour, Elaine, and Nancy M. Hewitt, *Talking about Leaving: Why Undergraduates Leave the Sciences*, Westview Press, 1997, Boulder, Colorado.

[28] Seymour and Hewitt.

[29] GAO-04-639.

[30] Report of the Congressional Commission on the Advancement of Women and Minorities in Science, Engineering and Technology Development, *Land of Plenty: Diversity as America's Competitive Edge in Science, Engineering, and Technology*, September 2000.

[31] NAFSA: Association of International Educators, *In America's Interest: Welcoming International Students*, Report of the Strategic Task Force on International Student Access, January 14, 2003, Washington, D.C.

[32] GAO, *Border Security: Visa Process Should Be Strengthened as an Antiterrorism Tool*, GAO-03-132NI (Washington, D.C.: Oct. 21, 2002).

[33] GAO, *Border Security: New Policies and Increased Interagency Coordination Needed to Improve Visa Process*, GAO-03-1013T (Washington, D. C.: July 15, 2003).

[34] GAO, *Border Security: Improvements Needed to Reduce Time Taken to Adjudicate Visas for Science Students and Scholars*, GAO-04-371 (Washington, D.C.: Feb. 25, 2004).

[35] GAO-05-198.

[36] GAO, *Homeland Security: Performance of Information System to Monitor Foreign Students and Exchange Visitors Has Improved, but Issues Remain*, GAO-04-690 (Washington, D.C.: June 18, 2004).

[37] GAO, *Homeland Security: Performance of Foreign Student and Exchange Visitor Information System Continues to Improve, but Issues Remain*, GAO-05-440T (Washington, D.C.: March 17, 2005).

[38] Report of the Congressional Commission on the Advancement of Women and Minorities in Science, Engineering and Technology Development, *Land of Plenty: Diversity as America's Competitive Edge in Science, Engineering, and Technology*, September 2000.

Appendix I

[1] See Technical Paper 63RV:Current Population Survey—Design and Methodology, issued Mar. 2002. Electronic version available at http://www.censusgov/prod/2002pubs/tp63rv.pdf.

[2] See Technical Paper 63RV, page 11-4.

[3] Seymour, Elaine, and Nancy M. Hewitt, *Talking about Leaving: Why Undergraduates Leave the Sciences*, Westview Press, 1997, Boulder, Colorado.

In: Global Issues in Higher Education
Editor: Pamela B. Richards, pp. 341-391

ISBN: 978-1-60021-802-6
© 2007 Nova Science Publishers, Inc.

Chapter 13

HIGHER EDUCATION: SCHOOLS' USE OF THE ANTITRUST EXEMPTION HAS NOT SIGNIFICANTLY AFFECTED COLLEGE AFFORDABILITY OR LIKELIHOOD OF STUDENT ENROLLMENT TO DATE*

United States Government Accountability Office

WHY THIS STUDY?

In 1991 the U.S. Department of Justice sued nine colleges and universities, alleging that they had restrained competition by making collective financial aid determinations for students accepted to more than one of these schools. Against the backdrop of this litigation, Congress enacted a temporary exemption from antitrust laws for higher education institutions in 1992. The exemption allows limited collaboration regarding financial exemption applies only to aid practices with the goal of promoting equal access to education. The institutional financial aid and can only be used by schools that admit students without regard to ability to pay.

In passing an extension to the exemption in 2001, Congress directed GAO to study the effects of the exemption. GAO examined(1) how many schools used the exemption and what joint practices they implemented, (2) trends in costs and institutional grant aid at schools using the exemption(3) how expected family contributions at schools using the exemption compare to those at similar schools not using the exemption, and (4) the effects of the exemption on affordability and enrollment. GAO surveyed schools, analyzed school and student-level data, and developed econometric models. GAO used extensive peer review to obtain comments from outside experts and made changes as appropriate.

---

*Excerpted from http://568group.org/docs/gao.pdf

WHAT WE FOUND

Twenty-eight schools—all highly selective, private 4-year institutions—formed a group to use the antitrust exemption and developed a common methodology for assessing financial need, which the group called the consensus approach. The methodology used elements already a part of another need analysis methodology; schools modified this methodology and reached agreement on how to define those elements. By the 2004-2005 school year, 25 of 28 schools in the group were using the consensus approach. Schools' implementation of the approach varied, however, with officials from 12 of the 25 schools reporting that they partially implemented it, in part because they believed it would be costly to do so.

Over the last 5 years, tuition, room, and board costs among schools using the antitrust exemption increased by 13 percent compared to 7 percent at all other private 4-year schools not using the exemption. While the amount of institutional aid at schools using the exemption also increased—it did so at a slower rate. The average institutional grant aid award per student increased by 7 percent from $18,675 in 2000-2001 to $19,901 in 2005-2006.

There was virtually no difference in the amount students and their families were expected to pay between schools using the exemption and similar schools not using the exemption. While officials from schools using the exemption expected that students accepted to several of their schools would experience less variation in the amount they were expected to pay, GAO found that students accepted to schools using the exemption and comparable schools not using the exemption experienced similar variation in the amount they were expected to pay. Not all schools using the consensus approach chose to adopt all the elements of the methodology, a factor that may account for the lack of consistency in expected family contributions among schools using the exemption.

Based on GAO's analysis, schools' use of the consensus approach did not have a significant impact on affordability—the amount students and families paid for college—or affect the likelihood of enrollment at those schools to date. While GAO found that the use of the consensus approach resulted in higher amounts of need-based grant aid awarded to some student groups compared to their counterparts at schools not using the consensus approach, the total amount of grant aid awarded was not significantly affected. It was likely that grant aid awards shifted from non-need-based aid, such as academic and athletic scholarships, to aid based on a student's financial need. Finally, implementing the consensus approach did not increase the likelihood of low-income or minority students enrolling at schools using the consensus approach compared to schools that did not.

The group of schools using the exemption reviewed this report and stated it was a careful and objective report. However, they had concerns about the data used in GAO's econometric analysis, which GAO believes were reliable.

RESULTS IN BRIEF

Twenty-eight schools—all highly selective, private 4-year institutions—formed a group to use the antitrust exemption, and of the four collaborative activities allowed, the group has engaged in only one—development of a common methodology for assessing financial need, which the group called the "consensus approach." With respect to the other three activities allowed under the exemption, the schools either chose not to engage in the activities or piloted them on a limited basis. For example, three schools in the group attempted to share student-level financial aid data through a third party. However, the schools reported that because the effort was too burdensome and yielded little useful information, they chose not to continue. The consensus approach to need analysis developed by the group is based on elements already a part of another need analysis methodology that considers a family's income and assets to determine a student's ability to pay for college. Schools modified some elements of that methodology and reached agreement on how to define those elements. Although schools in the group agreed to the concept of the consensus approach, the schools varied in their implementation of the methodology. Schools that partially implemented or did not implement the consensus approach often cited concerns about potential increased costs associated with implementing the methodology. Twenty five of the 28 schools implemented the consensus approach methodology; three did not. Schools that chose to use part or all of the elements of the consensus approach did so between 2002 and 2005.

Over the last 5 years, tuition, room, and board costs at the group of schools using the exemption increased, and while the amount of grant aid these schools provided to students also increased, it did so at a slower rate. Between school years 2000-2001 and 2004-2005, tuition, room, and board increased by 13 percent, from $38,319 to $43,164, compared to a 7 percent increase at other private 4-year not-for-profit schools. Average institutional grant aid awards increased by 7 percent from $18,675 to $19,901 at schools using the exemption, and the percentage of students receiving such aid increased from 37 to 40 percent, from school years 2000-2001 to 2005-2006. Among students receiving institutional grant aid awards, the percent of students who received need-based institutional grant aid at schools using the exemption increased from 34 to 36 percent, and the percent of students receiving non-need-based institutional grant aid awards (i.e., academic or athletic scholarships) also increased slightly from 2 to 4 percent.

We found virtually no difference in the amounts students and their families were expected to pay at schools using the exemption compared to similar schools not using the exemption. Average expected family contribution (EFC) for students accepted at schools using the exemption was $27,166 and for those accepted at comparable schools not using the exemption was $27,395 in school year 2005-2006. While officials from schools using the exemption expected that students accepted to several of their schools would experience less variation in their EFC, we found that the variation in the EFC for a student who was accepted to several schools using the exemption was similar to the variation in EFC that same student received from schools not using the exemption. The variation in EFCs for these students was about $6,000 at both sets of schools. Not all schools using the consensus approach chose to adopt all the elements of the methodology, a factor that may account for the lack of consistency in EFCs among schools using the exemption. For example, seven schools chose not to use the consensus method for considering home equity that could have contributed to the variation in EFCs at schools using the exemption.

Based on our analysis, schools' use of the consensus approach did not have a significant impact on affordability—the amount students and families paid for college, which is measured by the total cost of attendance less total grant aid—or affect the likelihood of enrollment at schools using the exemption. While we found that the use of the consensus approach resulted in higher amounts of need-based grant aid awarded to some student groups (middle income, Asian students, and Hispanic students) compared to their counterparts at schools not using the consensus approach, the total amount of grant aid awarded did not significantly change. It is likely that because the change in total grant aid was similar compared to the change at schools not using the consensus approach, the increase in need-based grant aid was offset by a decrease in non-need-based aid, such as academic scholarships. We also found that low income students at schools using the consensus approach, compared to those at schools not using the consensus approach, received a significantly higher amount of total aid, which includes both grants and loans. However, the amount of grant aid that these students received did not significantly change, which suggest they likely received more aid in the form of loans, which they would need to repay. Additionally, implementing the consensus approach did not affect the likelihood of low-income or minority students enrolling at schools using the consensus approach compared to schools that did not. Because we have data for only one year after implementation, it is possible that some eventual effects of the consensus approach may not be captured. The effects of using the consensus approach could be gradual, rather than immediate, and therefore may not be captured until later years.

We provided the group of schools using the antitrust exemption, Secretary of Education, and Attorney General with a copy of our draft report for review and comments. The group of schools using the exemption reviewed a draft of this report and stated it was a careful and objective report, but raised concerns about the data used in our econometric analysis and the report's tone and premise. We believe that the data we used were reliable to support our conclusions. The group of schools using the exemption also provided technical comments, which we incorporated where appropriate. The group's written comments appear in appendix IV. The Department of Education reviewed the report and did not have any comments. The Department of Justice provided technical comments, which we incorporated where appropriate.

BACKGROUND

Legal History of Antitrust Exemption for Higher Education Institutions

In the early 1990's the U.S. Department of Justice (Justice) sued nine universities and colleges, alleging that their practice of collectively making financial aid decisions for students accepted to more than one of their schools restrained trade in violation of the Sherman Act [1]. By consulting about aid policies and aid decisions, through what was known as the Overlap group, the schools made certain that students who were accepted to more than one Overlap school would be expected to contribute the same towards their education. Thus, according to Justice, "fixing the prices" students would be expected to pay. All but one school, Massachusetts Institute of Technology (MIT), settled with Justice out of court, ending the activities of the Overlap group. The District Court ruled that MIT's joint student aid decisions in the Overlap group violated the Sherman Act. On appeal, the Third Circuit Court of Appeals agreed with the District Court that the challenged practices were commercial activity subject to the antitrust laws. However, it reversed the judgment and directed the District Court to more fully consider the procompetitive and noneconomic justifications advanced by MIT during the court proceedings and whether social benefits attributable to the practices could have been achieved by means less restrictive of competition [2]. In recognition of the importance of financial aid in achieving the government's goal of educational access, but also mindful of the importance of antitrust laws in ensuring the benefits of competition, the Congress passed a temporary antitrust exemption [3]. In 1994, Congress extended the exemption and specified the four collective activities in which schools that admit students on a need-blind basis could engage [4]. The exemption was extended most recently in 2001, and is set to expire in 2008 [5].

Determining a Student's Financial Need

For many students, financial aid is necessary in order to enroll in and complete a postsecondary education. In school year 2004-2005, about $113 billion in grant, loan, and work-study aid was awarded to students from a variety of federal, state, and institutional sources [6]. Need analysis methodologies are used to determine the amount of money a family is expected to contribute toward the cost of college and schools use this information in determining how much need-based financial aid they will award. For the purposes of awarding federal aid, expected family contribution (EFC) is defined in the Higher Education Act of 1965, as amended, as the household financial resources reported on the Free Application for Federal Student Aid, minus certain expenses and allowances. The student's EFC is then compared to the cost of attendance to determine if the student has financial need. (see figure 1)

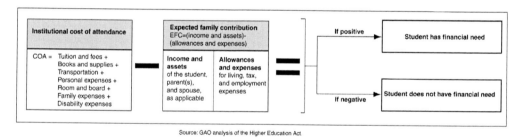

Figure 1. Determining a Student's Financial Need.

While the federal methodology is used to determine a student's eligibility for federal aid, some institutions use this methodology to award their own institutional aid. Others prefer a methodology developed by the College Board (called the institutional methodology) or their own methodology [7]. Schools that use the institutional methodology require students to complete the College Scholarship Service/Financial Aid PROFILE application and the College Board calculates how much they and their families will be expected to contribute toward their education. Schools that use these alternative methodologies feel they better reflect a family's ability to pay for college because they consider many more factors of each family's financial situation than the federal methodology. For example, the institutional methodology includes home and farm equity when calculating a family's ability to pay for college, while the federal methodology excludes them. See table 1 below for a comparison of the federal methodology to the institutional methodology.

Twenty-Eight Schools Used the Antitrust Exemption to Develop a Common Methodology for Assessing a Family's Financial Need

Twenty-eight schools formed a group under the antitrust exemption and engaged in one of the four activities allowable under the exemption. School officials believed that the one activity—development of a common methodology for assessing financial need—would help reduce variation in amounts students were expected to pay when accepted to multiple schools and allow students to base their decision on which school to attend on factors other than cost. In developing the common methodology, called the consensus approach, schools modified an existing need analysis methodology and reached agreement on how to treat each element of the methodology. While the schools reached agreement on a methodology, implementation of the methodology among the schools varied.

Table 1. Comparison of the Federal Methodology and the College Board's Base Institutional Methodology for Need Analysis

	Federal methodology	Institutional methodology
Home equity	Not included.	Included.
Family farm equity	Not included.	Included.
Student assets	Included, 35 percent of student's net worth expected to be used for college costs. Minimum contribution from student expected.	Included, 25 percent of student's net worth expected to be used for college costs. Minimum contribution from student expected.
Family assets	Excluded the assets of families whose income fell below $50,000 and who filed a simple tax return.	Included a fuller range of family assets, such as home equity, other real estate, and business and farm assets.
	12 percent of assets expected to be used towards college.	5 percent of assets expected to be used towards college.
Divorced and separated families (Noncustodial parent contribution)	Excluded noncustodial parent income and assets.	Included noncustodial parent income and assets.
Total income	Included only the adjusted gross income reported on federal tax returns, plus various categories of untaxed income.	Included in total income any untaxed income and any paper depreciation and business, rental, or capital losses that artificially reduced adjusted gross income.
Medical/elementary and secondary school expenses	Not included.	Included.[a]
Cost of living variance	Not included.	Not included.[b]
Number of siblings in college	Included—divides the parental contribution by the number of siblings enrolled in college.	Included—instead of dividing by the number in college, parental contribution per student reduced by 40 percent for 2 in college and by 55 percent for 3.

Highly Selective Private 4-Year Colleges and Universities Formed a Group to Participate in Activities Allowable under the Exemption

Twenty-eight schools, all of which have need-blind admission policies as required under the law, formed the 568 Presidents' Group in 1998 with the intent to engage in activities allowed by the antitrust exemption [8]. Members of the group are all private 4-year schools that have highly selective admissions policies. One member school dropped out of the group because the school no longer admitted students on a need-blind basis. (See table 2 below for a list of current and former member schools.)

Membership is open to colleges and universities that have need blind admissions policies in accordance with the law. Member schools must (1) sign a certificate of compliance confirming the institution's need-blind admissions policy and (2) submit a signed memorandum of understanding that indicates willingness to participate in the group and adhere to its guidelines. Additionally, members share in paying the group's expenses.

In addition to the group's 28 members, 6 schools attended meetings of the group to observe and listen to discussions, but have not become members [9]. In order to attend meetings, observer schools were required to provide a certificate of compliance stating that they had a need-blind admission policy. Observer schools explained that their participation was based on a desire to be aware of what similar schools were thinking in terms of need analysis methodology, as well as have an opportunity to participate in these discussions. Despite these benefits, observer schools said they preferred not to join as members because they did not wish to agree to a common approach to need analysis or they did not want to lose institutional independence.

Table 2. Schools Using the Antitrust Exemption, as of May 2006

Amherst College	Middlebury College
Boston College	Northwestern University
Brown University	Pomona College
Claremont McKenna College	Rice University
Columbia University	Swarthmore College
Cornell University	University of Chicago
Dartmouth College	University of Notre Dame
Davidson College	University of Pennsylvania
Duke University	Vanderbilt University
Emory University	Wake Forest University
Georgetown University	Wellesley College
Grinnell College	Wesleyan University
Haverford College	Williams College
Massachusetts Institute of Technology	Yale University

Source: GAO analysis.
Note: Bowdoin College and Macalester College were once members of the group.

Other institutions with need-blind admissions reported that, although eligible to participate in activities allowed by the exemption, they were not interested or not aware of the group formed to use the antitrust exemption. Some told us that they did not understand how students would benefit from the schools' participation in such activities. Others cited limited funding to make changes to their need analysis methodology and concerns that they would lose the ability to award merit aid to students [10].

Participating Schools Agreed to a Common Methodology for Assessing Financial Need, but Schools Varied in Their Implementation of the Methodology

Of the four activities allowed under the antitrust exemption, the 28 schools engaged in only one—development of the consensus approach for need analysis. With respect to the other three activities allowed under the exemption, the schools either chose to not engage in the activities or piloted them on a limited basis. For example, three schools in the group attempted to share student-level financial aid data through a third party. However, they reported that because the effort was too burdensome and yielded little useful information, they chose not to continue. The group also expressed little need or interest in creating another common aid application form as such a form already existed. Schools also decided to leave open the option to award aid on a non-need basis.

According to the officials representing the 28 schools, the main purpose of the group was to discuss ways to make the financial aid system more understandable to students and their families and commit to developing a common methodology for assessing a family's ability to pay for college, which they called the consensus approach. Developing an agreed upon common approach to need analysis, according to school officials, might help decrease variation in what families were expected to pay when accepted to multiple schools, allowing students to base their decision on what school to attend on factors other than cost. School officials also believed that agreeing to a common need analysis methodology would produce expected family contributions that were reasonable and fair for families and allow schools to better target need-based aid. The group did not address the composition of a student's financial aid package; specifically, what combination of grants, loans, or work-study a student would receive.

In developing the consensus approach for need analysis, the schools modified elements already in the College Board's institutional methodology, but member schools agreed to treat these elements the same when calculating a student's EFC. Some of the modifications that the group made to College Board's institutional methodology were later incorporated into the institutional methodology. The consensus approach and the institutional methodology similarly treat income from the non-custodial parent, and both account for the number of siblings in college in the same manner when calculating a student's expected family contribution. However, there are differences in how each methodology treats a family's home equity and a student's assets. For example, the institutional methodology uses a family's entire home equity in its assessment of assets available to pay for college, while the consensus approach limits the amount of home equity that can be included. According to one financial aid officer at a member school, including the full amount of a family's home equity was unfair to many parents because in some areas of the country the real estate market had risen so rapidly that equity gains inflated a family's assets. Officials representing some member schools stated that adjustments to home equity would likely affect middle and upper income families more than lower income families who are less likely to own a home. Table 3 below further illustrates the differences and similarities between the consensus approach and the institutional methodology.

In addition, under the consensus approach schools agreed to a common calendar for collecting data from families. Members continue to maintain the ability to exercise professional judgment in assessing a family's ability to pay when there are unique or extenuating financial circumstances.

Twenty-five of 28 schools implemented the consensus approach; 3 did not. While 13 schools implemented all the elements of the consensus approach, the remaining schools varied in how they implemented the methodology. As shown in table 4 below, seven schools chose not to use the consensus approach method for accounting for family loan debt, home equity, and family and student assets.

The 25 schools that implemented the consensus approach did so between 2002 and 2005. Member schools reported that they preferred to use the consensus approach as opposed to other available need analysis methodologies because it was more consistent and fairer than alternative methodologies. Moreover, according to institution officials, they believed the new methodology had not reduced price competition and had resulted in the average student receiving more financial aid. In some cases, if using the consensus approach lowered a student's EFC, the institution would then allocate more money for financial aid than it would have if it had used a different need analysis methodology. For some schools the consensus approach was not that different from the methodology their institution already had in place, but other schools said that fully implementing the consensus approach cost their school more money. Among schools that partially implemented the consensus approach, many explained they did not fully implement the new methodology because it would have been too costly.

Table 3. Comparison of Consensus Approach Developed by Schools Using the Antitrust Exemption Compared to the College Board's Institutional Methodology

	Institutional methodology	Consensus approach
Home equity	Included. No limit on amount considered asset available to pay for college.	Included. Home value is capped at 2.4 times income minus mortgage debt.
Family farm equity	Included.	Included.
Student and family assets	Included, but assets counted separately. 25 percent of student's net worth expected to be used for college costs. 5 percent of parent's assets expected to be used for college costs.	Included. In general student assets—such as prepaid and college savings plans are combined with family assets. 5 percent of family assets expected to be used for college. Trust funds will be considered on a case by case basis.
Divorced and separated families (Noncustodial parent)	Included. Expects noncustodial parent to contribute towards college costs.	Same as IM.
Total income/adjusted gross income	Included in total income any untaxed income and any paper depreciation and business, rental, or capital losses which artificially reduced adjusted gross income.	Excluded business and rental losses from calculation of income.
Medical/elementary and secondary school expenses	Included.[a]	Included.
Cost of living variance	Excluded.[b]	Adjusted living expenses based on geographic location. Takes into consideration that it is more costly to live in some areas of the country.
Number of siblings in college	Included—considers number of children enrolled in college, but instead of dividing by the number in college, it reduced the parental contribution for each student by 40 percent if 2 in college and by 55 percent if 3.	Same as IM.
One-time income adjustment	Not included.[c]	Excluded income that was not received on an annual basis, such as unemployment income or capital gains.
Family debt	Not included.	Made allowance for debt payments on loans incurred by parents for student's education.

Source: GAO analysis. Note: The consensus approach is being compared to the base institutional methodology. Schools may choose to implement other options available under the institutional methodology when assessing a student's financial need.

[a]Private elementary and secondary school tuition allowed at the option of the institution.

[b]As an option schools can adjust living expenses based on geographic locations.

[c]This is not in the base IM; however, a financial aid officer can adjust for this on a case-by-case basis, consistent with professional judgment.

As the Cost of Attendance at Schools Using the Exemption Rose, the Amount of Institutional Grant Aid They Provided to Students Increased at a Slower Rate

The cost to attend the schools participating under the exemption rose over the past 5 years by over 10 percent while cost increases at all other private schools rose at about half that rate. At the same time, the percentage of students receiving institutional aid increased and institutions increased the amount of such aid they provided students, although at a slower rate than cost increases.

Table 4. Number of Schools That Did Not Implement Certain Consensus Approach Options in School Year 2005-2006

Options in the consensus approach	Number of schools that did not implement option[a]
Number of siblings in college	1
One-time income adjustments	2
Elementary and secondary school tuition expenses	3
Medical expenses	3
Cost of living variances	5
Divorced and separated families	6
Family and student assets	7
Home equity	7
Family loan debt	7

Source: GAO analysis of schools' survey responses.

[a] A total of 25 member schools used part or all of the consensus approach.

Cost of Attendance Increased at Schools Using the Exemption Corresponding to Increases at Other Private Schools

During the past 5 years, the cost of attendance—tuition, fees, room, and board—at schools using the exemption increased by approximately 13 percent from $38,319 in school year 2000-2001 to $43,164 in school year 2004-2005, a faster rate than other schools [11]. For example, at other private 4-year schools there was a 7 percent increase in these costs, from $25, 204 to $27, 071.[12]. Additionally, as figure 2 illustrates, among a set of schools that were comparable to the schools using the exemption, costs increased by 9 percent from $40,238 to $43,939 over that same time period [13].

Percentage of Students Receiving Institutional Grant Aid and the Amount Schools Provided Them Increased

Over the same time period, the percentage of students who received any form of institutional grant aid at schools using the exemption increased by 3 percentage points, from 37 to 40 percent, as illustrated by figure 3.

Among students receiving institutional grant aid, the percentage of students receiving need-based grant aid increased from 34 to 36 percent from 2000 to 2006. The percentage of students receiving non-need-based grant aid also increased slightly, from 2 to 4 percent. Non-need-based aid is awarded based on a student's academic or athletic achievement and includes fellowships, stipends, or scholarships. The majority of schools using the exemption did not offer any non-need-based institutional grant aid in school year 2005-2006. However, in 2005-2006 some schools did, allocating non-need-based grant aid to between 16 to 54 percent of their students.

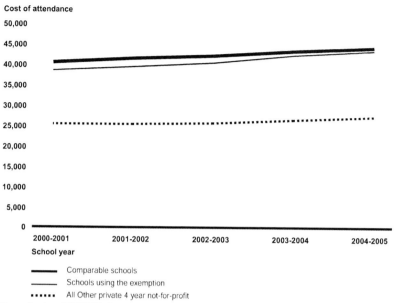

Source: GAO analysis of IPEDS data.

Note: Comparable schools include the seven schools selected as control schools for our econometric analysis.

Figure 2. Average Tuition, Fees, and Room and Board at Schools Using the Antitrust Exemption Compared to All Other Private 4-Year Not-For-Profit Schools and Comparable Schools, School Years 2000 to 2005.

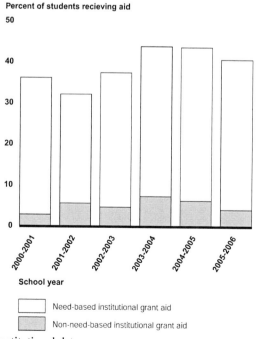

Source: GAO analysis of institutional data.

Note: Data collected from 26 of the 28 schools using the antitrust exemption.

Figure 3. Percentage of Students at Schools Using the Antitrust Exemption Receiving Various Types of Institutional Grant Aid from 2000 to 2006.

As the cost of attendance and percentage of students receiving institutional aid rose, participating institutions increased the amount of such aid they provided students, although the percentage increases in aid were smaller. As shown in figure 4, the average need-based grant aid award across the schools using the exemption increased from $18,925 to $20,059, or 6 percent. The average amount of non-need-based grant aid awards dropped slightly from $12,760 in 2000-01 to $12,520 in 2005-06, or 2 percent. Overall, the average total institutional grant aid awarded to students, which included both need and non-need-based aid, increased from $18,675 in 2000-01 to $19,901 in 2005-06, or 7 percent.

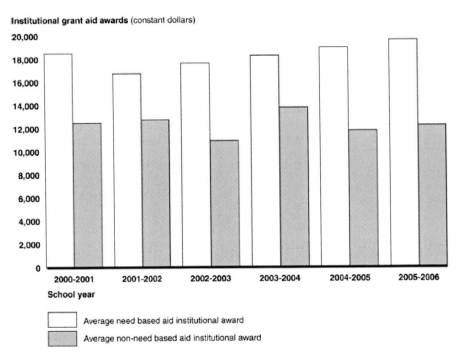

Figure 4. Average Amount of Various Institutional Grant Aid Awards at Schools Using the Antitrust Exemption from 2000 to 2006.

Students Accepted to Both Schools Using the Exemption and Comparable Schools Had No Appreciable Difference in the Amount They Would Be Expected to Contribute Towards College

There was virtually no difference in the amounts students and their families were expected to pay between schools using the exemption and similar schools not using the exemption. Average EFC was $27,166 for students accepted at schools using the exemption, and $27,395 for those accepted at comparable schools not using the exemption in school year 2005-2006. Moreover, the variation in the EFC for a student who was accepted to several schools using the exemption was similar to the variation in EFC that same student received from schools not using the exemption. The variation in EFCs for these students was about

$6,000 at both sets of schools [14]. Because the number of such students was small, we also analyzed variation in EFCs for students who were accepted only at schools using the exemption and compared it to the variation for students who were only accepted at comparable schools not using the exemption [15]. We found slightly greater variation among EFCs for students who were accepted at schools using the exemption; however, because we could not control for student characteristics, factors external to the exemption could explain this result, such as differences in a family's income or assets.

Although officials from schools using the exemption expected that students accepted at several of those schools would experience less variation in the amounts they were expected to pay, none of our analyses confirmed this. The lack of consistency in EFCs among schools using the exemption may be explained by the varied implementation of the consensus approach. As previously mentioned, not all schools using the consensus approach chose to adopt all the elements of the methodology. For example, seven schools chose not to use the consensus approach to home equity, which uses a percentage of the home equity in calculating the EFC. Using another method for assessing a family's home equity could significantly affect a student's EFC. For instance, we estimated that a family residing in Maryland with an income of $120,000 and $350,000 in home equity would have an EFC of $58,243 if a school chose not to implement the home equity option in the consensus approach. Under the consensus approach, the amount of home equity included in asset calculations would be capped and only $38,000 of the home's equity would be included in the calculation of EFC. The same family would then have an EFC of $42,449 if the school chose to implement the option.

Implementation of a Common Methodology Has Not Significantly Affected Affordability or Enrollment at Schools Using the Exemption

Based on our econometric analysis, schools' use of the consensus approach did not have a significant impact on affordability, nor did it cause significant changes in the likelihood of student enrollment at schools using the consensus approach compared to schools that were not using the consensus approach [16]. As shown in table 5, while we found that the consensus approach resulted in higher need-based grant aid awards for some student groups (middle income, Asian students, and Hispanic students) compared to similar students at schools that were not using the consensus approach, this increase was likely offset by decreases in non-need-based grant aid, such as academic or athletic scholarships [17]. Thus, total grant aid awarded was not affected by the consensus approach because the increase in need-based aid was likely offset by decreases in non-need-based grant aid [18].

A different effect was found when low-income students at schools using the consensus approach were compared to their counterparts at schools not using the consensus approach. As shown in table 5, low income students at schools using the consensus approach received, on average, a significantly higher amount of total aid—about $12,121, which includes both grants and loans. However, the amount of grant aid that these students received did not significantly change, suggesting that that they likely received more aid in the form of loans, which would need to be repaid, or work-study. Our analysis of the effects of the consensus approach on various racial groups showed no effect on affordability for these groups compared to their counterparts at schools not using the consensus approach. While Asian, white, and Hispanic students received more need-based grant aid compared to their counterparts at schools not using the consensus approach, their overall grant aid awards did not change.

Finally, as shown in table 5, there were no statistically significant effects of the consensus approach on student enrollment compared to the enrollment of students at schools not using the consensus approach. In particular, the consensus approach did not significantly increase the likelihood of enrollment of low-income or minority students or any student group.

Table 5. Estimated Changes in Amount Paid, Financial Aid, and Enrollment at Schools Using the Consensus Approach Compared to Schools Not Using the Exemption

Student group	Estimated changes of using the consensus approach on:				
	Amount students paid	Total grant aid	Need-based total grant aid	Total aid (grant, loans, work-study)	Probability of enrollment
All students			$6,125[b]		
	$3,021	-$749	[$239, $12,011]	-$2,886	38%
Financial-aid applicants	2,177	n/a	n/a	n/a	22
Low-income				12,121[b]	
	-4,061	3,688	1,956	[1,837, 22,404]	59
Lower-middle income	8,089[c]	-3,671	6,556	-7,776	95
Middle income			20,221[a]		
	2,320	1,618	[6,718, 33,724]	1,178	26
Upper-middle income	-1,048	-973	2,769	-3,054	18
High income	3,699	-714	4,687[c]	-3,856	31
Asian students			14,628[a]		
	-376	5,726	[5,051, 24,206]	3,694	1
Black students	4,468	-1,227	4,332	-6,542	-26
Hispanic students			9,532[b]		
	1,168	1,520	[1,006, 18,059]	3,648	108
White students			6,017[b]		
	2,588	-491	[178, 11,856]	-2,879	19

Source: GAO analysis (see table 16 in app. II).

[a]Result is statistically significant at the 1 percent level or lower. [b]Result is statistically significant at the 5 percent level or lower. [c]Result is statistically significant at the 10 percent level or lower.

Notes: The estimates in brackets are the confidence levels of the estimates that are significant at the 5 percent or lower level.

n/a means not applicable because of data limitations.

All the monetary values are in 2005 dollars.

Amount students paid is defined as tuition, room, board, fees, and other expenses minus grant aid.

Total grant aid includes both need- and non-need-based aid from federal, state, institutional and other sources.

Total aid includes grants, loans, and work-study aid from federal, state, institutional, and other sources.

The effect of the consensus approach on need-based institutional grant aid was $6,020, significant at the 5 percent level, with confidence interval between $512 and $11,528.

The value of the effect of the consensus approach on institutional grant aid was $1,331, but not statistically significant.

Our econometric analysis has some limitations that could have affected our findings.[19] For example, we could not include all the schools using the consensus approach in our analysis because there were no data available for some of them. However, there were enough similarities (in terms of "best college" ranking, endowment, tuition and fees, and percentage of tenured faculty) between the included and excluded participating schools that allowed for a meaningful analysis. (See table 6 for a list of schools included in our analysis).

Table 6. Schools Included in Analysis of Effects of Exemption

Schools using the consensus approach	Comparable schools not using the consensus approach
Cornell University	Brandeis University
Duke University	Bryn Mawr College
Georgetown University	New York University
University of Notre Dame	Princeton University
Vanderbilt University	Tulane University
Wake Forest University	University of Rochester
Yale University	Washington University at St. Louis

Source: GAO analysis.

Moreover, the data for our post-consensus approach period was collected in 2003-2004—the first or second year that some schools were using the consensus approach. Because we have data for only one year after implementation, it is possible that some eventual effects of the consensus approach may not be captured. The effects of using the consensus approach could be gradual, rather than immediate, and therefore may not be captured until later years.

Concluding Observations

By providing an exemption to antitrust laws enabling schools to collaborate on financial aid policies, the Congress hoped that schools would better target aid, making college more affordable for low income and other underrepresented groups. The exemption has not yet yielded these outcomes. Nor did our analysis find an increase in prices that some feared would result from increased collaboration among schools. Initial implementation of the approach has been varied; some schools have not fully implemented the need analysis methodology, and many schools are still in the initial years of implementation. As is often the case with new approaches, it may be too soon to fully assess the outcomes from this collaboration.

Agency Comments

We provided the group of schools using the antitrust exemption, the Secretary of Education, and the Attorney General with a copy of our draft report for review and comments. The group of schools using the exemption provided written comments, which appear in appendix IV. In general, the group stated that our study was a careful and objective report, but raised some concerns about the data used in our econometric analysis and the report's tone and premise. Specifically, they raised concerns about the selection of treatment and control schools for our econometric analysis. As we noted in the report, we selected schools for selection in treatment and control groups based, in part, on the availability of student-level data in the NPSAS. Some schools that used the consensus approach were not included because there were no data available for them. However, we believe there were enough similarities between the included and excluded schools to allow for a meaningful analysis. The group also stated that a number of conclusions were based on a very small number of observations. In appendix II, we acknowledge the small sample size of the data could make the estimates less precise, especially for some of the subgroups of students we considered. However, we performed checks to ensure that our estimates were reliable and believe that we can draw conclusions from our analysis. With respect to the tone and premise of the report, the group raised concerns about using low income students as "a yardstick for judging the success of the Consensus Approach." When passing the exemption, Congress hoped that it would further the government's goal of promoting equal access to educational opportunities for students. Need-based grant aid is one way to make college more affordable for the neediest students to help them access a post-secondary education. The group also highlighted several positive outcomes from their collaboration, including a more transparent aid system and more engagement by college presidents in aid-related discussions, topics which our study was not designed to address. The group provided technical comments, which we incorporated where appropriate. Education reviewed the report and did not have any comments. The Department of Justice provided technical comments, which we incorporated where appropriate.

APPENDIX I:
STATISTICAL ANALYSIS OF EXPECTED FAMILY CONTRIBUTIONS AT SCHOOLS USING THE EXEMPTION AND COMPARABLE SCHOOLS

We compared variation in expected family contributions (EFCs) between students who were admitted to both schools using the exemption and comparable schools that did not. We collected data on student EFCs from 27 of the 28 schools using the exemption and 55 schools that had similar selectivity and rankings as schools using the exemption. The data included the student's EFC calculated by the schools as of April 1, 2006, based on their need analysis methodology. We determined that these data would most likely reflect the school's first EFC determination for a student and thus would be best for comparison purposes. We then matched students across both sets of schools to identify students accepted to more than one school (which we call cross-admits).

Our sample consisted of data for the following three types of cross-admit students:

1. Students accepted to several schools using the exemption and several schools that were not (type 1 students);
2. Students accepted to only schools using the exemption (type 2 students); and
3. Students accepted to only schools not using the exemption (type 3 students).

Data from the type 1 sample provided the most suitable data for our analysis because it controlled for student characteristics. However, because this sample was relatively small, we used the other samples to supplement the analysis.

Once the cross-admits were identified, the EFCs for each student were used to evaluate the mean and median as measures of location and the standard deviation and range as measures of variation. Given the potential scale factor, the variation measures were standardized. The standard deviation was standardized by dividing it by the mean, and the range was standardized by dividing it by the median. The two resulting variation measures were the coefficient of variation (V1) and its robust counterpart (V2), respectively.

These two measures of variation were estimated for each and every student. The estimates were grouped for both sets of schools. We labeled schools using the exemption as "568 schools" and comparable schools that were not as "non-568 schools."

Table 7 reports various estimates averaged over students in each group. The table generally shows similar group averages for the mean, standard deviation, median, and range that were used to compute V1 and V2. The values reported are the averages for all the students in each group. There are fewer observations for the 568 schools than for the non-568 school, except for type 1 students where the number of observations were equal because the students were in both groups of colleges. In addition, we imposed the following three conditions:

- First, for the coefficient of variation V1, we excluded all observations where the standard deviations were zero. The zero standard deviations are excluded because some of the non-568 schools that use only the federal methodology to calculate EFCs report the same EFCs for a student and are likely to bias the results. None of the observations with zero standard deviations that we excluded involved a 568 school.
- Second, for the coefficient of variation V2, we excluded all observations where the medians were zero because we could not construct this measure that was obtained by dividing the range by the median.
- And, third, for the coefficient of variation V2, we excluded observations where the standardized variation exceeded 3 based on the observed distributions of the data.

The test results were similar when none of those conditions were imposed.

Table 7. Summary Statistics of Expected Family Contributions

Students	Schools using the exemption (568 schools)		Comparable schools (Non-568 schools)	
Statistic	Type 1 students	All students	Type 1 students	All students
Standard deviation	$6,188	$6,447	$6,190	$7,035
Mean	$27,166	$31,640	$27,395	$28,747
	[$22,576, $31,757]	[$30,380, $32,900]	[$22,293, $32,497]	[$27,924, $29,571]
Coefficient of variation 1 (V1)	0.27	0.24	0.36	0.35
Range	$12,200	$12,886	$9,671	$8,813
Median	$30,374	$31,677	$29,225	$31,075
	[$25,380, $35,367]	[$30,394, $32,961]	[$23,858, $34,593]	[$30,314, $31,836]
Coefficient of variation 2 (V2)	0.47	0.49	0.52	0.37
Number of students	N1=79	N1=1,158	N1=79	N1=2,866
	N2=76	N2=1,150	N2=76	N2=3,653

Source: GAO analysis.
Notes: Coefficient of variation 1 (V1) equals standard deviation divided by mean.
Coefficient of variation 2 (V2) equals range divided by median.
Type 1 consists of students with multiple offers from 568 colleges as well as offers from non-568 colleges. For the 568 colleges, all students consist of type 1 and type 2—students with multiple offers from only 568 colleges. And for the non568 colleges, all students consist of type 1 and type 3—students with multiple offers from only non-568 colleges.

The values in brackets are the 95 percent lower and upper bounds (confidence intervals).
N1 is the sample size for coefficient of variation 1 (V1) and N2 is sample size for coefficient of variation 2 (V2).

Denoting the estimates of V1 and V2 for the two groups by $\hat{V}1$ and $\hat{V}1$, and $\hat{V}2$ and $\hat{V}2$, the empirical distribution of $\hat{V}1$ was $_{non\ 568}$ then compared with the empirical distribution of $\hat{V}1_{non568}$ to examine whether $\hat{V}1$ and $V1$ had identical distributions (that is EFCs for 568 schools were similar in variations to those for non-568 schools). A similar comparison was made using the robust measures $\hat{V}2,\ _{568}$ [1]. To more closely examine the difference between the $non568$ variations in EFCs of cross-admit students for 568 and non-568 schools, we performed the Kolmogorov-Smirnov test. The test examines whether the distributions of the variation measures $\hat{V}1_{568}$ and $V1_{non568}$ were the same.

Table 8. Tests of Variations in Expected Family Contributions

Variable	Student Data	Alternative hypothesis	Test-statistic, D	p-value	Conclusion
Coefficient of variation 1 (V1)	Type 1 N1=79 N2=79	Non-568 EFCs are smaller	0.1013	0.445	EFCs are similar
		Non-568 EFCs are larger	-0.1519	0.162	EFCs are similar
					Overall—EFCs are similar
Coefficient of variation 2 (V2)	Type 1 N1=76 N2=76	Non-568 EFCs are smaller	0.1447	0.203	EFCs are similar
		Non-568 EFCs are larger	-0.1053	0.431	EFCs are similar
					Overall—EFCs are similar
Coefficient of variation 1 (V1)	All N1=1,158 N2=2,866	Non-568 EFCs are smaller	0.1724	0.000	Non-568 EFCs are smaller
		Non-568 EFCs are larger	-0.1788	0.000	Non-568 EFCs are larger
					Overall—Inconclusive
Coefficient of variation 2 (V2)	All N1=1,150 N2=3,653	Non-568 EFCs are smaller	0.3970	0.000	Non-568 EFCs are smaller
		Non-568 EFCs are larger	-0.0399	0.061	EFCs are similar
					Overall—Non-568 EFCs are smaller

Source: GAO analysis.
Notes: Coefficient of variation 1 (V1) equals standard deviation divided by mean.
Coefficient of variation 2 (V2) equals range divided by median.
All means students with multiple offers from 568 schools as well as offers from non-568
     schools (type 1), students with multiple offers from only 568 schools (type 2), and students with multiple
offers from only non-568 schools (type 3).
The p-values are for the Kolmogorov-Smirnov tests of equality of distribution functions. All tests reinterpreted using the 5 percent or lower level of significance.
N1 is the sample size for coefficient of variation 1 (V1) and N2 is sample size for coefficient of variation 2 (V2).

The same analysis was done for the V2 measures. The test was reported for both samples, consisting of type 1 students and all students. The results reported in table 8 suggest that there was no difference in EFC variations across the two groups, using type 1 students. The results using all students, however, are inconclusive for the V1 estimate, but suggest that non-568 schools have smaller EFC variation for the V2 estimate. The results based on the type 1 sample are more useful as a stand-alone descriptive finding, because this sample controls for student characteristics. The finding based on the combined data requires further analysis to control for student characteristics that we were unable to perform due to data limitations.

APPENDIX II: ECONOMETRIC ANALYSIS OF EFFECTS OF THE HIGHER EDUCATION ANTITRUST EXEMPTION ON COLLEGE AFFORDABILITY AND ENROLLMENT

To estimate the effects of schools' implementation of the consensus approach to need analysis on affordability (measured by price) and enrollment of freshmen students, we developed econometric models. This appendix provides information on theories of the exemption effects on student financial aid, the data sources for our analyses and selection of control schools, specifications of econometric models and estimation methodology, our econometric results, and limitations of our analysis.

Theories of the Effects of the Consensus Approach on Financial Aid

Two theories exist about the effects the consensus approach on student financial aid. It is important to note that the award of grant aid represents a discount from the nominal "list price", which lowers the price students actually pay for college. So, any decision to limit grant aid would be an agreement to limit discounts to the list price, and thus may raise the price some students would pay. It is also important to note that schools admit only a limited number of students. One of the theories suggests that allowing schools a limited degree of collaboration could reduce the variation in financial need determination for an individual student and reduce price competition among colleges vying for the same students. While the reduced competition would imply lower financial aid (hence higher prices) for some students, schools could thus devote more financial aid resources to providing access to other students, especially disadvantaged students. This "social benefit theory" assumes that under these conditions disadvantaged students would receive more grant aid and as a result, pay less for school. Also, an implicit assumption of this theory is that the exemption would essentially result in redistribution of financial aid without necessarily changing the amount of financial aid resources available. Moreover, because costs to students and their families would change for some students, enrollment of such students would be affected.

An opposing theory is that the exemption will allow schools to coordinate on prices and reduce competition. This "anti-competitive theory" essentially views coordination by the group as restraining competition. Specifically, under this theory, allowing an exemption would result in less grant aid and higher prices on average, especially for students that schools competed over by offering discounts on the list price. As a result, the amount of financial aid available to some students would likely decrease. If prices are higher on average, it could cause a decrease in enrollment, particularly of disadvantaged students since they would be less able to afford the higher prices.[1] Our analyses allowed us to test these two theories with the data available.

Sources of Data for the Model

To construct our model, we used data from:

- National Postsecondary Student Aid Study (NPSAS): These data, available at the student-level, served as the primary source for our study because we were interested in student outcomes of the exemption. Data were published every 4 years during the period relevant to our study; hence, we have data for academic years 1995-1996, 1999-2000, and 2003-2004. The data contained student-level information for all freshmen enrollees in the database, including enrollment in school, cost of attendance, financial aid, Scholastic Aptitude Test (SAT) scores, household income, and race. The number of freshmen in the database for our study was 1,626 in 1995-1996, 272 in 1999-2000, and 842 in 2003-2004.
- Integrated Postsecondary Education Data System (IPEDS): These data, available at the school level, included tuition and fees, faculty characteristics, and student enrollment for 1995-1996 and 2003-2004, there were no data published for 1999-2000. However, some of the data for 1999-2000 were reported in the subsequent publications. We were able to construct some data for 1999-2000 through linear interpolation of the data for 1998-1999 and 2000-2001 or using the data for either year depending on availability; we believed this was reasonable because data for these institutions did not vary much over time [2]
- National Association of College and University Business Officers (NACUBO): This source provided data on school endowment from 1992 through 2004 [3]
- GAO Survey: The survey collected data on the activities of the schools using the higher education antitrust exemption, including when schools implemented the consensus approach methodology.

Selection of Control Schools

Determining the effects of the exemption required both a treatment group (schools using the exemption) and a control group (a comparable set of schools that did not use the exemption). To find a comparable set of schools we used data on school rankings based on their selectivity from years 1994 to 2004 from the *U.S. News and World Report (USNWR)*. We selected control schools similar to schools using the antitrust exemption that had comparable student selectivity and quality of education using the "best schools" rankings information in the *USNWR*.[4]. The combined control and treatment schools were matched to school-level data from IPEDS, and student-level data from NPSAS. We selected the control schools based on their ranks in the years prior to the implementation of the consensus approach—1995-1996 and 1999-2000—and after the implementation of the consensus approach—2003-2004. The *USNWR* published its "best schools" rankings annually in August or September. Thus, the 2004 publication reflected the selectivity of the schools during 2003-2004. However, because publications in prior years—2002 and 2003—provided relevant information to students who enrolled in 2003-2004, we considered the rankings published from 2002 through 2004 as important input into decisions made by students and the schools for 2003-2004. Similarly, the publications from 1994 through 1996 were used to determine the selectivity of the schools in 1995-1996, and the publications from 1998 to 2000 were used to determine school selectivity for 1999-2000.

The *USNWR* published separate rankings for liberal arts schools and national universities. The schools using or affiliated with the exemption consisted of 28 current members, two former members, and six observers [5]. These 36 schools comprised the treatment schools used initially to select the comparable control schools. All 36 treatment schools were private; 13 were liberal arts schools and 23 were national universities [6]. To ensure there were enough control schools for the treatment schools, we initially selected all the schools ranked in tier 1 (and tier 2 when available) in the *USNWR* rankings for each of the two types of institutions—liberal arts schools and national universities [7]. This resulted in 250 schools, including all 36 treatment schools, for nine selected years (1994 to 1996, 1998 to 2000, and 2002 to 2004). All the treatment schools were ranked in each of the nine years (except for one school that was not ranked in 2002). The initial list of 250 schools was refined further to ensure a proper match in selectivity between the treatments and controls.

Although we were interested in obtaining an adequate number of control schools to match the treatment schools, we refined the selection process to ensure they were comparable using the following conditions. First, we limited the selection of all the schools (controls and treatments) to those that were ranked in tier 1. This reduced the sample of schools from 250 to 106 schools, comprising all 36 treatment schools and 70 control schools. Second, the list of 106 schools was used to match school-level data from the IPEDS in each of the three academic years [8]. Third, these data were then matched with the IPEDS data for each of the three academic years to student-level data from NPSAS. From the NPSAS, we selected data for cohorts who entered their freshmen year in each of the three academic years [9]. Fourth, since we used a difference-in-difference methodology for the analysis, we wanted data for each school in at least two of the three academic years—one in the pre-treatment and one in the post-treatment period. We therefore initially constructed four samples of schools, depending on whether there were matches between all three academic years, or between any two of the three academic years. This resulted in 30 schools with data in all three academic years 1995-1996, 1999-2000, and 2003-2004 (referred to as sample 1). There were 34 schools with data in 1995-1996 and 2003-2004 (sample 2); 35 schools with data in 1999-2000 and 2003-2004 (sample 3); and 37 schools matched between 1995-1996 and 1999-2000 (sample 4) [10]. Finally, we limited the selection to private schools because all of the treatment schools are private. We did this because the governance of private schools generally differed from state-controlled public schools and these differences were likely to affect affordability and enrollment at a school.

Determination of the Appropriate Time Periods for Assessing Effects and Classification of Schools that Only Attended the Meetings

We also determined the academic year(s) data that would be used to represent the period before and the period after the implementation of the consensus approach. Since we had data for only1995-1996, 1999-2000 and 2003-2004, and given that the consensus approach was implemented in 2003-2004 (or in the prior year by some schools) we selected 1995-1996 as the pre-consensus approach period and 2003-2004 as the post-consensus approach period. Although the 1999-2000 data were relatively current for the pre-consensus approach period, it is possible that the 1999-2000 data may offer neither strong pre- nor post-consensus approach information since the period was very close to the formation of the 568 President's Group in 1998. Furthermore, the institutional methodology, which is a foundation for the consensus approach and used by some of the control schools in 2003-2004, was revised in 1999. We therefore investigated whether it was appropriate to include 1999-2000 in the pre-consensus approach period or in the post-consensus approach period. We also investigated in which group (control or treatment) the schools that only attended the 568 President's Group meetings, but had not become members of the group or implemented the consensus approach, belonged.

Table 9. Control and Treatment Schools for Analyzing Effects of the Consensus Approach Implementation

Academic years	Control school (Non-CA)	Treatment school (CA)
1995-1996 1999-2000 & 2003-2004	Sample 1: Brandeis University New York University Princeton University[b] Tufts University[a,b] Tulane University University of Rochester Washington University at St. Louis	Samples 1, 2, or 3: Boston College[a] Cornell University[b] Duke University Georgetown University Massachusetts Institute of Technology[a,b] University of Notre Dame University of Pennsylvania[a,b] Vanderbilt University Wake Forest University Yale University[b]
1995-1996 & 2003-2004	Sample 2—All of Sample 1 Plus: Bryn Mawr College[b] Yeshiva University[e]	
1999-2000 & 2003-2004	Sample 3—All of Sample 1 Plus: Colgate University Lehigh University Whitman College	
1995-1996 & 1999-2000	Sample 4—All of Sample 1 Plus: Carnegie Mellon University Johns Hopkins University	Sample 4—All of Above Plus: Columbia University[b]

Source: GAO analysis.

[a]Schools were excluded because there were no data for SAT scores for 2003-2004. [b]Member of the former Overlap group.[c]Members of the 568 Group that had not implemented the consensus approach.[d]Were not members of the 568 Group but attended meetings.[e]Former member of the 568 Group.

Notes: Schools that Only Attended 568 Group Meetings: Sample 2: Stanford Universityd, University of Southern Californiaa,d and Sample 4: Case Western Reserve Universitye. ember schools that had not implemented the consensus approach: Sample 2: Brown University[b,c] Sample 3: Dartmouth College[b,c].Other 568-Affiliated Schools: Amherst College,[b] Bowdoin College,[b,e] California Institute of Technology,[d] Claremont McKenna College, Davidson College, Emory University, Grinnell College, Harvard University,[b,d] Haverford College, Macalester College[e] Middlebury College,[b] Northwestern University, Pomona College, Rice University, Swarthmore College, Syracuse University,[d] University of Chicago, Wellesley College,[b] Wesleyan University,[b] Williams College[b].

Using the Chow test for pooling data, we determined that 1999-2000 should be excluded from the pre-consensus approach period as well as from the post-consensus approach period. We also determined that schools that only attended the 568 President's Group meetings could not be regarded as control schools or treatment schools in analyzing the effects of the consensus approach [11]. Therefore, the treatment schools consisted of the group members that implemented the consensus approach, and the control schools consisted of the schools that were not members of the 568 Group and did not attend their meetings. Based on the analysis above, we used the data in sample 2, which excluded data collected in 1999-2000, for our baseline model analysis; the period before the consensus approach is 1995-1996 and the period after is 2003-2004; the control schools that did not use the consensus approach (non-CA schools) are Brandeis University, Bryn Mawr College, New York University, Princeton University, Tulane University, University of Rochester, and Washington University at St. Louis, and the treatment schools that used the consensus approach (CA schools) are Cornell University, Duke University, Georgetown University, University of Notre Dame, Vanderbilt University, Wake Forest University, and Yale University. The complete list of the schools is in table 9.

Specifications of Econometric Models and Estimation Methodology

We developed models for analyzing the effects of the implementation of the consensus approach (CA) on affordability and enrollment of incoming freshman using the consensus approach [12]. We used a difference-indifference approach to identify the effects of implementation of the consensus approach. This approach controlled for two potential sources of changes in school practices that were independent of the consensus approach. First, this approach enabled us to control for variation in the actions of schools over time that were independent of the consensus approach. Having control schools that never implemented the consensus approach allowed us to isolate the effects of the exemption and permitted us to estimate changes over time that were independent of the consensus approach implementation. Second, while we had a control group of schools that did not use the consensus approach, but were otherwise very similar to treatment schools, it is possible that schools using the consensus approach differed in ways that would make them more likely to implement practices that are different from those of other schools [13]. The difference-in-difference approach controlled for this possibility by including data on schools using the consensus approach both before and after its adoption. Controlling then for time effects independent of the consensus approach as well as practices by these schools before adoption, the effect of the use of the consensus approach could be estimated.

Compared to the schools that did not use the consensus approach, we expected that the implementation of the consensus approach would have a significantly greater impact on the schools using the consensus approach because its use has potential implications for affordability and enrollment of students in these schools.

Modeling the Effects of the Consensus Approach Methodology for Financial Need on Affordability and Enrollment

The basic tenets of financial need analysis are that parents and students should contribute to the student's education according to their ability to pay. The CA schools used the consensus approach for its need analysis methodology and to determine the expected family contribution (EFC) for each student based on that methodology. Conversely, the non-CA schools primarily used a need analysis methodology called the institutional methodology (IM). The difference between the cost of attendance (COA) and the EFC determines whether a student has financial need. If so, the school then develops a financial aid package of grants, loans, and work study from various sources. The actual amount that students and families pay depends on how much of the aid received is grant aid. Therefore, the implementation of the consensus approach was expected to affect the price paid and the financial aid received by students, and by implication, their enrollment into schools.

Dependent Variables

The study examined the effects of the implementation of the consensus approach on two key variables: affordability (measured by price) and enrollment of freshman. We also estimated other equations to provide further insights on affordability— tuition, total grant aid, need-based grant aid, and total aid. All the dependent variables were measured at the student level, except tuition. Also, all monetary values were adjusted for inflation using the consumer price index (CPI) in 2005 prices [14]. The dependent variables were defined as follows:

- Price ($PRICE_{ijt}$): Price, in dollars, actually paid by freshman i who enrolled in school j in an academic year t. The variable was measured as the cost of attendance less total grant aid. The cost of attendance consisted of tuition and fees, on-campus room and board, books and supplies, and other expenses such as transportation. Total grant aid consisted of institutional and non-institutional grant aid; it excluded self-help aid (loans and work study).

The other dependent variables that we estimated to help provide more insights into the results for affordability were:

- Tuition ($TUITION_{ijt}$): The amount of tuition and fees in dollars charged by school j to freshman i who enrolled in an academic year t. [15].
- Total grant aid ($AIDTGRT_{ijt}$): The amount of total grant aid received, in dollars, by a freshman i who enrolled in school j in an academic year t. The counterpart to grant aid was self-help aid [16].
- Need-based grant aid ($AIDNDTGRT_{ijt}$): The amount of need-based grant aid received, in dollars, by freshman i who enrolled in school j in an academic year t. The counterpart to need-based aid was non-need-based aid, which consisted mainly of merit aid [17].Total aid package ($AIDTOTAMT_{ijt}$): The amount of total aid received, in dollars, by freshman i who enrolled in school j in an academic year t. The total aid consisted of total grants (from the school, the various levels of

government—federal, state—and other sources) and self-help (includes loans and work-study).

- Student enrollment (ENRCA$_{ijt}$): An indicator variable for student enrollment into a CA school (ENRCA$_{ijt}$). It equals one if a freshman i enrolled in an academic year t in school j that was a school using or later the consensus approach, and zero otherwise. Thus, at t=0 (1995-1996), a school was designated as a CA school if it implemented the consensus approach in period t=1 (2003-2004). Students who enrolled in a non-CA school were assigned a value of zero. In other words, ENRCA takes a value of one for every student enrolled in a CA school in any time period (1995-1996 or 2003-2004), and zero otherwise.

Explanatory Variables

Several variables could potentially affect each of the dependent variables identified above. The explanatory variables we used were based on economic reasoning, previous studies, and data availability.[18] All the equations used were in quasi reduced-form specifications. The key explanatory variable of interest was the exercise of the exemption through the implementation of the consensus approach by the 568 Group of schools. We were also interested in the effects of the implementation of the consensus approach on affordability and enrollment of disadvantaged students. In order to isolate the relationships between the consensus approach implementation and each of the dependent variables, we controlled for the potential effects of other explanatory variables. The following is a complete list of all the explanatory variables we used:

- Exemption indicator: EMCA$_{jt}$ [19]. The exemption was captured by the implementation of the consensus approach by a school [20]. EMCA equals one if school j has implemented CA by academic year t, where t is 2003-2004 and zero otherwise.
  We used other explanatory variables in our equations, in addition to the exemption indicator for the implementation of the consensus approach. These variables included school-level characteristics, school specific fixed-effects, time specific fixed-effects, and student-level characteristics.
- School-level characteristics [21]
  The school variables or attributes varied across the schools *(j)* and over time *(t)*, but did not vary across the students *(i)*. The school characteristics may capture the quality of the schools, expenditures by the schools that may compete with financial aid for funding, revenue sources for financial aid, or the preferences of the students.[22] The variables used were:
- ENDOWSTU$_{jt}$: The interaction between the 3-year average endowment per student and the 3-year average percentage rate of return on endowment per student at school j for an academic year t. The inclusion of the rate of returns from endowments helped minimize the possibility that developments in financial markets could bias the results especially if the average endowment per student differed across the two groups of schools.

- RANKAVG$_{jt}$: The average "best schools" rank of school j for an academic year t. Although we used this variable to select the control schools that were comparable in selectivity to the treatment schools before matching the data to the NPSAS data, this variable was included, due to data limitations, to control for the possibility that the two groups of schools used in the sample may differ in selectivity.
- ENROLUG$_{jt}$: The 3-year average growth rate (in decimals) of undergraduate enrollment at school j for an academic year t.
- TENURED$_{jt}$: The percentage (in decimals) of total faculty at school j that was tenured in an academic year t.
- Time specific fixed-effects: These variables captured differences over time that did not vary across the schools, such as increases in national income that could increase affordability of schools. This was an indicator variable for the academic years (time): AY1995$_t$: Equals one for the academic year1995-1996, and zero otherwise AY2003$_t$: Equals one for the academic year 2003-2004, and zero otherwise.

Student characteristics: [23].

All the student-level variables or attributes generally varied across students *(i)*, across schools *(j)*, and across time *(t)*. The student characteristics indicated the preferences of the students for a school as well as the decisions of the schools regarding the students they admitted. The variables used were:

- FINAID$_{ijt}$: Equals one if a freshman i who enrolled in school j in an academic year t applied for financial aid, and zero otherwise.
- RACE: Equals one if a freshman i who enrolled in school j in an academic year t is:

  Asian—ASIAN$_{ijt}$, and zero otherwise.
  Black—BLACK$_{ijt}$, and zero otherwise.
  Hispanic—HISPANIC$_{ijt}$, and zero otherwise.
  White—WHITE$_{ijt}$, and zero otherwise.
  Foreigner—FOREIGN$_{ijt}$, and zero otherwise.
  None of the above—OTHER$_{ijt}$, and zero otherwise [24].

INCOME: Equals one for a freshman i who enrolled in school j in an academic year t has household income in the following quintiles: INCLO$_{ijt}$: Below or equal to the 20th percentile, and zero otherwise. These were low-income students, and the median income for the group was $13,731 in 2005 dollars.

INCLOMD$_{ijt}$: Above the 20th and below or equal to the 40th percentile, and zero otherwise. These were lower-middle income students, and the median income for the group was $40,498 in 2005 dollars.

INCMD$_{ijt}$: Above the 40th and below or equal to the 60th percentile, and zero otherwise. These were middle-income students, and the median income for the group was $59,739 in 2005 dollars.

INCUPMD$_{ijt}$: Above the 60th and below or equal to the 80th percentile, and zero otherwise. These were upper-middle income students, and the median income for the group was $88,090 in 2005 dollars.

INCHI$_{ijt}$: Above the 80th percentile, and zero otherwise. These were high-income students, and the median income for the group was $145,912 in 2005 dollars.

Since we included minority students (Asian, black, and Hispanic students) as well as lower income groups (low income and lower-middle income students) to measure needy students, the minority variables likely captured nonincome effects [25]

EFC$_{ijt}$: Expected family contribution for a freshman i who enrolled in school j in an academic year t. Although this variable captured the income of the students, it also reflected other factors that affect financial aid, such as the number of siblings in collage [26]

SCORESAT$_{ijt}$: The combined scholastic aptitude test (SAT) scores for math and verbal of freshman i who enrolled in school j in an academic year t.

Tables 10 and 11 show summary statistics for the variables listed above for treatment and control schools in sample 2 (as listed in table 9) [27]. In general, the values of the variables were similar between the two groups of schools.

Table 10. Summary Statistics of Variables Used in Regression Analysis, 1995-1996 and 2003-2004: CA Schools

Variable	Mean	Std	Min	Max
School-level				
TUITION	$26,245	$3,557	$18.910	$31,152
ENDOWSTU	$227,213	$230,768	$44,061	$1,146,129
RANKAVG	16	9	2	27
ENROLUG	2%	6%	-1%	21%
TENURED	56%	13%	25%	75%
Student-level				
PRICE	$30,792	$11,144	$1,065	$52,354
AIDTGRT	$7,133	$9,866	$0	$40,658
AIDNDTGRT	$5,526	$8,722	$0	$35,321
AIDNONDTGRT	$1,607	$4,360	$0	$30,403
AIDTOTAMT	$12,465	$13,566	$0	$43,195
AIDSELFPLUS	$4,794	$8,155	$0	$36,730
EFC	$24,486	$22,268	$0	$115.090
SCORESAT	1301	144	790	1600
FINAID	76%	n/a	n/a	n/a
ASIAN	9%	n/a	n/a	n/a
BLACK	5%	n/a	n/a	n/a
HISPANIC	7%	n/a	n/a	n/a
FOREIGN	2%	n/a	n/a	n/a
OTHER	5%	n/a	n/a	n/a
WHITE	71%	n/a	n/a	n/a
INCLO	5%	n/a	n/a	n/a
INCLOMD	11%	n/a	n/a	n/a
INCMD	13%	n/a	n/a	n/a
INCUPMD	17%	n/a	n/a	n/a
INCHI	54%	n/a	n/a	n/a
Schools	Cornell University, Duke University, Georgetown University, University of Notre Dame, Vanderbilt University, Wake Forest University, Yale University			
Number of observations				241

Table 11. Summary Statistics of Variables Used in Regression Analysis, 1995-1996 and 2003-2004: Non-CA Schools

Variable	Mean	Std	Min	Max
School-level				
TUITION	$27,031	$2,259	$24,571	$31,714
ENDOWSTU	$256,147	$329,513	$27,909	$1,504,930
RANKAVG	23	12	1	43
ENROLUG	1%	1%	-2%	4%
TENURED	56%	12%	26%	72%
Student-level				
PRICE	$28,815	$10,305	$4,569	$50,726
AIDTGRT	$10,869	$9,792	$0	$32,803
AIDNDTGRT	$8,573	$9,132	$0	$31,487
AIDNDTGRT	$2,296	$5,419	$0	$27,919
AIDTOTAMT	$16,487	$13,875	$0	$48,572
AIDSELFPLUS	$5,293	$7,686	$0	$48,041
EFC	$21,717	$21,724	$0	$105,095
SCORESAT	1268	151	740	1590
FINAID	80%	n/a	n/a	n/a
ASIAN	12%	n/a	n/a	n/a
BLACK	5%	n/a	n/a	n/a
HISPANIC	4%	n/a	n/a	n/a
FOREIGN	3%	n/a	n/a	n/a
OTHER	3%	n/a	n/a	n/a
WHITE	74%	n/a	n/a	n/a
INCLO	10%	n/a	n/a	n/a
INCLOMD	9%	n/a	n/a	n/a
INCMD	12%	n/a	n/a	n/a
INCUPMD	21%	n/a	n/a	n/a
INCHI	48%	n/a	n/a	n/a
Schools	Brandeis University, Bryn Mawr College, New York University, Princeton University, Tulane University, University of Rochester, Washington University at St. Louis			
Number of Observations				277

Note: All values are (probability) weighted averages, and the monetary values are in 2005 dollars.

Table 12. CA and Non-CA Schools: Price and Financial Aid

	CAS chools			Non-CAS chools		
All students	1995-1996	2003-2004	Percentage difference	1995-1996	2003-2004	Percentage difference
Price^a	$28,039	$35,488	27%	$28,068	$30,838	10%
Tuition & fees	24,062	29,967	25	25,770	30,447	18
Total observations	150	91		198	79	
Financial-Aid Applicants Only						
Student Applied for Financial Aid						
Price^a	$25,845	$32,897	27%	$24,960	$29,705	19%
Total grant aid	9,142	9,775	7	13,391	13,960	4
Need-based total grant	7,771	6,439	-17	11,863	8,122	-32
Institutional grant aid	7,073	6,529	-8	11,297	11,116	2
Total aid	16,604	16,046	-3	19,827	22,255	12
Loans (incl. PLUS)	5,954	4,849	-19	5,271	6,669	27
Work study	710	866	22	986	715	-27
Number of observations	112	72		152	73	
Student Did Not Apply for Financial Aid^b						
Price^a	34,645	44,504	28	37,714	44,292	17
Number of observations	38	19		46	6	
Total observations	150	91		198	79	

Source: GAO analysis. ^aPrice equals cost of attendance less total grant aid. Cost of attendance equals tuition and fees, plus expenses (including room and board, and books).^bFinancial aid data were not available for students who did not apply for financial aid. otes: All values are (probability) weighted averages, and the monetary values are in 2005 dollars.

Comparison of Prices and Financial Aid in CA and Non-CA Schools

Table 12 shows summary statistics on price and financial aid before and after the implementation of the consensus approach in 2003-04 at the CA and non-CA schools in sample 2. Similarly, table 13 shows the summary statistics by income and racial groups [28]. It is important to note that the summary information on the observed differences before and after the implementation of the consensus approach for the CA and non-CA schools are heuristic and do not conclusively determine the potential effects of the implementation of the consensus approach. It is also important to note that, for any given variable, it is possible that there are other factors than implementing the consensus approach that are responsible for the observed differences, including differences between CA and non-CA schools' student populations or differences in the characteristics of the schools, or both. For instance, the price paid by middle-income students increased more in CA than in non-CA schools. While this may reflect the effect of consensus approach, it is possible that other factors are responsible for the differences. For example, the racial composition of middle-income students might also be different between the two groups, or there may be systematic differences in endowment growth between the CA and non-CA schools that affect financial aid to middle-income students. Thus, to assess the effect of consensus approach, it is necessary to study the effects of consensus approach while controlling simultaneously for all factors that influence price and aid policies.

Table 13. CA and Non-CA Schools—Financial Aid Applicants Only: Price and Financial Aid

	CA schools			Non-CA schools		
	1995-1996	2003-2004	Percentage difference	1995-1996	2003-2004	Percentage difference
Income level						
Low income						
Price[a]	$12,566	$10,095	-20	$18,950	$21,886	15
Total grant aid	$23,429	$27,020	15	$19,093	$21,861	14
Need-based total grant	$21,422	$21,191	-1	$16,849	$17,756	5
Institutional grant aid	$17,278	$12,597	-27	$14,060	$17,447	24
Total aid	$27,385	$35,956	31	$24,772	$26,523	7
Number of observations	9	3		26	8	
Lower-middle income						
Price[a]	$17,613	$30,437	73	$17,623	$20,546	17
Total grant aid	$17,531	$14,793	-16	$20,598	$23,014	12
Need-based total grant	$15,762	$12,949	-18	$20,417	$15,456	-24
Institutional grant aid	$11,735	$9,667	-18	$15,742	$19,386	23
Total aid	$24,025	$18,409	-23	$28,462	$30,509	7
Number of observations	13	12		22	5	
Middle income						
Price[a]	$22,146	$30,156	36	$21,240	$25,279	19
Total grant aid	$12,277	$12,076	-2	$17,173	$17,336	1
Need-based total grant	$8,293	$10,767	30	$16,053	$9,048	-44
Institutional grant aid	$11,096	$9,936	-10	$16,000	$13,854	-13
Total aid	$18,811	$20,743	10	$24,261	$25,176	4
Number of observations	16	10		20	12	
Upper-middle income						
Price[a]	$23,759	$31,631	33	$26,905	$29,524	10
Total grant aid	$10,410	$10,374	-0.3	$12,030	$13,478	12
Need-based total grant	$9,732	$5,864	-40	$10,289	$6,593	-36
Institutional grant aid	$8,694	$7,719	-11	$10,900	$7,198	-34
Total aid	$16,926	$19,277	14	$19,425	$20,769	7
Number of observations	21	13		32	11	

Table 13. (Continued)

	CA schools			Non-CA schools		
	1995-1996	2003-2004	Percentage difference	1995-1996	2003-2004	Percentage difference
High income						
Price[a]	$31,776	$37,127	17	$30,184	$33,806	12
Total grant aid	$3,493	$5,468	57	$7,941	$10,331	30
Need-based total grant	$2,810	$1,694	-40	$6,185	$5,377	-13
Institutional grant aid	$2,532	$3,430	35	$7,062	$8,884	26
Total aid	$12,393	$10,850	-12	$13,300	$19,797	49
Number of observations	53	34		52	37	
Total observations	**112**	**72**		**152**	**73**	
Race[b]						
Asian						
Price[a]	$28,082	$28,756	2	$25,642	$27,624	8
Total grant aid	$8,371	$16,265	94	$10,827	$17,834	65
Need-based total grant	$7,675	$13,129	71	$9,900	$14,646	48
Institutional grant aid	$6,906	$11,607	68	$7,771	$13,376	72
Total aid	$14,343	$23,037	61	$15,513	$27,425	77
Number of observations	11	5		23	13	
Black						
Price[a]	$12,702	$22,935	81	$13,530	$17,375	28
Total grant aid	$21,360	$19,958	-7	$23,296	$25,010	7
Need-based total grant	$19,836	$8,932	-55	$18,517	$15,631	-16
Institutional grant aid	$15,046	$17,404	16	$18,582	$21,231	14
Total aid	$29,572	$24,950	-16	$29,121	$26,707	-8
Number of observations	10	3		8	4	
Hispanic						
Price[a]	$21,177	$21,529	2	$20,282	$16,694	-18
Total grant aid	$15,432	$18,586	20	$17,028	$25,993	53
Need-based total grant	$13,514	$13567	0.4	$14,684	$18,611	27
Institutional grant aid	$11,960	$13,813	15	$13,187	$17,998	36
Total aid	$20,110	$25,576	27	$22,446	$32,732	46
Number of observations	7	8		11	2	
White						
Price[a]	$27,032	$35,099	26	$25,736	$30,952	20
Total grant aid	$6,711	$7,382	10	$13,028	$12,512	-4
Need-based total grant	$5,271	$4,284	-19	$11,645	$6,249	-46
Institutional grant aid	$5,105	$4,240	-17	$11,378	$10,187	-10
Total aid	$14,635	$14,130	-3	$20,042	$21,005	5
Number of observations	81	48		103	49	
Total observations	**112**	**72**		**152**	**73**	

Source: GAO analysis.

[a]Price equals cost of attendance less total grant aid. Cost of attendance equals tuition and fees, plus expenses (including room and board, and books).

[b]Data for other race, including Native American, unidentified race, and foreign students were too few to report.

Notes: All values are (probability) weighted averages, and the monetary values are in 2005 dollars.

Model Specifications and Estimation Methodology

Our econometric analysis is based on panel data, which pooled cross-sectional and time series data. The cross-sectional data were based on freshmen who enrolled in CA schools and non-CA schools, and the time series data were for academic years 1995-1996 and 2003-2004. Where feasible, we used panel-data estimation appropriate for cross-sectional and time series data. Also, we used fixed-effects estimation instead of random-effects estimation because the observations were not randomly chosen and there were likely to be unobserved school-specific effects [29]. The reported estimates were based on the fixed-effects estimators, using probability weights, and the standard errors were robust [30].

Price, Tuition, and Financial Aid Equations

Let Y_{ijt} be the dependent variable for freshman i's outcomes at the chosen school j in academic year t, where the main outcome variable studied is affordability represented by price ($PRICE_{ijt}$).[31]. The regression equations were specified generally as follows:

$$Y_{ijt} = \alpha + \sum_{t=2}^{T} \psi_t + \sum_{j=2}^{J} \theta_j + I_{jt}\beta + S_{ijt}\rho + EMCA_{jt}\delta + EMCA_{jt} I_{jt}\eta$$
$$+ EMCA_{jt} S_{ijt} \gamma + \varepsilon_{ijt}$$

(1)

where I and S are vectors of school (institution)-level and student-level variables, and EMCA represents the consensus approach implementation; ψ (time specific fixed-effects) and θ (school specific fixed-effects) are scalar parameters, and α and ε are the constant and the random error terms, respectively. There are interactions between EMCA and the school-level variables and between EMCA and the student-level variables [32].

We were primarily interested in the total effects of the implementation of the consensus approach on affordability, as well as the effects that were specific to particular groups of students, such as low-income and minority students, and students who applied for financial aid.

Using equation 1, the total effect of the CA implementation on price was estimated by $\delta^\wedge$ $+I\eta^\wedge +S\gamma^\wedge$, where I and S are averages of I and S taken over the observations for the CA schools during the period of the consensus approach implementation (2003-2004) [33]. This measures the effect of the consensus approach implementation on CA schools, relative to non-CA schools, controlling for time invariant differences in schools and other variations over time that are common to both groups. The coefficient $\delta^\wedge$ measures the unconditional effect of the consensus approach implementation on price, while $\eta^\wedge$ and $\gamma^\wedge$ measure the conditional effects of the consensus approach implementation on price through the school-level variables and student-level variables, respectively.

The expression for the total effects of the consensus approach implementation can be evaluated for particular groups of students by averaging I and S over that particular subset of students. For example, the effects of the consensus approach implementation on prices paid by low-income (INCLO) students can be estimated by $\delta + I^{INCLO}\eta^\wedge + S^{INCLO}\gamma^\wedge$, where the school-level and student-level variables are averaged over the low-income students. More specifically, the second term is the coefficient estimates of each school-level variable multiplied by the school-level variable averaged over the subset of low-income (INCLO) students attending CA schools after the consensus approach implementation; similarly the average is taken for the third term, which is for the student-level variables.

Alternatively, we can use equation 1 to illustrate the effects of the consensus approach implementation for particular groups. Consider a simple example in which there are two student characteristics, F and A, where F is an indicator variable equal to one if the student is a financial aid applicant and zero otherwise, and A is an indicator equal to one if the student is black, and zero otherwise. Then, using equation 1, the equation for this example is:

$$Y_{ijt} = \alpha + \sum_{t=2}^{T} \psi_t + \sum_{j=2}^{J} \theta_j + I_{jt}\beta + F_{ijt}\rho_F + A_{ijt}\rho_A + EMCA_{jt}\delta$$
$$+ EMCA_{jt} I_{jt} \eta + EMCA_{jt} F_{ijt} \gamma_F + EMCA_{jt} A_{ijt} \gamma_A + \varepsilon_{ijt} \qquad (1.1)$$

Now consider a white student who is a financial aid applicant in school j at time t. [34]. The predicted price for a white student if j is a CA school is:

$$\hat{\alpha} + \hat{\psi}_t + \hat{\theta}_j + I_{jt}\hat{\beta} + \hat{\rho}_F + \hat{\delta} + I_{jt}\hat{\eta} + \hat{\gamma}_F \qquad (1.2)$$

and the predicted price if j is not a CA school is:

$$\hat{\alpha} + \hat{\psi}_t + \hat{\theta}_j + I_{jt}\hat{\beta} + \hat{\rho}_F \qquad (1.3)$$

The effect of the consensus approach implementation for a financial aid applicant at school j is then the difference between equations 1.2 and 1.3, which is:

$$\hat{\delta} + I_{jt}\hat{\eta} + \hat{\gamma}_F \qquad (1.4)$$

The coefficient $\hat{\delta}$ measures the effect of adopting the consensus approach that is invariant across school and student type, the term $I\hat{\eta}$ captures the differential effect of adopting the consensus approach for a school with characteristics I_{jt}, and the third term, $\hat{\gamma}$, captures the differential effect of adopting the consensus approach for a white student who is a financial aid applicant. Repeating the exercise above for a black student who is a financial aid applicant, the predicted effect of adopting the consensus approach would be:

$$\hat{\delta} + I_{jt}\hat{\eta} + \hat{\gamma}_F + \hat{\gamma}_A \qquad (1.5)$$

The first three terms in equation 1.5 are the same as equation 1.4, while the fourth term captures the differential effect of the consensus approach implementation for a black student. In this example, then, the estimated effect of the consensus approach implementation on financial aid students would be the weighted average of the terms in equations 1.4 or 1.5, with weights corresponding to the proportions of white and black financial-aid students across all schools j that adopted the consensus approach at time t, respectively.

Another estimate of the consensus approach's effect on a particular group is the estimated *differential* effect on a group, given by $\hat{\gamma}$, holding everything else constant. For example, one can ask how a low-income student as compared to a high-income student would be affected by the consensus approach implementation, assuming all other characteristics of the student and the student's school are held constant. This estimated effect is simply given by the element of the vector in $\gamma\hat{}$ that corresponds to INCLO. This differs from the total effect of the consensus approach implementation discussed above by taking as given the consensus approach implementation, and by abstracting from the likelihood that low-income students will have other characteristics and attend different schools than non low-income students. We will also discuss the coefficient $\rho\hat{}$, which captures the value of the dependent variable for the particular group in both CA and non-CA schools before the consensus approach implementation, where necessary.

The total effect of the exemption on price as well as its specific effects on particular groups will depend on which theory of the exemption is supported by the data. In particular, we expect price to be lower for disadvantaged students if the social benefit theory is valid; on the other hand, price will increase if the anti-competitive theory is valid. Similarly, the effects of the student-level variables would depend on the theories of the effects of the exemption. For the effects of the school-level variables, ENDOWSTU should be negative because with more resources there is less need to raise tuition and there will be more funds for grant aid. RANKAVG should be negative because as the quality of the school decreases tuition as well as grant aid should decrease. ENROLUG would be negative if higher growth in student enrollment perhaps means more revenues and less need to raise tuition. On the other hand, if students' education is on net subsidized by other sources of school income then ENROLUG would be positive as increased enrollment increases the costs to the school of providing education. And TENURED should be positive if more tenured faculty implies higher quality [35].

We estimated equation 1 for price, as well as for tuition and the financial aid variables, using probability-weighted regression and robust standard errors, as well as the fixed-effects estimator for panel data [36]. See the regression estimates for price and tuition in table 14, and those for the financial aid variables in table 15 [37].

The regression models for the price, tuition, and financial aid variables are all highly significant using the F-values of the models. See tables 14 and 15. Furthermore, the school-level variables generally have the expected effects. In particular, for the price equation, a student enrolled in a school with an endowment per student (ENDOWSTU) of $250,000 paid about $5,000 lower price [38]. Also, a student paid about $464 less for a school with a unit drop in its selectivity (RANKAVG). Although the effect is not significant, the positive sign for ENROLUG suggests that an increase in enrollment growth may result in a higher price paid, implying that education is net subsidized and increases in enrollment increases the cost of providing education; and vice versa. Finally, a student enrolled in a school with 10 percent higher tenured faculty (TENURED) paid about $3,310 higher. As discussed earlier, the effects of the student-level variables depend on which theory of the effects of the higher education exemption is relevant [39].

Student Enrollment Equation

The regression equation for enrollment into a CA school (ENRCAijt) would depend on student characteristics. Generally, enrollment is the outcome of decision-making that included application, admission, and acceptance of the admission offer. The first and third decisions are made by the student, and the second decision is made by the school. Therefore, in general, both student-level variables and school-level variables would be relevant. However, our approach, as indicated in equation 2, treated the CA schools essentially the same and likewise for the non-CA schools, with differences between the two groups other than the consensus approach implementation captured by the constant term in the regression. The enrollment equation was thus specified as follows, excluding school-level variables as regressors:

$$Prob(ENRCA_{ijt} = 1) = \Phi(\alpha + S_{ijt}\,\rho + AY2003_t\,\delta + AY2003_t\,S_{ijt}\,\gamma)$$

$$(2)$$

Φ is the standard normal cumulative probability distribution function. Similar to equation 1, equation 2 includes student characteristics (with coefficients ρ), time fixed-effects captured by AY2003, and the interaction of the time variable AY2003 with student characteristics (with coefficients γ) [40].

The time specific fixed-effect for AY2003 captures any shift, which is constant across students, toward or away from the CA schools, after the consensus approach implementation, while the interaction terms between the AY2003 and the student characteristics capture shifts toward or away from the CA schools by students with specific characteristics [41].

The marginal effect of the consensus approach implementation is captured by the effects of AY2003 on enrollment in CA schools. Specifically, this equals, *d [Prob(ENRCA =1)] / d(AY 2003) =(δ+S γ)ϕ(.),* where ϕ is the standard normal probability density function. It should be noted that if AY2003 affects the probability of enrollment in CA schools, it would be a valuable suggestive evidence about the potential impact of the consensus approach implementation. However, it would not establish that the consensus approach implementation caused the shift. This is because it is possible that such effects might be due to changes in other factors at CA schools versus non-CA schools (e.g., more rapid endowment growth in the latter than the former). The effect of the consensus approach implementation is the change in the probability of enrollment in CA schools relative to non-CA schools as a result of the consensus approach implementation. The overall effect of the CA implementation as well as the effects of the consensus approach implementation on particular groups of students, such as low-income students and those who applied for financial aid, can be obtained similar to the discussion above for the price.

The marginal effect of the student characteristics is captured by the effects of S on enrollment in CA schools. Specifically, this equals, *d [Prob(ENRCA =1)] / dS =(ρ+AY 2003 γ)ϕ(.).* The effect of the consensus approach implementation on how the probabilities of enrollment of low-income and minority students, and those who applied for financial aid, are affected can be obtained similar to the discussion for the price.

Similar to the discussion for the price equation, the effects of the exemption and the student-level variables on enrollment into CA schools will depend on which theory of the exemption is valid. In particular, the social benefit theory will imply increased likelihood of enrollment into CA schools, especially of low-income students, because prices will be lower. While the opposite will occur with the anti-competitive theory because average price will be higher. We estimated equation 2 for student enrollment using the probit estimation, with probability weights and robust standard errors [42]. The regression estimates are in table 14.

Table 14.Regression Estimates of Effects of Consensus Approach Implementation on Price, Tuition, and Enrollment

Variable	Price	Tuition	Enrollment
EMCA	43,743.75[a] [0.002]	-1,720.72 [0.512]	n/a
AY2003	12,133.55[a] [0.000]	5,650.28[a] [0.000]	0.25751 [0.631]
Student-level			
FINAID	-7,573.33[a] [0.000]	n/a	0.01292 [0.854]
FINAID*	190.21 [0.911]	n/a	-0.30976[b] [0.015]
ASIAN	1,084.13 [0.363]	n/a	-0.01069 [0.910]
ASIAN*	-7,109.66[c] [0.055]	n/a	-0.08486 [0.613]
BLACK	-9,444.68[a] [0.000]	n/a	0.19398 [0.129]
BLACK*	-566.20 [0.921]	n/a	-0.20422 [0.339]
HISPANIC	-4,686.31[a] [0.007]	n/a	0.06790 [0.574]
HISPANIC*	-1,610.12 [0.588]	n/a	0.35354[b] [0.021]
FOREIGN	3,398.09 [0.230]	n/a	-0.25968 [0.221]
FOREIGN*	10,588.17[b] [0.026]	n/a	0.36734[c] [0.054]
OTHER	-2,047.09 [0.407]	n/a	0.02366 [0.887]
OTHER*	-1,077.16 [0.727]	n/a	0.30781[c] [0.059]
EFC	0.10871[a] [0.000]	n/a	2.30e-06 [0.190]
EFC*	-0.00745 [0.872]	n/a	-3.43e-06 [0.219]
INCLO	-8,427.06a [0.000]	n/a	-0.15253 [0.196]
INCLO*	-6,507.64 [0.274]	n/a	-0.15185 [0.489]
INCLOMD	-8,696.19[a] [0.000]	n/a	-0.03045 [0.797]
INCLOMD*	-1,789.68 [0.593]	n/a	0.16593 [0.384]
INCMD	-4,804.25[a] [0.000]	n/a	0.06859 [0.506]
INCMD*	945.64 [0.771]	n/a	-0.16166 [0.303]
INCUPMD	-1,434.39 [0.163]	n/a	-0.03378 [0.689]
INCUPMD*	-1,715.73 [0.522]	n/a	-0.07025 [0.657]
SCORESAT	-2.48 [0.430]	n/a	0.00024 [0.227]
SCORESAT*	-7.82 [0.383]	n/a	0.00013 [0.764]
School-level			
ENDOWSTU	-0.01935[a] [0.001]	-0.00401[c][0.008]	n/a
ENDOWSTU*	-0.01056[b] [0.044]	0.00038 [0.831]	n/a
RANKAVG	-464.33[c] [0.051]	-151.06[c] [0.064]	n/a
RANKAVG*	-798.05[a] [0.000]	36.28 [0.792]	n/a
ENROLUG	19,038.16 [0.785]	35,553.57 [0.133]	n/a
ENROLUG*	-45,843.9 [0.518]	-44,159.24[c] [0.095]	n/a
TENURED	33,100.97[a] [0.000]	-610.06 [0.492]	n/a
TENURED*	-25,823.9[b] [0.014]	4,632.48 [0.315]	n/a
Constant	29,651.89[a] [0.000]	28,746.01[a] [0.000]	n/a
Test statistic of model[d]	22.97[a] [0.000]	375.71[a] [0.000]	37.68[b] [0.050]
R-squared	0.62	0.99	0.06
Sample size	518	28	518
Joint test for EMCA	2.85[a] [0.000]	1.15 [0.460]	18.70[b] [0.133]
Linear restriction test for EMCA[e]	1.18 [0.240]	-0.59 [0.586]	n/a

Source: GAO analysis.

[a]Statistically significant at the 1 percent level or lower. P-values are in brackets. [b]Statistically significant at the 5 percent level or lower. P-values are in brackets.[c]Statistically significant at the 10 percent level or lower. P-values are in brackets. [d]F-statistic values for the price and tuition equations, and chi-square values for the enrollment equation. [e]t-statistic values for the price and tuition equations, and z-statistic values for the enrollment equation.

Notes: N/A means data are not available or applicable. *means interaction terms with EMCA for price and tuition equations, and interaction terms with AY2003 for the enrollment equation. Estimates of price and tuition are obtained using fixed-effects models. Estimates for enrollment are the marginal effects from a probit model.

Table 15. Regression Estimates of Effects of Consensus Approach Implementation on Financial Aid

Variable	Total grant aid	Need-based grant aid	Total aid
EMCA	-28,705.63^c [0.066]	-15,512.93 [0.178]	-50,805.28^b [0.016]
AY2003	2,159.46 [0.348]	-1,511.37 [0.522]	7,385.03^c [0.062]
Student-level			
FINAID	n/a	n/a	n/a
FINAID*	n/a	n/a	n/a
ASIAN	-722.86 [0.649]	-740.76 [0.590]	-2,638.73 [0.221]
ASIAN*	6,970.89 [0.142]	6,546.91^c [0.066]	8,275.76 [0.221]
BLACK	7,914.65^a [0.000]	4,796.63^b [0.026]	8,425.58^a [0.000]
BLACK*	2,546.02 [0.656]	-2,267.21 [0.514]	965.32 [0.862]
HISPANIC	4,709.93^b [0.023]	2,826.32 [0.140]	2,281.05 [0.389]
HISPANIC*	2,038.96 [0.570]	206.79 [0.947]	2,606.82 [0.622]
FOREIGN	-5,754.55^b [0.031]	-4,634.40 [0.132]	-11,961.86^a [0.002]
FOREIGN*	-10,965.98^b [0.032]	-10,414.55^b [0.032]	-11,659.21^c [0.068]
OTHER	4,656.42 [0.169]	5,229.39 [0.129]	4,196.89 [0.349]
OTHER*	-2,813.57 [0.481]	-1,725.88 [0.667]	-4,098.47 [0.496]
EFC	-0.16058^a [0.000]	-0.149889^a [0.000]	-0.187923^a [0.000]
EFC*	0.044382 [0.397]	0.03185 [0.472]	0.006624 [0.929]
INCLO	7,178.94^a [0.000]	7,932.99^a [0.000]	3,276.04 [0.177]
INCLO*	7,346.13 [0.239]	6,955.88^c [0.096]	14,970.89 [0.020]
INCLOMD	8,227.84^a [0.000]	8,747.21^a [0.000]	7,153.01^a [0.001]
INCLOMD*	2,830.62 [0.395]	3,585.08 [0.198]	3,678.72 [0.359]
INCMD	5,084.33^a [0.000]	3,488.27^b [0.015]	4,116.59^b [0.040]
INCMD*	1,835.35 [0.617]	4,773.69 [0.134]	5,366.73 [0.339]
INCUPMD	2,215.09^c [0.093]	1,699.48 [0.161]	1,643.62 [0.419]
INCUPMD*	600.56 [0.851]	-473.12 [0.873]	2,503.61 [0.632]
SCORESAT	1.23 [0.729]	-0.51436 [0.882]	-3.05 [0.561]
SCORESAT*	10.81 [0.306]	1.97 [0.775]	18.18 [0.170]
School-level			
ENDOWSTU	0.00684 [0.317]	0.01056 [0.144]	-0.00583 [0.512]
ENDOWSTU*	0.001786 [0.774]	0.00272 [0.644]	0.015595^c [0.092]
RANKAVG	88.79 [0.773]	406.70 [0.114]	58.30 [0.888]
RANKAVG*	140.56 [0.571]	38.06 [0.859]	566.66 [0.178]
ENROLUG	-36,447.82 [0.623]	-238,689.4^a [0.004]	-12,713.12 [0.922]
ENROLUG*	30,780.66 [0.683]	246,969.5^a [0.003]	32,081.77 [0.807]
TENURED	-4,340.32 [0.545]	5,070.34 [0.486]	8,685.55 [0.530]
TENURED*	15,405.02 [0.204]	16,399.34 [0.103]	11,726.97 [0.514]
Constant	8,727.25 [0.375]	-1331.71 [0.878]	17,640.66 [0.209]
F value of model	14.81^a [0.000]	16.36^a [0.000]	8.79^a [0.000]
R-squared	0.55	0.54	0.36
Sample size	409	409	409
F value of joint test	1.13 [0.328]	1.83^b [0.026]	1.60^c [0.067]
t value of linear restriction	n/a	2.05^b [0.041]	0.64 [0.525]

Source: GAO analysis.

^{a}Statistically significant at the 1 percent level or lower. P-values are in brackets. ^{b}Statistically significant at the 5 percent level or lower. P-values are in brackets. ^{c}Statistically significant at the 10 percent level or lower. P-values are in brackets. Notes: n/a means data are not available or applicable.

*Means interaction terms with EMCA.

The regression model for enrollment in table 14 is significant using the chi-square of the model. As indicated earlier, we expect the estimation results will enable us to determine if the likelihood of enrollment into schools implementing the consensus approach by various student groups is more consistent with the social benefit theory or the anti-competitive theory of the effects of the higher education exemption.

Estimation Results of the Effects of Attending Meetings and Implementing the Consensus Approach [43]

The results of estimating equations 1 and 2 for the total effects of the CA implementation on affordability and enrollment are summarized in table 16, based on the regression results in tables 14 and 15. The results for price and enrollment in table 16 contain the key findings of the entire study, with the other variables (tuition and financial aid) providing information that supplements the findings for price. [44]

Total Effects of Implementing the Consensus Approach (from table 16)

Prices [45]

For the average student, the consensus approach implementation did not significantly change the prices paid by students in CA schools compared to non-CA schools, including the effects on low-income and minority students and students who applied for financial aid.[46]

Tuition [47]

The CA schools, compared to non-CA schools, did not significantly change the tuition they charged students as a result of the consensus approach implementation.

Total Grant Aid [48]

The consensus approach implementation did not significantly change the amount of total grant aid received by students in CA schools compared to non-CA schools.

Need-Based Total Grant Aid [49]

The consensus approach implementation increased the amount of need-based total grant aid received by students in CA schools compared to non-CA schools by about $6,125, with a confidence interval of between $239 and $12,011.[50] The amounts of need-based grant aid received by students in CA schools compared to non-CA schools were higher for middle income students by about $20,221, with a confidence interval of between $6,718 and $33,724. Asian students received higher need-based grant aid of about $14,628, with a confidence interval of between $5,051 and $24,206; Hispanic students received higher need-based grant aid of about $9,532, with a confidence interval of between $1,006 and $18,059; and white students received higher need-based grant aid of about $6,017, with a confidence interval of between $178 and $11,856.

Total Aid [51]

The consensus approach implementation did not significantly change the amount of total aid received by students in CA schools compared to non-CA schools. However, low-income students in CA schools received higher total aid of about $12,121, with a confidence interval of between $1,837 and $22,404 [52].

Table 16. Estimates of Effects of Consensus Approach Implementation on Affordabili ty and Enrollment in CA Schools Relative to Non-CA Schools

Total effect of consensus approach on...	Price	Tuition	Total grant aid	Need-based total grant aid	Total aid	Probability of enrollment
All students	$3,021	-$433	-$749	$6,125[b]	-$2,886	38%
	[-$2,026, $8,068]	[-$2,465, $1,599]	[-$6,967, $5,470]	[$239, $12,011]	[-$11,805, $6,034]	[8%, 67%]
Financial-aid applicants	$2,177	n/a	n/a	n/a	n/a	22%
	[-$3,319, $7,673]					[-11%, 54%]
Low income	-$4,061	n/a	$3,688	$1,956	$12,121[b]	59%
	[-$15,583, $7,461]		[-$8,511, $15,887]	[-$5,232, $9,144]	[$1,837, $22,404]	[-52%, 170%]
Lower-middle income	$8,089[c]	n/a	-$3,671	$6,556	-$7,776	95%
	[-$263, $16,441]		[-$12,487, $5,145]	[-$2,145, $15,257]	[-$19,776, $4,224]	[6%, 184%]
Middle income	$2,320[d]	n/a	$1,618	$20,221[a]	$1,178	26%
	[-$8,043, $12,682]		[-$11,221, $14,457]	[$6,718, $33,724]	[-$19,616, $21,971]	[-41%, 93%]
Upper-middle income	-$1,048	n/a	-$973	$2,769	-$3,054	18%
	[-$7,641, $5,545]		[-$7,801, $5,855]	[-$3,986, $9,524]	[-$13,177, $7,068]	[-47%, 82%]
High income	$3,699	n/a	-$714	$4,687[c]	-$3,856	31%
	[-$824, $8,222]		[-$6,905, $5,476]	[-$449, $9,824]	[-$12,817, $5,104]	[-6%, 68%]
Asian students	-$376	n/a	$5,726	$14,628[a]	$3,694	1%
	[-$10,426, $9,674]		[-$5,671, $17,123]	[$5,051, $24,206]	[-$13,693, $21,082]	[-78%, 80%]
Black students	$4,468	n/a	-$1,227	$4,332	-$6,542	-26%
	[-$7,452, $16,387]		[-$13,238, $10,783]	[-$4,992, $13,657]	[-$20,353, $7,269]	[-142%, 91%]
Hispanic students	$1,168[d]	n/a	$1,520	$9,532[b]	$3,648	108%
	[-$6,744, $9,079]		[-$8,300, $11,341]	[$1,006, $18,059]	[-$8,981, $16,278]	[-6%, 222%]
White students	$2,588	n/a	-$491	$6,017[c]	-$2,879	19%
	[-$2,403, $7,578]		[-$6,766, $5,784]	[$178, $11,856]	[-$11,922, $6,164]	[-14%, 52%]
Number of observations	518	28	409	409	409	518

Schools

CA Schools: Cornell University, Duke University, Georgetown University, University of Notre Dame, Vanderbilt University, Wake Forest University, Yale University

Non-CA Schools: Brandeis University, Bryn Mawr College, New York University, Princeton University, Tulane University, University of Rochester, Washington University at St. Louis

Source: GAO analysis. [a]Statistically significant at the 1 percent level or lower. bStatistically significant at the 5 percent level or lower. cStatistically significant at the 10 percent level or lower. d Effects were negative when data for only financial aid applicants were used.

Notes: The values in brackets are the 95 percent confidence intervals for the estimates that are significant at the 5 percent level or lower. "n/a" means data are not available or applicable.

All the monetary values are in 2005 dollars. Results are based on tables 14 and 15. δ ˆ Iη ˆ Sγ ˆ ,

The calculated values are based on where the average values are for all students. ˆ k kThe estimates are based on δI η ˆ S γ ˆ, where the average values are for the relevant k subgroup of students.

Enrollment

The consensus approach implementation did not significantly change the overall likelihood of enrollment into CA schools compared to non-CA schools, for all types of students.

Prior Levels and Differential Effects of the Consensus Approach on Affordability and Enrollment for Students with Particular Characteristics [53]

We discuss the estimates of affordability and the likelihood of enrollment in both the schools that adopted the consensus approach and those that did not, of students with particular characteristics, before the consensus approach was implemented. The estimates are reported in table 17, based on tables 14 and 15. These estimates could help explain the extent to which the consensus approach affected particular groups of students. For instance, if certain students were receiving higher financial aid awards prior to the consensus approach, they may be less likely to receive much higher awards as a result of its adoption. We also discuss the differential effects on students with particular characteristics that the consensus approach may have had on affordability and enrollment at those schools. The estimates are reported in table 18, based on tables 14 and 15. As already discussed, these estimates indicate how the consensus approach affected students with particular characteristics, assuming all the other characteristics of the students are held constant.

Prices
Some students paid lower prices prior to the CA implementation; in particular, financial aid applicants relative to non-financial aid applicants; low income, lower-middle income, middle-income students relative to high-income students; and black and Hispanic students relative to white students. But there were no significant differential effects of implementing the consensus approach on prices paid by these groups of students in CA schools.

Total Grant Aid
Some students received higher total grant aid prior to the consensus approach implementation; in particular, low-income, lower-middle income, middle-income, black, and Hispanic students.

Need-Based Total Grant Aid
Some students received higher need-based aid prior to the consensus approach implementation; in particular, low-income, lower-middle income, middle-income, and black students. But there were no significant differential effects of implementing the consensus approach on prices paid by these groups of students.

Total Aid
Some students received higher total aid prior to the consensus approach implementation; in particular, middle-income, and black students. But lower-middle income students received lower total aid prior to the consensus approach implementation.

Only low-income students in CA schools received higher aid, compared to high-income students, as a result of implementing the consensus approach.

Table 17. Estimates of Affordability and Enrollment before the Consensus Approach Implementation for Particular Groups of Students in Both CA and Non-CA Schools

Students	Price	Total grant aid	Need-based total grant aid	Total aid	Probability of enrollment
Financial-aid applicants[d]	-$7,573[a]	N/A	N/A	N/A	1%
Low income[e]	-$8,427[a]	$7,179[a]	$7,933[a]	$3,276	-15%
Lower-middle income[e]	-$8,696[a]	$8,228[a]	$8,747[a]	-$7,153[a]	-3%
Middle income[e]	-$4,804[a]	$5,084[a]	$3,488[b]	$4,117[b]	7%
Upper-middle income[e]	-$1,434	$2,215[c]	$1,699	$1,644	-3%
High income	N/A	N/A	N/A	N/A	N/A
Asian students[f]	$1,084	-$723	-$740	-$2,639	-1%
Black students[f]	-$9,445[a]	$7,915[a]	$4,797[b]	$8,426[a]	19%
Hispanic students[f]	-$4,686[a]	$4,710[b]	$2,826	$2,281	7%
White students	N/A	N/A	N/A	N/A	N/A
Number of observations	518	409	409	409	518
Schools	CA Schools: Cornell University, Duke University, Georgetown University, University of Notre Dame, Vanderbilt University, Wake Forest University, Yale University				
	Non-CA Schools: Brandeis University, Bryn Mawr College, New York University, Princeton University, Tulane University, University of Rochester, Washington University at St. Louis				

Source: GAO analysis.

[a]Statistically significant at the 1 percent level or lower. [b]Statistically significant at the 5 percent level or lower. [c]Statistically significant at the 10 percent level or lower. [d]The estimates are relative to non-financial aid applicants. eThe estimates are relative to high income students. [f]The estimates are relative to white students. Notes: Results are from tables 14 and 15, based on the coefficient $\hat{\rho}$ in equations 1 and 2. For instance, the value for price for financial-aid applicants is based on the estimated coefficient FINAID in table 14. N/A means data are not available or applicable. All the monetary values are in 2005 dollars.

Table 18. Differential Effects of Consensus Approach Implementation on Affordability and Enrollment in CA Schools for Particular Groups of Students

Students	Price	Total grant aid	Need-based total grant aid	Total aid	Probability of enrollment
Financial-aid applicants[d]	$190	N/A	N/A	N/A	-31%[a]
Low-income[e]	-$6,508	$7,346	$6,956[c]	$14,971[b]	-15%
Lower-middle income[e]	-$1,790	$2,831	$3,585	$3,679	17%
Middle income[e]	$946	$1,835	$4,774	$5,367	-16%
Upper-middle income[e]	-$1,716	$601	-$473	$2,504	-7%
High income	n/a	n/a	n/a	n/a	n/a
Asian students[f]	-$7,110[c]	$6,971	$6,547[c]	$8,276	-9%
Black students[f]	-$566	$2,546	-$2,267	$965	-20%
Hispanic students[f]	-$1,610	$2,039	$207	$2,607	35%[b]
White students	n/a	n/a	n/a	n/a	n/a
Number of observations	518	409	409	409	518
Schools	CA Schools: Cornell University, Duke University, Georgetown University, University of Notre Dame, Vanderbilt University, Wake Forest University, Yale University				
	Non-CA Schools: Brandeis University, Bryn Mawr College, New York University, Princeton University, Tulane University, University of Rochester, Washington University at St. Louis				

Source: GAO analysis.

[a]Statistically significant at the 1 percent level or lower. [b]Statistically significant at the 5 percent level or lower. [c]Statistically significant at the 10 percent level or lower. [d]The estimates are relative to non-financial aid applicants. [e]The estimates are relative to high income students. [f]The estimates are relative to white students. Notes: Results are from tables 14 and 15, based on the coefficient $\hat{\gamma}$ in equations 1 and 2. For instance, the value for price for financial-aid applicants is based on the estimated coefficient FINAID* in table 14. N/A means data are not available or applicable. All the monetary values are in 2005 dollars.

Enrollment

Students generally were not more or less likely to enroll in a CA school prior to the consensus approach implementation. However, implementing the consensus approach lowered the likelihood of enrollment of financial-aid students, compared to non-financial aid applicants, while the likelihood of enrollment of Hispanic students increased, compared to white students, in CA schools.

Limitations of the Study

Sample Selection Bias

The findings of the study could be limited by the potential of selection bias if the CA schools had characteristics that we could not control for that made them more inclined to adopt the consensus approach and independently influenced the outcome variables. We believe that this is not a serious problem with the estimation since the difference-indifference approach includes CA schools before the implementation of the CA, implying the latter selection problem would require significant change over a short time span in the character of these schools. Furthermore, a key factor that might motivate schools to join the 568 Group is the legacy of the Overlap group. The 568 Group has objectives that are similar to those stated by the Overlap group—to be able to offer financial aid to more needy students. Our test indicated that the chances of a former Overlap group member joining or not joining the 568 Group did not differ between the two groups of schools in our sample.[54] Thus, the similarity between the two groups, in terms of a school joining the 568 Group, implied the potential for selection bias may be small.

Measures of Price

In our analysis, the total grant aid does not include self-help aid (loans and work study). However, if the true amount of total grant aid should include some proportion of self-help aid, then its exclusion would lead to an underestimation of total grant aid. Nonetheless, we believe this did not significantly affect our results since we found that the consensus approach implementation did not affect self-help aid.

Early Decision Admissions

It may be that early admit students pay higher prices because early decision admission might be used by need-blind schools as a screening mechanism to indirectly identify a student's willingness-to-pay. Under the early decision process a non-financial aid student is therefore more likely to be admitted than a financial-aid student of comparable quality.[55] We did not expect the early decision process to affect our results because while the process might help identify a student with a higher willingness to pay, it is the student's ability to pay that determines the need-based aid offered by the 568 Group. Furthermore, the total probability of enrollment of a financial-aid applicant was similar to that of a non-financial aid applicant both before and after the consensus approach implementation, even though the consensus approach implementation tended to decrease the likelihood of enrollment of financial-aid students.

Excluded Schools of Comparable Selectivity

We could not include all the schools affiliated with the 568 Group in the analysis because of data limitations. (See the list of unmatched treatment schools in table 9.) However, there were several similarities (in terms of "best college" ranking, endowment, tuition and fees, and percentage of tenured faculty) as well as differences (in terms of freshmen enrollment) between the included and excluded CA colleges.

Table 19. Comparison of Observed and Predicted Price and Financial Aid Variables in CA and Non-CA Schools: Pre— and Post—Consensus Approach Implementation Period

	CAS chools			Non-CAS chools		
	1995-1996	2003-2004	Difference	1995-1996	2003-2004	Difference
Price						
All students						
Observed	$28,039	$35,488	$7,449	$28,068	$30,838	$2,770
Predicted	$30,791	$37,171	$6,380	$25,386	$27,882	$2,496
Financial-aid						
Observed	$25,845	$32,897	$7,052	$24,960	$29,705	$4,745
Predicted	$28,222	$34,352	$6,130	$22,347	$27,330	$4,983
Non financial-aid						
Observed	$34,645	$44,504	$9,859	$37,714	$44,292	$6,578
Predicted	$38,771	$46,625	$7,854	$35,127	$34,973	-$154
Low income						
Observed	$12,566	$10,095	-$2,471	$18,950	$21,886	$2,936
Predicted	$14,272	$11,389	-$2,833	$13,613	$18,106	$4,493
Lower-middle-income						
Observed	$19,220	$30,437	$11,217	$17,623	$20,546	$2,923
Predicted	$20,650	$32,075	$11,425	$15,156	$19,501	$4,345
Middle-income						
Observed	$24,785	$34,201	$9,416	$22,560	$26,069	$3,509
Predicted	$26,035	$36,438	$11,838	$21,092	$20,764	-$328
Upper-middle-income						
Observed	$26,285	$32,310	$6,025	$29,429	$34,305	$4,876
Predicted	$31,423	$35,121	$3,698	$26,566	$27,616	$1,050
High income						
Observed	$32,616	$39,496	$6,880	$33,137	$34,138	$1,001
Predicted	$35,538	$41,043	$5,505	$31,129	$32,582	$1,453
Financial aid—						
All students						
Total grant aid						
Observed	$9,142	$9,775	$633	$13,391	$13,960	$569
Predicted	$10,285	$11,877	$1,592	$12,181	$13,194	$1,013
Need-based grant aid						
Observed	$7,771	$6,439	-$1,332	$11,863	$8,122	-$3,741
Predicted	$7,443	$6,170	-$1,273	$12,277	$9,151	-$3,126
Total aid						
Observed	$16,604	$16,046	-$558	$19,827	$22,255	$2,428
Predicted	$17,998	$17,957	-$41	$18,425	$20,127	$1,702

Limited Data Availability

The data were available for only one academic year period after implementation of the consensus approach. This could mask potential effects of the consensus approach since these effects could be gradual, rather than immediate, and therefore take time to for the effects to be captured. Also, the small sample size of the data could make the estimates less precise, especially for some of the subgroups of students we considered. However, we checked to ensure that the estimates were consistent with the data by estimating the predicted values corresponding to the observed mean values for price, the key variable of interest, and the financial aid variables. The results, presented in table 19 above, show that the predictions of our model are consistent qualitatively with the observed data.

APPENDIX III:
CLASSIFICATION OF 1999-2000 ACADEMIC YEAR AND SCHOOLS ONLY ATTENDING THE 568 GROUP MEETINGS

We conducted tests to determine whether to use data collected in academic year 1999-2000 and whether schools that attended meetings of the 568 President's group but did not implement the consensus approach could be included in our analysis. First, the academic year 1999-2000 was very close to the establishment of the 568 President's Group, which occurred in 1998. The 1999-2000 academic year might have been a transitional period, and it would therefore not be appropriate to use the data as part of the period before the 568 Group implemented the consensus approach. Second, there were five schools, among the schools with data available for our econometric analysis, that either only attended the 568 Group meetings (Case Western Reserve University, Stanford University, and University of Southern California) or were members of the 568 Group but had not implemented the CA as of 2003 (Brown University and Dartmouth College). We therefore investigated which group—control or treatment—each of the five schools belonged.

Does Academic Year 1999-2000 belong to the Pre– or Post– Consensus Approach Implementation Period?

We used the data for sample 4 to investigate if data collected in 1999-2000 belonged in the pre-CA period (with data collected in 1995-1996). Although both samples 1 and 4 have data for 1995-1996 and 1999-2000, we chose sample 4 because it was the larger sample. See table 9 in appendix II for the list of the schools in each sample and the academic years for which data were available.

The tests were performed using the Chow test, which is of the form: [1] (1) $y = \beta 01 + \beta 11$ $x1 + \beta 21\ x2 + u$, $u \sim N(0,\sigma2)$, for group = 1995-1996 (g1), and (2) $y = \beta 02 + \beta 12\ x1 + \beta 22\ x2 + u$, $u \sim N(0,\sigma2)$ for group = 1999-2000 (g2).

Pooling the two groups of data we estimated, (3) $y = \beta 01 + \beta 11\ x1 + \beta 21\ x2 + (\beta 02 - \beta 01)g2 + (\beta 12 - \beta 11)g2x1 + (\beta 22 - \beta 21)g2x2 + u$, where g2 is an indicator variable.

The test examines the hypothesis that the added coefficients are jointly zero: $(\beta 02 - \beta 01) = (\beta 12 - \beta 11) = (\beta 22 - \beta 21) = 0$.

An insignificant test statistic (a small test statistic and a large p-value) suggests that the above equality holds, and there is no difference between the estimates for 1999-2000 and the group with which it is compared (1995-1996). On the other hand, a significant statistic (a large test statistic and a small p-value) suggests that the above equality does not hold and the 1999-2000 is different from the group with which it is compared (1995-1996).

We combined 1999-2000 with 1995-1996 and tested if the coefficients for 1999-2000 differed from that of 1995-1996, using sample 4. The tests were done for price, the key variable affecting student outcomes for schools. We performed a joint test that the added coefficients in equation 3 are jointly zero. The F-value is 1.71, and significant with a p-value of 0.0375. This implied that data collected in 1999-2000 did not belong to with the 1995-1996 data in the pre-CA period [2].

Similarly, we examined if 1999-2000 belonged to the post-CA period by combining 1999-2000 with 2003-2004, using sample 3. The F-value of the joint test is 8.36, and significant with a p-value of 0.0. This implied that 1999-2000 data did not belong to with the 2003-2004 data in the post-CA period.

These results suggest that it was more appropriate to exclude 1999-2000 from the analysis, implying that samples 1 and 2, which have data for the pre-CA period (1995-1996) and the post-CA period (2003-2004) would be more appropriate. However, because sample 2 was larger than sample 1, our subsequent analysis used sample 2.

Do the Schools That Only Attended the 568 group Meetings belong to the Control or Treatment Group?

We performed an analysis similar to that described above to determine whether schools that only attended meetings—Brown University, Case Western Reserve University, Dartmouth College, Stanford University, and University Southern California (USC)—belonged in the treatment or control group. We determined whether the behavior of each of these schools was more consistent with the control schools or the treatment schools after the consensus approach implementation, using data for 2003-2004. Since we had determined from the above analysis that samples 1 and 2 are more appropriate for our subsequent analysis, we focus on sample 2, the larger sample, for these tests [3].

To Which Group Did Brown Belong—Control or Treatment?

Similar to the analysis in section above, we included Brown in the control group and tested if the coefficients for Brown differed from the control group. We performed a joint test and obtained an F-value of 25.68, significant at 0.00. This implied that Brown did not belong to the control group. For the treatment group test, the F-value was 7.37, significant at 0.00. This also implied that Brown did not belong to the treatment group. Thus, Brown did not belong to either the control or treatment group.

To Which Group Did Stanford Belong—Control or Treatment?

The F-value for the control group test was 19.16, significant at 0.00, and the F-value for the treatment group test was 5.59, significant at 0.00. This implied that Stanford did not belong to either the control or treatment group.

To Which Group Did USC Belong—Control or Treatment?

We tested for which group USC belonged by excluding the SAT scores variable (SCORESAT) from the model since the data were not available for 2003-2004. The F-value for the control group test was 23.23, significant at 0.00, and the F-value for the treatment group test was 12.54, significant at 0.00. This implied that USC did not belong to either the control or treatment group.

Based on the above analysis, we determined that the best data for our analysis was sample 2, and we excluded all five schools that only attended the 568 Group meetings but did not implement the consensus approach.

APPENDIX V:
CONSULTANTS AND PEER REVIEWERS

Hashem Dezhbakhsh,
Ph.D. Professor of Economics Emory University

Dennis Epple, Ph.D.

Thomas Lord
Professor of Economics Graduate School of Industrial Administration Carnegie Mellon University

Janet Netz,
Ph.D. Founding Partner ApplEcon LLC

Richard Romano, .D.

Gerald L. Gunter
Professor of Economics Department of Economics Warrington College of Business University of Florida

Lawrence White, Ph.D.

Arthur E. Imperatore
Professor of Economics Department of Economics Leonard N. Stern School of Business New York University

Gordon C. Winston, Ph.D.
Orrin Sage Professor of Political Economy, Emeritus
Director of the Williams Project on the Economics of Higher Education Department of Economics Williams College

BIBLIOGRAPHY

Avery, C. and C. Hoxby."Do and Should Financial Aid Packages Affect Students' College Choices?" *National Bureau of Economic Research Working Paper,* No. 9482. 2003.

Bamberger, G., and D. Carlton."Antitrust and Higher Education: MIT Financial Aid (1993)." Case 11. *The Antitrust Revolution* (Third Edition: 1993).

Carlton, D., G. Bamberger, and R. Epstein. "Antitrust and Higher Education: Was There A Conspiracy to Restrict Financial Aid?" RAND *Journal of Economics*, vol. 26, no. 1 (Spring 1995): 131-147.

Epple, D., R. Romano, S. Sarpca, and H. Sieg. "Profiling in Bargaining Over College Tuitions," unpublished paper. January 21, 2005.

Hill, C., and G. Winston. "Access: Net prices, Affordability, and Equity At a Highly Selective College." unpublished paper. December 2001.

Hill, C., G. Winston, and S. Boyd. "Affordability: Family Incomes and Net Prices at Highly Selective Private Colleges and Universities." *The Journal of Human Resources*, vol. XL, no. 4 (2005): 769-790.

Hoxby, C. "Benevolent Colluders? The Effects of Antitrust Action on College Financial Aid and Tuition." *National Bureau of Economic Research Working Paper*, No. 7754. June 2000.

Kim, M. "Early Decision and Financial Aid Competition Among Need-Blind Colleges and Universities." unpublished paper. May 1, 2005.

Morrison, R. "Price Fixing Among Elite Colleges and Universities," *The University of Chicago Law Review*, vol. 59 (1992): 807-835.

Netz, J. "Non-Profits and Price-Fixing: The Case of the Ivy League." unpublished paper. November 1999.

Netz, J. "The End of Collusion?: Competition After Justice and the Ivy League Settle." unpublished paper. Fall 2000.

Salop, S., and L. White. "Antitrust Goes to College," *Journal of Economic Perspectives*, vol. 5, no. 3 (Summer 1991): 193-2002.

Shepherd, G. "Overlap and Antitrust: Fixing prices in a Smoke-Filled Classroom," *The Antitrust Bulletin*. Winter (1995): 859-884.

Winston, G., and C. Hill. "Access to the Most Selective Private Colleges by High-Ability, Low-Income Students: Are They Out There?" unpublished paper. October 2005.

REFERENCES

[1]   The schools sued were: Brown University, Columbia University, Cornell University, Dartmouth College, Harvard College, Massachusetts Institute of Technology, Princeton University, University of Pennsylvania, and Yale University.

[2]   *U.S. v. Brown*, 5 F.3d 658 (3rd Cir. 1993). The Department of Justice and MIT subsequently entered into a settlement agreement in which MIT agreed to certain "Standards of Conduct."

[3]   Pub. L. No. 103-325 (1992).

[4]   Pub. L. No. 103-382 (1994).

[5]   Pub. L. No. 107-72 (2001).
[6]   Some financial aid is awarded to students based on merit rather than financial need.
[7]   The College Board is a not-for-profit membership association composed of more than 5,000 schools, colleges, universities, and other educational organizations. In conjunction with financial aid professionals and economists, the College Board developed its own methodology to measure a family's ability to pay for college.
[8]   568 refers to the section in the Improving America's Schools Act of 1994 where the exemption is contained.
[9]   These schools were: California Institute of Technology, Case Western University, Harvard University, Stanford University, Syracuse University, and University of Southern California.
[10] Participation in the 568 Presidents' Group, however, does not prohibit members from awarding merit aid.
[11] All dollar amounts are in 2005 dollars. Data presented for schools using the exemption was collected from 26 of the 28 schools using the exemption.
[12] Other private 4-year schools include not-for-profit institutions and do not include for-profit institutions. This set of schools includes schools that do not have need-blind admission policies and therefore would not be able to participate in activities allowed under the exemption.
[13] Comparable schools include the seven schools selected as control schools for our econometric analysis.
[14] Variation was measured by the standard deviation of the EFCs.
[15] For a more detailed discussion of our analysis see appendix I.
[16] GAO's econometric analysis was focused on the mandate from Congress that requires us to examine the effects of the exemption. It is different from a market-specific analysis conducted in an antitrust investigation, and is not intended to address whether or not conduct may be taking place that might violate the antitrust laws in the absence of the exemption.
[17] The results were similar for need-based institutional grant aid.
[18] The discussed effects of the consensus approach are statistically significant (i.e., different from zero) at the 5 percent significance level or less.
[19] For a more detailed discussion on our econometric models and the limitations of our analysis see appendix II.

Appendix I

[1]   We used the KSMIRNOV command in *Stata* to perform the tests.
[2]   Student enrollment data was obtained through linear interpolation, and faculty data was based on 1998-1999 data.

Appendix II

[1]   This theory is consistent with the idea that non-profit organizations have an incentive to exercise market power despite not directly capturing profits, because the extra resources

from exercising market power allow them to invest in other areas they deem important; e.g., schools may charge high prices to students because it could enable them to offer higher salaries to attract high-caliber faculty.

[2] Where necessary, the data were supplemented by data from IPEDS.

[3] Schools were ranked annually based on various criteria (including selectivity, faculty and financial resources, graduation rate, and alumni satisfaction) in various publications—particularly in the USNWR, the Peterson's Four-Year Schools, and the Barron's Profiles of American Schools. The rankings of the schools by the different publishers were generally similar, but since the data were readily available in the USNWR we chose its rankings. Using the published rankings helped avoid a possible bias from arbitrarily picking the schools. Furthermore, these rankings were widely used and generally stable over time.

[4] Although the observers were not members they attended the group's meetings. The former members were Bowdoin College and Macalester College.

[5] Liberal arts schools emphasize undergraduate education and award at least half of their degrees in the liberal arts discipline, and most are private. National universities offer a wide range of undergraduate majors as well as master's and doctoral degrees, and many emphasize research.

[6] The number of schools in the two tiers for each type of school was between 50 and 90 for each year.

[7] We also used endowment data from NACUBO, and school-level data from GAO's survey of the schools.

[8] We used data for students who were enrolled as freshmen, as of October of the academic year, in the NPSAS database.

[9] Although the sample periods used by Hoxby (2000) and Netz (2000) are much earlier than what we used, our list of schools is reasonably consistent with theirs. Similarly, our list of schools was consistent with the schools in the Consortium for Financing Higher Education (COFHE), which are some of the most selective private schools in the U.S.

[10] See appendix III for details of the tests.

[11] We did not separate the effects of the CA into the effects of only attending the 568 Group meetings and the effects of only implementing the CA, although some schools only attended meetings and had not implemented the CA, because in table 9 there are only three schools in sample 2 that would serve as treatments or serve as controls if we investigate the effects of only attending meetings or the effects of only implementing the CA, respectively.

[12] In addition to having the control schools, we also controlled for a number of school characteristics that are discussed below. It is only the possibility of changes in differences between treatment and control schools that were not measurable or not observable that might lead to bias in estimating the effects of the consensus approach implementation. For example, schools adopting the consensus approach might differ in their objectives concerning their preferred student body. As discussed next in the text, the difference-indifference approach provided controls for such possibilities.

[13] All the dependent variables were from NPSAS, except tuition, which was from IPEDS. We used the general price level instead of the price index for higher education to adjust the monetary values because the former better reflected potential substitution effects

between college education and other expenditures by households. Furthermore, sector-specific price indexes generally tend to be more volatile.

[14] The tuition amount was the same for all freshmen in a private school.

[15] We also estimated an equation for institutional grant aid (*AIDINSTGRT*) and self-help aid (*AIDSELFPLUS*).

[16] We also estimated an equation for need-based institutional aid (*AIDNDINST)* and non-need-based grant aid (*AIDNONDTGRT*), which was the difference between total grant aid and need-based aid. However, we did not have enough data to estimate merit-only aid.

[17] We relied on several previous studies, including Avery and Hoxby (2003), Carlton et al. (1995), Bamberger and Carlton (1993), Epple et al. (2005), Hill et al. (2005), Hoxby (2000), Kim (2005), Netz (1999, 2000), Hill and Winston (2001), Morrison (1992), Salop and White (1991), Shepherd (1995), and Winston and Hill (2005).

[18] This variable was from the GAO survey of the CA and non-CA schools.

[19] [20]The CA schools are the 568 schools that have either implemented the consensus approach fully or in part by implementing some of the options under that need analysis methodology for financial aid. Of the seven CA schools in sample 2 in table 9, only three had not fully implemented the consensus approach (Georgetown, Vanderbilt, and Wake Forest).

[20] All the school-level variables are from IPEDS.

[21] The school specific fixed-effects were estimated using the fixed-effects estimator, where feasible. This effect captured differences among the schools that did not vary over time, such as location, memberships in athletic conferences and other organizations such as the former Overlap group. Also, several school-level variables could not be used in the models because the variables did not vary over time, and were therefore expected to be captured by the school specific fixed-effects.

[22] All the student-level variables were from NPSAS.

[23] We included Native Americans in *OTHER* because of their relatively small numbers.

[24] To avoid the dummy-variable trap in the estimation, we excluded white students from the racial groups, and high-income students from the income groups.

[25] The *EFC* is the federal calculation, which differs significantly from the *EFC* calculated by the CA schools, and to some extent from the *EFC* calculated by the non-CA schools. We found a negative relationship between the number of siblings and *EFC* using the limited data on siblings, although the link was not strong.

[26] The reported values are probability-weighted.

[27] The reported values are probability-weighted.

[28] The panel data were unbalanced because there were different observations on the freshmen for each school in each academic year. An important purpose in combining cross-sectional and time series data was to control for individual school-specific unobservable effects, which may be correlated with the covariates in the models. An advantage of using the fixed-effects estimator was that there was no need to assume that the unobserved school-specific effects were independent of the covariates. However, unlike the random-effects estimator, the fixed-effects estimator did not allow the inclusion of time-invariant variables, such as the former Overlap group and membership in sports associations, as covariates.

[29]   The weights are the probability weights from the number of students in the sample for each school, and the robust estimates of the standard errors are based on the Huber/White sandwich estimator. All estimates were obtained using *Stata*.

[30]   The same model specification is used to estimate the financial aid equations, and tuition equation, which excludes the student-level variables.

[31]   In the estimated equations, the interaction terms between *EMCA* and other variables have the suffixes "*;" for example *ENDOWSTU** is the interaction term between *ENDOWSTU* and *EMCA*.

[32]   This effect can be tested as a linear restriction if the joint test of significance of *EMCA* and the terms involving *EMCA* is significant.

[33]   White students are excluded from the race groups in the estimation to avoid the dummy trap.

[34]   The effects of these variables on tuition were expected to be similar to that of price. On the other hand, the effects of these school-level variables on the financial aid variables were expected to be opposite to that of price.

[35]   The statistical procedure we used is *AREG* in *Stata*.

[36]   The regression estimates for the financial aid variables excluded non financial-aid applicants, which reduced the number of observations but not the number of schools. Similar results were obtained for the price equation when the estimates were based on only financial-aid applicants. The regression estimates for tuition were obtained by excluding student-level variables because students at a school were charged the same tuition.

[37]   The $4,800 decrease is approximately equal to $250,000 x –(0.01935).

[38]   As discussed earlier, similar arguments can be obtained for the tuition and financial aid variables.

[39]   The model could not be estimated with school specific fixed-effects because they predict successes or failures perfectly.

[40]   In the estimated equations, the interaction terms between AY2003 and other variables have the suffixes "*;" for example INCLO* is the interaction term between INCLO and AY2003.

[41]   We could not use the panel data estimation technique for probit (*XTPROBIT*) because of lack of convergence. Similar results were obtained when the estimates were based on only students who applied for financial-aid.

[42]   Due to lack of sufficient data, we could not obtain separate estimates of the effects of attending meetings only or the effects of implementing the consensus approach only because it involved only two schools—Brown and Stanford. Also, we could not obtain separate estimates of the effects of implementing fully or partly the consensus approach because only three of the seven CA schools in sample 2 (Georgetown, Vanderbilt, and Wake Forest) had not fully implemented the CA.

[43]   All tests are performed using the 5 percent or lower level of significance.

[44]   The results were similar when we limited the data to only students who applied for financial aid.

[45]   The effect of the consensus approach implementation on lower-middle income was positive and significant at the 10 percent level. We performed several tests for the total effects of the consensus approach on prices. First, the effect was significant at the 5 percent level when data for only students who applied for financial aid were used.

Second, the total effect of the CA on prices was $3,488 and significant at the 5 percent level when ENROLUG and ENROLUG* were excluded from the model. Third, because prices are bounded at the lower end at zero and at the upper end at the cost of attendance, we also estimated the price equation using Tobit regressions. The total effect of the consensus approach on prices was negative and insignificant (at the 10 percent level). Unlike the fixed-effects estimates, the Tobit estimates were unweighted and the standard errors were not robust.

[46] The results are based on the seven CA and the seven non-CA schools in tables 11 and 12. Similar results were obtained when we included the schools that had no SAT scores in AY 2003-2004—three CA schools (Boston, MIT, and Pennsylvania) and two non-CA schools (Tufts and Yeshiva).

[47] The value of the effect of the CA on institutional grant aid was $1,331, but not significant.

[48] The effect of the CA on need-based institutional aid was generally similar to need-based total grant aid. The effect was about $6,020 and significant at the 5 percent level, with a confidence interval of between $512 and $11,528.

[49] The value of the effect of the CA on non-need-based grant aid was estimated to be about -$6,873, though not significant; the F-test of the joint significance of EMCA and its interactive terms had a p-value of 14 percent, and the test of the total effect of the CA had a p-value of 2.1 percent.

[50] The value of the effect of the CA implementation on self-help aid (loans, including PLUS, and work study) was $1,034, but not significant.

[51] The value of the total effect of the CA on total aid was estimated to be about $7,140, though not significant; the F-test of the joint significance of EMCA and its interactive rms had a p-value of 20 percent, and the test of the total effect of the CA had a p-value of 1.4 percent.

[52] The results for financial aid applicants are relative to non financial aid applicants, those for the income groups are relative to the high-income students, and those for the racial groups are relative to the white students.

[53] We tested for the equality of the proportions of CA schools and non-CA schools that were members of the former of the Overlap group. We used the 11 CA schools and the 14 non-CA schools in samples 1 through 4 in table 9. The CA schools had 5 Overlap members and the non-CA schools had 3 Overlap members.

[54] See Kim (2005).

Appendix III

[1] See http://www.stata.com/support/faqs/stat/chow3.html for details.

[2] As expected, the estimates from the pooling (equation 3) are the same as for the separate estimates (equations 1 and 2). Also the residual variances from equations 1 and 2 were similar, suggesting that the pooling was appropriate. This applies to all the other Chow tests we performed.

[3] The test was not performed for Case Western Reserve and Dartmouth because they are in samples 4 and 3, respectively. Samples 3 and 4 cannot be used because there are no data for 1995-1996 and 2003-2004, respectively.

INDEX

A

academic motivation, 106
academic performance, 105, 215, 234, 235
academic success, 100, 113, 115, 116, 292
academic tasks, 106, 107, 178
academics, 60, 62, 63, 68, 74, 75, 77, 78, 80, 81,
    130, 135, 137, 140, 143, 145, 150, 153, 154, 155,
    157, 158, 159, 164, 168, 169, 183, 186, 188
access, x, 2, 23, 24, 53, 62, 86, 89, 91, 129, 140, 155,
    159, 160, 173, 182, 227, 260, 266, 278, 294, 341,
    345, 356, 359
accommodation, 2
accountability, 10, 130, 150, 178, 186, 187
accounting, 200, 201, 218, 348
accuracy, 93, 96, 247, 251, 263
achievement, 101, 102, 103, 104, 108, 109, 110, 111,
    114, 115, 116, 121, 122, 123, 124, 125, 179, 238,
    239, 241, 242, 253, 261, 266, 272, 295, 350
acquisition of knowledge, 245
action research, 10, 61
activation, 103, 106, 111, 237
activity level, 203, 207
activity theory, 82
adaptation, 1, 5, 33, 106
administrators, 1, 7, 176, 181, 182, 185, 269, 297,
    304, 305
adolescents, 124
adult education, 73
affective dimension, 23
affective reactions, 114
Africa, 157
African American(s), 270, 274, 279, 282, 288, 289,
    303
age, 1, 42, 45, 47, 54, 92, 158, 159, 160, 182, 210,
    218, 223, 264, 302
agent, 59, 75, 103, 168
aging, 1, 143

aging population, 1
agriculture, 41, 43, 238
AIDS, 309
Alaska, 274, 289, 306, 338
Alaskan Native, 279
alertness, 243
alternative, x, 7, 141, 161, 166, 167, 174, 181, 200,
    221, 246, 345, 349
ambiguity, 181
American Educational Research Association, 81, 83
American Indian(s), 274, 279, 289, 338
American Psychological Association, 125
analytical framework, 58
annotation, viii, 85, 86, 88, 92, 94, 97
ANOVA, 219
antitrust, 341, 342, 344, 346, 347, 351, 355, 360, 387
anxiety, 21, 26, 106, 109, 111, 112, 113, 121, 123,
    125
appendix, 269, 272, 275, 281, 282, 283, 284, 288,
    289, 298, 301, 344, 355, 359, 383, 387, 388
applied research, 11, 174, 181, 183
aptitude, 100, 367
argument, 69, 176, 186, 196, 197, 258
Aristotle, 243
arithmetic, 46, 47
articulation, 109, 139, 185, 190
aspiration, 264
assault, 177
assessment, 2, 10, 11, 12, 14, 16, 18, 19, 20, 21, 22,
    23, 24, 25, 26, 27, 29, 30, 31, 86, 92, 96, 120,
    141, 155, 178, 186, 218, 222, 239, 247, 257, 291,
    301, 348
assets, 343, 348, 350, 353
assignment, viii, 25, 85, 86, 90, 91, 94, 111, 154,
    198, 201, 206, 218
assimilation, 241, 252, 253, 262, 263
assistive technology, 2, 3
assumptions, 44, 179, 259
asynchronous communication, 196, 211

attachment, 299

attention, x, 7, 10, 19, 21, 51, 107, 110, 118, 120, 173, 174, 183, 184, 187, 228, 244, 252, 258, 264, 292

attitudes, 27, 100, 106, 206, 208, 237, 239, 241, 249, 254, 255, 256, 260, 261, 262, 263, 264, 265, 266

Attorney General, 344, 355

attribution, 114, 265

auditing, 270, 299

Australia, 101, 120, 128, 144, 145, 149, 157, 158, 160, 171, 174, 293

Austria, 265

authenticity, 62, 83

authority, x, 151, 152, 157, 163, 167, 168, 174, 187, 246, 256

autonomy, 6, 59, 82, 157, 176, 178, 188

availability, 25, 134, 140, 177, 355, 360

averaging, 33, 371

avoidance, 107, 108, 121, 123

awareness, 68, 75, 88, 95, 102, 106, 115, 165, 246

B

bachelor's degree, 51, 268, 272, 276, 283, 289, 337

background information, 197, 200, 202

banks, 151, 155

barriers, 129, 141, 180, 184, 190

BEA, 53

behavior, ix, 99, 100, 102, 103, 104, 111, 152, 187, 188, 238, 242, 243, 246, 254, 260, 261, 262, 384

behavioral disorders, 13

behavioral sciences, 242

beliefs, 14, 18, 21, 22, 24, 25, 34, 75, 102, 103, 104, 105, 106, 110, 111, 112, 114, 121, 122, 123, 124, 125, 154, 215, 216, 234

benchmarking, 182

benchmarks, 188

beneficial effect, 221

benign, 80

beverages, 155

bias, 33, 45, 357, 365, 381, 388

biotechnology, 274

blind spot, 83

blogs, 30

blood, 240, 252, 261, 262

border security, 268

bounds, 174, 301, 322, 357

boys, 292

brain, 2

brand image, 162

breakdown, 62

Britain, 146, 176

broadband, 239

budding, 78

bureaucracy, ix, 7, 149, 150, 151, 152, 153, 158, 163, 169

bureaucratization, 153, 154

business management, 152

C

calculus, 291

caliber, 388

Canada, 57, 58, 62, 81, 174, 182, 293

candidates, 10, 140, 144

capitalism, 130, 146, 153, 185

career development, 63

case study, ix, 12, 146, 149, 157, 165, 233

cast, 4

catalyst, 52

categorization, 272, 301

category a, 132

category d, 115

causal attribution, 106, 113, 114

causality, 258

CCR, 310

Census, 42, 43, 55, 56, 272, 302, 305

certificate, 281, 318, 322, 346, 347

certification, 272, 291

chain of command, 163

changing environment, 157

channels, 151

charities, 143

children, 124, 238, 248, 265, 272, 291, 298

China, 184, 186, 293

chunking, 19, 26

citizenship, 278, 298

classes, 16, 29, 105, 124, 154, 156, 160, 291, 294

classification, 181, 203, 241, 264, 302, 303

classroom(s), vii, 9, 12, 16, 25, 26, 30, 31, 33, 34, 82, 85, 86, 97, 101, 119, 120, 121, 122, 123, 124, 125, 209, 210, 237, 240, 243, 244, 246, 248, 249, 250, 251, 252, 255, 256, 257, 260, 262, 264, 266, 291, 292, 294

classroom management, 31

classroom practice, 210

classroom settings, 210

clients, 14, 179, 186, 217, 218

closure, 134

coaches, 19, 87

codes, 224, 302, 303

coding, 30, 33, 62, 65, 91, 224, 257

coefficient of variation, 356, 357, 358

coercion, 197

cognition, 102, 103, 104, 111, 121, 123

cognitive abilities, 265

cognitive activity, 216
cognitive function, 104
cognitive level, 30, 226, 250
cognitive models, 104
cognitive perspective, 104, 125
cognitive process, 100, 101, 102, 103, 119, 219
cognitive processing, 219
cognitive psychology, 103
cognitive style, 103
coherence, 20, 21, 22, 23, 24, 64, 65, 188
cohort, 24, 25, 30, 128, 221
collaboration, x, 6, 143, 179, 195, 196, 197, 198, 199, 201, 203, 204, 205, 206, 207, 208, 209, 211, 212, 223, 229, 271, 298, 341, 355, 356, 359
College Entrance Examination, 97
college students, 121, 123, 125, 234, 278, 291, 292
colleges, 54, 130, 146, 153, 158, 177, 184, 186, 269, 272, 274, 294, 295, 297, 299, 304, 305, 306, 337, 341, 344, 346, 357, 359, 382, 387
combined effect, 190, 234
commerce, 134, 140
commodity, 129, 161
communication, 17, 30, 85, 100, 120, 184, 189, 196, 197, 199, 202, 204, 206, 209, 217, 220
communication skills, 217
communication strategies, 184
community, 58, 60, 61, 62, 63, 64, 65, 66, 67, 68, 69, 70, 71, 72, 73, 74, 75, 76, 78, 79, 86, 87, 175, 180, 182, 193, 210, 295
comparative research, 179
compensation, 7
competence, 100, 105, 106, 107, 108, 109, 111, 112, 121, 123, 124, 217, 222, 223, 225, 226, 227, 229, 231, 259
competition, 128, 131, 150, 161, 163, 168, 179, 245, 293, 341, 345, 359
competitive advantage, 161, 267, 268, 296
complement, 228
complexity, 22, 23, 58, 72, 88, 169, 171, 187, 189, 210, 263
compliance, 76, 187, 338, 346, 347
components, ix, 14, 15, 18, 22, 24, 99, 101, 103, 104, 105, 106, 110, 118, 123, 211, 235, 240, 246, 254
composition, 200, 348, 369
compounds, 72
comprehension, viii, ix, 99, 101, 107, 117, 187, 258, 260
computer labs, 2
computer technology, 249, 274
computers, 2, 3, 155, 239, 240, 241, 249, 254, 255, 256, 257, 263, 264, 265, 291, 292
computing, 13
concentrates, 128, 140, 197, 262

concentration, 136, 143, 153
conception, 78, 103, 104, 150, 152, 155, 158, 161, 163, 166, 168, 180
conceptual model, 184
conceptualization, 105, 116, 186, 242
concrete, 78, 80, 115, 228, 231
concretion, 119
conditioning, 180
confidence, 221, 259, 269, 281, 282, 283, 288, 289, 301, 303, 305, 318, 319, 320, 322, 323, 324, 325, 326, 327, 354, 357, 377, 378, 391
confidence interval, 269, 281, 282, 283, 288, 289, 301, 303, 305, 318, 320, 322, 323, 324, 325, 326, 327, 354, 357, 377, 378, 391
configuration, 114, 177, 185
conflict, 79, 197, 208, 230
confusion, 21, 27, 69
Congress, iv, 268, 299, 341, 345, 355, 356, 387
consciousness, 162
consensus, 38, 51, 166, 342, 343, 346, 347, 348, 349, 350, 353, 354, 355, 359, 360, 362, 363, 364, 365, 369, 371, 372, 374, 376, 377, 378, 379, 381, 382, 383, 384, 385, 387, 388, 389, 390
consent, 63
consolidation, 238, 254
Constitution, 72
constraints, 145, 156, 184, 188, 197, 248
construction, viii, 43, 45, 57, 58, 62, 75, 79, 83, 101, 116, 117, 182, 196, 210, 225, 238
constructivist learning, 212
consultants, 183
consulting, x, 173, 180, 229, 344
consumer price index, 364
consumers, 39, 129, 155
consumption, 155, 156, 161
content analysis, 221, 257, 258, 259, 264, 265, 266
contingency, 17
continuity, 62, 152
control, 6, 46, 87, 88, 89, 94, 95, 96, 102, 103, 106, 107, 108, 111, 112, 113, 114, 118, 120, 154, 155, 166, 169, 177, 178, 181, 188, 216, 237, 243, 245, 247, 251, 258, 304, 351, 353, 355, 359, 360, 361, 362, 363, 366, 367, 381, 383, 384, 385, 387, 388, 389
control group, 355, 360, 363, 384, 385
convergence, 5, 6, 40, 41, 43, 44, 50, 192, 390
conversion, 134
cooking, 155
corporations, 155
correlation(s), 215, 224, 225, 227, 249, 257, 258, 259, 260
costs, 38, 39, 41, 51, 52, 53, 128, 137, 150, 152, 155, 161, 270, 279, 292, 341, 342, 343, 350, 359, 373

costs of compliance, 150
counsel, 167
counseling, 265
course content, 16, 228
course design, 17, 25, 32
course work, 92
Court of Appeals, 344
coverage, 129
covering, 223
creative potential, 7
creativity, 140, 242, 248, 249
creativity tests, 248
credentials, 291
credibility, 175
credit, 155, 222, 224
criticism, 135
crystallization, 263
cues, 95
culture, 6, 7, 30, 62, 63, 70, 71, 129, 145, 157, 159,
    206, 227, 228, 305
curiosity, 243, 248
curriculum, 2, 10, 11, 24, 61, 75, 78, 80, 116, 155,
    156, 159, 246, 247, 248, 255, 260, 264, 291, 294
customers, 155, 156, 183
cycles, 12, 31, 115, 125
Czech Republic, 185

D

danger, 33, 183
data analysis, vii, 9, 18, 32, 35, 141, 150, 160, 203,
    226
data availability, 365
data collection, 10, 18, 32, 218, 258
data set, 49, 64, 67, 301
database, 89, 175, 248, 249, 274, 300, 360, 388
death, 169
debt, 53, 74, 348, 350
decision makers, 189
decision making, 179, 184, 250, 252, 253, 254, 256,
    261, 262, 263, 265
decision-making process, 176, 180, 188, 207
decisions, ix, 6, 10, 12, 16, 17, 18, 19, 20, 22, 23, 24,
    25, 28, 29, 30, 32, 33, 34, 38, 40, 61, 72, 81, 99,
    102, 152, 153, 163, 165, 166, 167, 168, 188, 199,
    201, 207, 247, 250, 252, 253, 256, 259, 262, 263,
    267, 268, 269, 271, 289, 290, 291, 292, 293, 296,
    297, 299, 304, 306, 344, 361, 366, 373
defense, 73
defensive strategies, 113
deficiency, 26
deficit, 104

definition, 35, 45, 161, 169, 175, 197, 200, 201, 216,
    241, 242, 247, 248, 250, 251, 258, 262, 263
delivery, 2, 11, 12, 16, 17, 25, 27, 28, 33, 89, 128,
    129, 155, 168, 180, 184, 252
demand, 5, 6, 128, 134, 143, 144, 146, 153, 156,
    179, 189, 223, 247
democracy, 245
demographic characteristics, 301
demographics, 186
Department of Agriculture, 270, 275, 306
Department of Commerce, 55, 56, 271, 275, 307,
    329
Department of Defense, 269, 300
Department of Energy, 275, 307
Department of Health and Human Services, 271,
    275, 296, 297, 308, 331
Department of Homeland Security, 268, 273, 275,
    294, 310, 337, 338
Department of Justice, 341, 344, 356, 386
Department of the Interior, 275, 310
dependent variable, viii, 37, 41, 44, 45, 48, 49, 219,
    364, 365, 371, 373, 388
depression, 77
deregulation, 129
designers, 27, 31, 34, 228
desire(s), viii, 76, 85, 127, 154, 271, 293, 347
developed countries, vii, 41, 135, 162
development policy, 185
developmental process, 59
deviation, 225, 356
devolution, 38, 137
dieting, 155
differentiation, 40, 41, 108, 156
diminishing returns, 41
disability, 1, 2
disadvantaged students, 359, 360, 365, 373
discipline, viii, 40, 57, 58, 60, 61, 62, 63, 65, 66, 67,
    68, 71, 74, 77, 78, 80, 82, 115, 138, 140, 144,
    159, 174, 183, 190, 216, 247, 388
discourse, 7, 78, 87, 96, 105, 129, 138, 211
dispersion, 187
dissatisfaction, 136, 181
distance education, 266
distance learning, 196, 210, 241, 256, 257, 258, 260,
    261, 262, 263, 265, 266
distribution, 39, 202, 206, 221, 228, 291, 358
distribution function, 358
divergence, 250
diversification, x, 173
diversity, x, 3, 65, 150, 173, 246, 258, 269, 304
division, 76, 116, 240, 262
doctors, 134, 303
domain-specificity, 234

downsizing, 155
draft, 15, 17, 18, 19, 21, 23, 25, 26, 27, 30, 63, 73,
    87, 92, 93, 151, 271, 278, 279, 296, 297, 298,
    344, 355
dualism, 223, 229
due process, 167
duplication, 298
duration, 115
duties, 151
dynamic systems, 11

E

earnings, 40, 55
ears, 124
earth, 291
East Asia, 311
Eastern Europe, 176
econometric analysis, 342, 344, 351, 353, 354, 355,
    370, 383, 387
economic activity, viii, 37, 38, 41, 42, 44, 45, 47, 48,
    50
economic change, 185
economic development, 54, 135, 146, 175, 176, 182
economic growth, vii, 37, 39, 40, 41, 43, 44, 45, 50,
    51, 54, 55
economic growth model, 45
economic resources, 159
economic status, 249
economic theory, 40, 44
economics, 40, 50, 51, 52, 53, 54, 55, 56, 174, 238,
    242, 252, 262, 337
economies of scale, 178
ecosystem, 131
educational attainment, 39, 56, 303
educational objective, 11
educational policies, 5
educational policy, 130
educational programs, 267, 268, 270, 274, 299
educational psychology, 13, 21, 25, 122
educational quality, 278
educational research, 62, 174, 176, 258
educational services, 155
educational settings, 12, 196
educational system, 5
educators, 1, 26, 92, 115, 116, 117, 267, 268, 269,
    277, 297, 299
efficiency criteria, 54
ego, 105, 107, 123
elaboration, 212, 228
elementary school, 124, 264, 265
email, 10, 14, 16, 17, 18, 19, 25, 26, 28, 30
emergence, x, 129, 169, 174, 176, 178, 187, 189

emerging issues, 62
emotion(s), 77, 79, 106, 111, 114, 124, 211
emotional reactions, 106, 113
emotional state, 111
emotional well-being, 107, 111, 112
employability, 139, 140
employees, 1, 7, 143, 155, 161, 169, 267, 268, 269,
    270, 280, 281, 287, 288, 289, 296, 297, 299, 300,
    302, 327
employment, 82, 134, 135, 141, 143, 269, 270, 274,
    281, 289, 296, 302
EMU, 187
encouragement, 166, 292
enculturation, 161
endogeneity, 45
energy, 46
engagement, 2, 60, 102, 107, 108, 110, 111, 113,
    123, 175, 203, 257, 356
England, 137, 139, 144, 146, 157
English Language, 128
enrollment, 26, 41, 56, 271, 273, 281, 283, 298, 301,
    304, 341, 342, 343, 354, 359, 360, 361, 363, 364,
    365, 366, 373, 374, 375, 376, 377, 378, 379, 381,
    382, 387
enthusiasm, 290
entrepreneurs, 164, 166
entrepreneurship, 157, 164
environment, ix, x, 1, 2, 61, 63, 82, 103, 104, 127,
    137, 140, 160, 168, 174, 186, 189, 199, 200, 201,
    202, 203, 208, 211, 238, 243, 244, 245, 248, 249,
    258, 260, 262, 264, 265, 266, 305
Environmental Protection Agency, 268, 271, 275,
    296, 297, 300, 308
EPA, 268, 308
epistemology, 122
equality, 177, 178, 358, 383, 391
equity, 39, 343, 345, 348, 350, 353
erosion, 187
ESL, 19
EST, 160
estimating, 43, 47, 377, 382, 388
ethical standards, 79
ethics, 83
ethnic background, 52
ethnic groups, 52, 272, 279, 288
ethnicity, 1, 274, 289, 305
EU, x, 132, 174, 187, 188, 189, 190
Europe, x, 101, 173, 174, 175, 176, 177, 178, 182,
    189, 190, 192, 193
European Commission, x, 173, 187
European Court of Justice, 187
European integration, 187, 192
European Monetary Union, 187

European Social Fund, 217
European Union, 5, 129, 187, 188, 189, 190, 192
evolution, vii, 5, 9, 11, 12, 28, 101, 109, 245
examinations, 153, 248
exclusion, 38, 381
excuse, 113
executive function(s), 188
exercise, 79, 120, 151, 188, 203, 204, 206, 207, 208,
    209, 348, 365, 372, 387
expenditures, 55, 365, 389
expertise, 152, 153, 175, 178, 182, 187, 198, 215,
    218, 219, 224, 229, 233
exposure, 142, 291
external benefits, vii, 37, 38, 39, 41, 50, 51, 52
external environment, 62
external influences, 244
externalities, 51
extraction, 46
extrinsic motivation, 112
eyes, 65

F

facilitators, ix, 149, 167, 169
failure, 104, 113, 114, 124, 177, 211, 240, 249, 260,
    262, 265
family, 61, 198, 227, 238, 243, 246, 302, 341, 342,
    343, 345, 348, 353, 356, 364, 367
fast food, 154, 155, 162
fatigue, 140
fear, 6, 106, 111, 249
federal funds, 296
federal government, 131, 267, 268, 272, 295
feedback, viii, 2, 14, 17, 23, 27, 29, 30, 34, 73, 85,
    86, 87, 88, 89, 91, 92, 93, 94, 95, 96, 97, 103,
    117, 118, 119, 189, 204, 205, 209, 257, 258, 260
feelings, 74, 80, 113, 239, 244, 260
females, 131
finance, vii, 37, 38, 43, 53, 54, 55
financial crisis, 178
financial markets, 365
financial resources, 154, 296, 297, 345, 388
financial support, 277, 295
financing, vii, 6, 37, 38, 53, 55, 56, 130, 184
Finland, 157, 182, 195, 209, 211, 215, 218
firms, 151, 157, 158
fish, 210
flexibility, 1, 157, 197, 248, 249
floating, 187
flooding, 256
focus groups, 61, 62, 67, 71, 76, 304
focusing, viii, 33, 57, 58, 94, 105, 177, 180, 184, 305
food, 162, 243

foreign language, 337
fortitude, 166
France, 54
freedom, 76, 151, 153, 199, 201, 246, 259
friction, 152
frustration, 74, 76, 77, 113, 118
fulfillment, 151, 188
funding, 3, 7, 38, 57, 58, 59, 71, 72, 74, 130, 135,
    137, 138, 139, 143, 144, 150, 155, 156, 157, 158,
    161, 162, 178, 275, 276, 279, 295, 299, 306, 307,
    308, 309, 310, 311, 312, 338, 347, 365
fundraising, 157
funds, 6, 7, 135, 138, 158, 162, 275, 276, 295, 373
futures, 67

G

gender, 131, 133, 145, 284, 305, 318
gender balance, 131
gene, 11
generalization, 117, 119
generation, 11, 142
genre, 97
geography, 337
geology, 291
Georgia, 174, 269, 304, 306
Germany, 154, 171, 176, 178
germination, 243
gestures, 260
gifted, 264
giftedness, 125
girls, 291, 292
global competition, 128, 143, 145, 293
global markets, 161
global village, 83
globalization, iv, x, 144, 161, 174, 185, 186
goal setting, 206, 216
goals, x, 22, 23, 25, 27, 34, 61, 62, 77, 87, 89, 101,
    102, 103, 104, 105, 106, 107, 108, 109, 110, 113,
    118, 121, 122, 123, 124, 161, 168, 169, 173, 179,
    180, 196, 206, 207, 220, 231, 238, 239, 240, 246,
    247, 250, 251, 252, 253, 259, 260, 261, 262, 263,
    270, 272, 275, 277, 279, 292, 299, 338
governance, 5, 159, 185, 187, 188, 189, 191, 192,
    361
government, vii, 6, 37, 38, 40, 43, 128, 130, 131,
    135, 136, 137, 139, 140, 143, 155, 156, 157, 158,
    160, 161, 162, 164, 175, 176, 178, 181, 182, 184,
    185, 186, 187, 188, 270, 279, 295, 299, 337, 365
Government Accountability Office, vi, 267, 341
government policy, 6
grades, 247, 260, 289, 290, 295, 305
grading, 86, 218, 248

graduate education, 295, 298
graduate students, 17, 61, 71, 72, 277, 280, 306, 337
grains, 243
grants, 41, 51, 344, 348, 353, 354, 364
grassroots, 72
Greece, 212
greed, 344
grids, 198, 200
group activities, 19, 196
group membership, 21, 23, 24
group processes, 204
grouping, 23, 197
groups, xi, 19, 22, 23, 24, 27, 29, 67, 87, 101, 115, 143, 156, 157, 160, 164, 169, 180, 195, 196, 197, 200, 201, 203, 204, 206, 207, 208, 209, 210, 217, 219, 222, 227, 249, 254, 264, 270, 271, 275, 277, 278, 295, 298, 303, 353, 355, 357, 358, 359, 365, 366, 367, 369, 371, 373, 374, 379, 381, 383, 389, 390, 391
growth, vii, viii, 7, 11, 37, 38, 39, 40, 41, 42, 43, 44, 45, 46, 48, 49, 50, 51, 52, 71, 88, 128, 130, 131, 133, 134, 141, 142, 143, 169, 175, 177, 186, 223, 245, 262, 277, 283, 337, 366, 369, 373, 374
growth rate, 39, 366
growth theory, 41
guidance, 18, 197, 198, 209, 211, 293
guidelines, vii, 3, 9, 14, 31, 32, 95, 137, 139, 142, 188, 199, 201, 248, 304, 328, 347
guilt, 112

H

hands, 153, 246, 295
happiness, 113
Hawaii, 170, 307
HE, ix, 127, 128, 129, 130, 131, 135, 137, 138, 141, 143
health, 13, 25, 155, 272, 303
health care, 155, 303
health insurance, 303
hegemony, 182
heroism, 152
heterogeneity, 161
heteroskedasticity, 44, 48, 49, 50, 56
high school, 10, 13, 24, 40, 42, 45, 47, 52, 53, 125, 237, 249, 266, 271, 289, 291, 294
high scores, 249
higher education, iv, vii, viii, ix, x, 9, 37, 38, 39, 40, 42, 45, 47, 49, 50, 51, 52, 53, 54, 55, 56, 78, 81, 82, 83, 88, 99, 101, 103, 124, 127, 130, 139, 144, 145, 146, 147, 149, 156, 158, 160, 162, 173, 174, 175, 176, 177, 178, 179, 180, 181, 182, 183, 184, 185, 186, 188, 189, 190, 191, 193, 195, 196, 198, 201, 203, 209, 211, 212, 215, 233, 234, 268, 277, 305, 341, 360, 373, 376, 388
higher quality, 96, 373
hip, 389
hiring, 135, 144, 168
Hispanics, 52
HM Treasury, 146
homogeneity, 161
hospitals, 205
House, 264, 266
household income, 360, 366
households, 302, 389
human capital, 40, 41, 42, 44, 45, 47, 49, 50, 51, 55
human capital theory, 40, 44, 50
human nature, 167
human resource development, 217, 223, 233
hybrid, 174
hypothesis, 41, 249, 257, 383

I

identification, 19, 22, 23, 24, 26, 27, 60, 221, 226, 227
identity, viii, 36, 57, 58, 59, 60, 61, 64, 65, 66, 74, 75, 77, 78, 79, 80, 81, 82, 83, 150
ideology, 128
images, 3
imagination, 35
Immanuel Kant, 246
immigrants, 338
impairments, 1
implementation, vii, x, 9, 12, 16, 17, 18, 20, 25, 26, 28, 31, 32, 33, 34, 100, 114, 173, 174, 178, 180, 188, 189, 193, 198, 237, 253, 255, 268, 342, 343, 344, 346, 353, 355, 359, 360, 362, 363, 364, 365, 369, 371, 372, 373, 374, 377, 378, 379, 381, 382, 384, 388, 390, 391
incentives, 145, 295
incidence, 12, 115
inclusion, 3, 45, 46, 116, 192, 365, 389
income, 38, 40, 51, 52, 53, 129, 156, 157, 164, 295, 302, 342, 343, 348, 350, 353, 354, 355, 356, 366, 367, 369, 371, 372, 373, 374, 377, 379, 380, 389, 390, 391
income tax, 302
increased workload, 135
independence, 6, 347
independent variable, viii, 37, 42, 44, 45, 46, 48, 49
indexing, 304
India, 134, 293
Indians, 308
indicators, 100, 145, 188, 225
individual action, 206

individual differences, 121
individual students, 38, 40, 41, 51, 218
individualism, 179
individuality, 151
individualization, 182
induction, 71
industrial sectors, viii, 37, 38, 41, 42, 43, 46, 49
industry, vii, 41, 43, 53, 55, 135, 138, 140, 143, 146, 147, 156, 159, 160, 162, 223, 279, 302
inefficiency, 54
inequality, 131
inequity, 54
inertia, 156, 158
infancy, 175
inferiority, 259
inflation, 42, 289, 364
information processing, 101, 102, 103, 104, 257
information sharing, 204, 205, 209, 293
information technology, 1, 218, 219, 288
infrastructure, 41, 150, 278
initial state, viii, 37, 42
innovation, 32, 188, 255, 256, 267, 268
input, 41, 58, 88, 141, 261, 361
insight, 30, 62, 63, 75, 95, 198
inspectors, 183
inspiration, viii, 85, 86, 179, 224
instability, 175
institutional change, 6
institutional reforms, 177
institutions, 1, 3, 12, 13, 38, 40, 41, 51, 77, 129, 135, 136, 137, 139, 143, 144, 146, 153, 158, 176, 177, 178, 179, 181, 182, 184, 185, 186, 188, 189, 268, 269, 270, 276, 277, 295, 301, 304, 305, 337, 338, 341, 342, 345, 347, 350, 352, 360, 361, 387
instruction, vii, 1, 2, 9, 10, 12, 18, 23, 30, 32, 35, 105, 116, 117, 118, 119, 121, 122, 153, 197, 209, 211, 216, 228, 233, 245, 248, 250, 255, 265, 289, 295
instructional activities, 255
instructional design, 11, 13, 14, 16, 17, 21, 25, 29, 35, 198, 210
instructional materials, 18, 23
instructional methods, 119
instructors, viii, 2, 10, 12, 13, 17, 21, 30, 33, 85, 86, 87, 88, 90, 92, 96, 97, 153, 260
instruments, 179, 187, 188, 189, 190, 192, 238, 249, 257, 266
insurance, 43
integration, 105, 192, 228, 232, 237, 239, 240, 241, 248, 252, 256, 257, 259, 261, 262, 263, 293
integrity, 88
intellectual property, 157
intelligence, 104, 215, 250, 264

intensity, 105, 241
intentionality, 79
intentions, 60, 61, 74, 75, 76, 87, 101, 109, 111
interaction(s), 2, 59, 60, 63, 65, 66, 75, 76, 80, 101, 104, 116, 118, 122, 188, 189, 196, 197, 198, 207, 209, 210, 212, 220, 243, 244, 245, 251, 252, 257, 258, 259, 260, 262, 265, 266, 293, 365, 371, 374, 375, 376, 390
interaction effect, 220
interactivity, 265, 266
interface, 30, 88, 89, 197
internal consistency, 11
internal influences, 244
international standards, 3
international students, 26, 28, 158, 268, 269, 270, 271, 272, 274, 280, 282, 283, 287, 293, 296, 297, 298, 304
internationalization, 186
internet, 239
internship, 68
interpersonal communication, 210, 246
interpersonal interactions, 60
interpretation, viii, 33, 82, 99, 101, 180, 182, 212, 243, 244, 260
interrelations, 59, 153
interval, 218, 288, 301, 303, 322, 327, 377
intervention, 11, 26, 32, 33, 34, 86, 105, 114, 118, 120, 121, 244
intervention strategies, 86
interview, 202, 219, 220, 223, 224
intrinsic motivation, 104, 112, 219
intrinsic value, 110
investment, vii, viii, 37, 38, 39, 40, 42, 45, 47, 49, 50, 51, 52, 53, 54, 55, 165, 240, 261, 264
investors, 41, 161
iron, 154, 167
isolation, 6, 74, 80, 293
Israel, 237
Italy, 160
iteration, 33

J

Japan, 182
job insecurity, 130
jobs, 131, 293
judges, 238
judgment, 51, 166, 247, 262, 344, 348, 349
judiciary, 151
junior high school, 278
justification, x, 39, 173, 174

K

key indicators, 163
Keynes, 145
kindergarten, 271, 272, 278, 289, 290, 294, 295, 305
knowledge acquisition, 244
knowledge construction, 196, 204, 206, 209, 213, 223, 225, 229
knowledge economy, 135, 145
knowledge transfer, 157

L

labeling, 22
labor, 39, 40, 42, 45, 46, 56, 174, 178, 179, 181, 229, 268, 272, 288
labor force, 39, 40, 42, 45, 46, 56, 268, 272, 288
labour, 76, 145
labour market, 145
land, 13, 25
language, 3, 13, 14, 22, 26, 60, 85, 86, 112, 177, 202, 241, 272, 337
language acquisition, 26
Latin America, 157
laws, 151, 153, 187, 188, 245, 341, 344, 355, 387
LEA, 211
leadership, ix, 53, 54, 130, 141, 144, 145, 149, 150, 158, 160, 161, 165, 166, 167, 168, 169, 171, 174, 175, 182, 188, 279, 295
leadership style, ix, 149, 158, 160, 161, 166, 167, 168, 169
learners, ix, 2, 16, 21, 22, 25, 99, 102, 105, 106, 113, 122, 123, 125, 196, 207, 209, 210
learning, vii, viii, ix, x, 1, 2, 3, 6, 9, 10, 11, 12, 13, 14, 16, 18, 20, 21, 22, 23, 24, 25, 26, 28, 29, 31, 32, 34, 35, 36, 53, 58, 61, 69, 75, 78, 80, 81, 82, 83, 86, 88, 92, 97, 99, 100, 101, 102, 103, 104, 105, 106, 107, 108, 109, 110, 113, 114, 115, 116, 117, 118, 119, 120, 121, 122, 123, 124, 125, 129, 135, 153, 156, 173, 176, 186, 195, 196, 197, 198, 199, 200, 201, 203, 204, 205, 208, 209, 210, 211, 212, 213, 215, 216, 217, 218, 219, 220, 221, 222, 223, 224, 225, 226, 227, 228, 229, 230, 231, 232, 233, 234, 235, 237, 238, 239, 240, 241, 242, 243, 244, 245, 246, 247, 248, 249, 250, 251, 252, 256, 257, 258, 259, 260, 261, 262, 263, 264, 265, 266, 270
learning activity, 14, 103, 108, 219
learning disabilities, 121, 124
learning efficiency, 186

learning environment, x, 3, 195, 196, 198, 203, 209, 211, 212, 217, 222, 243, 244, 246, 247, 258, 260, 264
learning outcomes, 10, 197, 217, 220, 223, 224, 226, 227, 230, 231, 257, 258, 266
learning process, ix, x, 99, 100, 102, 103, 106, 118, 120, 195, 196, 209, 216, 237, 239, 240, 241, 242, 243, 244, 245, 247, 249, 251, 252, 257, 259, 261, 262
learning skills, 121, 122
learning styles, 1, 121
learning task, 14, 16, 18, 21, 22, 24, 28, 29, 105, 109, 115, 198, 212, 246, 257
legality, 152
legislation, 1, 184
leisure, 155
lens, 78, 79, 80
liberal education, 130
lifetime, 40
likelihood, 342, 343, 353, 354, 373, 374, 376, 378, 379, 381
limitation, 26, 44, 45, 68, 76, 161, 305
links, 12, 17, 20, 23, 24, 128, 159, 168, 175, 176, 257
literacy, 27, 45, 121, 123
literacy rates, 45
litigation, 341
livestock, 243
loans, 38, 53, 130, 145, 344, 348, 353, 354, 364, 365, 381, 391
local authorities, 187
local community, 65
local government, 157
location, 70, 177, 257, 356, 389
locus, 113, 167
love, 153
lower prices, 379

M

major cities, 237
Malaysia, 160
management, x, 5, 7, 12, 32, 34, 35, 86, 89, 97, 128, 130, 131, 138, 140, 144, 150, 151, 152, 155, 157, 159, 165, 166, 167, 173, 174, 175, 177, 178, 179, 181, 182, 185, 186, 187, 199, 216, 217, 218, 220, 227, 228, 257
management practices, 130
mandates, 1, 77
manpower, 244
manufacturing, 41, 43

market(s), ix, 6, 7, 46, 51, 127, 128, 142, 143, 144, 145, 150, 159, 160, 161, 168, 174, 176, 178, 179, 181, 186, 293, 348, 387
market failure, 51
marketing, 138, 144, 157, 163
marriage, 7
Marx, 232
mastery, 107, 108
mathematics, 27, 109, 122, 146, 248, 267, 268, 271, 272, 280, 284, 287, 289, 290, 291, 292, 294, 295, 299, 305, 306, 312, 318, 327, 337
matrix, 56, 178
maturation, 218
meanings, 101, 102, 177, 244
measurement, 39, 238, 239, 240, 242, 246, 247, 257, 262
measures, 6, 46, 134, 137, 150, 155, 215, 219, 226, 261, 281, 283, 293, 303, 356, 357, 358, 359, 371, 372
media, 19, 20, 23, 24, 25, 27, 28, 29, 34, 129
median, 218, 225, 289, 303, 356, 357, 358, 366, 367
Medicaid, 38
membership, 60, 63, 78, 79, 387, 389
memory, 244, 250
men, 133, 282, 284, 285, 288, 292, 303, 306, 321
mental capacity, 104
mental model, 223
mental processes, viii, 99, 101
mentor, 292
mentoring, 271, 289, 292, 295
messages, 77, 87, 202, 207, 208, 252, 260
meta-analysis, 116, 122, 124, 210
metacognition, 120, 234
metacognitive skills, 234
metaphor, 109
migration, 46
military, 151
mining, 43, 46
minorities, 131, 135, 268, 270, 271, 272, 280, 288, 289, 292, 295, 298, 338
minority, 164, 269, 270, 279, 280, 281, 282, 284, 296, 303, 304, 342, 344, 354, 367, 371, 374, 377
minority groups, 303
minority students, 270, 281, 282, 342, 344, 354, 367, 371, 374, 377
miscommunication, 184, 189
missions, 184
model specification, 390
modeling, 17, 63, 80, 117
models, x, 6, 11, 14, 18, 20, 23, 29, 34, 49, 87, 88, 92, 93, 96, 97, 102, 104, 113, 118, 120, 125, 177, 184, 195, 196, 197, 198, 216, 256, 261, 262, 263, 292, 341, 359, 363, 373, 375, 387, 389

modern society, 262
modules, 115
mold, 238
molecules, 242
money, 68, 129, 139, 162, 163, 164, 345, 349
monopoly, 187
mood, 111
moral behavior, 261, 263
moral judgment, 245
motivation, ix, 99, 101, 102, 103, 104, 105, 106, 107, 109, 110, 111, 112, 113, 114, 119, 121, 122, 123, 124, 125, 211, 216, 217, 219, 220, 234, 244, 245, 258, 261, 264
motives, 77, 83, 102, 107, 108, 109, 110, 121, 218, 224
movement, 72, 104
multidimensional, 171, 264
multimedia, 3, 24
multiplicity, 119, 181
music, 142
mutual respect, 2

N

naming, 66, 67, 72, 188
nation, 42, 54
National Aeronautics and Space Administration, 268, 271, 275, 276, 296, 297, 300, 310
National Assessment of Educational Progress, 291
National Center for Education Statistics, 42, 52, 53, 54, 268, 269, 291, 301, 336, 337, 338
National Center for Education Statistics (NCES), 269, 301
national income, 366
National Institutes of Health, 268, 270, 275, 300, 308
national product, 39
National Science Foundation, 3, 134, 146, 267, 268, 270, 271, 272, 275, 300, 301, 309, 310, 332, 336, 338
national security, 293
Native Americans, 279, 389
Native Hawaiian, 306
natural environment, 243, 244
natural science(s), 136, 242
NCES, 268, 269, 273, 301, 305
negative emotions, 106, 111, 112
negative relation, 389
negotiating, 61, 75, 79
negotiation, 65, 199, 206
neo-liberalism, x, 6, 7, 174
Netherlands, 55, 157, 176, 178, 185, 188, 193, 210
network, 75, 180, 233
networking, 222, 233

new media, 159
New South Wales, 159
New Zealand, 131, 144, 293
next generation, 137, 143
No Child Left Behind, 268, 272
non-citizens, 278
North America, 62, 135, 175
Norway, 185, 206
novelty, 255
nurses, 303
nursing, 141, 142, 145

O

objectivity, 264
obligation, 86, 244
observable behavior, 104
observations, 33, 44, 47, 289, 296, 297, 298, 356, 357, 370, 371, 389, 390
OECD, 50, 54, 129, 185
Office of Management and Budget, 280, 305
oil, 41, 46
openness, 183, 249
organ, 106, 187
organization(s), viii, x, 2, 29, 71, 72, 82, 88, 99, 101, 150, 151, 152, 153, 163, 165, 169, 173, 174, 177, 178, 179, 180, 181, 185, 186, 223, 230, 270, 273, 293, 294, 295, 298, 299, 301, 306, 387, 389
Organization for Economic Cooperation and Development, 54
orientation, 6, 14, 104, 106, 109, 115, 121, 122, 123, 125, 155, 158, 163, 200, 219, 224
originality, 249, 250
osmosis, 141
output, 30, 41, 51, 134, 261, 264
overload, 130
oversight, 59
ownership, 88

P

Pacific, 182, 279, 282, 289, 311, 338
Pacific Islander(s), 279, 282, 289, 338
parents, 1, 10, 100, 130, 155, 238, 292, 348, 364
partnership(s), 157, 218, 304
passive, 6, 55, 110, 117, 120, 156
password, 93
pathways, 109, 122, 157
pedagogy, 35, 59, 80, 305
peer review, 33, 73, 147, 188, 341
peers, 2, 17, 27, 29, 33, 73, 292
pensions, 303

per capita income, 41
percentile, 366, 367
perception(s), 12, 15, 18, 22, 23, 26, 30, 32, 75, 79, 80, 110, 118, 123, 127, 135, 143, 160, 161, 169, 211, 217, 219, 244, 255
performance indicator, 129, 169, 188
permit, 88
perseverance, 100
personal goals, 60, 118, 231
personal learning, 26, 201
personal values, 60, 109, 154
personality, 241, 244, 248, 254, 255, 256, 263, 265
personality traits, 254, 255
persons with disabilities, 279
persuasion, 167
Perth, 160
pessimism, 107, 113, 123
physical education, 13, 25
physics, 291, 295
planets, 216
planning, 2, 23, 32, 106, 111, 117, 133, 160, 179, 182, 184, 216, 247, 253, 265
Plato, 243
pleasure, 64, 67, 69, 71, 75, 79, 80, 110
policy choice, 179
policy maker(s), 39, 129, 135, 179, 182, 184, 185, 246, 296, 297
pools, 188, 189
poor, 134, 204, 292
population, vii, 6, 41, 43, 55, 56, 242, 261, 264, 272, 274, 292, 301, 302, 303, 322, 327
population growth, 41
portability, 5
portfolio, 31, 34
Portugal, 99, 173, 185
positive correlation, 259
positive relation, 110
posture, 156
poverty, 291
power, 28, 72, 73, 76, 150, 152, 153, 167, 168, 169, 170, 182, 187, 188, 243, 387
power relations, 188
practical knowledge, 142
predictability, 154
prediction, 223, 248
predictors, 124
preference, 249, 250
preparedness, 62, 135
preschool(ers), 204, 205
president, 71, 188
pressure, 130, 141, 182, 190, 242, 245
prestige, 177
prevention, 158

price competition, 349, 359
price index, 388
prices, 53, 344, 355, 359, 364, 371, 374, 377, 379, 381, 386, 388, 390
primacy, 177
primary school, 205
prior knowledge, 104, 244
private benefits, 38, 41, 54
private investment, 38
private sector, 135, 164, 182, 223
privatisation, 129
probability, 113, 116, 196, 301, 303, 322, 327, 368, 370, 371, 373, 374, 381, 389, 390
probability density function, 374
probability distribution, 374
problem solving, 187, 209, 223, 245, 246
problem-based learning, 197, 198, 199, 210, 211, 222
problem-solving, 119, 176, 183, 197, 210
problem-solving skills, 197
problem-solving strategies, 119
producers, 136
production, viii, ix, 12, 14, 35, 59, 62, 78, 79, 80, 85, 86, 94, 127, 128, 131, 135, 136, 138, 140, 143, 145, 152, 153, 161, 169, 185, 241, 250
productivity, vii, viii, 10, 37, 39, 40, 41, 42, 43, 44, 45, 46, 48, 49, 50, 51, 53, 54, 55, 78, 80, 154, 185, 186
productivity growth, 41
profession, 60, 137, 138, 238
professional careers, 156
professional development, 34, 231
professions, 159, 160
profit(s), 7, 228, 242, 261, 343, 387
program, viii, 11, 14, 20, 22, 24, 27, 29, 39, 57, 58, 59, 61, 62, 66, 68, 70, 75, 79, 81, 117, 124, 145, 163, 217, 222, 223, 224, 225, 226, 228, 229, 230, 231, 233, 258, 270, 271, 274, 276, 277, 279, 288, 294, 295, 296, 297, 298, 300, 302, 312, 337, 338
programming, 91, 97, 155, 218, 220, 289
progress reports, 72, 76
proliferation, 187
proposition, 140, 154
prosperity, 39, 237
prototype, 20, 22, 23, 24, 25, 27, 89
psychology, 122, 174, 233, 234, 250, 252, 261, 265, 282
public administration, 174
public expenditures, 41
public finance, 51
public investment, 40, 51
public policy, 38, 51, 53, 55, 179, 188
public schools, 13, 305, 361

public sector, vii, 6, 37, 38, 40, 44, 50, 51, 55, 129, 130, 143
publishers, 388
P-value, 375, 376

Q

qualifications, 305
qualitative concept, 261
qualitative differences, 114, 122, 305
qualitative research, 82
quality assurance, ix, 127, 169
quality control, 155, 305
quality of life, 69, 237
quantitative concept, 261
questioning, 7, 17, 87, 187, 203
questionnaires, 202, 217, 218, 254, 300

R

race, 1, 167, 281, 302, 305, 360, 370, 390
racial groups, 353, 369, 389, 391
range, viii, 1, 2, 3, 20, 23, 24, 34, 57, 60, 63, 75, 78, 79, 80, 88, 105, 154, 156, 186, 188, 196, 216, 260, 277, 297, 356, 357, 358, 388
rate of return, 365
ratings, 19, 20, 28, 91, 225
rationality, 151, 154
reading, 22, 26, 64, 65, 66, 87, 105, 111, 112, 114, 115, 200, 203, 224, 227, 228, 244, 248, 272, 337
real estate, 43, 348
reality, 74, 101, 165, 169, 211, 216, 237
reasoning, x, 195, 196, 203, 365
reasoning skills, x, 195, 196
recall, 103, 118, 202, 203, 226, 230, 250
recall information, 250
receptors, 189
recession, 56
recognition, 61, 74, 345
reconcile, 61, 62, 74, 75
recovery, 137
redistribution, 6, 359
reduction, 18, 32, 33, 63, 72, 152, 187
refining, 96
reflection, ix, 20, 24, 35, 63, 85, 99, 101, 113, 114, 117, 176, 183
reflective practice, 97, 125
reforms, vii, 5, 168, 187
regeneration, 138
regression, viii, 37, 41, 44, 45, 47, 49, 219, 371, 373, 374, 376, 377, 390
regression analysis, 44

regression equation, 42, 371, 373

regulation(s), 100, 103, 104, 105, 106, 111, 114, 120, 121, 123, 125, 151, 176, 178, 186, 211, 216, 219, 223, 224, 225, 228, 229, 233

regulators, 100, 104, 105

rehearsing, 66

rejection, 60, 292

relationship(s), x, 25, 41, 44, 48, 49, 50, 58, 67, 74, 76, 79, 81, 135, 140, 157, 161, 165, 166, 178, 181, 185, 189, 195, 202, 229, 257, 259, 265, 266, 273, 365

relevance, ix, 106, 110, 127, 143, 150, 178, 181, 182, 183, 184, 186, 190, 258

reliability, 33, 219, 252, 269, 300, 301

repair, 87

replacement, 6

representative samples, 305

reputation, 78, 158, 161, 162

research funding, 150, 161

resistance, 7, 38, 55, 62, 75, 83, 158, 164, 166, 167, 168, 256, 262

resource allocation, 168

resource management, 113, 217

resources, ix, xi, 2, 4, 6, 17, 23, 24, 25, 28, 39, 41, 51, 71, 72, 86, 87, 99, 100, 102, 111, 112, 130, 135, 153, 156, 160, 163, 164, 177, 179, 186, 187, 189, 195, 197, 200, 204, 209, 216, 217, 227, 244, 246, 271, 279, 280, 295, 296, 297, 299, 359, 373, 387

responsiveness, 179

restaurants, 155

restructuring, 130, 179

retail, 43

retention, 258, 293

returns, 41, 54, 156, 302, 365

returns to scale, 41

revenue, 40, 155, 156, 157, 161, 163, 164, 168, 365

rewards, 108, 111, 112, 128, 141

rhetoric, 38, 83, 165, 185, 186

rigidity, 157

risk, 54, 113, 118, 124, 144, 163, 165, 166, 168, 234, 254, 255, 265

risk management, 144

risk-taking, 254, 255, 265

robotics, 274

routines, 100, 117

royalty, 157

S

sabotage, 164

sadness, 113

safety, 2, 14

sample, 20, 22, 23, 47, 49, 50, 169, 229, 242, 249, 260, 269, 294, 298, 300, 301, 302, 303, 305, 322, 327, 356, 357, 358, 359, 361, 363, 366, 367, 369, 381, 382, 383, 384, 385, 388, 389, 390

sample design, 302, 305

sampling, 269, 300, 304, 327

sampling error, 269, 300, 304, 328

satellite, 10, 155, 251

satisfaction, 113, 135, 181, 217, 223, 224, 292, 388

savings, 41

scheduling, 27, 30

Scheffe test, 254

scholarship, 83, 138, 146, 153, 174, 185

Scholastic Aptitude Test, 360

school, vii, 5, 9, 10, 14, 24, 35, 42, 54, 86, 92, 101, 105, 106, 112, 115, 116, 121, 122, 123, 151, 157, 159, 174, 204, 205, 223, 237, 239, 240, 241, 244, 247, 251, 255, 256, 260, 262, 263, 265, 272, 274, 278, 280, 290, 291, 293, 294, 295, 305, 337, 341, 342, 343, 344, 345, 346, 347, 348, 349, 350, 351, 352, 353, 354, 355, 356, 357, 358, 359, 360, 361, 362, 363, 364, 365, 366, 367, 369, 370, 371, 372, 373, 374, 376, 377, 378, 379, 381, 382, 383, 384, 385, 386, 387, 388, 389, 390, 391

school enrollment, 293

school performance, vii, 9

school work, 105

schooling, viii, 36, 50, 85, 92

science department, 134

scientific knowledge, 34, 228, 239

scores, 216, 248, 249, 260, 360, 362, 367, 385, 391

search, 28, 40, 177, 179, 180, 186

searching, 1, 88, 89, 250

second generation, 142, 146

second language, 13, 27, 97, 291

secondary education, 356

secondary schools, 153

secondary teachers, 278, 290

security, 293, 294

selecting, 137, 165, 271

selectivity, 137, 356, 360, 361, 366, 373, 388

self-assessment, 18

self-concept, 103, 220, 221

self-confidence, 221, 259

self-efficacy, 102, 103, 104, 105, 106, 107, 110, 112, 114, 123, 125

self-esteem, 83, 114, 123

self-evaluations, 260

self-image, 107

self-knowledge, 106

self-monitoring, 105, 123

self-observation, 106

self-perceptions, 18

self-reflection, 191
self-regulation, 100, 102, 103, 104, 105, 106, 109, 110, 111, 113, 114, 117, 119, 120, 121, 122, 123, 124, 125, 181, 216, 217, 219, 220, 225, 227, 232, 233
self-reports, 221
semi-structured interviews, 219
Senate, 164
sensations, 113
September 11, 268, 293
sequencing, 19, 22, 25, 29
series, ix, 51, 61, 78, 102, 104, 106, 111, 113, 120, 127, 175, 217, 218, 247, 301, 370
settlements, 237
sex, 125, 302
shame, 112
shape, 24, 82, 96, 197, 261
shaping, 77, 86, 88, 245
shares, 38, 43, 52, 72, 188
sharing, 204
Sherman Act, 344
shortage, 6, 138
shoulders, vii, 37, 38
siblings, 348, 350, 367, 389
sign, 3, 202, 346, 373
signals, 46
significance level, 387
signs, 154
similarity, 160, 246, 381
simulation, 153, 156, 249, 253
Singapore, 146
skill acquisition, 217
skills, ix, 14, 27, 78, 100, 109, 110, 120, 121, 127, 135, 139, 140, 141, 142, 146, 159, 161, 187, 217, 220, 221, 222, 231, 234, 238, 245, 261, 290
social benefits, 39, 51, 53, 344
social context, 36
social desirability, 224
social evaluation, 6
social group, 60
social learning, 104
social learning theory, 104
social network, 141
social policy, 180
social psychology, 104
social relations, 257
social responsibility, 186
social roles, 246
social sciences, x, 57, 134, 135, 143, 144, 173, 261, 282
social skills, 217, 246
social structure, 60, 152
social theory, 212

socialization, 71, 104, 146
society, vii, 5, 6, 37, 38, 41, 51, 52, 53, 58, 66, 76, 128, 135, 140, 151, 152, 174, 175, 185, 238, 245, 246, 255, 261, 262
Socrates, 243
software, 2, 3, 30, 86, 88, 89, 91, 92, 93, 97, 98, 140, 160, 251, 265
solar system, 216
South Africa, 160, 185
South Korea, 182
Soviet Union, 295
Spain, v, 99, 120, 124
special education, 13, 25
specialization, 151, 180
specific knowledge, 111, 221
specificity, 116
spectrum, 247
speech, 3, 199
speed, 28, 152
sports, 389
stability, 44, 47, 49, 113
staff development, 255
stages, 21, 25, 31, 63, 207, 246, 247, 252, 263
stakeholders, 156, 158, 181, 229
standard deviation, 47, 50, 356, 357, 358, 387
standard error, 44, 48, 49, 50, 371, 373, 374, 390, 391
standards, 3, 25, 39, 108, 139, 144, 183, 208, 238, 270, 272, 299, 305
stars, 167
stasis, 143
statistics, 46, 49, 54, 93, 134, 170, 367, 369
stimulus, 243, 244
STM, 336, 337
stock, 42, 45, 49, 50
storage, 32, 88, 89, 250
strategic planning, 169
strategies, x, 28, 54, 55, 73, 74, 76, 100, 101, 102, 103, 104, 106, 107, 108, 109, 111, 112, 113, 114, 115, 116, 117, 118, 119, 121, 122, 123, 124, 125, 155, 168, 174, 206, 211, 215, 234, 244, 272, 279
strategy use, 113, 125
stratification, 145
streams, 163, 168, 181
strength, 33, 78, 79, 95, 237, 262
stress, ix, 19, 54, 127, 130, 144, 145, 146
stressors, 145
structuring, x, 17, 61, 180, 195, 198, 202, 248
student characteristics, 58, 353, 356, 359, 366, 371, 373, 374
student enrollment, 269, 283, 296, 301, 353, 354, 360, 365, 373, 374

student group, x, 66, 195, 198, 202, 203, 208, 227, 342, 343, 353, 354, 376
student motivation, 120, 122
student populations, 369
student retention, 305
subgroups, 356, 382
subjectivity, 82
subsidization, 52
substitution, 154, 388
substitution effect, 388
suffering, 130
summaries, 33, 64, 65, 205, 258
summer, 19, 20, 24, 25, 115
superiority, 152, 248
supervision, 58, 82, 108, 140, 151, 177, 178
supervisor, 62, 63, 66, 67, 68, 69, 70, 72, 73, 75, 76, 77, 78, 79, 135, 140, 227
supervisors, 63, 74, 79, 80, 216
supply, 6, 22, 54, 128, 134, 144, 145, 146, 244, 245, 246, 257, 258, 259, 305
surprise, 88, 137
sustainability, 190
Sweden, x, 101, 157, 173, 174, 176
synthesis, 65, 217, 224, 245
systems, 10, 30, 35, 75, 83, 89, 144, 154, 155, 175, 177, 178, 179, 181, 182, 184, 185, 186, 199, 217, 218, 220, 221, 227, 233, 237, 238, 239, 240, 241, 247, 250, 251, 252, 253, 254, 256, 257, 260, 261, 262, 263, 264, 268, 272, 289

T

talent, 245
target population, 299
targets, 87, 164
task difficulty, 110, 113
task performance, 109, 110
tax increase, 38
taxonomy, 115, 226, 250
teacher attitudes, 266
teacher effectiveness, 294
teachers, 7, 10, 14, 16, 19, 20, 22, 24, 25, 28, 31, 34, 88, 92, 97, 100, 101, 105, 116, 117, 118, 119, 120, 218, 221, 228, 232, 241, 255, 256, 258, 259, 260, 265, 272, 278, 289, 290, 291, 292, 294, 305
teaching, vii, viii, x, 1, 5, 6, 7, 9, 10, 11, 12, 13, 14, 15, 16, 17, 18, 19, 20, 21, 22, 23, 24, 25, 26, 27, 28, 29, 32, 33, 34, 35, 60, 63, 77, 78, 81, 82, 85, 86, 100, 103, 104, 108, 115, 116, 117, 118, 119, 120, 122, 123, 124, 125, 129, 130, 135, 153, 154, 155, 156, 160, 161, 162, 173, 176, 180, 186, 205, 211, 233, 237, 238, 239, 240, 241, 244, 245, 246, 247, 248, 249, 250, 251, 252, 253, 254, 255, 256, 257, 258, 259, 260, 261, 262, 263, 265, 272, 292, 298
teaching experience, 13, 28
teaching process, 241, 253, 254, 256, 259, 262
teaching quality, 104
teaching strategies, 25, 28, 29, 258
team members, 218
technological advancement, 186
technology, 3, 10, 13, 14, 19, 20, 24, 25, 26, 27, 28, 29, 34, 35, 41, 86, 88, 92, 96, 128, 129, 133, 140, 146, 154, 155, 159, 196, 197, 212, 240, 250, 251, 252, 255, 256, 267, 268, 272, 274, 282, 284, 287, 294, 295, 298, 299, 306, 312, 318, 327
technology transfer, 274, 294
telephone, 10
television, 10, 251, 266
temperature, 242
tension, 60, 64, 66, 67, 74, 140, 164, 228
tenure, vii, 9, 10, 68, 79, 154, 184
test statistic, 44, 47, 383
theory, ix, 10, 40, 41, 44, 50, 51, 53, 54, 55, 97, 104, 110, 113, 120, 122, 124, 125, 142, 149, 168, 169, 182, 184, 186, 192, 198, 200, 201, 203, 210, 232, 234, 241, 242, 243, 245, 250, 265, 359, 373, 374, 376, 387
thinking, 16, 22, 23, 26, 27, 29, 30, 62, 76, 79, 80, 81, 85, 118, 226, 242, 243, 244, 245, 246, 251, 252, 261, 262, 263, 347
threat, 134, 154
three-dimensional model, 216
threshold, x, 173, 174, 175, 178, 234
time, vii, viii, 6, 10, 12, 19, 20, 21, 22, 25, 26, 27, 28, 29, 31, 32, 33, 34, 41, 43, 44, 47, 49, 50, 57, 60, 61, 63, 64, 68, 72, 76, 77, 80, 85, 86, 87, 88, 95, 104, 109, 113, 114, 117, 118, 122, 131, 132, 134, 135, 136, 137, 138, 139, 141, 143, 152, 155, 156, 162, 166, 168, 178, 184, 187, 189, 196, 204, 206, 207, 209, 215, 216, 217, 222, 223, 226, 227, 228, 230, 240, 243, 263, 274, 279, 282, 283, 292, 293, 294, 300, 301, 305, 349, 350, 360, 363, 365, 366, 370, 371, 372, 374, 381, 382, 388, 389
time frame, 113, 300
time periods, 43, 47, 49
time series, 370, 389
Title IX of the Education Amendments of 1972, 338
trade, 43, 344
trading, 78
tradition, 6, 51, 143, 175, 176, 183
traditional authority, 152
traditionalism, 255
training, ix, 2, 3, 5, 6, 10, 13, 14, 36, 40, 45, 104, 115, 116, 117, 120, 127, 135, 137, 139, 140, 141, 142, 143, 144, 151, 152, 153, 180, 182, 186, 201,

217, 222, 223, 224, 225, 226, 227, 228, 229, 230,
231, 233, 234, 245, 260, 265, 270, 276, 290, 291,
292, 294, 295
training programs, 6, 115, 116, 120, 224, 227, 233,
270, 276
traits, 161, 166, 259
trajectory, 79
transcripts, 63, 64, 65, 66, 203, 224
transformation(s), 101, 144, 157, 166, 185
transition, 135, 205, 255
translation, 152
transmission, 6, 239, 240, 264
transparency, 130
transport, 243
transportation, 43, 272, 364
treaties, 187
tree plantings, 159
trend, 6, 38, 105, 178, 179, 180, 182, 185
trial, 243, 244, 245
trial and error, 243, 244
tribes, 175
triggers, 196
tuition, 38, 54, 55, 137, 167, 292, 342, 343, 349, 350,
354, 360, 364, 368, 370, 373, 375, 377, 382, 388,
389, 390

U

U.S. Geological Survey, 310
UK, v, ix, x, 82, 83, 101, 121, 127, 128, 129, 130,
131, 132, 133, 134, 135, 136, 137, 138, 139, 141,
142, 143, 144, 145, 146, 147, 173, 174, 185, 189,
192, 293
undergraduate, viii, 85, 86, 92, 94, 95, 138, 143, 156,
281, 291, 295, 301, 306, 318, 322, 366, 388
undergraduate education, 388
unemployment, 302
UNESCO, 185, 193, 265
uniform, 130, 146
unit cost, 156
United States, vi, 28, 30, 39, 56, 150, 154, 158, 177,
267, 268, 271, 272, 274, 283, 290, 293, 296, 336,
337, 338, 341
universe, 305
universities, ix, x, 5, 6, 7, 12, 74, 78, 82, 83, 127,
128, 129, 130, 131, 135, 136, 137, 141, 142, 143,
144, 145, 146, 149, 150, 151, 153, 154, 155, 156,
157, 158, 159, 160, 161, 162, 163, 165, 166, 168,
169, 173, 176, 177, 178, 180, 184, 186, 237, 266,
269, 270, 271, 272, 274, 278, 289, 290, 291, 292,
293, 294, 295, 297, 299, 304, 306, 337, 341, 344,
346, 361, 387, 388
university education, 100, 177, 217

university students, 124, 217, 237, 265
updating, 139
USDA, 270, 276
user-interface, 89
users, 89
Utterances, 202

V

vacuum, 216
validation, 125, 257
validity, 33, 252, 253
values, 10, 33, 45, 50, 59, 61, 66, 77, 79, 80, 87, 103,
110, 121, 124, 130, 131, 150, 153, 157, 161, 181,
184, 238, 245, 301, 303, 322, 327, 354, 357, 358,
364, 367, 368, 370, 373, 375, 376, 378, 380, 382,
388, 389
variability, 300
variable(s), x, 42, 43, 44, 45, 49, 50, 103, 109, 113,
195, 202, 221, 223, 224, 225, 232, 239, 240, 241,
244, 247, 249, 250, 253, 254, 255, 256, 257, 258,
260, 261, 262, 263, 364, 365, 366, 367, 369, 371,
373, 374, 377, 381, 383, 384, 385, 389, 390
variance, 43, 216, 225, 245, 249, 254, 304, 327
variation, 41, 44, 47, 49, 65, 67, 78, 207, 342, 343,
346, 348, 352, 353, 356, 357, 358, 359, 363
vector, 373
vertigo, 182
visa system, 293
visas, 272, 274, 288, 293, 296, 297, 337, 338
vision, 27, 226, 228
vocabulary, 26
voice, 60, 61, 62, 63, 64, 65, 66, 67, 68, 69, 70, 71,
72, 73, 74, 75, 76, 77, 78, 79, 80, 199

W

wages, 154, 269, 289, 303, 327
walking, 160
war, 167
weakness, 182
wealth, 130
web, vii, 9, 16, 17, 19, 20, 23, 24, 25, 26, 27, 28, 29,
30, 31, 53, 56, 89, 140, 202, 203, 207, 210, 212,
222
web pages, 17, 20, 27, 30
websites, 3, 24
welfare, 178, 179, 180, 205
welfare state, 178
well-being, 111
Wellesley College, 347, 362
Western Europe, 176, 177, 178, 181, 191, 192

wheat, 243, 244
wheat germ, 243
wholesale, 43
winning, 108
women, 131, 133, 135, 268, 269, 270, 271, 272, 280,
    281, 282, 284, 285, 288, 289, 292, 295, 296, 303,
    304, 306, 320, 321
word processing, 86
work environment, 140
work roles, 219, 220
work study, 364, 381, 391
workers, 40, 46, 153, 274
working conditions, 6
working groups, 280
working hours, 151
workload, 131
workplace, 75, 77, 82, 131, 142, 197, 230, 234
World Bank, 182, 193
worldview, 150, 245

writing, viii, 14, 29, 62, 63, 70, 73, 78, 80, 82, 85,
    86, 87, 88, 92, 95, 96, 97, 100, 115, 118, 122,
    132, 142, 204, 245, 248, 252
WWW, 12, 13

X

XML, 89, 91, 93

Y

yield, 40, 44, 51, 161, 242

Z

zero growth, 38